Seminars in Consultation Liaison Psychiatry

College Seminars Series

For details of available and forthcoming books in the College Seminars Series please visit: www.cambridge.org/series/college-seminars-series

Seminars in Consultation-Liaison Psychiatry

Third Edition

Edited by

Rachel Thomasson
Manchester Centre for Clinical Neurosciences

Elspeth Guthrie
Leeds Institute of Health Sciences

Allan House
Leeds Institute of Health Sciences

Shaftesbury Road, Cambridge CB2 8EA, United Kingdom

One Liberty Plaza, 20th Floor, New York, NY 10006, USA

477 Williamstown Road, Port Melbourne, VIC 3207, Australia

314–321, 3rd Floor, Plot 3, Splendor Forum, Jasola District Centre, New Delhi – 110025, India

103 Penang Road, #05–06/07, Visioncrest Commercial, Singapore 238467

Cambridge University Press is part of Cambridge University Press & Assessment, a department of the University of Cambridge.

We share the University's mission to contribute to society through the pursuit of education, learning and research at the highest international levels of excellence.

www.cambridge.org
Information on this title: www.cambridge.org/9781911623540

DOI: 10.1017/9781911623533

First published 1996
Second edition 2012
Third edition 2024

A catalogue record for this publication is available from the British Library

Library of Congress Cataloging-in-Publication Data
Names: Thomasson, Rachel, editor. | Guthrie, Elspeth, editor. | House, Allan, editor.
Title: Seminars in consultation-liaison psychiatry / edited by Rachel Thomasson, Manchester Centre for Clinical Neurosciences, Elspeth Guthrie, Leeds Institute of Health Sciences, Allan House, Leeds Institute of Health Sciences.
Other titles: Seminars in liaison psychiatry.
Description: Third edition. | Cambridge, United Kingdom ; New York, NY : Cambridge University Press, 2023. | Series: CGSS College seminars series | Revised editon of: Seminars in liaison psychiatry / edited by Elspeth Guthrie, Sanjay Rao. 2nd edition. 2012. | Includes bibliographical references and index.
Identifiers: LCCN 2023027790 (print) | LCCN 2023027791 (ebook) | ISBN 9781911623540 (paperback) | ISBN 9781911623533 (ebook)
Subjects: LCSH: Consultation-liaison psychiatry.
Classification: LCC RC455.2.C65 S46 2023 (print) | LCC RC455.2.C65 (ebook) | DDC 616.89–dc23/eng/20230912
LC record available at https://lccn.loc.gov/2023027790
LC ebook record available at https://lccn.loc.gov/2023027791

ISBN 978-1-911-62354-0 Paperback

....

Contents

List of Contributors vii

1 **The Assessment Process in Consultation-Liaison Psychiatry** 1
Caroline Buck

2 **Notes on Training Pathways in Consultation-Liaison Psychiatry** 19
Faye Stanage and Gregory Carter

3 **Nursing in Consultation-Liaison Settings** 32
Kate Chartres and Sarah Eales

4 **Psychological Reaction to Physical Illness** 48
Elspeth Guthrie and Marc Mandell

5 **Self-Harm and Suicidal Thoughts** 61
Allan House

6 **Depression in Medical Settings** 78
Elspeth Guthrie

7 **Functional Somatic Symptoms** 97
Constanze Hausteiner-Wiehle and Peter Henningsen

8 **Alcohol Misuse** 117
Rachel Thomasson and Ashokkumar Shishodia

9 **Substance Misuse** 134
Matthew Kelleher

10 **Psychosis in General Hospital Settings** 158
Seri Abraham, Daniel Kaitiff, Samira Malik, Annalie Clark and Rachel Thomasson

11 **Acute Behavioural Disturbance in the General Hospital** 172
Ankush Singhal, Sridevi Sira Mahalingappa, Deepa Bagepalli Krishnan and Rachel Thomasson

12 **The Neurology–Psychiatry Interface** 189
Annalie Clark and Rachel Thomasson

13 **Perinatal Psychiatry** 210
Sarah Jones, Aaron McMeekin, Ipshita Mukherjee and Laura Murphy

14 **Paediatric Consultation-Liaison Psychiatry** 232
Rachel Elvins, Louisa Draper, Neelo Aslam and Ruth Marshall

15 **Psychological Treatment** 250
Elspeth Guthrie

16 **Legal and Ethical Issues in Consultation-Liaison Psychiatry** 271
Elena Baker-Glenn and Annabel Price

17 **Social Aspects of Consultation-Liaison Psychiatry** 288
Max Henderson

18 **Education for Acute Hospital Staff** 301
Mathew Harrison and Max Henderson

19 **Considerations in the Planning and Delivery of Consultation-Liaison Psychiatry Services** 318
Allan House

20 **Outcome Measurement in Consultation-Liaison Psychiatry** 328
Allan House

21 **The Evidence Base for Consultation-Liaison Psychiatry** 345
Elspeth Guthrie

22 **Primary Care Consultation-Liaison Services** 356
Chris Schofield and Philippa Bolton

23 **Emergency Department Psychiatry** 373
Alex Thomson and Rikke Albert

24 **Setting Standards for Consultation-Liaison Psychiatry Services** 389
Jim Bolton

25 **Policy to Practice: Developing Consultation-Liaison Psychiatry Services** 401
Peter Aitken and William Lee

26 **Consultation-Liaison Psychiatry: Four International Perspectives** 413
Gregory Carter, Wolfgang Söllner, James Levenson and Kathleen Sheehan

Index 448

Contributors

Seri Abraham, Consultant Liaison Psychiatrist, Pennine Care NHS Foundation Trust, Ashton-under-Lyne, UK.

Peter Aitken, Consultant Liaison Psychiatrist, Devon Partnership NHS Trust, UK; Honorary Associate Professor, University of Exeter College of Medicine and Health, Exeter, UK.

Rikke Albert, Consultant Nurse, Mental Health Liaison Team, East London NHS Foundation Trust, London, UK.

Neelo Aslam, Consultant Child and Adolescent Psychiatrist, Royal Manchester Children's Hospital, Manchester University NHS Foundation Trust, Manchester, UK.

Elena Baker-Glenn, Consultant Psychiatrist and Clinical Director for Crisis Pathway, East London NHS Foundation Trust, London, UK.

Jim Bolton, Consultant Liaison Psychiatrist, Department of Liaison Psychiatry, St Helier Hospital, South West London and St George's Mental Health NHS Trust, London, UK.

Philippa Bolton, Consultant Liaison Psychiatrist, Tees, Esk and Wear Valleys NHS Foundation Trust, York, UK.

Caroline Buck, Specialist Trainee in General Adult and Later Life Psychiatry, Greater Manchester Mental Health NHS Foundation Trust, Manchester, UK.

Gregory Carter, Professor of Psychiatry, Faculty of Health Sciences, University of Newcastle, Callaghan, Australia; Senior Staff Specialist and Acting Director of

Consultation-Liaison Psychiatry, Calvary Mater Newcastle Hospital, Waratah, Australia.

Kate Chartres, Nurse Consultant, Sunderland Liaison Mental Health Service, Cumbria, Northumberland, Tyne and Wear NHS Foundation Trust, Durham, UK.

Annalie Clark, Specialist Trainee in Adult Psychiatry, Greater Manchester Mental Health NHS Foundation Trust, Manchester, UK.

Louisa Draper, Consultant Child and Adolescent Psychiatrist (Paediatric Liaison), Clinical Health Psychology Services, Alder Hey Children's NHS Foundation Trust, Liverpool, UK.

Sarah Eales, Lead Matron in Mental Health, University Hospital Southampton NHS Foundation Trust, Southampton, UK.

Rachel Elvins, Consultant Child and Adolescent Psychiatrist, Royal Manchester Children's Hospital, Manchester University NHS Foundation Trust, Manchester, UK; Training Programme Director, Core Psychiatry HEE(NW), Greater Manchester Mental Health Trust, Manchester, UK.

Elspeth Guthrie, Professor of Psychological Medicine, Leeds Institute of Health Sciences, School of Medicine, University of Leeds, Leeds, UK.

Mathew Harrison, Medical Psychotherapist and Consultant Liaison Psychiatrist, Lead Clinician for the Liaison Psychiatry Outpatients Service, Leeds and

York Partnership NHS Foundation Trust, Leeds, UK.

Constanze Hausteiner-Wiehle, Professor of Psychosomatic Medicine, Department of Psychosomatic Medicine and Psychotherapy, Technical University of Munich, Munich, Germany; Psychosomatic Consultation-Liaison Service, BG Trauma Center, Murnau, Germany.

Max Henderson, Associate Professor and Consultant Liaison Psychiatrist, Leeds Institute of Health Sciences, University of Leeds, Leeds, UK.

Peter Henningsen, Professor of Psychosomatic Medicine, Department of Psychosomatic Medicine and Psychotherapy, Technical University of Munich, Munich, Germany.

Allan House, Emeritus Professor of Liaison Psychiatry, Leeds Institute of Health Sciences, School of Medicine, University of Leeds, Leeds, UK.

Sarah Jones, Consultant Perinatal Psychiatrist, Greater Manchester Mental Health NHS Foundation Trust, Manchester, UK.

Daniel Kaitiff, Consultant Adult Psychiatrist, Pennine Care NHS Foundation Trust, Ashton-under-Lyne, UK.

Matthew Kelleher, Consultant Psychiatrist, Strategic Command, HQ Defence Medical Services, Whittington, UK; The ADHD Centre, London, UK.

Deepa Bagepalli Krishnan, Consultant Perinatal Psychiatrist, Nottinghamshire Perinatal Mental Health Service, Nottinghamshire Healthcare NHS Foundation Trust, Nottingham, UK.

William Lee, Consultant Liaison Psychiatrist, Cornwall Partnership NHS Foundation Trust, Bodmin, UK.

James Levenson, Rhona Arenstein Professor of Psychiatry and Professor of Medicine and Surgery, Virginia Commonwealth University School of Medicine, Richmond, VA, USA.

Sridevi Sira Mahalingappa, Consultant Psychiatrist, South London and Maudsley NHS Foundation Trust, London, UK; Honorary (Consultant) Assistant Professor, University of Nottingham, Nottingham, UK.

Samira Malik, Specialist Trainee in General Adult Psychiatry, Greater Manchester Mental Health NHS Foundation Trust, Manchester, UK.

Marc Mandell, Consultant Older Adult Psychiatrist (retired); Member of the Executive Committee of the Faculty of Liaison Psychiatry, Royal College of Psychiatrists, London, UK.

Ruth Marshall, Consultant Child and Adolescent Psychiatrist, Galaxy House, Royal Manchester Children's Hospital, Manchester University NHS Foundation Trust, Manchester, UK.

Aaron McMeekin, Consultant Perinatal Psychiatrist, Greater Manchester Mental Health NHS Foundation Trust, Manchester, UK; Honorary Senior Clinical Teacher, Academic Unit of Medical Education, Western Bank, University of Sheffield, Sheffield, UK.

Ipshita Mukherjee, Consultant Perinatal Psychiatrist, Greater Manchester Mental Health NHS Foundation Trust, Manchester, UK.

Laura Murphy, Consultant Perinatal Psychiatrist, Greater Manchester Mental Health NHS Foundation Trust, Manchester, UK.

Annabel Price, Consultant in Liaison Psychiatry for Older Adults, Addenbrooke's Hospital, Cambridge, UK; Associate Specialist Director for Palliative Care, Cambridge Institute of Public Health, Cambridge, UK; Chair, Faculty of Liaison Psychiatry, Royal College of Psychiatrists, London, UK.

Chris Schofield, Consultant Liaison Psychiatrist, Nottinghamshire Healthcare NHS Foundation Trust, Nottingham, UK.

Kathleen Sheehan, Clinician Investigator, Centre for Mental Health, University Health Network, Toronto, Canada; Assistant Professor, Department of Psychiatry, University of Toronto, Toronto, Canada.

Ashokkumar Shishodia, Consultant Psychiatrist Department of Psychiatry Abu Dhabi, UAE.

Ankush Singhal, Consultant Liaison Psychiatrist, Oldham Psychological Medicine Service and Mental Health Liaison Team, Pennine Care NHS Foundation Trust, Ashton-under-Lyne, UK.

Wolfgang Söllner, Professor Emeritus of Psychosomatic Medicine and Psychotherapy, Paracelsus Medical University, Nuremberg, Germany.

Faye Stanage, Consultant Liaison Psychiatrist, St George's Hospital, South West London and St George's NHS Trust, London, UK.

Rachel Thomasson, Consultant Neuropsychiatrist, Department of Neurology, Manchester Centre for Clinical Neurosciences, Manchester, UK.

Alex Thomson, Consultant Liaison Psychiatrist, Northwick Park Hospital, Central and North West London NHS Foundation Trust, London, UK.

The Assessment Process in Consultation-Liaison Psychiatry

Chapter **1**

Caroline Buck

Introduction

It is well established that people suffering from a mental disorder have poorer physical health outcomes, including increased mortality, than those without such a disorder (1). In addition, people with severe mental illness are more likely to be admitted to non-psychiatric medical services, have longer admissions and present with more emergencies (2). The mental health consultation-liaison (CL) team is perfectly placed to ensure holistic assessment and integrated care of this population, with the opportunity to improve both physical and mental health outcomes. There is evidence that mental health CL teams improve a number of outcomes, including decreased mortality and readmission rate and increased patient satisfaction and quality of life (3), in addition to the potential economic benefits of reducing unnecessary admissions and reduced length of stay (4). By offering consultation, the CL practitioner has the advantage of taking a holistic view of a person, plus adequate time to establish a person's priorities and any barriers to accessing the best care. The roles of the CL practitioner are many but centre around the concepts of patient advocacy, communication with acute colleagues, flexibility and holistic assessments. This chapter aims to outline the practicalities of performing an assessment from start to finish, maximising integration and contribution to positive patient outcomes.

Assessment Overview

It is important to note that CL practitioners cover a range of areas in the hospital. The assessment process is tailored to the environment, but this chapter is focused on an assessment on the general wards. The principles can easily be translated to any CL assessment. The full process is summarised in Figure 1.1.

Preparation: Processing Referrals

Does It Meet Our Referral Criteria?

The assessment begins at the point of the referral. Different teams have different approaches to triaging referrals (5) and to handover requirements (6). Many organisations will accept and assess all referrals. The benefit of this approach is that it does not expect non-experts to ask pertinent questions, much like it might be unfair to expect a psychiatrist to know how to triage the urgency of a new heart murmur. Behind every referral there is a concern for patient welfare, so value can usually be added to a patient's experience by routine assessment

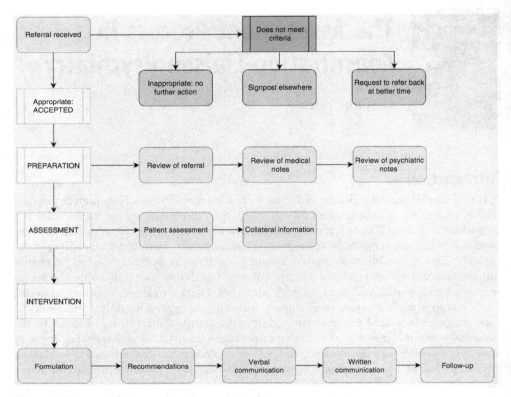

Figure 1.1 Summary of the mental health consultation-liaison assessment process.

of all referrals. Some teams apply triage criteria before deciding whether to see a referral. The commonest are:

a. **Severity**: Some services do have a triage function and do not routinely see all referrals themselves, instead signposting to other services such as primary care, psychology services or substance misuse services. The Royal College of Psychiatrists suggests that CL services have a role in accepting all referrals that indicate a mental health problem which is moderate to severe and/or impairing physical healthcare (7). In theory, there are many referrals which will not meet this threshold and the standard operating procedure of the service may dictate that these cases are best dealt with elsewhere.

b. **Age**: Different services cater to different populations. Some CL services are 'ageless', providing care all the way from children and adolescents to older adults. Other areas have specific older adult and general adult teams, and many areas have entirely different services for under 16s. This will depend on the specific services which are commissioned in individual healthcare providers. If age is a part of the referral criteria, it is important to first check that the patient is with the right team. Flexibility may be required to ensure the patient is seen by the practitioners with the skillset most appropriate for their needs; for example, a 55-year-old patient with early onset dementia may be better cared for by an older adult team (7).

c. **Are they 'medically fit'?**: Another part of the referral criteria, which differs between teams, is at which point in the journey the patient is accepted as suitable to be assessed.

There has been a tradition that patients are not assessed until they are 'medically fit' and some teams still use this model. There are certain circumstances in which it may be appropriate to defer assessment for medical reasons, for example if a patient is too unwell to engage or is acutely intoxicated. Sometimes patients can experience significant changes during their admission, for example when receiving bad news or undergoing significant procedures, which clearly cause fluctuations in their mental state. For these reasons some teams choose to wait until the patient is 'medically fit', which will minimise the variability in the patient's presentation secondary to external factors such as their current illness.

However, there is a strong argument for parallel assessment. Firstly, being in hospital can be very challenging. Patients are away from their families and routine, usually suffering with some sort of pain or discomfort, facing uncertainty and being told distressing news with potentially life-changing consequences. While all staff have a duty to listen and be empathetic, mental health professionals can have an invaluable role in offering psychological and emotional support and getting to the heart of the patient's priorities. This sort of support cannot be delivered if patients are only seen at the point of discharge. Assessing patients from the start of their admission, alongside the medical teams, also ensures that appropriate planning can take place that prevents delays to the patient journey. It gives an opportunity to ensure thorough assessments without the pressure of an imminent discharge. Very importantly, it fosters positive working relationships with colleagues in the acute wards, and a desire for more parallel working is often stated by acute staff (8).

Encouraging Helpful Referral Requests

Although there are no specific data for CL services, the literature regarding primary care physician referrals to various specialties demonstrates that there is inadequate information 'fairly often' or 'very often' (5), missing key areas such as those detailed in the next paragraph. These referrals can take time away from more pressing needs and sometimes subject patients to a psychiatric assessment which is not needed and not asked for by the patient. Identifying trends in the referral structure creates a shared platform for clarifying what information is helpful to the team and how it can be embedded routinely in referrals.

There is often very little or missing clinical information; insufficient preliminary assessment with no working diagnosis or impression; limited understanding of the purpose of the referral (what is the question being asked?); and the desired outcome of the assessment is unclear (how can the mental health CL team help?).

The CL team's aims and expectations can be advertised through regular educational events and training sessions. In addition, publication of the roles and remit of the team, as well as expected referral criteria, can be advertised on hospital electronic systems and team policy documents or included on the referral form itself. The principles of SBAR (situation, background, assessment, recommendations) can be used to make a robust referral to any specialty team (6). An example of using SBAR is demonstrated in Figure 1.2.

Organisational Aspects of the Referral; Prioritising and Allocating

Once the referral has been accepted, there are some pieces of information which help to triage its priority and plan the assessment. Firstly, we need to know where the referral is coming from. Most referrals will come either from the wards or from the emergency

SITUATION:	BACKGROUND:	ASSESSMENT:	RECOMMENDATION:
47-year-old lady on the general surgical ward admitted with perforated duodenal ulcer 2 weeks ago. On IV antibiotics.	History of depression. Was being treated with sertraline by her GP. Has had counselling in the past. Lives with husband and 12-year-old daughter. Teacher.	On the ward, presenting as very low and tearful. Struggling with nutrition and mobilisation.	I would appreciate some advice regarding treatment of low mood; perhaps medications or talking therapy. Goal is to improve recovery to aid discharge home.

Figure 1.2 Example of referral using SBAR (situation, background, assessment, recommendations).

department (ED). Assessments for patients in the ED need to be started within 1 hour from the point of referral and within 24 hours for ward referrals (7). There will occasionally be urgent referrals from the wards which require a prompter response, for example a patient with mental illness and risks to self who is asking to self-discharge.

It is also important to know who is referring the patient. This not only helps on a practical level to ensure good communication and feedback after the assessment but also gives some important information which may help to anticipate the priorities of the referral. This will help to allocate the assessment to the appropriate practitioner if available. For example, a referral from a social worker requesting support with discharge planning may be best taken by a mental health social worker, whereas a consultant geriatrician may ask for medication advice which is best given to a doctor or a non-medical prescriber.

Alternative Sources of Referrals

There are occasionally referrals from other sources. Sometimes referrals come from the outpatient clinic, for example when a patient incidentally presents with unusual behaviour or expresses suicidal ideation when attending for a routine medical appointment. In this circumstance, different organisations will have different protocols, but they usually involve the CL team arranging to see the patient either in a designated room in the outpatient clinic or in the ED. If the patient is reluctant to attend the ED or speak with a member of the CL team, the mental health practitioner may have to support the staff in the outpatient clinic to risk-assess the situation and make appropriate onward plans, for example asking the primary care physician to monitor the patient's mental state or to assess whether a more urgent intervention is required.

Similar phone calls may be received from other agencies outside of the hospital. In some services the mental health hotline, crisis team or single point of access may manage these calls, but in other healthcare providers the CL team may be required to provide advice. Paramedics may call expressing concerns about a patient who is refusing to come to hospital for assessment. The role of the CL practitioner would be to support the referring clinician in risk-assessing and assessing the patient's capacity to refuse to come for assessment. Primary care physicians may also call for advice. The role of the CL team is to support assessment of urgency and to signpost to the relevant team for further assessment, whether this is a recommendation to attend the ED, make a referral to the crisis team, speak to the on-call psychiatrist for out-of-hours medication advice or make a routine referral to community services, among other options.

The police are another agency that have very frequent contact with the CL team. They may simply be calling for collateral information or may be bringing a patient for a mental health assessment either voluntarily or under a police holding power (Section 136 in England). If the police are bringing a patient under a Section 136, it is important to establish several things. *Firstly, what is going to happen if the patient is not deemed to need mental health admission? Can they be discharged or do they need to go back to police custody? Are they under the influence of any substances or alcohol?* If they are intoxicated and at risk of withdrawals, the patient needs to attend the ED rather than a Section 136 Suite, as there is instant access to medical care. *Is there any suspicion of an overdose or a medical illness?* Again, they will need to go to the ED for medical management in parallel with psychiatric assessment. *Is the person particularly aggressive or agitated?* This helps to establish if they are best managed in the Section 136 Suite or the ED, whether the police are going to be asked to stay until the outcome of the assessment, whether the assessment needs to be performed in pairs and whether additional security measures will be required. Although the mental health law is explicit about the use of police holding powers, the practicalities of these assessments vary geographically. These are only preliminary considerations and it is best to consult local policies for the procedural aspects of managing patients detained by police.

Preparation: Distilling Key Questions and Reviewing Background Information

As previously discussed, a helpful referral will be asking a specific question or presenting a specific dilemma. It is important to understand what is being asked; if this is not clear, it is prudent to seek clarity from the referring team so that the emphasis of the assessment is appropriate. It is also interesting to know why the question is being asked now. *What has changed? Is a mental health concern creating a potential barrier to recovery?* It may be straightforward to carry out an assessment acknowledging someone is depressed. The real skill of the CL practitioner is to understand what is contributing to this depression (long hospital admission, missing one's partner, etc.) and how low mood is impacting their engagement with physiotherapy and thus preventing discharge. The question needs to be clear prior to assessment so the consultation can be goal-orientated and contribute to problem-solving. The literature on specific referrals received is limited (9); based on the experience of our team, common examples are summarised in Table 1.1.

Review of Medical Notes

Prior to seeing the patient, it is good to gather as much information as possible. One place to start is exploring the patient's current hospital admission. Not all hospitals have entirely electronic systems and not all CL services have access to the full electronic patient record (EPR), but this is the case for many services and should be aspired to for others, as there is much information which will support diagnostically and with management planning. Those services which do not have access to the EPR will have to rely on exploration of the paper medical notes and looking at bedside information, such as drugs charts and observations. Verbal handover with the medical teams will also be paramount in these circumstances to ensure all relevant background is available for the assessment. As access to the EPR is the standard to be aspired to, I will proceed as though this is a given, but the following information can be gained through the other means mentioned.

Table 1.1 Common referrals to consultation-liaison services

Older adult wards	• Cognitive deficit: diagnostic assessment (delirium versus dementia) – support prognostically and for discharge planning
	• Known dementia with troublesome behavioural and psychological symptoms of dementia: medication advice
	• Troublesome delirium: medication advice
	• Known dementia and no longer managing at home: advice regarding capacity and placements
	• Poor engagement with rehab or nutrition: diagnostic assessment +/– treatment of mood (particularly social isolation or long hospital admissions)
General medical wards	• Suicidal ideation or self-harm – either prompting admission or during admission: risk assessment
	• Long admission and concerns about mood: medication advice and signposting to psychology
	• Patients with severe mental illness with community mental health team input or patients admitted medically from psychiatric hospital: general review of mental state and responding to concerns
	• Issues with compliance with treatment plan: support with capacity assessments (mainly to determine if evidence of underlying mental disorder)
	• Adjustment disorders: planning advice and community referrals
Accident and emergency	• Self-harm or suicidal ideation/acts
	• Relapse mental illness
	• First-presentation mental illness

Tip

Paramedic notes are often overlooked and can give you vitally important information about how a patient presented medically and from a mental health point of view prior to arrival in hospital.

Current Presentation

When did the patient come to hospital and why did they come? Is this an acute illness or has there been a gradual deterioration? Did they call for help themselves or has someone else expressed concern? It is important to know whether they have been admitted for a primary psychiatric reason, a primary medical reason or something in between. This may give an indication as to the patient's current health priority, providing a focus for the assessment. From a practical point of view, it also helps as a guide to how long a patient is likely to be in hospital, as uncomplicated primary psychiatric presentations do not usually need to be in the general hospital for very long. This helps to prioritise referrals and organise timings of assessments.

Progress throughout Admission

You can then proceed to understanding the patient's journey in hospital so far. Patients can have very long admissions by the time they come to the attention of the CL team, so it is not always practical or time efficient to read all the medical notes. It is, however, very helpful to know all the major events during the admission. Not only does this give longitudinal information for diagnostic purposes, it also helps to understand what the patient has experienced and can be helpful if the patient has questions. If the CL practitioner has the competencies to do so, they may be able to give broad details to the patient, such as 'you are waiting for test results' or 'you have been treated for an infection', which the treating team may not have had the opportunity to communicate well previously. Helping patients understand what we would consider small details can be hugely therapeutic. The knowledge that a person has been in intensive care, has received a diagnosis of cancer or has been in hospital away from their partner for three months can begin a formulation as to why the patient is experiencing difficulties. This information can be quickly obtained by reading the ED assessment or admission clerking, post-take ward round and the most recent ward round entry, though further notes may need to be consulted for clarity.

Multidisciplinary Team (MDT) Notes

Occupational therapists and physiotherapists have often already taken collateral information from relatives. They will also usually have taken very detailed social histories. They are usually the members of the team who comment on motivation and engagement. They also often complete cognitive tests when concerned. Social workers may have provided information about current care arrangements or care placements. Nursing staff spend the most time with patients and often document behaviours well, including out of hours. They may also have developed the best rapport with patients and so are privy to more intimate and personal details. Make sure to look for notes about discussions with relatives, as this can provide a lot of information, give an idea as to a person's support in the community and help to understand the most pressing concerns and anxieties affecting a family. Although we have one primary patient, a good deal of therapeutic work is supporting people *and* their loved ones.

Investigations

Depending on the clinical scenario, it is usually appropriate to look at a patient's investigations. The reasons for looking at these investigations clearly differ, but common scenarios will help to demonstrate. For example, a patient may have presented with confusion and the ward want a diagnostic opinion. A significant proportion of the assessment will be about good history-taking and gathering collateral information, but investigations can provide meaningful supporting evidence. The blood tests may show raised inflammatory markers, indicating infection, or deficits in vitamin B12 or folate, or hypothyroidism, among other changes. Likewise, septic screens in the form of chest x-rays, lumbar punctures and urinalysis may indicate the presence or absence of an infection. These lend weight to a diagnosis of delirium. The bloods and septic screen may be normal but delirium still present, so this is not diagnostic; it is merely supporting. In addition, brain imaging may show chronic vascular changes or atrophy beyond expected for the patient's age, which may raise suspicion of an underlying dementia. Another scenario that highlights the utility of appraising investigation results is the referral requesting medication advice regarding psychotropics such as lithium and antipsychotics. It is imperative to look at baseline blood tests – possibly drug levels and ECGs. Blood tests, including drug levels, can also help to ascertain compliance with medication, which again can contribute meaningfully to the risk assessment. In cases of overdoses of medication such as paracetamol, investigations help to give an indication of the severity of the overdose, which not only guides medical management but also contributes meaningfully to the risk assessment.

Medication Chart

The next source of information to be examined is the medication chart. This can offer a wealth of information. *Firstly, what are the regular medications the patient is prescribed?* This gives an indication of their past medical and psychiatric history. There may also be regular medications which are potential contributors to the current presentation, such as medication with profound anticholinergic effects in a case of confusion. It is important to also know what is new, as these are the most likely offenders. Numerous medications prescribed in the acute setting have psychiatric consequences, such as steroid-induced psychosis, depression associated with some antiepileptics and perceptual abnormalities associated with dopamine agonists. Although medication reconciliation is not the primary role of the CL practitioner, the assessment is another opportunity to ensure that vital medications are not being missed. Depot injection medications have a high risk of being missed as they will not come with the patient in their medicines box and are not always on the primary care physician medications list. Another very important part of reviewing the medication chart is to review medication compliance, as previously mentioned.

Primary Care Physician Care Record

Yet another source of information is the primary care physician care record. Not all areas have an integrated care record, but where it is available it can be a good source of collateral information. It is likely to give some idea of the patient's baseline and may provide information regarding the onset of the current illness, as well as confirming medications, past medical history and so forth. If there is no integrated care record and the patient is not known to mental health services, it is imperative to get some collateral information from the primary care physician by direct contact.

Medical State on the Day and Barriers to Progress

The next questions pertain to the patient's current medical status and the barriers to further improvement. The patient may now be medically optimised but awaiting psychiatric review prior to discharge. This patient should be prioritised for review as they could potentially return home. Patients may simply still need ongoing medical treatment as they are still unwell or commonly may be medically optimised but awaiting social care packages. In these cases, there may be a little more time to review, gather further information and organise a management plan. The CL team is often recruited during this time as there are perceived barriers to the patient's recovery. For example, a common question is whether low mood is affecting patient motivation to engage with physiotherapy and whether an intervention to improve mood would promote their engagement.

Another common question is whether a patient is likely to recover from their confusion (delirium) or whether discharge planning needs to take into account a longitudinal cognitive issue (dementia). Providing this diagnostic assessment contributes meaningfully to their care plan. In essence, understanding the current medical situation and barriers to recovery helps to focus the input of the CL team such that a meaningful contribution can be made to advancing the patient's journey. It also gives an idea of the length of time available to deliver interventions and support. If a patient is to remain in hospital for a while, we can do some short-term psychological work, commence and monitor medication or do serial cognitive tests. The expectations of the management plan would be more streamlined if the patient is likely to go home in the next couple of days, with the emphasis on ensuring onward community referrals.

Review of Psychiatric Notes

Psychiatric notes can be extensive, but there are key pieces of information that can be rapidly distilled (Table 1.2). *Firstly, is the patient known to mental health services?* An absence of notes on the psychiatric care record does not necessarily mean the patient has no past psychiatric history. It is important to get collateral information. An obvious source is the primary care physician, as previously mentioned. It is also often necessary to contact mental health services in other local areas. For example, some CL services are based in tertiary centres where patients come from a huge geographic area, so their psychiatric services will also be based out of the area. Some patients have a pattern of presenting to numerous different ED departments, particularly in population-dense areas where there are

Table 1.2 Summary of preparatory work prior to assessment

Medical records	Reason for and circumstances of current admission
	Progress throughout admission
	Multidisciplinary team notes
	Investigations
	Medication chart
	Presentation on the day of assessment
Primary care physician records	Any recent contact with primary care physician
	Confirmation of medications and diagnosis
	Baseline mental state
Psychiatric records	Diagnosis/formulation
	Do they have a team? Do they have a care coordinator?
	Previous admissions? Under section? Informal? When was last admission? Are they on a community treatment order?
	Risk history and severity of previous risks
	Recent circumstances and stressors
	Any indication of worsening of mental state
	Do they have a care plan? Do they have a crisis plan?

several large hospitals in very close proximity that may belong to different healthcare providers and organisations. Additionally, patients may have recently moved into the area, so their historical records are based elsewhere.

When examining the psychiatric care record or asking for salient collateral information from another mental healthcare provider, there are a few key pieces of information to look out for. *Does the person have a diagnosis or a formulation? Are they under a community mental health team and what level of support do they receive from the team? Do they have a care coordinator?* If they do, it is usually helpful to speak with them, as they should have the best historical knowledge of the patient, as well as an up-to-date appraisal of the patient's recent mental state and any current concerns. It is also important to know what level of support can be reasonably expected by the care team in the community to help facilitate discharge planning.

There are several important historical factors to look for in the notes. *Are there previous diagnostic formulations and treatment regimens, including adverse effects? Has the patient had previous admissions or periods under home-based treatment teams? Are they on a community treatment order? What are the major historical risks and how severe have they been? Are there any forensic implications?* Not only does this help to build a picture of a person, but it will also help when deciding how to conduct the assessment in the ED or on the ward. If there are significant risks, considerations need to be made, such as assessments in pairs, the presence of security, the particulars of the assessment room and so forth. *Are they a frequent attender of the ED? What usually helps?* Once these key historical details have been distilled, it is important to ascertain the current circumstances. Look at the most recent contacts or clinic letters. *Have concerns arisen about deteriorating mental state? Have there been concerns about medication adherence or engagement with the community team? Have there been any significant social changes or stressors? What is the current care plan? Is there a crisis care plan or any indication of what helps this particular person in times of need?*

Assessment

Although the foregoing sounds like a lot of preparation, it is a fairly swift process, especially once well practised. Taking the time to do the preparation demonstrates to a patient that you are interested and have taken care to learn about them, prevents patients having to repeat potentially traumatizing chunks of their history and contributes to a holistic and patient-centred assessment. It allows the CL practitioner to shape the focus of the assessment before meeting the patient, which should lead to a well-structured and concise review.

Where to Carry Out the Assessment

The final part of preparation is working out where to do the assessment. In an ideal assessment, a space should be provided which offers privacy and is safe. In the ED there should be a dedicated room or set of rooms which meet a certain standard for safety and privacy, for example being free of ligature points and potential missiles, with multiple entries and exits, and equipped with alarms (10). If all these rooms are in use, it is very likely that a non-specialist room will be used, so all efforts should be made to ensure safety, for example orientation of the room and proximity to the door, access to personal alarms, reviews in pairs or with security available and letting colleagues know where you are. In the general ward, patients can often be seen in the day room or family room and similar considerations have to be made. There are many circumstances where this is not possible, however, such as unwell older patients with dementia or delirium who are bedbound. The assessment then has to be undertaken at the bedside but should be performed sensitively with consideration of the fact that curtains are not soundproofed.

Handover from Nursing Team or One-to-One Staff

At this juncture, take a handover from the nurse looking after the patient that day or the support staff if they are being nursed on a one-to-one basis. This will give the most up-to-date assessment of the patient's health and behaviour, as well as highlighting any risks or new concerns. If patients do have a member of staff carrying out one-to-one observations with them, it is usually appropriate to ask the staff member to leave while you conduct the assessment to maintain privacy. If there are significant risks, however, this will not be possible. On some occasions, family members may also be present. Again, unless there is a clear reason not to, it is prudent to see patients alone in the first instance and then invite family to join later with the patient's consent. The patient should always be given the opportunity for a private assessment, even if they ultimately choose to request their family members remain.

Patient Assessment

Finally, we have reached the point of assessment. Once you are with the patient, it is important to introduce yourself and your role and explain why you have come to do an assessment. Although patients should always be made aware that they have been referred to the CL team and should always have consented if they have capacity, this is not always the case. For some, even the mention of mental health can hold stigma, so it is sometimes necessary to contextualize your role and explain how you might be able to help. It helps to ascertain if now is the best time to see the patient. *Does the patient have plenty of time to talk before lunch? Are they imminently going for a scan? Are they in pain or nauseated? Have they just received bad news that they need time to process?* This can usually be determined by checking with the patient that they feel comfortable and are happy to engage in a conversation right now. Make sure to take a chair and sit with the patient. This demonstrates that you are not just hovering for a few minutes but are committed to spending time with them. It is usually a good idea to let a patient know that you have a general idea of their background, so they do not feel the burden of having to explain everything all over again.

The assessment itself is no different from psychiatric assessments (Table 1.3) in any other setting but, as previously mentioned, there are certain areas which may take more of the focus than others and this will be led by the patient. Be open in your questioning style and allow patients to discuss their priorities. Some specific information will be needed, such as risk assessment, and this can be introduced sensitively by explaining that there are certain questions which are routinely asked. Once the assessment part of the encounter is concluded, a plan needs to be established with the patient. Always ask the patient what they think will help. This is not always possible or achievable as some may simply not know and some may not be able to communicate their needs; finding out what is important to a person is vital when forming a plan. There is a huge range of options of interventions and different services will approach follow-up differently. Capacity assessments are dealt with in more detail in Chapter 16.

Table 1.3 Basics of a psychiatric history and mental state examination

Psychiatric history	Mental state examination
Presenting complaint	**Appearance and behaviour:** Self-care, eye contact, agitation, appropriate clothing, psychomotor activity, guarded/engaged
History of presenting complaint	**Speech:** Rate, tone, rhythm, volume
Past psychiatric history	**Mood:** Subjective, objective
Past medical history	**Thought:** Form and content
Medications	**Perceptions:** All five modalities; subjective, objective
Drugs and alcohol	**Cognition:** Formal or informal; memory, orientation, attention, concentration
Family history	**Insight:** Good, limited, poor, none
Social history	**Capacity:** Decision- and time-specific (see Chapter 19)
Personal history	
Forensic history	
Pre-morbid personality	

Tip

Although it is tempting in a time-pressured environment to record a list, if you are reviewing a patient with a chronic condition, it is worth spending some time asking them about their journey with the condition. This can provide valuable information regarding adjustment to any role loss or change and level of resilience, coping strategies, hopes/fears both now and for the future, how mental health difficulties may have become shaped by the condition or indeed triggered by living with it and whether relationships with family and friends have changed (see Chapter 4).

Getting Collateral

It is usually best to get collateral from family and friends after seeing a patient. By this point, the CL practitioner will have the best sense of who to talk to and also be able to discuss this with the patient. Consent is not required to simply gather information, and sometimes it is necessary to go against a person's wishes if there are risks involved. However, the patient is at the centre of their care, so it makes sense that they should be asked about this part of their care plan. If specific consent is given to share information, it can be very reassuring for family members, rather than calling simply to take information without giving anything back. The COVID-19 pandemic has been particularly challenging for patients and relatives because of the suspension of visiting in hospitals. Relatives rely on staff for updates about their loved ones, so some of the role of taking a collateral history may actually be about providing information and reassurance where appropriate.

A lot of collateral information will already have been gained by this point from the primary care physician, psychiatric and medical notes, members of the multidisciplinary team and observation in hospital, but families are usually the most persistently involved in a person's everyday life and hopefully understand their priorities and wishes best. Relatives can be asked to corroborate information already given by the patient and express their concerns about the patient's mental state or ability to manage prior to admission. For patients who cannot currently communicate because of their illness, families are often vital participants in best-interests discussions in order to formulate treatment plans.

Assessments in Specialist Circumstances

Certain assessments will require some modifications because of specific communication difficulties. Patients may speak limited, if any, English and an interpreter will then be required. All efforts should be made to acquire a face-to-face interpreter, but this is not always achievable and telephone interpretation may have to be used. Using family or friends as interpreters is not good practice as it introduces the risk of misinterpretation, either deliberately or accidentally. Assessments with interpreters will always take more time, so this needs to be planned for when organising the assessment. Make sure to speak to your patient, not the interpreter. It is still possible to build good rapport and engagement by ensuring good eye contact, using the appropriate tone of voice and demonstrating non-verbal communication and active listening.

Some people may have a disability or different communication preferences, which means modifications must be made. Make sure people have their hearing aids or their false teeth in if appropriate to maximise their ability to communicate. If people have speech or hearing impairments but no major cognitive deficit, written communication may be more appropriate, using whiteboards or pens and paper. Speech and language therapists and occupational therapists may be able to support with advice about specific communication aids. It may be helpful to recruit family members, who will be more familiar with a person's communication preferences. All efforts should be made to maximise a person's potential to communicate their needs.

Acquired brain injury, dementia, learning disabilities and autism spectrum disorders can be associated with cognitive impairment and/or nuanced communication styles, which may require sensitive reframing of questions and information to maximise understanding. Family members are often good at helping to shape questions into a format that will be understood, as well as interpreting response patterns. Aim for short, clear, simple phrases that require fairly closed answers until you get a better sense of your patient's communication style, and be aware of the possibility of indiscriminate yes/no answers.

Intervention

Feeding Back to the Treating Teams: Verbal and Written Communication

Once the assessment has finished, it is important to have clear communication with the treating team to share your impression and suggest interventions. It is best practice to have a verbal handover, particularly where urgent matters or risk are involved. Verbal communication also allows questions and concerns to be shared mutually and fosters good working relationships between the CL and medical/surgical teams.

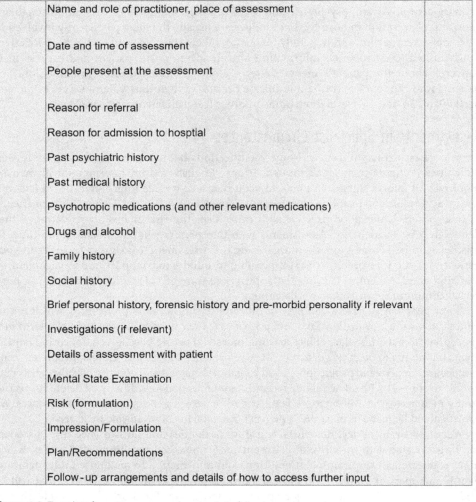

Name and role of practitioner, place of assessment

Date and time of assessment

People present at the assessment

Reason for referral

Reason for admission to hosptial

Past psychiatric history

Past medical history

Psychotropic medications (and other relevant medications)

Drugs and alcohol

Family history

Social history

Brief personal history, forensic history and pre-morbid personality if relevant

Investigations (if relevant)

Details of assessment with patient

Mental State Examination

Risk (formulation)

Impression/Formulation

Plan/Recommendations

Follow-up arrangements and details of how to access further input

Figure 1.3 Template for writing a comprehensive note following assessment.

A clear and robust written note is also required after each assessment and an example document can be seen in Figure 1.3. While this is an important source of information, it is often impractical for medical and nursing staff on busy wards to read a document of this length. As such, a brief summary paragraph at the *beginning* of your documentation should be included with clearly defined headings (diagnostic impression, salient risks identified, management plan, follow-up arrangements).

Many patients disclose very personal and intimate details, so be mindful that what is being written will be seen by many and some details are not necessary. Where particularly sensitive information is being shared in a consultation, it is good practice to let a patient know what you intend to write in the notes and to ask whether they would prefer some details to be omitted. Unless there is a risk issue, this can be a perfectly reasonable request.

Table 1.4 Approach to a bio-psycho-social-spiritual formulation

	Likely to see in consultation-liaison setting	Others
Biological	Chronic illness Current illness Medications Substances Family history	Family history Birth history Genetics
Psychological	Impact of illness on quality of life Psychological impact of a new diagnosis Adjustment disorder	Past psychiatric history Past trauma
Social	Being away from family Reduced ability to do activities of daily living Loss of routine	Housing issues Debt or financial issues Social isolation Limited support network
Spiritual	May be facing end of life or lifelimiting illness Limits of illness on meaningful activity Hope or hopelessness	Faith Organised religion

Formulation

The summing-up of your documentation will be a formulation or impression. This will already have been informally discussed with the patient during the consultation, but a more structured written formulation can help with communication and shared understanding. We very frequently use the bio-psycho-social model in psychiatry, or even a bio-psycho-social-spiritual model, with spirituality not referring to religion but the way a person finds meaning in life (11). Table 1.4 shows some examples of contributors to a bio-psycho-social-spiritual formulation.

Case example: Mary has been in hospital for 12 weeks with pneumonia (biological). She has been very unwell and has suffered from physical deconditioning over the course of the admission (biological). She misses her husband (social) and being in hospital reminds her of her mother passing 10 years ago (psychological). She is desperate to get home but is very upset that she will not be able to look after her husband anymore (social/spiritual). She worries about the meaning of her life now that she cannot do as much (spiritual). This has contributed to her feeling low in mood and hopeless. She will not engage with physiotherapy as she does not see the point.

The interventions required need to focus on Mary's belief that she has lost meaning/purpose, helping her find a new meaning or a way to understand that she is still a meaningful partner even if her role has changed. Psychological interventions can help her to understand that the contributing factors of being in hospital, away from husband and where her mum died, are temporary and there is potential reversibility in her deconditioning. A formulation helps to understand why she feels like this and give a goal-orientated approach to encourage engagement and eventually returning home.

Table 1.5 Approach to the Five Ps formulation

Presenting issue	What is the problem?
Predisposing factors	What makes this person at risk of becoming unwell? Examples: coping strategies, previous trauma, family history, chronic illness, lack of social support
Precipitating factors	What has contributed to the presentation now? What is the trigger? Examples: acute illness, major stressor such as loss of job, homelessness, bereavements
Perpetuating factors	What is keeping the problem going? Examples: maladaptive coping strategies, resistant social issues (such as debt, probation, relationships), ongoing substance use
Protective factors	What keeps a person going? What gives their life meaning?

Another way to approach formulation is the 'Five Ps' (Table 1.5) (12). This can be used either for general formulation or for risk formulation. These Five Ps (presenting issue, predisposing factors, precipitating factors, perpetuating factors, protective factors) can in turn be broken down into a bio-psycho-social framework. Some authors advocate for a bio-psycho-social-spiritual formulation where appropriate (11). Again, using formulation gives a much more nuanced impression, helps to understand an individual's specific needs and helps to work out goal-orientated solutions.

Example: Mary is feeling low in mood. She has no significant past psychiatric history and has had consistent and supportive relationships with her family and her husband. Sadly, her mum died 10 years ago and since then she has been more prone to feeling low (predisposing). Mary started to feel low 6 weeks into admission, as she misses her husband and is feeling very unwell with pneumonia (precipitating). She continues to feel unwell and needs to stay in hospital, and this is preventing her getting back home to her husband and routine (perpetuating). This in turn is making her feel hopeless; she cannot find the motivation to engage in physiotherapy and so sees no progress towards going home (perpetuating).

Recommendations

Broadly speaking, the interventions that are likely to be offered are medications advice; recommendations regarding investigations; referrals to inpatient psychology; referrals to chaplaincy; referrals to community care, whether in primary or secondary care services; referrals to support services for social activation; social care plans; and even possibly psychiatric inpatient admission, to name but a few. There is always room for advocating for patients and it may be that the main intervention is about expressing to the treating team that the patient is not eating as they only eat tomato soup or that they desperately need to get home to look after their aged cat. CL practitioners often have the most time to get to know what is meaningful to a person and this cannot be underestimated.

Follow-Up: Inpatient

For some patients, a single consultation and advice is all that is required, but many will need ongoing input from the CL team throughout their admission. It is important to explain to the patient whether they are likely to be reviewed again to manage expectations, and also to let them know how to access further support while on the ward (clinical psychology, chaplaincy, alcohol and substance misuse CL nursing). Ensure that the ward staff are aware of your plans for follow-up and have a contact number to request further support if needed in the future.

Arranging Follow-Up on Discharge

This requires careful thought and services will vary considerably depending on geographic location. Inpatient admission, brief stays in crisis houses (it is worth checking to see if there are any local to the patient if this is relevant to the presentation) and interventions from home-based treatment teams are generally reserved for severely unwell patients and/or those with salient risk issues that cannot be managed with less intensive input. For patients that require outpatient follow-up, not all will be suitable for community mental health team input, which is generally reserved for patients with affective and psychotic disorders and anxiety disorders (some teams also have a personality disorder pathway). For patients with functional disorders, difficulties adjusting to physical illness or psychiatric sequelae as a result of organic disease, options in the UK generally include clinical health psychology, CL outpatient clinics in both primary and secondary care, specialist functional disorder clinics and neuropsychiatry. Service commissioning for these patient groups is somewhat complex and disjointed across the UK, and as such it is worth making enquiries locally, regionally and even nationally sometimes as neighbouring regions can differ widely in terms of provision.

References

1. World Health Organization. Excess mortality in persons with severe mental disorders. Geneva; 2015.

2. Ronaldson A, Elton L, Jayakumar S et al. Severe mental illness and health service utilisation for nonpsychiatric medical disorders: A systematic review and meta-analysis. *PLoS Med.* 2020;**17**(9): e1003284.

3. National Institute for Health and Care Excellence. Consultation-liaison psychiatry emergency and acute medical care in over 16s: Service delivery and organisation. London; 2017.

4. Parsonage M, Fossey M, Tutty C. Liaison psychiatry in the modern NHS. London; 2012. www.centreformentalhealth.org.uk/sites/default/files/2018-09/Liaison_psychiatry_in_the_modern_NHS_2012_0.pdf.

5. Imison C, Naylor C. Referral management: Lessons for success. London; 2010.

6. NHS Improvement. SBAR Communication Tool: Situation, background, assessment, recommendation. London; 2018. https://improvement.nhs.uk/documents/2162/sbar-communication-tool.pdf.

7. Royal College of Psychiatrists. College Report 183 Liaison Psychiatry for every acute hospital: Integrated mental and physical healthcare. London; 2013.

8. Becker L, Saunders R, Hardy R, Pilling S. The RAID model of consultation-liaison psychiatry: Report on the evaluation of four pilot services in East London. London; 2016.

9. Guthrie E, McMeekin A, Thomasson R et al. Opening the 'black box': Consultation-liaison psychiatry services and what they actually do. *BJPsych Bulletin.* 2016;**40**(4):175–80.

10. Baugh C, Blanchard E, Hopkins I. Psychiatric Consultation-Liaison

Accreditation Network (PLAN) Quality Standards for Consultation-Liaison Psychiatry Services, 6th ed. London; 2020.

11. Saad M, Medeiros R de, Mosini AC. Are we ready for a true biopsychosocial–spiritual model? The many meanings of 'spiritual'. *Medicines*. 2017;4(4):1–6.

12. Macneil CA, Hasty MK, Conus P, Berk M. Is diagnosis enough to guide interventions in mental health? Using case formulation in clinical practice. *BMC Med*. 2012;10:111.

Chapter

2

Notes on Training Pathways in Consultation-Liaison Psychiatry

Faye Stanage and Gregory Carter

Introduction

Consultation-liaison (CL) psychiatry was first recognised as a subspecialty of adult psychiatry in the UK in the 1980s (1). Training in psychiatry (as for all specialties) is overseen by the General Medical Council (GMC) and the curriculum in CL psychiatry is designed by the Royal College of Psychiatrists (RCPsych). It is subject to regular review and update. It provides a framework and identifies competencies which need to be achieved in order to attain credentials to practise independently. In this chapter we will explore the UK curriculum in detail and consider ways in which trainees could evidence how they achieve their competencies through their Personal Development Plan (PDP) and RCPsych portfolio. We will also briefly discuss training in CL psychiatry in a number of other countries around the world (see also Chapter 26 in this volume). All psychiatry training curricula in the UK have recently been revised (August 2022).

Training in Psychiatry: The Pathway from Medical School Graduate to Consultant

In order to become an independently practising consultant psychiatrist in the UK, one must first complete a two-year foundation programme on graduation from medical school. The foundation programme (2) covers a broad range of medical and surgical specialties (not necessarily including psychiatry) and after the first year leads to full registration with the GMC, the medical regulatory body. Following foundation programme completion, trainees can apply for specialty training. In psychiatry this is separated into core and higher training. Selection for both is competitive and based on an application form and interview. Applicants are ranked nationally and successful candidates 'matched' to their programme of choice.

Core training is a three-year full-time equivalent scheme whereby trainees rotate through six separate six-month placements in several subspecialties of psychiatry. These provide the trainee with a broad range of psychiatric experience and the fundamentals of the discipline. It is expected that during this time the trainees will complete the RCPsych exams for membership of RCPsych. This exam and completion of core training are the minimum requirements for eligibility for higher training.

In the UK there are higher training opportunities in six psychiatric subspecialties (general adult psychiatry, old-age psychiatry, child and adolescent psychiatry, forensic psychiatry, medical psychotherapy, and psychiatry of intellectual disability). Following completion of core training, trainees must choose which subspecialty in which they would like to complete their higher training. It is also possible to complete dual training, where two subspecialties are chosen, although opportunities for this do vary around the country.

Higher training in a single subspecialty is also completed over three years and consists of three 12-month placements. One of the placements in general adult psychiatry can be completed in a subspecialty (addiction psychiatry, rehabilitation psychiatry and CL psychiatry), which leads to an endorsement for this particular skillset. It is also possible to complete an endorsement in CL psychiatry when completing higher training in old-age psychiatry.

Higher trainees seeking an endorsement in CL psychiatry will undertake their year-long placement in an RCPsych-approved post. It is important to note that trainees are expected to follow both their chosen specialty (general adult or old-age psychiatry) and CL curricula, as they are still expected to show progression in the former at the Annual Review of Competencies Panel at the end of their training year. These meetings assess whether trainees have demonstrated satisfactory achievement of competencies over the course of the year and the panel make a recommendation on whether they can progress to the next stage of training.

Completion of a GMC-approved training programme leads to the award of the Certificate of Completion of Training (CCT) and entry on to the GMC Specialist Register. This gives the clinician the eligibility to commence the role of consultant psychiatrist and work as an independent practitioner in both the public and private sectors.

Obtaining a Credential in Consultation-Liaison Psychiatry after Completing Training

There is currently a framework approved by the GMC for consultant psychiatrists to undertake a standardised post-CCT credential in liaison psychiatry (10). The curriculum for this is broadly similar to the new curriculum for the endorsement other than the omission of the outcomes that the doctor would have already met, and evidenced, in order to complete their training. This allows psychiatrists to further subspecialise after their training is complete in their original specialty.

Curriculum Structure

The current CL psychiatry curriculum was published in August 2022 (3). A review was undertaken to ensure that the most up-to-date standards set by the GMC were being met (4, 5) and to ensure that training programmes are kept in line with the principles of the 'Shape of Training' review (6). For instance, 'education and training should be based on the demonstration of capabilities, not simply time served, although time and experience remain important elements' (6). It was also felt that transparency in training outcomes was essential for others to understand the level of competency that doctors have attained.

This most recent revision of the CL psychiatry curriculum is based on the GMC's Generic Professional Capabilities Framework (7) which replaces the CanMEDS structure used previously (8). This document outlines what are considered to be the 'essential generic capabilities needed for safe, effective and high quality medical care in the UK' and applies to all clinical specialties. Educational outcomes are based on the principles and professional responsibilities that all doctors are required to possess. There are nine educational outcomes, or 'Generic Professional Capabilities (GPC) domains', which have been incorporated into the new curriculum (Table 2.1).

Each of these nine domains is linked to a High-Level Outcome. These are the overarching objectives a trainee needs to complete over the course of specialty training. These link

Table 2.1 Overview of the 2022 consultation–liaison psychiatry curriculum

	GPC domain	High-Level Outcome
1	Professional values and behaviours	Demonstrate the professional values and behaviours required of a consultant psychiatrist, with reference to good medical practice, core values for psychiatrists (CR204) and other relevant faculty guidance.
2	Professional skills	Demonstrate advanced communication and interpersonal skills when engaging with patients, their families, carers of all ages, their wider community, colleagues and other professionals.
		Demonstrate advanced skills in the psychiatric assessment, formulation, diagnosis and person-centred holistic management of an appropriate range of presentations in a variety of clinical and non-clinical settings within liaison psychiatry.
		Apply advanced management skills within liaison psychiatry in situations of uncertainty, conflict and complexity across a wide range of clinical and non-clinical contexts.
3	Professional knowledge	Apply advanced knowledge of relevant legislative frameworks across the UK to safeguard patients and safely manage risk within liaison psychiatry.
		Work effectively within the structure and organisation of the NHS and the wider health and social care landscape.
4	Health promotion and illness prevention	Demonstrate leadership and advocacy in mental and physical health promotion and illness prevention for patients within liaison psychiatry and the wider community.
5	Leadership and teamworking	Demonstrate effective team working and leadership skills to work constructively and collaboratively within the complex health and social care systems that support people with mental disorder.
6	Patient safety and quality improvement	Identify, promote and lead activity to improve the safety and quality of patient care and clinical outcomes of a person with mental disorder.
7	Safeguarding vulnerable groups	Lead on the provision of psychiatric assessment and treatment of those who are identified as being vulnerable within liaison psychiatry.
		Demonstrate advocacy, leadership and collaborative working around vulnerability and safeguarding in patients, their families and their wider community.
8	Education and training	Promote and lead on the provision of effective education and training in clinical, academic and relevant multidisciplinary settings.
		Demonstrate effective supervision and mentoring skills as essential aspects of education to promote safe and effective learning environments.
9	Research and scholarship	Apply up-to-date advanced knowledge of research methodology, critical appraisal and best practice guidance to clinical practice, following ethical and good governance principles.

into Key Capabilities under each domain. These are mandatory requirements trainees are expected to achieve by the end of their training and can be found in full within the CL psychiatry curriculum (3). Trainees are also encouraged to consult the RCPsych report on core values for psychiatrists (9).

The Personal Development Plan

Given the time-limited nature of training, it is very unlikely that any trainee will be able to demonstrate competence in every Key Capability in the curriculum. It is therefore essential that they are instead able to demonstrate a broad range of competencies (11). At the start of each post, trainees should review the curriculum and begin to plan which competencies they would like (and are likely to be able) to demonstrate – and how to set about doing this – by creating some learning objectives. Integral to this process is the construction of a PDP. Not only does this help the individual to identify their own learning needs, it can also be used to set out how they are going to achieve their desired goals, and by when.

At the start of every placement, trainees are expected to develop their PDP with their assigned educational supervisor. In order to provide the best care for patients, it is essential to ensure that individual learning needs are constantly re-appraised and developed. The PDP effectively serves as a learning map for the coming year – a plan that can be set out, by the trainee, of desired achievements in the workplace, whether professional or personal, and how to reach them in the form of learning objectives. By reflecting on strengths and weaknesses (perhaps from previous assessments, PDPs or through discussion with colleagues), trainees can work these into their PDP while considering which outcomes would be relevant. It is also useful to set up a meeting with their clinical supervisor in order to explore opportunities that may be available during the placement. These do not need to be confined exclusively to the workplace, and indeed can include opportunities such as courses, conferences, special interest sessions and e-learning modules.

For UK trainees, this PDP is created within the RCPsych portfolio (12). This free, online portfolio is available to all members, affiliates and pre-membership psychiatric trainees of RCPsych. It allows trainees to complete an electronic record of their professional activities, development and achievements (12). This allows evidence of completion of certain activities, such as during workplace-based assessments (WPBAs), to be linked directly to learning objectives in order to demonstrate competence.

Constructing the Personal Development Plan

At the time of writing, the RCPsych portfolio PDP stipulates three components to each individual learning objective – a description of the learning objective, how it will be achieved and a target date for completion (12).

Table 2.2 presents a collection of examples for both trainees and supervisors that can be utilised to construct a PDP for a liaison psychiatry post. These examples are relevant to both the current and proposed curricula. Included here is an example of a PDP that a higher trainee in liaison psychiatry may keep. Indeed, it is simple to maintain a basic PDP, but it takes more thought to maintain one which will provide maximum benefit; for instance, including how a learning objective can help an individual's development and perhaps even reflecting on this following completion of the learning objective.

The target date for completion can be in the short, medium or long term, depending on the individual learning objective.

Table 2.2 Examples of Personal Development Plan objectives

Learning objective (GPC 2)	Learn about the varied presentations of delirium and demonstrate both the use of this knowledge and the skill in assessing and managing them. This is to include common overlapping of symptoms with psychiatric disorders such as depression and psychosis.
How it will be achieved	I will evidence this through the completion of case logs of patients with delirium, case-based discussion and completing supervised assessment of a patient with acute confusion to obtain feedback on my diagnostic approach.
Target date for completion	December 2023.
Learning objective (GPC 8)	Demonstrate the ability to provide clinical supervision to colleagues, as I want to develop this skill in preparation for consultant practice.
How it will be achieved	To be evidenced by completing a workplace-based assessment (being supervised in providing a session of supervision to a doctor in training) and completing at least one reflection on this provision. This may also be evidenced through my mini-Peer Assessment Tool (PAT).
Target date for completion	November 2023.
Learning objective (GPC 6)	Identify, and learn about, resources for supporting patients and their families with medically unexplained symptoms. I am not aware of any resources currently. This will help both myself and colleagues who I will be able to share the information with.
How it will be achieved	To be evidenced by the creation of/updating an existing Patient Information Leaflet that can be distributed in clinics/on the ward.
Target date for completion	January 2024.

Collecting Evidence for the Personal Development Plan

There are multiple forms of workplace assessments used within the UK RCPsych trainee portfolio (12). Examples of how these assessments, and others, can be used alongside the learning objectives in the curriculum can be found in Table 2.3. Other competencies which require evidencing, but which are not included in the trainee's development plan, can also be linked directly to assessments. Multiple assessments can be linked to the same Key Capabilities, allowing triangulation of evidence and demonstration of competence, and each assessment can be linked to multiple Key Capabilities in order to demonstrate multiple competencies.

Obtaining audit and research competencies can often be a source of anxiety. Early discussion during the liaison training post between trainee and supervisor enables timely identification of an audit topic and/or ideas for achieving research competencies. Common themes include audits on referral and assessment timelines, screening prescribing charts of referred patients for polypharmacy and anticholinergic burden, auditing lithium and clozapine monitoring in the general hospital setting, provision of care plans for patients presenting with self-harm, adherence to trust policies on management of patients with

Table 2.3 Mapping curriculum objectives to different types of workplace assessment

Curriculum domain	Examples of workplace assessments that could be used
1	Professional values and behaviours	Mini-PAT (peer assessment)
		Clinical supervisor's report
		Reflection
2	Professional skills	*Communication skills:*
	Considers practical skills, communication and interpersonal skills, dealing with complexity and uncertainty, clinical skills	Mini-PAT
		Mini-ACE of specialised assessments such as patients with oropharyngeal disease or neurological illness
		Explain psychological skills:
		CbD of the use of a psychological treatment relevant to the management of a patient in liaison psychiatry
		DONCS
		Patient assessment
		ACEs and CbDs of patients who have been fully assessed, including a collateral history from family/ friends/staff/involved agencies
		Mini-ACE of further specialised assessments such as of cognitive function
		CbD focusing on risk assessment in a complex patient, or discussion of management of psychiatric emergency while on call
		DONCS of arranging/chairing a multi-professional meeting/MDT for a complex case
		SAPE of undertaking a supervised psychotherapy case
		Complexity and uncertainty
		ACEs and CbDs of complex patients with diagnostic uncertainty, with a focus on management
		Attend Balint groups if available, or indeed consider setting one up in an appropriate setting with support where required
3	Professional knowledge	ACE and CbD of assessment and management of patient under the Mental Health Act while on call
	Professional requirements, national legislative requirements, the health service and healthcare system	CbD around the management of a patient on a medical/ surgical ward requiring application of a legal framework such as the Mental Capacity Act or the Mental Health Act

4	Capabilities in health promotion and illness prevention	Mini-PAT – collaborative working with colleagues in the physical healthcare setting Clinical supervisor report – challenging stigma within the physical healthcare setting
5	Capabilities in leadership and team working	Mini-PAT DONCS chairing meeting DONCS leading morning meeting and delegating jobs/assessments Provide clinical supervision to nursing team/junior colleagues where appropriate
6	Capabilities in patient safety and quality improvement	Undertake a quality improvement project DONCS on Serious Incident investigation
7	Capabilities in safeguarding vulnerable groups	Mini-PAT CbD of complex case involving capacity assessment/mental capacity legislation DONCS of involvement in Best Interest Meeting
8	Capabilities in education and training	Undertake locally offered courses, i.e. in Teaching and Learning/PGcert in Medical Education Keep a PDP AoT of providing liaison/psychiatry teaching to staff/medical students
9	Capabilities in research and scholarship	Undertake a research project

ACE – Assessed Clinical Encounter; AoT – Assessment of Teaching; CbD – Case-based Discussion; DONCS – Direct Observation of Non-Clinical Skills; mini-ACE – mini Assessed Clinical Encounter; mini-PAT – mini Peer Assessment Tool; SAPE – Structured Assessment of Psychotherapy Expertise (Royal College of Psychiatrists).

delirium, dementia or alcohol dependence, and utilising National Institute for Health and Care Excellence (NICE) standards for auditing assessment and treatment pathways. Research projects may be ongoing in the department; other avenues for developing competencies are preparing manuscripts for case reports, case series, systematic reviews and pilot studies (e.g. standardising documentation for patient reviews and handovers or offering outreach to a particular medical specialty for a fixed period of time).

'Must-See' Cases in Consultation-Liaison Psychiatry

In addition to collecting necessary evidence for the trainee portfolio, the training placement in CL psychiatry presents a unique opportunity to assess patients presenting both acutely and sub-acutely in the general hospital setting. Some of these cases might be encountered while covering general hospitals as part of out-of-hours duties but a dedicated training placement maximises the opportunity to acquire experience in assessment and management of these patients, with the option of follow-up reviews to appraise the impact and efficacy of clinical decision-making and consultation skills. Below is a list that can be used as a broad scaffold for collecting case exposure during the training placement. This is by no means exhaustive.

Acute presentations:

- of anxiety, depression, mania and psychosis
- personal or social crisis – especially with suicidal thoughts
- presentation after an episode of self-harm
- acute behavioural disturbance
- acute complications of alcohol or substance misuse (intoxication and withdrawal states).

Common conditions:

- problems with adjustment (examples include change in life circumstances; physical illness; the physically unwell patient with depressed mood)
- delirium: common dementias and how they present in the general hospital setting (examples include confusion, falls, and self-neglect); understanding how these presentations differ and also how they overlap and present comorbidly
- eating disorders (complications from anorexia, orthorexia, bulimia and binge eating disorder)
- somatoform disorders including cases which stimulate thinking about the concepts of somatisation, hypochondriasis, central sensitisation and functional overlay
- Factitious disorders and malingering.

Specialist management advice:

- assessment of mental capacity in collaboration with the medical or surgical team
- medication management including medication-related symptoms, and decisions about inpatients taking clozapine, lithium, methadone or depot injections.

International Examples of Training in Consultation-Liaison Psychiatry

The Royal College of Physicians and Surgeons of Canada, the American Medical Association, the Academy of Consultation-Liaison Psychiatry (USA) and The Royal Australian and New Zealand College of Psychiatrists have useful online resources detailing training pathways and curricula. Here is a brief overview of training in these regions.

Canada

In contrast to psychiatric training in the UK where training programmes are overseen by centralised bodies, Canada's residency programmes are administered by universities. There are 17 universities in Canada, and at the time of writing all offer residency training in general psychiatry (13). Residency training is generally for five years and can be applied for immediately following completion of the initial medical degree. There is no foundation programme (or equivalent). A resident is the North American equivalent to a core/higher UK trainee.

In order to attain certification from the Royal College of Physicians and Surgeons of Canada, doctors must successfully complete their residency programme, as well as their College portfolio and examination in psychiatry. Similarly to the UK, residents progress through training by demonstrating competencies, although these are set by individual institutions rather than centrally. There are four stages to their training, but, unlike the UK, they are not set to a specific timescale, although there is a recommended time limit on their completion (14).

Programmes generally offer between three and four 4–6-week rotations in CL psychiatry and many also offer between placements of between 3 and 6 months placements for senior residents, during their fourth or fifth year of training (13). These are at two universities which offer post-residency fellowships in CL psychiatry – McGill University and the University of Toronto (13).

The USA

The model of training in the USA is similar to that of Canada in that residency programmes are run by individual universities. Thus, a medical graduate applies directly to each institution in order to be considered for a post. The general length of psychiatric residency is four years. In order to be accredited by the Accreditation Council for Graduate Medical Education (ACGME), a psychiatric residency programme must offer a minimum 2-month full-time equivalent placement in CL psychiatry, although many do offer more than this (15).

In order to achieve certification in CL psychiatry, following completion of their residency, psychiatrists then undertake a year-long fellowship in their subspecialty. Again, the doctor applies to multiple potential placements and is matched following interview. Certification follows the completion of this fellowship, as well as a written examination (16).

Australia and New Zealand

Training Requirements

All training requirements are set and monitored by the Royal Australian and New Zealand College of Psychiatrists (RANZCP). The RANZCP training programme uses locally delivered educational programmes linked to a bi-national curriculum and a series of clinical rotations based on an 'apprenticeship' training model, with specified mandatory training experiences and minimum training periods, coupled with a competency-based curriculum and assessment procedures and a series of written and viva examinations. International training standards were influential on local training programmes (17, 18) and the competency-based curriculum and assessment component was heavily influenced by the Canadian model (19). The introduction to the RANZCP of a competency-based fellowship programme for psychiatry in Australia and New Zealand was influenced by CL psychiatrists from both countries (20).

Workforce

A recent RANZCP workforce and training report was approved by the Commonwealth and all state and territory health ministers (21), and reported a likely shortfall of available places in CL psychiatry for the 6-month basic training rotations required for Stage 1 and Stage 2 (first 36 months of training) and for the two years of Advanced Training in Stage 3.

Basic Training

Stage 2 Basic Training requires a minimum of 24 months' full-time equivalent training and mandatory rotations in child and adolescent psychiatry (6 months) and CL psychiatry (6 months).

Two Entrustable Professional Activities for each of the following areas must be completed:

(1) Child and adolescent: manage an adolescent, pre-pubertal child
(2) CL: delirium, psychological distress
(3) Addiction: intoxication and withdrawal, comorbid substance use
(4) Old age: behavioural and psychological symptoms in dementia, medication for patients aged 75 years or older.

Advanced Training

The requirements for completion of Advanced Training (Stage 3) are:

(1) Duration: 24 months (full-time equivalent) in accredited CL posts
(2) Experiences:

  (a) 12 months' attachment to a CL service offering consultation across an entire general hospital including emergency work
  (b) one or more liaison-style attachments to a unit providing medical or surgical treatment (at least one day per week full-time equivalent for at least 12 months)
  (c) an outpatient experience, including longitudinal follow-up of patients with chronic physical illness (at least one half-day per week full-time equivalent for at least 12 months)
  (d) a maximum of 30% of standard work hours in an emergency department.

(3) Attainment of eight Stage 3 Entrusted Professional Activities
(4) Completion of one Observed Clinical Activity during each 6-month clinical rotation
(5) Completion of an approved formal CL psychiatry teaching programme

  (a) Section of Advanced Training in CL Psychiatry will recommend relevant, upcoming local and international scientific meetings, conferences, workshops and so on that trainees will be encouraged to attend as part of the teaching programme.

(6) Successful completion of a scholarly project; 3,000–5,000 words in length
(7) Presentation of a scholarly project at an approved meeting or conference
(8) Completion of 20 case summaries of 300–500 words for each case.

Teaching Methods for Trainees

There have been multiple areas of inquiry into aspects of training in general with implications for CL psychiatry: reports identifying the characteristics of 'good' supervisors using qualitative techniques with trainee informants (22), supervisors' perceptions of their own role (23), trainee perceptions on improving training experiences (24), a method of trainee evaluation of the supervision and training experience (25), trainee impressions of subspecialty training in neuropsychiatry (26), trainee experiences in rural New South Wales (27, 28), the implementation of the 2004 Indigenous Mental Health Training By-Laws within Victoria (29), how research skills are taught to psychiatrists-in-training across Australasia (30), supervision of trainee scholarly projects (31), a systematic review of empirical studies relating to the outcomes of supervision contracts (32), and a hierarchical, structured approach to clinical reasoning (Bloom's Taxonomy) needed for psychiatric formulation (33). Rarely, papers are published that specifically address the aspects of training in CL psychiatry (34).

References

1. Aitken P. Psychosomatic medicine: The British experience. In Leigh H. (ed.), *Global Psychosomatic Medicine and Consultation-Liaison Psychiatry: Theory, Research, Education, and Practice*. New York; 2019, p. 195.

2. UK Foundation Programme. Foundation programme. https://foundationpro gramme.nhs.uk/programmes/2-year-foundation-programme/ukfp.

3. Royal College of Psychiatrists. Sub-specialty endorsement in Liaison Psychiatry Curriculum. www .rcpsych.ac.uk/docs/default-source/train ing/curricula-and-guidance/2022-curricula/liaison-psychiatry-curriculum-final-16-june-22.pdf?sfvrsn=bf898b0_2.

4. General Medical Council. Good medical practice. 2020. www.gmc-uk.org/-/media/ documents/good-medical-practice–english-20200128_pdf-51527435.pdf.

5. General Medical Council. Excellence by design: Standards for postgraduate curricula. 2017. www.gmc-uk.org/education/post graduate/standards_for_curricula.asp.

6. General Medical Council. Shape of training: Securing the future of excellent patient care. 2013. www.gmc-uk.org/-/me dia/documents/shape-of-training-final-report_pdf-53977887.pdf.

7. General Medical Council. Generic professional capabilities framework. 2017. www.gmc-uk.org/-/media/documents/gen eric-professional-capabilities-framework–2109_pdf-70417127.pdf.

8. Frank JR, Snell L, Sherbino J (eds.). CanMEDS: Better standards, better physicians, better care. Royal College of Physicians and Surgeons of Canada. 2015.

9. Royal College of Psychiatrists. Report CR204: Core values for psychiatrists. 2017. www.rcpsych.ac.uk/docs/default-source/ improving-care/better-mh-policy/college-reports/college-report-cr204.pdf?sfvrsn= 5e4ff507_2.pdf.

10. General Medical Council. Credentialing. www.gmc-uk.org/education/standards-guidance-and-curricula/projects/ credentialing.

11. Longson D. The liaison psychiatry curriculum. In Guthrie E, Rao S, Temple M (eds.), *Seminars in Liaison Psychiatry*. London; 2012, p. 20.

12. Royal College of Psychiatrists. Portfolio online. https://training.rcpsych.ac.uk/home.

13. Gagnon, F. Canadian consultation-liaison psychiatry/psychosomatic medicine: A discipline still waiting for official recognition and patient care accessibility. In Leigh H. (ed.), *Global Psychosomatic*

Medicine and Consultation-Liaison Psychiatry. Theory, Research, Education, and Practice. New York; 2019, p. 536.

14. Royal College of Physicians and Surgeons of Canada. Psychiatry training experiences. 2020. www.royalcollege.ca/rcsite/ibd-search-e?N=10000033+10000034+4294967084&label=Psychiatry.

15. Accreditation Council for Graduate Medical Education. ACGME program requirements for graduate medical education in psychiatry. 2020. www.acgme.org/Portals/0/PFAssets/ProgramRequirements/400_Psychiatry_2020.pdf?ver=2020-06-19-123110-817.

16. Rabinowitz T. Why consider a CLP fellowship? 2020. www.clpsychiatry.org/residents-fellows/resident-information/why-consider-clp-fship.

17. Ford CV, Fawzy FI, Frankel BL, Noyes R. Fellowship training in consultation-liaison psychiatry. *Psychosomatics.* 1994;**35**(2):118–24. doi: 10.1016/s0033-3182(94)71784-9.

18 Gitlin DF, Schindler, BA, Stern TA et al. Recommended guidelines for consultation-liaison psychiatric training in psychiatry residency programs: A report from the Academy of Psychosomatic Medicine Task Force on Psychiatric Resident Training in Consultation-Liaison Psychiatry. *Psychosomatics.* 1996;**37**(1):3–11. doi: 10.1016/s0033-3182(96)71591-8.

19. Iobst WF, Sherbino J, Cate OT et al. Competency-based medical education in postgraduate medical education. *Medical Teacher.* 2010;**32**(8):651–6. doi: 10.3109/0142159X.2010.500709.

20. Jurd S, de Beer, W, Aimer M et al. Introducing a competency based fellowship programme for psychiatry in Australia and New Zealand. *Australas Psychiatry.* 2015;**23**(6):699–705. doi: 10.1177/1039856215600898.

21. Australian Department of Health. Australia's future health workforce: Psychiatry report. 2016. www1.health.gov.au/internet/main/publishing.nsf/Content/Australias-future-health-workforce%E2%80%93psychiatry.

22. Chur-Hansen A, McLean S. Supervisors' views about their trainees and supervision. *Australas Psychiatry.* 2007;**15**(4):273–5. doi: 10.1080/10398560701441695.

23. Chur-Hansen A, McLean S. Trainee psychiatrists' views about their supervisors and supervision. *Australas Psychiatry.* 2007;**15**(4):269–72. doi: 10.1080/10398560701441703.

24. Stephan A, Cheung G. Clinical teaching and supervision in postgraduate psychiatry training: The trainee perspective. *Australas Psychiatry.* 2016;**25**(2):191–7. doi: 10.1177/1039856216679539.

25. Clarke DM. Measuring the quality of supervision and the training experience in psychiatry. *Aust NZJ.* 1999;**33**(2):248–52. doi: 10.1046/j.1440-1614.1999.00551.x.

26. Rego T, Eratne D, Walterfang M, Velakoulis D. Trainee experiences in a specialist neuropsychiatry training position. *Australas Psychiatry.* 2019;**28**(1):95–100. doi: 10.1177/1039856219871894.

27. de Moore G, Smith K, Earle M. From golden beaches to the heartland: Reflections of NSW Rural Trainees. *Australas Psychiatry.* 2006;**14**(1):72–5. doi: 10.1080/j.1440-1665.2006.02249.x.

28. Nash L, Hickie C, Clark S, Karageorge A, Kelly PJ, Earle M. The experience of psychiatry training in rural NSW. *Australas Psychiatry.* 2014;**22**(5):492–9. doi: 10.1177/1039856214543086.

29. Duke M, Ewen S. Social and emotional wellbeing training of psychiatrists in Victoria: Preliminary communication. *Australas Psychiatry.* 2009;**17**(1_suppl):S100–S103. doi: 10.1080/10398560902948522.

30. Andrews L, Coverdale J, Turbott S. Training directors' and registrars' views on research training in Australasian psychiatry. *Australas Psychiatry.* 2001;**9**(1):20–4. doi: 10.1046/j.1440-1665.2001.00307.x.

31. Cheung G, Friedman SH, Ng L, Cullum S. Supervising trainees in research: What does it take to be a scholarly project supervisor? *Australas Psychiatry.* 2017;**26**

(2):214–19. doi: 10.1177/1039856217726696.

32. Lu D, Suetani S, Cutbush J, Parker S. Supervision contracts for mental health professionals: A systematic review and exploration of the potential relevance to psychiatry training in Australia and New Zealand. *Australas Psychiatry.* 2019;27 (3):225–9. doi: 10.1177/1039856219845486.

33. de Beer WA. Original opinion: The use of Bloom's Taxonomy to teach and assess the skill of the psychiatric formulation during vocational training. *Australas Psychiatry.* 2017;25(5):514–19. doi: 10.1177/1039856217726692.

34. Hatcher S. Why do advanced training in CL? *Aust NZJ.* 2007;41(1_suppl):A28. doi: 10.1080/14401614070410s142.

Chapter 3

Nursing in Consultation-Liaison Settings

Kate Chartres and Sarah Eales

Introduction

Liaison mental health nurses are the single largest professional group in consultation-liaison psychiatry. Liaison nurses frequently work as part of large, multidisciplinary teams but they regularly make independent admission and discharge recommendations. Liaison nurses require a large repertoire of competencies to fulfil such roles and understandably this comes from a variety of post-registration experiences. This chapter sets out the competencies required of liaison mental health nurses. The chapter also outlines the unique and important role a nurse consultant can play in a liaison team. Liaison mental health nursing continues to expand as a professional group within consultation-liaison mental healthcare. Mental health nursing has a workforce shortage, and this chapter also looks at how to develop or 'grow your own' liaison nurses by employing nurses at the point of registration and developing sound liaison nurses over a 12- to 18-month period.

The Development of Liaison Mental Health Nursing

Liaison mental health nursing is an internationally recognised specialist area of mental health nursing practice. The origins of mental health nurses practising in general hospital settings can be found in the USA in the 1960s. Liaison mental health nursing first came to prominence in the UK in the early 1990s with mental health nurses offering direct consultation to patients and staff in accident and emergency departments, particularly bio-psychosocial assessment following self-harm and suicide attempts, cancer care and HIV services. Throughout the 1990s and 2000s liaison mental health nursing grew (acknowledging a few bumps in the road) and developed to serve many aspects of physical healthcare and also became evident globally, including in Australia, Iran, Saudi Arabia and Scandinavia. The developments in the UK have primarily become part of multidisciplinary collaborative teams with a vast array of service titles. Regel and Roberts in 2002 (1) presented a seminal text on liaison mental health nursing, in which Roberts reiterated his 1998 model of liaison mental health nursing that we argue remains valid today. The model encapsulates the importance of working both directly to assess and plan with patients, who are referred by our medical and nursing colleagues, and of what Roberts terms indirect consultation, where the focus of work is just direct patient care but also the education and support of the acute hospital workforce. The model draws on the community psychiatry work of Caplan in 1970. At a similar time, Eales and Hart (2) produced the first edition of the liaison mental health nursing competencies. Liaison nurses have chosen to identify with the term mental health rather than psychiatry for a variety of reasons, including the following.

- Liaison is about prevention, not just treatment, of mental illness (1).

- Our work is not always with those who have a formal diagnosis of mental illness, for example acute mental distress leading to an attempt to take one's own life (1).
- Liaison mental health nursing was identified as replacing psychiatric nursing in the 1994 review of the field of nursing (1).
- Liaison mental health is a term that can readily be attached to teams or services and other professional groups, acknowledging the multi-professional collaborative nature, whereas liaison psychiatry is rooted in the medical profession (1).
- Recent UK government guidance on acute care pathways recognises the endeavour of liaison mental healthcare rather than liaison psychiatry.

Liaison Mental Health Nursing Competencies

Competencies for liaison mental health nursing were originally developed in the UK between 2002 and 2004 to articulate the roles and responsibilities of liaison nursing (2). This was a time of significant development in the liaison mental health nursing profession with the emergence of nurse consultant roles, 24-hour services and the implementation of Agenda for Change as a banding structure for nursing and allied health professionals. A forum existed (the London-Wide Liaison Nurses Special Interest Group), which was supported by the Royal College of Nursing, and the original competencies were developed by that group under the guidance of Chris Hart, a London-based nurse consultant in liaison mental health.

There have been two subsequent revisions to the competencies to ensure that they remain contemporary. The first in 2014 came at a time when liaison mental health teams had seen significant expansion across the UK. The competencies were being used across professional groups and the range of bandings and experience of nurses and other allied health professionals working in liaison required a more comprehensive set of competencies. The content expanded to cover not just liaison-specific competencies, such as working with medically unexplained or persistent physical symptoms, but also competencies covering the core expectations of the mental health nurse (3), such as assessment in liaison settings. A third iteration of the liaison mental health nursing competencies is in process and reflects a broadening remit of liaison nurses, for example including non-medical prescribers and the addition of autism as an identified area where competence is required.

Liaison nursing competencies have always acknowledged exposure to a broad range of clinical presentations, such that liaison nurses can be asked to assess, support and plan for a dynamic group of people. It is generally accepted that not every liaison nurse will possess highly specialist levels of competence in every area. Therefore, the competence document reflects varying levels of competence using a performance rating scale. This ranges from an individual not being able to perform an activity satisfactorily (0), to being able to perform it with no assistance but with supervision (3), to being able to deliver it at an expert level in special situations and being able to lead others (6). Expert levels of competence are required for the front-door emergency department work of liaison nurses because they make independent discharge decisions about people in mental health crisis. Identifying the correct treatment decisions from signposting to local/national services to crisis and home treatment/inpatient care requires very well-developed assessment and formulation skills and a high level of freedom to act under UK Agenda for Change criteria. Over time, such decisions have been delegated to band 6 nurses, having been very much the remit of band 7 and above at the start of the Agenda for Change job-matching process in 2004. This appears to be an erosion of recognition for the expectation of competence that is required of the liaison mental health nurse.

The competencies are used in clinical practice collaboratively; self-appraisal is enhanced by live clinical supervision from a clinical lead and collaborative discussion, leading to an individual nursing development plan, which can then be used confidentially with the rest of the team to develop a team training programme.

Opportunities to enhance skills include shadowing colleagues within and outside the liaison team. Many services have found that adding in opportunities to shadow other specialist nurses (e.g. stroke/cardiac) is helpful, as is spending time working in the emergency department or medical assessment unit or with the crisis team. Training packages that include opportunities to simulate events and assessments add a huge amount to learning, enabling appraisal of what to say and how to say it and how body language comes across. The debrief itself should take longer than the simulation to offer adequate refection time (4).

Respect for equality or diversity is not identified as a separate competency because it is inherent in all of the 19 competencies. The liaison nurse always has a role in breaking down stigma about mental healthcare needs. Understanding that diversity and inequalities may impact upon when/how people present to healthcare services and the impact that minority status may have or have had upon individual experience of treatment and care is an essential component of the liaison nursing skill set.

Domains of Liaison Nursing Competency

1. Providing Mental Health Nursing Assessment and Consultation

Many nurses struggle at first to use the bio-psycho-social approach, particularly where patients are presenting with complexity and an interaction between physical and psychological components (5, 6). More information on conducting the clinical interview can be found in Chapter 1 in this volume. For nurses and other allied health professionals, demonstrating up-to-date knowledge of mental health problems is key to achieving this competency. Focus on presentations which are common within an acute hospital setting, for example personality disorder, psychosis, depression and anxiety, is strongly encouraged. Liaison skills are required to ensure that the assessment is enhanced by collaborating with family, the staff on the ward, community services and the voluntary sector where involved. Clear, comprehensive documentation is key with respect to communicating core findings from the assessment with the ward and the patient. A minimum standard for writing in the acute trust record is as follows (7).

(1) What the problem/s is/are (diagnosis or formulation).
(2) The legal status of the patient and their mental capacity for any decision to be made if relevant.
(3) Clear documentation of the mental health risk assessment – immediate and medium term.
(4) Whether the patient requires any further risk management, for example observation level.
(5) A management plan including medication or other therapeutic intervention.
(6) Advice regarding contingencies, for example what to do if the patient wishes to self-discharge.

(7) A clear discharge plan in terms of mental health follow-up.

In the case of frequent attenders, many of whom are complex in their presentation, a review is often necessary. It is not uncommon to find care plans that effectively rule out further assessment as unhelpful or imply assessment might make a crisis worse. Given that we are tasked with identifying the subtle changes in presentation to understand which crisis situation might be the one that leads to someone taking their own life (8), *contact should be offered for every presentation and every engagement opportunity taken to enhance and develop a safety plan.* Teams should also ensure support is offered to the treating clinical team as often these patients provoke much concern and anxiety. A disengaged liaison nurse or team could damage integrated working (9).

2. Assessment of Risk Including Self-Harm

Nurses working in liaison mental health are often making the decision to discharge clients directly after assessment. While many services operate some kind of daily multidisciplinary meeting (or at a minimum on weekdays), the actual decision about what happens in terms of follow-up and ongoing support is made by the assessing clinician. This is a significant responsibility for many nurses and an aspect of the role that they often struggle with when initially transitioning into the field of liaison mental health. Skilled assessment of risk is needed to ensure that decisions are safe and that development of a collaborative safety plan that promotes independence is facilitated (8). The ability to arrive at a clear formulation and mitigation plan that can be concisely documented is a competency that is developed over time.

3. Assessment and Advice on Capacity Issues

Capacity assessments must be completed by the treating team; specialist support from the liaison nurse where mental health issues are present may be needed. This requires up-to-date knowledge of mental capacity legislation and adherence to the principles of assessing capacity. The skills that are required include an ability to explain the rationale for assessing capacity, ensuring advanced decisions are adhered to where appropriate, sharing this information if it is present in the mental health clinical record and being able to clearly document this in the acute hospital records, including what to do if the clinical presentation changes. The role of the liaison nurse is to support effective communication to enable the patient to make an informed decision.

4. Identifying and Considering Ethical Issues

The liaison nurse is frequently called upon to act as an advocate for patients with mental health needs and/or their family/carers in the acute hospital. Nurses may identify inconsistency in clinical practice, for example regarding a lack of parity of esteem (10) for those with mental health needs. Paternalistic or dismissive attitudes may represent contributing factors. The complexity of working across multiple organisations with different policies, behaviours and legal concerns often presents difficulties in gaining consensus. Clinical forums have developed for liaison nurses and other practitioners (e.g. in the northeast of England), presenting an opportunity to discuss shared complex problems to support development of consensus. Frequently the requirements of competencies 3, 4 and 5 are interwoven in complex decision-making. Acute hospitals will have ethics committees who can be consulted by the multidisciplinary team where decisions are complex and/or consensus is lacking.

5. Providing Nursing Advice on Legal Issues

Nurses are required to have up-to-date knowledge of the relevant legislation utilised in mental healthcare so that advice and support can be offered to our acute hospital colleagues. This includes local procedures, the roles and responsibilities of different partners and ensuring that advocates are requested and utilised where needed. Mental Health Act legislation tends not to be designed with the acute hospital trust in mind, and the liaison nurse will need a well-developed understanding of the Acts of Parliament, subsequent case law and codes of practice that support decision-making. Liaison nurses may act as an advocate for a patient where concerns arise in terms of clinical care, particularly where an action or omission breaches local policy or legal frameworks. This helps to safeguard appropriate reporting and ensure duty of candour is followed (11).

6. Interventions Used in Liaison Mental Health Nursing

The use of clinical interventions in liaison nursing is diverse and may include cognitive behavioural interventions, dialectical behavioural informed practice and collaborative safety planning (12). Dementia-specific interventions are frequently utilised, including reminiscence work and positive behavioural support. Therapeutic interventions include planning care and disseminating this to the ward team with the aim of encouraging a shared understanding of an individual's clinical presentation and strategies to minimise distress and enhance engagement with healthcare. Education on an ad hoc basis to enhance the skill set of our acute hospital nursing colleagues also allows opportunities to prevent stigma, to reduce the likelihood of a 'fear' of delivering care to the person with co-morbid mental health and physical health needs (9). Interventions in liaison mental health nursing should be co-produced with the patient and underpinned by recovery-focussed care (13).

7. Admission and Discharge of Patients

Acute liaison teams generally provide 24/7 services for the acute hospital, which means decisions about admission and discharge need to be made safely in the moment. These clinical decisions are made considering risk mitigation/safety/acting in accordance with ongoing community treatment plans. It is therefore necessary to ensure any new liaison practitioners gradually accumulate knowledge and understanding of safe decision-making. On occasion, the decision cannot and should not be made by the assessing nurse, and in these cases involvement of medical colleagues might be required. It is therefore important that liaison mental health nurses (and Allied Healthcare Practitioners (AHPs)) have good self-awareness of their limitations in making what are sometimes sensitive decisions around complex cases.

8. Maintaining Accurate Records, Documentation and Report Writing

There is an art to delivering complex information about all aspects of a clinical presentation to the acute hospital in a concise manner. This is an under-recognised skill which tends to develop over time, but it is important that an acceptable degree of competence is acquired via induction and relevant training as soon as possible. We know the majority of people that we communicate with require clear information that succinctly demonstrates the reason for presentation, the relevant clinical background, what the assessment demonstrated, the relevant risks, how they are being mitigated and any plan/recommendation. Development routes include reading through previously completed high-standard assessments, live supervision and receiving feedback on documentation standards. Completion of local mental healthcare provider records, which may be inaccessible to those currently responsible for the care of the patient, must not take precedence over timely completion of the host provider documentation (14).

9. Providing Nursing Advice on the Management and Care of Patients with Complex Psychosocial and/or Challenging Presentations

Patients with complex needs are often perceived as 'a clinical challenge' when presenting to the acute hospital. It is important that a compassionate approach is developed when navigating the complex issues surrounding this for inpatient teams. At times it is not simply an assessment that is required; rather, a response is needed where support can be given to the treating team which ensures care is delivered in the least restrictive way. Often a better understanding of what is driving a particular behaviour for the patient and for the care providers is essential. Liaison mental health nurses (and AHPs) should get involved, work with the team to avoid using security staff to manage behaviour and work towards enabling healthier communication. Nursing teams are often affected by specific cases where things have gone wrong in the past and not always as a direct response from that patient (9). Liaison nurses, particularly when new to the role, will often focus on 'getting the assessment done' rather than looking at the wider implications of being helpful to the ward in supporting the management of challenging behaviours. It is important that any team training/induction allows for this. This can include looking at the environment, the communication style being used, when the behaviour occurs and so on.

10. Providing Nursing Advice on Medication, Including Non-Medical Prescribing in Liaison Mental Health

Historically, when many liaison services were nurse-led, nurses and others were expected to and do currently give advice around medication. It is important that any prescribing decisions are made by individuals that are appropriately skilled and trained in independent prescribing (15). The most recent iteration of the competency framework (2) includes a subsection on independent prescribing in liaison psychiatry. Nurses who are not prescribers should ensure they only offer assistance regarding possible side effects and the impact on mental state from a variety of psychotropic medications, and should involve pharmacy/prescriber colleagues where needed.

11. Working with People with Specific Physical Illnesses

Psychological morbidity is frequently associated with physical illnesses, with many people suffering mood or anxiety problems as a direct impact of having a long-term condition (16). Liaison nurses and AHPs, particularly when new to the area, believe that they do not hold the right skill set to help this group of people. In many cases they already hold the relevant skills. Examples of good practice include teaching people mindfulness skills or breathing exercises to manage distress in the moment, something we frequently do for the agitated patient in the emergency department but that we seem to forget might be useful for the patient who has just had a stroke (17), or for the patient with an exacerbation of chronic obstructive pulmonary disease (COPD) (18). It is important to reiterate that the skills obtained as a community mental health nurse or ward nurse are transferable (19). A sound understanding of common physical health problems, blood results and their meanings can be taught and learned, but we must always remember we are working as part of a wider team and can ask about the components of the presenting concern that we do not know.

12.   Working with Older Adults

Liaison teams in England are required to have dedicated services for older people (20). For some services this might include a separate arm of the service, but for most it is generically skilled clinical staff and with specialists in the form of a liaison psychiatrist and clinical leads. Nurses and others coming into liaison mental health need to have a good understanding of the impact of dementia and delirium in this client group. An enhanced understanding of the impact of frailty is also needed, particularly around the effects of psychotropic medication and of polypharmacy. More so, but not solely, there is often a greater need to liaise with social services and family around care needs and gaining collateral information to enhance any assessment, particularly when planning ongoing care. Documents such as This is Me (21) are often underutilised and can be crucial in supporting effective care in acute hospital admissions.

13.   Working with People with a Substance Misuse Problem Including Alcohol

Maintaining up-to-date knowledge of the ever-evolving range of substances that can potentially be abused is an important aspect of working within this clinical area. *A history of drug or alcohol ingestion should not be used as a reason for not assessing the client; rather, assessment should be completed in parallel with the medical team* (19). Many people who are dependent on substances, whether alcohol or drugs, might be entirely capable of engaging in an assessment and their assessment may not need to be delayed. Where a full assessment is not possible because of the level of intoxication, risk management should be developed collaboratively with the clinical team and repeat reviews arranged every 2 hours or so until a full assessment formulation and plan is possible. Knowledge of availability and close working with community drug services and acute hospital alcohol care teams (22) can facilitate effective care and ensure specialist knowledge is available to the team.

14.   Working with People with Persistent Physical Symptoms

Many of the people described as frequent attenders at the acute hospital are presenting with chronic, recurring physical symptoms. This creates frustration for the client and the team delivering care. The role of the liaison nurse in this circumstance is to validate concerns from both the patient and the treating team. Displaying a positive attitude to the client and their carers and providing education around the specific symptoms, both to the client and the care team, allows an opportunity to improve quality of life. Increased understanding of the impact of stress on the body, related symptoms and when they occur can help to alleviate distress. As with any other clinical presentation to the liaison team, collaboration here is key; time should be taken within the assessment process to understand the experience of the client, including symptoms, triggers and patterns, using a bio-psycho-social approach and gently exploring insight. The language used should be carefully considered as engagement is a key factor in improving quality of life; if the client feels they are not being heard, this opportunity might be lost. In-depth discussion around working with people with persistent physical symptoms and functional disorders is available in Chapter 7 in this volume.

15. Working with People with Learning Disabilities and Autism

The majority of acute hospitals now have some degree of service provision specifically for people with learning disabilities and the core liaison mental health team may be contacted when there is concern about co-existing mental health symptoms. Knowledge of increased mortality due to physical and co-morbid mental health problems in people with learning disabilities (23) is therefore an important component of the liaison nursing skill set. There needs to be clear consideration in assessing risk, particularly around vulnerability, when working with this client group. Sensory impairment should be considered, along with environmental factors in consultation with the ward team, to try to reduce the frequency, severity and duration of any potentially distressing stimuli (24). Communication aids might be required to maximise understanding and expression of needs and wishes; this might be carried out in collaboration with speech and language therapists.

16. Working with Mothers and Babies

Perinatal mental health services have developed significantly over the last decade, and many teams will offer in-reach services to acute hospitals. These services are not available outside of working hours and so liaison teams are often asked to support the new mother presenting with mental health concerns. When completing nursing development plans utilising the competency framework, this area of practice seems to provoke increased concern. It is important to consider the increased risk of suicide among this client group and the fact that suicide is one of the leading causes of death in the first postnatal year to set these concerns in context (25). Chapter 13 in this volume gives detailed information on perinatal mental health. Options to enhance the skills of interested clinicians include accessing enhanced training, for example, the Solihull package (26), and ensuring that all nursing staff have a solid knowledge of risk factors presenting in the perinatal period, the risk of relapse for those with a known mental illness, and local, regional and national resources available. Nursing team members will generally utilise the support of the team as needed and should be aware of their own limitations.

17. Working with Children and Young People

This competency aligns with contemporary considerations of ageless services. This creates opportunities for liaison teams to expand their remit and include provision to those aged under 18. This competency also supports staff in hospitals that have already established child and adolescent/paediatric liaison teams. However, as these are currently unlikely to be 24-hour services, competence may be required for adult services, particularly where they are commissioned for 16–18-year-olds. Knowledge about specific groups that are more vulnerable to mental illness is important, for example, looked-after children, the impact of adverse childhood events (ACEs) and how brain development affects presentation. Nurses are encouraged to be a little more risk-averse with this client group and where possible involve the child's family in the assessment process. This caution is reflected by National Institute for Health and Care Excellence (NICE) guidance for self-harm which continues to stipulate that good practice is to admit under 16s for an assessment the following day (27). Most geographic areas comply with this. We are aware of several services in the UK who safely and effectively assess and discharge from the emergency department; much depends on the availability and responsiveness of community-based Child and Adolescent Mental

Health Services (CAMHS) to support the young person. Paediatric wards require support in skills development to care for those with mental health needs, particularly teenagers. Use of the *We Can Talk* training package (28) and young people-specific safety planning are helpful tools (29) to support non-CAMHS specialists. Young people may choose the adult care pathway where competent to do so and again cause anxiety in the treating team because of their age and the nuances of maintaining safety; the above packages can prove useful here too. For more information on working with children and young people in liaison mental health, see Chapter 14 in this volume.

18.   Education, Training, Research and Supervision

At least a third of what we do in liaison psychiatry should include education, whether formal and informal. Recently revised standards for pre-registration nursing education – the Future Nurse Standards (30) – set increased expectations in relation to parity of esteem (31) for all nurses, irrespective of field, requiring much better-developed mental health skills. While this may provide a more skilled workforce in the future, there remains the need to support the current nursing workforce to upskill in relation to mental health needs within their patient groups. The Nursing and Midwifery Council (NMC) Code (11) states that 'all nursing staff should be able to recognise deterioration of mental and physical health', and yet many liaison teams still struggle to gain consistent commitment from acute hospitals to release staff for formal training. Liaison nurses therefore frequently focus on informal approaches while also working strategically to develop buy-in for more focussed education plans.

Informal opportunities include:

- gentle challenging of negative views/stigma
- viewing every interaction as a potential educational activity
- ensuring feedback about patient assessment (develops knowledge for the referrer by providing a rationale for decisions)
- working collaboratively/jointly in clinic settings
- offering mental health drop-in/reflective practice groups on an ongoing basis or as part of a debrief process.

Clinical liaison nurses tend not to be primary investigators in funded research projects or their related publications. In line with an increased number of senior nursing posts, including liaison nurse consultants, engagement in research needs to develop. Wherever possible, nursing colleagues should be actively engaged in key research grant applications to reflect the multidisciplinary nature of liaison mental healthcare. As liaison nurses develop their careers, they should look to develop connections to local universities to develop research collaborations. At the very minimum, engagement with up-to-date research and its critical application to practice is expected. Engaging with research and dissemination should be evident at all levels of liaison nursing to ensure that we share good practice nationally and internationally and develop the evidence base of liaison mental health nursing.

Expert clinical supervision is key to maintaining effective practice. All nurses practising in the complex field of liaison mental health should be receiving regular supervision. This should not be overlooked and can help to maintain positive working practice in what can sometimes be very challenging environments.

19. Evaluating and Improving Liaison Mental Health Nursing Provision

Knowledge of different tools used to evaluate liaison nursing provision is required; this should include a working understanding of the clinical outcome measures detailed in Chapter 20 in this volume. It is important for liaison nurses at all levels to have a good understanding of what data are collected and why, and furthermore how this should influence practice and service development. The Framework for Routine Outcome Measures in Liaison Psychiatry (32) clearly and succinctly captures key data. Many UK liaison teams choose to engage with the national accreditation process. The UK Psychiatric Liaison Accreditation Network standards are set collaboratively and based on national guidelines. This process of accreditation involves peer review and service user/carer scrutiny of services.

Nursing Leadership in Liaison Psychiatry

Development of the Service and Nursing Influence

Nurse leaders influence the development and structure of liaison services, which are often nurse-led in the sense that nurses complete initial assessments and make decisions on admission and discharge around the clock. Teams require systems centred around work-load, which ideally translates to adequate staffing for emergency department work, liaison work (wards and departments) and outpatient work. In reality, staff move flexibly between roles during any given day or week according to service needs.

In the Emergency Department and Wider Hospital

Responding within an hour to mental health presentations to accident and emergency services is vastly improved from response times even a decade ago. Services that have developed are vast and varied, with nursing staff often leading on specialist projects, which vary depending on what is commissioned. Some examples of projects the authors have been involved in include the following.

- Nurse-led clinics for long-term conditions (LTCs), for example, COPD. Four- to six-hourly sessions of low-grade cognitive behavioural interventions led by a clinical lead nurse and support worker staff with supervision provided by team consultants (nurse and medic). Sessions are mainly delivered as home visits to improve attendance.
- Self-harm follow-up clinics (generally two to three times a week for first-episode cases or those that need follow-up and are not open to other services, delivered by band 6 nurses and clinically supervised by lead nurses (clinical leads or nurse consultant)).
- Dementia/delirium follow-up clinics (delivered by nurses to review the need for an ongoing referral to memory clinic a few weeks post-discharge to meet delirium pathway requirements (33)).
- Post-intensive care review and follow-up. This pathway was developed to offer a comprehensive assessment to people being followed up by the rehabilitation after critical illness team, who review people three months post-discharge. The team screened for post-traumatic stress disorder (PTSD), with referral into liaison outpatients for those scoring as 'likely to have PTSD'. Referrals enabled a full trauma assessment, with treatment arranged either by liaison outpatients or by referring to Improving Access to Psychological Therapies (IAPT).

- Persistent physical symptoms including functional neurological disorders and medically unexplained/chronic abdominal pain. Referrals came into a central point in outpatients and were treated by the relevant clinician. Within the nurse consultant clinic, eye movement desensitisation and reprocessing (EMDR) interventions were used with this client group where clinically indicated (34).
- Stroke care pilot, working closely with stroke nurses to develop and deliver screening for all new admissions to the stroke ward. Assessments were initially carried out by liaison mental health staff and then, after education and support, by the team themselves. The aim was to ensure that patients needing treatment (pharmacological or cognitive therapy) were not missed. The education plan was delivered by psychiatrists, a nurse consultant and clinical leads and a band 6 member of staff regularly attended the multidisciplinary team meeting. These interventions served to enhance the knowledge base of the stroke team, meaning only the most complex cases required liaison input. This is a good example of speculating to accumulate over a limited time period.

Outpatient clinics provide the following functions.

- Allow a review of the patient at the optimum time, be that a few days after an unplanned presentation with self-harm or after suicidality, or to offer an appointment two to three months post-delirium to see if it is resolved.
- A full assessment of mental health utilising a full bio-psycho-social assessment and signposting to a service for ongoing support.
- Enhanced safety planning: checking what is working and supporting what is not (8).
- Brief psychological interventions.
- An opportunity to review the plan that was put in place, hopefully at a time when things have somewhat reduced in intensity.
- Many liaison services signpost to the 'best-fit' service for ongoing support. For example, anxiety associated with an LTC may be referred on to primary care psychological therapy services. Liaison clinics enable a short, structured piece of therapeutic work that can be tailored to the individual patient.

Sadly, because of the nature and acuity of their clinical presentation or because of the complexity of their physical health condition, people presenting to acute hospitals often do not meet the criteria for community mental health input. For patients ensconced in recurrent cycles of admission and discharge where the relationship between their physical and mental health has not been addressed, liaison clinics could represent an effective setting in which to deliver a short intervention to manage frequent attendance. Nurses are great enablers for this work as they can deliver focussed intervention and link collaboratively with specialist nurses in the field, for example, within the community stroke service. This work allows an osmosis of skills over time, ensuring that liaison services only get involved with the most complex cases while supporting specialist physical health nurses to provide good standards of mental healthcare (3).

The Role of the Nurse Consultant in Liaison Psychiatry

Nurse consultant roles subject to nationally agreed job descriptions are broadly divided into four key roles, with clinical practice taking the lion's share (50%) and the other three components (research, leadership and teaching) sharing equal parts of the remainder.

Expert Clinical Practice

(1) Non-medical prescribing is complex, capitalising upon relevant medical knowledge and discussion with pharmacy where required to enable careful prescribing. Nurses tend to make very safe prescribers, for example, taking time to review possible contraindications (2).

(2) The nurse consultant contributes to the daily multidisciplinary team to provide senior nursing leadership and ad hoc teaching, and offers alternative perspectives for ongoing care for those seen within the last 24 hours in the emergency department pathway.

(3) Nursing leadership should be provided to nursing groups within the acute hospital, including support to break down stigma within teams and developing nursing policies and care plans around mental health and dementia/delirium pathways (3).

(4) Complex cases within liaison psychiatry require innovative treatment plans to create sustainable improvement and communication/care planning with diverse teams. The nurse consultant plays a key role in enabling this type of work.

(5) Another cornerstone of the nurse consultant role is supporting the wider team to develop practice and capability in setting up and diversifying outpatient clinics.

Professional Leadership and Consultancy, Including Clinical Supervision

(1) Leadership across the mental healthcare provider, acute hospital, links with commissioning and influencing at a national level have been central to the success and reputation of liaison services within the author's organisation.

(2) Influencing has included the development of the local service and the liaison psychiatry agenda at regional and national forums.

(3) Clinical supervision: nurses in clinical lead roles tend to provide supervision for band 3–6 nursing staff. In turn, the nurse consultant supervises the clinical leads within the team, and so provides overall leadership for the clinical supervision structure within the nursing team.

(4) Clinical supervision can also be provided to specialist nurses in an informal way to support development of their working knowledge base with respect to mental health.

(5) Informal supervision is also provided to visiting junior medical staff.

Education, Training and Development of Staff, Statutory and Non-Statutory Agencies in Management and Treatment Services for People Presenting to the Acute Hospital

(1) Examples include offering continuing professional development for the team, designing training packages that team members can utilise to deliver training in the acute hospital and developing specialist training packages for specific teams within the acute hospital to enhance their skill set in terms of managing distress, such that referrals into liaison psychiatry are focussed mainly on complex cases (examples include stroke, intensive care, trauma and rehabilitation). Training can also be offered to the wider mental healthcare provider.

(2) Role modelling locally, regionally and nationally – enhancing the reputation of the growing nursing workforce within the field of liaison psychiatry.

Research into Various Aspects of Service Provision and Service Evaluation Which Involves This Client Group

(1) Service outcomes; development of clinician-reported outcome measures (CROMs), patient-reported outcome measures (PROMs) and patient-reported experience measures (PREMs). Research development around the financial benefits of liaison psychiatry to ensure that the service continues to develop year on year in terms of outcomes in its widest sense and eventually within a stagnant financial envelope (Framework for Routine Outcome Measures in Liaison Psychiatry – FROM-LP) (32).

(2) Looking for and influencing opportunities to develop patient advocates with 'lived experience' who may follow treatment support in enhanced understanding about the impact of living with an LTC or with unexplained persistent physical symptoms across the wider health economy.

Growing Your Own Liaison Nurses

It has been necessary, given the shortage of staff at all levels of nursing, to develop innovative ways of growing your own liaison nurses. One option is to offer newly qualified preceptorship nurses an opportunity to develop a unique set of skills in liaison mental healthcare. Liaison mental health is a specialist field and so there is a requirement to develop the nurse's skill set.

From the authors' experience, the role would include the following key areas.

- Start and continue in line with a local induction which is based around the psychiatric liaison accreditation networks standards.
- Provider-wide induction of two to three days.
- The liaison provider-wide induction is increased to a week by working half-time across each part of the service, where we have a separation of emergency and liaison in some teams; in others the split is around age. We are keen for people to have a specialist interest while holding a generic liaison skill set to deliver an initial assessment and formulation to any presenting individual.
- Assessments are initially completed jointly with new staff, first as an observer; then, as skills develop, they may start to take the lead with support.
- Brief psychological interventions are acquired over time; with training, these become available in-house, delivered specifically for services such as COPD/stroke. These include dialectical behavioural therapy-informed skills training and basic cognitive behavioural therapy training.
- The induction experience could be further enhanced by opportunities to work with other specialities within the acute hospital, for example, specialist respiratory nurses.
- The second edition of the Liaison Nurse Competency Framework is used in conjunction with other preceptorship documents with the view that establishing a level 3 in all areas is suggestive of an individual's readiness to start applying for a band 6 role (35).

Key Points at the End

Liaison mental health nursing is a dynamic area that develops year on year. It is therefore critical that liaison nurses maintain their knowledge and clinical skills and remain up to date.

(1) Liaison nurses are required to have a diverse set of clinical skills and knowledge and be capable of assessing people across chronological age ranges and with a multitude of clinical presentations.

(2) The field of liaison nursing requires a high level of freedom to proactively decide on the best course of action, where people need to be signposted to a diverse range of statutory and voluntary sector services.

(3) Liaison nurses should not become overly focussed on *getting the assessment done*; rather, they should see the role as supporting the patient and the clinical team in communicating effectively and fostering parity of esteem regarding physical and mental health.

(4) In the case of frequent attendance, opportunities should be taken to support the patient to understand what is going on, to review the safety plan and to mitigate the risk.

(5) Liaison nurses can support innovation in developing enhanced skills and knowledge in their peers by working closely and developing and delivering training packages.

(6) The inception of a nurse consultant role within a liaison team allows for significant enablement of the wider nursing team, develops the team skills and capability and offers a clear career development pathway.

(7) Taking opportunities to effectively grow your own liaison nurses offers significant benefits in developing this specialist role.

References

1. Roberts D. Working models for practice. In Regel S, Roberts D (eds.), *Mental Health Liaison: A Handbook for Nurses and Health Professionals*. Edinburgh; 2002, pp. 23–42.

2. Eales S, Chartres K. (eds.). *A Competency Framework for Liaison Mental Health Nursing*. London; 2021.

3. Health Education England. Mental health nursing competence and career framework. 2020. www.hee.nhs.uk/sites/default/files/documents/HEE%20Mental%20Health%20Nursing%20Career%20and%20Competence%20Framework.pdf.

4. Jaye P, Thomas L, Reedy G. The Diamond: A structure for simulation debrief. *The Clinical Teacher*. 2015;**12**(3):171–5.

5. Royal College of Psychiatrists. The role of liaison psychiatry in integrated physical and mental healthcare. PS07/19. 2019. www.rcpsych.ac.uk/docs/default-source/improving-care/better-mh-policy/position-statements/ps07_19.pdf?sfvrsn=563a6bab_2.

6. Trenoweth S, Moone, N. Overview of assessment in mental health care. In Trenoweth S, Moone, N (eds.), *Psychosocial Assessment in Mental Health*. Los Angeles, CA; 2017, pp. 3–13.

7. National Confidential Enquiry into Patient Outcome and Death. Mental health in general hospitals: Treat as one. 2017. www.ncepod.org.uk/2017mhgh.html.

8. Cole-King A, Lepping P. Suicide mitigation: Time for a more realistic approach. *Br J Gen Pract*. 2010;**60**(570):e1–e3.

9. Foye U, Simpson A, Reynolds L. 'Somebody else's business': The challenge of caring for patients with mental health problems on medical and surgical wards. *J Psychiatr Ment Health Nurs*. 2020;**27**(4):406–16.

10. Her Majesty's Government. No health without mental health: A cross-government mental health outcomes strategy for people of all ages. 2011. www.gov.uk/government/publications/no-

health-without-mental-health-a-cross-government-outcomes-strategy.

11. Nursing and Midwifery Council. The Code: Professional standards of practice and behaviour for nurses, midwives and nursing associates. 2018. www.nmc.org.uk /standards/code.

12. Staying Safe from Suicidal Thoughts. https://stayingsafe.net.

13. Perkins R, Morgan P. Promoting recovery throughout our lives. In Trenoweth S (ed.), *Promoting Recovery in Mental Health Nursing*. Los Angeles, CA; 2017, pp. 79–90.

14. Waldock H. Essential mental health nursing skills: Writing and keeping records. In Callaghan P, Gamble C (eds.), *Oxford Handbook of Mental Health Nursing*, 2nd ed. Oxford; 2016, pp. 35–78.

15. The Royal Pharmaceutical Society. A competency framework for all prescribers. 2016. www.rpharms.com/Port als/0/RPS%20document%20library/Open %20access/Professional%20standards/Pres cribing%20competency%20framework/pre scribing-competency-framework.pdf.

16. Sartorius N. Comorbidity of mental and physical diseases: A main challenge for medicine of the 21st century. *Shanghai Arch Psychiatry*. 2013;**25**(2):68–9.

17. Cohen BE, Edmondson D, Kronish IM. State of the art review: Depression, stress, anxiety, and cardiovascular disease. *Am J Hypertens*. 2015;**28** (11):1295–302.

18. Breland JY, Hundt NE, Barrera TL et al. Identification of anxiety symptom clusters in patients with COPD: Implications for assessment and treatment. *Int J Behav Med*. 2015;**22**(5):590–6.

19. Brown S, Eales S, Hood S et al. Side by side: A UK-wide consensus statement on working together to help patients with mental health needs in acute hospitals. 2020. www.rcpsych.ac.uk/docs/default-source/members/faculties/liaison-psychiatry/liaison-sidebyside.pdf.

20. NHS England. Implementing the Five Year Forward View for Mental Health. 2016.

www.england.nhs.uk/publication/imple menting-the-fyfv-for-mental-health.

21. Alzheimer's Society. This is me. 2017. www .alzheimers.org.uk/sites/default/files/2020-03/this_is_me_1553.pdf.

22. Public Health England and NHS England. Optimal Alcohol Care Teams as part of an effective alcohol treatment system. 2019. www.longtermplan.nhs.uk/wp-content/up loads/2019/11/ACT-what-are-we-proposing-and-why-011119.pdf.

23. Cooper SA, McLean G, Guthrie B et al. Multiple physical and mental health comorbidity in adults with intellectual disabilities: Population-based cross-sectional analysis. *BMC Family Practice*. 2015;**27**(16):110.

24. Gordon C, Lewis M, Knight D et al. Mental health practice: Differentiating between borderline personality disorder and autism spectrum disorder. 2020. htt ps://juiceboxcreative-autismwa.s3.ap-southeast-2.amazonaws.com/wp-content/ uploads/2021/01/12192827/BPD-vs-ASD-article.pdf.

25. MMBRACE-UK. Saving lives, improving mothers' care: Lessons learned to inform maternity care from the UK and Ireland Confidential Enquiries into Maternal Deaths and Morbidity 2015–17. 2019. www .npeu.ox.ac.uk/assets/downloads/mbrrace-uk/reports/MBRRACE-UK%20Maternal% 20Report%202019%20-%20WEB%20VER SION.pdf.

26. Douglas H, Ginty M. The Solihull Approach: Changes in health visiting practice. *Community Practitioner*. 2011;**74** (6):222–4.

27. National Institute for Health and Care Excellence. Clinical guideline 16: Self-harm in over 8's – Short-term management and prevention of recurrence. 2004. www .nice.org.uk/guidance/cg16.

28. We Can Talk. 2022. https://wecantalk .online/online.

29. Papyrus. Self-harm safety planning tool. www.papyrus-uk.org/wp-content/uploads/ 2018/10/Suicide-Safety-Plan-Template-1 .pdf.

30. Nursing and Midwifery Council. Standards of proficiency for registered nurses. 2018. www.nmc.org.uk/standards/standards-for-nurses/standards-of-proficiency-for-registered-nurses.

31. Mental Health Foundation. Parity of esteem. 2021. www.mentalhealth.org.uk/a-to-z/p/parity-esteem#:~:text='Parity%20of%20esteem'%20is%20defined,improve%20the%20quality%20of%20care.

32. The Royal College of Psychiatrists. The Framework for Routine Outcome Measures in Liaison Psychiatry (FROM-LP). 2015. www.rcpsych.ac.uk/docs/default-source/members/faculties/liaison-psychiatry/framework-for-routine-outcome.pdf?sfvrsn=6df8b8e9_2.

33. National Institute for Health and Care Excellence. Clinical guideline 103. Delirium: Prevention, diagnosis and management. 2023. www.nice.org.uk/guidance/cg103.

34. National Institute for Health and Care Excellence. Clinical guideline 116. Post-traumatic stress disorder. 2018. www.nice.org.uk/guidance/ng116.

35. Eales S, Wilson N, Waghorn, J. London-wide liaison nurses special interest group: A competency framework for liaison mental health nursing. 2014. https://eprints.bournemouth.ac.uk/32294/7/A%20Competence%20Framework%20for%20Liaison%20Mental%20Health%20Nursing%202014%20v2.pdf.

Chapter 4

Psychological Reaction to Physical Illness

Elspeth Guthrie and Marc Mandell

Introduction

Physical illness is stressful; however, given time and support, most people manage to adjust and cope with serious physical illness without the need for psychological intervention. Psychological reaction to physical illness refers to a set of cognitive, emotional and behavioural responses which are triggered by the development of physical symptoms or a diagnosis of a physical condition by a healthcare professional. Experiencing and living with illness is a dynamic process and it takes time to assimilate new information, manage feelings and make appropriate adjustments to family and social circumstances. Chronic physical illness usually involves having to make a sequential series of psychological adjustments as the disease progresses.

There are many different ways of understanding psychological reactions to physical illness based upon cognitive, behavioural, social and psychodynamic theories, and some knowledge of these different theoretical approaches can be helpful for professionals working in liaison settings. This chapter is co-authored by a former consultant psychiatrist, Dr Marc Mandell, who developed a severe stroke in middle age, and it includes a personalised account of his lived experience of illness and recovery. It provides a unique insight into the process of psychological adjustment to illness from a personal and professional perspective, which complements and illuminates the theoretical understanding of this topic.

Meaning of Illness

One of the most influential psychiatrists to study people's reaction to physical illness was Lipowski (1), who began writing about this field over 50 years ago. He described psychological reaction to illness as a set of responses to illness-related information, whereby the person appraises the information, consciously and unconsciously, and arrives at its personal meaning for them.

By 'meaning', Lipowski referred to the subjective significance for the person of all the illness-related information to which they were privy. This information would then be appraised, based upon people's prior personal experience, knowledge, values, beliefs and needs. Lipowski described four common reactions to physical illness: seeing illness as a challenge or threat; experiencing illness as a loss; feeling gain or relief; or feeling punished. Although these may seem rather crude categories, it is not uncommon to come across these reactions in clinical practice.

Viewing illness predominantly as a threat is likely to elicit anxiety or fear or sometimes anger. It is quite common for people to talk of cancer as if they are fighting or combatting disease. Many people view illness in terms of loss, both concrete and symbolic. Loss can involve loss of function or loss of a body part or a sensory organ, but it can also involve a loss of self, particularly if the person loses self-independence. Loss inevitably involves a sense of grief and sadness, which can be mistaken for depression. For some people, illness can involve some kind of relief as it offers a respite from social demands or a situation which is difficult and challenging. Some people regard illness as a punishment which can either feel unjust ('why me?') or just ('I deserve to be punished'). The latter group may passively accept the condition and not fully engage in treatment.

Adjustment to Chronic Disease

Chronic disease requires adjustment across multiple life domains, and adjustment unfolds over time often in a stepwise fashion. There is considerable heterogeneity in the different ways that people adjust to chronic illness. Adjustment encompasses multiple components that cross interpersonal, cognitive, emotional, physical and behavioural domains and interact with each other. Although adjustment varies from person to person, a positive outcome includes five key factors: mastery of disease-related adaptive tasks; preservation of functional status; perceived good quality of life in several domains; absence of psychological disorder; and low negative affect (2). Other factors that have been discussed in the literature include maintaining personal worth, maintaining or restoring relationships with important others, resolution of a search for meaning, negotiating the healthcare environment, maintaining satisfactory relationships with healthcare professionals and resumption of employment if possible. A satisfactory adjustment to illness does not imply that an individual has to have a relentlessly cheerful mood or an unwavering stoic attitude. Expressions of distress, disappointment, irritation, frustration or sadness in response to physical illness events are to be expected and should not be pathologised.

Adjustment As a Dynamic Process

Adjusting to chronic illness is a dynamic and changeable process. Most people with chronic illness have at least two illnesses, and many people have multiple conditions that they must manage. Chronic illnesses vary in their prognosis and course. Some, like many cancers, carry an ongoing threat to life; others are characterised by a rapid deterioration and severe disease progression; others may be characterised by flares that then resolve; others have a downward stepwise path; others begin with a deterioration which is followed by significant improvement (e.g. hip replacement in people with osteoarthritis); and others may involve a severe sudden catastrophic event (e.g. a severe hemiplegia or severe trauma following a road traffic accident). The variety of patterns and variations in disease progression are manifold but most involve a fairly continuous process of adjustment across many life domains.

Illness can have positive benefits and it is not uncommon for individuals to report that their illness has resulted in enhanced personal relationships, a greater appreciation of life, enhanced personal strength, sharpened awareness of priorities and deeper spirituality.

Theories of adjustment to chronic illness are often derived from more general conceptual frameworks about adjustment to stressful experiences. Two of the most prominent in health research are the stress and coping theory by Lazarus and Folkman (3) and the self-regulation theory of Leventhal (4).

Stress and Coping

Coping has been described as cognitive and behavioural efforts to manage specific external and or internal demands that are appraised as taxing or exceeding the resources of the person (5). Within the concept of coping is the notion of emotion regulation, which has been defined as the processes responsible for monitoring, evaluating and modifying emotional reactions, especially their intensive and temporal features, to accomplish one's goals (6). Coping refers to general strategies people use to cope with difficulties, whereas emotion regulation refers specifically to ways in which they moderate their emotional experience. Table 4.1 shows some examples of coping and emotion regulation strategies that are associated with an adaptive response to illness, while Table 4.2 shows examples of strategies that are associated with maladaptive responses to illness and draw upon findings from a meta-analytic review of illness representations, coping and outcomes (7) and a review of coping, emotion regulation and well-being (8).

The Common-Sense Model of Self-Regulation and Illness Perception

Illness perceptions are frameworks or working models that people construct to make sense of their symptoms and medical conditions. They comprise a number of interrelated beliefs about an illness and what it means for the person's life. The major components include how the illness was caused, how long it will last, what the consequences of the illness are for the person's life and family, the symptoms that are part of the illness and how the condition is controlled or cured (9). Individuals' perceptions of illness were first examined in the 1960s in research about health threat communications.

Subsequent research led to the development of Leventhal's common-sense model of self-regulation (4), which has become one of the most well-known theories concerning individuals' response to illness. The theory describes a parallel response model in which people process emotional/feeling responses to illness and cognitive representations of illness relatively independently. These feelings and cognitions cause people to use specific behaviours to regulate their emotions and cope with the illness. Following adoption of these behaviours, people appraise the effects on illness and the self-system, and this can then result in changes to their feelings and cognitive representations in a feedback loop. The perceptions are regarded as being multi-level in that they are shaped by prior personal experience and are derived from prototypes of self, illness and treatment.

The model consists of five core constructs that concern perceptions that are activated in response to somatic and functional changes. These domains are: (1) identity: the symptom pattern, severity and location; (2) timeline: the rate of progression of the illness and the perception of illness duration; (3) consequences: the functional, social and financial impact of the symptoms; (4) control: how far treatment goes in controlling the illness or pain; and (5) cause: the mechanism underlying the illness and how treatment links to this.

Research has demonstrated that patients' perceptions of their illness along these domains vary widely, even between patients with similar illnesses or injuries. People build models of their illness based on previous personal or family experiences with their disease or information they may have received from medical staff or the general media. These illness models may be specific to the individual and may differ considerably from those of the clinicians providing a diagnosis or giving treatment.

Table 4.1 Examples of adaptive coping and emotion regulation strategies

Type of coping	Description
Cognitive re-appraisal	Cognitive efforts to acknowledge the illness, accept initial responses to it and then take on board a broader context
Problem-solving: general	Actively engaging in actions to help address optimum ways to manage illness (e.g. lose weight and exercise)
Problem-solving: specific	Engage in specific illness-related coping behaviours (e.g. take medication or monitor blood glucose)
Seeking social support	Reaching out to appropriate family and friends for practical help and emotional support
Emotional expression	Being able to put into words how you feel about the illness and communicate this to appropriate others
Emotional processing	Attempts to psychologically adjust to the illness and understand one's emotional responses

Table 4.2 Examples of maladaptive coping and emotion regulation strategies

Type of coping	Description
Cognitive avoidance	Mental disengagement and avoidance of thinking about the illness
Behavioural avoidance	Disengagement with behaviours that are necessary for investigation, control or treatment of the illness (e.g. not monitoring blood sugar in diabetes)
Denial	Acting as if the illness does not exist
Thought blocking	Efforts to keep negative thoughts about illness out of conscious awareness
Harmful behaviours	Using alcohol or drugs to avoid dealing with illness
Worry	Uncontrollable repeated intrusive thoughts about negative aspects of the illness
Catastrophisation	Overwhelming extreme negative thoughts imagining the worst possible outcome of the illness or disease
Rumination	Repetitive thoughts and focus on a particular aspect of the illness or treatment
Social avoidance	Shunning support that is offered by family and friends

One of the best-known measures of illness perception is the Brief Illness Perception Questionnaire (10); measure items include perceived consequences, timeline (acute–chronic), amount of perceived personal control, perceived control over treatment, identity (symptoms), concern about the illness, coherence of the illness and emotional representation.

A large body of literature has shown that patients' illness perceptions are related to a range of important health outcomes, including functioning, healthcare utilisation, adherence and mortality. For example, worse consequence and identity beliefs are consistently associated with worse physical, role and social functioning, higher distress and lower well-being and vitality (11). Higher control beliefs are consistently associated with better social functioning and well-being, lower distress, higher vitality and better disease state. Longer timeline beliefs are associated with higher distress, lower role and social functioning and lower vitality.

Patient drawings have been used in research as a more personal way to access illness perceptions than the use of a questionnaire. For example, in one study of patients with heart disease, participants were asked to draw their hearts. The drawings provided indications of how damaged patients felt their hearts were, and how likely treatment (such as heart surgery) was going to have a positive outcome. Patient drawings have been shown to be associated with important outcomes such as time to return to work and functional status. More organ damage drawn and larger drawing size are associated with worse illness perceptions and poor illness outcome (12).

Other Relevant Psychological and Social Models of Health Behaviour

There are several other psychological and social models of health behaviour such as the Illness Action Model (13) and the Network Episode Model (14). The former emphasises individualistic and cognitive processes in decision-making about treatment, while the latter recognises the importance of individual actions but seeks to understand them in the context of social networks with which people interact. Another relevant model is Andersen and Newman's Framework of Health Services Utilisation (15), which divides determinants of healthcare use into three categories: predisposing characteristics, enabling resources and need factors. This model includes symptom response but also suggests that health seeking can be driven by other factors including poverty or isolation. Attachment theory also provides a framework for understanding health seeking in the context of a need for interpersonal care (16).

Differential Effect of Chronic Diseases

Diseases vary in their course, prognosis, threat to life, toxicity of treatment, degree of associated pain or disability, requirement for lifestyle changes and predictability. The differential impact of chronic diseases has been most clearly explored in relation to physical function in large prospective cohort studies. A recent study used data from three large cohorts (NHS: 121,701 nurses aged between 30 and 55 years in 1976; NHS II: 116,686 female nurses aged between 25 and 42 years in 1989; and Health Professionals Follow-up Study: 51,530 male health professionals aged between 40 and 75 years in 1986) (17).

Physical function in the three populations decreased year on year by small increments for both men and women and, on average, participants had a mean of 3.3 chronic diseases. Among the most common diseases, the impact on physical function varied considerably with differences of more than 10-fold between some of the conditions. The five most common conditions (at least 15,000 participants) with the highest impact on physical function were osteoarthritis, herniated disc, rheumatoid arthritis, chronic obstructive pulmonary disease and diabetes. Less common conditions with very high impacts on physical function were multiple sclerosis, Parkinson's disease, knee replacement surgery, lung cancer, stroke, peripheral vascular disease and hip replacement surgery. Conditions with relatively low impacts were high cholesterol, hypertension, asthma, cataracts, prostate cancer, osteoporosis and basal cell carcinoma. A weighted index was developed by the study authors to account for the impact of multiple co-morbid conditions on physical function. On average men had higher weighted scores than women, suggesting poorer physical function.

The Importance of Relationships

Supportive interpersonal relationships have been shown to help ameliorate the negative impact of chronic disease. Relationships can provide a forum for emotional expression, a sense of connectedness, practical support, a sense of being loved and valued, reinforcement of positive health behaviours and minimisation of adverse behaviours. Individuals who receive more support tend to show more effective coping, higher self-esteem and life satisfaction and fewer depressive symptoms. Effective social support partially explains trajectories of psychological adjustment to chronic illness. In patients with breast cancer, maladaptive coping mechanisms and poor social support were independently associated with patients who had the greatest emotional, cognitive and physical decline (18).

Absence of social support predicts poorer outcome in a variety of chronic conditions, as does the perception that others are unsupportive or unreceptive to a person's needs. Couple relationships have been shown to be both helpful and unhelpful in relation to adjustment to chronic illness, depending upon the quality of the relationship. Marital dissatisfaction predicts poorer cancer-related adjustment over time. In diabetes, patients who felt supported by their partners compared with those who felt unsupported reported more positive mood states and were more likely to engage in exercise and follow dietary advice (19). In breast cancer, greater social support is associated with lower depressive symptoms, which in turn are associated with higher adherence to cancer treatment (20).

Attachment theory also provides a framework for understanding health seeking in the context of a need for interpersonal care (16). Attachment theory proposes that internal working models that we have of ourselves and others are developed from early childhood parental/carer relationships around themes of worthiness and trust. People with a positive sense of self and an ability to trust others are considered to have a secure attachment style, whereas people who either have a negative view of themselves or find it difficult to trust others (or both) have an insecure attachment style. Insecure attachment has been linked to a variety of poor health outcomes in physical disease, including poor adherence to treatment, poor quality of life, more complications, greater physical morbidity and increased mortality (21).

Spirituality

Spirituality and religious faith are important aspects of some people's lives. Religious faith refers to a person's association with a specific religious institution or teaching, whereas spirituality is a broader concept involving ideas about divinity, nature, transcendence, meaning, hope and connectedness that are not necessarily linked to religious ideas. Clinicians often ignore the impact of spiritual beliefs and practices on health, although people often make sense of illness, healing and death through religious precepts and spiritual practice. Being ill often creates emotional and existential problems that lead people to question or search for a meaning to their lives and a need to draw upon something 'bigger' than themselves to help them cope.

A recent qualitative study identified four interrelated dimensions of spirituality and faith that were important to people living with diabetes and/or cardiovascular disease (22). Coping involved a feeling of regaining control over the illness through meditation, prayer or bible-reading. Support included attendance at religious services, prayer or bible groups, or a sense of greater autonomy because people felt they were supported by God. Acceptance included a sense of acceptance, peace and letting go of stress or blame, an increased capacity to cope and transcendence. Healing involved a sense of recovery, feeling good, reconciliation and comfort and increased self-worth.

Faith or belief in God may not necessarily be the key component of spirituality which conveys benefit for people with chronic physical illness. In a large study of multi-ethnic cancer survivors, three facets of spirituality were studied over a nine-year period: faith, a sense of peace and meaning. Patients who reported lower levels of peace and meaning but not faith were more likely to develop depressive symptoms over time. Higher faith also predicted higher levels of depression in the context of lower meaning. These findings suggest that cancer survivors with greater meaning and peace appeared to be better able to integrate the cancer experience into their lives, but not necessarily those with the strongest faith beliefs (23).

Most hospitals have on-site multi-faith, religious departments who offer support and religious guidance to staff and hospital inpatients. It is helpful for liaison teams to make links with such services, who often include skilled counsellors, so that patients can have access to this form of support if religion or spirituality plays an important role in their lives.

Resilience

The concept of resilience has developed from psychoanalytic theory and originates from the concept of ego-resiliency introduced by Block and Block (24). It is seen as the ability to have adaptive responses to adversity and stressful life situations, including chronic illness. There is no universally agreed definition of resilience. One recent review defined it as 'the process of effectively negotiating, adapting to, or managing significant sources of stress or trauma'. Assets and resources with the individual, their life and environment facilitate this capacity for adaptation and 'bouncing back' in the face of adversity. Across the life course the experience of resilience will vary (25). Measures of resilience include such concepts as mastery, resourcefulness, perseverance, adaptability, equanimity or balance, flexibility, a balanced perspective on life, self-reliance and independence (26).

Resilience has been studied as an aspect of personality and as a dynamic process. Research on adults tends to focus on the concept as a personality trait, whereas longitudinal studies in childhood have considered developmental aspects. Many studies of physical disease refer to resilience in terms of returning to or maintaining normal function, although this is clearly not possible in conditions that are progressive or involve some form of severe physical incapacity (e.g. a spinal injury resulting in paraplegia). Studies have also examined the relationship between resilience and mental illness in people with physical illness. Higher resilience is associated with better mental health across a wide range of differing physical health conditions (27).

Previous Experiences

Previous experience of illness shapes and informs people's response to illness. Childhood experience of illness in parents is an independent risk factor for later unexplained symptoms, and unexplained symptoms in childhood are also associated with later development of unexplained symptoms as an adult (28). Attitudes about illness and illness concerns are passed from adults to children. Craig and colleagues showed that health anxieties of mothers with unexplained symptoms were reflected in their children who were more likely to have worries and concerns about their own health (29). Other negative life events such as parental death are also associated with a greater risk of unexplained symptoms as an adult. The quality of parental and peer relationships in adolescence predicts adult mental and functional somatic health as much as 26 years later (30).

Interactions between health staff and patients also shape the way people respond to illness, how they appraise it and future use of services. Recursivity describes how future demand for services, and the process of help-seeking, is determined by a patient's previous experiences (31).

Formulation

Liaison psychiatrists are often asked to assess patients who are struggling to adjust to and/or cope with physical illness. An understanding of relevant theories can help determine when poor adjustment morphs into mental illness and how best to help the individual concerned. Most people go through a process of adjusting to illness without the help of a psychiatrist and it is important not to interfere with a normal adjustment process by over-pathologising it. It is not uncommon for patients to be referred to liaison mental health services because they have seemed distressed in a ward or outpatient setting. This distress may be entirely normal and part of their adjustment process.

Psychiatrists are taught to formulate cases in terms of predisposing, precipitating and maintaining factors. We have outlined some steps to take in the following paragraphs that may help with formulation when there are concerns as to whether the person is making a normal adjustment to illness.

1. Establish the Nature of the Distress, Its Duration and Its Relationship with Physical Health

Encourage the person to tell you about their experience in their own words and use gentle prompts to elicit more detail. Be sure you establish the depth or severity of their distress and its timeline. Be concerned if the distress seems very severe or there is no sense of it gradually reducing in severity over time, or it is increasing in severity. Establish the relationship of the distress to physical illness – it may or may not be related. If the distress is illness related, explore the person's beliefs and perceptions about their illness. Are they exaggerated or realistic? What are they based upon? Have they been given appropriate information and time to assimilate that information? Further explanation and clarification from medical staff regarding aspects of their illness or care may be warranted.

2. Relationships with Healthcare Staff

Try to establish the degree of trust between the individual and the staff involved in their healthcare. This is a two-way process and problems can arise from either staff or the patient or both. Hospitals are stressful and alien environments for most people. Their clothes and belongings are removed, access to loved ones is severely restricted, information is sometimes difficult to come by, key staff constantly change, people may be moved from one ward to another, they may witness distress or behavioural disturbance in other hospital inpatients, food is often poor, usual ways of controlling anxiety such as cigarettes or alcohol are restricted, there is a regimented system to which the person has to adhere, the person may be in pain or suffering from embarrassing symptoms, there is a lack of privacy, sleep may be difficult, and bathing and toilet facilities have to be shared with strangers. Healthcare staff often fail to appreciate how unnerving and destabilising hospital admission can be for people, even those without any cognitive impairment. For people who have difficulty trusting others, hospital admission can be especially challenging, particularly if staff fail to recognise they are struggling with the ward environment.

3. Past History of Physical Illness

Previous experience of illness (both in ourselves and significant others) shapes our response to current illness. Try to get a picture of how the person has coped with illness before, especially any illness in childhood, either in themselves or parents and other family members.

4. The Person

Try to get to know the person you are seeing. How do they normally cope with adversity? How do they normally get on with people? What kind of support systems do they have in place? What do they normally do in relation to diet and fitness? You are trying to establish an understanding of the attachments they form, their usual coping strategies and their resilience.

5. The Meaning of the Illness

This could be included in the first point, but it is usually discussed later on in the assessment. It is not related to symptoms or distress but rather to the impact of the illness on the person's sense of their own self. Lipowski's original ideas about illness can be helpful in considering 'meaning', although there are many more categories than the ones he described.

6. Past History of Mental Health Problems or Childhood Adversity

As with mental health conditions, a prior history of anxiety/depression or childhood neglect and adversity are powerful predictors of a poor adjustment regarding physical health. The bi-directional relationship between physical and mental problems often means cyclical patterns develop which can be difficult to interrupt.

7. Family

Family can play a crucial role in facilitating or impeding (often unintentionally) adjustment to physical illness. Both overprotectiveness and under-concern can limit or impede recovery.

A Personalised Account of Illness and Recovery

In this section Dr Marc Mandell, consultant psychiatrist for older adults (retired) and a member of the Faculty of Liaison Psychiatry Executive Committee, describes the process of his personal adjustment to a catastrophic sudden illness.

A Personalised Account of My Experience of Illness and Recovery

I would like to be clear that I can only describe my own experience of illness, not the experience of those who suffer from relapsing and remitting illness. My illness was, by its nature, of sudden onset and has left me with a static set of disabilities.

My stroke was a result of a carotid aneurysm which was caused by a road traffic accident, where a white van hit my car head on.

I have full recall of the accident itself. My injuries seemed minor, but I then lost consciousness in hospital where I suffered a stroke in the accident and emergency department. The next thing I knew I was waking up in the Intensive Care Unit, very confused and delirious, with no idea that I'd had a stroke. All I knew was that I was being given CPAP (continuous positive airway pressure) to reduce my risk of a chest infection. It felt like I was being suffocated. My delirious brain interpreted this as torture; I was convinced I was in Germany back in World War II. This got so bad that I wasn't certain I wanted to continue being alive.

The stroke had caused left-sided hemiplegia; unfortunately for me, I used to be left-handed. I also had a communication impairment including articulatory dyspraxia and aphasia. I was unable to express my needs, my feelings or to connect to others verbally or in writing, which left me feeling very isolated.

When you have a communication impairment, it is very frustrating to be asked the same questions on multiple occasions when the act of answering is a huge effort. Especially when you know that the answers are in the medical notes!

After I found out I had suffered a stroke, I went on an emotional rollercoaster, starting with an adjustment reaction. It took time to take on board the implication of the news. Obviously, I had prior knowledge of stroke, so I was aware of the long-term implications.

This was followed by low mood which was made worse by the communication impairment. My speech and my writing were unintelligible; I couldn't express my basic needs, let alone my emotions.

I experienced anger with the other driver and the situation I found myself in. I tried to channel the anger into my neurorehabilitation. You don't want to direct the anger towards your family and friends or the staff who are helping you. So, I tried to direct this emotional energy towards attaining my rehab goals. It fuelled my determination to keep working hard.

The next emotion I experienced was guilt about what others had to do for me – things which I knew I would have previously done for myself.

Recovery can become like Groundhog Day; it can be very wearing. I have to remind myself daily that I am not dead yet! The worst aspect of it is waking up after a dream about having no disability only to find it was a dream. But I want to point out the value of humour. It can be an effective coping strategy for some patients and their families. I knew I was back on track with my family when they felt comfortable taking the piss out of me, as usual! The reason this is important is because it shows they don't see me as someone who is fragile or someone to pity. I don't want pity.

Every day is a battle between me and my limitations to gain control over my life, which can be exhausting. There are some days I am so tired just from the effort in getting ready for the day that I want to go back to bed! But I definitely noticed a link between my progress in my rehab and my mood as I regained my independence and started to recover my identity.

I would like to turn to the subject of identity – having a disability has impacted on my self-image, and how others treat me, which can be very different from before the accident. You can find yourself being ignored by people who act like you aren't there. This can be like 'does he take sugar?' and having your wheelchair pushed out of the way by a stranger who sees you as an obstacle. This can negatively impact on how you see your value to society. It can feel like you are treated with less respect. Sometimes it feels like there is a lack of common decency. There is also a fine line between being helpful and infantilising someone.

Identity is bound up in the roles we play in society (employment, family roles). There can be a loss of role which can negatively impact on self-identity. So, I struggled with both the loss of my roles as a doctor and as a father who would do all the practical things for my children but now has to accept help from them.

I have found I often compare myself to how I was before the stroke. It is a double-edged sword. It can be a good source of motivation in rehab and yet it can cause frustration, magnifying the sense of loss. In some ways it feels like someone stole my future – all my plans were snatched away from me in an instant.

The next phase was my search for my new identity. I was trying to take back control of my life from my disabilities, rather than them controlling me. And trying to give some meaning to what I went through. If my experience can be of benefit to others, then it will have had some useful purpose. This is why I agreed to write this account.

I would like to thank my family and all my friends and colleagues for their support. This support has been invaluable in my recovery.

Summary

Psychological reaction to physical illness is an individualistic process, as illustrated by Marc's account, that varies from person to person. It a process that evolves over time and usually does not require involvement from mental health professionals. Many theories have been developed to help explain human reactions to illness. A knowledge of some of the most common ones are helpful to guide understanding and formulation of clinical scenarios. However, the most important thing is to recognise and try to understand the personal experience of each person you are asked to see, being aware of any potential difficulties they may have in communicating that experience to you.

References

1. Lipowski ZJ. Physical illness, the individual and the coping processes. *Psychiatry Med.* 1970;1(2):91–102.

2. Stanton AL, Sworowski LA, Mahwah NE. Adjustment to chronic illness: Theory and research. In Baum A, Singer JE (eds.), *Handbook of Health Psychology*. Mahwah, NJ; 2001, pp. 387–403.

3. Lazarus RS, Folkman S. *Stress, Appraisal, and Coping*. New York; 1984.

4. Leventhal HBY, Benyamini Y, Brownlee S et al. Illness representations: Theoretical foundations. In KJ Petrie (ed.), *Perceptions of Health and Illness: Current Research and Applications*. Reading; 1997, pp. 19–45.

5. Lazarus RS. Psychological stress and coping in adaptation and illness. *Int J Psychiatry Med.* 1974;5(4):321–33.

6. Thompson RA. Emotion regulation: A theme in search of a definition. *Monogr Soc Res Child Dev.* 1994;**59**:25–52.

7. Hagger M, Orbell S. A meta-analytic review of the common-sense model of illness representations. *Psychol Health.* 2003;**18**(2):141–84.

8. Marroquín B, Tennen H, Stanton AL. *Coping, Emotion Regulation, and Well-Being: Intrapersonal and Interpersonal Processes.* New York; 2017.

9. Petrie KJ, Weinman J. Patients' perceptions of their illness: The dynamo of volition in health. *Curr. Dir. Psychol.* 2012;**21**:60.

10. Broadbent E, Petrie KJ, Main J, Weinman J. The brief illness perception questionnaire. *J Psychosom Res.* 2006;**60**(6):631–7.

11. Broadbent E, Wilkes C, Koschwanez H, Weinman J, Norton S, Petrie KJ. A systematic review and meta-analysis of the Brief Illness Perception Questionnaire. *Psychol Health.* 2015;**30**(11):1361–85.

12. Broadbent E, Schoones JW, Tiemensma J, Kaptein AA. A systematic review of patients' drawing of illness: Implications for research using the Common Sense Model. *Health Psychol Rev.* 2019;**13**(4):406–26.

13. Dingwall R. *Aspects of Illness.* Farnham; 2001.

14. Pescosolido BA. Illness careers and network ties: A conceptual model of utilization and compliance. *Adv Med Sociol.* 1991;**2**:161–84.

15. Andersen RMNJ. Societal and individual determinants of medical care utilization in the United States. *Milbank Memorial Fund Quarterly: Health and Society.* 1973;**51**:95–124.

16. Adshead GGE. The role of attachment in medically unexplained symptoms and long-term illness. *BJPsych Advances.* 2015;**21**:167–74.

17. Wei MY, Kawachi I, Okereke OI, Mukamal KJ. Diverse cumulative impact of chronic diseases on physical health-related quality of life: Implications for a measure of multimorbidity. *Am J Epidemiol.* 2016;**184**(5):357–65.

18. Dura-Ferrandis E, Mandelblatt JS, Clapp J et al. Personality, coping, and social support as predictors of long-term quality-of-life trajectories in older breast cancer survivors: CALGB protocol 369901 (Alliance). *Psychooncology.* 2017;**26**(11):1914–21.

19. Helgeson VS, Mascatelli K, Seltman H, Korytkowski M, Hausmann LR. Implications of supportive and unsupportive behavior for couples with newly diagnosed diabetes. *Health Psychol.* 2016;**35**(10):1047–58.

20. Bright EE, Stanton AL. Prospective investigation of social support, coping, and depressive symptoms: A model of adherence to endocrine therapy among women with breast cancer. *J Consult Clin Psychol.* 2018;**86**(3):242–53.

21. Jimenez XF. Attachment in medical care: A review of the interpersonal model in chronic disease management. *Chronic Illn.* 2017;**13**(1):14–27.

22. Unantenne N, Warren N, Canaway R, Manderson L. The strength to cope: Spirituality and faith in chronic disease. *J Relig Health.* 2013;**52**(4):1147–61.

23. Bamishigbin ON, Stein KD, Leach CR, Stanton AL. Spirituality and depressive symptoms in a multiethnic sample of cancer survivors. *Health Psychol.* 2020;**39**(7):589–99.

24. Block J, Block JH. Venturing a 30-year longitudinal study. *Am Psychol.* 2006;**61**(4):315–27.

25. G. W. What is resilience? A review and concept analysis. *Rev Clin Gerontol.* 2011;**21**(2):152–69.

26. Wagnild GM, Young HM. Development and psychometric evaluation of the Resilience Scale. *J Nurs Meas.* 1993;**1**(2):165–78.

27. Färber FRJ. The association between resilience and mental health in the

somatically ill: A systematic review and meta-analysis. *Dtsch Arztebl Int.* 2018;**115**:512–17.

28. Hotopf M. Childhood experience of illness as a risk factor for medically unexplained symptoms. *Scand J Psychol.* 2002;**43** (2):139–46.

29. Craig TK, Cox AD, Klein K. Intergenerational transmission of somatization behaviour: A study of chronic somatizers and their children. *Psychol Med.* 2002;**32**(5):805–16.

30. Landstedt E, Hammarström A, Winefield H. How well do parental and peer relationships in adolescence predict health in adulthood? *Scand J Public Health.* 2015;**43**(5):460–8.

31. Rogers KH, Nicolaas G. *Demanding Patients? Analysing the Use of Primary Care.* Buckingham; 1999.

Chapter

5

Self-Harm and Suicidal Thoughts

Allan House

Introduction

Lifetime prevalence of self-harm (self-poisoning or self-injury) is 5–6% in the UK adult population. Rates are increasing especially among young women, where lifetime prevalence is now 25%. The commonest immediate causes are social and interpersonal problems. The most commonly associated mental health problems are mood disorders and alcohol misuse. Assessment involves careful characterisation of the act of self-harm, the person who self-harms and their social circumstances, but should not entirely be focussed on risk. It should identify needs in mental health or physical health, social needs and psychological needs, and should be a therapeutic experience for the person who has self-harmed. The assessment itself may be helpful for some. Research into cost-effective treatment is limited, but even so it is reasonable to offer brief psychological therapies to everybody and longer-term therapies to those with severe repeated self-harm. Quality improvement activities should aim to improve the experience for people making contact with mental health and to increase the availability and accessibility of therapeutic interventions for self-harm.

Definition

The World Health Organization (WHO) defines self-harm as 'an act with non-fatal outcome, in which an individual deliberately initiates a non-habitual behaviour that, without intervention from others, will cause self-harm, or deliberately ingests a substance in excess of the prescribed or generally recognised therapeutic dosage, and which is aimed at realising changes which the subject desired via the actual or expected physical consequences'. More concisely, the National Institute for Health and Care Excellence (NICE) defines self-harm as 'any act of self-poisoning or self-injury carried out by a person, irrespective of their motivation' (1).

Neither definition includes a statement about motivation and especially no statement about intent to die. The WHO definition adds an unhelpful observation that the act is 'aimed at realising changes', while the NICE definition explicitly excludes motivation from its definition. These definitions are therefore at odds with the approach taken in the USA and followed by others, which is that there is a clear distinction between non-suicidal acts and suicidal behaviour – the former are usually associated with self-injury in the widely cited *Diagnostic and Statistical Manual of Mental Disorders* (DSM) 5 diagnostic category of non-suicidal self-injury (NSSI) (2).

The suicidal intent of an act of self-harm can be defined as the degree to which the individual undertaking a particular act reports that at the time their intention was to end their life. It is tempting to infer suicidal intent from the nature of an act (sometimes called *implicit intent*) from its potential lethality, the degree of planning or the attempts made to avoid interruption. This approach can have value in clinical practice but the risk of error must be acknowledged – acts that are not medically dangerous can be associated with strong suicidal intent and life-threatening acts may be unplanned. It would be better to call the result of this exercise *inferred intent* rather than implicit intent, thereby flagging the role of a third party in attribution.

Criticism of this dichotomising approach has been broadly along three lines (3). One criticism points out that non-suicidal intent has been over-identified with self-injury, as if non-suicidal self-poisoning does not exist. A second line of criticism is that so-called non-suicidal self-injury is associated with suicidal thoughts and is indeed a risk for suicide: this is not a fundamental criticism of how to describe an individual act because a person at high risk of suicide who thinks often of suicide may yet undertake a non-suicidal act. In fact, people will report that a deliberately non-fatal act can be a means of averting suicide. Much more to the point is the criticism that it simply is not possible to attribute intent so neatly: intent scores on standardised measures are not bi-modally distributed and expressed desire to die is often ambivalent or unclear. These ideas – that suicidal intent cannot be regarded as simply present or absent but can be thought of as present to various degrees and can co-exist with a desire not to die – are long established but not captured by the practice of describing acts as straightforwardly suicidal or non-suicidal.

Identification of suicidal intent is also likely to be unreliable because individual reports of intent change over very short periods of time and as time passes after an episode. Clinical experience tells us that stated intent changes over time as changing circumstances and emotions lead to reattribution.

Giving too much salience to reported intent has a further disadvantage in that it over-emphasises the suicide risk residing in a particular act rather than residing in the individual. Use of the distinction persists no doubt because clinical management decisions are very largely dichotomous – admit/don't admit, prescribe medication/don't prescribe and so on.

Overlapping Phenomena

Other intentional and harmful conditions include eating disorders and alcohol or drug misuse. They are usually regarded as separate because bodily harm is a secondary consequence rather than the primary aim of the individual's actions. However, their frequent co-occurrence with self-harm suggests they have at least some shared origins.

There are other intentional actions the primary aim of which is to damage the body in some way, but which are not included in the definition of self-harm: extensive scarification, piercing and other sorts of body modification are usually regarded as separate because they are not seen as evidence of psychological problems but rather are socially sanctioned, if only by a selected sub-group of the population. However, when taken to extremes they do suggest psychological disorder, so again the distinction is not clear-cut – the boundaries of any categories used in health and healthcare are inevitably blurred.

Epidemiology

In the UK, there are three main sources of information about population patterns of self-harm. First, and longest established, there are reports from NHS services that give information about people who go for treatment. Most of these studies have been based upon hospital attendances, especially in the emergency department, although recent studies have also reported on contacts made in general practice. The statistics behind these reports came in the UK from a body now called NHS Digital (https://digital.nhs.uk). The figures also come from primary care physician computerised records. A second source of information comes from the results of large-scale surveys like the Adult Psychiatric Morbidity Survey (https://digital.nhs.uk/data-and-information/publications/statistical/adult-psychiatric-morbidity-survey) and the Millennium Cohort Study (https://cls.ucl.ac.uk/cls-studies/millennium-cohort-study), which are funded by government and cover many topics, of which one is self-harm. Our third source of information about self-harm is academic research studies, especially those aimed at identifying people who self-harm but do not present to health services for help. This has been an important source of information about self-harm in young people of school age, for example.

Each of these sources has its own biases – hospital and primary care statistics miss those who do not present to health services, while surveys and research studies miss those who are not willing to report their actions to a third party. There are also differences in definition – for example, the Adult Psychiatric Morbidity Survey asks a series of questions about what people have done, why they did it and what help they sought, whereas the Millennium Cohort Study asks only one question about whether the respondent has hurt themselves 'on purpose in some way'. Notwithstanding these recording problems, there are some common findings.

Self-harm is common in the UK and getting commoner. There are an estimated 200,000 hospital attendances in England for self-harm made by approximately 160,000 people per year (4) and at least double this number of episodes in primary care. About 5% of the adult population have harmed themselves at some time in their life.

Age

Self-harm is rare before puberty, becoming increasingly common in the years immediately afterwards up to the mid-20s. Age-standardised rates of hospital-presenting self-harm are 362 per 100,000 population for men and 441 per 100,000 population for women. In the UK the annual incidence is highest in 16–24-year-olds; thereafter incidence rates fall to barely more than a tenth of that figure.

Gender

Self-harm has been consistently found to be commoner in females than males, particularly during adolescence and young adult life – around 25% of young women 16–24 years old have self-harmed on at least one occasion, more than double the male rate. This gender gap is widening and in recent years there has been a dramatic increase in the number of girls presenting with self-harm to both hospital and their primary care physician, over and above the increase seen in adolescent boys. In truth, very little is known about the causes of this female preponderance.

It is important not to stereotype self-harm as solely a problem of young women. The gender ratio across the whole population is about 60:40, and something like a third of all episodes are accounted for by people over 35 years.

Socio-economic Status

As anybody who works in liaison services is aware, self-harm presentations are commoner from areas of greater deprivation. This is not just a question of differences in likelihood of presentation – economic deprivation and other aspects of socio-economic status (like unemployment and low educational attainment) are risks for self-harm.

Ethnicity

Some of the risks for self-harm in minority-ethnic groups are specific to their social position – minority-ethnic status in the UK, as in many countries, brings exposure to racism and for those with a relatively recent immigration history there can be intergenerational tensions. In other ways the important factors are similar to those faced by young people everywhere – material deprivation, concerns about future security, difficulties in relationships. Not surprisingly, therefore, rates of self-harm are higher in people of South Asian and African Caribbean heritage (5). There are exceptions – for example, men of South Asian heritage present much less often. Rates of repetition are lower in people from South Asian and African Caribbean backgrounds: one explanation might be lower rates of alcohol use and misuse in those populations.

Outcomes Following Self-Harm

Something like 1.5–2% of people who present to hospital following self-harm will die by suicide in the next 12 months, and one in 25 will kill themselves within the next 5 years (6). Approximately half of all people who die by suicide have previously self-harmed. In the UK, 30% of those who attend hospital after self-harm will repeat within six months and 50–60% in the next five to six years.

Self-harm is important not just because it is a risk for suicide. Follow-up studies indicate that other outcomes are poor – persistent mood symptoms and poor quality of life, high rates of drug and alcohol misuse, lower levels of educational attainment and high rates of unemployment. People, and especially the young, with a history of self-harm are over-represented in the so-called NEET population (Not in Education, Employment or Training).

Associations with Self-Harm

Mental Disorder

Mental illnesses that are known to be associated with an increased risk of suicide are substantially over-represented in populations of people seen after self-harm, but they account for only a small minority of cases. A recent systematic review found prevalences of less than 10% for bipolar illness (6%), other psychoses (6%) and eating disorders (7%). For the overwhelming majority of those who are given a psychiatric diagnosis, it is for a disorder of mood: depression (49%), anxiety (35%) or adjustment disorder (26%). These are essentially diagnoses for states of distress and, as judged by rates of referral to psychiatric services for treatment, many are not regarded as ill enough to require specialist treatment. Substance misuse, mainly involving alcohol, is also commonly diagnosed (34%) either alone or in combination with one of these other diagnoses (7).

There are predictable differences in children and adolescents: psychosis (2%) is rarer while disorders usually only diagnosed in childhood, such as attention deficit hyperactivity disorder (ADHD) and conduct disorder, feature with frequencies influenced very much by the sample studied.

Figures from the Adult Psychiatric Morbidity Survey suggest that self-harm in learning disability is twice as common as in the general population, although here – as with autism – true rates have been difficult to ascertain historically because of a tendency to see self-harm as a different phenomenon – sometimes called 'self-injurious behaviour' – in these populations.

Self-Harm and Personality Disorder

The latest versions of the two main diagnostic systems – the International Classification of Diseases (ICD) 11 and DSM 5 – take different approaches to the diagnosis of personality disorder but both require evidence of persistent or recurrent impairment of social and interpersonal function. Since many people who self-harm give an explanation that involves recurrent relationship and social difficulties, it is perhaps not surprising that a diagnosis of personality disorder is often made, particularly when the history is of repeated self-harm. In the review of Hawton et al. (7) the pooled estimate was 30% prevalence.

There are particular problems with diagnosing personality disorder in this setting. Most assessment involves a single contact in stressful circumstances and it is difficult to attribute personal and relationship problems to the individual's actions, which is one explanation for considerable variability and unreliability in diagnosis. As discussed later, diagnosis, and particularly one of borderline personality disorder, is disliked by those to whom it applies and can lead to stigmatising by health professionals.

Psychological Characteristics

A recent review of the psychology of suicidal behaviour (8) summarised 32 key psychological risk and protective factors and 11 models of suicidal behaviour that attempted to synthesise these factors into an explanatory framework, suggesting a field too unwieldy to be of much use to the clinician. For practical purposes the most robust findings fall into three broad categories:

Negative thinking including negative thoughts about the future, hopelessness, pessimism; negative thoughts about the self, including low self-worth and perceived burdensomeness; and negative thoughts about relationships, including a sense of isolation and what has been called thwarted belongingness.

Unhelpful approaches to problems including problem-solving deficits, brooding (rumination) and cognitive rigidity, and impulsivity.

Attitudes to self-harm and suicide including familiarity arising from personal experience or acts of close others, and apparent lack of fear of injury or death.

Life Events and Difficulties

When asked about the reasons for an episode of self-harm, some people initially mention an aspect of mental state – depressive ideas, for example – but most give an account of social and personal adversity (9). The details are as diverse as is human experience; commonly they fall into one of the following groups.

Problems in relationships – in the family, with peers or in romantic relationships. Because stable and supportive relationships are protective against adversity, long-standing difficulties in important relationships are often present and related to an immediate precipitating event.

Experience of abuse or neglect – either physical or sexual. Perhaps most immediate and pressing is to recognise abuse that is taking place in person, with the perpetrator known to the victim and still in contact. A more recently identified form of abuse takes place online, for example through cyber-bullying or trolling, when the perpetrator may be known but may be completely anonymous or using a false identity.

Practical difficulties – with housing, money, employment or education.

Physical illness – which can have a direct effect if, for example, it causes pain or disability or other social or personal problems.

These adversities are recognisably stressful, with the specific nature of the stress derived from the meaning given them by the individual. Losses, threats and apparently insoluble dilemmas are all common and can give rise to feelings of hopelessness and inability to find resolution – either by their very nature or because of the psychological and social characteristics of the person experiencing them.

Management of Self-Harm

Guidelines for the management of self-harm in the UK are provided by NICE (1). The outline here is aimed at liaison psychiatrists and therefore primarily at acute hospital practice rather than work in other settings where self-harm may be common, such as schools, primary care, social services or prisons.

NICE recommends assessment with two main aims – assessment of risk and assessment of need – with the assessment then forming the basis for a jointly agreed management plan that addresses safety for the individual, social and interpersonal problems and the role of psychological therapy.

Assessment

In recent years, there has been a focus on risk assessment following self-harm which has resulted in some instances of a checklist approach to the problem, a rather defensive clinical practice mentality and little endeavour to focus on what might actually be helpful or therapeutic for the person being seen.

Risk assessment is aimed at estimating the likelihood of repeated self-harm or of suicide and at identifying the risk factors for either outcome with a view to mitigation. The standard clinical assessment performs rather poorly at identifying risk. The problem is that there are a number of well-known risks but each individually contributes only modest effect, and each can therefore be present in individuals at low risk. The result is that success in using combinations of these risks to identify individuals who go on to future repetition (high sensitivity) is bought at the expense of identifying many who do not (low specificity). This is especially a problem in suicide prediction because the low incidence leads to a low positive predictive value, which unlike sensitivity and specificity is dependent upon the frequency of the phenomenon being studied; any response set up to deal with high-risk cases will therefore be swamped by misidentified low-risk cases.

Because the problem resides mainly in the nature of known risks rather than poor practice in applying risk assessment, the use of standardised assessment tools does little to improve this situation. The dilemma is this: many of the risks identified are not amenable to intervention and risk assessment is too inaccurate as a tool for selecting whom to treat when service capacity is limited; and yet common sense suggests that assessment of risk must have

Table 5.1 The main risks for suicide or repetition of self-harm after an episode of self-harm

Domain	Comment
The act	
Method used – self-injury; mixed self-poisoning + self-injury	Contrary to popular belief, self-injury is associated with a higher risk of suicide as well as self-harm
History of repeated self-harm	Also, commonly and mistakenly taken to indicate lower risk
High suicidal intent	Should be judged by circumstances, e.g. degree of planning, effort not to be interrupted, and not just by self-report
High lethality	The converse is not true – low lethality cannot be taken to mean no risk
The person	
Age and gender	Suicide is the commonest cause of death in middle-aged men in the UK
Mental health problems	
Depression	
Serious mental illness, e.g. psychosis	Relative risk is high, although absolute numbers are not
Recent or current psychiatric treatment	
Hopelessness	Bear in mind other negative ideas about self, e.g. worthlessness, sense of burdensomeness
Problematic alcohol or drug use	
Chronic physical illness and disability	Especially associated with chronic pain
The circumstances	
Living alone	Especially when associated with sense of loneliness, isolation, disconnectedness
Living in deprived area	
Recent losses, e.g. bereavement, separation	
History of sexual or physical abuse	

a place. A sensible approach is to ensure that the commonest and most robust known risks are actively identified. Rather than using risk to determine who is followed up, it can be used to inform a decision about *acuity of care*. That is, intervention after self-harm is aimed at meeting unmet needs, which determine the *form and content* of support, while risk is used to inform the *immediacy and intensity* of support. The important risks that can be identified in a standard clinical assessment are outlined in Table 5.1.

Assessment of needs will inevitably cover some of the same ground, especially in relation to mental and physical health and the social circumstances of the person being seen. However, understanding of social circumstances – especially recent stressful events and difficulties and the nature of personal relationships – needs more detail and individualisation than risk assessment provides.

An important consideration when thinking about the value of psychological therapy is to obtain an initial assessment of other aspects of psychological state that are relevant in self-harm but do not fit well into the format of conventional mental health assessment. One element of this is to identify psychological characteristics that are risks for further self-harm or suicide, such as poor problem-solving and impulsivity. There are standardised tests for both, but they are not readily applicable in the context of clinical assessment; instead, it is often possible to form a view from the history – which can reveal evidence of a limited repertoire of approaches to problems or a tendency to act impulsively, the latter sometimes obvious in the self-harm act itself.

The other way to approach this part of assessment is to consider what functions (purposes) are served by the self-harm. Answers to this question can shed light on the unmet needs or unfulfilled goals that are met (unsatisfactorily) by self-harm. There have been several reviews of the functions of self-harm (10–12) and particularly repeated self-harm, which can be summarised as follows (13).

Responding to distressing thoughts or memories – self-harm can temporarily obliterate such experiences through the effect of sedating drugs, or because the pain of self-injury displaces emotional pain.

Responding to negative feelings about self – either by self-punishment or by experiencing the cathartic or cleansing effect of the act.

Managing powerful feelings – typically either suicidal or aggressive in nature.

These functions all describe personal attempts to manage unpleasant psychological states and they should raise questions about the origins of those states. Sexual abuse is common and should be inquired about but not assumed: a history of current or previous experience of neglectful or abusive relationships of all sorts may not be immediately confided. Sensitivity is required in judging how far to explore, especially at a first meeting.

Communicating distress – while self-harm is often an intensely private affair and many people do not disclose it to anybody they know, it can also be a means of communication. Sometimes this has a help-seeking function, sometimes one that is more self-validating – simply finding out if acceptance from others is possible. Self-harm has been called a language that cannot be put into words and in fact the 'communication' may be with self, a way of acknowledging what is happening and who one is.

This communicative function is not to be labelled as attention-seeking but is to be recognised as a reflection of a need for understanding that cannot be articulated in other ways and requires further exploration.

Generating Positive Feelings – For some, self-harm serves not just to manage negative feelings; it can generate positive feelings. These include a sense of warmth or relaxation, or powerfulness, or being in control; at times even a sense of arousal or excitement during the build-up to an act. What this experience of the 'positive' aspects of self-harm points to is a lack of opportunities to achieve similar feelings in other ways. Such an idea can be explored by determining what goals or values a person has, the fulfilment of which could generate similar feelings. The elements of assessment of needs are outlined in Table 5.2.

Table 5.2 The common needs of people seen after self-harm

Domain	Comment
Mental health needs	
Accessing new treatment	For example, of previously unrecognised depressive disorder
Optimising existing treatment	
Facilitating contact with services	Disengagement from services should be explored and rectified where possible
Physical health needs	
Optimising existing treatment	
Tackling social impacts of disability	
Social needs	
Finding practical support for living	For example, debt support, housing
Accessing intervention and protection in abusive relationships	
Identification of, and planning the response to, current life events and difficulties	
Psychological needs	
Learning problem-solving and other self-management skills	
Dealing with distressing thoughts and memories	
Managing suicidal ideas	
Establishing supportive relationships	
Identifying and pursuing positive goals	

Of course, not all these ideas can be explored in a brief assessment – typical clinical assessments after self-harm last 20–40 minutes – but it is usually possible to identify areas for further exploration at the same time as checking on somebody's interest in taking the discussion further.

Assessment That Acknowledges Diversity

Increasingly, we are called upon to recognise the degree to which clinical practice has failed to be sensitive to the diversity of modern societies. Self-harm is common in people with characteristics typically thought of as making them marginal or not part of mainstream society: for example, minority sexual orientation or gender identity; disability including sensory disability and intellectual disability; autism; and minority-ethnic status. What people with these characteristics share is an experience of discrimination which is itself stressful and which can also be associated with secondary consequences such as employment difficulties. They are also likely to have an assessment that does not take into account their particular circumstances in the same way, and therefore to have problems accessing the full range of services.

Assessment of Resources and Assets

The nature of assessment in psychiatry has been to concentrate on problems and deficits rather than assets and resources. This is unfortunate because most people have at least some skills or resources they can turn to if encouraged. They include:

Personal resources – including information (or knowledge of where to obtain it) about current problems or available services to help. Questions about experience of coping in previous times of adversity that help to elucidate how somebody coped successfully (even if only partially) with a bereavement or unemployment, for example, may be a useful starting point.

Social support – can come from a number of sources: family, friends, third sector or peer-support organisations. An important consideration is the ability a person has to *confide* in their main source of support. Online support has an unusual status in this respect – access can be anonymous and the degree of confiding can be controlled. Although it can seem impersonal to others, this degree of detachedness can be helpful in the face of anxiety about intimacy. Support has been divided into the practical and the emotional, the former more useful when problems can realistically be resolved, the latter when accommodating to problems is more realistic. It is helpful to have more than one source of support, with different sources and types of support chosen according to each of the range of problems being encountered – so-called *matched support*.

Professional support – bear in mind that the most valued professional may not be one immediately identified, such as a key worker in a community mental health team or a primary care physician. It may instead be a different and even less experienced team member who is more consistently available or who is experienced as more approachable and sympathetic.

In Summary

These three elements of assessment can flow easily into each other with practice. An initial review of the nature of self-harm, its antecedents and the individual's current circumstances leads to a more detailed exploration of needs, what help has been sought already and what has been helpful or otherwise. All this then forms a platform for discussion about what future help might be available.

Near-Fatal Self-Harm

The majority of people who are admitted to a general hospital bed following self-harm require some form of medical/surgical treatment or monitoring of their physical status. Near-fatal self-harm has been used to describe a subset of these people with the most serious injuries or physical consequences of their self-harming behaviour. They present challenges to liaison psychiatry teams as many cannot be moved to a mental health unit, and their inpatient mental healthcare has to be delivered in a general hospital setting. Medical and surgical wards are not designed to manage people who are suicidal; they are busy, bustling places with a high throughput of people coming and going without any checks; and there are many potential ligature points and blind spots. Medical and nursing staff are unfamiliar with suicidal risk issues and can either greatly over- or under-estimate things, leading to either panic or failure to act when they need to. They are not skilled in assessing mental state or behaviour, so no regular assessments are conducted unless the person is receiving one-to one nursing from a mental health nurse. Even then, it is not unusual to find the patient is being 'nursed' by a security guard rather than a mental health nurse.

Hospital patients with near-fatal self-harm should be assessed by the liaison team as soon as it is practically possible to do so and this should not be left until they are 'medically fit for interview', as has been the case in the past in certain services. Even if the person is not well enough to engage in a psychiatric assessment, steps should be put in place to keep them safe. This may involve assessment of the ward environment (e.g. access to nearby ligature points, open windows, stairs), alerting ward staff about risk issues and deciding whether the person needs one-to-one mental health nursing care. A clear risk assessment (albeit incomplete) should be written in the case notes and discussed with the senior ward manager. Prior psychotropic treatment should be reinstated as soon as possible unless there are medical contraindications. Decisions regarding the appropriate legal framework to care for the patient should be clearly communicated to all staff involved in their care and acted upon. The liaison team should review the person regularly, at least daily. A full assessment should be conducted when it is feasible to do so with a collateral history from a friend or relative if possible.

The liaison team should work closely with the general ward staff, recognising any fears or concerns they may have and trying to address these as soon as possible (see Table 5.3).

Therapeutic Responses

Supported Self-Management and the Internet

Many people who self-harm do not seek professional help, finding instead ways of managing their own needs. First-hand accounts of what helps fall into two broad groups:

Breaking the link between self-harm and the circumstances, thoughts and feelings that usually prompt self-harm. This involves, for example, finding ways of interrupting thoughts about self-harm, of using alternative (substitute) actions instead of self-harm and of managing immediate circumstances (much as is used in anger management).

Building new foundations, which involves acknowledging that just stopping self-harm is not enough – a more positive future is needed. Planning for that future, goal-setting, tackling barriers to change and re-evaluating one's own role – all these can take place without getting stalled by the difficulty of immediately stopping self-harm.

An increasingly accessed resource for self-management is the online world. Much recent debate has centred on the unhelpful or damaging effects of the internet, and especially of social media sites, in relation to self-harm. A balanced view sees the potential for online support for those who do not want or cannot access therapy, and part of management should be to provide information about suitable resources. Because these things change so quickly, the way to access such information is not from textbooks but by developing a local repository of contacts and links.

Table 5.3 Examples of people with near-fatal self-harm admitted to a general hospital setting and the input from the liaison team

Case presentations	Case management
Man (aged 40–50) who jumped from 6th floor of building, became trapped in scaffolding on his way down to the ground. His leg had to be amputated at the scene. Homeless. Socially isolated. Estranged from his ex-partner and child. While in hospital, his flat was burgled and everything of value taken. He had left the door wide open when he left with the intention of ending his life. Multiple fractures to lower remaining limb and back.	At first assessment, he was judged to be immobile so one-to-one nursing was not required. Remained suicidal for several days following admission. Severely depressed. Started on antidepressant medication and provided with psychological support. Mood gradually improved. Contact made with ex-partner and arrangement made for regular access to his child discussed. Homeless team involved as he had lost tenancy of his flat. Benefits which he had been entitled to but had not claimed were instated. Fitted with prosthetic leg. When discharged 8 weeks post-admission, his mood had considerably improved. No suicidal thoughts.
25-year-old woman came to emergency department having tried to jump out of her flat window after taking ketamine. While in the emergency department absconded and was found hanging from a beam in another part of the hospital. Resuscitated but query anoxia and also damage to vocal cords.	Detained under Section 2 of the Mental Health Act. One-to-one nursing instated. Nursed in a side room, with secure window and no ligature points. Cognitive function gradually improved over 2. Mental state rapidly reverted to a euthymic state. Voice remained hoarse although damage to cords was thought to be minimal. Risks of future drug-taking discussed in depth. Section rescinded and discharged home to parents.
35-year-old man with schizophrenia admitted to acute surgical unit after cutting off his penis. Very psychotic. Refusing his regular renal dialysis. Clinical picture was mix of psychosis and confusion. Very aggressive and threatening to enucleate and flay himself. Religious delusional beliefs.	Detained under Section 3 of the Mental Health Act. Underwent surgical repair. Antipsychotic medication started. One-to-one nursing arranged with two nursing staff with him at all times. Renal dialysis was eventually given on the Intensive Care Unit, under the Mental Capacity Act. Liaison team reviewed him at least twice per day. Mental state gradually improved. He remained very psychotic but suicidal and self-harm thoughts diminished in intensity. After 2 weeks, he was able to be transferred to a mental health unit and return to having dialysis on the dialysis unit.

Talking Therapies after Self-Harm

Some Common Ingredients of Useful Responses

People with personal experience of therapy after self-harm report a number of features that are useful regardless of the specifics of what they were offered.

Therapist Factors

People who self-harm report it is important that therapists are non-judgemental and really listen to them, so they feel understood. This observation matches what is known about so-called common factors in therapy. They include warmth, empathy and building rapport. They are important to many people with self-harm who have a very negative experience of the NHS, including mental health professionals, and who feel stigmatised, criticised and fobbed off by emergency department staff and mental health teams.

Warmth involves conveying to the client a deep and genuine sense of caring for them as a person with human potentialities, a caring which is unaffected by evaluations of their thoughts, feelings or behaviours. Empathy is the ability of the therapist to accurately and sensitively understand the person's experiences and feelings and their meaning. Rapport is the degree to which the two parties get on with each other and are able to work together productively.

Knowledge and Experience Related to Self-Harm

It is helpful to see somebody who knows about self-harm, can respond to old and new events in a practical way and is experienced in helping people with self-harm. Therapy should in some obvious way be 'about' self-harm while at the same time it is important to show that therapy is responsive to the individual's needs – not all self-harm is the same.

Mutual Trust

Everybody needs to feel they can trust their therapist, who will work on the assumption that change is possible and that the person they are seeing wants to change. Diagnostic stereo-typing ('another borderline personality disorder') is mistrusted.

Practical Help Is Useful

People value practical advice, even while they may be exploring more underlying issues. However, they are sceptical of too much in the way of simple advice – about relaxing, using distraction and so on, which can feel dismissive. For example, safety planning may be part of every initial contact but it needs to be flexible and responsive to the individual person being seen: some may never have experienced safety planning, some people will already have safety plans and some may be weary of such plans and experience this sort of advice as trivialising.

Therapeutic Assessment

It cannot be overemphasised that the first contact with people after self-harm is not simply a fact-finding exercise. Even though there is a major element of assessment to this contact, there is reasonable evidence that a well-conducted contact can be beneficial for the person involved (14). The most likely explanation resides in the common ingredients just noted, and it is a sorry observation that they are not, therefore, universally experienced.

Ultra-Brief Interventions

The briefest of additional interventions take place during the single initial face-to-face contact on presentation, which is then supplemented by follow-up contact by telephone, email or postal messages. The additional content in the face-to-face meeting often involves some variant of safety planning; see Table 5.4 for one example of the output of this.

Follow-up may entail checking on well-being and reinforcing the messages about safety planning. It does not involve telephone or online delivery of therapy. The evidence is not strong that these very brief interventions are effective, but they are simple, not heavy on resources and do not have obvious undesired effects. Since many people currently receive no offer of follow-up, it seems reasonable to implement them unless they are supplanted by more extensive involvement.

Brief Psychological Therapies

The mainstay of therapeutic response to self-harm has been brief psychological therapy: although there are several variants, the most commonly used have been cognitive behavioural therapy (CBT) and psychodynamic interpersonal therapy (PIT).

CBT focusses on the negative thoughts that drive self-harm. More recent formats such as behavioural activation have included larger components of behavioural experiment aimed at increasing social participation. PIT addresses interpersonal difficulties to improve interpersonal functioning and social support, which have been shown to buffer the negative impact of stressful life events.

Pooled results from trials of psychological treatment from two recent systematic reviews (15, 16) suggest that both psychological treatments lead to a reduction in repetition of self-harm at 6 and 12 months in comparison with controls. Cochrane reviews also provide evidence for the benefit of brief therapies for depression and hopelessness on self-harm and may reduce suicidal thinking and behaviour. The latest NICE guidelines (1) rather conflate brief therapies into what they call a CBT-informed category, which means in essence that they are standardised (manualised), time-limited and include elements recognisable from CBT such as practical problem-solving.

More Intensive and Longer-Term Therapies

Brief therapies are not likely to be effective for more established repeated self-harm, and indeed the latest Cochrane review treats this group separately in its analysis. The two best-known therapies in this context are dialectic behaviour therapy (DBT) and mentalization-based therapy (MBT).

DBT focusses on four main targets: mindfulness; interpersonal effectiveness; distress tolerance; and emotion regulation. It is delivered in individual face-to-face sessions, group work with an emphasis on interpersonal and social skills, and telephone or ad hoc contact to help crisis management. MBT is a specific type of psychodynamically orientated psychotherapy. Its focus is helping people to differentiate and separate out their own thoughts and feelings from those around them.

These therapies are of long duration and are only available in specialist centres. Until recently, access has depended upon receiving a diagnosis of borderline personality disorder. Recent reviews have provided some evidence of effectiveness but it is not conclusive.

Table 5.4 A typical safety plan

Safety plan for:	Date:
If I am feeling overwhelmed and in danger of acting on suicidal thoughts, I will:	
Statement *Write a clear statement using 'I' that you can read and repeat to yourself: e.g. 'I will give myself time to try to take care of myself and help myself feel a bit better.'*	I will make a deal with myself not to act on this immediately and to follow my safety plan to reduce the risk of acting on these thoughts. I will …
Someone to call *I will call one of the following people: (It's a good idea to save these numbers in your phone contacts under a relevant heading like 'Help'. You could also see if one or more of the listed people would agree to keep a copy of your safety plan and help talk you through it if necessary)*	Friend: Parent/relative: Doctor: Samaritans: 08457 90 90 90 E: jo@samaritans.org HOPELine UK: T: 0800 068 41 41 SMS: 0776 209 697 E: pat@papyrus-uk.org Get connected: T: 0808 808 4994 Local Crisis Service: Other:
Remove dangerous items *Write down what you can do to make it more difficult for you to harm yourself (e.g. not drinking alcohol while you are feeling this way, not stockpiling medication, removing or locking away razor blades, knives, rope, etc.)*	I will make myself safe from acting impulsively by:
Distraction or soothing: *e.g. watch TV or a light-hearted DVD; read a book; write in a diary; tidy my room; have a soothing bath; go for a walk with upbeat music on my phone; focus on my breathing or listen to a relaxation or mindfulness tape*	I will choose something from my list of self-soothing distractions and focus on it for at least 20 minutes
Write down one or more coping statements that you can repeat to yourself: e.g. 'I have survived so far, and I will make a commitment to surviving for another hour/day.'	I will remind myself of my coping statements and what has helped me before
Write down places you may be able to go to if you still feel at risk, e.g. friend who has agreed to be available – check limits to this; halls welfare officer; campus emergency support services; nearest emergency department, remembering to tell them you feel you are a danger to yourself	If I still feel suicidal and at risk, a safe place I can go to is:

In Summary

Current practice is that something like 50–60% of people who present after self-harm in the UK will receive no therapy in response. Given its poor outcomes, that is surely unacceptable. Despite evidence that is not entirely conclusive, it is reasonable to suggest that at the very least everybody should receive a therapeutic assessment and the offer of a brief therapy such as PIT or CBT. For those who decline, a lighter-touch follow-up as in ultra-brief therapies is in order. For severe repeated self-harm, a longer-term therapy is justified despite the lack of conclusive evidence of cost-effectiveness. There is no place for medication as a therapeutic response to self-harm, as opposed to its possible use for treatment of associated mental illness.

Again, it is important to mention population diversity because it is a significant deficiency of current therapies that they are so inaccessible to the groups noted earlier. It is now a legal requirement that health services make reasonable adjustments to allow suitable treatment for all people with disabilities – a requirement that is widely ignored. Under pressure from recent wider societal changes, there is an increasing expectation of cultural competence among clinicians and therapists. There is still a long way to go in achieving equity for all these groups, but at least the issue is now recognised – a first step towards real change.

The Perspective of People with Personal Experience

The feedback from people with personal experience of contact with health services after self-harm is mixed. Some find the help offered useful, but it has to be acknowledged that there is a long history of comments about negative experiences. The main criticisms are about:

> *Brusqueness*, sometimes amounting to rudeness, from staff – as if dealing with somebody who has self-harmed is just too much trouble. Even if not explicitly stated, the person treated with this sort of social behaviour perceives that they are regarded as a time waster.
>
> *Insensitivity* – here meaning a lack of responsiveness to the needs of the person being seen rather than straightforward crudeness. A recurrent complaint is of stock questioning as part of risk assessment – which is sometimes literally done as box-ticking – as if the only job is to go through the motions of ensuring suicide risk is low.
>
> *Stereotyping* – especially a complaint from people who have been given a diagnosis of personality disorder. Recipients of these attitudes will sense that they are regarded as being wilfully difficult and just need to go away and take some responsibility for their own actions.

These criticisms might seem difficult to square with observations that assessment in the emergency department can be beneficial. There are two likely explanations. One is that not all mental health professionals behave badly and enough are helpful enough to produce good outcomes. The other is that the more disaffected people vote with their feet, so that outcome results are biased by loss to follow-up and non-response.

Lack of aftercare is the other frequent complaint: what is the point of assessment if it does not lead to an offer of help? There is some justification for this observation – in the UK about 50% of those who attend hospital after self-harm leave without a specialist assessment or plan for therapeutic follow-up; many community mental health teams will only offer appointments to those with a mental illness diagnosis, and psychological therapy services (including Improving Access to Psychological Therapies (IAPT)) will not see those deemed at risk of suicide.

Conclusion

There are well-established frameworks for the assessment and management of self-harm that are outlined here. Given how common self-harm is and how poor its outcomes, there is a pressing need for improvements in services to support this clinical work. There is also a need for action to eradicate the poor attitudes and practice that are still a cause for complaint from some who make contact with the mental health services after self-harm.

References

1. National Institute for Health and Care Excellence. Self-harm in over 8s: Long term management. NICE Guideline. September 2022; NG 225.

2. Mumme TA, Mildred H, Knight T. How do people stop non-suicidal self-injury? A systematic review. *Arch Suicide Res.* 2017;**21**(3):470–89.

3. House A, Kapur N, Knipe D. Thinking about suicidal thinking. *The Lancet Psychiatry.* 2020;**7**(11):997–1000.

4. Clements C, Turnbull P, Hawton K et al. Rates of self-harm presenting to general hospitals: A comparison of data from the Multicentre Study of Self-Harm in England and Hospital Episode Statistics. *BMJ Open.* 2016;**6**(2):e009749.

5. Al-Sharifi A, Krynicki CR, Upthegrove R. Self-harm and ethnicity: A systematic review. *Int J Soc Psychiatry.* 2015;**61**(6):600–12.

6. Carroll R, Metcalfe C, Gunnell D. Hospital presenting self-harm and risk of fatal and non-fatal repetition: Systematic review and meta-analysis. *PLoS One.* 2014;**9**(2):e89944.

7. Hawton K, Saunders K, Topiwala A, Haw C. Psychiatric disorders in patients presenting to hospital following self-harm: A systematic review. *J Affect Disord.* 2013;**151**(3):821–30.

8. O'Connor RC, Nock MK. The psychology of suicidal behaviour. *The Lancet Psychiatry.* 2014;**1**(1):73–85.

9. Townsend E, Ness J, Waters K et al. Self-harm and life problems: Findings from the Multicentre Study of Self-Harm in England. *Soc Psychiatry Psychiatr Epidemiol.* 2016;**51**(2):183–92.

10. Suyemoto K. The functions of self-mutilation. *Clin Psychol Rev.* 1998;**18**(5):531–54.

11. Nock MK, Prinstein MJ. A functional approach to the assessment of self-mutilative behavior. *J Consult Clin Psychol.* 2004;**72**(5):885.

12. Klonsky ED. The functions of deliberate self-injury: A review of the evidence. *Clin Psychol Rev.* 2007;**27**(2):226–39.

13. Edmondson AJ, Brennan CA, House AO. Non-suicidal reasons for self-harm: A systematic review of self-reported accounts. *J Affect Disord.* 2016;**191**:109–17.

14. Carroll R, Metcalfe C, Steeg S et al. Psychosocial assessment of self-harm patients and risk of repeat presentation: An instrumental variable analysis using time of hospital presentation. *PLoS One.* 2016;**11**(2):e0149713.

15. Hawton K, Witt KG, Taylor Salisbury TL et al. Psychosocial interventions for self-harm in adults. *Cochrane Database of Systematic Reviews.* 2016(**5**).

16. Hetrick SE, Robinson J, Spittal MJ, Carter G. Effective psychological and psychosocial approaches to reduce repetition of self-harm: A systematic review, meta-analysis and meta-regression. *BMJ Open.* 2016;**6**(9):e011024.

Depression in Medical Settings

Elspeth Guthrie

Depression is common in people with long-term physical conditions and those seen in medical settings. The actual prevalence varies according to the setting, type and severity of disease, the individual's perception of their condition and premorbid risk factors (e.g. childhood adversity). Depression has a bi-directional causal relationship with physical disease, so each can be a risk factor for the other. Depression and anxiety symptoms co-occur more often than as separate conditions and are often undetected or diagnosed by primary and secondary healthcare staff. People who experience depression and physical illness understand depression as part of their whole life experience and not just as being simply related to their physical health. Depression, and to a lesser extent anxiety, in the context of physical disease are associated with a range of poor outcomes, including poorer physical health outcomes and quality of life; increased hospitalisations, investigations and healthcare costs; and higher mortality. Treatment should be patient-focussed and guided by a detailed understanding of the person and their previous life experiences, past psychiatric history, social circumstances and interpersonal support, plus an understanding of the severity/complexity of their physical health problems. The National Institute for Health and Care Excellence (NICE) recommends treatment with psychological approaches initially, with antidepressants and associated drugs as second-line medications. Care is needed when prescribing psychotropic drugs in the context of physical illness and the potential for any drug interactions should be carefully considered.

Diagnosis and Detection

Depression refers to a wide range of mental health problems characterised by a negative affect and occurs more commonly together with anxiety than alone. Diagnostic criteria for the various depressive syndromes are available in the relevant diagnostic classification systems and will not be discussed further as specific diagnoses are rarely helpful in a liaison setting, unless to distinguish psychotic from non-psychotic conditions. In the context of physical disorder, depression is best understood in terms of a spectrum of severity and chronicity.

Depression in the context of physical disorder can be difficult to diagnose as many people with physical disease understandably feel down or anxious at times, and many physical symptoms that are characteristic of depression/anxiety are also common in physical disease. Greater reliance is therefore placed upon emotional and cognitive symptoms when diagnosing depression, as well as function: is the person's level of functioning commensurate with their physical disabilities? Box 6.1 lists the main non-somatic symptoms of depression in people with physical disease. A degree of caution should be exercised when determining whether wishes to die or stop life-sustaining treatment are symptoms of

Box 6.1 Symptoms of Depression in People with Physical Disease

Persistent low mood

Morning depression

Loss of interest

Withdrawn and uncommunicative

Mood unresponsive to social cues

Wanting to die (take account of context)

Wanting to stop life-sustaining treatment (take account of context)

Increased symptom reporting and reduced function not explained by illness

No positive feelings about the future

No desire to participate in treatment or rehabilitation

Hopelessness

Feeling a burden

Feeling worthless

Suicidal ideation

depression. In certain circumstances they may be entirely understandable (e.g. a patient with advanced terminal illness who has made a reasoned choice to stop treatment with the support of their family and in the absence of other major symptoms of depression), whereas in other circumstances they may be highly indicative of a depressed state (e.g. a young man who has undergone left-foot amputation following a road traffic accident who is failing to engage in rehabilitation and has a persistent severe low mood).

Persistent low mood is the key symptom of all depressive states and it drives many of the other symptoms. Most people, given time, can adjust to a change in their physical health, even if that change is severe. Therefore, failure to adjust to a physical condition should prompt concern as to whether the individual is depressed. Table 6.1 shows some questions that can be used to tease out the difference between a psychological reaction to illness and depression. Obviously answers to these questions from real patients can be more nuanced than those in the table, but they provide a useful starting point for the diagnostic assessment. It is important to note that most chronic physical illnesses consist of a series of downward steps in physical health; each step requires its own adjustment and over time many adjustments need to be made.

People's Understanding of Depression

Depression is still poorly understood among the wider public. Common terms used by people to describe depressive states include stress, blues, nerves, sadness, loneliness and emotional or mental disorder. Studies that have interviewed people with depression and physical illness provide greater insight into their experiences and understanding of depression (1). Most people do not understand depression in terms of a biological model and often attribute the cause to external negative life events or complex multifactorial causes. Depression is sometimes seen a spiralling process with episodes being both a consequence of previous depression

Table 6.1 Questions to help determine the difference between a psychological reaction to illness and depression

Questions	Psychological reaction	Depression
I wonder how you feel now compared to when you were diagnosed with cancer 3 months ago?	It was terrible, I felt dreadful but I'm beginning to accept things and manage things a bit better.	I feel terrible . . . just as bad . . . in fact . . . even worse.
And does anything make you feel a little better? Seeing friends or family, for instance?	It's hard to feel ok . . . but going out at the weekend definitely helped.	No nothing . . . I just don't want to do anything.
And when you are low . . . I wonder if you have any ideas about ending your life?	Oh no . . . I couldn't possibly do that.	I just want to it to be over. I . . . I just want to be left alone to die.
I wonder if sometimes you get spells, even briefly, when you feel ok?	Maybe yeah . . . when I am walking the dog I sometimes feel quite calm and alive . . . but it doesn't last for long.	No . . . I don't feel at all ok . . . .
The treatment's quite tough; how are you managing with it?	I know I've got to get through it and grit my teeth . . . but it wipes me out the next couple of days and I feel dreadful.	I just wish I could be left to die. I'm only continuing with the treatment because of my husband. I'd rather be left alone. I think I'd be better off dead.

and a cause of new-onset depression. For some people depression raises existential issues, defining them and being seen as a part of them and their personality. Suicidal thinking is seen as a sign of depression and something that would never be considered by 'normal people', if well. Blame and stigma are also important considerations. People describe the difficulty of talking about depression with others because of fears of being thought crazy, an idea that depression equates to weakness or a concern of being blamed for their mental state.

Many people with depression and physical disease find it difficult to acknowledge the need for help but also hold quite strong beliefs about what they think might be of help. In one study, people who had no prior experience of antidepressants were resistant to taking them for depression, but people who had received antidepressants in the past were more positive (2). People who had not received psychological treatment previously were quite positive about receiving it, but those who had previously had psychological treatment were actually uncertain of its benefits.

Pathogenesis

It is well recognised that there is a bi-directional relationship between depression and physical disease. Both are risk factors for each other, which has been demonstrated in several conditions, including diabetes, heart disease and inflammatory bowel disease. The relationship between physical and mental health, however, is more complex. Katon provides a useful summary (3).

Genetic vulnerability and childhood adversity are both potential pathways for the development of mental health problems and physical health problems as an adult. These pathways may be mediated via maladaptive attachment patterns, learned behaviour within families and continuing social adversity or disadvantage, and lead to biobehavioural risk factors for chronic physical disease which may include obesity, sedentary lifestyle, smoking, increased alcohol consumption, inflammatory processes and autonomic nervous system dysfunction, many of which are also risk factors for depression. Ongoing acute and chronic psychosocial stressors such as isolation, chronic work-related stress or acute psychological trauma also increase the risk of several chronic medical conditions as well as poor mental health. Depression and chronic physical illness each contribute to the worsening of the other condition via a variety of feedback loops.

Depression in the context of physical disease is harder to treat and has a poorer outcome than depression in the absence of physical disease. It is an over-simplification to regard depression in the context of physical disease as a co-existing separate entity that can be added or removed as a separate condition. As patients themselves report (see previous section), depression has to be understood in the context of the person's whole life, their premorbid and current psychosocial stressors and the nature of the physical condition itself.

Epidemiology

Psychological morbidity is two to three times higher in people with chronic physical illness than in those who do not have a physical illness and there is a dose-response relationship between the likely prevalence of depression and number of chronic physical conditions (one condition, 23%; two conditions, 27%; three conditions, 30%; four conditions, 31%; five conditions or more, 41% (4)). Rates of depression in patients with chronic obstructive pulmonary disease are two to three times higher than in control subjects and there is similar evidence for high psychological morbidity in asthma, diabetes coronary heart disease and other chronic physical health conditions.

From the age of 50 years onwards the majority of people with physical disease are multimorbid (they have at least two chronic conditions). From the age of 65 years, over half the population are multimorbid and this rises to three quarters by the age of 75 (5). Physical disease does not occur randomly in the population but conditions are clustered in particular individuals, so there is a smaller than expected number of sicker people with a greater than expected number of conditions. This is partly because certain diseases have shared causes and social deprivation has a major impact on disease prevalence with the highest rates in the most deprived areas of the country. The proportion of people in the population with multimorbidity has nearly trebled over the last 20 years. Although chronic physical disease is more common in older adults, multimorbidity is important in younger people since there are fewer older people in the population than those who are middle aged. Roughly half of all the people with multimorbidity are under 65 years of age. Although the prevalence of depression is higher in older people who are multimorbid, nearly two thirds of all people with a mental health condition (most likely depression) as part of their multimorbidity are under 65 years of age (5).

There is great variability between individual studies which have examined the prevalence of depression in people with chronic physical health problems due to a variety of different factors. The prevalence of depression tends to be higher in patients with more severe physical disease, those seen in an inpatient setting as opposed to primary care, those with conditions that affect the brain (e.g. Parkinson's disease) and those with terminal conditions. Higher rates of depression are generally recorded if self-report measures (which generate a score) are used as opposed to interview methods which generate diagnostic criteria. Rates of depression are also higher in people with premorbid histories of childhood adversity, premorbid depression and current severe psychosocial adversity than those without such factors. The way people perceive their condition also affects mood and outcome, with those who view their condition in a more negative way than others having a greater risk of depression and poorer outcome. Measures of depression that include somatic symptoms usually produce higher scores than measures which excluded somatic symptoms. A recent systematic review of 31 studies which had recorded levels of depression in general medical and surgical inpatients reported prevalence estimates ranging from 5% to 34% (6). The average reported prevalence of depression was 12% (95% confidence interval 10–15%). Another review of patients with severe advanced disease included 41 studies and reported a median prevalence of depression of 29% (interquartile range 19.50±34.25%), using a cutoff on a self-report measure, and a median prevalence of 15% of major depressive disorder (ranging from 5% to 26%) for studies that had used a structured research interview (7).

Course of Depression in Physical Disease

The course of depression and anxiety has been studied in several different chronic diseases with similar patterns emerging with groups of patients that have different outcomes. There are at least three to five different courses which include patients with: chronic high depression/anxiety symptom scores; consistently low symptoms of anxiety and depression; fluctuating symptoms; a recovery pattern; and a deteriorating pattern (8). The severity of baseline depression also predicts a poor outcome in terms of persistent depression, higher healthcare costs and poorer quality of life. Assessments of individuals that only focus on a score of depression at one point in time will not distinguish patients whose depression is likely to spontaneously improve without any formal intervention from those who will run a more chronic course and require treatment. A full history, looking for premorbid risk factors, concurrent psychosocial difficulties and a recent course of the depression, is required to determine the most appropriate course of action.

Older Adults

Rates of depression among older adults are higher in those with physical disease in comparison to those without. The presentation of depression in older adults can be different to that in younger adults and there may be an absence of mood symptoms. Instead, people may describe a lack of feeling or emotion, and reduced energy levels and fatigue are common. Agitation and irritability may be prominent, as well as cognitive deficits. Somatisation or hypochondriasis which starts late in life can also be a sign of an underlying depression. Depression is a risk factor for the subsequent development of dementia or may mask an already present underlying dementia. Older adults may be less likely to report symptoms of depression to healthcare professionals than younger adults, so depression may present late.

Physical illnesses associated with chronicity, pain and disability pose the greatest risk for the subsequent development of depression. Pharmacokinetic and pharmacodynamic age-related changes also contribute to an increased risk of medication-induced depression in older adults.

Physical illness is associated with a high risk of suicide in older adults. One well-conducted study reported an increased risk of suicide of sixfold for people over the age of 50 years who had physical illness in comparison with those without. Between 50% and 70% of older adults who die by suicide have had recent contact with healthcare professionals, including primary care and emergency departments, within 30 days of their death. In most cases, the last consultation or contact is for a physical condition.

Outcomes Associated with Depression in People with Physical Disease

Depression and anxiety are associated with a poor outcome in physical disease and there appears to be a stepwise relationship between the severity of symptoms and overall outcome. Patients with depression and physical disease have the poorest outcome, followed by patients with sub-threshold depression and physical disease, with patients with physical disease but no depression having the best outcome.

Emergency Hospital Admission

Depression is associated with a 50% increase in emergency hospital admissions in people with chronic physical disease and severe depression increases the risk by twofold (9). Other important independent predictors include prior hospital admission in the previous 12 months, having no partner and ongoing stress/threatening experiences.

Use of Unscheduled Care

Depression is associated with a 49% increase in the odds of urgent healthcare utilisation (10) in patients with chronic physical disease and is independent of the severity of physical illness and other relevant factors.

Poor Quality of Life

Chronic physical illness is associated with poor quality of life, but depression in the presence of chronic physical illness is associated with a further reduction in quality of life. A systematic review of 20 studies in patients with diabetes including 18 cross-sectional and two longitudinal found that all studies reported a negative association between depressive symptoms and at least one aspect of quality of life (generic and domain-specific measures were used) (11).

Poorer Response to Drug Treatment for the Physical Condition

In some diseases, depression contributes to a reduced chance of a positive response to drug treatment. In rheumatoid arthritis baseline depression contributes to 30% reduced odds of response to biological therapy. This includes both patients' subjective response (e.g. pain) and objective responses (e.g. inflammatory markers).

Maladaptive Effects

Depression can lead to an amplification of somatic symptoms, increased intolerance to pain, increased adverse health behaviours (e.g. smoking, overeating, sedentary lifestyle) and decreased self-care and adherence to medication regimes. For example, in coronary artery disease, patients with co-morbid depression in comparison with those without depression report taking medication as prescribed less often, forget to take their medication or decide to skip their medications more often, are less likely to adhere to daily low-dose aspirin and are more likely to drop out of cardiac exercise rehabilitation programmes. In diabetes, depression adversely affects adherence to self-care regimes, diet, exercise regimes and cessation of smoking. Chronic depression as opposed to shorter forms of depression has a particularly negative effect on adherence to treatment regimes.

Physiological Effects

Depression has a variety of physiological effects which may help to explain its complex association with physical disease. The most clearly elaborated pathway to date involves the relationship between depression and cardiovascular disease (12). Depression may act through an autonomically mediated increase in myocardial workload or ventricular irritability, diminished beat-to-beat heart-rate variability or increased atherogenesis, through effects on platelet function or hypercortisolaemia-mediated effects on other cardiovascular risk factors such as blood pressure or lipid levels.

Depression-related dysregulation of the sympathoadrenal system and hypothalamic–pituitary–adrenal (HPA) axis causes an increase in circulating catecholamines and serum cortisol, resulting in surges in heart rate and blood pressure, which increases the risk of atherosclerotic plaque rupture and acute coronary thrombosis (12). High levels of catecholamines also increase the irritability of the heart muscle, which can lead to ventricular arrhythmias and modify the function of circulating platelets. Increased cortisol may lead to inflammation, excessive clotting, metabolic syndrome, induction of hypercholesterolemia and hypertriglyceridemia.

Poor Interactions with Medical Staff

Depression is associated with poor communication between patients and medical staff. Patients with depression compared to those without are more likely to report poorer explanations from medical staff about their health and poorer responses from staff regarding treatment preferences.

Mortality and Suicide

The risk of mortality in people over 50 years of age increases in a stepwise manner with the duration of depression. This is partially explained by a variety of connected pathways, including the presence of physical illness, levels of physical activity, cognitive function and functional impairment (13). Depression has been shown to be associated with increased mortality in a variety of physical conditions including coronary artery disease, chronic obstructive airways disease, stroke and diabetes. In diabetes, depression is associated with an all-cause mortality risk of between 1.5 and 2.5. Depression in cardiac patients has been linked to the development and progression of coronary artery disease and in patients who suffer from an acute coronary syndrome it has been associated with a two- to threefold increased risk of mortality.

The risk of suicide is also elevated in people with depression and physical disease, for example cancer, chronic obstructive airways disease, diabetes, multiple sclerosis and heart failure. In cancer, the risk of suicide is particularly high in the first 90 days after initial diagnosis for specific types of cancer and advanced cancer. A large UK study of patients with physical disease in a primary care setting found a general increased risk of suicide in people with depression and physical disease, but an unexpected higher risk (twofold) of suicide in women with cancer, coronary heart disease, stroke, chronic obstructive pulmonary disease and osteoporosis (14). The risk was greater in younger women with a physical illness and older women with multimorbidity. A recent study of over 1 million people in Northern Ireland found that individuals with physical illness and substantial activity limitation were over three times more likely to die from suicide in comparison to people with no limitations. This suggests that the effect of physical illness on limiting people's activity may be more important than the nature of the physical condition itself in relation to suicide (15). The findings of these studies highlight the importance of detection and treatment of people with physical illness and low mood.

The Association between Depression and Inflammatory Conditions

Recently, there has been growing interest in the roles of inflammation in contributing to the development of depression in people with physical illness, particularly conditions associated with inflammation such as cardiovascular disease, diabetes and rheumatoid arthritis. Several different associations have been observed, including the following: (i) depression is associated with an increase in biomarkers of inflammation, including c-reactive protein (CRP), interleukin 1 (IL-1) (IL-6, IL1-β and TNFα), interleukin 6 (IL-6) and tumour necrosis factor alpha (TNF-α) in clinical and community populations; (ii) chronic inflammatory diseases are also associated with rises in proinflammatory cytokines, such as interleukin-1β (IL-1β), TNF-α and IL-6; (iii) higher plasma levels of CRP are associated with treatment-resistant depression, suggesting perhaps that those with inflammatory burden are most likely to be non-responsive to conventional antidepressants; (iv) interferon-alpha, which greatly increases the level of inflammatory mediators, is associated with development of major depression in up to one third of patients; and (v) drugs that have a powerful anti-inflammatory effect have been shown to have a small but significant positive impact on mood.

Screening for Depression

Several self-report instruments can be used to screen for depression in medical settings including the Hospital Anxiety and Depression Scale (16), the Patient Health Questionnaire-9 (PHQ-9) (17) and its shorter form the PHQ-2 (18). If used alone, however, case finding or screening questionnaires for depression have little or no impact on the detection and treatment of depression by clinicians. NICE Guidelines for the management of depression in chronic physical illness suggest using the two questions from the PHQ-2 to help detect depression (19). If the person responds 'yes' to either question, then a full assessment is recommended.

- During the last month, have you often been bothered by feeling down, depressed or hopeless?
- During the last month, have you often been bothered by having little interest or pleasure in doing things?

Depression Caused by Medications Commonly Used to Treat or Manage Chronic Physical Disease

A variety of medications are said to lead to depressive symptoms either directly by altering levels of neurotransmitters or indirectly via their side effects (e.g. fatigue, loss of appetite, nausea) (20). However, it is often difficult from a clinical perspective to determine whether a particular drug is causal or contributing to a patient's depression. Patients with chronic medical disease have high rates of depression/anxiety irrespective of treatment regimens for their physical health problems. Much of the evidence regarding the depressogenic effect of drugs is based on case reports or small, potentially biased samples.

Rheumatoid Arthritis

Older case reports suggest that patients taking biologic DMARDs (disease-modifying antirheumatic drugs such as infliximab) and hydroxychloroquine have high rates of depression and suicidal ideas in comparison to patients' treatment with methotrexate and leflunomide. However, evidence from more recent trials suggests that most drugs used to treat rheumatoid arthritis have a small but significant positive effect on depressive symptoms.

Hypertension

Most classes of antihypertensive drugs including angiotensin antagonists, calcium channel blockers and thiazide diuretics are associated with a small increase in the risk of major depression, particularly beta-blockers. Propranolol may be associated with an increased long-term risk of mood disorders.

Epilepsy

Most anticonvulsants have been associated with the development of depression, but historically three in particular have been implicated. These are phenobarbitone (and other barbiturates), vigabatrin and topiramate, and all affect the y-aminobutyric acid (GABA) neurotransmitter system. Phenobarbitone is known to have long-term depressogenic effects. Depression can occur at any time during treatment with vigabatrin, although it commonly starts following initiation of the drug. Depressive symptoms associated with topiramate are dose-dependent so at-risk patients should be started on a slow-dose titration schedule. All patients taking any of these three drugs should be monitored for depressive symptoms. More recently, the α-amino-3-hydroxy-5-methyl-4-isoxazolepropionic acid (AMPA) antagonist Perampanel has caused concern regarding the emergence of depressive symptoms and suicidal thoughts and the SV2A antagonist levetiracetam has also been associated with the development or re-occurrence of depressed mood.

Parkinson's Disease

Although L-dopa has been associated with a small increased risk of depression, most medications used to treat Parkinson's disease do not appear to depress mood and some may even improve it.

Hepatitis C

Interferon-alpha is used in combination with ribavirin for the treatment of hepatitis C. Interferon has been strongly linked to depression and also disrupts sleep. Patients who are treated with interferon-alpha should be assessed beforehand and patients at high risk of depression should be started on prophylactic antidepressant medication. If depression develops during treatment, it is usually responsive to antidepressant treatment. Interferon-beta 1a and 1b are commonly used in the treatment of multiple sclerosis but are not considered to be associated with depressive effects.

Anti-Inflammatory Drugs

Corticosteroids are used to treat a wide variety of conditions in medicine and are associated with depression plus other neuropsychiatric side effects. If possible, they should be stopped or avoided if a patient has a prior history of depression associated with steroid use. Of course, this is not always possible and antidepressant medication should be used to try to mitigate any effects, unless the patient has had a steroid-induced elevated mood.

Antiretroviral Drugs

Although some antiretroviral drugs have been linked with neuropsychiatric side effects, there is no clear evidence that they cause depression or lower mood.

Chemotherapy Drugs

A variety of chemotherapy agents have been linked to depression, including interleukin-2, mitotic inhibitors, L-asparaginase, vinca alkaloids, antimetabolites, hormonal agents and corticosteroids. Individual cancer drugs should be checked for their association with depression if symptoms develop in a patient and are commensurate with the timeline of drug treatment.

Catatonia

Catatonia is a neuropsychiatric syndrome characterised by particular motor and behavioural signs, including stupor, rigidity, immobility, mutism, agitation, staring, grimacing and posturing. The most common psychiatric causes are delirium and severe depressive/affective states but it can also be associated with many other psychiatric and neurological conditions. The prevalence is low in a general hospital setting but most services with high turnovers will see several patients per year. The prevalence in older adults referred to liaison services is 9%, 4% on the intensive care unit and 1–2% on general wards. Catatonia is difficult to diagnose but is treatable with lorazepam (usually 1–3 mg per day over several days) if detected early, and rarely requires electroconvulsive therapy. One study has suggested that mortality in patients with catatonia in a general hospital setting which is under-diagnosed is much higher than in patients in which the condition is diagnosed (13% vs. 4%)

Box 6.2 Case Example of a Patient with Catatonia

A man between the age of 40 and 50 years was admitted to a medical ward with confusion. He had a history of pancreatitis and severe heart disease. He had been found lying on the floor of his flat by a neighbour who called an ambulance. He was noted to be dehydrated on admission and was severely underweight, but there was no evidence of infection or a flare-up of his pancreatitis, stroke or a recent cardiac event. He was treated with fluids and a plan to carefully start re-feeding was instituted. As his confusion cleared, he began to voice ideas that he was rotting and people could smell him. He appeared very low in mood and over a period of a few hours he became mute, immobile and unresponsive with a staring gaze, and with marked rigidity of muscle tone. He was referred to liaison psychiatry and a diagnosis of catatonia secondary to a severe depressive disorder was made based on the history and his current mental and physical state. Further investigations showed a mildly raised creatinine kinase. The primary care physician was contacted and confirmed that the man had no prior exposure to neuroleptics but did have a prior history of severe depression in his 20s. He was started on lorazepam 1.5 mg per day and slowly responded to this treatment.

(21). Also, patients in whom an underlying psychiatric condition is suspected are less likely to be fully investigated compared to those without a suspected underlying psychiatric condition.

Detection can be improved by use of the Bush-Francis Catatonia Rating Scale (BFCRS) (22), which screens for the 14 most common catatonic signs (excitement, immobility/stupor, mutism, staring gaze, posturing/catalepsy, grimacing, echopraxia/echolalia, stereotypies, mannerisms, verbigeration, rigidity, negativism, waxy flexibility and withdrawal). Two or more signs of catatonia need to be present for at least 24 hours for a suspected diagnosis.

Several symptoms help distinguish catatonia from neuroleptic malignant syndrome (NMS), which can also present with increased muscle tone. NMS is associated with a recent exposure to antipsychotic symptoms, marked muscle rigidity and markedly raised serum creatinine kinase levels. Catatonia is not usually associated with neuroleptics; there may be mild muscle rigidity and mildly raised levels of creatinine kinase. Both conditions are associated with a pyrexia, sweating and tachycardia. NMS is more usually associated with a delirium-type picture. Box 6.2 describes a case of a man with catatonia who presented with a delirium (rather untypical of catatonia), which was found to be secondary to dehydration linked to poor fluid intake and a severe depressive state. The two conditions can be difficult to distinguish in a clinical setting and both are thought to be linked to a massive dopamine blockade.

Treatment and Management

Collaborative Care

There is a strong evidence base that collaborative care improves depression outcomes in patients with depression and chronic illness, with less robust evidence that physical outcomes improve following treatment. The term collaborative care has been used to describe a wide variety of different interventions with different levels of intensity. Table 6.2 shows

Table 6.2 Examples of different forms of collaborative care

Authors and participants	Components of collaborative care
Katon et al. 2010 (31) Depression, poorly controlled diabetes, coronary artery disease or both	12-month programme with pharmacotherapy to control depression, hyperglycaemia, hypertension and hyperlipidaemia monitored every 2 weeks by nurses following target to treat protocols with guided adjustments according to depression scores and glycated haemoglobin, blood pressure levels and low-density lipid cholesterol. Nurses received weekly supervision from a psychiatrist, primary care physician and psychologist to review new cases and track patient progress. Physicians recommended medication changes which were implemented by the nurses who also offered problem-solving, goal-setting for improved medication adherence and promotion of self-care management.
Camacho et al. 2018 (32) Primary care patients with diabetes and/or coronary artery disease and depression	Brief low-intensity treatment (8 sessions) delivered by psychological well-being practitioners employed by Improving Access to Psychological Therapy services. Behavioural activation, graded exposure, cognitive restructuring and/or lifestyle changes. 10-minute session with practice nurse during sessions 2 and 8 aimed to facilitate integration of care. Psychological well-being practitioners were expected to liaise with primary care physician about medication.
Langer et al. 2014 (26) Primary care patients with depression and at least one of the following: diabetes, chronic obstructive airways disease, asthma or coronary heart disease	Primary care intervention delivered by a mental health nurse and social worker. Review of medication (both for mental and physical health) with rationalisation and increase in antidepressant treatment if indicated (supervised by a consultant psychiatrist); low-intensity psychological treatment as in Camacho et al. 2018; smoking cessation; exercise and diet plans with active engagement; empathic support and building of the therapeutic alliance based on psychodynamic principles; social interventions – identifying state benefits to which patient may be entitled, helping patient complete applications for benefits, bus pass and disability parking badge, writing to utility companies to have debts written off, application for grants for essential household items, identification of charities and application to relevant charities for support regarding finances; practical support – liaison with local services to effect practical adaptations in the home; signposting to health trainers, disability taxi services, good neighbour schemes, local support groups and charities; education and information – checking patients using medications in the right way, information about their illness, answering questions about illness.

three examples of collaborative care, one of which describes the original model developed in the USA by Katon and colleagues; the other two are UK versions. In general, better effects have been seen in the USA than in the UK, where the interventions have tended to be shorter and less intense.

A systematic review of 74 trials of collaborative care for depression included 16 studies in which participants with a chronic physical health condition and depression were targeted (23). Overall, collaborative care was shown to increase the outcomes and process of care for depression. Interventions which included a psychological therapy, either alone or with antidepressant treatment, conferred additional benefit. Trials that included patients with chronic physical conditions reported increased use of antidepressant medication. No separate analysis of trials which included patients with chronic physical disease was undertaken, although other evidence suggests that collaborative care is effective for people with depression and chronic physical disease, and the benefits derived do not differ across people with different types of physical condition (24). Scheduled clinical supervision of practitioners also resulted in better outcomes. Recurrence of symptoms was common but patients who continued treatment with antidepressants reduced the risk of recurrence by 70%. Few patients responded to a starting dose of antidepressant medication and only 40% of patients achieved remission after receiving full therapeutic dosages. Sixty out of the 72 studies were conducted in the USA.

Considerable cost savings have been reported from some trials in the USA, whereas in the UK treatment has been termed cost-effective at internationally accepted willingness-to-pay thresholds; in other words, the interventions do not lead to a reduction in costs but are considered worth paying for.

Exercise

A large evidence base supports the use of exercise for the treatment of depression in chronic physical disease. Graded exercise should be included in most treatment plans with specific time devoted to helping the patient establish an appropriate exercise plan. A recent systematic and meta-analysis which included 122 studies of exercise treatment interventions in a variety of brain disorders (including Parkinson's disease, multiple sclerosis and Alzheimer's disease) showed that exercise had a large effect on depression (effect size 0.78) as well as positive effects on quality of life, memory and psychomotor speed (25). The amount of exercise in term of minutes per week was strongly associated with the degree of improvement in depressive symptoms. Similar positive effects for exercise have also been recorded for the treatment of depression in other chronic physical diseases, including heart disease, chronic obstructive pulmonary disease and patients undergoing haemodialysis.

Psychosocial Interventions

The social circumstances of people with chronic disease and depression are often overlooked when developing treatment plans, as they are often regarded as being beyond the scope of traditional mental health interventions. However, helping people replace damp and mouldy carpets or enabling them to write off debts from utility companies may have an enormous impact on their psychological well-being. Table 6.2 shows the key components from an intervention that was developed to treat depression in chronic physical illness and reduce use of urgent care (26). The intervention was delivered by a mental health nurse and a social worker in a primary care setting. The fundamental approach was based upon collaborative care and the use of low-intensity psychological treatments but, in addition, incorporated a strong social component and drew upon psychodynamic principles to facilitate a strong therapeutic alliance between the mental health worker and their client. Box 6.3 provides an example of a psychosocial intervention in a patient with physical disease, anxiety/depression and poor social circumstances.

Box 6.3 A Case Example of a Psychosocial Intervention for Depression and Chronic Physical Disease

A woman between the age of 70 and 80 years (widowed) with diabetes (type 2), coronary heart disease, chronic obstructive airways disease and depression/anxiety lived in a small terraced house. Over the previous year, since her husband's death, she had become increasingly unsteady on her legs, had become low in mood and constantly worried about falling at home. She had stopped going out for fear of falling and had lost contact with two important friends. She had no prior history of depression but had contemplated suicide at times, as she could see no way out of her predicament. She did not have access to social media and also had poor eyesight because of diabetic complications which compounded her concerns about going out. A recent review by the primary care physician did not find a cause for her unsteadiness. On assessment by the liaison mental health team who visited her at home, she was found to be low in mood and very anxious. The stairs in her home were very steep and there were no additional aids to help her get up or down them. Her electricity meter was at the top of the stairs at a height that required her to stand on a stool to put money in it. A combination of her poor eyesight, fear of falling and unsteadiness meant that she often could not face putting money in the meter and sat in the dark and cold for many hours. Her husband had always been the person who topped up the meter as he was taller than her and did not need a stool to stand on. She had become so anxious about filling the meter that the anxiety had generalised to most other areas of her life. She had suffered a leak in the house the previous winter and her carpets were damp and had never properly dried out. She did not know how to access any kind of help and had not mentioned the problem to the primary care physician.

Intervention

A grant was arranged to replace her damp carpets.

The electricity company was contacted and the meter was removed. She was switched to the cheapest payment plan and signed to a company who would switch her provider to the cheapest tariff on a regular basis.

Her benefits and financial situation were reviewed and she was found to be eligible for more support.

Stair guide rails were fitted and additional support rails in the bathroom.

A local charity was contacted who offered to take her to meet her friends twice a week.

A behavioural intervention was instituted with a view to increasing her level of physical activity and ability to leave the home safely.

Psychological sessions also encouraged her to talk about the loss of her husband followed by brief behavioural activation with a goal to increase her social contacts and ability to use social media.

A review at the diabetic clinic was organised as she had missed the last two appointments and transport arranged to enable her to attend.

Response of Physical Symptoms to Psychological/Psychotropic Treatment

The evidence for strong effects on physical symptom outcome for mental health interventions is limited. A recent Cochrane review of 35 studies in coronary heart disease involving psychological treatment interventions found little evidence that interventions had an impact on mortality, the risk of revascularisation procedures or the rate of non-fatal further myocardial infarction (27). Two of the best-known trials of psychological interventions in patients with physical disease are the TEAMcare trial (27) and the ENRICHd trial (28).

TEAMcare targeted patients with depression and/or diabetes and coronary heart disease and used an intensive collaborative care approach. At 12 months after the start of the trial, there were significant improvements for the intervention versus control group in terms of depression, glycated haemoglobin, lipids and blood pressure, but at the 24-month follow-up only improved depression remained significantly different. The ENRICHd trial is one of the largest studies of psychological treatment in physical disease. Nearly 2,500 patients were recruited and the treatment intervention which was tested was cognitive behavioural treatment plus citalopram in patients post-myocardial infarction. The intervention showed a positive effect on mood but no impact on cardiac events.

Older Adults with Multiple Diseases

There is some evidence to that coordinated care improves primary and secondary outcomes in older adults with multimorbidity, including those with chronic obstructive pulmonary disease and depression and diabetes and depression.

Primary/Community Care

In England, Improving Access to Therapy Services (IAPT) have been given a remit to treat patients with depression and co-morbid long-term conditions. The evidence to date suggests these patients require more intensive treatment than routine referrals to IAPT and also have poorer outcomes than people with depression without a long-term condition (29).

Antidepressant Treatment in Primary Care

Antidepressants are used widely in primary care to treat depression, but recent evidence suggests that much antidepressant treatment in general practice is for people with minimal or mild symptoms, while people with moderate or severe depression may miss out. There is considerable scope to improve the management of people with depression and those with depression and chronic physical illness in primary care (30).

NICE Guidelines

NICE produced a National Clinical Practice Guideline for the treatment of depression in people with physical illness entitled 'Depression in Adults with a Chronic Physical Health Problem' (19). NICE recommends a stepped-care approach to the treatment of depression in people with depression and chronic physical illness, which is summarised in Table 6.3. The guidance is probably of most help to non-specialists rather than those working in a liaison psychiatry setting.

Table 6.3 Summary of NICE Guidelines for the treatment of depression in people with chronic physical illness

Severity of depression	Recommended intervention
Low-level symptoms	Sleep hygiene Active monitoring
Sub-threshold symptoms	Low-intensity psychological intervention Structured group physical activity programme Group support Individual guided self-help Computerised cognitive behavioural treatment
Sub-threshold symptoms that persist	More structured and tailored interventions delivered more frequently Structured group physical activity programme Group support Individual guided self-help Computerised cognitive behavioural treatment
Recognised depression	Consider antidepressant if person has not responded to low-intensity intervention High-intensity cognitive behavioural treatment
Severe depression	Combination of antidepressant and cognitive behavioural treatment

General Treatment Approaches

Liaison psychiatrists will tend to see people with severe or chronic depression in the context of physical illness, where it is particularly important to carry out a detailed assessment and formulation of the person's problems. Ward referrals can include patients who have been admitted with significant weight loss, anorexia or gross neglect where the underlying cause is a severe undiagnosed depressive illness.

The value of a full assessment should not be underestimated as it can help an individual begin to understand the relationship between their physical and mental health and identify factors which improve or exacerbate their mood. Gathering contextual information can be particularly helpful. Examples include previous adverse life events and how someone coped with these, history of mental health problems and current social circumstances. Most people do not understand their depression in the context of physical illness according to a medical model, so coming to a shared understanding of the relationship between their mood, physical health and other aspects of their life is very important.

It is also important to explain to medical and nursing staff the links between physical and mental health rather than just presenting a diagnosis, as they too can actively encourage or facilitate behaviours which improve mood. Improving activity, particularly exercise (if possible), should always be included in part of a treatment intervention and there may be occupational therapists or physiotherapists on the ward who can help with this.

Treatment with antidepressants should be considered and time spent with the person to fully explain the rationale for this, the likely benefits and any side effects. A lot of people do not respond to antidepressants because they do not take them. Consider starting at a very low dose (below the usual starting dosage) to improve acceptance and tolerance to the drug but then titrate up quickly, according to response.

Psychological treatment should be considered but realistically it is not always available or there may be a long waiting list. People need to be able to concentrate and feel reasonably well to actively participate in psychological treatment, so it may not be suitable for people who have impaired concentration or severe nausea (or other debilitating symptoms). Some liaison services offer outpatient psychological treatment which is delivered by experienced therapists, familiar with treating people with physical disease. Clinical or health psychology services may also be available.

If treatment is started in the general hospital setting, when the person is an inpatient, it can all fall apart after the person is discharged home or to a community setting unless the primary care physician is closely involved and understands the comprehensive treatment plan. Pressures on community mental health teams mean very few people can be followed up after discharge by mental health services unless liaison teams offer outpatient follow-up or there are primary care liaison teams. Most people seen by liaison services will not meet the criteria for admission to community mental health teams, which tend to focus on people with severe mental illness. The case for liaison services for people with complex physical and mental health is still one that needs to be made to government, as in most parts of the country it is erroneously assumed that such people can be treated by Improving Access to Psychological Therapies (IAPT).

Summary

Depression is common in physical disease and often goes undetected. The relationship between depression and physical disease is complex and influenced by shared genetic and psychosocial premorbid pathways and bi-directional feedback loops. Depression is associated with a variety of poor outcomes in physical disease. Treatment results in an improvement in mood but not generally an improvement in physical parameters. If physical parameters do improve, these tend to be short-lived. Treatment should be tailored to the individual and their circumstances but should include an appropriate mix of psychological, social and pharmacological treatment. Exercise or increased physical activity should always be considered as part of a comprehensive treatment plan that should be shared with the relevant medical team or primary care physician.

References

1. Alderson SL, Foy R, Glidewell L, McLintock K, House A. How patients understand depression associated with chronic physical disease: A systematic review. BMC Fam Pract. 2012;13:41.

2. Alderson SL, Foy R, Glidewell L, House AO. Patients' understanding of depression associated with chronic physical illness: A qualitative study. BMC Fam Pract. 2014;15:37.

3. Katon WJ. Epidemiology and treatment of depression in patients with chronic medical illness. Dialogues Clin Neurosci. 2011;13.

4. Gunn JM, Ayton DR, Densley K et al. The association between chronic illness, multimorbidity and depressive symptoms in an Australian primary care cohort. Soc Psychiatry Psychiatr Epidemiol. 2012;47 (2):175–84.

5. Guthrie B, Wyke S, Gunn J et al. *Multimorbidity: The Impact on Health Systems and Their Development*. Paris; 2011.

6. Walker J, Burke K, Wanat M et al. The prevalence of depression in general hospital inpatients: A systematic review and meta-analysis of interview-based studies. *Psychol Med*. 2018;**48**(14):2285–98.

7. Hotopf M, Chidgey J, Addington-Hall J, Ly KL. Depression in advanced disease: A systematic review. Part 1: Prevalence and case findings. *Palliat Med*. 2002;**16**(2):81–97.

8. Palacios J, Khondoker M, Mann A, Tylee A, Hotopf M. Depression and anxiety symptom trajectories in coronary heart disease: Associations with measures of disability and impact on 3-year health care costs. *J Psychosom Res*. 2018;**104**:1–8.

9. Guthrie EA, Dickens C, Blakemore A et al. Depression predicts future emergency hospital admissions in primary care patients with chronic physical illness. *J Psychosom Res*. 2016;**82**:54–61.

10. Dickens C, Katon W, Blakemore A et al. Does depression predict the use of urgent and unscheduled care by people with long term conditions? A systematic review with meta-analysis. *J Psychosom Res*. 2012;**73**(5):334–42.

11. Schram MT, Baan CA, Pouwer F. Depression and quality of life in patients with diabetes: a systematic review from the European depression in diabetes (EDID) research consortium. *Curr Diabetes Rev*. 2009;**5**(2):112–19.

12. Charlson FJ, Stapelberg NJ, Baxter AJ, Whiteford HA. Should global burden of disease estimates include depression as a risk factor for coronary heart disease? *BMC Med*. 2011;**9**:47.

13. White J, Zaninotto P, Walters K et al. Duration of depressive symptoms and mortality risk: The English Longitudinal Study of Ageing (ELSA). *Br J Psychiatry*. 2016;**208**(4):337–42.

14. Webb RT, Kontopantelis E, Doran T et al. Suicide risk in primary care patients with major physical diseases: A case-control study. *Arch Gen Psychiatry*. 2012;**69**(3):256–64.

15. Onyeka IN, Maguire A, Ross E, O'Reilly D. Does physical ill-health increase the risk of suicide? A census-based follow-up study of over 1 million people. *Epidemiol Psychiatr Sci*. 2020;**29**:e140.

16. Zigmond AS, Snaith RP. The hospital anxiety and depression scale. *Acta Psychiatr Scand*. 1983;**67**(6):361–70.

17. Kroenke K, Spitzer RL, Williams JB. The PHQ-9: Validity of a brief depression severity measure. *J Gen Intern Med*. 2001;**16**(9):606–13.

18. Kroenke K, Spitzer RL, Williams JB. The Patient Health Questionnaire-2: Validity of a two-item depression screener. *Med Care*. 2003;**41**(11):1284–92.

19. National Institute for Health and Care Excellence. *Depression in Adults with a Chronic Physical Health Problem: Recognition and Management*. London; 2009.

20. Celano CM, Freudenreich O, Fernandez-Robles C et al. Depressogenic effects of medications: A review. *Dialogues Clin Neurosci*. 2011;**13**(1):109–25.

21. Llesuy JR, Medina M, Jacobson KC, Cooper JJ. Catatonia under-diagnosis in the general hospital. *J Neuropsychiatry Clin Neurosci*. 2018;**30**(2):145–51.

22. Bush G, Fink M, Petrides G, Dowling F, Francis A. Catatonia: I. Rating scale and standardized examination. *Acta Psychiatr Scand*. 1996;**93**(2):129–36.

23. Coventry PA, Hudson JL, Kontopantelis E et al. Characteristics of effective collaborative care for treatment of depression: A systematic review and meta-regression of 74 randomised controlled trials. *PLoS One*. 2014;**9**(9):e108114.

24. Panagioti M, Bower P, Kontopantelis E et al. Association between chronic physical conditions and the effectiveness of collaborative care for depression: An individual participant data meta-analysis. *JAMA Psychiatry*. 2016;**73**(9):978–89.

25. Dauwan M, Begemann MJH, Slot MIE et al. Physical exercise improves quality of life, depressive symptoms, and cognition across chronic brain disorders: A transdiagnostic systematic review and meta-analysis of randomized controlled trials. *J Neurol.* 2021;**268**(4):1222–46.

26. Langer S, Chew-Graham CA, Drinkwater J et al. A motivational intervention for patients with COPD in primary care: Qualitative evaluation of a new practitioner role. *BMC Fam Pract.* 2014;**15**:164.

27. Katon W, Russo J, Lin EH et al. Cost-effectiveness of a multicondition collaborative care intervention: A randomized controlled trial. *Arch Gen Psychiatry.* 2012;**69**(5):506–14.

28. Froelicher ES, Miller NH, Buzaitis A et al. The Enhancing Recovery in Coronary Heart Disease Trial (ENRICHD): Strategies and techniques for enhancing retention of patients with acute myocardial infarction and depression or social isolation. *J Cardiopulm Rehabil.* 2003;**23**(4):269–80.

29. Delgadillo J, Dawson A, Gilbody S, Bohnke JR. Impact of long-term medical conditions on the outcomes of psychological therapy for depression and anxiety. *Br J Psychiatry.* 2017;**210**(1):47–53.

30. Davidson SK, Romaniuk H, Chondros P et al. Antidepressant treatment for primary care patients with depressive symptoms: Data from the diamond longitudinal cohort study. *Aust NZJ Psychiatry.* 2020;**54**(4):367–81.

31. Katon WJ, Lin EH, Von Korff M et al. Collaborative care for patients with depression and chronic illnesses. *N Engl J Med.* 2010;**363**(27):2611–20.

32. Camacho EM, Davies LM, Hann M et al. Long-term clinical and cost-effectiveness of collaborative care (versus usual care) for people with mental-physical multimorbidity: Cluster-randomised trial. *Br J Psychiatry.* 2018;**213**(2):456–63.

Functional Somatic Symptoms

Constanze Hausteiner-Wiehle and Peter Henningsen

Introduction

In the absence of defined disease, but also on top of it, functional somatic symptoms indicate subjective distress. They have multidimensional, individual origins and their course is heterogeneous. We do not understand their exact psychophysiological pathways yet, but we know that stressors, attention/expectation and the way we handle them matter a lot. This applies especially to consultation-liaison psychiatry, where patients rarely have one single and simple problem, and there are frequent mismatches between the subjective symptom burden and objective findings.

Management of functional somatic symptoms should be interdisciplinary, mixing diagnostic and therapeutic, physical and psychological techniques. Treatment is based on empathy, psychoeducation, activation and the development of a bio-psycho-social explanatory model. Symptom relief and co-morbid illness can require medication, but passive interventions should only be temporary, with weighted risks and benefits. More severe cases need a multimodal approach or psychotherapy, carefully addressing the embodied self with all its experiences, attitudes and resources.

Functional somatic symptoms are common, sometimes impressive illustrations of the close interactions between body and mind, person and environment, present and past. They should receive more attention in medical education and care. In the future, more valid diagnostic concepts, suitable healthcare structures and effective therapies need to be established.

Background

Somatic Symptoms in the Population, in Different Cultures and in History

Somatic symptoms are everyday experiences. Cross-sectional surveys in the general population consistently show high background-point prevalences of 50–80%, with the most common symptoms being pains (of various locations, with back pain being the global frontrunner for many years), fatigue and functional disturbances such as dizziness or digestive troubles. There are overlapping clusters of gastrointestinal, cardiovascular, musculoskeletal pain and general symptoms. Typical symptoms and symptom clusters exist within certain cultural groups; for example, troubling back pain is twice as common in Germany compared to the UK. There are also 'culture-bound syndromes' such as Dhat in South Asia or Susto in Latin America. In mass psychogenic illness, symptoms are 'transmitted' within communities, closely related to the assumption of (modern) threats. Somatic symptoms are also historic phenomena: there are characteristic symptoms from certain times, eras or circumstances, such as neurasthenia in the nineteenth century. The most tragic historically embedded symptoms are related to human catastrophes, such as shell shock in the First World War. In 'modern times' there are 'modern illnesses': new, enigmatic phenomena with new explanatory models according to the spirit of the respective age, such as 'multiple chemical sensitivities'. They grab a lot of attention – and often disappear after a while.

The phenomenon of 'high symptom reporting' (somatisation) can be found across the human population, in all age groups, ethnocultural groups and societies. It is associated with all kinds of somatic co-morbidity such as endocrine, dermatological, rheumatological, cardiological, neurological and gastroenteric disorders, and cancer. High symptom reporting is also associated with female gender, older age, lower educational level, unemployment, loneliness, lack of social support, functional impairment, adverse life events and all kinds of psychological distress (depression, anxiety including health anxiety, irritability, tension, problems with sleeping). Notably, its association with higher healthcare utilisation and future impaired health is independent of somatic illness and classic risk factors.

Persistent and Distressing Somatic Symptoms in Clinical Practice: The Problem of Subjectivity, Causality and Co-morbidity

When somatic symptoms are multiple, persistent or distressing, when they are interpreted as threatening and when barriers in the healthcare system are low enough, people will seek a medical opinion more readily than when they are experiencing psychological distress. As presumed indicators of defined disease, symptoms are immediately traced and sorted. With targeted treatment in mind, medicine tries to find single specific 'mental' or 'organic' causes. However, attributing particular symptoms to particular causes is difficult, often impossible and sometimes needless: Symptoms often do not match textbook knowledge or fit neatly into dualist (psychological/mind vs. organic/body – see Box 7.1) stereotypes; they are subjective, culturally framed and ambiguous.

- Laboratory testing and imaging are subject to errors, norm variants and incidental findings. Experts can disagree, and we do not have reliable tests for everything.
- Whether there is major disease or not: some people do not complain about or do not even notice bodily signals; others can be extremely bothered by minor changes.
- People rarely have only one single symptom. They can have many symptoms, from several minor and major, current and former illnesses, or from functional disturbances or normal psychophysiological stress reactions only.
- People can have both 'explained' and 'unexplained' symptoms at the same time, and even a single symptom can be partly 'explained' or partly 'unexplained' (e.g. fatigue).
- Likewise, symptoms can be both 'somatic' and 'psychological' at the same time, for example, fatigue.
- Symptom phenomenology and narration can be vague, figurative, non-anatomical or with an affective colouring ('brain fog', 'puppet limbs', 'upper-body numbness', 'devastating pain').
- Memory of inciting events, symptom history and frequency is strongly biased.

Box 7.1 Functional Somatic Symptoms: A Disambiguation

- 'Symptoms' represent variations from normality. They are usually startling or unpleasant but can also have a positive connotation (if someone experiences symptoms of recovery, for example). In contrast to signs, which are recognisable to others (such as the examiner), symptoms are almost exclusively apparent to the symptomatic individual, who may recognise them, feel them and report them as subjective salient signals from *within*.
- 'Somatic' means 'belonging to' or 'coming from the physical body'; 'soma' is also the biological term for cell body. The term has been coined as the opposite of 'psychological' and 'psyche', but such a 'soma–psyche' or 'body–mind' dualism continues to be one of the biggest challenges in philosophy, biology and medicine.
- 'Function' describes an object's mechanisms, tasks and effects as opposed to its form, material and structure. 'Functional' (as opposed to 'structural') means 'concerning (an object's) procedural use', often in a chain or a system of objects functioning together.
- 'Distress' is an aversive state of insufficient adaptation to agents, conditions, stimuli or events ('stressors'), expressing itself in maladaptive reactions on many different levels including bodily and behavioural changes.
- Thus, the term 'functional somatic symptoms' (FSS) describes subjective bodily signals that derive from functional disturbances rather than structural lesions. The concept of 'bodily distress' subsumes distressing FSS with relevant impact on individual functioning.

Which Term Fits It All?

The paraphrase 'medically unexplained (physical) symptoms' (MU(P)S) is widely used in the medical literature. But instead of being a relief for patients, this negative definition (by an absence of explanations) is arbitrary, unsettling and not well accepted among patients (1). It neither implies reassurance nor any constructive latitudes. It ignores that of course these symptoms have somatic correlates in the body and the brain. It denies integrated, psychosocial approaches a place in medicine. The alternative term 'persistent physical symptoms' offers more aetiological neutrality, but also carries no psychophysiological concept (2,3). Among patients, it is better accepted than MUS (1).

The International Classification of Diseases (ICD)-10 still uses the term 'somatoform' for a group of disorders characterised by persistent and distressing physical symptoms for which no organic cause can be found (see later). Like 'psychosomatic', it is often equated with 'psychogenic' and felt to be offensive (1). It did not become widely accepted, and its successor, 'somatic symptom disorder', appears to regarded as offensive as well (1).

A different approach is to regard the symptoms as 'functional': as irregularities in an organism's functions, mechanisms and effects (instead of its structures), usually within systems or chains. This indicates that symptoms can also *have* functions. They can, for example, point towards a general problem of energy, capacity or motivation, enable rest or communicate the need for help to oneself and to others. 'Functional' is well accepted by patients as well as medical professionals (1, 4). Functional symptoms can represent the organism's answer to stressors; that is, dynamic whole-body reactions to its needs and challenges. When stressors are overwhelming, or the organism weakened, existing adaptation mechanisms can be insufficient and symptoms arise (bodily distress). Both terms open the door to concurrent general medical and psychological treatment; they will be preferably used in this chapter and we suggest they should also be used with colleagues and patients.

Functional Somatic Symptoms

Aetiology and Psychophysiology

The human organism is a complex, highly adaptive and creative self-regulating system. Perception and action are formed by active multimodal integration according to all current sensory input as well as presumed needs and motives; above all, adaptation and survival. Based on what it expects to perceive, or what should be done, the brain can prioritise strong expectations over the actual incoming sensory input, allowing for increasing or decreasing, emerging or disappearing symptoms (2, 3, 5–7). Salient stimuli that contradict expectation provoke immediate alert and attentional focussing ('what is that? It might be dangerous'), followed by some kind of action to verify and eventually correct expectations ('looking upwards makes me dizzy; I'll change my position – now it should feel better'). If expectations are very potent, for example due to intense fear or adverse experiences, perception can be distorted to meet expectations ('dizziness can indicate a stroke – I think my speech is blurred now, too'). The early phases of (preconscious) motor planning are also influenced by involuntary predictions about bodily states as well as their emotional valence. Thus, symptoms can be modulated by regulation or suggestion (e.g. in placebo analgesia or nocebo hyperalgesia), fade with distraction, increase with gain or catastrophisation or, as in phantom pain, become disproportionately intense even without adequate stimuli. Under extreme (life-threatening) stress, sensory input and motor output can even be completely shut off (dissociative analgesia, playing dead).

Symptom processing comprises various structures (from proprioceptors and nociceptors to a mesolimbic network), various functions (from extinction, inhibition and habituation to conditioning, amplification and sensitisation) and various directions (bottom-up and top-down within the nervous system, cross-system with immune and endocrine systems and between organisms and their external environments). This allows for high individuality and flexibility.

At the same time, symptom processing confers the risk of errors and dysfunctions; for example, through structural damage, persistent threat, pharmacological manipulation or cognitive bias. This explains why functional somatic symptom type, localisation and severity is so manifold, non-specific and ambiguous, and why they can occur in organically healthy organisms but also in addition to physical and mental illness. There is no single, one-dimensional or monocausal aetiology of FSS. It is rather a complex interplay of biological including genetic, psychological including attentional and motivational and social including cultural factors that can make a particular person fatigued, environmentally sensitive, aching all over, suddenly dizzy or paralyzed, or their digestion so irritable. Manifold determinants act as predispositions, triggers and maintaining factors, individually weighed and sometimes in merging roles (Figure 7.1).

Different types of FSS have shared risk factors and predictors, above all female sex, general medical disorders, disturbed sleep, anxiety, depression and somatisation,

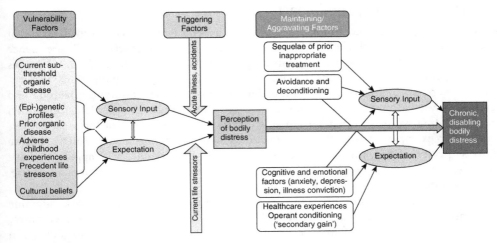

Figure 7.1 The dynamic aetiology of functional somatic symptoms (8 with permission by S. Karger AG).

frequent medical consultations, stress related to chronic ill health and poor perception of general health. There are shared cognitive behavioural features such as increased catastrophisation. There may be precipitating events shortly before onset such as infection preceding chronic fatigue and irritable bowel syndrome, or physical injury preceding fibromyalgia and functional neurological disorders. Special importance is attached to life adversities and interpersonal distress, but these are the most difficult to assess – and to reverse, naturally.

In principle, the human organism is shaped by all sorts of events and difficulties, in childhood as well as recently, either all of a sudden or over a long time, and sometimes during especially vulnerable periods of life. Violence, neglect, grave illness and accidents are especially prone to scarring the body and to scarring the soul. Notably, according to an embodied neuroscience, the body can be scarred and the soul can be scarred alike, and it is anyway hard to tell the difference (9).

There is a robust association between psychological trauma and neglect, post-traumatic stress disorder and various functional somatic syndromes such as fibromyalgia syndrome, irritable bowel syndrome, functional neurological disorders and chronic fatigue syndrome (10–12). But not all patients report such stressors. Incriminating memories are difficult to share; they can be preconscious or suppressed, or on the other hand overrated or even false. In addition, the association of adversities and trauma with FSS is not specific; there is, for example, also an association with cardiometabolic disease (13).

Therefore, adverse and conflicting experiences and events are neither necessary nor sufficient for an assignment of somatic symptoms as 'functional', 'somatoform' or 'dissociative'. They are no longer required for diagnosis and should not be overrated (7). It is nevertheless important, especially in consultation-liaison psychiatry, to remember the close relationship between adversities, symptom burden and general health; to recognise any according signs in a particular patient (such as hyperarousal or difficulties with emotion recognition, stress regulation or interpersonal relationships) and to enable coping with *current* as well as *preventing further* distress.

Clinical Presentation and Impact

FSS are among the most common, distressing (for patients and their care providers) and at the same time most overlooked problems in medicine. In general practice, their prevalence is about 20–25%; in somatic specialty clinics up to 50% of patients have FSS (4, 8, 14). Just as in the general population, the most common FSS are pains, fatigue and functional disturbances. There is a high variability of individual symptom presentation, interpretation and course. Polysymptomatic presentations are common, often as clusters (see later), and often the presenting symptom is neither the only nor the most persistent nor the most bothersome. For example, in patients with functional neurological disorders (FNDs), fatigue affects quality of life more than motor symptoms. Remarkably, FSS appear to have a higher impact on quality of life than similar symptoms due to well-defined organic disease, also when they appear co-morbidly or with mixed aetiology.

There is a high co-morbidity, above all with anxiety and depression, but also migraine and various other 'functional, 'mental' and 'organic' illnesses, for example of dissociative seizures with epilepsy and of non-specific chest pain with coronary heart disease (2, 5, 7). In elderly people, it is especially challenging to differentiate structural pathology from functional mechanisms.

The course of FSS is usually favourable, but about 30% (more in FNDs, for example, up to 78% of functional dystonias) persist or even deteriorate. Many take waxing-and-waning courses; others occur all of a sudden, in a dramatic and alarming manner (especially cardiovascular and nervous system symptoms such as chest pain, shortness of breath, paralysis, seizures and sensory disturbances including loss of vision and speech). These are especially prevalent in emergency departments. Together with the number of co-morbidities and the understanding of one's own illness, these symptoms are predictive of visits to accident and emergency departments. The total somatic symptom burden is a good predictor of outcome, since it is associated with lower health-related quality of life, more functional impairment, higher healthcare utilisation and a worse prognosis. Suicidal ideation is an especially relevant problem in the presence of pain and anger. Increased mortality has been reported in patients experiencing dissociative seizures.

Functional Somatic Symptoms As 'Illnesses in Their Own Right': Barriers and Prospects

For all kinds of physical symptoms, such as for new-onset headache or tremor, there are specific physical examinations and procedural workups – but not for FSS. Because of medical due diligence, and financial as well as legal concerns, there is much over-investigation of FSS. This can become associated with increased risk of helplessness, chronicity and even disability *because of* recurrent, unnecessary medical interventions. During prolonged organ-focussed workups, psychological aspects go unnoticed and unresolved, hence obstacles to recovery are often overlooked. Instead, the patient's requirement for physical findings and explanations is detrimentally increased ('iatrogenic somatisation'). When no pathology can be found, doctors can feel overused, helpless or even misled because their medical training taught them to find and fight somatic disease. There is often incomprehension and reservation towards FSS; they may be considered subordinate and illegitimate. Patients are vilified as 'annoying', 'hysterical', 'frequent flyers' or 'malingerers', and such disinterest and stigmatisation can lead to amplified symptoms. Many physicians avoid making functional diagnoses because they presuppose a requirement for psychological 'causes'. There is discomfort and a lack of familiarity with 'private' questioning, and 'psychological' interventions are beyond their remit. Thus, a substantial portion of functional somatic symptom chronicity is 'homemade', and consultation-liaison psychiatrists are often contacted quite late in their course.

There is a lot of unsettledness on the patients' side, too. Most patients are anxiously convinced to suffer from physical illness. They travel long medical journeys, with a lot of negative experiences. Most patients do not have a single, irrevocable explanation, nor do they expect one from their doctor – they just want sufficient medical validation of their symptoms, emotional support and information about what can be done next (14, 15). There are also patients whose previous experiences have contributed to them feeling insecure, being hard to reassure and having unrealistic expectations regarding retirement.

When a functional diagnosis is made, doubts can remain on both the patient's and the doctor's side, especially when symptoms do not subside with treatment. In 0.4% (with good workup) to 8.8% (without), symptoms are misinterpreted as functional when in fact there is defined illness. Thus, a thorough workup is mandatory. Much more often, however, there are incorrect organic diagnoses. The rate is especially high in emergency situations, such as epilepsy and stroke. This can have serious consequences in conditions with bleak prognoses such as Alzheimer's disease or cancer (7).

Current Diagnostic Concepts

The classification of FSS is subject to continuous debate: should they be seen as 'mental' or 'organic'? Is it more useful to assign them to an overarching concept of bodily discomfort, regardless of the particular type of symptoms ('lumping')? Or should there be separate diagnostic categories for each symptom or organ system ('splitting')? Is it better to define diagnoses by distressing symptoms only or is their validity increased by additional criteria, for example regarding their aetiology or accompanying psychobehavioural features? In summary, things are getting better, but there is still considerable confusion.

Somatoform Disorders

For the diagnosis of a 'somatoform disorder' in the ICD-10, there must be a 'repeated presentation of physical symptoms together with persistent requests for medical investigations, in spite of repeated negative findings and reassurances by doctors that the symptoms have no physical basis'. If any physical disorders are present, 'they do not explain the nature and extent of the symptoms or the distress and preoccupation of the patient'. There are several subgroups and neighbours with regard to symptom types (F45.0 for severe, multiple and early-onset symptoms; F45.2 for health anxiety; F45.3 for autonomous symptoms; F45.4 for pain; F44 for dissociative disorders, usually disturbances in motor or sensory function or consciousness, such as sudden-onset paralysis, numbness, stupor or seizures; F48 for neurasthenia/fatigue). F44 suggests 'insoluble problems or interpersonal difficulties' as triggers to symptom onset. But both the absence of organ pathology and the causality of conflicts are difficult to prove.

Bodily Distress Disorder and Somatic Symptom Disorder

The ICD-11 will abandon 'somatoform disorders' and introduce 'bodily distress disorder' (BDD; 6C20) instead, equivalent to the Diagnostic and Statistical Manual of Mental Disorders (DSM) 5's 'somatic symptom disorder' (SSD). Both are diagnosed if there are one or many bodily symptoms that are present on most days for at least several months that are distressing to the individual and excessive attention is directed towards the symptoms that is not alleviated by appropriate clinical examination, investigations and appropriate reassurance. The symptoms, associated distress and preoccupation must impact the individual's functioning. Thus, positive psychobehavioural criteria are required – but no longer evidence of psychological causes or conflicts, or the absence of organic illness. Therefore, they can be diagnosed more readily now, and co-morbid to other illnesses. BDD houses neurasthenia, which will disappear from the ICD, but it is separated from 'dissociative disorders', and 'hypochondriasis', the latter being classified as a subtype of obsessive compulsive disorders. DSM 5 SSD, on the contrary, is categorised next to conversion disorder ('functional neurological symptom disorder'), 'illness anxiety disorder', 'factitious disorder' and 'psychological factors affecting other medical conditions' ('somatic symptom and related disorders'). In the general population, the prevalence for DSM 5 SSD is 4.5–7%.

Bodily Distress Syndrome

The primary care diagnosis of a 'bodily distress syndrome' (BDS) is simply based on typical symptom clusters. It does not ask for 'somatic' versus 'psychological' causes for the symptoms or for psychobehavioural concomitants, but the exclusion of relevant differential diagnoses is recommended. BDS is differentiated into 'single-organ' (one or two clusters) and 'multi-organ' (more than two clusters) subtypes; the prevalence is estimated at 9.6–15.1% and 1–1.3%, respectively.

Functional Somatic Syndromes

Circumscribed symptom clusters can also be called 'functional somatic syndromes'. Many medical subspecialties define their own functional somatic syndromes, such as fibromyalgia (FM), irritable bowel syndrome (IBS), chronic fatigue syndrome or multiple chemical sensitivity, but their phenotypes overlap considerably. FM (MG30.01), for example, defined by widespread musculoskeletal pain, unrefreshing sleep, subjective cognitive disturbances and depressed mood, affects about 2–4.6% of the general population; 32–80% of patients with FM also have IBS (DD91.0), characterised by abdominal pain related to defecation, a change in frequency of stool and/or a change in form/appearance of stool. Its general prevalence is estimated at 3.6–11%. Only few functional somatic syndromes are listed in the ICD-10 and -11, but the latter will include several FNDs (for example, functional tremor 8A04.4). FNDs also have an increased co-morbidity with FM (16%) and IBS (12–36%). They are the second commonest reason for new neurology consultations; for example, up to 8% of suspected strokes are 'functional stroke mimics'.

Dissociative Disorders

In the ICD-11, there will be a partly parallel classification of FNDs (as disorders of the nervous system) and 'dissociative neurological symptom disorder' (6B60) (as mental, behavioural or neurodevelopmental disorders). The latter will be characterised by an impairing, complete or partial involuntary disruption or discontinuity in the normal integration of identity, sensations, perceptions, affects, thoughts, memories, control over bodily movements or behaviour. In contrast to the ICD-10, 'a psychogenic origin, being associated closely in time with traumatic events, insoluble and intolerable problems, or disturbed relationships', is no longer required.

Chronic Primary Pain

As a new multifactorial concept for pain in one or more anatomical regions, the ICD-11 will introduce 'chronic primary pain' (MG30.0), with visceral, musculoskeletal, headache/oro-facial and widespread subtypes, the latter including fibromyalgia. It is neutrally located in the ICD-11 section 'general symptoms'. It emphasises the commonalities of its subtypes – that is, emotional or functional disability – independently of identified biological or psychological contributors. However, it ignores other manifestations of bodily distress than pain, such as fatigue, dizziness and cardiovascular or gastrointestinal symptoms (4).

Functional Somatic Disorders

Therefore, an overarching concept has been introduced recently (4): 'functional somatic disorders' cover persistent and troublesome physical symptoms, with several subtypes (multisystem/single system/single symptom; gastrointestinal/musculoskeletal/nervous system/cardiorespiratory/genito-urinary/fatigue-related). Its core pathology is assumed mal-adaptive central/cognitive functioning with according bodily/behavioural changes, but there are no diagnostic criteria regarding aetiology or onset. Psychobehavioural character-istics can be specified but are not necessary for diagnosis. Another specifier enables the diagnosis of a functional somatic disorder together with 'same system physical disease', such as functional musculoskeletal symptoms in a patient with rheumatoid arthritis.

Other Possibilities

Sometimes, more time and information are needed before a diagnosis can be made or rejected. For these cases, ICD-10 and ICD-11 provide symptom categories such as R42/MB48, 'dizziness and giddiness'.

Another possibility is to code 'factors influencing health status and contact with health services' (ICD-10 Z; ICD-11 24), such as, 'problems related to social environ-ment'. If FSS clearly complicate the course of concomitant disorders but do not warrant a diagnosis on their own right, they can be classified as 'psychological factors affecting other medical conditions' (ICD-10 F54.0, ICD-11 6E40). In consultation-liaison psychiatry, there are probably more patients fitting these categories than in classic psychiatry hospitals (see Chapter 4 in this volume).

FSS should not be confused with the deliberate symptom production in factitious disorder, with psychotic sensory disturbances or with malingering. Nevertheless, there is some shared dysfunctionality of the sick role in functional and factitious disorders; some-times there are mixed motives.

Management in Consultation-Liaison Psychiatry

Similar to primary care physicians in the outpatient setting, consultation-liaison psychi-atrists function as counsellors and translators for patients with FSS, as pilots and gatekeepers. They convey medical information to patients and improve communication between patients and medical professionals. They advise the medical team about FSS management and lay the foundation for further treatment. In the following, we will illustrate general management strategies and provide an outlook on more specific examples. Recommendations are based on current international clinical guidelines and reviews for the general management of FSS (6, 8, 14–18). Several focus on specific FSS and cover symptom-targeted *as well as* generalised strategies, for example for FND (7), IBS (20) and FMS (21).

Making and Communicating the Diagnosis

Screening

Screening for symptom type, count and severity is advisable in most clinical situations, with *all* of the patients' symptoms being listed. In everyday practice, direct questioning should be preferred (Table 7.1). Self-assessment screening devices such as the Patient Health Questionnaire (PHQ-15) or the Somatic Symptom Score (SSS-8) can be economic alternatives. Based on the amount, variety and persistence of symptoms, Rosendal et al. suggest a simple prognostic estimation ('multiple symptoms, multiple systems, multiple times') (6).

Examination and Workup

Most FSS do not disclose at first sight, and general hospital settings usually have other diagnostic targets in mind. Nevertheless, since FSS are so common, heterogeneous and intertwined with other illness, they should be considered from the beginning and throughout all medical workups in all fields of medicine. Alertness paired with restraint enables a broad diagnostic perspective without premature fixation on one single diagnosis or cause (Table 7.1).

Table 7.1 Basic management of functional somatic symptoms: practical tips and examples

Task	Example
Setting the agenda	How can I help you? What is it that brought you to hospital/to clinic today? What is your main concern about this symptom? We have about X minutes for this consultation today so I'll keep it quite focussed, but we can set up another appointment in X weeks.
Screening	What's bothering you the most at present? Is there anything else? Do you have any other discomfort or pains anywhere? How are you sleeping? Have you had any blackouts or trouble concentrating?
Broadening the lens	Ok, let me see. You have a history of X yourself, and a family history of Y. Plus, there is this problem at work. Have you ever noticed your symptoms decreasing over the weekends?
Framing investigations	This is a routine procedure and I think the results will be reassuring. Your EEG shows steady, healthy brain activity.
Watchful waiting with interdisciplinary cooperation	We have ruled out all the urgent and dangerous possibilities such as epilepsy or cancer. I am quite sure that your symptoms will subside as soon as there's less stress at your workplace. We don't need any further investigations now, but I suggest you see your primary care physician in 2 weeks in case the symptoms persist.
Diagnosis as treatment	Did you notice that the strength in your leg came back to normal briefly when you lifted up the other one? Shall I show you that again? This is most likely functional weakness (7).

Table 7.1 (cont.)

Task	Example
Validation and reassurance	I can see how distressing this is for you and the impact it is having on your life.
Making sense of symptoms	Sample models to aid discussion include: intact hardware but faulty software (many patients struggle with this analogy, but in some groups it might particularly resonate); (2) the brain and body are not communicating with each other smoothly; (3) the structure of the body is okay but there is a problem with how signals are being sent and received; (4) an interruption of the connection between the mind and body.
Framing expectations and goals	Regarding your symptoms and activities, it's better to take small, focussed, realistic steps: 'Being able to take a bus again' versus 'getting healthy', which is a bit less focussed; 'going to the bowling club tonight' versus 'training for a 10K run', which might be a bit too much just yet. How about your aims in life, your dreams? Is there something you really want to achieve? Could it be done by working towards it in small, gradual steps?
Self-efficacy and self-help	With functional somatic symptoms, less medicine is more. There are many ways for you to be your own doctor. Here is a good guideline for patients with functional somatic symptoms (e.g. neurosymptoms. org). For example, I have several patients who benefited from yoga or mindfulness-based stress reduction, which train the body *and* the mind.
Passive somatic treatment	I think it would be helpful for you take sedating antidepressants for a short period of time (weeks to months depending on the presentation and indication). It could help you to get more refreshing sleep, perform better at work and feel less distressed and distracted by your symptoms/these events that are stressful.
Active body–mind treatment	I can understand your fear of moving your back. I recommend physiotherapy. There are some helpful exercises that will enable you to regain your strength, balance and regular movement patterns.
Motivation for multimodal or psychotherapy	Many people benefit from psychotherapy, also those with physical illness. It can help you with coping and re-focussing on your goals. And sometimes it's good to have someone professional to talk to.

Symptom presentation and body language can point towards a functional dimension of symptoms, for example unusual, dramatic descriptions, reluctance to perform certain movements, a tense posture, a pressed, anxious or bitter voice, or more or less direct indication of psychosocial needs – but these are not at all specific and can occur in all kinds of illness and personalities. However, there are several particular clinical findings that are clear positive signs specifically for FND (Table 7.2) (7). Hopefully reliable clinical signs for other types of FSS will be found in the future.

Table 7.2 Exemplary clinical signs for FND (7)

Functional seizure	Eyes closed and hyperventilation during event, waxing and waning, resistance to eyelid opening, crying after event
Functional leg weakness	Hip extension strength becomes normal with contralateral hip flexion against resistance (Hoover's sign); hip abduction is weak to direct testing, but strength becomes normal with contralateral hip abduction against resistance (hip abductor sign)
Functional tremor	When the patient copies the examiner making rhythmic pincer movements of thumb and forefinger with their better side, the tremor stops or entrains to the same rhythm as the examiner (tremor entrainment test)
Functional dystonia	Fixed position with fixed muscular contraction (clenched fist, inverted ankle)
Functional visual disturbances	Tubular field defects are the same at different widths (instead of increasing with distance). Goldman perimetry constricts spirally the longer the tests go on

So far, there are no laboratory or imaging techniques that prove FSS. Therefore, any further investigations (as well as prescriptions and procedures) should be chosen wisely, based on earlier and current findings. Redundant procedures only to reassure the doctor and the patient should be avoided. If investigations are necessary, they should be framed in a reassuring manner. When discussing the results with the patient, the wording should be comprehensible and reassuring (Table 7.1). Occasional summarising of all previous findings enables an all-encompassing (re-)evaluation of medical results. As long as there is a sufficiently clear picture of findings and co-morbidities, and as long as red flags are ruled out, 'watchful waiting' is justifiable. Most patients will accept uncertainty concerning their symptoms to some degree, as long as they perceive their doctors' diligence and empathy.

Symptom Conditions, Contexts and Consequences

Patients should be carefully and impartially listened to, observed, asked *and* examined. The resulting multidimensional picture of conditions, contexts and consequences allows for a balanced assessment of the clinical relevance of FSS and at the same time provides clues for tailored treatment (Table 7.3). It is important to keep the diagnostic lens as broad as possible: sometimes there is a single event that appears pivotal, such as a recent loss or an accident, but that may only be the last straw in symptom aetiology or an additional burden and not necessarily its major cause.

Delivering the Diagnosis

Diagnosis-telling is not only a matter of 'if' but also of 'how' (Table 7.1). Regardless of the symptoms' severity, it is an early and effective element of FSS treatment: the positive message of legitimate and very common symptoms, a comprehensible psychophysiological model and the prospect of potential reversibility provides relief, which can itself reduce bodily distress. Plus, it reveals therapeutic starting points.

Table 7.3 Symptom conditions, context and consequences – and therapeutic starting points

Structural and biochemical changes	Gather and review old notes and investigations and make well-considered choices regarding further investigations Watch out for red flags – but do not overrate incidental findings
Co-morbidity	Watch out for all kinds of co-morbid illness, especially anxiety and depression
Timeline and variability	Ask for onset and course of symptoms, exacerbating and relieving factors, limitations, a typical day, good and bad days, medical experiences, previous results and treatments
Dysfunctional cognitions	Ask for and observe fear, catastrophising or negative appraisals (e.g. 'physical work breaks your back', 'I should avoid movements and exertion')
Dysfunctional illness behaviour	Observe avoidance, concealment, aggravation, dramatised symptom presentation, (medical) activism, a pronounced sick role (e.g. avoidance behaviour, anxious body scanning, identification with other sick patients, compensation claims) Ask for lifestyle and health behaviour (e.g. social withdrawal, excessive workload, dietary restrictions, excessive smoking, dysfunctional alcohol use)
Stressors, precursors, triggers and sequelae	Ask for current problems and predicaments with family, health, work, money, law, recent losses Ask for physical triggers such as injury or migraine Ask about family history of illness when patient was a child, also illness in the patient during childhood and any admissions to hospital when a child Tactfully enquire about childhood adversity and neglect both within and outside the home. Be vigilant regarding clues for preceding experiences with violence, neglect or parental illness, but consider the risk of re-traumatisation
Explanatory model and expectations	Ask for the patient's own explanatory model ('this might as well be cancer', 'I think there are toxins in my office', 'I've been cursed') Ask for future expectations ('I will stay disabled', 'I want to retire')
Individual resources	Ask for and observe individual strengths, hobbies, trust, humour, goals, allies

If diagnostic criteria are not met, patients should be informed about the commonness of FSS in a normalising, non-repellent and non-trivialising manner. Symptoms should be explained as short-term disturbances of well-being, balance or rhythm which are part of everyday health regulation. If there is a diagnosis, patients should be told and reassured. They should be told that medicine is familiar with such cases; that there are other patients with similar problems; that there are therapeutic standards and a normal life expectancy. Just as in many other conditions such as migraine or depression, communicating a diagnosis does not require a determination of its causes – it rather needs an explanation of mechanisms and solutions.

Treatment

Communication, Cooperation and Commitment

First, consultation-liaison psychiatrists play a key role in counselling and training patients and clinicians on functional somatic symptom management. As patients seek recognition and a shared understanding and treatment of their symptoms, good communication in the consultation is essential. Watchfulness and commitment can be signalled by offering further contacts and cooperations, including, for example, a short conference with or a consultation letter for their primary care physician at home, a second consultation-liaison appointment or a joint ward round visit together with the rest of the medical team.

Second, consultation-liaison psychiatrists should reflect upon their own role. Experienced consultation-liaison psychiatrists often have good antennae for the psychodynamics of FSS, but even they may be wrong. Plus, withdrawing patients from somatic medicine and pressing a (possibly insufficient) psychological explanation on them can lead to more defence and more symptoms. The patient's psychological mindedness cannot be presumed, especially if there is relevant organic co-morbidity, if they have already been 'iatrogenically somatised' by previous caregivers and if they do not realise psychological distress (e.g. due to alexithymia). It is essential to recognise the patient's symptoms, to take their perspective and pace and to work in close cooperation with the medical team (Table 7.1).

Making Sense of Symptoms

The development of an individual explanatory model is the bridge between diagnosis-making and treatment. A comprehensible, blame-free model can contain both psychosocial (such as a recent divorce) and physiological contributors (such as a recent gastrointestinal infection), without necessarily answering the 'chicken-and-egg' question. It should be developed by doctor and patient *together*, based on the patient's own context and findings, their own experience and previous causal interpretations (even if they may seem oversensitive, one-sided or implausible), and psychophysiological facts about FSS. It can make use of new scientific findings, for example, the power of attention/distraction, placebo/nocebo responses or the positive effects of sports. Graphic material can help, especially explaining bodily manifestations of stress, 'false alarms', blockages, domino effects and vicious circles (Table 7.1).

Framing Expectations and Goals

To interrupt typical cycles of passivity, hope and frustration in FSS, it is important to frame expectations clearly. With good information, most patients understand that there is no single, rapid pharmacological or surgical intervention. They understand why it is important to cut down on medical procedures and turn towards more functional tasks instead.

Personal goals of patients with FSS should be concrete, realistic and small-step (Table 7.1). Therapeutic goals should first and foremost be feasible and applicable at home, such as yoga practices or relaxation techniques. They should be picked according to individual resources and preferences and re-evaluated during the course of the treatment.

When patients are embedded within a sick role, they are also partners, employees, parishioners, sportmates. Plus, FSS treatment requires some personal commitment and activity, and thus needs rewards. Therefore, there should also be superordinate values and motivators ('what is all this for?'): visions and aims in life such as closer contact with one's grandchildren, a holiday or an honorary post can serve as 'lighthouses' for long-term healing. Even if they may cost some energy, they provide distraction, integration, self-worth and meaning.

Self-Efficacy and Self-Help

Even if consultation-liaison psychiatrists (as well as other physicians and therapists) offer a counselling role, most of the 'hard work' is done by the patients themselves. Simple leisure activities and home remedies can be first steps to increase well-being and decrease distress, as long as they are self-determined and active. A stronger focus should be set on self-governed measures to escape passivity and the sick role, and to regain autonomy and self-regulation (Table 7.1) – which can eventually be reinforced in subsequent psychotherapy:

- Self-help literature and self-help groups can be helpful (as long as they offer empowerment and support beyond medical interventions and victimhood). By combining current information, practical tips and experience from fellow sufferers, they foster self-care and self-compassion, which may have previously become hidden or never learnt. Patients who become involved in self-help groups often mobilise amazing organising or altruistic abilities. The internet helps a great deal in terms of scope, accessibility and diversity, in many languages.
- By focusing on procedures and interventions, medicine promotes patient passvity. Even if they are usually suggested by doctors, and not requested by patients, there can be a lot of pressure from anxious, helpless or aggressive patients. Thus, medical decision-making should consider patient beneficence (and non-maleficence) as well as autonomy (i.e. their will and preferences). If patients are extremely demanding or manipulative, for example regarding opioids or an amputation, a factitious disorder should be considered.
- For patients with FSS, there are two important facets of health behaviour: first, a balanced use of healthcare service, avoiding under- and especially over-use. Second, a healthy lifestyle outside the health system (physical activity, balanced nutrition, cessation of smoking and drinking, getting enough exercise and rest). Hospitalisations should be avoided if possible.
- Training the body, training the mind: beyond a generally healthy lifestyle, patients with FSS can actively work on body–mind regulation and stress management. Aerobic exercise, grassroots sport or body–mind techniques such as Feldenkrais, yoga or mindfulness-based stress reduction can help to increase strength, body positivity, self-steering, relaxation, resilience and acceptance. At the same time, they can enable distraction and social contacts.
- Finally, by becoming more active (sports, a journey; see earlier), patients can shape their lives according to their own superordinate goals. Ideally, they learn that these goals can be pursued without, with some, with or in spite of symptoms ('I won't let the pain keep me from living') and have a fulfilled life.

Bio-psycho-social Treatment in the Somatic Setting

What can medicine offer these patients? It has become clear that in FSS management, less is more. However, some patients need medical help and guidance. The integration of psychosocial treatment elements in usual medical treatment has been referred to as 'enhanced (primary) care'; well-situated outpatient networks but also hospitals with rehabilitation, psychological or consultation-liaison psychiatry services provide some valuable offerings.

- Although medical interventions should not (again) become the only focus, bio-psycho-social treatment of FSS includes good control of both somatic and mental co-morbidities (examples include cancer, multiple sclerosis, migraine, inflammatory bowel disease, depression, anxiety, addiction, etc.).

- Passive measures are preferred by some patients. Some of these can alleviate symptoms, such as passive physiotherapy, massage or complementary interventions (e.g. acupuncture and phytotherapy). They usually have no or only mild side effects. Symptom-targeted peripherally acting treatments, such as analgesics, probiotics or anti spasmodics, may be taken for initial symptom relief and thus help with return to normal functioning. Centrally acting psychopharmacological agents (such as antidepressants, sedatives, anxiolytics, rarely antipsychotics) can improve mood or sleep, according to individual co-morbidities. Examples include tricyclics for sleep and pain, selective serotonin reuptake inhibitors (SSRIs) for pain and mood, and pregabalin for anxiety and pain. As long as their specific roles and effects are explained, and their risks (including side effects and addiction) are evaluated regularly, these adjuncts may be considered as part of a patient's treatment plan.

- There are numerous active therapies, aiming at harmonisation and regulation of psychological and physical strength, reactivity and sensitivity, and also at new experiences and insights. They help patients understand the close interactions between 'physical' and 'psychological' processes and, if necessary, facilitate the transition to psychotherapy exercise therapy. Physiotherapy and exercise therapy can focus on bodily dysfunctions, such as loss of use and strength, malpositions, dysfunctional movement or breathing patterns. They can, usually in a graded and often in a distractive, playful manner, enable patients to re-experience their bodily self as active, robust and productive, and to rediscover functional-or give up dysfunctional-operations. For FND, there are physiotherapy consensus recommendations (21). Occupational therapy is centred on helping people overcome the effects of their symptom profile through practical support to improve performance in activities of daily living, thereby reducing dependence. This may involve re-training normal movement within function, increasingly including imagery and virtual reality techniques, graded re-introduction to daily activities such as personal care, domestic activities, childcare, community or leisure activities, aids and adaptations to improve access to home, education, work or community environments, anxiety management and the re-establishment of structure and routine. The person is supported to take ownership of their rehabilitation and develop an internal locus of control, rather than placing control in the hands of clinicians and family members. For occupational therapy in FNDs, consensus recommendations have recently been published (22). Balneotherapy, a mixed passive–active treatment comprising simultaneous stimulation, relaxation and exercise, has been shown to be effective in fibromyalgia (20).

– Active, positive, body-centred therapies contain a lot of psychological, mostly motivational and distracting effectors. In addition, there are more specific psychological interventions that do not need the setting, intensity and duration of psychotherapy, usually aiming at psychoeducation, reappraisal/reattribution, relaxation and acceptance. Guided stress, pain and conflict management can improve coping with daily hassles and release tension and anger. Biofeedback and relaxation techniques can help to steer and calm physiological responses, for example by reducing sympathetic arousal. Meditative body–mind approaches allow for a broader, non-focussed, non-appraising perception of the steady flow of bodily as well as environmental signals; they can moderate implicit, non-verbal stress reactions to salient stimuli and memories. Hypnotherapy can be valuable to break through symptom perception and generation; it has been shown to be efficacious in IBS (19).

Combining physical and psychological techniques creates a 'multimodal' approach. In certain countries like Germany, multimodal inpatient programmes are provided in psychosomatic (with more psychological interventions, one-to-one and in groups) and in rehabilitation hospitals (with more physical interventions, one-to-one and in groups). In multimodal treatment, patients complete several weeks of a scheduled programme including psychological counselling, group psychotherapy (e.g. for pain management) and different types of mostly active and partly body–mind physical exercise under medical supervision. It is also possible to arrange outpatient multimodal treatment, for example by co-creative cooperation of primary care physicians, neurologists, psychotherapists, physiotherapists and psychologists.

Psychotherapy

Psychotherapy should be reserved for patients with profound problems with their physical or psychological symptoms, associated, for example, with persistent inability to work, disturbed relationships, difficult experiences in the medical system or mental comorbidity. Psychotherapy addresses the patient more individually than other treatment, with sensitively tailored aproaches and goals. Because most patients perceive and express *bodily* rather than psychosocial distress, the first treatment goal is often focussed on increasing motivation to engage with psychotherapy. This can already be pursued by previous care providers, including the consultation-liaison psychiatrist.

Outpatient psychotherapy provides a medium- to long-term professional and at the same time confidential relationship. It provides psychoeducation, support and a safe ground for self-exploration and new experiences. Individual resources, and on the other hand dysfunctional models and patterns, can be identified and modified with respect to affect regulation as well as cognitive distortions, dysfunctional attitudes, behaviours and interactions. This includes the relationship to one's own body, especially the experience and handling of physical boundaries, pain and arousal, as well as interpersonal relationships. Specifically, cognitive behavioural therapy tackles unhelpful misattributions and avoidance of all sorts, and psychodynamic and interpersonal therapy (PIT/IPT) tackles more interpersonal questions (see Chapter 15 in this volume). But irrespective of the method, psychotherapy in FSS must stay close to the patient's bodily experience and expression.

During the course of psychotherapy, with the body remaining in focus, more individual and more delicate aspects can be tackled. Biography, personality and implicit bodily (including traumatic) experiences can be observed, explored, put into perspective and carefully modified, for example by developing a basic sense of trust, reduced helplessness and self-incrimination and more self-defence, eventually by confronting with and recovering from traumatic experiences. Bodily integration and agency schemas as well as their aberrances (such as dissociation, apotemnophilia, dysmorphophobia or self-harm) are important to be recognised and addressed. Especially when it has been neglected, abused, hurt or experienced threatening illness in itself or significant others, psychotherapy can increase consciousness and care for the embodied self.

Current evidence supports several psychotherapeutic, psychosocial and multimodal approaches to different kinds of FSS. There are well-established psychodynamic, interpersonal, cognitive behavioural and imaginative concepts. The same is true for such interventions for other illnesses, for example for fatigue in multiple sclerosis or for chronic pain, which again questions dualistic causal attributions. Their overall efficacy is only small to moderate, and though sustained effects are small, there is some evidence for improved functioning, but not on the symptoms themselves. Treatment motivation and adherence are moderate; drop-out rates are high. Better strategies with higher acceptance and higher efficacy are needed.

Key Points

- Are generated by perceptual dysregulation and dysfunctional stress responses. That means that they are 'real', not imagined or made up. They are involuntary, not 'faked'.
- Because of their highly individual and situational aetiology, FSS are polymorphic and do not fit monocausal, unidirectional explanations. There are various risk factors, albeit few objective indicators. Stressors, expectations and our way of handling them matter a lot.
- FSS can be transient and mild, but also severely disabling, putting a considerable burden on both the patient and the health system – even in the absence of defined disease. Very often they occur co-morbidly to somatic and/or mental illness, so broad diagnostic vigilance is important. Suicidality should not be missed.
- FSS need multidimensional, stepped and individually tailored management. Interdisciplinary cooperation is mandatory for effective assessment and treatment.
- Much is achieved by avoiding typical mistakes such as recurrently medicalising symptoms and fostering learned helplessness, chronicity and even additional disability as a result of recurrent interventions. Watchful waiting increases the possibility of spontaneous remissions and decreases the risk of iatrogenic chronicity.
- Treatment should be preferably active, both physical *and* psychological, and aim at self-efficacy. As in diagnostics, the individual context should be considered, with a focus on understanding, coping and functioning.
- Psychoeducation, the development of a blame-free, individual explanatory model and activation are the cornerstones of treatment. Self-regulation including, stress management and improvement of sleep as well as the pursuit of personal goals can be promising starting points. Severe cases benefit from psychotherapy addressing the 'embodied self'.

References

1. Ding JM, Kanaan RA. What should we say to patients with unexplained neurological symptoms? How explanation affects offence. *J Psychosom Res* 2016;**91**:55–60.

2. Henningsen P, Gündel H, Kop WJ et al. EURONET-SOMA Group. Persistent physical symptoms as perceptual dysregulation: A neuropsychobehavioral model and its clinical implications. *Psychosom Med.* 2018;**80**(5):422–31.

3. Kube T, Rozenkrantz L, Rief W, Barsky A. Understanding persistent physical symptoms: Conceptual integration of psychological expectation models and predictive processing accounts. *Clin Psychol Rev* 2020;**76**:101829.

4. Burton C, Fink P, Henningsen P, Löwe B, Rief W. EURONET-SOMA Group. Functional somatic disorders: Discussion paper for a new common classification for research and clinical use. *BMC Med* 2020;**18**(1):34.

5. Köteles F, Witthöft M. Somatosensory amplification: An old construct from a new perspective. *J Psychosom Res.* 2017;**101**:1.

6. Rosendal M, Olde Hartman TC, Aamland A et al. 'Medically unexplained' symptoms and symptom disorders in primary care: prognosis-based recognition and classification. *BMC Fam Pract.* 2017;**18**(1):18.

7. Stone J, Burton C, Carson A. Recognising and explaining functional neurological disorder. *BMJ.* 2020;**371**:m3745.

8. Henningsen P, Zipfel S, Sattel H, Creed F. Management of functional somatic syndromes and bodily distress. *Psychother Psychosom.* 2018;**87**(1):12–31.

9. Popkirov S, Carson AJ, Stone J. Scared or scarred: Could 'dissociogenic' lesions predispose to nonepileptic seizures after head trauma? *Seizure.* 2018;**58**:127–32.

10. Afari N, Ahumada SM, Wright LJ et al. Psychological trauma and functional somatic syndromes: A systematic review and meta-analysis. *Psychosom Med.* 2014;**76**(1):2–11.

11. Ludwig L, Pasman JA, Nicholson T et al. Stressful life events and maltreatment in conversion (functional neurological) disorder: Systematic review and meta-analysis of case-control studies. *Lancet Psychiatry.* 2018;**5**(4):307–20.

12. Kaleycheva N, Cullen AE, Evans R et al. The role of lifetime stressors in adult fibromyalgia: Systematic review and meta-analysis of case-control studies. *Psychol Med.* 2021;**51**(2):177–93.

13. Suglia SF, Koenen KC, Boynton-Jarrett R et al. American Heart Association Council on Epidemiology and Prevention; Council on Cardiovascular Disease in the Young; Council on Functional Genomics and Translational Biology; Council on Cardiovascular and Stroke Nursing; and Council on Quality of Care and Outcomes Research. Childhood and adolescent adversity and cardiometabolic outcomes: A scientific statement from the American Heart Association. *Circulation.* 2018;**137**(5):e15–e28.

14. Roenneberg C, Sattel H, Schaefert R et al. Functional somatic symptoms. *Dtsch Arztebl Int.* 2019;**116**(33–4):553–60. www.awmf.org/leitlinien/detail/ll/051-001.html.

15. Chitnis A, Dowrick C, Byng R et al. Guidance for health professionals on medically unexplained symptoms. London; 2011. https://dxrevisionwatch.files.wordpress.com/2013/06/guidance-for-health-professionals-on-mus-jan-2011.pdf.

16. van der Feltz-Cornelis CM, Hoedeman R, Keuter EJW, Swinkels JA. Presentation of the multidisciplinary guideline Medically Unexplained Physical Symptoms (MUPS) and somatoform disorder in the Netherlands: Disease management according to risk profiles *J Psychosom Res.* 2012;**72**(2):168–9.

17. Rosendal MSKK, Christensen KS, Agersnap L et al. Functional disorders: Clinical guideline for general practitioners. Copenhagen; 2013. www.eapm.eu.com/wp-content/uploads/2018/06/clinical-guideline-functional-disorders-dsam-2013.pdf.

18. Olde Hartman TC, Rosendal M, Aamland A et al. What do guidelines and systematic reviews tell us about the management of medically unexplained symptoms in primary care? *BJGP Open.* 2017;1(3):bjgpopen17X101061.

19. Layer P, Andresen V, Pehl C et al. Deutschen Gesellschaft für Verdauungs- und Stoffwechselkrankheiten; Deutschen Gesellschaft für Neurogastroenterologie und Motilität. (Irritable bowel syndrome: German consensus guidelines on definition, pathophysiology and management). *Z Gastroenterol.* 2011;49(2):237–9. www.awmf.org/leitlinien/detail/ll/021-016.html.

20. Deutsche Schmerzgesellschaft. Definition, Pathophysiologie, Diagnostik und Therapie des Fibromyalgiesyndroms. 2019. www.awmf.org/leitlinien/detail/ll/145-004.html.

21. Nielsen G, Stone J, Matthews A et al. Physiotherapy for functional motor disorders: a consensus recommendation. *J Neurol Neurosurg Psychiatry.* 2015;86(10):1113–9.

22. Nicholson C, Edwards MJ, Carson AJ et al. Occupational therapy consensus recommendations for functional neurological disorder. *J Neurol Neurosurg Psychiatry.* 2020;91(10):1037–45.

23. Agarwal V, Nischal A, Praharaj SK et al. Clinical practice guideline: Psychotherapies for somatoform disorders. *Indian J Psychiatry* 2020;62(suppl. 2):S263–S271.

24. The Danish Committee for Health Education. Information about functional disorders. 2012. https://funktionellelidelser.dk/fileadmin/www.funktionellelidelser.au.dk/patient_Pjecer/When_the_body_says_stop.pdf.

25. Stone J. Functional Neurological Disorder (FND): A patient's guide. 2015. http://neurosymptoms.org/welcome/4594357992.

26. NHS. What is IBS? 2017. www.nhs.uk/conditions/irritable-bowel-syndrome-ibs.

Alcohol Misuse

Rachel Thomasson and Ashokkumar Shishodia

Complications of alcohol misuse are frequently encountered in the general hospital setting, as well as primary care and outpatient clinics. It is an essential part of the skillset of a consultation-liaison (CL) psychiatrist to be able to competently assess the scale of the problem, to offer advice and guidance on acute issues which may arise during intoxication and withdrawal and to orchestrate appropriate support and follow-up if a patient is willing to engage. This chapter aims to equip the reader with relevant epidemiology, some clinically useful biology and mathematics and a scaffold for building on previously acquired basics in terms of assessment and management of alcohol-related problems in the general hospital setting.

Alcohol Misuse: Some Facts and Figures

Alcohol misuse is a major cause of morbidity and mortality in many countries, and as such is ranked by the World Health Organization as one of the leading causes of disease burden. Harmful use of alcohol is associated with 3 million deaths per year worldwide (1).

Europe is the heaviest drinking region in the world. In the UK Office for National Statistics report of adult drinking habits in 2017, men were more likely to drink than women and those aged 45–64 were the most likely to drink, while those aged 16–24 were the least likely to drink. Since 2005, teetotalism has increased among those aged 16–44 but has fallen by 5% for those aged 65 and over (2).

In England there are an estimated 602,391 dependent drinkers, and less than 20% of this cohort are receiving treatment (3). Twenty-four per cent of adults in England and Scotland regularly drink over the Chief Medical Officer's low-risk guidelines (4, 5), and 27% of drinkers in Great Britain binge drink on their heaviest drinking days (over 8 units for men and over 6 units for women) (2).

In 2018–19 in England, 75,555 people were in treatment at specialist alcohol misuse services, a fall of 18% since 2013–14 (6). Females represent 40% of those in treatment, although only 23% of females in the population have problematic alcohol use. Eighty-five per cent of people engaged with treatment for alcohol misuse are White British, 4% are other White ethnicities and 7% are from non-White ethnic groups. Approximately 61% of clients starting treatment were self-referrals. Twenty-four per cent were from health services and social care, which includes 14% from primary care physicians (6). Fifty-four per cent of people in alcohol treatment also require mental health treatment, with 19% of them not receiving any relevant interventions (8). Thirty-one per cent of people in alcohol treatment in England in 2018–19 disengaged before successfully completing treatment (6).

A recent digital NHS report on adult health-related behaviours (7) estimates 358,000 admissions to UK hospitals in 2018–19 where the principal reason for admission to hospital was attributed to alcohol. This was 6% higher than 2017–18 and 19% higher than 2008–9. Of all hospital admissions, 7.4% are attributable to alcohol being either the main driver for presentation or a secondary diagnosis linked with alcohol. According to the Office for National Statistics, there were 8,974 alcohol-specific deaths in England in 2020, which is an increase of 18.6% from 2019. The alcohol-specific age-standardised death rate is twice as high in males (8).

Patients presenting with apparent alcohol intoxication can be a complex and challenging group in terms of assessment and treatment. Acute behavioural disturbance is common, as are co-morbid injuries, attempted self-harm and medical conditions that require attention. Common presenting complaints associated with alcohol intoxication have been summarised below and reflect hospital data reported from Australia, New Zealand, the USA and the UK (9).

- Head injury
- Falls and collapses
- Victim/perpetrator of assault
- Possible seizure
- Hypoglycaemia
- Behavioural disturbance
- Acute confusional state/psychosis
- Other mental health problems – suicidality, deliberate self-harm (alcohol often co-ingested)
- Chest pain, suspected cardiomyopathy
- Gastrointestinal presentations – gastritis, liver disease, pancreatitis.

The Pharmacology of Alcohol

Pharmacokinetics

Ethyl alcohol is a small, water-soluble molecule that is rapidly and efficiently absorbed into the bloodstream from gastric (20%) and intestinal (80%) mucosa. The presence of food can delay gastric emptying time. It is rapidly distributed throughout the body, reaching peak concentrations 20–60 minutes after ingestion.

Approximately 10 ml (1 UK unit) of ethanol is metabolised per hour. In the liver, alcohol is broken down by alcohol dehydrogenase (ADH) and mixed function oxidases such as P450IIE1 (CYP2E1). Levels of CYP2E1 may be increased in chronic drinkers, which represents a putative mechanism for tolerance. ADH activity represents a rate-limiting step in alcohol metabolism as it is affected by the quantity and rate of alcohol consumption and genetic polymorphisms which affect its intrinsic efficiency. Rapid consumption of a large amount of alcohol saturates the conversion system as it follows zero-order kinetics (constant amount oxidised per unit of time), resulting in high levels of blood alcohol. Uncomplicated intoxication usually subsides within a matter of hours. Genetic polymorphisms resulting in reduced enzyme efficiency are commoner in Asian populations; severe, rapid intoxication with modest alcohol consumption is common in ALDH2*2 carriers and there is an increased risk of alcohol poisoning.

Pharmacodynamics

Alcohol consumption causes central nervous system (CNS) depression via enhanced gamma-aminobutyric acid (GABA-A) transmission and reduced N-methyl-D-aspartate (NMDA) transmission. Chronic ingestion leads to downregulation of GABA-A receptors and upregulation of NMDA and α-amino-3-hydroxy-5-methylisoxazole-4-propionic acid (AMPA) receptors. Abrupt reduction of alcohol consumption or stopping entirely renders the brain hyperexcitable because of the above changes. Upregulation of glutamatergic, dopaminergic and noradrenergic transmission could account for propensity for withdrawal seizures, hallucinations and autonomic overdrive, respectively. Repeated withdrawals can lead to a 'kindling effect', increasing the risk of severe complications during withdrawal (10). It becomes clear why benzodiazepines and anticonvulsants form the mainstay of treatment during alcohol withdrawal.

Alcohol by Numbers: Percentages and Units

In the UK, the measure of alcohol consumption used is the alcoholic unit. A unit of alcohol is defined as 10 millilitres (8 grams) of pure alcohol. This definition is independent of the strength (% ABV) and amount (volume) of any individual alcoholic beverage. The number of units of alcohol in a bottle or can (and, optionally, the number of units in a typical serving) is indicated on the drink container. Typical servings deliver 1–3 units of alcohol (see Table 8.1).

Calculating alcohol consumption in units:

units = percent alcohol (ABV) × volume in ml / 1000

Worked example: a 750-ml bottle of wine at 12% strength: 12 × 750 / 1000 = 9 units

Recommended limits at the time of writing (in UK units):

UK – 14 units per week

Ireland – women 14 units, men 21 units per week

Table 8.1 Reference guide for alcohol units

Quantity	Strength	Units
Standard bottle of wine = 750 ml	12%	9
Standard glass of wine = 175 ml	12%	2.1
Large bottle of spirits = 750 ml	38–40%	28.5–30
Quarter-bottle of spirits = 250 ml	38–40%	9.5–10
Single measure of spirits = 25 ml	38–40%	1
Can of lager = 440 ml	4%	2
Small bottle of lager = 330 ml	4–5%	1.3–1.7
Pint of bitter = 568 ml	3.8%	2.2
Can of super-strength lager = 500 ml	9%	4.5
Can of strong 'white' cider = 500 ml	7.5%	3.75
Bottle of normal strength cider = 2000 ml	5%	10

USA – women 12 units, men 24.5 units per week

Australia – 2.5 units per day

New Zealand – women 12.5 units, men 19 units per week

Screening for Harmful, Hazardous and Dependent Drinking

In addition to the assessment framework outlined in Chapter 1, Focused questions pertaining to alcohol use can help to identify harmful and dependent drinking. A pre-screening question about any alcohol use can be used before easing into usual frequency, type and quantity of alcohol consumed in the previous 30 days, followed with more comprehensive timeline and a more formal screening tool. The UK National Institute for Health and Care Excellence (NICE) recommends use of a screening tool such as the Alcohol Use Disorders Identification Test (AUDIT) (11), and for further questioning of severity of alcohol misuse, the Severity of Alcohol Dependence Questionnaire (SADQ) (12) can be helpful. The physical, psychological and social impact of drinking should be explored, as well as previous withdrawal complications such as seizures or delirium tremens (DT), historical attempts to address alcohol use and whether the patient is currently ready to make changes and/or accept support in terms of working towards reducing intake or remaining abstinent.

It is important to note that patients presenting with acute intoxication and withdrawal syndromes are often unable to engage in a comprehensive assessment of alcohol use until acute concerns have been dealt with and they are sober and stabilised on a withdrawal regimen where necessary. Timing of these questions requires careful thought to maintain rapport and maximise chances of engagement.

Common Acute Presentations

Intoxication

As highlighted earlier, the CL team may be asked to get involved in a broad spectrum of presentations related to alcohol consumption. The acutely intoxicated patient will require rapid, systematic assessment for potentially life-threatening injuries and other physical health issues that require prompt treatment. While this will be carried out by medical and nursing staff in the emergency department, the CL team should be vigilant for any evolving signs of physical health complications related to alcohol intoxication. Other assessment priorities include confirming alcohol intoxication or identifying and treating the condition resembling it and screening for mental and physical health complications associated with chronic alcohol use.

Consider how much time has elapsed since the patient was originally picked up (if several hours ago, their presentation should have improved at least in part). Paramedic notes/collateral – where was the patient picked up? Was any alcohol found in their possession? Did they smell of alcohol? Was their presentation at that time suggestive of alcohol intoxication? Are there any presenting features on the paramedic history sheet that appear to have resolved or have things got worse (consider peak alcohol levels emerging, withdrawal or an evolving physical health problem)? Is there a history of previous presentations – if so, what for? Is there a documented or collateral history of heavy alcohol use or illicit substances? Is there any psychiatric, medical or medication history that might provide clues to an alternative diagnosis or co-morbidities that should not be overlooked?

Typical characteristics of alcohol intoxication are summarised in sections F1 and F10 of the World Health Organization's *International Classification of Diseases* (ICD-11) (13). Presenting features include disinhibition, argumentativeness, aggression, mood lability, impaired attention and judgement *plus* one or more of unsteady gait, difficulty in standing, slurred speech, nystagmus, decreased level of consciousness, flushed face and conjunctival injection. Hypotension, hypothermia and hypoglycaemia may also be apparent on examination.

It becomes clear that features of alcohol intoxication do overlap with some of the symptoms and signs suggestive of mental health problems such as mania and schizophrenia, but disturbed level of consciousness and cerebellar motor features are usually absent in these conditions. There are other conditions, however, that mimic behavioural and motor features of alcohol intoxication and these should not be missed. Intoxication with benzodiazepines or opioids can be mistaken for alcohol intoxication or they may have been co-ingested; it is important to try to confirm this as specific treatments exist that can rapidly reverse life-threatening features of intoxication. Other conditions that resemble alcohol intoxication are outlined later in this section.

Alcohol levels may be measured by sampling blood, exhaled breath, saliva or urine. Blood and/or breath measurements are most commonly reported. Results may be reported as mcg/L, mcg/100 ml, mg/L or mg/dL but some breathalyser machines convert to estimated blood alcohol percentages. There are also online calculators that convert breath readings to equivalent blood alcohol concentrations. Alcohol intoxication is defined by clinical manifestations of impairment that occur after alcohol consumption. At a blood alcohol concentration between 20 mg% and 99 mg%, loss of muscular coordination begins, and changes in mood, personality and behaviour occur (14). Although a level of 80 mg% is considered legal intoxication, many people may have significant impairment below that level.

Policies for measuring alcohol levels in patients presenting to emergency departments vary widely both within and between different countries according to whether measurements are taken and whether blood or breath measurements are preferred. Breath measurements are rapid and efficient estimates but require a degree of co-operation and coordination from the patient. Table 8.2 outlines common symptoms and signs associated with increasing alcohol levels. A degree of variation exists according to age, gender, weight, recent food consumption and, most importantly, how much alcohol is consumed on a regular basis. A regular heavy drinker without liver disease will appear far less intoxicated with a blood alcohol level of 100 mg/100 ml than an occasional drinker and will metabolise any ethanol consumed at a faster rate. Someone who is intoxicated with a blood alcohol level of 20 mg/100 ml is unlikely to be dependent.

A common question is whether blood/breath alcohol measurements can help to indicate when someone is ready for psychiatric assessment in the emergency department. Clinical judgement should be exercised first and foremost according to current risks and the symptoms and signs detailed in Table 8.2. If the patient is highly tolerant to alcohol, they may appear sober despite much higher breathalyser readings.

The irritable, drowsy patient who smells strongly of alcohol and vomit, with slurred, rambling speech and a broad-based, unsteady gait, will often be correctly diagnosed with uncomplicated alcohol intoxication and may need no further input from the emergency department, with symptoms and signs resolving in a matter of hours as blood alcohol levels fall. Given the frequency of co-morbid presentations and conditions that mimic alcohol intoxication, however, it makes sense to consider a checklist of common co-morbidities and alternative diagnoses.

Table 8.2 Stages of alcohol intoxication

9 mcg/100 ml breath	Relaxed, mild euphoria, mild impairment of judgement.
22 mcg/100 ml breath	Less inhibited, talkative, impaired concentration.
35 mcg/100 ml breath	Impaired balance, speech, depth perception and peripheral vision, reaction time and hearing, judgement, reasoning and memory. Impaired judgement and self-control.
44–54 mcg/100 ml breath	Mood swings – anger and tearfulness. Staggering gait, slurred speech, blurred vision, impaired gross motor control and reaction times, vomiting.
88 mcg/100 ml breath	Confusion and dizziness, requires help to stand and walk. Stuporose, impaired gag reflex, possible loss of consciousness.
132 mcg/100 ml breath	Unconsciousness common, even coma.
198 mcg/100 ml breath	Respiratory arrest will occur in most individuals.

Initial Assessment Scaffold for the Intoxicated Patient

What is the reason for presentation to hospital (e.g. seizure, injuries, drowsy and unsteady, aggression, suicidality or self-harm attempt, psychotic symptoms)?

Are there any immediate risk issues (agitation, aggression, refusing investigations and treatment, attempting to leave the hospital)?

Did police accompany the patient and if so, why? (E.g., concerns for safety and well-being, in custody, Section 136.)

Are there any atypical or additional features that warrant further assessment beyond a working diagnosis of alcohol intoxication? While investigating mimics may be the primary remit of the treating medical team, it is often helpful for the mental health practitioner to have a list of alternative or parallel possibilities to alcohol intoxication to encourage comprehensive assessment and also to ensure we keep an open mind about the presentation (see Boxes 8.1 and 8.2).

Head injury deserves special consideration as it is a common co-morbid presentation and sometimes the correct underlying diagnosis in an apparently intoxicated patient. In the UK, NICE and the Scottish Intercollegiate Guidelines Network (SIGN) have constructed guidelines to assist healthcare professionals making decisions in both pre-hospital and hospital settings on patients with suspected head injury. This includes guidance on whether a patient requires neuroimaging after head injury and how urgently this should take place (15).

Common reasons for requesting an assessment from the CL team include aggression, confusion, symptoms suggestive of psychosis or concerns about suicidality. If agitation or frank aggression is the source of concern (see also Chapter 11), briefly observe the patient and determine whether level of agitation is low, moderate or high. How does agitation manifest (motor restlessness, distressed or hostile verbal communication, physically

Box 8.1 Co-morbidities Not to Miss

Aspiration and respiratory tract infections

Cardiomyopathy

Gastritis

Pancreatitis

Hepatitis/cirrhosis

Coagulopathy

Head injury, including concussion

Other traumatic injuries (falls, altercations, deliberate self-harm)

Seizures

Wernicke's encephalopathy

Hallucinosis

Suicidality

Ingestion of illicit drugs

Box 8.2 Mimics of Alcohol Intoxication

Post-ictal states

Cerebellar/brain stem vascular event or inflammation (cerebellitis/multiple sclerosis)

Meningitis

Encephalitis

Encephalopathy (Wernicke's, hypoxic-ischaemic, hepatic, uraemic)

Traumatic brain injury

Hypoglycaemia/diabetic ketoacidosis

Hypo/hypernatraemia

Myocardial infarction

Drug overdose – benzodiazepines, phenytoin, carbamazepine, gabapentin, phenobarbital, lithium, amiodarone, ciclosporin

threatening or aggressive behaviour or a combination)? Does agitation/arousal escalate or settle when you attempt to talk with the patient? Consider early whether staff who are trained in restraint and delivering intramuscular injections, security or the police need to be involved. A short-acting benzodiazepine and neuroleptic may be required and should be prescribed in oral and intramuscular form.

Confusion in an apparently intoxicated patient is a common presentation with a potentially diverse range of underlying causes. Wernicke's encephalopathy is a key consideration given high rates of mortality and morbidity for what is a treatable condition.

Relapse of primary mental health disorders such as bipolar affective disorder and psychosis should be considered alongside reversible physical health causes. A complicating factor is that presentations may co-exist such as the patient with schizophrenia who is relapsing and intoxicated; the alcohol-dependent patient who is intoxicated and septic; the patient with young-onset dementia whose cognitive and behavioural symptoms have become exacerbated because of intoxication. Careful history-taking and review of results from the 'acute confusion screen' (physical examination and observations, routine blood tests, urine dipstick, a chest x-ray and head computerised tomography) will often yield diagnostic clarity. This paves the way for focussed input from the CL team in terms of risk management, symptomatic treatment and onward planning (involvement of community mental health team, memory services, alcohol liaison services).

Psychotic symptoms can be related to DT or alcohol-related hallucinosis. Morbid jealousy also has a recognised association with chronic, heavy alcohol use. What are the key concerns? Is the patient actively responding to non-apparent stimuli? Are they suspicious, agitated or frightened? Try to establish whether there is an association between heavy drinking and development or worsening of symptoms or whether the patient has recently become abstinent. Is there a previous history of schizophrenia, schizoaffective disorder, mood disorder with psychosis, drug-induced psychosis (culprit drug?), alcoholic hallucinosis (worsens with heavy drinking) or DT? If there is a history of a psychotic disorder, try to establish whether the patient is compliant with their medication regimen, whether they find it effective or whether they sometimes use alcohol to reduce the impact of distressing hallucinations and delusional beliefs.

Depressed mood, suicidal thoughts and attempted self-harm are common co-morbid features of alcohol associated presentations to the emergency department. Assessment of self-harm is covered in detail elsewhere, but specific aspects of assessment in the patient presenting with intoxication are detailed here. Establish the severity of depression and associated risks. If the patient has ongoing suicidal thoughts and they are thinking of or have recently acted on these thoughts, they should be under one-to-one observation. Do suicidal thoughts intensify when intoxicated? Have these thoughts ever led to self-harm – was the patient intoxicated at the time and was self-harm planned, impulsive or accidental? Does the patient harbour any concern for their own safety when intoxicated (could provide a window of opportunity for intervention)? Is there a temporal relationship between development of depressed mood/anxiety and alcohol misuse? (Try to establish which came first.) Is there a history of significant life events that precipitated either low mood or alcohol misuse? Does alcohol help to blot out difficult feelings and memories, quell anxiety or aid sleep? Are mood, appetite and energy levels better when abstinent from alcohol?

Important questions to ask after the initial assessment are whether risks have been identified and contained, and whether any contributing factors from mental health problems require further assessment and treatment planning and, if so, who will return to review the patient and when. There may be important questions still to be asked that were not possible while the patient was acutely intoxicated and it is important the treating team are kept informed of any requirement for repeat assessment from the CL team.

Alcohol Withdrawal Syndromes

In medically or surgically hospitalized patients, withdrawal contributes to higher post-operative complications and mortality and a longer stay (see Table 8.3). Studies have

Table 8.3 Alcohol withdrawal severity

Severity category	Associated CIWA-Ar range	Treatment
Mild	CIWA-Ar ≤10	Pharmacological treatment generally unnecessary unless history of DT (consider use of ancillary scales such as PAWSS) but consider current medical status
Moderate	CIWA-Ar 11–15	Treatment recommended to prevent progression to severe withdrawal
Severe	CIWA-Ar 16–19	Immediate treatment essential, often with higher doses of benzodiazepine (30–40 mg four times daily)
Complicated	CIWA-Ar > 19	Urgent and comprehensive management plan required to treat or reduce risk of hallucinosis, delirium, seizures, malignant hypertension, coma

shown that about 20% of patients admitted to the hospital have an alcohol use disorder, and the rate among those admitted for acute trauma or for conditions related to high alcohol intake, such as head and neck cancers, is even higher. Patients requiring more than small amounts of medication for withdrawal symptoms need an individualised assessment by clinicians experienced in the management of withdrawal.

Recognising patients in a withdrawal state is a vital skill during CL assessments. Patients may have been referred for entirely different reasons and withdrawal may only become apparent several days into a hospital admission. For patients already identified as being in an acute withdrawal state, common requests for CL input include management of the withdrawal state itself, acute behavioural disturbance, escalating anxiety, consideration of medicolegal aspects of refusal of treatment and/or preference to leave hospital before investigations and treatment have taken place, and assessment and treatment of psychotic symptoms and confusion.

In patients with physiological dependence on alcohol, the clinical manifestations of alcohol withdrawal begin 6 to 24 hours after the last drink, sometimes arising before the blood alcohol level has returned to zero. Early withdrawal signs and symptoms include anxiety, agitation, sleep disturbances, anorexia, nausea and headache. Physical signs include tachycardia, hypertension, hyperreflexia, sweating and mild pyrexia. These signs may be masked in a patient taking beta blockers. A tremor, best brought out by extension of the hands or tongue, may appear. This resembles an exaggerated physiological tremor. The severity of these symptoms varies, but in a majority they are mild and transient, peaking at 12–30 hours and passing within 1 to 2 days (16). In terms of formal diagnostic criteria, the *Diagnostic and Statistical Manual of Mental Disorders* (DSM 5) requires two of autonomic hyperactivity (sweating or tachycardia); increased hand tremor; insomnia; nausea or vomiting; transient visual, tactile or auditory hallucinations or illusions; psychomotor agitation; anxiety; and tonic–clonic seizures (17).

Structured withdrawal severity assessments scales are useful to objectively quantify withdrawal and to guide treatment. The most commonly used and extensively studied is the Clinical Institute Withdrawal Assessment – Alcohol, or CIWA, and a concise version known as the CIWA-A Revised (CIWA-Ar) (18). The CIWA-Ar has well-documented reliability, reproducibility and validity compared to ratings of withdrawal severity by experienced clinicians and requires limited patient co-operation. While treatment is not generally recommended for patients scoring in the mild category, severely medically unwell patients are at risk of developing severe withdrawal; as such, consider whether the potential benefits of a benzodiazepine prescription outweigh the risks. When a patient has unexpectedly mild withdrawal symptoms, there also may be utility in using a predictability scale to bolster confidence in using prophylactic treatment. The Prediction of Alcohol Withdrawal Severity Scale (PAWSS) is one example (19).

Typical monitoring requirements are 4-hourly for patient scoring 0–9, 2-hourly if scoring 10–15 and hourly for scores higher than this. It is important that staff responsible for the patient's care are trained in using the CIWA-Ar. Although it is not a diagnostic instrument for alcohol withdrawal, it is helpful for guiding treatment for alcohol withdrawal. Withdrawal scales can also contribute to appropriate triage of patients because it has been shown that high scores early in the course of withdrawal are predictive of the development of seizures and delirium. Marked autonomic hyperactivity, serum electrolyte abnormalities and acute medical co-morbidities, particularly infection and trauma, are associated with an increased risk of DT or severe withdrawal.

In more severe cases of withdrawal, mild perceptual distortions or misperceptions may evolve into frank hallucinations. Visual hallucinations are the most common and frequently involve animals. Auditory hallucinations may begin as unformed sounds (such as a click, humming or buzz) and may progress to verbal narrative. Tactile hallucinations, if present, often involve a sensation of insects crawling on or under the skin.

Withdrawal seizures usually begin within 8 to 48 hours after the patient's last drink and may occur before the blood alcohol level has returned to zero. Like hallucinosis, seizures can sometimes occur with no or very few symptoms of withdrawal. Seizures peak 24 to 48 hours after the last drink. There is increased risk of seizure in those with previous history of withdrawal seizures and those undergoing concurrent withdrawal from benzodiazepines or other sedative–hypnotic drugs.

For most patients, withdrawal does not progress beyond mild to moderate symptoms. In a small number of patients, the clinical presentation can progress to withdrawal delirium, subsequently leading to DT. DT generally appears 48 to 96 hours after the last drink. The presentation is hallmarked by severe dysautonomia, anxiety, global confusion, disorientation to place and time and sleep–wake cycle disturbance. Hallucinations are frequent and marked psychomotor agitation may develop. Malignant hypertension, seizures and coma contribute to a 5% mortality rate (10, 20).

Management of Alcohol Withdrawal

As with intoxication states, treating teams should keep an open mind regarding the differential diagnosis and possible co-morbidities. Treatment of withdrawal may be guided by serial assessments using the CIWA scale in addition to maintaining adequate fluid and electrolyte balance and addressing nutritional deficiencies (thiamine and B complex vitamins including folate). Supportive non-pharmacological care is an important and useful component in the management of all patients undergoing withdrawal. Interventions such as reassurance about symptom management, nursing in a well-lit, low-stimulus environment and frequent re-orientation can be helpful.

While it may or may not be the primary remit of all CL teams to prescribe withdrawal treatment plans depending on service specifications, it is certainly helpful to have an understanding/refresher as to what standard regimens look like and the rationale for selecting particular medications. Individual hospitals will usually have their own policies. In terms of pharmacological management of withdrawal, it is postulated that the provision of benzodiazepines can alleviate the acute deficiency of GABA neurotransmitter activity that occurs with sudden cessation of alcohol use. Longer-acting agents such as diazepam and chlordiazepoxide may be more effective at preventing seizures. Longer-acting agents also may contribute to smoother withdrawal course, with a reduction in breakthrough or rebound symptoms. In individuals with liver disease, shorter-acting agents are preferable such as oxazepam, temazepam and lorazepam (21). Sample regimens are included in Tables 8.4 and 8.5. Treatment of severe dependence may require a fixed-dose regimen of 30–50 mg chlordiazepoxide four times daily, gradually reduced over 7–10 days. Treatment may have to be individualised further (it is helpful to calculate the 24-hour requirement on day 1 and to give this in four divided doses on day 2, reducing from that point) and medication prescribed as required depending on how the clinical presentation evolves.

It is critically important when assessing patients receiving withdrawal treatment to be vigilant for signs of over-sedation and respiratory depression prior to receiving additional doses and to withhold additional doses if such signs or symptoms are present (21).

Alternatives to giving medication on a fixed schedule include front-loading and symptom-triggered therapy. The risk of benzodiazepine toxicity is high during the initial phase of front-loading regimens as patients are given very high doses of benzodiazepines at the outset, with gradual reduction over a period of a few days. Although there is evidence to suggest the treatment course is shorter and there could be marginal benefit in reducing the risk of severe withdrawal (22), these regimens are often impractical in busy general hospital environments outside of intensive care settings because of the intensity of monitoring required in the initial loading phase and the grave risks of benzodiazepine toxicity if left unchecked.

In symptom-triggered therapy, the patient is monitored through the use of a structured assessment scale and given medication only when symptoms cross a threshold of severity, typically when the CIWA-Ar score is above 8–10 (23). Although symptom-triggered therapy enables delivery of large amounts of medication quickly to patients with rapidly escalating withdrawal, thereby reducing the risk of undertreatment that may arise with the use of fixed doses, again it is often impractical in busy general hospital environments because of the frequency of required assessments.

Management of Delirium Tremens

DT is a serious yet treatable complication of alcohol withdrawal, characterised by dysautonomia and fluctuating disturbance of attention, level of consciousness and cognition. Psychotic symptoms are also common. Timely diagnosis is critical as there are well-established treatment regimens that provide rapid symptomatic relief. The principles of successful treatment involve adequate sedation with benzodiazepines, use of neuroleptics where appropriate and careful management of fluids and electrolytes. DT is often encountered in patients admitted for acute medical problems whose alcohol dependence was not recognised and/or whose withdrawal symptoms were not adequately treated. DT occurs in 5% of patients undergoing alcohol withdrawal with a 15–20% mortality rate in inappropriately managed patients; this reduces to 1–5% with timely and appropriate treatment.

Table 8.4 Sample Fixed-dose regime: chlordiazepoxide

Medication	01	02	03	04	05	06	07
Chlordiazepoxide	20 mg four times daily PLUS 20–30 mg as required	15 mg four times daily PLUS 20–30 mg as required	10 mg four times daily	10 mg three times daily	5 mg three times daily	5 mg twice daily	5 mg nocte
Thiamine	Pabrinex three times daily	Pabrinex three times daily	Pabrinex three times daily	300 mg once daily	300 mg once daily	300 mg once daily	300 mg once daily
B vitamins	Vitamin B compound strong – two tablets three times daily						

If using oxazepam, use equivalent dose; for example, 20 mg chlordiazepoxide = 30 mg oxazepam = 2 mg lorazepam. Tapering should not begin until the patient is stable and CIWA-Ar scores are consistently below 10.

Table 8.5 Sample Fixed-dose lorazepam (dosing in patients with liver damage)

Medication	01	02	03	04	05
Lorazepam	2 mg four times daily	2 mg four times daily	1.5 mg four times daily	1 mg four times daily	0.5 mg four times daily

In addition, prescribe 1–2 mg when required.

DT can be missed easily. Beware the patient with new-onset psychosis or delirium felt to be secondary to intercurrent illness. A CL assessment for behavioural disturbance opens up a window of opportunity to diagnose DT and to advise on pharmacological and non-pharmacological management.

DT usually emerges between day 2 and 3 (occasionally up to day 5). Core features include those listed for alcohol withdrawal (dysautonomia, agitation, anxiety, psychosis, seizures) in addition to the presence of delirium (fluctuating disturbance of perception and cognition).

Prevention of the onset of DT is a key priority. Most cases of DT can be prevented by prompt initiation of appropriate treatment. Risk factors for DT include:

(a) Previous history severe withdrawal/delirium

(b) Tachycardia >100 bpm

(c) CIWA-Ar > 15 with high breathalyser alcohol reading > 0.5

(d) Intercurrent infection such as chest infection/urinary tract infection or other significant medical co-morbidity

(e) Older age

(f) Concomitant misuse of other CNS depressants.

While medical and surgical teams are familiar with recognising and treating DT, and will often orchestrate the treatment process, it can prevent delay if the assessing Consult-Liaison psychiatrist who diagnoses DT is able to recommend treatment as time is of the essence here. Most guidelines suggest benzodiazepines as a first-line choice. Examples include oral lorazepam 1–4 mg (start with 1 mg), depending on the severity of symptoms, repeating every 10–30 minutes until the patient is calmer and signs of dysautonomia have started to subside *or* oral diazepam 10–20 mg hourly. Parenteral options include intravenous diazepam every 10 minutes (5 mg, 5 mg, 10 mg, 10 mg, 20 mg thereafter) until the patient is calmer. Neuroleptics such as haloperidol 1–5 mg or olanzapine 5–10 mg may be required as adjunct medications if psychotic symptoms are prominent and response to benzodiazepines has been partial. The usual precautions about use of intramuscular lorazepam and olanzapine apply. Once the patient settles, a tapered withdrawal regimen can be drawn up or the previous regimen optimised in light of development of DT. In rare cases where a patient appears to be refractory to benzodiazepines, liaison with intensivist colleagues is essential to look at alternatives such as propofol, phenobarbital and dexmedetomidine.

Management of Wernicke's Encephalopathy

Patients with chronic alcohol misuse are at risk of thiamine deficiency, which may lead to Wernicke's encephalopathy (WE) and subsequently Korsakoff syndrome (KS). If there is impaired intake, absorption and storage, thiamine stores deplete relatively quicky (the human body has about 18 days' worth in storage), leading to metabolic derangement and neuronal cell death. WE is an acute neurological emergency characterised by oculomotor dysfunction, gait disturbance and confusion (it should be noted, however, that this clinical triad is absent in 90% of patients). KS is a late neuropsychiatric complication of untreated WE, characterised by short-term memory impairment with frequent confabulation. Other late complications include seizures and spastic paraparesis. Chronic alcoholism is a principal risk factor for WE, but malnutrition, malignancy, immunodeficiency syndromes, liver disease and hyperthyroidism can also increase the likelihood of developing it.

WE is a clinical diagnosis. Aside from the history outlining risk factors, nystagmus is common in addition to gaze palsies and sluggish pupillary reflexes. Look also for a broad-based gait and truncal instability. Drowsiness and disorientation may be present. Routine blood tests and a magnetic resonance brain scan may not yield any further pointers towards WE (thalamic, mamillary body, cerebellar vermis and periaqueductal grey-matter changes are sometimes apparent).

Treatment should commence immediately to prevent or reduce the prospect of irreversible neuronal damage; moreover, WE carries a 15% mortality rate. A standard regimen involves two pairs of intravenous ampoules of high-potency B complex vitamins (e.g. Pabrinex) thrice daily for three days to evaluate response. Other B vitamins, magnesium and folate should also be given as per local policy. Oculomotor dysfunction usually responds first, followed by ataxia and finally cognitive impairment, though improvement in the latter will be poor in up to 50% of patients. If there is a response within the first three days, then intravenous B vitamin therapy should be continued until there is a plateau in the clinical presentation. A dietetics referral is often helpful in these cases.

The Role of CL Psychiatry in Patients with Chronic Alcohol Misuse

So far, we have discussed management of acute alcohol-related emergencies, but what of the patient struggling with chronic harmful or dependent drinking and co-morbid mental health problems who requires ongoing support in hospital or community-based support? Joint working between alcohol liaison nursing and the CL team is often helpful for these patients. Shared insight into the intersection between alcohol misuse and mental health problems can pave the way for meaningful intervention that aims to reduce the impact and complications of both. Shared priorities include:

• Screening for harmful and dependent drinking
• Opportunistic mental and physical health screening
• Offering counselling and brief interventions
• Signposting to community-based alcohol services.

Screening tools for alcohol use have been covered elsewhere in this chapter. Joint working with the admitting medical/surgical team enables routine physical screening for nutritional status, altered bowel habit and continence, presence of liver disease, pancreatitis, gastritis, bone health, neuropathy and myopathy. Assessment of mental health, social care needs and cognitive status along with results from physical health screening enables early involvement of allied healthcare professionals such as dietetics, occupational therapy and social work.

Alcohol risk reduction work may be undertaken by a broad range of professionals across different health and social care settings and there are online resources such as those provided by NHS Scotland (24, 25). Key principles include giving information and advice (risks and benefits), enhancing motivation and perceived sense of self-efficacy, building confidence and coping strategies and offering a scaffold of options for moving forwards (ideas for cutting down, keeping a schedule, setting realistic goals and pleasant distractions, etc.). The FRAMES counselling approach is a useful concept in this type of work (feedback, responsibility, advice, menu of options, empathy, self-efficacy) (27). Motivational interviewing is a useful therapeutic technique for patients contemplating behavioural change. Patients are encouraged to explore the discrepancy between their current behaviour and personal goals as a vehicle for motivating change. Goals are patient led and the practitioner is encouraged to 'roll with resistance' rather than imposing a paternalistic view on the correct way forward. Evidence is mixed but there does appear to be some benefit in terms of reducing alcohol consumption and repeat presentations to the emergency department (28).

Close working relationships with alcohol liaison specialist nurses are essential for any of the clinical scenarios outlined in this chapter. Services are sometimes integrated within the CL service but may also be stand-alone teams employed by the same healthcare provider. Alcohol liaison services carry out screening, health promotion and staff education, advise during alcohol withdrawals and associated complications in conjunction with developing clinical pathways and guidelines, offer interventions such as those outlined earlier and organise onward referral to appropriate services. Evidence suggests these services reduce the length of hospital stays and readmission rates but provision is patchy across the UK.

A Final Word: Alcohol-Related Brain Damage

Alcohol-related brain damage (ARBD) is a descriptive term which embodies the spectrum of neurological and psychiatric complications associated with chronic alcohol misuse. Although the severe end of the spectrum (Wernicke-Korsakoff syndrome) is well represented in training programmes and texts such as this, the milder but more prevalent end of the spectrum can go unnoticed. This generally presents as frontal-lobe dysfunction and tends to surface between the third and fifth decade of life. It is important to screen for ARBD in patients who have a history of chronic alcohol misuse; with appropriate support and care, up to three quarters of cases will achieve some degree of remission over a three-year period. There are few dedicated services in the UK, highlighting the importance of CL psychiatry teams and alcohol liaison services engaging in interface work, whether in the emergency department or on hospital wards. Goals include detection of alcohol withdrawal and ARBD, reducing the risk of withdrawal toxicity by offering guidance on administration of benzodiazepines and thiamine, and determining whether readiness for change is apparent and, if so, delivering brief interventions and signposting to community services for ongoing support. Readers are directed to the Royal College of Psychiatrists report (CR185) for further insights into ARBD.

References

1. World Health Organization. Global status report on alcohol and health. Geneva; 2018. www.who.int/publications/i/item/9789241565639.

2. Office for National Statistics. Adult drinking habits in Great Britain: 2017. www.ons.gov.uk/peoplepopulationandcommunity/healthandsocialcare/drugusealco holandsmoking/datasets/adultdrinking habits.

3. Public Health England. Alcohol dependence prevalence in England. 2021. www.gov.uk/government/publications/alcohol-dependence-prevalence-in-england.

4. Public Health England. The public health burden of alcohol: Evidence review. 2018.

www.gov.uk/government/publications/the-public-health-burden-of-alcohol-evidence-review.

5. Scottish Government Cabinet Secretary for Health and Social Care. Scottish Health Survey 2018 – revised 2020: volume one – main report. Chapter 3 – Alcohol. 2020. www.gov.scot/publications/scottish-health-survey-2018-volume-1-main-report/pages/30.

6. Public Health England. Adult substance misuse treatment statistics 2018 to 2019: Report. 2023. www.gov.uk/government/collections/alcohol-and-drug-misuse-and-treatment-statistics.

7. NHS Digital. Health Survey for England, 2018: Adults' health related behaviours report. 2019. https://files.digital.nhs.uk/B5/771AC5/HSE18-Adult-Health-Related-Behaviours-rep-v3.pdf.

8. Office for National Statistics. Alcohol specific deaths in the UK registered 2020. 2021. www.ons.gov.uk/peoplepopulationandcommunity/healthandsocialcare/causesofdeath/bulletins/alcoholrelateddeathsintheunitedkingdom/registeredin2020.

9. Thomasson R. The apparently drunk patient. In Mackway-Jones K (ed.), *Acute Psychiatric Emergencies*. New York; 2020, pp. 37–50.

10. Mirijello A, D'Angelo C, Ferrulli A et al. Identification and management of alcohol withdrawal syndrome. *Drugs*. 2006;**75**(4):353–65.

11. Saunders JB. The alcohol use disorders identification test. https://auditscreen.org.

12. Stockwell T, Murphy D, Hodgson R. The severity of alcohol dependence questionnaire: Its use, reliability and validity. *Br J Addict*. 1983;**78**(2):145–55. www.mdapp.co/severity-of-alcohol-dependence-questionnaire-sadq-calculator–518.

13. *International Statistical Classification of Diseases and Related Health Problems*, 11th ed.; ICD-11; World Health Organization. Geneva; 2019.

14. Strategies for managing alcohol withdrawal. In Fishman MJ, Shulman GR, Mee-Lee D (eds.), *ASAM Patient Placement Criteria: Supplement on Pharmacotherapies for Alcohol Use Disorders*. Philadelphia, PA; 2010, p. 32.

15. National Institute for Health and Care Excellence. Head injury: Assessment and early management. 2019. www.nice.org.uk/guidance/cg176.

16. Psychiatric emergencies. In Ramrakha P, Moore K, Sam S (eds.), *Oxford Handbook of Acute Medicine*, 4th ed. Oxford; 2019, pp. 711–38.

17. American Psychiatric Association. *Diagnostic and Statistical Manual of Mental Disorders*, 5th ed. Arlington, VA; 2013.

18. Sullivan JT, Sykora K, Schneiderman J et al. Assessment of alcohol withdrawal: The revised clinical institute withdrawal assessment for alcohol scale (CIWA-Ar). *Br J Addict*. 1989;**84**(11):1353–7.

19. Maldonado JR, Sher Y, Das S et al. Prospective Validation Study of the Prediction of Alcohol Withdrawal Severity Scale (PAWSS) in medically ill inpatients: A new scale for the prediction of complicated alcohol withdrawal syndrome. *Alcohol*. 2015;**50**(5):509–18.

20. Mayo-Smith MF, Beecher LH, Fischer TL et al. Management of alcohol withdrawal delirium: An evidence-based practice guideline. *Arch Intern Med*. 2004;**164**(13):1405–12.

21. Bird RD, Makela EH. Alcohol withdrawal: What is the benzodiazepine of choice? *Ann Pharmacother*. 1994;**28**(1):67–71.

22. Muzyk AJ, Leung JG, Nelson S et al. The role of diazepam loading for the treatment of alcohol withdrawal syndrome in hospitalized patients. *Am J Addict*. 2013;**22**:113–18.

23. Jaeger TM, Lohr RH, Pankratz VS. Symptom-triggered therapy for alcohol withdrawal syndrome in medical inpatients. *Mayo Clin Proc*. 2001;**76**(7):695–701. doi: 10.4065/76.7.695.

24. Public Health Scotland. Alcohol brief interventions (ABI) training manual part 1.

2011. www.healthscotland.com/uploads/documents/16720-ABI_TrainingManual Part1.pdf.

25. Public Health Scotland. Alcohol brief interventions (ABI) training manual part 2. 2011. www.healthscotland.com/uploads/documents/16720-ABI_TrainingManual Part2.pdf.

26. Public Health England. Adult substance misuse treatment statistics 2018 to 2019: Report. 2023. www.gov.uk/government/co llections/alcohol-and-drug-misuse-and-treatment-statistics.

27. Miller WR, Sanchez VC. Motivating young adults for treatment and lifestyle change. In Howard G (ed.), *Issues in Alcohol Use and Misuse by Young Adults*. Notre Dame, IN; 1993, pp. 55–82.

28. Davey CJ, Landy MS, Pecora A. et al. A realist review of brief interventions for alcohol misuse delivered in emergency departments. *Syst Rev*. 2015;4:45.

Substance Misuse

Matthew Kelleher

Summary

This chapter focusses on substances other than alcohol (see Chapter 8). The purpose is to introduce the reader to the wide variety of substances that are abused by explaining why people may use them, why the use can be harmful and broadly how this is managed. Liaison psychiatry is the bridge between inpatient care and community care and this complex relationship is demonstrated herein when discussing the management of these cases that require the input of a variety of clinicians. The substances detailed are further subdivided to cover background information, acute intoxication, toxicity, withdrawal states and other management advice. 'Top tips' are included where appropriate, which are practical considerations to make based on day-to-day experience working in the field.

General Assessment for Addiction Patients

A thorough addictions assessment should cover all of the diagnostic criteria for dependence syndromes and harmful use to ascertain which diagnosis is most suitable as this will impact the risk assessment, outcome and management options.

Substance Misuse History

It is important to make sure that the patient is aware that disclosure of using substances will not result in reports to the police and they are encouraged to be as honest as possible. It is helpful to remind patients that we are limited in what we can achieve if we do not have the full picture.

It is also very important to systematically ask about all possible drugs of abuse. Some patients seem not to consider cannabis as a 'proper drug' and often forget to mention it. Likewise, overusing a prescription drug or something available legally over the counter may also be overlooked.

For example: 'Do you ever use any street drugs? That includes cannabis, by the way, and what about using over-the-counter medications?' Once there is evidence that this person uses substances, it feels more natural to ask about specific drugs, as in the list below.

The most common drugs of abuse or with potential for dependence are, in no particular order:

- Tobacco
- Alcohol
- Cannabis
- Cocaine

- Opiate or related drugs including heroin, morphine and synthetic opioids
- Stimulant drugs including ecstasy, amphetamines and methylphenidate
- Gamma-hydroxybutyrate/gamma-butyrolactone
- Benzodiazepines
- Anabolic steroids
- Gabapentinoid drugs including gabapentin and pregabalin
- Novel psychoactive substances (NPS).

You will note the wide variation in the colloquial terms used in common parlance by patients. It is important to understand what they mean, displaying you are skilled in this area, but using them yourself as a clinician is best avoided as it could come across as unprofessional.

It is also worthwhile checking that your understanding of the colloquialisms as they may differ by region to some extent.

PATIENT: 'I had two bags of white and one of brown.'

DOCTOR: 'Okay, so just to check, you had two bags of cocaine and one bag of heroin?'

For each substance reported it is important to know the following details:

- Which substance?
- Route of administration (ingestion, inhalation, insufflation, injection)?
- Frequency of use?
- Quantity used?
- Do they have a history of overdose with that substance?
- How long have they used the substance for?
- Do they use this substance with another at the same time?
- When was the last time they used that substance?
- Have they ever achieved a period of abstinence with that substance? How did they achieve this? Did they suffer withdrawal symptoms?
- Would they like to stop using this substance?

Wherever possible, a drug urine screen should be part of a routine assessment. This works both ways in regard to mutual trust and the rationale should be explained clearly. The test is not merely to see if the patient is being truthful, although this is part of the boundary setting within the therapeutic relationship. A urine drug screen allows a safe means to understand what has recently been used in order to facilitate *safe prescribing* and may highlight batches of drugs that have been adulterated with other substances.

Urine drug screens show which drugs have been used recently. Each brand and specific test may test for different substances and the reading window will vary. Typically, a standard test used in a substance misuse service will test for the following as a minimum:

- Opiates (heroin and morphine)
- Methadone
- Cocaine
- Methamphetamines
- Benzodiazepines
- Cannabis.

If you are unfamiliar with a particular urine drugs screen, it would be sensible to either ask someone who is familiar to do it for you or to familiarise yourself with the product leaflet. You would not want to misinterpret the result, which is easy to do as they often just have a series of lines, and mistakes can happen.

The test for recent alcohol use is an alcohol breath analyser, similar to that used by the police for a roadside check. Again, familiarise yourself with its function, in particular how to attach the disposable breathing tubes.

Top Tip

There is potential for a challenging conversation when the urine drug screen is not as expected following a detailed history. The test may indicate that other substances are present which were either not disclosed or that the patient was not aware of.

DOCTOR: 'The urine drug screen has indicated that you have other drugs in your system that I was not expecting. Do you know why that may be?'

PATIENT: 'I don't know, doctor. Are you saying I'm a liar?'

DOCTOR: 'No, I wouldn't suggest that, but it's important we know why this has happened so we can treat you safely. Is it possible you took something else when you were "high"? Has your supplier changed? Did it feel different when you used recently; could it have been cut with something else?'

The following are possible examples of when a mental health professional may come across patients that misuse substances in a liaison setting.

In the emergency department:

- Acute intoxication of any illicit substance or alcohol
- Drug-induced psychosis, hallucinatory effects related to drugs
- Acute withdrawals of any illicit substance or alcohol
- Patients presenting for the first time seeking support with a substance or alcohol use.

In a liaison capacity you may see the following variations of the above:

- Acute withdrawals of substances that take longer to present or as a result of being admitted and therefore abstinent
- Known patients with a strong history of substance or alcohol misuse
- Patients displaying drug-seeking behaviour while admitted
- Patient admitted to the intensive care unit or recently stepped down in which substance misuse or dependence was related to the medical problems.

Regardless of the reason to see the patient, it is important to remember that *this may be the only time you interact with this patient.* A thorough history with a good approach may encourage this patient to seek further support when discharged. It is common for patients seeking help from drug and alcohol services in the community to disengage quickly, which may in part be related to the interactions with the clinicians as well as a symptom of dependence itself.

As the liaison psychiatrist, you may need to advise, support and train colleagues in the specialism of substance misuse. Often this patient group may present challenges which require specialist advice in order for the other team's plan to work effectively.

Heroin (Diamorphine)

Background Information

Brown, Smack, China-White

The origin of heroin use can be traced to the nineteenth century when opium was used to treat a variety of ailments and often without a prescription. The US Civil War resulted in a large increase in the use of morphine as a battlefield analgesic and many of those treated with it became dependent on it, referred to colloquially as 'The Soldier's Disease'. Since then, the sale and use of heroin have increased dramatically. Heroin is produced from opium from poppy plants.

Mechanism of Action

Heroin is a mu-opioid receptor agonist but has a lower affinity for the receptor in this form. Heroin undergoes metabolism that eventually converts it to morphine which has a higher affinity for the receptor. Morphine (and other opioids) also has agonistic activity on four other endogenous neurotransmitters: beta-endorphin, dynorphin, leu-enkephalin and met-enkephalin. Heroin is usually 'cut' with other substances, including baking soda and powdered milk, through to more toxic substances such as detergents and rat poison. As such, there can be significant unpredictability between batches. Heroin can be used in several ways depending on the knowledge of the user, preference and available equipment. The routes of administration are different around the world and have changed over time. Currently smoking and insufflation ('snorting') are the most common, but many users still inject.

Acute Intoxication

Sense of happiness and possibly euphoria described as a 'rush'

Sense of relaxation

Cutaneous flushing

Decreased respiratory rate

Itching

Nausea and vomiting

Slurred speech

Toxicity

Vomiting

Reduced muscle tone – limp limbs

Pinpoint and unreactive pupils

Loss of consciousness

Shallow or cessation of breathing

Bradycardia, peri-arrest pattern or cardiac arrest

Emergency Management of Toxicity

In a hospital setting, prescribed opiates may have caused an overdose or toxicity. Overdose from heroin use may occur accidentally when their tolerance has decreased, including recommencing use after a period of abstinence. Accidental overdose can also occur if they have used a new supplier with different potency. It is also important to consider whether the overdose was intentional.

Immediate action is required. The management of opioid toxicity is naloxone hydrochloride. The intravenous (IV) route is preferred for speed of onset, but subcutaneous, intramuscular and intranasal (spray) preparations are also available.

The speed of onset is approximately 1 minute via IV administration and slightly longer (and variable) in other routes.

IV dosing:

1st dose: 400 micrograms, then wait 1 minute

2nd dose: 800 micrograms, then wait 1 minute

3rd dose: 800 micrograms, then wait 1 minute

4th dose: 2 milligrams, then wait 1 minute.

If a total of 4 milligrams has been administered and the patient has either not responded or has briefly improved and then deteriorated, the diagnosis must be reviewed and consideration given to continuous IV infusion.

During the 1-minute period between dosing, the clinician or responder should assess the patient for response including change in level of consciousness, increased breathing rate, increased pulse and pupillary changes.

In a hospital environment, as this is an emergency situation with possibly life-threatening consequences, you must always request help from colleagues and consider if the environment is suitable; that is, does the patient require a department with more monitoring such as the High-Dependency Unit or Intensive Care Unit (ICU).

Some patients may be agitated or assaultive upon response to naloxone, depending on the context of the overdose, so remember your own personal safety as is taught in any emergency scenario – you cannot help if you become incapacitated yourself.

In a community setting, patients or bystanders will have less access to medication to assist. Heroin or opiate users known to addiction services or primary care should be given intramuscular naloxone to carry on their person, especially when they intend to use heroin on their own.

Community Dosing

Dose 1: 400 micrograms IM immediately. Call for help and request an ambulance. Wait 2–3 minutes.

Dose 2: 400 micrograms, wait 2–3 minutes.

Further doses: continue to administer naloxone IM until no doses are left or professional help arrives. Perform CPR if safe and competent to do so.

Complications of heroin or opiate misuse:

- Dependence syndrome
- Acute opiate toxicity
- Viral infections (hepatitis, HIV) indirectly through exposure by shared needles

- Chronic obstructive pulmonary disease when smoking
- Increased exposure to criminality and violence.

Withdrawal State

Withdrawal states occur when a dependent patient is not/has not been intoxicated with heroin or other opiates for several hours and can be very unpleasant. Withdrawal may occur because a user is attempting to stop using or their supply has been disrupted, for example, lack of money, incarceration or admission to hospital.

Signs and symptoms of withdrawal may appear within 6 hours after the patient last used but this depends on the level of physical dependency.

Signs and symptoms are as follows.

Typically seen within the first 12 hours:

- Psychological craving and drug-seeking thoughts
- Anxiety
- Yawning
- Diaphoresis
- Lacrimation
- Rhinorrhoea and or sneezing
- Restlessness
- Irritability.

Typically seen after the first 12 hours and could last a few days:

- Exacerbation of the symptoms above
- Mydriasis
- Goose-flesh skin (cutis anserina)
- Tachycardia
- Muscle ache
- Abdominal cramping
- Tachypnoea
- Increased blood pressure
- Diarrhoea
- Anorexia
- Nausea and vomiting.

In a hospital setting the Clinical Opiate Withdrawal Scale (COWS) should be used to allow objective and repeatable assessment of a potentially dependent and withdrawing patient. Local policy may use the COWS score to suggest treatment options but, if in doubt, this should be discussed with someone familiar with managing opiate withdrawals. Overzealous management of opiate withdrawal could lead to acute intoxication or toxicity, so caution is advised.

How Is Opiate Dependence Managed?

Generally, heroin is the main reason for the use of opiate substitution therapy (OST) but it can be used at the clinician's discretion for other opioid-drugs (prescribed or illicit) and synthetic opioids.

OST is almost always a choice between methadone or buprenorphine, but a *very small* number of patients nationally may be prescribed 'injectables'; that is, prescribed heroin (diamorphine). The latter should only be initiated by a consultant experienced in treating drug dependence and who is also authorised to do so by the Home Office under the 'The Misuse of Drugs (Supply to Addicts) Regulations 1997'.

Methadone

Methadone is routinely prescribed as a liquid in strengths of 1 mg/1 ml but is also sometimes prescribed as 10 mg/1 ml – but the risk of accidental overdose is higher. Methadone is started only once opioid dependency is confirmed including a positive urine drug screen. Methadone is titrated slowly over the period of a week or few weeks until the patient is neither withdrawing nor intoxicated; in effect, a like-for-like equivalent. Before a prescription is started that day, the patient must not be intoxicated with any substance including alcohol. They will usually be reviewed daily or a minimum of three times a week during the titration.

Patients treated with methadone compared to those not current on treatment for OST were four times less likely to die of opiate-related causes (1). This is a very important statistic to remember. Methadone is readily available and cost-effective; OST should be offered to suitable patients with opiate dependency.

It is also worth noting that methadone, being a substitute for heroin, can always be addictive in itself. Patients may ask what the benefit is of switching from one addictive medication to another. Methadone is significantly safer than heroin, and when stability is reached and the patient is ready, it can be gradually reduced. Patients engaged with health providers on methadone prescriptions have less need to associate with drug dealers and other users, which hopefully makes it easier for them to kick old habits.

Buprenorphine

Buprenorphine is usually prescribed in tablet form, but sublingual preparations and depot intramuscular forms are now available. Buprenorphine's mechanism of action is complicated but is thought to involve mixed partial-agonist and antagonist activity at different receptors. Buprenorphine is a partial agonist at the mu-opioid receptor which causes a partial response such as analgesia. Buprenorphine is also an antagonist at the kappa-opioid receptors (2) which prevents morphine from binding to it, hence its use in maintenance therapy.

Top Tip

It is essential that patients do not take buprenorphine it until they are withdrawing. If the patient is not withdrawing from opioids prior to taking buprenorphine, they will be pushed into precipitated withdrawal and buprenorphine will compete with and remove any attached opioids. Precipitated withdrawals are an intense and accelerated withdrawal with severe symptoms which are very unpleasant, although not dangerous. Patients experiencing this may be dissuaded from using this medication. A common cause of precipitated withdrawal is patients taking it prematurely when withdrawal symptoms start; patients should be supported and educated about this risk and encouraged to wait until the correct time.

Ideally a patient would abstain from opiate-based drugs from midnight the day before to reduce the changes of precipitated withdrawals. Patients who have abstained from opiates but who are still not withdrawing fully when they are assessed could either be seen again later that day as symptoms progress, or they can be given one tablet to take home, to use at their discretion. Buprenorphine protects patients against opiate intoxication and is overdose-safe by a process called the 'ceiling effect' (3).

Naltrexone

Naltrexone may be prescribed to assist abstinence for certain groups of patients. This may be for those who have undergone withdrawals and do not wish to have OST but also acknowledge they are likely to relapse without some pharmacological intervention. Broadly, this is an opiate antagonist medication but is usually initiated by a specialist and is out of scope for this liaison textbook.

Harm Minimisation

Patients with known opioid dependence and in particular those prescribed OST should also be prescribed and trained in the use of naloxone as a harm minimisation strategy.

Treatment in a Liaison Setting

Initiating OST in the inpatient setting is rarely appropriate. Patients acutely withdrawing from opiates in hospital should be managed symptomatically and if further treatment is needed upon discharge, they should be referred to a local drug and alcohol service.

Patients already receiving OST may wish to continue their prescription while admitted to avoid withdrawals or relapse. There are risks associated with OST with patients you do not routinely treat. Patients can be poor historians, and this may be worse in this population, often having a chaotic lifestyle. With this in mind, a patient's account of their recent OST prescription and compliance with it cannot be taken at face value. It is critical *to check that the patient's prescription* has been *issued and collected* before continuing the prescription. This reduces the likelihood of an iatrogenic overdose. Involving the hospital pharmacist at this stage is helpful.

Some patients are on 'daily pickup' or 'daily supervised consumption'. This means that the patient must attend the dispensing pharmacy daily to collect their OST and ingest it under supervision. Contacting the dispensing pharmacy prior to continuing a prescription will allow you to check that the patient has recently been compliant and therefore it is safe to continue the prescription.

Patients who are more stable may collect their prescription less frequently – that is, twice weekly or once weekly – and take OST home with them for administration without supervision. Urinalysis can be used to confirm the presence of recently used substances including for the metabolites of heroin, methadone and buprenorphine. Rapid drug urinalysis may not be available in all hospital settings and staff may be unfamiliar with their interpretations and limitations.

If the prescriber and hospital pharmacist is satisfied that the OST in the community has been complied with and it is safe to continue while an inpatient, your role will be to communicate this to the ward and ensure it is prescribed correctly. In due course the patient's discharge summary should clearly state that OST was continued including the dosage and frequency to avoid disruption of their supply upon discharge.

> **Top Tip**
>
> Patients with an opioid-abusing history who are currently in pain may present some challenges. These patients may require higher than usual doses of opiate-based analgesics to manage their pain due to their increased tolerance.
>
> Patients currently prescribed buprenorphine will not respond to opiate-based analgesics because of the blockade effect. A decision will need to be made about alternative medications or if buprenorphine is discontinued. This should be the decision of the treating team, but you may have input in addressing the patient's concerns about this. Some patients who have managed abstinence will be fearful of returning to illicit use once exposed to opiates again.
>
> It is unfortunate but possible that some staff may assume the patient is simply 'drug-seeking', which is unhelpful and stigmatising. If these ideas are being expressed by staff, it may be part of your role to carefully manage this in a supportive and non-judgemental way.
>
> The key message for inpatient OST: *it is easy to overdose a patient with OST, which could be fatal, so a cautious approach is prudent.*

Onward Referral

Even if patients have not engaged well during their inpatient stay, it is important to offer advice on accessing community drug and alcohol services. Most services do not need a formal referral letter and patients can turn up and ask for help.

Some users who are not ready or currently able to make changes to their drug use may choose not to engage with community teams. Although this can be quite disheartening for a concerned clinician, a careful and compassionate approach, even if just offering 'signposting', may go some way to show people that there are teams ready to help them when the time is right.

Benzodiazepines

Background Information

Benzos, Valium, Xanax, Downers

The positive effects of benzodiazepines are relaxation and reduced anxiety. Therefore, those suffering from an anxiety disorder may attain almost instant relief from their distress and patients may become dependent on benzodiazepines from either prescribed or illicit means.

Benzodiazepines are prescribed for muscular spasms, anxiety and insomnia, although this should be on a short-term basis. If the patient has remained on a prescription for too long, they can build a tolerance and physiological dependence.

With that in mind, not having access to benzodiazepines may be very difficult, leading to people who may not ordinarily source substances illicitly to do so. Illicit benzodiazepines are available on the street and internet, neither of which offer any safeguards to the quality of the medication. This is all relevant, as it explains why there is no 'typical' benzodiazepine-abusing or -dependent patient.

Mechanism of Action

Benzodiazepines exert their effect through their action as positive allosteric modulators on the gamma aminobutyric acid (GABA)-A receptor (4). GABA is an inhibitory neurotransmitter which is why it is broadly described as a central nervous system (CNS) 'depressant' and responsible for the sedative and anxiolytic properties that are desired.

> **Top Tip**
>
> Patients may take varying amounts of benzodiazepines, so it is helpful to ask them to provide a diary of their use. This should include the name benzodiazepine, strength, time of ingestion and ideally why they felt they needed it (feeling anxious? Withdrawal symptoms? etc.).
>
> Patients may also take a variety of different benzodiazepines depending on how they source it; that is, they use what they can get hold of. Since benzodiazepine strengths vary significantly, it is often necessary to convert their use into an equivalent of diazepam. The equivalent dose of diazepam will help clinicians to consider a gradual reduction in the community or for a 'detox'.

Acute Intoxication

- Reduced anxiety/calming effect
- Sedation
- Drowsiness

Toxicity (5)

- Slurred speech
- Ataxia
- Altered mental state (variable and could be minor)
- Usually unremarkable vital signs
- Respiratory compromise (unlikely unless very significant overdose or unless taken with other CNS depressants)
- Very severe toxicity could present as a comatose patient.

A specific toxicity is associated with IM or IV preparations of lorazepam and diazepam because of the propylene glycol used in these forms of the medication (6). The toxicity is related to the preparation rather than the action of the benzodiazepines. This particular toxicity is most likely to occur with infusions of benzodiazepines since most illicit and prescribed forms are usually in oral form.

Management of Toxicity

As with any emergency situation, standard life support assessment and measures should be followed. It may be a primary measure to offer airway support before considering an antidote.

Flumazenil is licensed to treat benzodiazepine toxicity. Clinicians should decide if it is necessary to treat if symptoms are mild as the benefit must outweigh the possible risks. (Flumazenil may precipitate seizures in benzodiazepine-dependent patients as they could in effect be put into a severe, acute withdrawal state.)

Dosage

First dose: 200 micrograms IV given over 15 seconds.

Additional doses: 100 micrograms every minute.

The usual dose is 300–600 micrograms in total. Maximum of 1 milligram licensed per course in the UK.

Dependence Syndrome and Withdrawal State

In an inpatient liaison setting, the medical team is best placed to manage a benzodiazepine withdrawal. The consequences of withdrawal could include seizures and death. If the medical team is not particularly experienced with dealing with these patients, your role may be to advise them to seek the opinion of the on-call neurologist or intensive care team if there are more severe symptoms such as seizures.

A detailed history of the duration of benzodiazepine use, dosage, source of medication and a history of previous withdrawals/seizures and current alcohol use are crucial. It is likely that a patient who has abused low-dose benzodiazepines for a few months may be more medically straightforward than someone who has abused high doses for years.

If the patient is only expected to be in hospital for a short duration, then the team's role may only be to prescribe benzodiazepines to avoid a withdrawal state and referral to a community drug and alcohol team upon discharge. If either the patient is expected to remain in hospital for some time and/or they wish to reduce or stop their benzodiazepine use, you may be required to support a benzodiazepine detox.

It is important to note that in the community, patients who have used benzodiazepines long-term may need a detox lasting several months in order to detox slowly enough to avoid withdrawal symptoms or rebound insomnia and anxiety. In an inpatient setting this could be completed more quickly if the team is skilled and equipped to manage this. There is currently no evidence base to support maintenance prescribing for benzodiazepine-dependent patients.

Harm Minimisation

- Inform patient of potential harms of benzodiazepine abuse and dependency.
- Discourage illicit supply where possible.
- Discourage mixing benzodiazepines with other sedatives or alcohol.
- Avoid abrupt cessation of benzodiazepines if dependent.

GBL/GHB

Background Information

'G', Liquid Ecstasy and Others

GHB (gamma hydroxybutyrate) and GBL (gamma butyrolactone) are often used interchangeably. GBL is the pro-drug or precursor which is converted into the active form GHB upon ingestion. Herein they shall both be referred to as GBL for ease.

GBL is currently legal to purchase and possess for legitimate purposes. The intended use of these chemicals includes industrial cleaning and to remove nail varnish, paint and enamel. Most examples seen by the author have come with serious warning labels about the potentially fatal consequences if swallowed.

GBL is usually swallowed and is said to have a 'chemical taste'. It can be ingested in its pure form but is often mixed with soft drinks, particularly in a social setting. GBL may also be used in 'booty bumping' where the liquid is put into the rectum and is absorbed by the mucous membranes. It is possible to snort and inject GBL, though these are infrequent and the latter incredibly dangerous.

Mechanism of Action

The pharmacology of GHB is complicated. GHB acts on both CNS GHB receptors and also GABA-B. Stimulation of the GHB receptor leads to dopamine release, whereas GABA-B stimulation leads to inhibitory actions of GABA, as described elsewhere.

Acute Intoxication

Broadly, GBL can be described as a 'depressant'. Much like alcohol, in small doses GBL can produce:

- Euphoria
- Increased confidence
- Decreased inhibitions
- Increased libido.

However, in slightly higher amounts, possibly only 1–2 ml more, the dose could be sedating and/or lethal.

This explains why ingesting alcohol and GBL at the same time could be very dangerous as the sedative effects of each could potentiate each other. *As a liaison psychiatrist, just offering the advice to avoid using these substances together could save someone's life.*

How Much GBL Do People Use?

Doses of GBL on average are in the range of 0.5–2 ml. This average refers to a non-dependent user, using it in one sitting recreationally. Patients who have developed a dependence syndrome to GBL may use this amount every 1–2 hours as withdrawal symptoms may develop in between. Imagine the inconvenience and risk associated with needing to use GBL that frequently.

GBL users will often know how much they use because it is measured out in a syringe. Although this method is safer than guessing or drinking it from the bottle, it is prone to error, especially if the patient is already intoxicated.

Patients may present to hospital in acute GBL withdrawal, which is serious and potentially fatal and therefore a *medical emergency*. If, for some reason, this patient is referred to liaison psychiatry first, your role will be to liaise with the medical team for assistance and admission.

Toxicity (7)

- Reduced consciousness
- Irritability
- Respiratory depression

- Cardiac abnormalities
- Death.

Withdrawal State

It may be helpful to view a GBL withdrawal as similar to a very significant acute alcohol withdrawal. The symptoms are as follows:

- Anxiety/irritability
- Insomnia
- Tremor
- Tachycardia
- Hypertension
- Confusion
- Hallucinations: auditory and visual
- Diaphoresis.

Less common and indicative of severe withdrawal state:

- Seizure
- Rhabdomyolysis
- Death.

GBL withdrawal presentations vary widely in the rate of symptom progression and symptom severity. Patients with significant withdrawal symptoms may need an ICU admission. The onset of withdrawal can occur in as little as 30 minutes from the last dose but more typically it is within a few hours.

GBL withdrawal symptoms can last from 3 to 21 days and this must be factored into any discharge planning from an acute hospital (8). Discharging a patient with 'mild' withdrawal symptoms after a few days may mean they continue to deteriorate at home, away from medical expertise.

Managing GBL withdrawal as a medical emergency is not the ideal way to manage these patients; it is far better to work with patients and plan a reduction or detox. There is debate about how best to manage a planned medically assisted withdrawal from GBL – that is, a planned hospital admission or a planned community intervention – and this will depend on a variety of factors.

Onward Referral

The liaison psychiatrist will likely facilitate a patient's referral to a community drug and alcohol team, although the patient needs to be motivated to change and they should ideally refer themselves. Given the potential severity and risks associated with GBL use, it is prudent to write directly to the primary care physician and drug and alcohol team to make them aware of this patient.

Harm Minimisation

- Never mix GBL with other substances, especially alcohol or benzodiazepines, because of the compound sedative and CNS depressant effect.
- Use your own supply of GBL that you are familiar with rather than using someone else's that may be of a different potency.

- Measure the amount of GBL you are using, ideally with a pipette, or less desirably a syringe. You should avoid drinking GBL directly from the bottle, or from a pre-mixed drink from someone else.
- Avoid injecting GBL as this is more likely to lead to overdose.
- Keep track of your GBL use by making an entry on your phone or writing it down so you can check how much you have used in that session.
- Avoid using alone, just in case you overdose.
- If you or someone else has used too much GBL, you should seek emergency medical attention, which may mean calling 999.
- Keep GBL out of the reach of children and adults. Someone may drink it by accident. Label it or add food colouring to make it obvious that it is not water or vodka.
- If you are using GBL in the 'chem sex' environment, remember to party with people you can trust and practise safe sex. If you think you may have engaged in risky sexual practices, see your primary care physician or genitourinary medicine (GUM) clinic for help.

Cocaine

Background Information

Coke, Charlie, White

Cocaine is made from the coca plant leaves, but some use it in its unrefined form by simply chewing on the leaves themselves. Cocaine was previously thought of as a 'rich person's drug' in the Western world, but this no longer seems to be the case. That being said, the price often correlates with the purity or quality of the drug. In London, 1 gram of 'good-quality' cocaine could cost £100, but cheaper, lower-quality alternatives can be found for £50–60.

Mechanism of Action

Cocaine is a CNS stimulant which mainly exerts its action on dopamine systems. By blocking the dopamine transportation, dopamine accumulates in the synaptic cleft and stimulates post-synaptic dopamine receptors. Dopamine is involved in the 'reward pathway' which is common to many addictive and rewarding processes (9), so it is understandable why accumulations of dopamine contribute to cocaine being highly addictive and pleasant to use.

How Is Cocaine Used?

- Usually insufflation (snorted)
- Smoked (crack cocaine)
- Ingested
- Injected (infrequent and particularly dangerous).

The route may be determined by personal preference, familiarity, tolerance and availability of equipment. Cocaine users may describe the amount of use in either 'bags', 'lines' or how much it cost. Clearly there is potential for error here, so try to get as much detail as you can.

Cocaine can be used on its own, but it is often used together with alcohol and for some patients with heroin (speed balling). Speed balling is very dangerous because of the competing physiological effects they both have. Heroin as a CNS depressant can reduce the respiratory rate, whereas cocaine as a stimulant can increase oxygen demand. Simultaneously needing more oxygen while reducing oxygen intake can place strain on many end organs, especially the heart and brain.

Mixing cocaine and alcohol is potentially very dangerous because of the formation of cocaethylene. Many people use cocaine and alcohol at the same time because of its availability in venues that serve alcohol, reduced inhibitions while intoxicated and inexperience. Some users may use them together, deliberately thinking that either substance may prevent the hangover or 'comedown' of the other.

The formation of cocaethylene in the liver is a very serious consequence of the metabolism of both substances. Cocaethylene is an active metabolite of cocaine with a three to five times increased plasma half-life compared to cocaine, therefore its pleasurable (user-intended) effects last longer, as does the potential for end-organ damage. There is up to a 25-fold increased risk of sudden death when alcohol and cocaine are used together (10).

Crack Cocaine

'Crack' is not simply 'regular' cocaine but smoked. It is a specific mixture of powered cocaine, baking soda and water. This mixture is then boiled so the water evaporates, leaving a highly concentrated cocaine/baking soda mix. Smoking this mixture produces cracking sounds, hence the name.

It is possible to smoke crack with a specific crack pipe (glass pipe with a glass ball at one end which is heated) or with hollow glass tubes. If a specific pipe is not used, crack is placed onto a piece of foil and then heated with a lighter; when the fumes are given off, the fumes are sucked up.

The term 'chasing the dragon' is often used in this context; as the crack heats up and liquifies, it can move around the foil in a motion similar to a dragon costume seen at Chinese New Year celebrations.

Acute Intoxication

- Euphoria
- Increased confidence/increased sociability
- Reduced inhibitions
- Hypersexuality
- Increased heart rate.

Toxicity (11)

- Chest pain
- Dyspnoea
- Hypertension
- Epistaxis
- Agitation and aggression

- Acute psychotic features
- Hyperthermia
- Diaphoresis.

In severe toxicity there may be additional and more significant signs, including:

- Significant CNS disturbance: altered mental state, coma and areflexia
- Significant cardiac disturbance: arrythmias, myocardial infarction, cardiac arrest.

Withdrawal State

The vast majority of cocaine withdrawal symptoms are psychological. Imagine a drug that makes you euphoric, very social and hypersexual, and taking this away – the 'down' after acute intoxication is quite dramatic but once this has become habitual, the impact is exacerbated.

Symptoms include:

- Low mood
- Fatigue
- Restlessness
- Anxiety
- Suicidal ideation
- Increased appetite.

Unlike other substances with a clear withdrawal state, no medication is currently licensed to manage these symptoms. Patients may express a desire for medication to assist them and sensitively explaining this without making them feel unsupported is a key intervention.

Psychological interventions to help could include:

- Clear goal setting
- Working on possible reasons for the use in the first place, for example, depression or social anxiety
- Promoting self-efficacy through reaching certain achievements
- Groups for others struggling with cocaine use and withdrawal.

If psychological symptoms of withdrawal persist and are consistent with another established diagnosis, for example clinical depression, it may be appropriate to treat that in the usual way with anti-depressant medication and structured psychotherapy.

Risks of Chronic Use

- Cocaine dependence syndrome
- Nasal septum cartilage damage through insufflation
- Higher risk of cardiovascular disease and complications (stroke, hypertension, aortic dissection, myocardial damage, cardiomyopathy and arrhythmias) (12).

Risks Specific to Crack Use

- Higher likelihood of developing a dependence syndrome
- Lung damage related to inhalation of fumes from crack, glass and foil.

Cannabis

Background Information

Ganja, Green, Pot, Weed, Skunk, Marijuana, Grass, Dope, Hash

Cannabis remains in wide use within the UK and worldwide. It is seen as a 'softer drug' than many others mentioned within this chapter, suggesting it is more acceptable, and some users do not see it as a drug at all. Cannabis comes from the *Cannabis sativa* plant.

Cannabis can be:

- Smoked
- Ingested.

Cannabis is mainly smoked but can also be consumed within food products, often called edibles. Cannabis can be smoked in a joint like a rolled cigarette, with a bong or in a pipe.

Edibles could technically be any food product with added cannabis but typically these are baked into cakes or brownies. It is common for people to underestimate the potency of some edibles, especially if they have not produced them themselves. People can consume edibles and believe that they've 'not had enough' because the effects take longer to present. If they eat more to compensate, they may end up having far more cannabis than they intended.

Cannabis or weed is also a broad term to describe the drug but the exact strain and potency of cannabis depends on a variety of factors, including the strain of plant used and the form it is in, for example leaves or resin. The infamous variant of cannabis known as 'skunk' is particularly psychoactive with a high tetrahydrocannabinol (THC) concentration. Ideally a liaison psychiatrist would have a rough idea of the cannabis available within the local area and if it is known to be particularly strong.

Mechanism of Action

For the purpose of simplification, only the two main chemicals within cannabis are discussed: THC and cannabidiol (CBD). The exact mechanisms appear to not be fully understood as the current evidence does not entirely explain the effects cannabis has on the body. THC acts upon the cannabinoid receptors – CB_1 and CB_2 – which are both coupled to G-proteins. CB_1 receptors are found in both the CNS and peripheral nervous system. The highest concentrations of CB_1 receptors are found in the hippocampus, cortex, olfactory areas, basal ganglia, cerebellum and spinal cord (13). CBD acts on the cannabinoid receptors as well as $5\text{-}HT_{1A}$ receptors as an agonist (14).

Acute Intoxication

Users will describe being 'stoned' or 'high'. Unlike many of the substances in this chapter, there is significant variation in the responses people will have with cannabis. One's response is likely a complex interplay between their personality and current situation and the type and strength of cannabis being used. Below is a list of the common possible symptoms and effects but these can vary person to person and even with the same person if their mood or supply is different.

- Feeling happy and laughing a lot
- Feeling anxious or paranoid

- Lethargy
- Subjective sense of time slowing down
- Hallucinations in any modality
- Increased appetite (the 'munchies')
- Conjunctival injection
- Dry mouth.

Toxicity

A significant overdose or toxicity with cannabis alone as a distinct process is unlikely. It is more likely that users will experience the above symptoms to a more substantial degree, for example symptoms of anxiety becoming more like a panic attack.

- Panic attacks
- Reduced consciousness
- Vomiting
- Pallor (when associated with vomiting, referred to as 'whitey')
- Intense perceptual disturbance including psychotic experiences, derealisation and depersonalisation.

Withdrawal Syndrome

There is evidence to suggest a psychological sequalae when chronic users stop their use. Cannabis withdrawal symptoms can begin within hours or days but can occur for several weeks. It is during this prolonged period that users may relapse, so adequate support is crucial in promoting abstinence.

Symptoms include (15):

- Sleep disturbance
- Decreased appetite (+/− associated weight loss)
- Irritability
- Anger
- Low mood
- Anxiety symptoms.

Patients with a cannabis use disorder can be seen by addiction services within hospital liaison teams or in the community. It is important that the liaison psychiatrist knows that help is available, though it could be considered less substantial than what is on offer for opiates dependency.

Currently no medication is available to help produce cannabis use specifically or any replacement or substitution therapy. The main provisions within addiction services would be to offer supportive help and possibly psychology input. Sometimes the patient just needs assistance with making a plan to gradually reduce their intake and sometimes psychology input may be useful if the patient is using cannabis as a form of self-medication. Psychology input is not available in all addiction services and patients may find themselves declined from NHS psychology, such as Improving Access to Psychological Therapies (IAPT), if they have disclosed substance misuse previously.

Associated Risks

It is important to highlight that when smoking cannabis with tobacco the risks of smoking generally remain but could be higher if a filter is not being used. It is also important to remind patients that cannabis itself being psychoactive is associated with a higher risk of various mental disorders, including schizophrenia and drug-induced psychoses.

Harm Minimisation

- If rolling joints, consider using a filter to reduce the harmful fact of tobacco.
- Carefully select which type of cannabis they intend to smoke, ideally avoiding higher THC-containing cannabis.
- Keep a record of their use, such as making a note on their smartphone. This will allow users to keep track of use and notice if this increases over time.
- Users are discouraged from using other substances while intoxicated with cannabis.

Novel Psychoactive Substances

Background Information

NPS are products that have gained popularity in recent years. Although a variety of options exist, a product that was particularly harmful and unfortunately particularly popular was called 'spice'. There have been several incidents of death and serious harm resulting from the use of NPS in prison settings as well as in the community generally.

NPS were at one point legal to purchase and were colloquially referred to as 'legal highs'. They were freely available in a variety of shops and gaining some popularity. Gradually it became apparent that the contents of such substances vary greatly, along with the potency and potential risk. The government was made aware of the potential harms and these were then banned for sale.

It is difficult to give specific advice on the use of NPS because the term is so broad. The main input a liaison psychiatrist or substance misuse service can have is to highlight some of the risks of the use involved; namely, that it is unclear what exactly is in these products and what the risks may be. Patients may be unaware of the risks they are exposing themselves to. Much like any other interaction, if a patient feels their use is difficult to control or there are obvious harmful consequences, they should be supported to try and reduce their intake.

Stimulants

Background Information

Ecstasy, Pills, E, MDMA, Powder

Stimulants is another broad term for a variety of drugs which are taken for their mood-elevating, energising and pro-social effects. Typically they are taken in a party scene but their use is widespread.

Examples of stimulants include:

- Ecstasy/MDMA
- Prescribed stimulants, such as methylphenidate.

They can be taken by:

- Ingestion (as a tablet or swallowed as powder)
- Insufflation.

Ecstasy and MDMA are often referred to in a way that suggests they are different drugs when they are actually the same chemical in different forms. Ecstasy comes in a pill or tablet form, whereas MDMA is the powdered form from which 'pills' are made.

The risks associated with stimulant use depend on the exact drug being taken. When somebody purchases a pill or tablet, how do they know what it is? Does the dealer or person providing the drug even know what it is?

Acute Intoxication

The acute effects are very similar to that of cocaine and include:

- Feelings of happiness and euphoria
- Increased sociability
- Increased energy
- Reduced inhibitions
- Feelings of anxiousness
- Feeling paranoid.

Toxicity

Toxicity is a difficult topic with stimulants of this nature because what the 'pills' or 'powder' actually contain can vary a great deal. To some extent, it depends on the true chemical compounds within these powders and tablets may be the cause of toxicity.

Rather than viewing this section as a toxic syndrome of overdose, it may be more helpful to consider the potentially harmful acute effects.

Risks Associated with Chronic Use

- Depression
- Anxiety
- Anything related to the chemicals used to cut tablets.

Ketamine

Background Information

Ket, K, Special K

Ketamine is an anaesthetic medication for humans and animals. In its medicinal form it is available in a solution for injection for either IM or IV injection and as a nasal spray in some countries.

Ketamine is chemically similar to phenyl cyclohexyl piperidine (PCP), which is uncommon in the UK but it should be considered a possible differential diagnosis. People taking ketamine illicitly tend to obtain it in its powder form and usually snort it for ease. It can also be ingested or injected by users.

Mechanism of Action

The mechanism of action of ketamine appears to be only partially understood currently. It is accepted that there is an *N*-methyl-D-aspartate (NMDA) receptor antagonism that explains the majority of its intended effects. It appears that other pathways are also involved (aminergic, dopaminergic, glutamatergic and opioid).

Acute Intoxication

Considering that the intended medicinal use of ketamine is for anaesthetic purposes, it is no surprise why users may choose to take it. The symptoms include (16):

- Feeling relaxed
- Feeling worry-free
- Sense of detachment from surroundings
- Altered perceptions of surroundings
- Altered perception of time
- Analgesia
- Abdominal cramping.

Risk of Acute Use

- Altered perception and feeling very relaxed may impair one's awareness of immediate risk, such as hazards around them.
- Analgesia may prevent users from realising they have come to harm by preventing the normal response to painful stimuli.
- K-hole: a sense of paralysis which can be very frightening.

Risk of Chronic Use

- Psychological dependence. A physical dependence syndrome is not thought to exist but patients may still crave the pleasant effects and have a strong desire to continue to use it.
- Ketamine bladder syndrome (17) (frequency, incontinence, haematuria, upper-tract obstruction and papillary necrosis).
- Depression.
- Unpleasant flashback-type intrusive thoughts relating to the experiences while intoxicated.

Toxicity

Toxicity in a substance misusing setting would mostly likely be due to overdosing or mixing other drugs with ketamine.

The serious signs and symptoms of toxicity include:

- Respiratory depression
- Bradycardia
- Hypotension
- Cardiac arrest (related to possible myocardial infarction and other cardiovascular compromise)

- Reduced consciousness
- Coma
- Seizure.

Harm Minimisation

- Patients should be made aware of the potential risks and harms from both infrequent and chronic use.
- Encourage patients to use this drug ideally in a group setting to ensure a degree of safety from harm from other people or dangerous surroundings.
- Discourage mixing ketamine with other drugs.
- Discourage IV use as it is associated with a higher risk of overdose and other harms related to injecting generally.

Nitrous Oxide

Background Information

Hippie Crack, Laughing Gas or 'Gas and Air'

Small canisters contain nitrous oxide under pressure and when pierced they release the gas. Typically, people do not inhale nitrous oxide directly as the pressure will likely lead them to cough and waste the product; there is also the theoretical potential of barotrauma depending on the pressure and volume of inhaled gas.

Often, the canister is opened so that the gas escapes into a container like a balloon or bag, allowing the gas to be inhaled slowly or even shared among others. Using a bag by placing it over one's head is particularly dangerous if they lose consciousness as there is a risk of suffocation if the bag is not removed. 'Gas and air' is usually used to describe medical uses of nitrous oxide such as in labour and reduction of dislocations in the emergency department.

Acute Intoxication

- Happiness and euphoria
- Excessive and uncontrollable laughter
- Sense of relaxation
- Perceptual disturbance, typically auditory or visual hallucinations, which could be pleasant or unpleasant
- Headache.

Toxicity

Potential toxicity is mainly related to inhaling nitrous oxide rather than air and the potential for inadequate oxygen inhalation. Symptoms include:

- Headache
- Dyspnoea
- Tachypnoea
- Confusion

- Dizziness
- Collapse
- Cardiac dysrhythmias.

Consequences of Chronic Use

- Peripheral neuropathy due to demyelination or myelopathy (18)
- Megaloblastic anaemia
- Thrombocytopenia.

Harm Minimisation

- Inform the patient of the harms associated with its use
- Discourage inhalation directly from the canister
- Discourage inhalation by using a bag over their head.

Other Considerations for Substance Misuse

Confidentiality is paramount for all clinical staff but so is the safety of patients and members of the public. Much in the same way that a variety of medication conditions may limit lawful activities and employment, the use of substances may also have implications. The Driver and Vehicle Licensing Agency (DVLA) lists a variety of restrictions for patient-abusing substances and this resource should be consulted.

Most adult patients are likely to use a private motor vehicle at some point and the DVLA may advise that this activity must stop for a period of time. Generally, the conditions and implications are more stringent for professional drivers such a lorry, bus or taxi drivers. A variety of other professions may also have occupational restrictions and their own guidelines, particularly those involved in safety-critical tasks such as the police, professional aviators and any employment involving the use of firearms such as the armed forces.

In accordance with current guidance from professional and defence bodies, patients should be informed of the rules and what actions they should take. Your advice should be clearly documented and communicated where appropriate. In instances whereby you may feel the need to break confidentiality in the interests of public safety, you are strongly recommended to discuss this with a senior colleague and/or medical defence organisation for advice.

Understandably, patients may be worried about the implications of their substance use. As a rule of thumb, it is fair to highlight that co-operation with the authorities is likely to be a better approach as it demonstrates a degree of insight and responsibility, whereas non-compliance could result in criminal charges.

References

1. Caplehorn J, Dalton M, Haldar F, Petrenas A, Nisbet J. Methadone maintenance and addicts' risk of fatal heroin overdose. Subst Use Misuse. 1996;31 (2):177–96.

2. Trescot A, Datta S, Lee M, Hansen H. Opioid pharmacology. Pain Physician. 2008;11:133–53.

3. Walsh S, Preston K, Stitzer M, Cone E, Bigelow G. Clinical pharmacology of

buprenorphine: Ceiling effects at high doses. *Clin Pharm Therap.* 1994;**55** (5):569–80.

4. Griffin C, Kaye A, Bueno F, Kaye A. Benzodiazepine pharmacology and central nervous system-mediated effects. *The Ochsner Journal.* 2013;**13**(2):214–23.

5. Kang M, Galuska M, Ghassemzadeh S. Benzodiazepine toxicity. 2021. www.ncbi.nlm.nih.gov/books/NBK482238.

6. Wilson K, Reardon C, Theodore A, Farber H. Propylene glycol toxicity: A severe iatrogenic illness in ICU patients receiving IV benzodiazepines – A case series and prospective, observational pilot study. *Chest.* 2021;**128**(3):1674–81.

7. Madah-Amiri D, Myrmel L, Brattebø G. Intoxication with GHB/GBL: Characteristics and trends from ambulance-attended overdoses. *Scand J Trauma Resusc Emerg Med.* 2017;**25**(1).

8. Abdulrahim D, Bowden-Jones O. Guidance on the management of acute and chronic harms of club drugs and novel psychoactive substances. 2015. http://neptune-clinical-guidance.co.uk/wp-content/uploads/2015/03/NEPTUNE-Guidance-March-2015.pdf.

9. Hummel M. D1 dopamine receptor: A putative neurochemical and behavioral link to cocaine action. *J Cell Physiol.* 2002;**191**(1):17–27.

10. Dasgupta A. *Alcohol, Drugs, Genes, and the Clinical Laboratory.* Amsterdam; 2017.

11. Richards J, Le J. Cocaine toxicity. www.ncbi.nlm.nih.gov/books/NBK430976.

12. Havakuk O, Rezkalla S, Kloner R. The cardiovascular effects of cocaine. *J Am Coll Cardiol.* 2017;**70**(1):101–13.

13. Kumar R, Chambers W, Pertwee R. Pharmacological actions and therapeutic uses of cannabis and cannabinoids. *Anaesthesia.* 2001;**56** (11):1059–68.

14. Resstel L, Tavares R, Lisboa S, Joca S, Corrêa F, Guimarães F. 5-HT1A receptors are involved in the cannabidiol-induced attenuation of behavioural and cardiovascular responses to acute restraint stress in rats. *Br J Pharmacol.* 2009;**156** (1):181–8.

15. Livne O, Shmulewitz D, Lev-Ran S, Hasin D. DSM-5 cannabis withdrawal syndrome: Demographic and clinical correlates in U.S. adults. *Drug Alcohol Depend.* 2019;**195**:170–7.

16. Orhurhu V, Vashisht R, Claus L, Cohen S. Ketamine toxicity. 2021. www.ncbi.nlm.nih.gov/books/NBK541087.

17. Srirangam S, Mercer J. Ketamine bladder syndrome: An important differential diagnosis when assessing a patient with persistent lower urinary tract symptoms. *BMJ Case Reports.* 2012;1–2.

18. Thompson A, Leite M, Lunn M, Bennett D. Whippits, nitrous oxide and the dangers of legal highs. *Pract Neurol.* 2015;**15**(3):207–9.

Chapter 10

Psychosis in General Hospital Settings

Seri Abraham, Daniel Kaitiff, Samira Malik, Annalie Clark and Rachel Thomasson

Introduction

Psychosis is a core area of practice across all psychiatric sub-specialties, each with its own challenges. This chapter illustrates some of the complexities involved in assessment and treatment of psychosis in general hospital settings. The intersection between schizophrenia and physical health risks is highlighted as a starting point before examining the approach to diagnosis and the range of presentations in different areas of the general hospital. Management of common queries is discussed, taking a bio-psycho-social approach. Finally, legal aspects of treating patients with psychosis are outlined using practical tips.

Epidemiology: Schizophrenia, Physical Health and the Role of the Consultation-Liaison Psychiatry Team

Schizophrenia has a pooled lifetime prevalence of 0.4%. Data from large Scandinavian registry studies consistently report poor physical health in this patient group and higher standardised mortality rates than the general population (1). Males with schizophrenia experience an average loss of 15–20 years from life expectancy and females 11–17 years. Physical health conditions are a major contributing factor to premature mortality, as evidenced from studies which partialled out contributions from suicide and accidents (1). The observed/expected mortality ratios for cardiovascular disease, respiratory disease, liver disease and cancer are increased two- to seven-fold, though data are often pooled across different serious mental health conditions. These physical health conditions are associated with modifiable risk factors such as obesity, smoking, type 2 diabetes, alcohol intake and side effects of neuroleptic medication. Data on general hospital admissions for this patient group are scarce, though a UK study reporting pooled data among patients with serious mental illness suggests admission rates to general hospital settings for physical health treatment are higher than the general population (2).

The role of the consultation-liaison (CL) psychiatry team in this patient group is broad in scope. Examples include optimising medication in light of metabolic risk factors and intercurrent physical illness, discussions and motivational interviewing about lifestyle and how this intersects with mental and physical health, and collaborating with the treating team with a view to educating on specific health risks in this patient group and the value of opportunistic health screening.

The following two sections discuss exploration of the causes of psychosis as part of the CL team's role in offering diagnostic clarity.

Assessment and Diagnosis

Psychosis is an umbrella term used to describe a cluster of symptoms and signs centred on hallucinations, delusional beliefs, disorganised speech and/or behaviour. Psychosis has its own inherent problems as a descriptive term as it can be applied to different symptom clusters in patients with different underlying conditions. A common misconception in general hospital settings is that psychosis equates to a diagnosis of schizophrenia. Psychotic symptoms may of course become apparent in other psychiatric conditions, a broad spectrum of medical conditions affecting the nervous system, as a side effect of medication or illicit substances and are commonly found in patients with delirium. There are nuances in the way psychosis presents across different conditions. Parallel assessment with the treating team is preferable to delaying assessments while investigations are taking place.

Positive symptoms of psychosis are the usual drivers for referrals to the CL psychiatry team but these requests also present an opportunity to screen for negative symptoms and how they may be impacting upon a patient's quality of life. It may also be possible to offer a differential diagnosis for negative symptoms and to shape treatment plans accordingly. Examples include organic apathy after acquired brain injury and/or depressive symptoms blurring the picture and presenting inherent diagnostic challenges for treating teams.

ICD-11 Diagnostic Criteria for Schizophrenia (3)

At least two of the following must be present most days for at least one month. At least one of the symptoms must be from items (a) through (d).

(a) Persistent delusions (e.g. grandiose delusions, delusions of reference, persecutory delusions).

(b) Persistent hallucinations (most commonly auditory, although they may be in any sensory modality).

(c) Disorganised thinking (formal thought disorder) (e.g. tangentiality and loose associations, irrelevant speech, neologisms). When severe, the person's speech may be so incoherent as to be incomprehensible ('word salad').

(d) Experiences of influence, passivity or control (i.e. the experience that one's feelings, impulses, actions or thoughts are not generated by oneself, are being placed in one's mind or withdrawn from one's mind by others, or that one's thoughts are being broadcast to others).

(e) Negative symptoms such as affective flattening, alogia or paucity of speech, avolition, asociality and anhedonia.

(f) Grossly disorganised behaviour that impedes goal-directed activity (e.g. behaviour that appears bizarre or purposeless; unpredictable or inappropriate emotional responses that interfere with the ability to organise behaviour).

(g) Psychomotor disturbances such as catatonic restlessness or agitation, posturing, waxy flexibility, negativism, mutism or stupor. Note: if the full syndrome of catatonia is present in the context of schizophrenia, the diagnosis of catatonia associated with another mental disorder should also be assigned.

The symptoms are not a manifestation of another medical condition (e.g. a brain tumour) and are not due to the effects of a substance or medication (e.g. corticosteroids) on the central nervous system, including withdrawal effects (e.g. from alcohol).

Making the Distinction between Schizophrenia and Other Causes of Psychosis

Sometimes it is unclear whether a patient has an established diagnosis of schizophrenia and one should certainly keep an open mind in any patient who has a relatively recent onset of psychotic symptoms, apparent treatment resistance or where the presentation is atypical. Importantly, a history of a previous psychotic episode does not exclude the possibility of an organic cause.

A summary of findings that raise suspicion for atypical presentations of psychosis is given in the box below (4, 5).

Factors That Should Prompt Consideration of Organic Drivers for Psychosis

Patient Factors

Older age

Intellectual disability

Illness Factors

Rapid onset or progression of psychosis

Infectious symptoms preceding onset of psychotic symptoms

Systemic symptoms suggestive of malignancy

Other systemic symptoms occurring around the same time as onset of psychotic symptoms

Relevant Factors in Medical History

Malignancy

Autoimmune disorder

Neurological disease

Epilepsy

Head injury

Central nervous system infection

Congenital cardiac defect

Atypical Symptoms

Prominent visual hallucinations

Examination Findings

Focal neurological signs on examination

Movement disorder

Decreased consciousness

New cognitive impairment

Aphasia, mutism or dysarthria

Autonomic disturbance

Dysmorphic features

Treatment Factors

Insufficient response to antipsychotics/treatment resistance

Adverse response to antipsychotics (e.g. neuroleptic malignant syndrome)

The differential diagnosis of organically driven psychosis is broad but a basic scaffold is provided in the box below. It can be helpful to consult with neuropsychiatrist colleagues locally where services exist for further guidance on tailoring investigations on a case-by-case basis.

Examples of Organic Drivers for Psychosis

Neurogenetic syndromes: Clues include dysmorphic facies, intellectual disability, cardiac, renal and other organ-based anomalies. Examples include 22q11 and 9q34 deletion syndromes.

Inborn errors of metabolism and deposition syndromes: Examples include Niemann Pick C, Cobalamin C disease, Porphyria, Brain copper (Wilson's), iron (neuroacanthocytosis, PKAN) and calcium (Farr's) deposition syndromes. All of these conditions carry a neurological footprint (examples include cerebellar ataxia, posterior column signs, neuropathies and extrapyramidal syndromes).

Endocrine disorders: glucocorticoid excess, hyperparathyroidism, thyroid disease.

Neuroinflammatory disorders: neuronal antibody-mediated encephalitis; psychiatric complications of systemic (lupus, sarcoidosis) and central nervous system-specific auto-immune disease.

Neoplastic disease: tumours causing distortion, oedema/haemorrhage into or destruction of brain parenchyma or distantly located tumours with known paraneoplastic tendency.

Acquired brain injury: strategic infarcts and tumours, traumatic brain injury (usually as delirium).

Epilepsy: interictal and postictal psychosis usually occurs after many years of poorly controlled temporal lobe epilepsy.

Infection: tertiary syphilis, HIV, herpes simplex virus encephalitis, Whipple's disease, Prion disease.

Neurodegenerative disorders: dementias, Huntington's disease, Parkinson's disease.

Presentations of Psychosis in Different General Hospital Settings

Patients with psychotic symptoms are encountered in all parts of the general hospital and represent a common reason for referral or request for advice. Examples are given below.

The Emergency Department

Common presentations include:

- Patients presenting with acute/subacute relapse of a previously diagnosed mental health condition
- First presentation of psychosis – is it psychosis and, if so, what is causing it?

- Psychosis presumed related to alcohol or illicit drug misuse
- Psychosis as part of delirium.

Concerns are often centred on limited or lack of insight, self-neglect, distress, agitation and/or aggression, risks associated with both positive and negative symptoms and refusal to accept care interventions.

Case 1 – Tim is 28 years old, diagnosed with schizophrenia five years ago. Medical history includes asthma. He is brought into the emergency department (ED) with his social worker who is concerned about self-neglect, confused thinking and command hallucinations to harm himself. He is usually well on risperidone 3 mg twice daily. Collateral history from his family suggests he stopped his medication a month ago because of side effects. Tim is clearly agitated and distressed and has bruising on his scalp. Parallel work with ED staff was implemented because of new-onset confusion and possibility of head injury. Routine blood tests and computed tomography (CT) head did not reveal a new reversible cause. Tim was willing to accept informal admission to a psychiatric inpatient unit.

Case 2 – Pam is 52 years old and was brought to the ED via ambulance after she was found on the pavement outside her apartment block. Approximately 8 hours prior to this, the patient had contacted the police to report that there were 'men in balaclavas' in her apartment. The police contacted the warden who could not find any evidence of a break-in or people in her apartment.

Her neighbours contacted emergency services to state that the patient had told them that she had jumped out of her apartment to escape the intruders. The paramedics did not find any evidence of traumatic injury but could not complete a thorough examination as Pam was agitated. In the ED, Pam reported that she had been seeing 'men wearing balaclavas staring at her, rabbits with large eyes and faces in the walls' for the past two days. She was frightened that the men would follow her to the hospital. She stated that she had jumped out of her window because she was feeling increasingly unsafe in her apartment. She was orientated to place but not to time. The patient also reported pain in her hip and constipation.

Pam has a past history of schizoaffective disorder and was on flupentixol decanoate injections 40 mg every four weeks. A referral was sent to the CL team to rule out a psychotic relapse. The team were able to ascertain that her last psychiatric admission was three years ago and the patient had received her depot injection five days prior to the admission. Her inflammatory markers were raised and urine analysis revealed infection. The working diagnosis was delirium. Psychotic symptoms resolved once the infection was treated and further investigation revealed hip fracture, which was treated conservatively. Pam was eventually discharged back to her flat with continued input from mental health services.

Intensive Care Unit (ICU) and Medical and Surgical Wards

Ward-based referrals range from commonly encountered requests to once-in-a-career conundrums. Examples are given below.

The challenge of separating delirium and/or other organic presentations from an existing psychiatric diagnosis.

Patients with established diagnosis of psychosis as part of a primary psychiatric disorder:

- Admitted after a suicide attempt.
- Struggling to settle into the ward environment.
- Reluctant to or refusing care interventions, investigations and/or treatment or wishing to leave against medical advice.
- Showing signs of relapse.
- Tracheostomy in situ or after ear, nose and throat surgery and so requiring alternative medication routes.
- Queries regarding electrolyte disturbance, ECG changes, new medications and how these intersect with prescribed neuroleptic medication.

Case 1 – Kwame is 32 years old with a history of schizoaffective disorder. He was admitted after a serious self-harm attempt. Ingestion of bleach led to oesophageal rupture requiring emergency surgical repair. He is now two days post-op with a tracheostomy and gastrostomy tube in situ. Staff are concerned that he 'seems suspicious in his eyes' and reluctant to accept certain care interventions. CL assessment using non-verbal communication reveals Kwame has active depressive symptoms and marked adjustment difficulties regarding his mental health diagnosis. There are no active psychotic symptoms but there is marked anxiety about his ICU surroundings. He is concerned he may catch a hospital-acquired infection or that he might see someone die on the ward. Kwame is reassured these are legitimate concerns. He deeply regrets the self-harm but it was carried out with lethal intent. Kwame's medications were tailored for administration through the gastrostomy tube with addition of an anxiolytic. Staff were encouraged to assist Kwame to use non-verbal communication techniques and to provide repeated reorientation and reassurance. Kwame receives daily reviews from the CL team and has one-to-one nursing care on the ICU. Observation requirements will be reviewed when he is due to step down to the ward which is less intensively nursed.

Case 2 – Andrew is 24 years old and has a history of polysubstance misuse. He was admitted to the ICU following suspected overdose. Three separate attempts to sedate him were unsuccessful and he continued to be markedly paranoid and physically aggressive towards medical and nursing staff. Concerns were raised regarding staff safety and urgent advice and intervention was sought. Andrew had previously been treated for an unspecified psychotic illness using low-dose risperidone (2.5 mg daily), although treatment adherence may have been poor. Andrew had a forensic history but this did not involve any violent crimes and his partner suggested this behavioural repertoire was very atypical.

Rapid decision-making was required as to which neuroleptics and/or mood stabilisers would be trialled, specifics of loading doses, additional benzodiazepine requirements and type and amount of support required from security staff. The CL team provided daily reviews to tailor the treatment plan as his presentation evolved.

Maternity Wards

Provision of community perinatal mental health teams, mother and baby units and midwives with specialist interests in mental health have expanded across England in recent years (6, 7), leading to improved access to specialist care. The CL team form part of the network of care for women in hospital presenting with psychosis in the puerperium and will often be asked to lead on psychiatric aspects of clinical decision-making where a rapid response is required.

Key examples include:

- Assessment of patients brought in for natural delivery, induction or caesarean section where there are concerns about mental state.
- Assessment of patient in the early postnatal period usually centred on mental state and/or advice regarding medication and breastfeeding (see Chapter 13 for further detail).

Less common but challenging scenarios include:

- Women who become reluctant to give birth in the middle and later stages of labour due to delusional beliefs. Rapid, coordinated decision-making between obstetrics and psychiatry is key here and will often involve consultation with the hospital legal team.
- Women admitted for late termination of pregnancy due to fatal foetal abnormalities; women who have experienced stillbirth. The CL team will occasionally be asked to explore concerns related to hallucinosis and unusual ideas and to give an opinion as to whether these experiences reflect the process of adjustment and grieving and/or relapse indicators.
- Liaison with police and children's social care where an emergency protection order has been sought to remove a child and maternal mental health is thought to be relevant.

Case 1 – Leanne is 31 years old with a history of bipolar affective disorder. She has had one previous episode of puerperal psychosis after the birth of her second child three years ago. She is known to her local community mental health team and the perinatal mental health service. She is four days postnatal and there are concerns from ward staff regarding anxiety and poor sleep. Clinical review from CL psychiatry reveals that her anxiety baseline is raised and contributing to poor sleep. Anxiety is centred on anxious thoughts about the risk of becoming unwell and the impact on the baby. Leanne is currently euthymic; there are no psychotic symptoms currently and no thoughts of harm to self, baby or others. This is a high-risk period and daily reviews are put in place. Goals include psychological support, serial monitoring of mental state and treatment plan for managing anxiety and poor sleep. Liaison with obstetric team and perinatal psychiatry regarding optimising medication postnatally and plan for follow-up on discharge from maternity ward.

Liaison Outpatients

CL psychiatry outpatient services in the UK are patchily distributed and differ in clinical remit and specialist interests (8). The central diagnostic challenge of determining whether psychotic symptoms are organically driven, medication- or substance-induced or part of a primary mental health disorder is evident across inpatient and outpatient CL services. An additional challenge in clinic is how to ensure patient safety at the end of the appointment and tight networking with local mental health services is essential in this respect.

Case 1 – Neil is 52 years old and is 11 months post-liver transplant. He has developed paranoid delusional beliefs about his family threatening his personal safety. There is no previous history of psychosis and no family history. Routine blood tests and neuroimaging do not reveal an obvious cause. He had recommenced tacrolimus approximately three weeks before symptoms surfaced. Discussion with transplant team led to his treatment plan being consolidated. Neil responded well to risperidone and his immunosuppressant was changed to ciclosporin. He was weaned off risperidone six months later.

Aspects of Management

Clinical Aspects

Mental health diagnoses are not always recorded in the patient's medical notes. Mansour and colleagues analysed patient general hospital records in a UK study and found recording rates for schizophrenia were 56% (9). This raises questions about continuity of care, patients accessing treatment while in hospital and appropriate services being alerted upon discharge.

If a diagnosis of schizophrenia is made or confirmed, the CL team is ideally placed to ensure the treating team have an appropriate understanding of the condition, how it is manifesting in this particular patient (current level of symptom control, relapse indicators, degree of insight and adjustment, willingness to engage with support networks) and how staff can provide a safe and supportive ward environment. The CL team also plays a key role in terms of facilitating better data-sharing between practitioners in mental and physical health and facilitating appropriate follow-up care arrangements in the period leading up to discharge.

A study looking at ways to combat stigma associated with mental health conditions in the general hospital suggested education, along with clear clinical communication, and the provision of high-quality CL services are the most effective ways to reduce stigma (10).

Psychological Factors

The psychotic patient can be challenging to manage in the already busy general ward environment. Many factors including the patient's associated risks, lack of insight or social withdrawal can raise difficult dynamics between staff and patient. There is the risk of these patients being ostracised into side rooms where they often lose the benefits of the staff–patient therapeutic relationship. The CL mental health team has a key role in breaking down commonly held negative beliefs. The ability to acknowledge and openly discuss integrated stigma can help dispel myths around diagnosis and is usually welcomed by treating teams. It is important to provide psychoeducation explaining the outcome benefits of maintaining the patient's autonomy, practices and healthy coping mechanisms during admission. Developing care plans collaboratively looking at day-to-day management will ease ward anxieties and perceived stigma. It can be beneficial to leave psychoeducation leaflets in the nursing notes and with the offer of further support as required.

Social Aspects

Psychosis can have a profound effect on independent social functioning. It is important to address concerns regarding employment, accommodation and maintaining the balance between personal autonomy and accepting social care. Positive and negative symptoms of psychosis can both pose barriers to accepting care on the ward and at home. While in hospital, patients may worry about their income and are often willing to work towards addressing these concerns. Providing support can be a way to ease anxieties and build trust. Where this support will come from can vary depending on individual circumstances and level of functioning: social workers, occupational therapists, the citizens advice bureau, trained designated benefit advisors, care-coordinators, local charities, family and friends can all have a role. General hospitals have discharge support teams who can advise on suitability for ongoing accommodation but the availability of temporary accommodation through this route is scarce. Joint efforts are often required, and CL teams can provide cohesion between medical and community teams to ensure that available services are explored and potential delays to discharge are reduced.

Biological Aspects

Medication management for patients on antipsychotic medications requires liaison between various teams and professionals (medicine, nursing, pharmacy). Physician colleagues often rely on prescribing expertise within CL psychiatry teams because of potential diagnostic uncertainty, risks, complexity with medical comorbidity, the need for follow-up or limited expertise in this area. Common referrals for advice include patients who are taking more than one antipsychotic medication, decision-making regarding commencement of medication for psychotic symptoms, management of depot antipsychotics and patients taking clozapine.

General Prescribing Considerations in Physically Unwell Patients

When prescribing antipsychotics in patients with liver disease, general principles such as clinical and biochemical monitoring for worsening liver disease, reducing polypharmacy, starting at lower doses with slower dose increases, avoiding drugs with high protein binding, long half-lives and those requiring extensive hepatic metabolism lay useful groundwork for safe prescribing (11, 12). Sedating, highly anticholinergic, QT-prolonging and/or constipating antipsychotics should also be avoided where possible. Similar principles apply when prescribing antipsychotics in patients with renal impairment (11, 12).

Liver Disease

Antipsychotics of choice: amisulpiride/sulpiride (renally excreted), paliperidone if depot injection required.

Proceed with caution and use lower maximum doses: aripiprazole, olanzapine, quetiapine, risperidone, lurasidone, brexipiprazole.

Antipsychotics to try and avoid: clozapine, flupenthixol, zuclopenthixol, phenothiazines, asenapine, iloperidone and cariprazine in severe disease.

Renal Disease

Suggested choice: aripiprazole; olanzapine 5 mg daily or haloperidol 2–6 mg daily.

Dose as normal in patients with glomerular filtration rate >10: asenapine, haloperidol, trifluoperazine, zuclopenthixol (oral), flupenthixol, fluphenazine.

Proceed with caution and use lower maximum doses: paliperidone, risperidone, quetiapine, lurasidone.

Antipsychotics to try and avoid: all depot injections (some leeway with risperidone and olanzapine in the literature), amisupiride/sulpiride (renally excreted), pipotiazine, clozapine in severe renal disease.

Arrhythmias

Antipsychotics are associated with the prolongation of corrected Q-T interval (QTc) which can lead to fatal arrythmias (11). Common risk factors for QTc prolongation include cardiac (bradycardia, ischaemic heart disease, myocardial infarction, left ventricular hypertrophy, myocarditis), metabolic (hypokalaemia, hypomagnesaemia, hypocalcaemia), anorexia nervosa and culprit medications. It is necessary to obtain an ECG before commencing antipsychotics and to repeat at regular intervals, ideally within a week of reaching the therapeutic dose of treatment. High-risk drugs such as pimozide are not routinely prescribed for psychosis in the UK. Amisulpiride, chlorpromazine, haloperidol and quetiapine carry a moderate risk of QTc prolongation.

If the QTc is raised (>440 msec in men and >470 msec in women), the first steps should be to review all medications. QTc prolongation is associated with many non-psychotropic drugs including common antibiotics, antiarrhythmics, methadone, tamoxifen, amantadine and ciclosporin.

Common Side Effects Masquerading as Physical Health Complaints

Aside from appraising the clinical effectiveness of a patient's antipsychotic medication, reviewing patients in general hospital settings also enables identification of side effects and how these dovetail with the patient's current physical health status. The obese patient who has type 2 diabetes, appears sedated and somewhat confused, has postural hypotension, is constipated and has urinary hesitancy requires scrutiny for anticholinergic, antihistaminergic and antiadrenergic effects of antipsychotic medication.

Depot Injections and Clozapine

Medical teams will have less experience of prescribing of antipsychotics to treat primary psychotic disorders and will need clear guidance on monitoring, test doses, administration sites if a depot injection is being used and potential side effects. The CL team can facilitate rapid communication with the patient's community mental health team to ascertain depot injection type, dose and last date of administration to ensure continuity of treatment. The olanzapine depot injection is associated with its own post-injection delirium/sedation syndrome, which is reported to occur in 1.4% of patients (13), and the patient will require observation for three hours post-dose.

Patients prescribed clozapine require special consideration in general hospital settings and it is preferable if all useful information for nursing, medical and pharmacy staff is encapsulated within a provider-wide policy document. Early contact with the prescribing team is essential to establish dosing and monitoring requirements and history of any previous adverse effects. Patients who are acutely unwell with physical health conditions may have developed contraindications to receiving clozapine. Careful thought needs to be given to blood monitoring requirements, drug interactions (carbamazepine, Macrolides, any drugs causing constipation), smoking status and any breaks in treatment that will necessitate re-titration (48 hours or more). Education around identifying early signs and symptoms of potentially harmful sequelae such as fever, chest pain, breathlessness, reduced bowel movements, ECG changes, hypotension and a drop in neutrophil count is essential in order to provide safe, effective care. Tools such as the Glasgow Antipsychotic Side-Effects Scale for

Clozapine (GASS-C) help identify and monitor clozapine-related issues in a broad range of settings (14).

Medicolegal Aspects of Management

Assessment of Capacity in Patients with Active Symptoms of Psychosis

Assessment of capacity is covered in detail in Chapter 16 but we offer further comment here relevant to patients with psychosis and to provide further clinical application. Patients who are mentally and/or physically unwell are commonly asked to consent to relevant investigations and treatment trials as part of the iterative process of achieving diagnostic clarity and successful treatment. This is often a collaborative process between the patient and the treating team, but when a patient refuses a particular investigation or trial of treatment or wishes to leave hospital before these iterations have taken place, assessment of mental capacity is sometimes required if the proposed investigation or treatment is felt to be in their best interests and there are no mutually agreeable alternatives.

Decisions regarding capacity are time- and issue-specific; as such, patients who are experiencing symptoms of active psychosis may still be able to make an informed decision on investigations and treatment, depending on how psychosis dovetails with the issue at hand. For example, if a patient who has longstanding delusional beliefs about government conspiracy and being monitored by cameras is being asked to consent to endoscopy, the reasons for refusing the procedure require careful exploration to determine whether psychotic symptoms are influencing decision-making versus the patient being primarily concerned with the risk of perforation and sepsis and wishing to explore alternatives such as CT imaging. The CL team will often work in tandem with the patient, the treating team, an independent mental capacity advocate, next of kin and/or an attorney. These scenarios provide opportunities to deconstruct assumptions surrounding mental illness equating to global lack of capacity. Conversely, detailed assessment of capacity may also expose impaired decision-making despite the patient being able to maintain a reasonable social façade.

The Mental Health Act

Assessment and treatments under the Mental Health Act (MHA) (15) constitute a significant proportion of interventions undertaken in liaison psychiatry for patients presenting with psychotic symptoms (16). These interventions accounted for a significant number of contacts, including face-to-face contacts. The independent MHA review undertaken by the Centre for Mental Health in 2018 (17) showed that 43% of patients with lived experience of MHA assessments had a diagnosis of a psychotic illness and/or bipolar disorder.

The CL psychiatrist often acts as a responsible clinician (RC) for patients detained on the acute wards. Although they may be employed by a separate healthcare provider, it is good practice for psychiatrists working in acute trusts to have an honorary contract while acting as an RC. Colleagues in medical and surgical settings may have limited awareness regarding the responsibilities of the RC and this can lead to difficulties understanding and accommodating protracted timelines for transfers, discharge, arranging appeals and so on. Other challenges include provision of Section 17 leave and limited access to the wider multidisciplinary team that would be available on inpatient psychiatric wards. Furthermore, acute wards are often open and mixed gender with limited access to staff with formal training in managing violence and aggression and limited access to medication choices such as depot antipsychotics. These factors must be acknowledged when deciding on the most appropriate setting for assessment and treatment.

Common scenarios in the general hospital setting include:

Scenario 1. A patient with psychotic symptoms is acutely agitated and wishes to leave hospital. Urgent action is required to try to prevent this from happening as the patient is deemed to be at risk. The CL team is tasked here with advising doctors whether use of the Mental Capacity Act versus Section 5(2) MHA is appropriate, depending on what is driving the agitation and what the treatment priorities are. Section 5(2) is essentially a temporary holding power that can be used while a formal assessment for detention under the Act can be arranged. It is important to note that doctors in their first year of training in the UK at the time of writing are not on the General Medical Council register and therefore cannot carry out these assessments. Advice is often sought as to where the relevant paperwork can be found and filed (18). The process should also trigger formal referral for assessment for detention under the MHA.

Scenario 2. A patient in the ED is floridly psychotic. The ED team confirm they do not require admission to a medical ward and they are refusing admission to a psychiatric inpatient unit. Section 5(2) cannot be used in hospital emergency departments, and in practice Section 4 as a temporary holding power is very rarely used. As such, these scenarios often trigger an assessment for detention under Section 2 of the Act. In some circumstances where the diagnosis is already established and the patient is well known, a direct application for detention under Section 3 is made. CL psychiatrists will be involved in the assessment if the service covers work in the ED or the team will help to signpost ED staff to the individuals assigned to cover these assessments in the ED (this is often a trainee psychiatrist covering an on-call rota).

Scenario 3. The patient who is floridly psychotic and is either an inpatient in the general hospital or who requires admission to this setting from the ED. Initial considerations centre on use of the Mental Capacity Act versus the MHA as in scenario 1. If the MHA is appropriate, decisions need to be made regarding application for detention under Section 2 or 3 as in scenario 2. The nuance here is that the patient may be detained to the general hospital as opposed to a psychiatric inpatient unit if they are not cleared for discharge from a medical setting or if a bed is not available for transfer out of the general hospital. In this case, one of the medical consultants of the CL team assumes the role of RC and paperwork for detention is filed with a designated administrator in the general hospital.

Scenario 4. A patient with acquired brain injury and challenging behaviour is initially assessed and treated under the Mental Capacity Act. It becomes clear that the patient has persistent psychotic symptoms and will require ongoing treatment. Discharge planning centres around transfer to a neuro-behavioural unit for individuals with acquired brain injury. In these scenarios, discussions take place with the receiving team about the appropriate legislative framework and the MHA is sometimes deemed to be appropriate in these cases.

Scenario 5. A patient detained to the general hospital under Section 2 wishes to appeal. This involves liaising with designated hospital managers with a view to arranging a manager's hearing or supporting the patient to apply to an MHA Tribunal.

Scenario 6. A patient detained under Section 3 MHA who has pneumonia is transferred from a psychiatric inpatient unit run by the regional mental health trust to a medical ward on the same site run by an acute care trust to receive treatment with intravenous antibiotics. This requires the RC to authorise leave of absence from the psychiatric inpatient unit using Section 17 as the patient will technically be under the care of an additional healthcare provider. Practice points include effective communication between the CL team and the psychiatry inpatient team, transfer of appropriate legislative paperwork (relating to detention and consent to treatment), clinical handover and medication charts.

Section 19

In the above scenario, where a patient's physical condition deteriorates and treatment in the general hospital setting becomes prolonged, it may be appropriate for the CL team to assume clinical and medicolegal responsibility for the patient to effectively integrate care. Section 19 of the Act regulates transfer between healthcare providers/hospitals for patients who are detained under the Act for assessment or treatment in addition to formalising transfer of detention. This section of the Act is also utilised to transfer patients detained under the Act out of the general hospital setting to psychiatry inpatient units and to nursing homes and rehabilitation units which are registered to accept patients detained under the Act. The MHA office/administrator advises on completion of necessary transfer paperwork such as the H4 form, CTO4 and CTO6 and additional requirements for patients detained under Section 37/41/47/49.

Section 62

Electroconvulsive therapy (ECT) is sometimes administered under Section 62 for patients with catatonic schizophrenia, often following an unsuccessful lorazepam challenge. Second opinion authorising doctor (SOAD) input under Section 58 would be required if the patient lacks capacity to consent to ECT and psychiatric treatment. This is a relatively infrequent occurrence on medical wards. Close coordination is required between the medical ward, CL team, MHA administration and ECT team in such instances. Clear communication regarding the location, frequency and timing of ECT sessions along with planning around staff accompanying the patient is vital. Often, patients have complex medical needs due to the severity of mental health difficulties impacting on oral intake, requiring interventions such as feeding tubes and monitoring. Therefore, a good working relationship across teams is key to optimise outcomes in these scenarios.

Summary

Patients with psychosis present various challenges across all settings within the general hospital. We have highlighted the requirement for a holistic approach to assessment and management and the importance of sound working knowledge of appropriate mental health legislation, and illustrated opportunities within these challenges to implement better working relationships across the interface between mental and physical health with a shared objective of improving outcomes for patients with psychosis.

References

1. Nordentoft M, Wahlbeck K, Hallgren J et al. Excess mortality, causes of death and life expectancy in 270,770 patients with recent onset of mental disorders in Demark, Finland and Sweden. *PLoS One*. 2013;8(1):e55176.

2. Jayatilleke N, Hayes RD, Chang CK, Stewart R. Acute general hospital admissions in people with serious mental illness. *Psychol Med*. 2018;48(16):2676–83.

3. World Health Organization. International Classification of Diseases – 11th revision. 2023. https://icd.who.int/browse11/l-m/en#/http%3a%2f%2fid.who.int%2ficd%2fentity%2f1683919430.

4. Pollak TA, Lennox BR, Müller S et al. Autoimmune psychosis: An international consensus on an approach to the diagnosis and management of psychosis of suspected autoimmune origin. *Lancet Psychiatry*. 2020;7(1):93–108.

5. Bonnot O, Herrera PM, Tordjman S, Walterfang M. Secondary psychosis induced by metabolic disorders. *Front Neurosci*. 2015;19(9):177.

6. NHS England. Implementing the Five-Year Forward View for Mental Health. 2017. www.england.nhs.uk/publication/implementing-the-fyfv-for-mental-health.

7. Royal College of Midwives. Specialist mental health midwives: What they do and why they matter. 2018. www.rcm.org.uk/media/2370/specialist-mental-health-midwives-what-they-do-and-why-they-matter.pdf.

8. Walker A, Barrett JR, Lee W et al. Organisation and delivery of liaison psychiatry services in general hospitals in England: Results of a national survey. *BMJ Open*. 2018;8(8):e023091.

9. Mansour H, Mueller C, Davis KAS et al. Severe mental illness diagnosis in English general hospitals 2006–2017: A registry linkage study. *PLoS Med*. 2020;17(9):e1003306.

10. Bolton J. 'We've got another one for you!': Liaison psychiatry's experience of stigma towards patients with mental illness and mental health professionals. *The Psychiatrist*. 2012;36(12):450–4.

11. Schizophrenia and related psychoses. In Taylor DM, Barnes TRE, Young HY (eds.), *The Maudsley Prescribing Guidelines*, 14th ed. Chichester; 2018, pp. 3–204.

12. Hepatic and renal impairment. In Taylor DM, Barnes TRE, Young HY (eds.), *The Maudsley Prescribing Guidelines*, 14th ed. Chichester; 2018, pp. 635–60.

13. Detke HC, McDonnell DP, Brunner E et al. Post-injection delirium/sedation syndrome in patients with schizophrenia treated with olanzapine long-acting injection, I: Analysis of cases. *BMC Psychiatry*. 2010;10:43.

14. Hynes C, Keating D, McWilliams S et al. Development and validation of a clozapine-specific side-effects scale. *Schizophr Res*. 2015;168(1–2):505–13.

15. Department of Health and Social Care. Code of practice: Mental Health Act 1983. 2017. www.gov.uk/government/publications/code-of-practice-mental-health-act–1983.

16. Guthrie E, McMeekin A, Thomasson R et al. Opening the 'black box': Liaison psychiatry services and what they actually do. *BJPsych Bull*. 2016;40(4):175–80.

17. Department of Health and Social Care. Modernising the Mental Health Act: Final report from the independent review. 2019. www.gov.uk/government/publications/modernising-the-mental-health-act-final-report-from-the-independent-review.

18. Department of Health and Social Care. Electronic forms for use under the Mental Health Act. 2020. www.gov.uk/government/collections/electronic-forms-for-use-under-the-mental-health-act.

Acute Behavioural Disturbance in the General Hospital

Ankush Singhal, Sridevi Sira Mahalingappa, Deepa Bagepalli Krishnan and Rachel Thomasson

Summary

Patients presenting with acute behavioural disturbance pose a significant challenge in terms of management of risk to the patient (particularly when there is potentially life-threatening illness and/or injury) and to others. The consultation-liaison (CL) team offers acute advice and expertise across the general hospital setting and has a key role in policy development in collaboration with medical colleagues to ensure timely and effective intervention for patients presenting with acute behavioural disturbance. This chapter explores aetiological factors contributing to presentations of acute behavioural disturbance and approach to assessment. Behavioural and pharmacological interventions are outlined along with guides for optimising assessment and management of patients with acute behavioural disturbance in the emergency department (ED).

Case Example

Joe is 34-year-old man with a history of schizoaffective disorder. He was brought to the ED by police as his neighbour was worried about him. Joe appears dishevelled; he is shouting and attempting to break his kitchen window. After an hour in the ED, Joe is becoming very restless and is refusing to stay in hospital. He is muttering to himself and appears suspicious. He admits to hearing voices of spirit advisors talking to him, saying that he should not waste time in hospital as he has a diamond mining corporation to attend to. He is becoming irritable and threatens to punch the attending nurse. He asks for help to leave and board a plane. Thirty minutes later, he assaults the nurse and absconds.

Key questions for this case centre on driving factors for his presentation, identifying priorities in terms of assessment, investigation, treatment and risk containment, strategies for de-escalation and reflecting on what could have been done to prevent the assault.

Introduction

Acute behavioural disturbance is an umbrella term rather than a clinical diagnosis as there are a variety of presenting features and underlying causes. It can be helpful to consider subtypes to stratify risk and to consider possible driving factors (1):

- Agitation with predominant physical aggression, such as fighting, throwing, snatching
- Agitation with predominant verbal aggression such as shouting, screaming

- Agitation with predominant physical (non-aggressive) manifestation such as pacing, restlessness
- Agitation with predominant verbal (non-aggressive) manifestation such as repeated questioning, talking over others.

Agitation and aggression are sometimes used as interchangeable terms but while motor restlessness, heightened responsivity to stimuli, irritability and repetitive motor activity or speech may be present in both of these states, aggression can be thought of as a dividing line that involves verbal or motor activity associated with an intent to harm (1).

There are limited data on the frequency of acute behavioural disturbance presentations in UK general hospitals. Of the 140 million patients who visited an ED in the USA in 2017, between 5% and 10% (7 to 14 million) were 'agitated patients', presenting with behavioural symptoms (2). In the USA, acute behavioural disturbance accounts for 4.3 million psychiatric emergency visits/year (3). Primary drivers include deliberate self-poisoning or self-harm (38%) and alcohol and illicit drug intoxication (33%), with patients who were medically or psychiatrically unwell or experiencing drug withdrawal representing the remainder (29%) (4).

Risk Factors

Acute behavioural disturbance represents a dynamic situation that can rapidly evolve from an anxious, distressed, restless patient to violent behaviour that confers immediate risk of harm (5). Knowledge of risk factors enables a degree of anticipation and forward planning but many of the demographic factors identified in the literature confer risk of reductionism. Young, single males with low educational attainment, lower socio-economic status and poor social support are identified as being at higher risk for presenting with agitation (6). Box 11.1 highlights other risk factors that are helpful in appraising risks when assessing a patient with acute behavioural disturbance.

Box 11.1 Risk Factors for Violence adapted from Garriga et al (6)

Previous history of physical violence or verbal threats – any previously established warning signs or trigger points?

History of multiple psychiatric admissions

Prolonged admissions

Detention under the Mental Health Act

Substance misuse (active intoxication, toxicity or withdrawal) – has it been historically associated with violence in this patient?

Psychosis (active thought disorder, paranoid delusions, command hallucinations)

Personality disorder involving antisocial behaviour, impulsivity, emotional instability, low frustration tolerance, external locus of control

Involvement in a violence devoted sub-cultural group

History of early adversity (abuse)

History of involvement with criminal justice services

Aetiological Considerations

Patients presenting with acute behavioural disturbance are generally classified into four aetiological groups, with acknowledgement that a combination of these may be actively contributing in any given clinical presentation:

- General medical conditions
- Medication-related effects (adverse effect, toxicity, withdrawal)
- Alcohol- or drug-related presentations (intoxication, toxicity, withdrawal)
- Primary psychiatric condition
- Undifferentiated agitation. This includes factors such as environmental triggers and social, familial and cultural contexts, and is beyond the scope of this chapter (7).

Agitation secondary to a general medical condition is generally caused by loss of central nervous system (CNS) substrate (oxygen, glucose), electrolyte abnormalities that affect neurotransmission, metabolic abnormalities, toxins that interfere with normal synaptic transmission (infection, medications/toxins, uraemia, ammonia) or CNS disease (trauma, vascular insult, seizures, infection, inflammation).

Routine blood tests and observations, standard septic screen, ECG and, where available, urine drug screen should be carried out. A computed tomography (CT) brain scan is often helpful if the presentation is not aligning with what is known about the patient's medical history or if there is any suspicion of vascular event, dementia or trauma. Recent changes to medication should also be reviewed, along with general polypharmacy burden and results from renal and liver function tests.

Alcohol and substance misuse are covered in detail in Chapters 8 and 9, respectively. It is worth mentioning pathological alcohol intoxication, which refers to symptoms of intoxication in the context of low blood alcohol levels. This is more commonly observed in patients with additional medical comorbidity and there may be subsequent amnesia for the episode of agitation on recovering.

Although acute agitation is commonly associated with presentations of psychosis, a broader differential diagnostic framework is helpful and should include mixed affective states, anxiety disorders, personality disorders, adjustment disorders and autism spectrum disorder.

Psychosis

Soyka and colleagues report that up to 14% of hospitalised patients with schizophrenia may initially present with acute behavioural disturbance (8), and up to 20% of this cohort will re-present with acute behavioural disturbance (9). Risks include first episode presentations, poor medication compliance, multiple previous admissions and active positive symptoms.

Affective Disorders

Acute behavioural disturbance is common in patients who are actively unwell with bipolar affective disorder. Agitation is estimated to occur in 87% of cases of mania, with up to 26% of patients having a documented episode of aggression within 24 hours of an inpatient admission (10).

Agitation can also present in patients who are depressed. Irritability may be a driving factor, along with an inner sensation of tension and restless. The agitation is less likely to be goal-directed and typically has a diurnal rhythm, being worst in the mornings (10, 11).

People Diagnosed with a Personality Disorder

Patients diagnosed with a personality disorder may present to the ED when in crisis. Patients diagnosed with borderline personality disorder form the largest proportion of this cohort and behavioural disturbance is multifaceted and relatively common (12). Examples include agitation, verbal and physical aggression, impulsivity, suicidal ideas and self-harm, and much of this is predicated upon severe psychological distress. Staff in the ED can find this patient group difficult to manage without training and support, resulting in limited attempts to de-escalate and validate the patient's emotional state. This can lead to further intensification of distress and its associated behavioural manifestations.

Clinical Tips

Tips include: offering practical problem-solving while setting boundaries and managing expectations regarding admission and medication; active listening – validating and reflecting to help your patient feel listened to and understood; monitoring and managing one's own counter-transference (the way you feel about the patient as the consultation progresses); and building awareness of any splitting tendencies (the patient may offer polarised views of individuals currently involved in the assessment process) and managing this collaboratively with other members of staff.

Approach to Assessment

The initial evaluation of a patient with acute behavioural disturbance requires a brief assessment to determine the most likely cause of the clinical presentation and the level of risk to the patient and others. A more extensive medical and psychiatric evaluation could take place once the patient is calmer or after sedation.

Case

Telephone call: 'We have a patient here in the ED, Luke, who is kicking off. He's punched and kicked staff and thrown a monitor across the bay. Can you come and see him?'

Preliminary Steps: Handover, Environment, Team Assembly

Initial contact with the referrer should be brief as the priority is to get to the scene as quickly as possible. It is helpful to establish the essentials:

- Whether any weapons are involved/suspected to be present (is there anything representing a potential weapon that can be removed from the scene?).
- Whether anyone else is immediately at risk (can they be removed/safer distance created?).
- Whether hospital security and/or police have been contacted/are present.
- If the police have brought the patient to the ED, what legal framework was used (arrest, Section 136, Mental Capacity Act)?
- Is there a room where Luke can be assessed? If so, ensure it is empty and clear of any obstructions.
- While you are en route, could the ED team try to establish why Luke is angry and what he wants?

- Is there any relevant history available (medical, psychiatric, forensic, risk alerts, alcohol or substance misuse)? If he arrived with police, can they disclose any helpful information to facilitate the assessment?
- Are there any staff present that have been trained in the use of restraint techniques? Make sure the hospital policy for rapid tranquilisation (RT) is readily available in case it is needed.

On arrival at the scene, obtain the information above, establish whether there are immediate risks to others and whether it is feasible to approach the patient or to secure the scene (this will involve removing other patients for their own safety and any immediately obvious potential weapons where possible); withdraw and await police presence. The latter situation is uncommon but is occasionally necessary. Verbal de-escalation can and should be attempted from a safe distance.

National guidance is available that outlines requirements for a designated room for mental health assessments in the ED (13). It is helpful to be aware of these requirements so that potential pitfalls within the assessment space can be considered if these requirements are not met (exit clearance is always mandatory):

✔ Fitted with an emergency call system, an outward opening door and a window for observation
✔ Contains soft furnishings and is well ventilated
✔ Contains no ligature points or furniture, fixtures and fittings that could be used as potential weapons
✔ *Exits clear of obstructions.*

Clinical Approach: Initial Observations

See the patient as soon as possible. If it's feasible, sit down as it is less confrontational. Maintain a safe distance and respect their personal space. Avoid prolonged or intense direct eye contact. Avoid sudden movements and minimise body language positions that can be considered confrontational and threatening (e.g. crossed arms or hands behind the back or hidden).

There are certain features that can serve to indicate arousal, which can precede aggression (Box 11.2).

Box 11.2 Features That Indicated Heightened Arousal

Restlessness or pacing

Clenched fists; clenched jaw

Loud speech, swearing and insults

Silence

Staring or avoiding eye contact

Verbal threats

Invading personal space

Tachypnoea, facial flushing

Threatening gestures – punching walls/banging on furniture

Rating scales are also available. The Behavioural Activity Rating Scale is a three-area (physical aggression, non-physical aggression and verbal agitation), 10-item scale that can be used for rapid assessment of level of aggression (14). The Brøset Violence Checklist is a six-item assessment tool for the prediction of imminent violent behaviour within the next 24 hours (15). The Violence Risk Screening-10 (V-RISK-10) has been reported as useful for acute psychiatric settings (16), and the Agitation Severity Scale is a 21-item scale that is useful for evaluation of agitated behaviour in acute settings (17).

Where possible, specific considerations should be made before assessing patients with cognitive impairment, speech and language difficulties and neurodevelopmental disorders such as autism spectrum disorders, and use of interpreters should be considered at the earliest opportunity for those in need, such as deaf patients and patients from culturally and linguistically diverse backgrounds.

Clinical Approach: Verbal De-escalation

The cardinal principle of management of acute behavioural disturbance is to treat the cause when possible, if known. However, as it is usually an emergency situation, the focus usually shifts to managing the patient to ensure everyone's safety, while definitive measures are taken to find the cause and/or to treat it. The least restrictive, non-pharmacological and non-coercive approach should be considered first, when clinically appropriate, minimising the impact on the therapeutic relationship. Treatment may need to be given under the relevant legal framework (e.g. common law, Mental Health Act or Mental Capacity Act) if informed consent is not available.

After initial management of acute behavioural disturbance, including monitoring as detailed below, the patient's overall care should be reviewed and regular treatment should be optimised as soon as possible. If no physical or psychiatric cause is suspected, and behaviour is dangerous or seriously irresponsible, consider informing security or the police for an appropriate action if they are not already present (18).

De-escalation is defined as 'an explicitly collaborative process involving a range of verbal and non-verbal interventions that aim to reduce agitation and distress, with the purpose of averting aggression or violence' (19). It is to help the patient to calm themselves. Project BETA group (20) recommends 10 domains of de-escalation summarised in Box 11.3.

Box 11.3 Ten Commandments for Safety: Domains of De-escalation

Respect personal space

Do not be provocative

Establish verbal contact

Be concise

Identify wants and feelings

Listen closely to what the patient is saying

Agree or agree to disagree

Lay down the law and set clear limits

Offer choices and optimism

Debrief the patient and staff

Put into practice, these tenets would place the assessing clinician more than two arms' length from the patient and close to an exit. The clinician introduces themselves clearly, gently and calmly without being patronising, challenging or confrontational. Luke is reassured the assessing clinician is here to keep him and others safe. Concise questions are asked, which identify the patient's needs/feelings:

'Hello Luke, I'm Dr B. I'm here to keep you and other people safe. The staff are worried about you. Can you tell me what's happening/what's wrong? I'd like to help you if I can.'

If Luke can't offer any clarity about his needs, listen to him and observe his body language to see if there are any clues and lead with this. Use short sentences and give him time to respond:

'Are you upset/angry about something?' 'Are you scared?' 'Could you tell me a bit more?'

Summarise and reflect back what Luke is saying to check your understanding and to confirm he is being listened to and understood:

'Can I check I've got it right – you're worried that your wife is not who she says she is and you think she might have poisoned you?'

Luke shows you a rash on his arm and asks if you believe what he is saying about being poisoned. He wants a whole-body PET scan to find the poison as it's hiding and multiplying in his body. Validating the patient's concern while avoiding collusion is key here, along with managing expectations about investigations while still offering hope that there is a way forward. There is also a window of opportunity here to collect some medical history and to carry out a basic examination +/− investigations.

'I can see why you are concerned about the rash and I think it's important that I ask you some more questions about your health. I'd like to keep an open mind about what is going on as I want to get to the bottom of it. There are some simple, practical tests I'd like to organise to check your health as a first step, if that's okay?'

If Luke's distress and level of aggression escalate, limits and boundaries should be set in a calm, 'matter-of-fact' way rather than as a threat. Offer kind, practical solutions:

'Luke, I need you to stop shouting/to work towards feeling calmer so that I can help you. Can I get you something to eat or drink? Do you want to try some medication to help you feel calmer?'

Any use of force, medication or restraint may damage trust and the therapeutic relationship, especially in an already volatile situation when the patient may feel paranoid, frightened and vulnerable. This may increase the risk of intensifying distress and further behavioural disturbance. Therefore, de-escalation should generally precede and accompany the use of RT. As-required medications can be used as part of a de-escalation strategy but their use alone is not de-escalation (13).

Clinical Approach: Restraint and Restrictive Practices

The National Institute for Health and Care Excellence (NICE) defines manual restraint as 'a skilled, hands-on method of physical restraint used by trained healthcare professionals to prevent patients from harming themselves, endangering others or compromising the therapeutic environment. Its purpose is to safely immobilise the patients'. It should be used only when de-escalation and other preventative strategies have failed (13). This should be the least restrictive option and proportionate to the risks. Due consideration should be given to patient' preferences, if known, their physical health, degree of frailty, presenting circumstances, available skillset for manual restraint and developmental age. The NICE guidance document further advises to avoid restraining the patient to the floor. However, if this is unavoidable, then the recommendation is to use the supine (face-up) position if possible for the shortest possible time (preferably no more than 10 minutes), ensuring no interference with the patient's airway, breathing, circulation, ability to communicate and dignity.

RT should be considered as an alternative to prolonged manual restraint. The Royal College of Emergency Medicine (RCEM) (21) endorses this advice and further adds that significant physiological derangements (acidosis, electrolyte abnormalities, cardiac arrhythmias, etc.) can occur due to the underlying condition (e.g. delirium) or as a result of resisting restraint and may be exacerbated by comorbidities (e.g. cardiac disease) or medication/illicit substances. If a patient is being restrained in the ED, even if the police are providing this intervention, ultimate responsibility for the patient's safety and well-being rests with the clinical team of the ED.

Clinical Approach: Pharmacological Management

Route of Administration

The oral route is preferable, where possible and appropriate. For rapid onset of action, orodispersible tablets (e.g. risperidone, aripiprazole and olanzapine), buccal (e.g. midazolam), sublingual and oral-inhaled absorption are alternative routes, when available, and can improve compliance as well. Generally, intravenous (IV) options must only be used in situations when other avenues are unavailable or inappropriate, in settings where resuscitation equipment and trained clinicians are available to manage medical emergencies. Note that the term Rapid Tranquilisation refers to parenteral administration in relevant NICE guidance.

Rapid Tranquilisation

The goal of RT is to achieve a state of calmness without sedation, sleep or unconsciousness, thereby reducing the risk to self and/or others while maintaining the ability of the patient to respond to communication, to facilitate an assessment. However, sedation may also help to manage acute disturbance, at least as an immediate step or interim strategy (19).

Following RT, a medical review (including checking medications administered over 24 hours) and risk assessment should be arranged. Patients should be closely monitored for physical health checks, as described below.

RT is different from as-required medication and hence should not be prescribed routinely. Judicious use of as-required medication can be extremely helpful in preventing incidents or managing the risks (and can prevent the use of RT), although it can lead to polypharmacy and subsequent unmonitored risk of adverse effects.

Medications Commonly Used in Management of Acute Behavioural Disturbance

Benzodiazepines – Benzodiazepines, alone or in combination (usually with antipsychotics), are the mainstay of most pharmacological regimens for treating acute behavioural disturbance. Most clinicians are familiar with commonly used benzodiazepines. Collectively they offer a broad range of pharmacokinetic options, multiple routes of administration and have a distinct advantage as flumazenil can be used to reverse any unwanted complications. A Cochrane review published in 2018 (22) found that benzodiazepines were equally effective as haloperidol for psychosis-related agitation, with lesser side effects; however, they were less effective than olanzapine.

Lorazepam is the most commonly used IM medication for RT in the UK. It has relatively quick onset and short duration of action, no active metabolite (hence it does not accumulate) and a good safety profile. IM lorazepam is recommended by NICE as a first-line choice for RT in the majority of patients (13).

IM midazolam is equally effective in treating acute agitation and can also be combined with antipsychotics for a faster and more enduring action in ED settings. In psychiatric emergencies, IM midazolam is more rapidly effective than IM haloperidol and promethazine in combination. However, active airway management might be needed with IM/IV midazolam, hence these routes should be restricted to acute medical settings with resuscitation facilities (13). In other settings, buccal midazolam can be used, but administration to acutely agitated patients can be tricky; bioavailability of midazolam using this buccal route is erratic and the evidence base for use in RT settings is limited (23).

Diazepam is rapid acting but long lasting and carries the risk of accumulation on repeated dosing. When given IM, it is painful with slow and erratic absorption. It is rarely used for RT in the UK and is not recommended by current guidelines. The IV route can used in appropriate circumstances with resuscitation facilities.

Benzodiazepines can cause over-sedation, drowsiness, ataxia, confusion and hypotension with the associated risk of falls. Potential respiratory depression is a significant concern, more likely with parenteral dosing, and the risk increases with repeated administration. Immediate access to flumazenil is recommended wherever parenteral benzodiazepines are prescribed.

Antipsychotics

Haloperidol – Haloperidol is effective for psychosis-induced acute disturbance (24). It is commonly used for RT in the UK, although practice is changing due to concerns regarding cardiotoxicity, extrapyramidal side effects (EPS) and impeding recovery after traumatic brain injury. Concurrent use of promethazine reduces the risk of EPS such as acute dystonia, while also adding to the tranquilising effect. An ECG is recommended before use as haloperidol carries a risk of QT interval prolongation. If IV administration is clinically necessary, this should be done only under continuous ECG monitoring for the detection of severe cardiac arrhythmias; this limits its utility (19).

Olanzapine – Oral olanzapine is commonly used in the UK to help with acute behavioural disturbance. Intramuscular olanzapine was commonly used for RT in the UK but is now limited to unlicensed use as it was withdrawn from the UK market for commercial reasons in 2013. Intramuscular olanzapine is as effective as IM haloperidol with lesser risk of extra pyramidal side effects and QT interval disturbance (25). Intravenous olanzapine has been used in ED and ICU settings. Both IV and IM routes pose the risk of respiratory depression and hypoxia (hence close monitoring is needed) and may require intubation in a minority of patients. The concomitant use of IM or IV olanzapine and benzodiazepines should also be avoided due to increased risk of hypotension, bradycardia and respiratory depression (6). There should be an interval of at least 1 hour between the two.

Droperidol – Droperidol was withdrawn in 2001 due to an association with QTc prolongation and carries a 'black box' warning by the US Food and Drug Administration (FDA). It is not FDA approved for psychiatric use and is only licensed for nausea and vomiting in the UK. However, more recent studies suggest that the cardiac risks are lower than previously thought. In ED settings, Calver and colleagues found QT prolongation in just 1.3%, with no cases of serious adverse cardiac events (27).

In psychiatric settings, IM droperidol (10 mg) was found to be as effective as IM haloperidol (10 mg). A 2016 Cochrane review supported its use to manage acute disturbance caused by psychosis (28).

Droperidol is currently endorsed by the RCEM for parenteral use in the ED when patients present with behavioural disturbance secondary to delirium (21). A baseline ECG is advised, similar to haloperidol, and consider alternatives in patients with acute traumatic brain injury.

Aripiprazole, Risperidone and Quetiapine – IM aripiprazole has been found to be as effective as IM haloperidol in patients with psychosis (but required more doses per unit time) but significantly less effective than IM olanzapine at reducing agitation. Because of limited available evidence, it is generally not recommended as a first-line agent. Similarly, the quality of evidence for both risperidone and quetiapine as agents for RT is insufficient to draw any firm conclusions or make any recommendations.

Loxapine – Loxapine is a first-generation antipsychotic which is structurally related to clozapine. The FDA approved its inhalatory formulation in acute behavioural disturbance associated with schizophrenia or bipolar I disorder in 2012. It has rapid onset of action and high bioavailability with a non-invasive route, although some cooperation from the patient is required. Although licensed, it is not commonly used for RT in the UK. It is contraindicated in patients with acute respiratory distress or with active airways disease as it can cause bronchospasm. A bronchodilator (e.g. salbutamol) should be available when used in such patients (29).

Haloperidol Plus Promethazine – The *tranquilização rápida-ensaio clínico* (TREC) studies are a collection of ageing yet methodologically robust, multicentre, pragmatic randomised controlled trials (RCTs). They evaluated the effectiveness of IM haloperidol (5–10 mg) plus IM promethazine (25–50 mg) ('the combination') versus IM midazolam, IM lorazepam, IM haloperidol or IM olanzapine for the purpose of RT in psychiatric emergencies (19). Collectively, the TREC studies concluded that IM haloperidol and promethazine in combination is more rapidly effective than IM lorazepam or IM haloperidol alone. When compared with IM olanzapine, the combination of IM haloperidol and promethazine was as rapidly effective and had a longer-lasting sedative effect. Only IM midazolam was more rapidly sedating than the combination, but respiratory depression was a concern. IM haloperidol alone was associated with an unacceptably high (6.4%) incidence of acute dystonia, in comparison to the combination.

These trials informed 2015 NICE guidance (13) and a 2016 Cochrane review, which concluded that a combination of IM haloperidol 5–10 mg plus IM promethazine 25–50 mg is an effective and safe strategy (26). A 2017 meta-analysis (24) also supported this combination, both for efficacy and safety, and it is currently endorsed by the British Association for Psychopharmacology (19).

Haloperidol Plus Lorazepam – This is a commonly used combination (in separate syringes) in the UK for RT. Two meta-analyses have reviewed the role of combination of haloperidol plus benzodiazepines in psychosis-induced aggression or agitation. Ostinelli and colleagues (24) focussed on haloperidol in 2017, while Zaman and colleagues (22) focussed on benzodiazepines in 2018. There was no clear difference in efficacy between using haloperidol alone or in combination. Antihistamines (such as promethazine) appear to be better adjuncts to haloperidol than benzodiazepines but adding lorazepam lowers the total dose required of haloperidol, thus reducing the risk of extra pyramidal side effects.

Other Medications

Ketamine – Ketamine is an *N*-methyl-D-aspartate (NMDA) receptor antagonist that is primarily used as an anaesthetic agent. However, over the last decade, it has been shown to be effective in severe acute behavioural disturbance, mostly in EDs or pre-hospital settings by paramedics. It has a rapid onset of action (less than 5 minutes) and causes few haemodynamic changes (30). Its use in EDs was endorsed in 2017 by the American College of Emergency Physicians and by the RCEM in 2022. The RCEM highlighted ketamine's rapid onset of action and wide therapeutic window without respiratory compromise but emphasised caution regarding its sympathomimetic activity conferring theoretical risk of exacerbating cardiovascular instability (21).

It is also associated with a high complication rate, including vomiting, hypersalivation, laryngospasm and emergence phenomena. It is associated with a relatively high requirement for airway management, with up to 30% of patients requiring intubation (31) and 20% requiring active airway management (32), most of which were in pre-hospital settings. It is primarily sedating as opposed to tranquillising and safer when used in environments where resuscitation facilities are present. Based on current evidence, parenteral ketamine is unlikely to be used for first-line RT in psychiatry settings (19). Intranasal ketamine is also being investigated as it may be safer and easier to use.

Promethazine – Promethazine is a sedating antihistamine with anticholinergic effects. IM promethazine (25–50 mg) can be a helpful sedative option as monotherapy in benzodiazepine-tolerant patients (33). IM promethazine has good evidence as an effective adjunct to IM haloperidol (26) and is also recommended by NICE (13).

Dexmedetomidine – Dexmedetomidine (IV infusion), a highly selective α2-adrenergic receptor agonist, has been shown to be effective in preventing or reducing the duration of delirium in intensive care units in general hospitals. Recent warnings from the European Medicines Agency emphasise caution however due to trial data suggesting increased risk of mortality in patients aged under 65 years (34). Sublingual Dexmedetomidine is currently under review as an alternative (35).

Choice of Specific Medications

Choice of medication should take into account the patient's preferences if known, pre-existing physical health problems or pregnancy, possible intoxication, previous response to medications including adverse effects, the potential for interactions with other medications and the total daily dose of medications prescribed and administered (13). The age of the patient, availability of resuscitation facilities, severity and suspected cause of acute behavioural disturbance, level of cooperation from the patient and familiarity of the clinician with the available drugs should also guide the choice of medication, along with local/national guidelines when present.

A systematic review and meta-analysis (36) of 53 RCTs for acute agitation in patients within a psychiatric setting concluded that olanzapine, haloperidol and promethazine or

Table 11.1 Usual doses of commonly used medications to manage acute behavioural disturbance

Name	Dose (oral)*	Dose (IM)*	Dose (IV)*	Additional remarks
Benzodiazepines				
Lorazepam	1–2 mg	1–2 mg	1–2 mg	May be repeated in 30–60 minutes
Midazolam	Buccal 5 mg	5 mg	2 – 5 mg	
Diazepam	5–10 mg	10 mg	5–10 mg (5 mg/minute)	May be repeated after 4 hours
Antipsychotics				
Haloperidol	5–10 mg (1–5 mg in delirium)	5 mg	5 mg	IM may be repeated in an hour
Droperidol	NA	5 mg	2.5 mg	Off-label use
Olanzapine	5–10 mg	5–10 mg	5 mg	IM/IV – off-label use
Risperidone	1–2 mg	1–2 mg	NA	
Other medications				
Ketamine	NR	2–4 mg/kg	1–2 mg/kg	Only for EDs
Promethazine	25–50 mg	25–50 mg	NR	Off-label use

NA = not applicable; NR = not recommended; *consider dose reductions of 50% in elderly patients.

droperidol are the most effective and safe for use as RT, with midazolam restricted to use within EDs in general hospitals (see Table 11.1).

Consensus guidelines produced by the World Federation of Societies for Biological Psychiatry (WFSBP) (6) and the BETA project (18) recommend:

- acute behavioural disturbance due to alcohol withdrawal, stimulant intoxication or non-psychotic agitation: benzodiazepines.
- acute behavioural disturbance due to a medical condition, alcohol intoxication or psychotic agitation: antipsychotics.

The NICE 2015 guideline (13) recommends:

- IM lorazepam alone or IM haloperidol plus IM promethazine for RT in adults.
- IM lorazepam is preferred if there is limited clinical information available, if the patient is antipsychotic naïve, if there is evidence of cardiovascular disease including a prolonged QTc or if no ECG has been carried out.
- If there is a partial response to IM lorazepam, a further dose is recommended. However, if there is no response, IM haloperidol plus IM promethazine is recommended for consideration (even if no ECG is available).

- Similarly, if there is a partial response to IM haloperidol plus IM promethazine, a further dose is suggested, but if there is no response, IM lorazepam is recommended if it has not already been used.

Rapid Tranquilisation during Pregnancy

Where necessary, an antipsychotic or a benzodiazepine with a short half-life should be considered at the minimum effective dose because of the risk of neonatal extrapyramidal symptoms (with antipsychotics) or floppy baby syndrome (with benzodiazepines). The Maudsley Prescribing Guidelines published in the UK (33) state that acute use of short-acting benzodiazepines such as lorazepam and of the sedative antihistamine promethazine is unlikely to be harmful.

Physical Health Monitoring after Rapid Tranquilisation

The process of RT confers various risks. These include adverse effects of medications, risks due to comorbid health conditions or other factors present (such as pregnancy, substance misuse) and risks due to polypharmacy and drug interactions, besides the potentially risky process of restraining and/or forcefully delivering the medications. This is in addition to the fact that medical causes of acute behavioural disturbance pose additional risks in terms of deterioration of physical health (21). Hence close monitoring after RT is essential.

The British Association of Psychopharmacology (19) recommends including all those physical health parameters as monitored by the National Early Warning Score (NEWS), namely temperature, pulse, systolic blood pressure, respiratory rate, oxygen saturation, level of consciousness and new confusion. Monitoring parameters recommended by NICE (13) also include hydration status. These parameters should be monitored at least every hour until there are no further concerns or every 15 minutes in the following circumstances:

- IM/IV route is used
- The British National Formulary maximum dose has been exceeded
- The patient appears to be asleep or sedated (continuous monitoring with pulse oximeter recommended)
- The patient has taken illicit drugs or alcohol
- The patient has a pre-existing physical health problem or has experienced any harm as a result of any restrictive intervention.

Fifteen-minute checks should be carried out for at least an hour and until there are no further concerns. An ECG should be obtained and an examination for extrapyramidal side effects should take place when parenteral antipsychotics (particularly haloperidol) are used.

If, following the use of benzodiazepines, respiratory rate falls below 10/min, flumazenil 200 µg IV should be given over 15 seconds. It can be repeated in 100-µg doses given over 15 seconds, if needed, after 1-minute intervals (usual dose 300–600 µg, max 1 mg in 24 hours). It is contraindicated in patients with epilepsy on long-term benzodiazepines (33).

In summary, de-escalation and least restrictive non-pharmacological management should precede use of medications if possible. Medications should be offered orally in preference to parenteral routes where possible. Although lorazepam and haloperidol-promethazine combination are the first-line recommended medications for RT by NICE guidelines, practice is evolving and the choice of medication depends on several factors, including individual patient characteristics and local policy recommendations. Any episode of RT must be followed by monitoring of physical health checks and ongoing review of the management plan.

Next Steps after De-escalation and Medication

Has a cause for acute behavioural disturbance been found? If not, and the patient is calmer, the ED and CL teams should complete parallel medical and psychiatric assessments. If there is no clear medical or psychiatric cause for the presentation, a discussion should take place about whether police involvement is necessary if property has been damaged or someone was assaulted during the assessment process. Where further evaluation is required, decisions should be made about (1) whether a general hospital or psychiatric inpatient setting is appropriate and (2) whether any legal frameworks need to be considered (Mental Health Act and Mental Capacity Act). Offer advice on behavioural management (low-stimulus environment, boundary-setting, awareness of trigger points) and prescribing advice so that the receiving team have a contingency plan if there is further behavioural disturbance. A timeline for repeat review should also be agreed if further input from the CL team is required.

Debriefing

Debriefing can sometimes be overlooked during a busy shift but it represents a valuable opportunity to support colleagues, build effective working relationships and improve services. Debriefing might include enquiring about staff well-being, thoughts on what went well and what could be improved, what people learned and how to plan for future incidents of acute behavioural disturbance. Debriefing with the patient provides a valuable opportunity for the patient to share their thoughts and feelings, to maintain therapeutic rapport and to reduce the risk of repeat escalation. Ask the patient how they were feeling and how they are currently. Take the opportunity to explain to the patient why staff members did what they did and reiterate that the focus is on trying to help and keep everyone safe. Collaborate on ways to prevent further escalation (asking for time out, a person to talk things through with, as-required medication) and ask how they would like the situation to be managed if they re-escalate.

Final Word: Ethnography and Impact Studies – Strategies for Reducing Violence in Acute Settings

A collaborative study between the Design Council and Department of Health outlined potential benefits of initiatives designed to reduce violence in NHS settings (37). These included tangible cost savings, improved staff confidence and job satisfaction, improved patient care through calmer environments and fostering a culture of mutual trust and respect between staff and patients. Design teams across the UK were invited to construct systems-based solutions for reducing violence in the ED. Proposals had to be easy to implement, non-provider-specific, retrofittable, flexible, affordable and effective. Ethnographic data were collected to identify staff, patient and environmental factors that could contribute to violence in the ED and existing data across a range of sectors were used to further inform the design process (hospitals, the criminal justice system, airports and transport organisations, bars, pubs and clubs). Factors contributing to violence in the ED included:

- Crowded waiting areas with people forced together by difficult circumstances, each undergoing their own stress and dealing with their own complex mix of clinical and non-clinical needs.
- Opacity and uncertainty of wait times to be seen and treated and perceived inefficiency, disorganisation and lack of focus.
- The ED as a busy, dehumanising and inhospitable environment, crowded with equipment and people.
- Staff emotional and physical fatigue juxtaposed with pressure for high patient turnover.

Design challenges included making the ED process more user-centred, diversifying spaces within the ED and placing safety at the centre of this, improving the waiting experience, using communication and design to reinforce positive behaviour and avoid aggression and violence, and making ED processes and pathways clearer and more transparent for patients.

Standards were set for the patient journey through the ED from pre-arrival, arrival and check in through to waiting, assessment, treatment and departure, with ethnographic data illustrating factors which negatively intersect with the journey (lack of information, disorientation, overcrowding, lack of privacy, noisy, etc.). Solutions were generated based on field data such as better signage, CCTV and security presence in the ED, staff welcoming role and better facilities in the waiting area.

Three distinct outputs were identified to improve patient and staff experience in the ED:

- Empowering patients by providing information about the department, waiting times and treatment practices by using environmental signage, patient leaflets, live and interactive digital platforms, map of patient's journey and so on.
- Providing person-centred training and reflective sessions for staff to regain their ability to provide compassionate care following a difficult experience.
- Providing NHS managers, designers and healthcare planners with information and guidance on providing an effective ED environment.

Practical detail is outlined in the report and the authors recommend it for any readers interested in this particular aspect of service development. Pilot studies at St George's Hospital, London and Southampton General Hospital demonstrated a significant reduction in aggression and violence in the ED. Furthermore, every £1 spent on design solutions generated £3 in benefits (38).

References

1. Lindenmayer JP. Pathophysiology of agitation. *J Clin Psychiatry*. 2000;**61** (suppl. 14):5–10.

2. Gottlieb M, Long B, Koyfman A. Approach to the agitated emergency department patient. *J Emerg Med*. 2018;54(4):447–57.

3. Marco CA, Vaughan J. Emergency management of agitation in schizophrenia. *Am J Emerg Med*. 2005; **23** (6):767–76.

4. Downes MA, Healy P, Page CB et al. Structured team approach to the agitated patient in the emergency department. *Emerg Med Australas*. 2009;21(3):196–202.

5. Citrome L, Volavka J. The psychopharmacology of violence: Making

sensible decisions. *CNS Spectr.* 2014;**19** (5):411–18.

6. Garriga M, Pacchiarotti I, Kasper S et al. Assessment and management of agitation in psychiatry: Expert consensus. *World J Biol Psychiatry.* 2016;**17**(2):86–128.

7. Nordstrom K, Zun LS, Wilson MP et al. Medical evaluation and triage of the agitated patient: Consensus statement of the American Association for Emergency Psychiatry Project Beta medical evaluation workgroup. *West J Emerg Med.* 2012;**13** (1):3–10.

8. Soyka M, Ufer S. Aggressiveness in schizophrenia: Prevalence, psychopathological and sociodemographic correlates. *Fortschr Neurol Psychiatr.* 2002;**70**(4):171–7.

9. Pilowsky LS, Ring H, Shine PJ, Battersby M, Lader M. Rapid tranquillisation: A survey of emergency prescribing in a general psychiatric hospital. *Br J Psychiatry.* 1992;**160**:831–5.

10. Swann AC, Lafer B, Perugi G et al. Bipolar mixed states: An international society for bipolar disorders task force report of symptom structure, course of illness, and diagnosis. *Am J Psychiatry.* 2013;**170** (1):31–42.

11. Schatzberg AF, DeBattista C. Phenomenology and treatment of agitation. *J Clin Psychiatry.* 1999;**60**(suppl. 15):17–20.

12. Moukaddam N, Flores A, Matorin A et al. Difficult patients in the emergency department: Personality disorders and beyond. *Psychiatr Clin North Am.* 2017;**40** (3):379–95.

13. National Institute for Health and Care Excellence. Violence and aggression: Short term management in mental health, health and community care settings. 2015. www .nice.org.uk/guidance/ng10.

14. Swift RH, Harrigan EP, Cappelleri JC et al. Validation of the behavioural activity rating scale (BARS): A novel measure of activity in agitated patients. *J Psychiatr Res.* 2002;**36**(2):87–95.

15. Woods P, Almvik R. The Brøset violence checklist (BVC). *Acta Psychiatr Scand Suppl.* 2002;**412**:103–5.

16. Bjørkly S, Hartvig P, Heggen FA et al. Development of a brief screen for violence risk (V-RISK-10) in acute and general psychiatry: An introduction with emphasis on findings from a naturalistic test of interrater reliability. *Eur Psychiatry.* 2009;**24**(6):388–94.

17. Bogner JA, Corrigan JD, Bode RK, Heinemann AW. Rating scale analysis of the Agitated Behavior Scale. *J Head Trauma Rehabil.* 2000;**15**(1):656–69.

18. Roppolo, LP, Morris, DW, Khan, F et al. Improving the management of acutely agitated patients in the emergency department through implementation of Project BETA (Best Practices in the Evaluation and Treatment of Agitation). *JACEP Open.* 2020;1–10.

19. Patel MX, Sethi FN, Barnes TR et al. Joint BAP NAPICU evidence-based consensus guidelines for the clinical management of acute disturbance: De-escalation and rapid tranquillisation. *J Psychopharmacol.* 2018;**32**(6):601–40.

20. Richmond JS, Berlin JS, Fishkind AB et al. Verbal de-escalation of the agitated patient: Consensus statement of the American Association for Emergency Psychiatry Project BETA de-escalation workgroup. *West J Emerg Med.* 2012;**13**(1):17–25.

21. Humphries C, Aw-Yong M, Cowburn P et al. Acute behavioural disturbance in the emergency department. London; 2022.

22. Zaman H, Sampson S, Beck A et al. Benzodiazepines for psychosis-induced aggression or agitation [published correction appears in *Schizophr Bull.* 2018;44(5):1166]. *Schizophr Bull.* 2018;**44** (5):966–9.

23. Parker C. Midazolam for rapid tranquillisation: Its place in practice. *Journal of Psychiatric Intensive Care.* 2015;**11**(1):66–72.

24. Ostinelli EG, Brooke-Powney MJ, Li X, Adams CE. Haloperidol for psychosis-induced aggression or agitation (rapid tranquillisation). *Cochrane*

Database Syst Rev. 2017;7(7):CD009377. doi: 10.1002/14651858.CD009377.pub3.

25. Kishi T, Matsunaga S and Iwata N. Intramuscular olanzapine for agitated patients: A systematic review and meta-analysis of randomized controlled trials. J Psychiatr Res. 2015;**68**:198–209.

26. Huf G, Alexander J, Gandhi P, Allen MH. Haloperidol plus promethazine for psychosis-induced aggression. *Cochrane Database Syst Rev.* 2016;**11.**

27. Calver L, Page CB, Downes MA et al. The safety and effectiveness of droperidol for sedation of acute behavioral disturbance in the emergency department. *Ann Emerg Med.* 2015;**66**(3):230–8.e1.

28. Khokhar MA, Rathbone J. Droperidol for psychosis-induced aggression or agitation. *Cochrane Database Syst Rev.* 2016;**12.**

29. de Berardis D, Fornaro M, Orsolini L et al. The role of inhaled loxapine in the treatment of acute agitation in patients with psychiatric disorders: A clinical review. *Int J Mol Sci.* 2017;**18**(2):349.

30. Tran K, Mierzwinski-Urban M. Ketamine for pharmacological management of aggression and agitation in pre-hospital settings: A review of comparative clinical effectiveness, safety and guidelines. Ottawa; 13 May 2019.

31. Mankowitz SL, Regenberg P, Kaldan J, Cole JB. Ketamine for rapid sedation of agitated patients in the prehospital and emergency department settings: A systematic review and proportional meta-analysis.*J Emerg Med.* 2018;**55**(5):670–81.

32. Sullivan N, Chen C, Siegel R et al. Ketamine for emergency sedation of agitated patients: A systematic review and meta-analysis [published correction appears in *Am J Emerg Med.* 2020;38(8):1702]. *Am J Emerg Med.* 2020;**38**(3):655–61.

33. Taylor, DM, Barnes TRE, Young AH. *The Maudsley Prescribing Guidelines in Psychiatry*, 13th ed. New York; 2018.

34. https://www.ema.europa.eu/en/docu ments/dhpc/direct-healthcare-profes sional-communication-dhpc-dexmedeto midine-increased-risk-mortality-intensive _en.pdf.

35. Hsiao JK. Sublingual dexmedetomidine as a potential new treatment for agitation. *JAMA.* 2022;**327**(8):723–5.

36. Bak M, Weltens I, Bervoets, C et al. The pharmacological management of agitated and aggressive behaviour: A systematic review and meta-analysis. *Eur J Psychiatry.* 2019;**57**:78–100.

37. Design Council, Department of Health. Reducing violence and aggression in A&E through a better experience. 2015. www .designcouncil.org.uk/fileadmin/uploads/ dc/Documents/ReducingViolenceAndAgg ressionInAandE.pdf.

38. Design Council. A&E design challenge: An evaluation summary. 2013. www .designcouncil.org.uk/our-work/skills-learning/resources/ae-design-challenge-impact-evaluation.

Chapter 12

The Neurology–Psychiatry Interface

Annalie Clark and Rachel Thomasson

The Psychiatry–Neurology Interface: Re-blurring the Landscape

Historically, the boundaries between neurology, neuropathology and psychiatry were somewhat blurred as clinicians were encouraged to see disorders of brain and mind as arising from a common organic denominator. It was not uncommon to see psychiatrists at the microscope making landmark discoveries (Alois Alzheimer and Solomon Carter-Fuller, to name just two of them), yet the twentieth century saw these three disciplines fractionate. Neurology and neuropathology retained collaborative threads as neurology became established as the speciality of organic brain disease, while psychiatry did not regain traction as a credible medico-scientific discipline for several decades. Thankfully, the boundaries between the three disciplines are once again blurred as it has become clear that many neurological conditions include symptoms commonly recognised and treated by psychiatrists. This chapter outlines how to approach assessment and diagnosis and gives an overview of psychiatric presentations in several core neurology topics including stroke, epilepsy, Parkinson's disease and autoimmune disorders.

Approach to Assessment 1: Known Neurological Diagnosis

Readers are directed to Chapter 1 for more detail on the basic assessment framework in consultation-liaison (CL) psychiatry. Where the neurological diagnosis is known, is this a first presentation or is the patient several years into their journey with this condition? If it is a repeat presentation, are there features that the patient considers to be new or atypical? Is there any comment on these features from the neurology team and, if so, are these features felt to be in keeping with the diagnosis or is there suspicion of either functional overlay or a parallel organic disorder? What is your own opinion? Consider whether you would anticipate a progressive, fluctuating, relapsing-remitting or static presentation for the diagnosed condition and over what time period. Acquired insults can include traumatic brain injury, vascular insult or status epilepticus; these typically present with abrupt onset of impairment, followed by varying degrees of recovery over weeks, months or even a year or two. Parkinson's disease can fluctuate but is progressive and motor neurone disease is relentlessly and often rapidly progressive.

One of the key reasons for considering the trajectory of disease is to look at how a patient might be adjusting to the condition and whether their insight and expectations regarding prognosis are influenced by factors such as fear, anger and resulting cognitive distortions (minimising, black-and-white thinking and catastrophising are examples). Equally importantly, if there is a temporal relationship between psychiatric symptoms and the pattern of progression, one has to ask whether symptoms are principally organically driven (anxiety when switched off in Parkinson's disease may be better treated by adjusting dopaminergic medications; post-ictal dysphoria and psychoses may require optimisation of the anticonvulsant regimen in addition to psychotropic medication, etc.).

Approach to Assessment 2: Is This a Primary Psychiatric Disorder or a Neurological Condition?

This is not always an easy question to answer. Some CL teams have a neuropsychiatrist as part of the team; where separate services exist, the authors advocate building collaborative relationships between the CL team and the neighbouring neuropsychiatry service. Cross-fertilisation of diagnostic opinions and case formulations can lead to meaningful progress in terms of drafting the roadmap for further investigation and treatment.

Constructing a differential diagnosis when patients present to general hospital settings with psychiatric symptoms can be challenging, particularly for depression and anxiety. Context is particularly important in terms of ancillary symptoms and signs in conjunction with what is known from investigation results.

The 'surgical sieve' is as relevant today as it was when the reader (and the authors, for that matter) was in medical school (1). It enables systematic consideration of the facts at hand, provides a method for expanding history-taking and examination and acts as a scaffold for considering relevant investigations. There are various permutations but a common working example is given below. Differential diagnoses under each of these subheadings can be extensive and it is beyond the scope of this chapter to discuss each of these in detail. Some pointers are given in what follows.

- **V:** vascular
- **I:** infective
- **T:** traumatic
- **A:** autoimmune
- **M:** metabolic/endocrine
- **I:** iatrogenic (medications/procedures)
- **N:** neoplastic
- **D:** degenerative

Vascular insults are often abrupt and may be recurrent/cumulative as in the case of amyloid angiopathy or Binswanger's disease. Vascular risk factors and focal neurology such as face or limb signs may or may not be apparent and imaging is often helpful for confirming one's suspicions. Thalamic infarcts, for example, are a lesser-known cause of drowsiness and aggression (2).

Infections often carry a history spanning days or weeks, though even in the era of highly active antiretroviral therapy (HAART), cases of untreated HIV infection can present years after seroconversion. These patients may present with insidious progression of neuro-psychiatric sequelae, acutely with encephalitis or progressive multifocal leukoencephalo-pathy (PML). Latent presentations of tertiary syphilis are commonly considered as an infective cause of neuropsychiatric presentations; a couple of lesser-known possibilities include subacute sclerosing panencephalitis, a rare and rapidly fatal complication of measles infection that often lays dormant for over a decade and can initially present with personality change and depression. Whipple's disease is an uncommon but important infective cause of diarrhoea, joint pain, cognitive impairment and psychosis.

Intracranial injury due to trauma may not be apparent in the history, possibly because of an unwitnessed fall or seizure with associated post-traumatic or post-ictal amnesia. Injuries sustained while intoxicated may not be subsequently recalled. Imaging is often helpful as the presentation may be non-specific (drowsiness, confusion, aggression) in the early stages of injury.

Psychiatric presentations due to autoimmune disease may stem from central nervous system (CNS) complications of systemic autoimmune disease such as Lupus or primary CNS inflammatory disorders such as multiple sclerosis. There is also an expanding number of anti-neuronal antibodies that can cause encephalitis, and some of these cases initially present with anxious and depressive symptoms, cognitive impairment, mania and psychosis (3).

Metabolic and endocrine causes of altered mental state may be confirmed or initially revealed using routine blood tests, parathyroid hormone and early morning cortisol levels. Common examples include electrolyte disturbance, thyroid disease and vitamin B12 deficiency. Wernicke-Korsakoff presentations should be considered in self-neglecting patients with no history of alcohol misuse and patients in young or middle adulthood with Parkinsonian, dystonia and/or cerebellar signs should be evaluated for brain copper (Wilson's disease), calcium (Fahr's disease) and iron (multiple) deposition syndromes. Presentations in later life are rare but not impossible (4). Relapsing-remitting attacks of porphyria can present with variable psychiatric symptoms and signs and ancillary clues such as gut disturbance, neuropathy and dysautonomia may be absent or transient. Bear in mind that treatment resistant seronegative autoimmune encephalitis or recurrent presentations of functional gut disorder might very occasionally represent this somewhat outmoded but genuine diagnostic possibility (5).

Clinical Tip

For the patient with severe traumatic brain injury 12 months ago who is struggling with depressed mood and lethargy, consider discussing the possibility of growth hormone deficiency with endocrinology colleagues (6).

The origins of psychiatric symptoms and signs in patients with neoplastic disease are complex. Brain parenchyma may be damaged or distorted by invasion, mass effect, oedema or haemorrhage. Autoimmune encephalitis may occur due to paraneoplastic disease. Radiotherapy and chemotherapy have been associated with disorders of mood and cognition (7, 8). Surgical resection can lead to loss of eloquent tissue and complications (stroke, seizures, infection) may present as delirium or more enduring cognitive impairment.

Expanding the Mental State Examination

Psychiatrists are experts when it comes to observing human behaviour. The goal here is not to feel under pressure to clinch small-print neurological diagnoses but to expand the range of observations and to comment on what might be atypical for a patient presenting with a primary psychiatric disorder so that the referring team receive valuable clues for furthering diagnostic pursuit.

Appearance: an opportunity to look for facial asymmetry, hypomimia (reduced facial expression) and reduced blink rate, orofacial dyskinesias. Gaze palsy may also be evident. Does the neck appear pulled backwards (retrocollis) or flexed forwards (antecollis)? Can the patient sit upright unsupported or is there truncal ataxia? Is gait normal; if not, what do you see (broad-based lurch, waddling, shuffling, legs scissoring in front of each other, one or both feet scuffing, to name a few examples)?

Behaviour: comment on level of alertness and whether it fluctuates. Is there a paucity of spontaneous speech and behaviour that resembles apathy or with patience; does it represent delayed response latency? If eye contact is poor, could this be due to poor attention or gaze palsy? When considering psychomotor status, is there an excess of movement resembling tremor or fidgeting that could be chorea or dyskinesia? Are there myoclonic jerks?

Speech: look for hypophonic speech seen in Parkinsonian disorders, dysarthria, word-finding difficulties and delayed response latency. Are there word errors; if so, are they sound-based (phonological) errors or semantic errors? If aphasia is present, is it expressive, receptive or both? Is there a right hemispheric lesion causing dysprosody?

Mood and affect: common referrals for depression or mania in patients with acquired brain injury or other neurological conditions actually pertain to mood lability, pseudobulbar affect or frontal lobe injury curtailing affectual range. It can be particularly helpful for patients to receive comment on whether the mood disturbance is organically driven, medication-related, part of an adjustment disorder or indeed reflective of a primary anxiety, depression or mania.

It is inevitable that there will be an adjustment process to experiencing physical illness and being diagnosed with a chronic, possibly progressive, neurological disorder. Patients may go through a process of grieving for various losses associated with their illness. A range of emotions may be experienced, including sadness, anger and guilt – these tend to become less intense as the individual adjusts to their symptoms and diagnosis, though may recur with progression of the illness or flares of symptoms (for further detail, see Chapter 4). Psychoeducation and reassurance are important to support this adjustment process. A 'normal' adjustment process needs to be distinguished from an adjustment disorder and a depressive disorder.

Adjustment disorder is a 'maladaptive reaction' to an identifiable psychosocial stressor (i.e. diagnosis of neurological illness) (9). It usually occurs within a month of the stressor but can be delayed. It is characterised by a preoccupation with the stressor and its implications, which impacts an individuals' functioning, but importantly none of the symptoms are of sufficient severity to meet the criteria of a more specific diagnosis (10). Depression tends to get worse with time and be associated with anhedonia and more pervasive negative cognitions. Psychomotor changes and frequent suicidal ideation are also suggestive of depression (for further detail, see Chapter 6). It should be noted, however, that research has found it can be difficult to differentiate these disorders; importantly, prognosis after six months may be similar, leading O'Keefe and colleagues to highlight the importance of focussing on biopsychosocial formulation of medically ill patients who present with symptoms along the spectrum of 'general distress syndrome' rather than wrangling over diagnostics labels (10).

Thought form and content: consider whether tangentiality, derailment and blocking are reflective of executive dysfunction or memory impairment. Are neologisms and word salad related to phonological errors and semantic impairment respectively? Delusional beliefs are observed in a broad spectrum of neurological conditions (stroke, epilepsy, multiple sclerosis, neurometabolic disorders and synucleopathies, to name a few); although not a discriminating feature for a particular condition, their presence warrants further scrutiny for organic drivers.

Perception: traditionally, the presence of visual or olfactory hallucinations led to pro-active search for organic causes, whereas now suspicions are raised for hallucinoses in any sensory modality. Abrupt onset, confinement to one hemifield, nostril or dermatome warrants further enquiry for an anatomical or pathological correlate (e.g. headache, seiz-ures, impairment of a special sense, history of stroke).

Cognition: desktop cognitive screens can be difficult to administer to an acutely unwell patient. The clinical interview can be used to survey different areas of cognitive function including memory, language, visuo-spatial function, praxis and frontal lobe function.

Stroke, Parkinson's disease, epilepsy and multiple sclerosis represent four of the largest zones of neurological practice and requests for psychiatric input are common. We present an overview of psychiatric presentations in each of these areas.

Core Neurology Topics for CL Teams 1: Stroke

Depression

Post-stroke depression (PSD) occurs in approximately 33% of stroke survivors (11). Rates are higher in the first year following stroke (12). It is associated with higher all-cause mortality and adverse outcomes, including severe disability, limitations in daily activities and slower functional recovery (13). It has also been associated with increased rates of anxiety, suicidal ideation and suicide attempts (11, 13).

Predictors of PSD are inconsistent across studies but generally include (11, 12):

- Female gender
- Family history of mental illness
- Comorbid anxiety
- Stroke severity, aphasia, dysphagia, combined physical and cognitive impairment
- Frontal lobe and basal ganglia infarcts, diffuse white matter change on imaging
- Pre-stroke depression and life events
- Dependence for activities of daily living
- Perceived lack of family and social support.

Assessment

PSD can present with more cognitive difficulties, less anhedonia and less sleep disturbance than depressive episodes in the general population (12). It can be difficult to partition somatic symptoms of depression from some of the physical effects of stroke (14). Exploring psychological symptoms of depression, such as guilt, hopeless-ness and worthlessness, can help to differentiate a depressive episode (12). Changes in facial expression and verbal communication can mask symptoms of depression (14). The Stroke Aphasic Depression Questionnaire and the Depression Intensity Scale Circles can be helpful in this respect.

Clinical Tip

Is it (solely) depression? Consider hypoactive delirium, apathy, pseudobulbar affect, catastrophic reactions and adjustment issues as alternatives and comorbidities.

Treatment of PSD

There is evidence that antidepressant treatment can reduce depressive symptom scores and increase remission rates, but a Cochrane review published in 2020 concludes that existing trials have methodological limitations impacting the quality of evidence (15). Antidepressant trials in PSD report increased rates of CNS and gastrointestinal adverse effects. In general, selective serotonin reuptake inhibitors (SSRIs) tend to be considered first-line for treatment of PSD due to the higher risk of significant adverse effects such as hip fracture with tricyclic antidepressants (TCAs). Data are mixed regarding risk of intracranial haemorrhage and use of SSRIs (16) and, as such, we recommend individual risk: benefit analyses, including consideration of type of stroke, current anticoagulation regimen, requirement for gastric protection and alternatives to standard SSRIs (nortriptyline, reboxetine, vortioxetine).

Prognostically, there is evidence that PSD is a chronically relapsing disorder (14), highlighting the importance of implementing early and effective treatment. Data are mixed regarding the efficacy of antidepressant prophylaxis after stroke. A 2021 Cochrane review specifically examining the effect of SSRIs on stroke recovery identified high-quality evidence that SSRIs reduce the risk of future depression but are also associated with increased bone fractures and seizures (17). In patients with risk factors for PSD, therefore, it certainly warrants consideration but is not without risk.

On review of data from studies using a variety of psychological treatment modalities, the Cochrane review cited earlier concluded that there was very low-certainty evidence that psychological therapy can increase remission rates in people with PSD (15). Cognitive behavioural therapy (CBT) alone or in combination with antidepressant medication has been shown to improve depressive symptoms in PSD (18). There is also evidence that behavioural activation is beneficial, particularly for individuals with verbal communication difficulties (12).

Anxiety

Post-stroke anxiety is common but is relatively under-recognised, under-treated and under-researched. The pooled prevalence of anxiety assessed by clinical interview has been estimated at 19%, although heterogeneity is high (95% CI 12.5%–24.9%) (19). Anxiety remains prevalent beyond the acute phase of stroke and may increase with time. It is associated with poor quality of life, increased dependence and reduced social participation three months after stroke (20). Risk factors for developing post-stroke anxiety include female gender, younger age, PSD, chronic pain, sleep disturbance, communication difficulties, lower socio-economic status and being unable to work after stroke (19, 20). There are few published trials of pharmacological or psychological interventions for anxiety disorders post-stroke and no placebo-controlled trials. As such, a 2017 Cochrane review concluded that there is not enough high-quality evidence to guide clinical practice (20).

Mania

Prevalence estimates of post-stroke mania are limited to case series but the consensus is that it is relatively uncommon (<2%) (14, 21). The clinical presentation after stroke is similar to primary mania, although occurring at an older age. Elevated mood was the primary symptom in 92% of patients. Common points in case histories included male gender, no family or personal history of psychiatric disorder and at least one vascular risk factor;

right-sided cerebral infarcts tended to predominate. Onset of manic symptoms occurred immediately post-stroke in 53% of patients, a further 23% within the first month, and some patients presented up to 24 months post-stroke (21). There are no placebo-controlled or double-blind clinical trials for treatment of manic symptoms post-stroke. There are few longitudinal data on the prognosis of post-stroke mania but recurrence of manic or hypomanic symptoms has been reported (21).

Psychosis

The prevalence of either delusions or hallucinations post-stroke has been estimated at around 5%, but this figure is pooled from studies in a number of different settings and time-points post-stroke (22). Average time to onset of psychotic symptoms over a 10-year period has been reported as 6.1 months but in 8% of cases it was the main presenting symptom at the time of stroke diagnosis. Delusional disorder was the most common presentation (31.1%), including delusional misidentification, persecutory delusions, delusional jealousy, reduplicative paramnesia and somatic delusions (22). Auditory and visual hallucinations also have been reported (14). The case literature trends towards right hemispheric lesions and it is noteworthy that psychosis can also surface after transient ischaemic attacks (22).

Given controversies regarding antipsychotic use and increased risk of stroke (23), it is unsurprising that there have been no controlled studies investigating treatment efficacy in post-stroke psychosis. Treatment with low-dose antipsychotic medication in case reports illustrates cross-sectional therapeutic benefits in terms of reducing distress and psychotic symptom burden but follow-up data are generally lacking. It is noteworthy that post-stroke psychosis is associated with adverse outcomes, including a higher 10-year mortality rate, with cardiovascular disease reported as the most common cause of death (22).

Core Neurology Topics for CL Teams 2: Parkinson's Disease

Depression

Depressive symptoms are common in Parkinson's disease (PD), occurring in 35% of patients, and 17% of patients will experience major depression at some point in the course of the disease (24). Depression in PD is reported as more common in women, those with early onset or advanced PD, cognitive impairment and patients with an external locus of control (25). It is associated with poor quality of life, greater cognitive and functional impairment, reduced adherence to medication, carer stress and increased mortality. There is also evidence that depression may detrimentally impact motor symptoms; untreated depression is associated with earlier initiation of dopaminergic therapy (26).

Assessment

If the patient experiences motor fluctuations secondary to PD medication, try to conduct the assessment during an 'on' phase to ensure accurate assessment. Use of a mood diary can be helpful to assess mood fluctuations as 75% of patients with motor fluctuations also experience anxious and depressive symptoms in the 'off' phase. These fluctuations may respond to adjustments in antiparkinsonian medications that smooth out fluctuations and limit 'off' periods.

Apathy is a common affective disturbance in PD (occurring in around 40% of patients) and it is generally unresponsive to antidepressant medication (24). It follows that 'decreased interest in things' does not always represent a core depressive symptom in this patient group. Common, treatable comorbidities such as anxiety, hypothyroidism and pain syndromes can contribute to low mood in this patient group and should be explored along with cognitive function (25).

Clinical Tip

Always complete a risk assessment – current suicidal ideation is reported in in 11% of PD patients (26).

Treatment

Trial data have generally been supportive of SSRIs, venlafaxine and TCAs (27). There is a theoretical risk of serotonin syndrome if SSRIs are prescribed for patients taking monoamine oxidase inhibitors such as rasagiline, but in clinical practice they are often co-prescribed cautiously without incident. TCAs are poorly tolerated due to anticholinergic and alpha-blocking effects (exacerbating cognitive difficulties, constipation and orthostatic hypotension). For non-serotonergic options, there is limited evidence that agomelatine may be beneficial for depression in PD and may result in improvement in global cognitive function and daytime sleepiness (25). CBT has also been found to be efficacious in patients with depression in PD (26). Electroconvulsive therapy (ECT) is considered to be relatively safe and effective in patients with PD (28). Implanted deep-brain stimulation electrodes do not generally pose a barrier if ECT is clinically indicated (29).

Anxiety

Anxiety disorders can occur at any time point in PD (see Box 12.1). Neurobiological theories posit that anxiety may be an early manifestation of PD-related brain changes (30). The average point prevalence of anxiety disorders in PD is 31% and approximately one third of patients have two or more comorbid anxiety disorders (31). Anxiety disorders in PD are associated with poor quality of life and lower self-perceived health status, higher levels of dependency and increased carer distress. Fluctuations in motor symptoms is the factor most consistently associated with anxiety in PD patients (30). Frequency of freezing has also been associated with the presence of panic disorder (32).

Box 12.1 Psychological Factors Contributing to Anxiety in PD

- Psychological reaction to diagnosis of chronic, progressive disease
- Impact of physical disability on functioning and social role
- Perceived lack of control relating to unpredictability of motor symptoms and of disease progression
- Feeling self-conscious or embarrassed of Parkinsonian symptoms can lead to distress and anxiety in social interactions.

Assessment

There are a number of anxiety symptoms specific to PD. Motor fluctuations can cause situational anxiety. Fear of falling negatively impacts upon quality of life. It should be noted that anxiety rating scales have limitations in patients with Parkinson's disease due to the overlap between somatic symptoms of anxiety and symptoms of PD (30).

Treatment

The evidence base for pharmacological treatments specifically for anxiety in PD is sparse, so treatment planning requires an individualized approach. SSRIs are often used; reports of worsening of parkinsonism have been reported but this is uncommon (32). Adjusting antiparkinsonian medications can be particularly important when there is a clear relationship between motor fluctuations and anxiety. Benzodiazepines may be considered for patients with anxiety and comorbid rapid eye movement sleep behaviour disorder but this requires careful risk–benefit evaluation on an individual patient basis due to the risk of impacting alertness, cognition and increasing risk of falls (38). Pregabalin represents an alternative. There is an equally limited evidence base for psychological treatment of specific anxiety disorders in PD, but there is evidence (primarily from small, non-controlled trials) that CBT improves anxiety symptoms in patients with PD (32).

Psychosis

Psychotic symptoms are common in PD, particularly as the disease progresses. Prevalence estimates depend on symptoms included and population studied; one UK study reported that 60% of patients experienced psychotic symptoms (excluding minor hallucinations) by the end of a 12-year follow-up period (33). They are associated with poorer quality of life, caregiver distress, increased risk of developing dementia, institutionalisation and mortality.

Clinical presentation and assessment

Psychotic symptoms in PD are varied and form a continuum over the course of the disease, which is thought to reflect the progression of Lewy body pathology from brain stem to forebrain systems (33). Minor hallucinations (presence and passage hallucinations, minor illusions) may even precede the onset of motor symptoms. These are generally less disruptive and may not be spontaneously reported. Visual hallucinations are most commonly reported in PD. These tend to be well-formed, recurring images of people or animals. In the early stages, hallucinations often occur during low ambient lighting and may last from seconds to minutes. Other modalities of hallucinations tend to co-occur with visual hallucinations. Delusions reported in PD are most commonly paranoid; other themes have been reported, however, including misidentification syndromes. Assessment should include a search for reversible organic causes as psychosis in PD can mimic delirium and vice versa. Review medication regimens as recent increases in dopaminergic medication can cause or exacerbate psychotic symptoms in PD. Anticholinergic and sedative medications also warrant scrutiny.

Pharmacological options for treating psychotic symptoms in PD centre on rivastigmine, quetiapine, pimavanserin (in the USA) and clozapine. Rivastigmine is generally used to treat visual hallucinosis, particularly in patients with cognitive impairment (34). Quetiapine is commonly used but the evidence base for efficacy is relatively weak as there are no high-quality randomised controlled trials that support its use (35). Sedation and orthostatic hypotension can occur, along with extrapyramidal side effects at higher (>75 mg) doses. Pimavanserin is an inverse 5-HT2A receptor agonist that is efficacious in the short term but trial data for longer term outcomes are lacking (36).

Low-dose clozapine has the best evidence base for treatment of psychosis in PD. It is usually started at 6.25–12 mg daily and titrated according to response (in the UK, the maximum recommended dose is 100 mg daily). Clozapine does not generally worsen motor symptoms; tremor reduction has also been reported (35). Sedation and orthostatic hypotension are commonly reported adverse effects. Neuroleptic malignant syndrome has also been reported.

A word on impulse control disorders:

Patients admitted to general hospital settings may have their anti-parkinsonian medications optimised due to deterioration in motor function. Increased dopaminergic load can lead to psychotic symptoms and also the emergence of impulse control disorders (ICDs) (for a recent review, see (37)). Binge eating and hypersexuality are more likely to be apparent than pathological gambling and spending in hospital settings but emergence of any new compulsive behaviours should raise suspicion of ICD. Treatment centres on reduction of dopaminergic medication (particularly dopamine agonists such as pramipexole and ropinirole); SSRIs are sometimes used as an adjunct to this strategy.

Core Neurology Topics for CL Teams 3: Epilepsy

Approximately 20–40% of people with epilepsy have a comorbid psychiatric condition and this is associated with increased healthcare use, reduced quality of life and premature mortality (38). Anxiety and depression symptoms have been found to explain more variance in health-related quality of life than seizure type or control (39). Suicide rates are high in people with epilepsy; 11.5% of deaths in epilepsy are due to suicide compared to 1% in the general population (40).

Principles for assessment of psychiatric comorbidity in people with epilepsy: careful history-taking is required to establish the temporal relationship of psychiatric symptoms with seizure activity. This is crucial to determine the correct treatment approach. Peri-ictal mental health problems may be more effectively treated by amendments to anticonvulsants or vagal nerve stimulator settings in addition to psychotropic medication, but do not overlook the psychological toll of experiencing seizures.

Psychosocial factors explain most of the variance in mood with people with epilepsy (38) and thus should receive due consideration. Iatrogenic factors should also be considered such as side effects of anticonvulsants and sequelae of epilepsy surgery. A risk assessment is vitally important given the suicide risk in this patient group.

Depression

Depression is common in people with epilepsy, with prevalence estimates of 15–50% depending on study population and definitions used (38). A number of screening tools for depression have been validated in epilepsy; the Neurological Disorders Depression Inventory for Epilepsy (NDDI-E) (41) is a six-item self-report questionnaire which has been designed to circumvent common side effects of anticonvulsants or cognitive problems seen in epilepsy and is gaining traction in UK neurosciences centres.

Peri-ictal mood disturbance is common. Transient dysphoria and suicidality have been reported post-ictally and are usually addressed by optimising seizure control. This is also important when considering inter-ictal depression as correlations exist between seizure frequency and recency of last seizure and risk of a major depressive episode (38). It is helpful to explore the temporal relationship of inter-ictal mood symptoms with any changes in medication, as anticonvulsants such as levetiracetam, zonisamide, topiramate and perampanel can adversely affect mood.

When considering antidepressants, SSRIs are recommended as first-line treatment of depression in people with epilepsy, as they carry a relatively low risk of reducing the seizure threshold (42). Monitor for hyponatraemia if carbamazepine or gabapentin are being prescribed. Fluvoxamine should be avoided due to enzyme-inhibiting effects, which could increase risk of anticonvulsant toxicity. Other antidepressants generally considered low to moderate risk include mirtazapine, reboxetine, vortioxetine, agomelatine, moclobemide and duloxetine. Venlafaxine is generally regarded as safe at therapeutic doses but pro convulsive in overdose. TCAs should be avoided where possible.

Mindfulness-based CBT and acceptance and commitment therapy have been associated with reduction of depressive symptoms burden in people with epilepsy, though evidence is mixed as to whether effects are sustained (38).

Anxiety

Anxiety disorders are common in people with epilepsy. A meta-analysis by Scott and colleagues found an overall pooled prevalence of anxiety disorders of approximately 20%, which is higher than the general population (43). Anxiety symptoms are associated with reduced quality of life and poorer seizure control. Factors contributing to anxiety in epilepsy include the unpredictability and lack of control of recurrent seizures, along with concern about injury during seizures. Anxiety is also a risk factor for suicidality in epilepsy (44).

Pooled prevalence of specific anxiety disorders varies across studies but generalised anxiety is generally the most common diagnosis (43). Patients experiencing spikes of anxiety and panic can be difficult to characterise diagnostically and epileptic prodromes, auras and seizures are sometimes misdiagnosed as anxiety and vice versa. Ictal panic is common in seizures arising from mesial temporal lobe structures and patients may have retained awareness. Ictal anxiety is normally brief and stereotyped, lasting seconds to minutes. It is also important to look for other features of temporal lobe seizures, such as olfactory hallucinations, epigastric rising sensation and déjà vu. Post-ictal anxiety (occurring within 72 hours of seizure offset) commonly includes agoraphobic and compulsive symptoms.

Inter-ictal anxiety is common and often intertwined with the prospect of having further seizures. It is important to explore avoidance and safety behaviours and to exclude a comorbid depressive disorder.

There is a dearth of literature and guidance specifically tailored towards treatment for anxiety in people with epilepsy. In clinical practice, SSRIs, beta blockers and pregabalin are used. It is not uncommon to find patients taking benzodiazepines as part of their anticonvulsant regimen developing tolerance to anxiolytic and sedative effects. Psychological therapy can be valuable for issues such as anticipatory anxiety regarding seizures, post-traumatic stress associated with hospital admission for status epilepticus and adjustment to role loss/change in terms of level of independence and effects of epilepsy on driving and employment status and participation in family life.

> **Box 12.2** Risk Factors for Psychosis in Epilepsy
> - Poorly controlled seizures
> - Left temporal epileptogenic focus
> - Hippocampal sclerosis
> - Neurodevelopmental disorders
> - Early age of epilepsy onset
> - History of status epilepticus
> - Family history of psychosis or affective disorder

Psychosis

Two to seven per cent of people with epilepsy develop psychosis and it is more common in temporal lobe epilepsy (10–15% prevalence) (45). There is often a delay in recognising and treating psychosis (5). Risk factors are shown in Box 12.2.

Ictal Psychosis

Ictal psychosis is characterised by brief bursts of psychotic symptoms that can resemble fluctuations in delirium. It is most commonly associated with focal onset and non-convulsive status epilepticus (46). Temporal lobe foci are usually implicated with occasional reports of seizures arising from frontal and cingulate cortices. The patient often has no recollection after the seizure as consciousness is impaired. Olfactory, gustatory, visual and auditory hallucinations can occur, with non-auditory hallucinations typically being more prominent (45). Delusions tend not to be systematised. There may be evidence of other seizure features, such as motor and oro-buccal automatisms in temporal lobe epilepsy. Ictal psychosis is not always associated with EEG changes.

Post-Ictal Psychosis

In post-ictal psychosis there is often a clear temporal relationship between a seizure and the onset of psychotic symptoms, though seizures are not always witnessed. Psychotic symptoms usually occur within three to seven days of a seizure (or cluster of seizures), typically after a lucid period. Insomnia can be the initial presenting symptom, followed by agitation and psychotic symptoms. Post-ictal psychosis is characterised by typical positive symptoms of psychosis. There can also be an affective component. Typically, symptoms last for days but can last weeks to months. Symptoms can resolve spontaneously but often recur with similar phenomenology (47). One in four cases progress to chronic psychosis (48).

Factors associated with increased risk of post-ictal psychosis:

- bilateral seizure foci, particularly limbic areas
- increased seizure frequency
- longstanding focal epilepsy
- secondary generalisation
- later age of onset of epilepsy
- personal or family history of psychosis
- history of encephalitis
- structural abnormalities on MRI brain.

Inter-ictal Psychosis

Persistent psychotic symptoms can occur independently of seizures and typically develop many years after the onset of epilepsy. Symptoms can have a relapsing-remitting or chronic course. Predominantly positive symptoms occur, with delusions and hallucinations occurring in clear consciousness. It can be challenging to differentiate inter-ictal psychosis from schizophrenia. Intellectual disability and poorly controlled temporal lobe epilepsy both increase the risk of developing inter-ictal psychosis.

Clues within the symptom profile include:

- later onset of symptoms compared to schizophrenia
- third-person auditory hallucinations less common
- personality relatively well preserved
- fewer negative symptoms
- less thought disorder and bizarre behaviour
- fewer affective changes.

Forced Normalisation

The CL team may be asked to assess patients with epilepsy that appear to have excellent seizure control yet psychotic or affective symptoms have surfaced. These patients may be on broad-spectrum anticonvulsants such as levetiracetam, have recently undergone resective surgery or had vagal nerve stimulator implantation. There is a reliable relationship in some patients between quiescence of epileptogenic activity and emergence of psychotic or affective symptoms, known as forced normalisation. Treatment with neuroleptic medication is not always successful, and lowering the seizure threshold, though controversial, is sometimes the most effective way to improve the patient's mental state (50).

Tips for Assessment

- Establish if person is presenting with new onset seizures or has an established diagnosis of epilepsy. Is the cause of epilepsy known (stroke, trauma, cortical dysplasia etc.)?
- Is there a parallel diagnosis or suspicion of non-epileptic attacks and can the patient distinguish between different seizure-type episodes?
- Clarify temporal relationship of psychiatric symptoms and any new neurological symptoms with seizures
- Level of current and historic seizure control, compliance with anti-epileptics, recent medication changes.

Treatment

Ictal psychosis is treated by optimising seizure control. Post-ictal psychosis may resolve with benzodiazepines but if this does not lead to rapid improvement, neuroleptics such as risperidone can be used (49). The speed at which antipsychotics can be tapered should be guided by the rate of symptom remission. If rapid remission is over a day or two, antipsychotics can be reduced over a few weeks. When symptoms last longer, a period of one to two months' complete symptom remission is recommended before tapering (42). Arranging clinical review after discharge to initiate tapering can be tricky; neuropsychiatry or liaison psychiatry outpatient clinics are ideally set up for this but where service provision is sparse, primary care and community mental health teams may agree to guide and support this process.

Inter-ictal psychosis should be treated with antipsychotics in the same manner as primary schizophrenia. The evidence base for the use of antipsychotics in patients with epilepsy and psychosis is sparse and there is no evidence to support specific antipsychotic drugs (49). Risperidone and olanzapine are generally well tolerated.

- Carbamazepine, phenytoin and phenobarbital increase clearance of most antipsychotic medications.
- Lamotrigine can increase risperidone levels.
- Valproate can increase clozapine levels; risperidone can increase valproate levels.

Core Neurology Topics for CL Teams 4: Neuroimmunology Autoimmune Encephalitis (AIE)

AIE refers to a heterogenous group of conditions driven by antibody–antigen interactions that have direct consequences on neuronal and glial function. The limbic system is a particular target in most of these conditions. There is variable association with malignancy (more common when antibodies against intracellular antigens are detected) and while phenotypic distinction is improving with respect to neurological features, psychiatric presentations associated with different antibodies show extensive overlap. N-methyl-D-aspartate (NMDA) receptor AIE has received the most coverage in literature regarding psychiatric manifestations, as patients commonly present with alterations in mental state as part of the initial presentation. The prototypical description of a young female patient with acute onset of affective and psychotic symptoms twinned with dyskinetic orofacial movements and catatonia is the most well characterised among neuropsychiatric presentations in AIE. Nuances exist, however, in presentations of NMDA receptor AIE, and the terms 'depression', 'anxiety', 'confusion', 'agitation', 'delirium' and 'psychosis' recur across the antibodies currently described in literature exploring symptomatic manifestations of AIE (51). Catatonia is an exception, being described mostly in patients with NMDA or gamma-amino-butyric-acid (GABA) antibodies.

A recent and useful clinical summary of different antibody syndromes is provided by Uy and colleagues (52). A broad-brushstrokes summary of *some* of these syndromes is presented in Table 12.1. The list is by no means exhaustive and any of the following syndromes can include psychotic, affective, cognitive and behavioural changes.

Psychiatric symptoms can be the presenting feature of AIE but usually within days to weeks, seizures, motor features and cognitive impairment surface and it is often the combination of these features that warrants the search for a culprit antibody and possibly a tumour. A more protracted course has occasionally been described with LGI1, CASPR2 and IgLON5 antibodies (52). MRI, EEG, serum and cerebrospinal fluid sampling are used in combination to yield culprit biomarkers but these are not always positive.

Different geographic regions will have different approaches to testing; it takes a considerable degree of skill to select one or two culprit antibodies and this is mostly based on distinct constellations of neurological features, some of which are elicited on examination. Other centres will test for antibodies en bloc (common order sets in the UK at the time of writing include anti-neuronal antibodies (Yo, Hu, Ma 1/2, Ri, CRMP5,

Table 12.1 Autoimmune encephalitis: clinical findings and biomarkers

	Clues – clinical presentation	Clues – history and investigations
NMDA	Dyskinesia (limb and orofacial), mutism and expressive dysphasia, dysautonomia, central apnoea, catatonia, coma	Ovarian teratoma; history of herpes simplex virus encephalitis
LGI1	Facio-brachial dystonic seizures, other focal seizures	Hyponatraemia, HLA-DRB1*07:01
CASPR2	Morvan's syndrome, peripheral nerve hyperexcitability, dysautonomia	Thymoma in 20%, HLA-DRB1*11:01,
AMPA	Cognitive impairment, seizures	Tumours in 70%
GABAa	Refractory seizures	Thymoma in 30%
GABAb	Refractory seizures	Tumours in 50% (mostly small-cell lung tumours)
Glycine	Stiff person syndrome, PERM (progressive encephalopathy with rigidity and myoclonus)	Electromyogram abnormal 60%, thymoma in 15%
DPPX	Tremor, myoclonus, hyperekplexia, gut symptoms	B-cell tumours in 10%
IgLON5	sleep disorder (rapid eye movement and non-rapid eye movement parasomnias, sleep apnoea) Bulbar features, progressive supranuclear palsy-like syndrome	HLA-DRB1*10:01/HLADQB*05:01 alleles in 87%. No history of autoimmunity or cancer in 91%
Hu	Painful sensory neuropathy, cerebellar ataxia	Small-cell lung cancer
Ma2	Diencephalic and brainstem involvement – narcolepsy, gaze paresis, cognitive impairment	Testicular germ cell tumours
CRMP5	Chorea, cranial nerve dysfunction, cerebellar ataxia	Small-cell lung cancer, thymoma
Amphiphysin	Stiff person syndrome	Female gender, breast cancer, EMG abnormalities

Ampiphysin, SOX1), NMDA, LGI-1, CASPR2, AMPA, GABA-A and B, Glycine and GAD, with others added if the phenotype is suggestive).

Some patients present with a cluster of symptoms and signs that are strongly suggestive of AIE but there is no culprit antibody on testing. Seronegative AIE is evolving as a disease entity and neurologist colleagues may opt to trial immunosuppressive treatment in these patients.

The role of the CL team in these cases includes:

(1) Remaining vigilant for AIE as a diagnostic possibility with a view to liaising with neurology and neuropsychiatry colleagues to discuss diagnostic possibilities,

investigations and to consider immunosuppression. Affective and/or psychotic symptoms twinned with seizures, cognitive impairment and/or motor symptoms raise the index of suspicion.

(2) Offering symptomatic treatment and psychological support for affective, psychotic and behavioural disturbance. While the principal mode of treatment in AIE centres on immunosuppression, psychotropic medication can be helpful to reduce symptom burden. There is no generic approach to this other than advising cautious use of neuroleptics in patients with NMDA encephalitis due to sensitivity. Neuropsychiatry colleagues based in regional neurosciences centres are often happy to discuss cases, offer relevant expertise and share perspectives and decision-making.

Core Neurology Topics for CL Teams 5: Multiple Sclerosis

Epidemiology

Neuropsychiatric abnormalities have been reported in up to 60% of patients with MS (53). In the majority of cases, psychiatric conditions occur after the initial diagnosis of MS, although psychiatric symptoms may form part of the initial clinical presentation. Psychiatric comorbidities are associated with reduced quality of life and reduced adherence with MS treatment (54).

Depression

Depression is the most common psychiatric comorbidity in MS. Almost half of all patients with MS will have a clinically significant depressive episode over the course of their life (after MS is diagnosed) (53). Avoidant and emotion-focused coping styles, negative cognitive illness appraisals and lower income have been associated with higher levels of depression (55). Rates of suicidal ideation and actual suicide rates are also higher than in the general population (29% with suicidal ideation and intent, 3% completed suicide (53)). Risk factors for parasuicide are shown in Box 12.3.

Aetiology

Depression in MS is thought to be multifactorial in origin. The neuropathological process of MS may contribute to depressive symptoms, both indirectly through inflammatory processes (with a correlation between depression and neuroinflammatory markers having been

---

Box 12.3 Risk Factors for Self-Harm in MS

Male gender

Young age of onset

Initial five years after MS diagnosis

Current or previous history of depression or self-harm

Social isolation

Recent functional deterioration

Substance misuse.

demonstrated) or directly due to specific brain lesions (56). Hypothalamic-pituitary-adrenal axis dysfunction has also been implicated (56). In terms of psychosocial factors, MS is a chronic, progressive and unpredictable disease which starts in young adulthood. It can detrimentally affect functioning in many areas of life, including employment, education, relationships and daily living activities. The unpredictable nature of the disease can be difficult to deal with due to uncertainty about health on a daily basis, while the progressive nature of the disease means that individuals have to constantly re-define their own self-image to overcome the limitations imposed by MS (56).

Assessment

As with many chronic neurological diseases, the overlap between symptoms of MS and biological symptoms of depression can make diagnosis difficult and contributes to depressive episodes being under-recognised and under-treated (53). Fatigue is particularly common. The Beck Fast Screen for Depression in Medically Ill Patients, the Hospital Anxiety and Depression Scale and the Beck Depression Inventory have all been validated for use in MS patients with depression (53).

Look for new medications that have been started, dose changes or abrupt discontinuation of medications. Disease-modifying medications, corticosteroids, baclofen, dantrolene and tizanidine have all been associated with emergence of depressive symptoms. Despite initial concern in case reports about beta-interferon inducing depression in patients with MS, there is no definite evidence of this association; depressive symptoms at baseline are one of the most important predictors of depression at follow-up (56).

Treatment

There is no research evidence to support use of a particular class of antidepressant medication and very little research examining the long-term efficacy of antidepressants in MS (57). It is recommended that medications should be titrated from an initial half-dose as patients with MS tend to have reduced tolerability of adverse effects.

SSRIs are generally regarded as first-line choices for depressive symptoms in MS (58). Amitriptyline and duloxetine may have been prescribed at low doses for pain; dose increase in these medications may negate the need for polypharmacy. Stimulant medications prescribed for fatigue can also enhance mood (53).

Data regarding the effectiveness of psychological interventions for depression in MS are limited, but there is reasonable evidence for a CBT-based approach (59). Data regarding ECT are based on case reports and require careful case-by-case consideration. The recent consensus is that it is efficacious in depressed patients with MS but long-term implications for cognitive function are uncertain, with the possibility of increased risks in patients with active disease and when using neuromuscular blocking agents during anaesthesia (60).

Bipolar Spectrum Disorders

Bipolar affective disorder is approximately twice as common in people with MS compared to the general population (53). The lifetime prevalence of Bipolar disorder in people with MS is around 8% (61). Furthermore, around one third of people with MS experience a cortico steroid or antidepressant-induced manic episode. Manic symptoms can occur before the onset of other neurological signs, but more commonly occur around a year after diagnosis (53).

Assessment

Culprit medications are similar to those increasing risk of depressive symptoms. Manic symptoms secondary to medications tend to occur early in treatment (within the first few weeks) and are dose-dependent.

Consider euphoria and pseudobulbar affect in patients with MS who appear manic. These are more common in patients with advanced disease and cognitive impairment (56). Euphoria in MS patients is described as an unusually persistent positive mood but without typical cognitive and behavioural disturbances seen in mania. Pseudobulbar affect refers to brief bursts of tearfulness and laughter without accompanying affective lability. It is associated with prefrontal cortex dysfunction and some patients respond to SSRIs and mirtazapine.

Treatment

In cases of drug-induced mania, close liaison with neurology colleagues is essential in order to engage in joint decision-making regarding reduction of culprit medications and adding a mood stabiliser (53). Lithium-induced polyuria can be problematic in patients with bladder disturbance and neuroleptics can exacerbate difficulties with fatigue, balance and coordination.

Anxiety

The lifetime prevalence of anxiety disorders in people with MS is higher than in the general population (55), with increased rates of generalised anxiety disorder, panic disorder, obsessive-compulsive disorder and social anxiety (58). Risk factors include female gender, limited social support and comorbid depression (56). Only 11% of people with MS who report anxiety symptoms receive treatment (62). It is important to prioritise managing anxiety in this population because it is associated with reduced quality of life and increased morbidity, including chronic pain, fatigue, somatic complaints, social impairment, increased alcohol consumption and suicidal ideation. The Hospital Anxiety and Depression Scale Anxiety subscale (HADS-A) has utility in detecting symptoms of anxiety in people with MS but full clinical evaluation is required to confirm diagnosis and guide management (62).

The evidence base for anxiety treatment in this specific population group is sparse. Pharmacological and psychological treatment of anxiety disorders should be treated using standard approaches, with due vigilance for parallel issues such as pain that could be effectively treated with anxiolytics such as pregabalin.

Psychosis

Psychosis is approximately three times as common in patients with MS compared to the general population, with a prevalence of 2–4% (53). Symptoms of psychosis occur *after* a diagnosis of MS in over 90% of patients and there is an association with temporal lobe lesions. An affective component may or may not be present. Low-dose atypical antipsychotics are generally recommended, particularly risperidone.

Cognitive Impairment

Cognitive dysfunction is a recognised feature of MS and is more common in older patients and those with progressive disease (56). Cognitive deficits resemble a fronto-subcortical syndrome (63). There is also evidence of impairments in social cognition (64).

References

1. Chai J, Evans L, Hughes T. Diagnostic aids: The Surgical Sieve revisited. *The Clinical Teacher*. 2016;**14**(4):263–7.

2. Pradeep R, Gupta D, Mehta A, Srinivasa R, Javali M, Acharya P. Wake-up sleepyhead: Unilateral diencephalic stroke presenting with excessive sleepiness. *J Neurosci Rural Pract*. 2019;**10**(1):145–7.

3. Endres D, Maier V, Leypoldt F et al. Autoantibody-associated psychiatric syndromes: A systematic literature review resulting in 145 cases. *Psychological Medicine*. 2020;Sep. 7:1–12.

4. Shah S, Mehta H, Fekete R. Late-onset neurodegeneration with brain iron accumulation with diffusion tensor magnetic resonance imaging. *Case Rep*. 2012;**4**(3):216–23.

5. Gerischer L, Scheibe F, Nümann A, Köhnlein M, Stölzel U, Meisel A. Acute porphyrias: A neurological perspective. *Brain and Behavior*. 2021;**11**(11).

6. Kgosidialwa O, Hakami O, Zia-Ul-Hussnain H, Agha A. Growth hormone deficiency following traumatic brain injury. *Int J Mol Sci*. 2019;**20**(13):3323.

7. Kramkowski J, Hebert C. Neuropsychiatric sequelae of brain radiation therapy: A review of modality, symptomatology, and treatment options. *Gen Hosp Psychiatry*. 2022;**74**: 51–7.

8. Hodgkiss A. Psychiatric consequences of cancer treatments: Conventional chemotherapy. In Hodgkiss A (ed.), *Biological Psychiatry of Cancer and Cancer Treatment*. Oxford; 2016, pp. 67–78.

9. World Health Organization. *International Statistical Classification of Diseases and Related Health Problems*, 11th ed. Geneva; 2019.

10. O'Keeffe N, Ranjith G. Depression, demoralisation or adjustment disorder? Understanding emotional distress in the severely medically ill. *Clin Med J R Coll Physicians London*. 2007;**7**(5):478–81.

11. Villa R F, Ferrari F, Moretti A. Post-stroke depression: Mechanisms and pharmacological treatment. *Pharmacol Ther*. 2018; **184**:131–44.

12. Medeiros G C, Roy D, Kontos N, Beach S R. Post-stroke depression: A 2020 updated review. *Gen Hosp Psychiatry*. 2020;**66**:70–80.

13. Cai W, Mueller C, Li YJ, Shen WD, Stewart R. Post stroke depression and risk of stroke recurrence and mortality: A systematic review and meta-analysis. *Ageing Res Rev*. 2019;**50**(January):102–9.

14. Hackett ML, Köhler S, O'Brien JT, Mead GE. Neuropsychiatric outcomes of stroke. *Lancet Neurol*. 2014;**13**(5):525–34.

15. Allida S, Cox K, Hsieh C, Lang H, House A, Hackett M. Pharmacological, psychological, and non-invasive brain stimulation interventions for treating depression after stroke (review). *Cochrane Database Syst Rev*. 2020;(**1**).

16. Liu L, Fuller M, Behymer TP et al. Selective serotonin reuptake inhibitors and intracerebral hemorrhage risk and outcome. *Stroke*. 2020;**51**(4):1135–41.

17. Legg LA, Rudberg AS, Hua X et al. Selective serotonin reuptake inhibitors (SSRIs) for stroke recovery. *Cochrane Database Syst Rev*. 2021;(**11**).

18. Wang S Bin, Wang YY, Zhang QE et al. Cognitive behavioral therapy for post-stroke depression: A meta-analysis. *J Affect Disord*. 2018;**235**(March):589–96.

19. Wright F, Wu S, Chun HY, Mead G. Factors associated with poststroke anxiety: A systematic review and meta-analysis. *Stroke Res Treat*. 2017;**2017**:2124743.

20. Knapp P, Campbell Burton CA, Holmes J et al. Interventions for treating anxiety after stroke. *Cochrane Database Syst Rev*. 2017;**2017**(5).

21. Santos CO, Caeiro L, Ferro JM, Figueira ML. Mania and stroke: A systematic review. *Cerebrovasc Dis*. 2011;**32**(1):11–21.

22. Stangeland H, Orgeta V, Bell V. Poststroke psychosis: A systematic review. *J Neurol Neurosurg Psychiatry*. 2018;**89**:879–85.

23. Zivkovic S, Koh CH, Kaza N, Jackson CA. Antipsychotic drug use and risk of stroke and myocardial infarction: a systematic review and meta-analysis. *BMC Psychiatry.* 2019;**19**(1):189.

24. Aarsland D, Påhlhagen S, Ballard CG, Ehrt U, Svenningsson P. Depression in Parkinson disease: Epidemiology, mechanisms and management. *Nat Rev Neurol.* 2012;**8**(1):35–47.

25. Marsh L. Depression and Parkinson's disease: Current knowledge. *Curr Neurol Neurosci Rep.* 2013;**13**(12):409.

26. Marsh L, McDonald WM, Cummings J et al. Provisional diagnostic criteria for depression in Parkinson's disease: Report of an NINDS/NIMH Work Group. *Mov Disord.* 2006;**21**(2):148–58.

27. Troeung L, Egan SJ, Gasson N. A meta-analysis of randomised placebo-controlled treatment trials for depression and anxiety in Parkinson's disease. *PLoS One*, 2013;**8** (11):e7951.

28. Borisovskaya A, Bryson WC, Buchholz J, Samii A, Borson S. Electroconvulsive therapy for depression in Parkinson's disease: Systematic review of evidence and recommendations. *Neurodegener Dis Manag.* 2016;**6**(2):161–76.

29. Peroski MS, Chu MM, Doddi SR, Regenold WT. The safety of electroconvulsive therapy in patients with implanted deep brain stimulators: A review of the literature and case report. *J ECT.* 2019;**35**(2):84–90.

30. Dissanayaka NNNW, White E, O'Sullivan JD, Marsh R, Pachana NA, Byrne GJ. The clinical spectrum of anxiety in Parkinson's disease. *Mov Disord.* 2014;**29**(8):967–75.

31. Broen MPG, Narayen NE, Kuijf ML, Dissanayaka NNW, Leentjens AFG. Prevalence of anxiety in Parkinson's disease: A systematic review and meta-analysis. *Mov Disord.* 2016;**31** (8):1125–33.

32. Chen JJ, Marsh L. Anxiety in Parkinson's disease: Identification and management. *Ther Adv Neurol Disord.* 2014;**7**(1):52–9.

33. Ffytche DH, Creese B, Politis M et al. The psychosis spectrum in Parkinson disease. *Nat Rev Neurol.* 2017;**13**(2):81–95.

34. Reading PJ, Luce AK, McKeith IG. Rivastigmine in the treatment of parkinsonian psychosis and cognitive impairment: Preliminary findings from an open trial. *Mov Disord.* 2001;**16**(6):1171–4.

35. Kyle K, Bronstein JM. Treatment of psychosis in Parkinson's disease and dementia with Lewy Bodies: A review. *Park Relat Disord.* 2020;**75**:55–62.

36. Seppi K, Ray Chaudhuri K, Coelho M et al. Update on treatments for nonmotor symptoms of Parkinson's disease: An evidence-based medicine review. *Mov Disord.* 2019;**34**(2):180–98.

37. Kelly MJ, Baig F, Hu MT, Okai D. Spectrum of impulse control behaviours in Parkinson's disease: Pathophysiology and management. *J Neurol Neurosurg Psychiatry.* 2020;**91**(7):703–11.

38. Elger CE, Johnston SA, Hoppe C. Diagnosing and treating depression in epilepsy. *Seizure.* 2017;**44**:184–93.

39. Scott AJ, Sharpe L, Hunt C, Gandy M. Anxiety and depressive disorders in people with epilepsy: A meta-analysis. *Epilepsia.* 2017;**58**(6):973–82.

40. Mula M. Depression in epilepsy. *Curr Opin Neurol.* 2017;**30**(2):180–6.

41. Gilliam FG, Barry JJ, Hermann BP, Meador KJ, Vahle V, Kanner AM. Rapid detection of major depression in epilepsy: A multicentre study. *Lancet Neurol.* 2006;**5** (5):399–405.

42. Kerr MP, Mensah S, Besag F et al. International consensus clinical practice statements for the treatment of neuropsychiatric conditions associated with epilepsy. *Epilepsia.* 2011;**52** (11):2133–8.

43. Scott AJ, Sharpe L, Hunt C, Gandy M. Anxiety and depressive disorders in people with epilepsy: A meta-analysis. *Epilepsia.* 2017;**58**(6):973–82.

44. Brandt C, Mula M. Anxiety disorders in people with epilepsy. *Epilepsy Behav.* 2016;**59**:87–91.

45. Maguire M, Singh J, Marson A. Epilepsy and psychosis: A practical approach. *Pract Neurol.* 2018;**18**(2):106–14.

46. Farooq S, Sherin A. Interventions for psychotic symptoms concomitant with epilepsy. *Cochrane Database Syst Rev.* 2015;**2015**(12).

47. Toone B. The psychoses of epilepsy. *J Neurol Neurosurg Psychiatry.* 2000;**69**(1):1–3.

48. Agrawal N, Mula M. Treatment of psychoses in patients with epilepsy: An update. *Ther Adv Psychopharmacol.* 2019;**9**:1–10.

49. de Toffol B, Trimble M, Hesdorffer DC et al. Pharmacotherapy in patients with epilepsy and psychosis. *Epilepsy Behav.* 2018;**88**:54–60.

50. Calle-López Y, Ladino LD, Benjumea-Cuartas V, Castrillón-Velilla DM, Téllez-Zenteno JF, Wolf P. Forced normalization: A systematic review. *Epilepsia.* 2019;**60**(8):1610–18.

51. Pollak TA, Lennox BR, Müller S et al. Autoimmune psychosis: An international consensus on an approach to the diagnosis and management of psychosis of suspected autoimmune origin. *Lancet Psychiatry.* 2020;**7**(1):93–108. doi: 10.1016/S2215-0366(19)30290-1.

52. Uy CE, Binks S, Irani SR. Autoimmune encephalitis: Clinical spectrum and management. *Pract Neurol.* 2021;**21**(5):412–23.

53. Murphy R, O'Donoghue S, Counihan T et al. Neuropsychiatric syndromes of multiple sclerosis. *J Neurol Neurosurg Psychiatry.* 2017;**88**:697–708.

54. Camara-Lemarroy CR, Ibarra-Yruegas BE, Rodriguez-Gutierrez R, Berrios-Morales I, Ionete C, Riskind P. The varieties of psychosis in multiple sclerosis: A systematic review of cases. *Mult Scler Relat Disord.* 2017;**12**:9–14.

55. Fisher PL, Salmon P, Heffer-Rahn P, Huntley C, Reilly J, Cherry MG. Predictors of emotional distress in people with multiple sclerosis: A systematic review of prospective studies. *J Affect Disord.* 2020;**276**:752–64.

56. Sá MJ. Psychological aspects of multiple sclerosis. *Clin Neurol Neurosurg.* 2008;**110**:868–77.

57. Koch MW, Glazenborg A, Uyttenboogaart M, Mostert JP, De Keyser J. Pharmacologic treatment of depression in multiple sclerosis. *Cochrane Database Syst Rev.* 2011;(2).

58. Multiple sclerosis. In Taylor DM, Barnes TRE, Young HY (eds.), *The Maudsley Prescribing Guidelines*, 14th ed. Chichester; 2018, pp. 709–12.

59. Thomas PW, Thomas S, Hillier C et al. Psychological interventions for multiple sclerosis. *Cochrane Database Syst Rev.* 2006(1).

60. Yahya AS, Khawaja S. Electroconvulsive therapy in multiple sclerosis: A review of current evidence. *Prim Care Companion CNS Disord.* 2021;**23**(2):20r02717.

61. Joseph B, Nandakumar AL, Ahmed AT et al. Prevalence of bipolar disorder in multiple sclerosis: A systematic review and meta-analysis. *Evid Based Ment Health.* 2021;**24**(2):88–94.

62. Litster B, Fiest KM, Patten SB et al. Defining the burden and managing the effects of psychiatric comorbidity in chronic immunoinflammatory disease. Screening tools for anxiety in people with multiple sclerosis: A systematic review. *Int J MS Care.* 2016;**18**(6):273–81.

63. Sumowski JF, Benedict R, Enzinger C et al. Cognition in multiple sclerosis: State of the field and priorities for the future. *Neurology.* 2018;**90**(6):278.

64. Cotter J, Firth J, Enzinger C et al. Social cognition in multiple sclerosis. *Neurology.* 2016;**87**:1727–36.

Perinatal Psychiatry

Sarah Jones, Aaron McMeekin, Ipshita Mukherjee
and Laura Murphy

Introduction

Perinatal mental illnesses are common and carry significant morbidity for the mother and infant, the family and wider society. Suicide remains a leading cause of maternal death. Pregnancy, childbirth and the transition into parenthood presents a unique life stage where a combination of physical, biological and psychological stressors can leave many women vulnerable to developing perinatal mental illness. This is a time where individuals often reflect on their own experiences of parenting and early life trauma can be reactivated. In addition, there is now consistent evidence that perinatal mental illness is not confined to maternal mental health problems. Approximately 10% of fathers experience postnatal depression and a recent study by the National Childbirth Trust has shown that 38% of all first-time fathers are concerned about their mental health.

The perinatal period is a time in a family's life when they are in contact with many health professionals. It is the responsibility of all professionals involved in the maternity journey to recognise perinatal mental illness. Early identification of perinatal issues, specialist assessment and management and effective liaison with all of the professionals involved in the care of the mother–infant dyad (including midwifery, obstetrics, health visiting, primary and secondary mental health services, psychology and social care) are key to achieving the best possible outcome for the family.

In this chapter, we outline the common perinatal mental health problems, discuss the challenges around prescribing and detail the specialist perinatal mental health resources. This will allow you to liaise with and advocate for women presenting in a psychiatric liaison setting.

Perinatal Mood Disorders

Baby Blues

Incidence and Prevalence

Baby blues is a common presentation following delivery but can be poorly understood and is ill defined by diagnostic criteria. Approximately 50% of women will experience baby blues post-delivery but the prevalence in research varies widely between 15% and 85% (1). The aetiology is uncertain but there is thought to be likely a link to changes in hormonal levels, specifically changes in oestrogen, progesterone and prolactin.

Presentation

The onset is approximately two to three days postpartum and can last for three to four days. If a woman is still experiencing symptoms two weeks following delivery, the presentation is unlikely to be consistent with baby blues and a comprehensive review for perinatal mental illness should be carried out in a timely manner.

The woman can experience tearfulness and increased emotional lability. Severe baby blues (reduced maternal self-esteem and pervasive worry when looking after baby) has been indicated as a precursor for depression (three times as likely) or postpartum psychosis (especially in predisposed women).

Management

Baby blues is self-limiting. Emotional support should be advised from friends and family. Ensure the mother's diet and hydration is maintained and emphasise protected refreshing sleep where possible.

Depression

Incidence and Prevalence

Global estimates of the overall adjusted prevalence of perinatal depression are 12% but women in lower-income countries may face a higher burden of depression (2). A recent review of 58 studies reported an incidence of postnatal depression at 12% and a prevalence of 17% (3).

Onset

The peak incidence for onset of symptoms is the acute postpartum period (4) but there is growing evidence that many women have onset of symptoms during pregnancy (5).

During pregnancy, episodes of depression occur more commonly in the first and third pregnancy trimester, possibly as the start of pregnancy and later incipient parenthood are significant life events and transition points (6) (Boxes 13.1 and 13.2).

Possibly most significantly, depression in pregnancy is one of the strongest predictors of depression postnatally. In women who have major depressive disorder, discontinuing antidepressant treatment prior to or soon after conception led to relapse rates of up to 70% (7).

Presentation

There are no independent diagnostic criteria for antenatal and postnatal depression. Professionals are advised to use International Classification of Diseases (ICD)-11 or the

---

Box 13.1 Factors That Place Women at a Higher Risk of Experiencing Depression during Pregnancy

- Maternal anxiety
- Life stress
- History of depression
- Family history of perinatal mood disorders
- Lack of support
- Domestic violence
- Unintended pregnancy

> **Box 13.2** Additional Risk Factors That Increase Risk of Experiencing Perinatal Depression
>
> - Low educational attainment
> - Lower income
> - Poor relationship with partner
> - Current or past pregnancy complications
> - Pregnancy loss

Diagnostic and Statistical Manual of Mental Disorders (DSM) 5 criteria regarding general depression with the additional perinatal specific questions outlined next.

It is important to elicit core depressive symptoms. These are low mood, low energy and anhedonia. Explore psychological changes, especially cognitions of guilt, worthlessness or hopelessness or thoughts of suicide. Explore the mother's viewpoint of herself as a mother and her bond with baby. Maternal guilt can be prominent but should be asked sensitively as it can be associated with shame and failure.

Explore biological symptoms. The mother may be experiencing reduced sleep, early morning wakening, reduced appetite, poor concentration and reduced libido. Be mindful these symptoms can be affected by normal pregnancy physiology. Sometimes the mother can experience psychomotor agitation or psychomotor slowing.

Sensitively explore the following points for perinatal depression:

- Low confidence as a mother.
- Lack of enjoyment when interacting with baby.
- Poor bond with baby (either complete absence of bond or protecting herself from previous feelings of loss or trauma, for example previous miscarriage).
- Feeling guilty about being a 'bad mother' or baby 'does not like her'. Women can idealise being a 'perfect mother', with anything less considered a failure. Consider the idea of the 'good enough' mother.
- Estrangement both emotionally and physically from pregnancy and unborn.

Depressed mothers are less likely to engage with antenatal services (35). Maternal depression has been linked to poor nutrition, weight gain, increased alcohol consumption, substance abuse and smoking (36).

Maternal depression has been associated with still birth and adverse neonatal outcomes including premature birth, low birth weight, low APGAR (Appearance, Pulse, Grimace response, Activity and Respiration) scores, smaller head circumference and major congenital anomalies. It is important to note, however, that study limitations were apparent and confounding factors such as smoking status were thought to account for a substantial proportion of the effect size.

In children born to women with perinatal depression, an increased risk of emotional problems, especially anxiety and depression in childhood, have been observed, as well as impaired cognitive development and symptoms of attention deficit hyperactivity disorder and conduct disorder. Again, it is important to think about possible confounding factors intersecting with these observations.

> **Box 13.3** Management of Maternal Depression
>
> - Mild episode: talking therapy, video interactive guidance, social prescribing, third-sector services (mother and baby groups, baby sensory, baby yoga)
> - Moderate episode: bio-psycho-social community approach, antidepressant and talking therapy, specialist mental health midwife (if pregnant), early attachment service (postnatally), consideration of specialist perinatal mental health team
> - Severe episode: bio-psycho-social intensive community approach or mother and baby unit admission

Postnatal depression is the strongest predictor of parenting stress and difficulties in the mother–infant relationship. As maternal depression is a risk factor for paternal depression in the postnatal period, a family can suffer the impact of both parents being unwell.

Management

The management of maternal depression is classified into a stepwise approach for mild, moderate and severe depressive episodes.

Mild episodes are treated through self-help, a form of talking therapy (e.g. cognitive behavioural therapy (CBT)) and social prescribing (e.g. community support mother and baby groups). In addition, significant benefits to parenting and child development in the context of perinatal depression have been achieved by interpersonal therapy, CBT, video interactive guidance, psychotherapeutic group support and massage (8).

In moderate to severe cases, an antidepressant would be indicated. The decision around prescribing will be influenced not only by the impact on the mother but also that on the mother–infant relationship, infant mental well-being and the wider family unit.

Sertraline is often used as first-line medication due to evidenced efficacy and the low rate of reported adverse effects on breastfed babies; sertraline may be appropriate for new episodes of depression (9). However, the prescriber should take into account a woman's previous response to medication; restarting an antidepressant that was previously effective may negate the need for future switching or augmentation. Careful monitoring of the infant is always important (10) (Box 13.3).

Anxiety Disorders

Prevalence

Anxiety during the perinatal period is common, with a recent meta-analysis suggesting a prevalence of 20.7% of women meeting the criteria for at least one or more anxiety disorder (11). In clinical practice it can be under-diagnosed and under-treated, possibly linked to difficulties differentiating between 'normal' anxiety related to a major life transition versus pathological anxiety. This should be carefully explored.

Generalised Anxiety Disorder

Prevalence

Generalised anxiety disorder (GAD) is a common perinatal presentation characterised by excessive, uncontrollable worry that can severely impact functioning with rates of 4.1% in pregnancy and 5.7% postnatally (12).

Presentation

Physical features of GAD such as fatigue and insomnia may be difficult to differentiate from pregnancy-related symptoms. Common themes include worries around the fetus (e.g. pregnancy loss, particularly after multiple miscarriages) or baby (e.g. sudden infant death syndrome), concern around maternal health or not achieving as a mother.

Management

Mild cases may respond to psychoeducation and signposting to self-care strategies, while moderate-severe cases typically benefit from psychology (e.g. CBT) and/or medication. In terms of medications, selective serotonin reuptake inhibitors (SSRIs) are the first-line choice, although as-required medications (e.g. promethazine, low-dose antipsychotics) may be required.

Obsessive Compulsive Disorder

Prevalence

Obsessive compulsive disorder (OCD) can affect approximately 1–2% of the general population. The perinatal period is associated with a higher risk of OCD with rates of around ~2% in pregnancy and 2–3% in the first postnatal year (13).

The risk of postpartum OCD is believed to be increased by stresses related to the transition to parenthood, a heightened sense of responsibility for a vulnerable infant, misinterpretation of intrusive thoughts (that the majority of the population can experience) and an over-estimation of perceived threat.

Presentation

OCD is characterised by obsessions and/or compulsions

Obsessions are recurrent, intrusive, unwanted distressing thoughts but may also be images, doubts, urges or bodily sensations. Obsessions in the perinatal period typically include fear of contamination (affecting baby), doubt that tasks have been completed correctly (sterilisation of bottles) or a drive for perfectionism ('perfect mother' role).

A common obsession concerns accidental or deliberate harm occurring to baby. Because of a fear of being judged or the involvement of social services, mothers typically find such thoughts difficult to discuss so this requires delicate exploration. It is important to note current evidence does not suggest that intrusive thoughts of harm to baby result in increased risk of harm to baby – in contrast to hallucinations or delusional ideas around baby related to psychotic disorders (13).

Compulsions are mental or behavioural acts completed to try and alleviate distress. This relief is typically short-lived; it can become time-consuming and impact daily function. The response to the obsession (rather than the obsession itself) may be more problematic with

> **Box 13.4** Perinatal Obsessive Compulsive Disorder: Points to Consider as a Consultation-Liaison Team
>
> Always ask about if intrusive thoughts or compulsions are related to or impacting on baby. This may present as overactivity with baby (repeatedly washing, checking, seeking reassurance). However, it may also present as underactivity, with mother so distressed and exhausted by the thoughts she will avoid her child.

potential for significant distress. Commonly women will report completing rituals such as over-cleaning baby equipment, repeatedly seeking reassurance (e.g. from family members, professionals or the internet) or avoidance of certain activities (e.g. spending time alone with baby can be distressing). Some mothers will report staying up all night to check baby is breathing in an attempt to reduce anxiety from intrusive thoughts (Box 13.4).

Management

Management of perinatal OCD includes CBT – exposure and response prevention treatment are particularly useful. An SSRI antidepressant may be considered. For cases that are more difficult to treat, switching to venlafaxine, clomipramine or augmentation with an antipsychotic such as aripiprazole or quetiapine may be required (6, 14).

Tokophobia

Prevalence

Tokophobia is a fear of pregnancy and childbirth. Primary tokophobia affects women who have no direct previous experience of childbirth. Secondary tokophobia affects women who have already had a delivery which has been experienced as traumatic. Secondary tokophobia is more prevalent. Maternal mild to moderate anxiety around childbirth is common (linked to concerns regarding pain, uncertainty and loss of control); there are estimates that up to 14% of women struggle with severe tokophobia (15).

Risk Factors

Risk factors include exposure to sexual trauma, a history of anxiety or depression, witnessing a traumatic delivery or suffering with a previous pregnancy loss.

Presentation

In women with secondary tokophobia, features of post-traumatic stress disorder (PTSD) are present and may include nightmares, flashbacks, ruminations and even avoidance of pregnancy. Avoidance may include eschewing any media mention of pregnancy and keeping away from people who are pregnant. Women may take steps to actively prevent pregnancy or consider a termination if they become pregnant.

Management

It is important to identify tokophobia early. This will ensure appropriate preconception support, psychoeducation, collaborative obstetric decision-making and consideration of options for psychological therapy (e.g. eye movement desensitisation and reprocessing (EMDR), trauma-focussed CBT) (14). During pregnancy, early discussions concerning mode of delivery and a clear birth plan can be helpful. Often women may express a preference for a planned Caesarean section which may be considered following an informed discussion with an obstetrician or within the context of a birth options clinic (16). Other helpful measures include continuity of care and visiting the maternity suite pre-delivery. Support for partners is also important to consider. The toolkit from the Pan-London Perinatal Mental Health Network provides a useful overview of tokophobia and helpful practical interventions (17).

Complex PTSD

Presentation and Prevalence

The diagnostic criteria for complex PTSD (CPTSD) includes the core elements of PTSD such as re-experiencing the traumatic event (e.g. flashbacks, nightmares), hypervigilance and avoidance of associated thoughts, memories or activities. Additional criteria include difficulties with affect regulation, pervasive feelings of shame/guilt and interpersonal problems. In sufferers there has typically been exposure to chronic trauma, especially childhood abuse. Estimates in high-income countries suggest that PTSD and CPTSD prevalence may vary between 2% and 12.7%, with higher rates found in lower-income countries.

There remains debate around this diagnosis and whether it may be a 're-brand' of the emotionally unstable/borderline personality disorder (EUPD) diagnosis in a way that potentially is less stigmatising. Those who argue that CPTSD is distinct from EUPD cite differences in presentation, particularly how patients with an EUPD diagnosis are more likely to engage in self-harming or suicidal behaviour and struggle more with idealisation and devaluation within their relationships with others (including services).

Management

Research is underway to understand the best way to treat CPTSD. Therapy rather than medication is likely to be key, with a focus on improving the individual's sense of safety, positive engagement in activities and relationships and reprocessing of trauma. Within the perinatal context, it is common that people generally think more about their own childhood experiences, including how they were parented, which may cause some destabilisation in mental health around this time. If there is a history of abuse, particularly sexual in nature, sensitive discussions about how the woman can be supported during delivery may be very helpful.

Bipolar Affective Disorder

Incidence and Prevalence

Bipolar disorder is a chronic relapsing and remitting illness characterised by episodes of depression and mania affecting approximately 1–3% of the population. Bipolar disorder carries high psychosocial and physical health morbidity and increased risk of suicide and attempted suicide. Women with a diagnosis of bipolar disorder are at risk of both depressive and manic relapses in the perinatal period. Women with bipolar disorder also have a greatly increased risk of severe postpartum episodes, including postpartum psychosis (20–30% compared to 0.1% in the general population) (18) and those with bipolar disorder *and* a family history of postpartum psychosis in a first-degree relative are at an even greater risk (74%) (18).

Box 13.5 Points to Consider: Bipolar Affective Disorder

- Patients with bipolar disorder are at higher risk of relapse postnatally
- Within this population relapse rates were higher for those not taking medication during pregnancy than for those on a medication regimen
- Mothers with bipolar disorder should have collaborative birth plans arranged, recognition of relapse indicators noted and risk support agreed

Risk of Relapse

The majority of research into bipolar disorder in the perinatal period has shown that women are more vulnerable to relapse in the postpartum compared to the antenatal phase. Di Florio and colleagues reported an approximately 50% risk of perinatal major affective episode per perinatal period in bipolar disorder, with approximately 90% of those occurring postpartum and approximately 80% within four weeks postpartum. Similarly, data from Danish registry studies (4) show that women with bipolar disorder were at greater risk of relapse postpartum than in pregnancy, with the highest readmission rates reported between days 10 and 19 postpartum (Box 13.5).

Women may also be at risk of relapse in the antenatal period. High relapse rates in the antenatal period have been reported particularly when women stop prophylactic medication. Analysis of relapse rates of women in pregnancy following discontinuation of mood stabilisers found recurrence risk in those discontinuing medication to be two-fold greater; median time to first recurrence was four-fold shorter and the number of weeks of illness during pregnancy was greater compared to women who remained on medication. Even for women who remained on medication, around one in four still experienced a mood episode in pregnancy.

Management

The management of bipolar disorder can be challenging due to several issues: patient presentation varies significantly, clinicians are required to manage episodes of both depression and mania, psychotropic medication used in the treatment of bipolar disorder is associated with adverse side effects and issues of non-adherence and perpetuating lifestyle factors are common.

The risk of relapse for both depressive and manic states is increased in the perinatal period, especially with medication discontinuation. Women with bipolar disorder need to be monitored carefully throughout the perinatal period and the risks of untreated illness, and therefore the benefit of medication must be weighed against the risks associated with treatment for both the mother and the developing fetus. An additional challenge in making these decisions is that there is a limited evidence base surrounding the risks associated with psychotropic medication.

A holistic approach is required involving both medication and psychological input, as well as psychoeducation programmes and psychosocial interventions. Women with a diagnosis of bipolar affective disorder require specialist support and a planned collaborative approach from preconception counselling to the end of the perinatal period.

Management should include assessing an individual's risk of relapse based on her past psychiatric history and family history. Early relapse signatures must be recorded and disseminated to all professionals. Modifiable risk factors should be optimised. A collaborative care plan outlining sleep preservation, professional monitoring (especially peri-delivery), medication options and identification of support networks should be developed. Women with bipolar disorder should be followed up and monitored closely, especially in the early postpartum period, by a specialist perinatal mental health team.

Postpartum Psychosis

Incidence

Postpartum psychosis is defined as a manic or psychotic illness that develops rapidly, with onset of symptoms often within the first few days post-delivery and usually within the first two weeks. The incidence of postpartum psychosis is approximately 1–2/1,000 maternities (live birth or still birth > 24 weeks gestation).

Presentation

The presentation has been described as 'kaleidoscopic', relating to the rapidly changing mixed affective states. In addition to mood symptoms, features of these episodes include confusion, disorientation, perplexity, strange beliefs, delusions and hallucinations (19).

Management

Postpartum psychosis is a psychiatric emergency and women require hospital admission and psychopharmacological treatment in the acute phase. Early identification and early initiation of antipsychotic medication are key. There can be diagnostic overshadowing between postpartum psychosis and delirium, and therefore full physical investigation is recommended in parallel to a psychiatric assessment. Women should preferably be admitted for psychiatric treatment with their infant to a specialised mother and baby unit.

Psychopharmacological treatment for postpartum psychosis usually involves antipsychotic medication and benzodiazepines and longer-term mood stabilisation depending on the presentation. Parent–infant bonding during more lucid period should be promoted and psychological input should be offered. Many women understandably report feeling distressed and traumatised by the experience of postpartum psychosis as the episode resolves and insight returns. Charitable organisations, for example Action on Postpartum Psychosis, and peer support can be beneficial in navigating the recovery.

Following the acute phase of postpartum psychosis, women are at an increased risk of developing a depressive episode. Discharge planning from a mother and baby unit (where there is intensive support) should include a graded leave plan, psychoeducation for the family, close liaison with the specialist community mental health team, input from a community psychiatric nurse regarding relapse prevention and close liaison with the family's health visitor +/– input from parent–infant mental health services to further support the parent–infant relationship. It is important to be mindful of the impact of an episode of postpartum psychosis on partners, fathers and co-parents, and family support, peer support and carers' interventions all need to be part of the care planning.

Women who are at particular risk of developing postpartum psychosis, for example those with a history of postpartum psychosis or a history of bipolar affective disorder, schizophrenia or schizoaffective disorder, need to be monitored carefully in the later stages of pregnancy and early postpartum. Modifiable risk factors, medication, psychological interventions, a specialist perinatal team and family support should be optimised in the later stages of pregnancy and the early postpartum period to reduce the risk of relapse. Some women, while asymptomatic in pregnancy, may choose to take prophylactic medication during the later stages of pregnancy to reduce the risk of relapse and some women at a very high risk of relapse may be offered a prophylactic mother and baby unit admission (Box 13.6).

Schizophrenia

Prevalence

Schizophrenia remains a worldwide serious mental illness (lifetime morbid risk approximately 0.7%). Beyond the accepted mental health burden, schizophrenia has consequences for a person's physical health, socio-economic status and ability to build relationships with others, including their children. Medications prescribed to alleviate the symptoms of schizophrenia are associated with side effects and negative physical health outcomes. Patients may find themselves on multiple medication regimens. These factors must be carefully considered by both patient and professionals when a person with schizophrenia wishes to or does become pregnant.

Women and men with schizophrenia have reduced fertility compared to the general population. Patients with schizophrenia have been found to have less than half as many children and half as many grandchildren. The course of the illness can affect a person's ability to find sexual partners and sustain relationships. Emotional responses may be flattened, sexual desire reduced and goal-orientated executive functioning diminished. Professionals are required to be sensitive to these issues when caring for women with schizophrenia within and outside of the perinatal period.

Risk Factors

Women with schizophrenia are at a higher risk of coercive relationships and sexual assault. As a result of their illness, they may undertake more risky behaviour with increased unwanted and unplanned pregnancies. Women with schizophrenia are more likely to be single mothers, experience social disadvantage and present towards the ends of the reproductive age spectrum (<20 and >35 years of age) (20).

Physical health may be poorer and women with schizophrenia are more likely to smoke, be older and take fewer antenatal vitamins. Women have increased risk of economic disadvantage and lack social support. Anxiety comes from stigma associated with their diagnosis, apprehension they could relapse and the constant underlying fear that baby may be removed. Women with pre-existing mental illness may avoid mental health services on this basis.

A diagnosis of schizophrenia in a mother is associated with adverse neonatal outcomes, including birth weight below the 10th percentile (even when the high rate of smoking among this cohort is accounted for). Obstetric complications include placental abnormalities (namely, placental abruption) and fetal distress (20). The need for augmentation of delivery significantly increases. Schizophrenia is an independent risk factor for congenital abnormalities (21). The risk of neonatal cardiovascular disorders significantly increases (20), as do conditions such as holoprosencephaly and microcephaly.

Onset and Presentation

During pregnancy psychotic relapse is rare, but following delivery women with paranoid schizophrenia have an increased risk of relapse and difficulties with parenting. For this cohort, onset of the relapse of psychosis is noted to be later and length of postnatal hospitalisation is longer compared to women with mood disorders. Women with non-affective psychosis have an increased risk of non-psychotic depression (which may be missed by professionals when the emphasis is on a psychotic relapse), leading to further difficulties bonding and mother–infant interaction. A 1996 study suggested the most important factor that predicted maternal separation from child or requirement of formal supervision was a schizophrenia diagnosis. The stress (and sleep deprivation) of looking after a child and managing a serious mental illness, against a background of reduced social and emotional support, has led to 50% of mothers with schizophrenia losing custody of their children.

Women with a diagnosis of schizophrenia can experience relapse during the perinatal period where positive symptoms and, in addition, negative symptoms and cognitive impairment associated with schizophrenia can impact the experience and ability to parent.

Management

Women with a diagnosis of schizophrenia require specialist support, psychoeducation and a planned collaborative approach from preconception counselling to the end of the perinatal period. Women with schizophrenia are routinely prescribed psychotropic medication during pregnancy, with 41% of women with schizophrenia on such a prescription. Understandably, the balance is a fine one between potential relapse of illness, effect on baby, impact on pregnancy and side effects (especially in the immediate postnatal period when looking after a newborn).

Preconception medication advice should focus on a collaborative review of antipsychotic medication, especially that which has been effective previously. All psychotropic medication should be reviewed with an aim, if possible, for a small number of effective medications (reducing fetal exposure). Folic acid and pregnancy vitamins should be advised (Box 13.7).

Box 13.7 Consultation-Liaison Team Considerations: Schizophrenia

- Schizophrenia is a severe mental illness that carries significant morbidity, including an increased risk of postpartum psychosis
- Positive, negative and cognitive symptoms associated with schizophrenia can affect the experience of parenting
- Specialist input and a planned collaborative approach to care from preconception to postpartum are key

Eating Disorders

Prevalence

Studies have estimated the prevalence of active eating disorders (EDs) during pregnancy to be between 1.47% and 7.5%. Depression, anxiety and a history of deliberate self-harm or attempted suicide are common among pregnant women with EDs (22).

Impact

A review of relevant literature revealed that EDs in pregnancy were associated with preterm birth in 36% of studies and small-for-gestational-age in 63% of studies. Anorexia nervosa increases the odds of a low-birth-weight baby, particularly when women enter pregnancy with a low body mass index (BMI). Binge eating disorder is positively associated with having a large-for-gestational-age infant, and bulimia nervosa is associated with miscarriage when symptomatic during pregnancy (23). There is high risk of relapse of the ED in the postnatal period, particularly in the first six months postpartum, as well as a higher risk of developing postpartum depression and anxiety.

Assessment

Useful screening questions include:

- History of ED?
- History of low BMI?
- Current low BMI (<17.5)?
- Are you using laxatives, appetite suppressants or diuretics?
- Do you have an intense fear of or aversion towards particular foods, vomiting or choking that affects how much you eat?
- Do you try to control your weight or shape in any way?

Also ask the SCOFF (Sick, Control, One, Fat, Food) questions:

- Do you make yourself sick?
- Do you worry that you have lost control over how much you eat?
- Have you recently lost more than one stone (6 kg) in a three-month period?
- Do you believe yourself to be fat when others say you are too thin?
- Would you say food dominates your life?

In perinatal ED, current BMI and weight loss are less important than failing to gain weight as expected during the pregnancy. Obtain a summary of physical health measures including temperature, blood pressure, pulse and BMI. In addition to routine bloods, request urea and electrolytes, liver function tests, glucose, HBA1C, amylase, bilirubin, thyroid function tests, lipid profile, vitamin D B12, folate, iron, bone profile, creatine kinase, magnesium and phosphate. Request an ECG if BMI < 16, there is self-induced vomiting and/or the patient is on any medications that can prolong corrected Q-T interval.

Management

Multidisciplinary collaboration is vital, involving the liaison, maternity, perinatal and ED services. Management depends on severity and risk factors and should be, whenever possible, administered by specialist ED services. Psychological treatments are still the treatments of choice at present (Box 13.8).

Box 13.8 Points to Consider: Eating Disorders

- EDs may be associated with adverse obstetric and infant outcomes
- Co-morbid psychiatric conditions are common
- Effective multidisciplinary liaison and collaboration are key

Box 13.9 Principles of Prescribing in Pregnancy

- The general principles of prescribing, such as adequate dose, efficacy and side-effect profile, should be followed in pregnancy. It is always pertinent to avoid unwarranted use of psychotropic medication in the first trimester, when the major organs develop.
- The decision to prescribe will be guided by a risk–benefit analysis. Only women suffering with a moderate to severe depressive disorder should be treated with medication, and prompt treatment of severe depression is important because of the associated risks. In those women with a history of a severe depression and where the risk of relapse is deemed to be high, continuation of antidepressant treatment will be necessary.
- Use the established antidepressant medication at the lowest effective dose; switching medication carries a risk of relapse, as well as potential effects on the fetus, so an increased level of monitoring will be required during these times.
- No psychotropic medication has a UK marketing authorisation specifically for women who are pregnant or breastfeeding. The prescriber should follow relevant professional guidance, taking full responsibility for the decision and obtaining and documenting informed consent.
- Discuss folic acid and pregnancy vitamins.

Psychotropic Medication

Decision-making regarding prescribing in pregnancy is difficult and complex. The prescriber has to consider the risk and benefits for two individuals at all times in the context of an evidence base that is limited and associated with multiple confounders (Boxes 13.9 and 13.10).

Antidepressants

For many women with moderate to severe depression, antidepressants will be necessary to improve outcomes. Untreated perinatal depression is associated with adverse maternal, obstetric and neonatal outcomes and it is important to bear in mind that suicide is a leading cause of maternal death. A risk and benefit analysis for women with moderate to severe depressive illnesses with associated risk may lead to a recommendation for antidepressant medication throughout pregnancy and the postnatal period. It is important to co-produce medication plans with women and their families and to be transparent around the challenges in interpreting the evidence base.

Congenital Malformations

The results from recent large meta-analyses suggest that the increased risk of congenital malformations with antidepressant exposure is as low as 1–2% above the background rate of 2–4% in the general population.

Box 13.10 Key Points for Weighing Risks versus Benefits When Discussing Prescribing in Pregnancy

- The potential benefits of any treatment, taking into account the severity of the disorder and response to any previous treatment
- The potential risks and harms of treatment
- The risks and harm associated with untreated mental illness
- The need for prompt treatment because of the potential impact of an untreated mental disorder on the fetus or infant
- The risk of relapse or deterioration associated with switching or stopping medication
- The risks associated with stopping medication abruptly
- The possibility that stopping or switching a drug with known teratogenic risk after pregnancy is confirmed may not remove the risk of malformation

Grigoriadis and colleagues (24) utilised sibling pairs discordant for maternal antidepressant use and congenital malformations to account for environmental and familial confounding factors when examining the teratogenicity of SSRIs and venlafaxine. Reassuringly, data suggest that the association between antidepressants in the study and congenital malformations is due to confounding factors and not the antidepressant exposure.

Persistent Pulmonary Hypertension of the Newborn

There is also an increased risk of persistent pulmonary hypertension in the neonate (PPHN) when the fetus is exposed in late pregnancy (after 20 weeks gestation), with the general population risk of PPHN of 1.9 per 1,000 live births increasing to 5.40 per 1,000 births (24). The absolute risk difference is 0.35%, with a number needed to harm (NNTH) of 286. The increased risk of PPHN is clinically small compared to the background rate; however, the clinical implications are life-threatening and individuals and families must be informed of this risk, although care should be taken in explaining the uncertainty around the clinical significance.

Autism and Autistic Spectrum Disorders

More recently, a number of studies have reported an association between SSRI exposure in pregnancy and autism and autistic spectrum disorders (1% vs. 2%); however, it may be that the increased risk is due to a more severe mood disorder in the treated population rather than the medication itself (25).

Choice of Antidepressants

In general, SSRIs are preferred to tricyclic antidepressants (TCAs) and venlafaxine due to the lower toxicity in overdose. Preference will depend on previous response and individual choice; however, women must be informed of the risk and benefits of each medication option.

An SSRI is first-line in women who have a first episode of antidepressant treatment or are known to be responders to SSRIs. Women who have a history of non-responsiveness to SSRIs should take the antidepressant that they are known to respond to. Venlafaxine may be associated with an increased risk of maternal high blood pressure at high doses and higher toxicity in overdose in the woman than SSRIs. There is a risk of discontinuation symptoms in the woman and neonatal adaptation syndrome in the baby with most TCAs, SSRIs and serotonin noradrenaline reuptake inhibitors (SNRIs). Paroxetine and venlafaxine are associated with increased severity of discontinuation symptoms in the woman and neonatal adaptation syndrome in the baby and TCAs have a higher fatal toxicity index than SSRIs in overdose.

Antipsychotics

Recently updated guidance in the UK (14) recommends antipsychotics as first-line in the treatment of mania and psychosis, and augmentation with antidepressants for severe depressive episodes and episodes of severe anxiety.

When choosing an antipsychotic for prophylaxis or treatment in women who wish to become or who are pregnant, the effect on fertility, the risk of gestational diabetes and weight gain must be considered. Hyperprolactinaemia is common with older antipsychotics and risperidone, sulpiride and amisulpiride and may affect a woman's chances of conceiving. Several antipsychotic drugs are associated with weight gain and metabolic syndrome, which can also impact on fertility and affect fetal outcome. Olanzapine and clozapine have been associated with weight gain as much as 7% above baseline with elevated triglycerides and new onset of metabolic syndrome or insulin tolerance. Some women may choose to switch antipsychotic to reduce the chance of hyperprolactinaemia and metabolic syndrome, particularly those with a history of gestational diabetes or diabetes mellitus.

The choice of antipsychotic will also depend on the side-effect profile of each drug, taking into consideration adverse effects including extrapyramidal side effects, sedation and tardive dyskinesia, as well as potential effects on Q-T interval. However, perhaps the most important issue to take into account in the choice of antipsychotic is an individual woman's history of medication response and history of side effects. National Institute for Health and Care Excellence (NICE) guidance recommends that if a woman is already taking an antipsychotic, is stable and at risk of relapse if untreated, then she should continue the current medication. Although there are few data on the use of depot medication in pregnancy, NICE guidelines recommend depots should be avoided unless there is a history of non-compliance with oral medication.

It is estimated that between 3,000 and 4,000 pregnancies in the UK are exposed to antipsychotics every year and antipsychotics are not thought to be major teratogens. One prospective study (26) identified 561 women exposed to second-generation antipsychotics and 284 exposed to first-generation antipsychotics and did not find evidence of teratogenicity. Some studies have reported increased risk of preterm delivery, low birth weight and small-for-gestational-age in infants exposed to first-generation antipsychotics; however, these data should be interpreted with caution as it is not clear whether the associated adverse outcomes are due to the medication, underlying psychopathology or uncontrolled confounding factors.

While there is no clear evidence of teratogenicity, a poor neonatal adaptation syndrome has been widely reported in neonates exposed to antipsychotics (27). The syndrome is characterised by tremors, irritability and somnolence; while common, it is self-limiting. Occasionally, infants will need to be monitored in hospital, although treatment is supportive only. Women should be advised to take folic acid when planning for pregnancy and prescribed an antipsychotic.

Lithium

The efficacy of lithium in the long-term management of bipolar disorder is well established and lithium is the one prophylactic medication that has been shown to be effective in the prevention of relapse in the perinatal period. Previously, retrospective studies reported high rates of cardiac abnormalities, especially Ebstein's anomaly, with some studies reporting a 400-fold increase in occurrence of the abnormality. More recent robust systematic reviews have reported a smaller increase in the risk of malformations. Women should be informed of the uncertainty around the risks associated with lithium therapy while considering the balance of risks of treatment versus non-treatment. On balance, for some women, the benefits of treatment with lithium may outweigh the risk, especially if there is good evidence of response and significant recurrence following previous discontinuation.

Because of the uncertainty around cardiac malformation and the dangers of lithium toxicity with the rapidly changing fluid balance around delivery, it is recommended to inform the obstetrician of first trimester exposure and consider additional fetal screening for cardiovascular anomalies. The recommendation from NICE and British Association for Psychopharmacology guidance is to measure plasma lithium levels monthly until 36 weeks pregnancy and then weekly until delivery. To prevent maternal and neonatal intoxication, lithium should be suspended for 24–48 hours before a planned Caesarean section or induction, and at the onset of labour and the lithium level should be measured 12 hours after the last dose. If levels are not above the therapeutic range, restart lithium on day 1 postnatal and check the level again after one week.

Mood Stabilisers

NICE guidance recommends the use of mood stabilisers in pregnancy only if antipsychotics are ineffective because of the teratogenic risks associated with mood stabilisers and the neurodevelopmental and neurobehavioral effects observed in infancy. Sodium valproate exposure in utero carries, associated with an 11% risk of congenital malformations, and adverse fetal outcome compared to the other mood stabilisers. Sodium valproate is singled out in the NICE guidance and recently updated guidance states that sodium valproate should no longer be prescribed to women of childbearing potential and is contraindicated in pregnancy.

In an absolute minority of cases, and only if there is a compelling case to prescribe, the woman needs to be fully informed of all the risks and engage with the Pregnancy Prevention Programme and undergo an annual review to assess the indication for ongoing prescription. Fetal exposure to sodium valproate has also been linked to adverse neurodevelopmental outcomes for some time. The relatively recent publication of data from the prospective observational study Neurodevelopmental Effects of Antiepileptic Drugs has provided robust evidence on the teratogenicity and adverse effects of exposure to mood stabilisers. Those infants exposed to sodium valproate had an IQ 7–10 points lower compared to unexposed peers at a six-year follow-up independent of maternal IQ, worse motor functioning and language skills (28), and impaired emotional and behavioural function.

Carbamazepine has also been associated with neurodevelopmental delay, although results appear to be more inconsistent than for sodium valproate. Lamotrigine may be a safer alternative. The International Lamotrigine Pregnancy Registry reported no consistent association between lamotrigine exposure in utero and congenital malformation in 1,558 cases. Care must be taken in prescribing lamotrigine in pregnancy as women are at risk of relapse if doses are not adjusted. Following delivery, lamotrigine levels rise and will need to be adjusted to prevent toxicity. There is also a risk of Stevens–Johnson syndrome which can be a life-threatening condition. Titration of lamotrigine should be carried out gradually according to British National Formulary guidance. Consideration should be given to measuring lamotrigine in pregnancy as levels can fall in the second and third trimester.

Anxiolytic and Hypnotics

There are limited data on the impact of anxiolytics and hypnotics on fertility, pregnancy and safety in breastfeeding. The risk and benefit analysis, therefore, is important as well as close monitoring of babies with mothers who are breastfeeding and taking these medications.

Benzodiazepines

Some studies have suggested an association between benzodiazepine exposure and oral cleft; however, subsequent studies have not replicated this finding (29). Some studies have suggested a poor neonatal adaptation syndrome post-delivery and therefore monitoring of the exposed neonate is recommended with supportive treatment.

The safety of benzodiazepines in breastfeeding is largely unknown. Given the uncertainty around the safety of benzodiazepines in pregnancy and breastfeeding, their use is rarely recommended.

Z-Drugs (Zopiclone and Zolpidem)

Information is limited about the safety of so-called Z-drugs in pregnant women. One study has suggested adverse obstetric outcomes, but it is unclear how much this is due to the Z-drug or an underlying disorder. Again, Z-drugs are not routinely recommended for women in the perinatal period.

Beta Blockers

Beta-blocker exposure in utero may be associated with fatal hypoglycaemia and intra-uterine growth restriction but this may be due to the underlying maternal hypertension and so, again, the safety of beta blockers in pregnancy is unclear. Use of beta blockers near term may result in neonatal beta adrenoceptor blockade, leading to neonatal bradycardia, hypotension and hypoglycaemia. Neonatal respiratory distress has also been reported.

For a full review of the safety evidence of antipsychotics, mood stabilisers and anti-depressants, readers are directed to comprehensive systematic reviews such as NICE guidance CG192 (14) and British Association of Psychopharmacology, Perinatal Guidelines (30). Further information and evidence on the reproductive safety of psychotropic medication can be found at the US Food and Drug Administration and Medicines Healthcare Products and Regulatory Agency.

Summary points:

- untreated perinatal mental illness can be associated with adverse outcomes for both the mother and developing fetus and infant
- there is much uncertainty around the evidence base for the safety of psychotropic medication in pregnancy and breastfeeding
- a careful risk and benefit discussion should be carried out to consider the individual case and the optimum time for this is preconception.

Perinatal Risk Assessment

Identification and Risk Assessment in the Perinatal Period

It is important to identify and support women with mental health issues in pregnancy and the postnatal period. Perinatal mental health illnesses are often predictable; therefore, early or preconception advice for women vulnerable to becoming unwell is important.

A range of guidance is available outlining the identification of risk factors within the perinatal period. These include NICE Clinical Guidance CG192 (14), Scottish Intercollegiate Guidelines Network SIGN (update is pending), Royal College of Obstetricians Good Practice No. 14 (31) and the Confidential Enquiry into Maternal Deaths, MBBRACE-UK (32).

Pregnancy does not protect against mental illness. There is a high risk of deterioration of existing serious mental illness and a resultant admission to a mental health hospital. Maternal suicide remains the leading direct cause of maternal death between six weeks and a year after delivery. In maternal suicide, the commonest diagnosis is recurrent depressive disorder.

It is essential to identify risks and discuss the management of mental health prior to a pregnancy. This allows time to plan medication and/or therapy, to optimise well-being (confronting alcohol, smoking or drug issues if present) and to improve physical health. Consideration should be given to preconception counselling for all women with serious mental illness in their reproductive years.

Women need to be asked about risk factors. The MBRRACE report identified that approximately 20% of women who died from completed suicide did not have recorded evidence of being asked about their mental health. It is essential this is a collaborative, supportive approach with the woman and she does not feel penalised or jeopardised because of her mental health.

Equally, professionals need to be aware and receive appropriate training to recognise initial insidious signs of perinatal mental health deterioration. The rapidity of onset and progression of illness should be highlighted.

At booking, women should be asked about:

- history of puerperal psychosis, psychosis, bipolar affective disorder and severe depression
- family history of puerperal psychosis or bipolar affective disorder.

Perinatal 'red flags' should be explored sensitively:

- new thoughts or acts of violent self-harm
- new and persistent expressions of incompetency as a mother
- estrangement from the infant
- recent significant changes in mental state or emergence of new symptoms
- repeated referrals of a mother to mental health services.

Disengagement from services should be regarded as concern of a potentially worsening mental state. Pro-active follow-up should be undertaken. In addition, judgements made based on psychosocial factors or certain diagnoses (especially those associated with impulsivity, substance misuse and social adversity) can result in self-harm and suicide risk being overlooked. Self-harm in pregnancy should always be explored. If red flags are identified, urgent referral is required to a perinatal mental health team with consideration of intensive support (mental health crisis teams) or admission to a mother and baby unit.

There should be a locally agreed protocol with safeguarding services if concerns or red flags are identified. This needs to be a collaborative approach; any professional considering a safeguarding referral should undertake an open conversation with the mother. Mental illness itself is not an indication for referral to safeguarding. Instead, a safeguarding referral should take place as a consequence of the information obtained from a thorough risk assessment.

The MBRRACE report outlines that there should not be an expectation to ask family members or partner to take the place of perinatal services. They are not trained in perinatal mental health conditions and may themselves be struggling or traumatised after the delivery. Family members do have a crucial role in supporting and caring for the mother. Therefore, education on relevant perinatal conditions is important as family members and partners will likely be the first people to recognise early changes in the mother's mental state.

Perinatal Care Planning

Perinatal Services

Between 2016 and 2021, as part of the five-year forward view, there has been a commitment of £365 million to support at least 30,000 more women each year to access timely, evidence-based specialist mental healthcare during the perinatal period that is closer to their homes and opening new mother and baby units.

Reports such as the National Maternity Review: Better Births have highlighted the need for services along the maternity journey to work together to provide personalised, holistic safe care. There is also increased recognition of the role of specialist mental health midwives. Based in many maternity units, and in addition to usual midwifery care, these specialist midwives play a vital role in liaising between maternity, mental health and other services to help provide optimum care for women struggling with mental health difficulties during their maternity journey.

The expansion of perinatal services has continued to be a priority in the Long-Term Plan (LTP) influenced by the '1001 critical days'. This recognises that the period from conception to two years old is critical for optimal child development. The LTP aims for women with moderate, severe and complex perinatal mental illness to be supported where needed for up to 24 months postnatal rather than the current 12 months postnatal. As well as further expanding therapy access (including parent–infant, couples and family interventions), there is also a focus on signposting partners to appropriate mental health support, with estimates that up to 20% of co-parents themselves experience perinatal mental health difficulties.

Preconception Counselling

There is increasing recognition that the preconception period is an ideal opportunity to optimise a woman's physical and mental health, thus improving outcomes for her, baby and the wider family (33). Women who are at high risk of relapse in the perinatal period should be offered referral to a perinatal psychiatrist for preconception counselling (14). During such appointments a full history is taken to allow a personalised care plan to be developed. This also provides the opportunity using the bio-psycho-social model to discuss support, including the use of medications in pregnancy and breastfeeding, and women can be counselled on the potential effect of medication on fertility as discussed. This is also an opportunity to discuss optimising modifiable risk factors including promoting antenatal engagement and physical health monitoring for co-morbidities, smoking cessation input, substance misuse support and advice on alcohol consumption.

Options for support such as input from the local perinatal mental health team, specialist mental health midwives and social care can be discussed, as well as organising a tour of the local mother and baby unit for those at high risk of severe illness in the perinatal period. There is also an opportunity to optimise physical health prior to pregnancy with psychoeducation around, for example, diet, pregnancy vitamins, alcohol, substance misuse and smoking, which all have a significant impact on obstetric and neonatal outcomes.

The Pan-London Perinatal Mental Health Network best practice toolkit for pre-birth planning includes a template that provides guidance on what should be considered in the planning and running of such a meeting (34).

References

1. Doyle M, Carballedo A, O'Keane V. Perinatal depression and psychosis: An update. *BJPsych Advances*. 2015;21(1):5–14.

2. Woody CA, Ferrari AJ, Siskind DJ et al. A systematic review and meta-regression of the prevalence and incidence of perinatal depression. *J Affect Disord*. 2017;219:86–92.

3. Shorey S, Chee CYI, Ng ED et al. Prevalence and incidence of postpartum depression among healthy mothers: A systematic review and meta-analysis. *J Psychiatr Res*. 2018;104:235–48.

4. Munk-Olsen T, Laursen TM, Mendelson T, Pedersen CB, Mors O, Mortensen PB. Risks and predictors of readmission for a mental disorder during the postpartum period. *Arch Gen Psychiatry*. 2009;66:189–95.

5. Biaggi A, Conroy S, Pawlby S et al. Identifying the women at risk of antenatal anxiety and depression: A systematic review. *J Affect Disord*. 2016;191:62–77.

6. Marchesi C, Ossola P, Amerio A et al. Clinical management of perinatal anxiety disorders: A systematic review. *J Affect Disord*. 2016;190:543–50.

7. Cohen MJ, Meador KJ, Browning N et al. Fetal antiepileptic drug exposure: Adaptive and emotional/behavioral functioning at age 6 years. *Epilepsy Behav*. 2013;29(2):308–15.

8. Letourneau, N, Dennis C, Cosic N et al. The effect of perinatal depression treatment for mothers on parenting and child development: A systematic review. *Depress Anxiety*. 2017;34 (10):928–66.

9. Lanza di Scalea T, Wisner KL. Antidepressant medication use during breastfeeding. *Clin Obstet Gynecol*. 2009 ep;52(3):483–97.

10. McAllister-Williams RH, Baldwin DS, Cantwell R et al. British Association for Psychopharmacology consensus guidance on the use of psychotropic medication preconception, in pregnancy and postpartum 2017. *J Psychopharmacol*. 2017;31(5):519–52.

11. Fawcett EJ, Fairbrother N, Cox ML et al. The prevalence of anxiety disorders during pregnancy and the postpartum period: A multivariate Bayesian meta-analysis. *J Clin Psychiatry*. 2019;80 (4):18r12527.

12. Dennis CL, Falah-Hassani K, Shiri R. Prevalence of antenatal and postnatal anxiety: Systematic review and meta-analysis. *Br J Psychiatry*. 2017;210 (5):315–23.

13. Russell EJ, Fawcett JM, Mazmanian D. Risk of obsessive-compulsive disorder in pregnant and postpartum women: A meta-analysis. *J Clin Psychiatry*. 2013;74:377–85.

14. National Institute for Health and Care Excellence. Antenatal and postnatal mental health: Clinical management and service guidance. 2020. www.nice.org.uk/guidance/cg192.

15. O'Connell MA, Leahy-Warren P, Khashan, A et al. Worldwide prevalence of tokophobia in pregnant women: Systematic review and meta-analysis. *Acta Obstetricia et Gynaecological Scandinavica.* 2017;**96**(8):907–20.

16. National Institute for Health and Care Excellence. Caesarean birth. 2021. www.nice.org.uk/guidance/ng192/chapter/Recommendations.

17. Healthy London Partnership, Pan-London Perinatal Mental Health networks. Fear of childbirth (tokophobia) and traumatic experience of birth: Best practice toolkit. 2018. www.transformationpartnersinhealthandcare.nhs.uk/wp-content/uploads/2022/08/Tokophobia-best-practice-toolkit-Jan-2018-update-for-website-2022-.pdf.

18. Jones I, Craddock N. Searching for the puerperal trigger: Molecular genetic studies of bipolar affective puerperal psychosis. *Psychopharmacol Bull.* 2007;**40**(2):115–28.

19. Di Florio A, Smith S, Jones I. Postpartum psychosis.*The Obstetrician & Gynaecologist.* 2013;**15**(3):145–50.

20. Jablensky A, Morgan V Zubrick, S et al. Pregnancy, delivery, and neonatal complications in a population cohort of women with schizophrenia and major affective disorders. *Am J Psychiatry.* 2005;**162**(1):79–91.

21. Hizkiyahu R, Levy A., Sheiner, E. Pregnancy outcome of patients with schizophrenia. *Am J Perinatol.* 2009;**27**(1):19–23.

22. Bye A, Nath S, Ryan, E et al. Prevalence and clinical characterisation of pregnant women with eating disorders. *European Eating Disorders Review.* 2020;**28**(2):141–55.

23. Charbonneau K, Seabrook J. Adverse birth outcomes associated with types of eating disorders: A review. *Can J Diet Pract Res.* 2019;**80**(3):131–6.

24. Grigoriadis S, VonderPorten EH, Mamisashvili L et al. The effect of prenatal antidepressant exposure on neonatal adaptation: A systematic review and meta-analysis. *J Clin Psychiatry.* 2013;**74**(4):e309–20.

25. Rai D, Lee BK, Dalman C, Golding J, Lewis G, Magnusson C. Parental depression, maternal antidepressant use during pregnancy, and risk of autism spectrum disorders: Population based case-control study. *BMJ.* 2013;**346**:f2059.

26. Habermann F, Fritzsche J, Fuhlbrück F et al. Atypical antipsychotic drugs and pregnancy outcome: A prospective, cohort study. *J Clin Psychopharmacol.* 2013;**33**(4):453–62.

27. Jansson LM, Velez M. Neonatal abstinence syndrome. *Curr Opin Pediatr.* 2012;**24**(2):252–8.

28. Shallcross R, Bromley RL, Cheyne CP, García-Fiñana M, Irwin B, Morrow J, Baker GA. In utero exposure to levetiracetam vs valproate: Development and language at 3 years of age. *Neurology.* 2014;**82**(3):213–21.

29. Ban L, Fleming KM, Doyle P et al. Congenital anomalies in children of mothers taking antiepileptic drugs with and without periconceptional high dose folic acid use: A population-based cohort study. *PLoS One.* 2015;**10**:e0131130.

30. British Association for Psychopharmacology. British Association for Psychopharmacology consensus guidance on the use of psychotropic medication preconception, in pregnancy and postpartum. 2017. www.bap.org.uk/pdfs/BAP_Guidelines-Perinatal.pdf.

31. Royal College of Obstetricians and Gynaecologists. Management of women with mental health issues during pregnancy and the postnatal period. 2001. www.rcog.org.uk/media/4gikqggv/managementwomenmentalhealthgoodpractice14.pdf.

32. MBRRACE-UK. MBRRACE-UK – Saving lives, improving mothers' care: Lessons learned to inform maternity care from the UK and Ireland confidential enquiries into

maternal deaths and morbidity 2018–20. 2022. www.npeu.ox.ac.uk/mbrrace-uk /reports.

33. Catalao R, Mann S, Wilson C et al. Preconception care in mental health services: Planning for a better future. *BJPsych*. 2020; **216**(4):180–1.

34. Healthy London Partnerships. Pan-London Perinatal Mental Health Network. Pre-birth planning: Best practice toolkit for perinatal mental health services. 2019. www .healthylondon.org/wp-content/uploads/ 2019/01/Pre-birth-planning-guidance-for -Perinatal-Mental-Health-Networks.pdf.

35. Dadi AF, Miller ER, Woodman R et al. Antenatal depression and its potential causal mechanisms among pregnant mothers in Gondar town: Application of structural equation model. *BMC Pregnancy Childbirth* 2020;**20**(168). https://doi.org/10 .1186/s12884-020-02859-2.

36. Marcus SM. Depression during pregnancy: Rates, risks and consequences – motherisk update 2008. *Can J Clin Pharmacol*. 2009;**16**: e15–e22.

Paediatric Consultation-Liaison Psychiatry

Rachel Elvins, Louisa Draper, Neelo Aslam and Ruth Marshall

Introduction

The aim of this chapter is to introduce the reader to the key conceptual and practical aspects of paediatric consultation-liaison psychiatry. The relationship between physical and mental illness in children and the wider implications for educational and social opportunities are discussed, along with comment on how this dovetails with the emergence of adversity. The need for dedicated paediatric liaison services becomes apparent, highlighting the value of interface work between community child and adolescent mental health services (CAMHs), the liaison psychiatry team and paediatric medical and surgical teams.

Practical tips on the nuances of assessing young people are outlined alongside common clinical presentations and mental health law in this patient group. Presentations to emergency departments are not covered as these generally fall outside the scope of dedicated paediatric consultation-liaison services. Finally, comments on service models and research are given to stimulate discussion within teams about service sustainability, development and quality improvement.

Relationship between Physical Illness and Psychiatric Disorders in Young People

There is a recognised imperative for paediatric and paediatric liaison services to work together to provide routine and systematic mental health screening in children and adolescents, anticipatory guidance, brief intervention for milder emotional or adjustment difficulties and triage to evidence-based treatment for particular disorders when needed. Why is this important in the twenty-first century?

- Chronic physical illness is on the increase and is estimated to affect a quarter of children worldwide (1).
- Developments in treatment have resulted in improved survival and life expectancy in children with a range of serious physical illness, a trend which has been apparent since the 1980s (2). These treatments are often not curative, resulting in an increased prevalence of chronic illness in childhood.
- Other non-developmental long-term childhood conditions such as asthma, obesity and diabetes are also on the rise (3).
- Psychological and behavioural disorders are common in childhood; 10% of children and young people (aged 5–16 years) have a clinically diagnosable mental health problem (1).
- Fifty per cent of mental health problems are established by age 14 and 75% by age 24.
- In any given year, 20% of adolescents may experience a mental health problem (1).

Given that both chronic physical illness and mental health problems are relatively common in childhood and adolescence, they are likely to co-occur and the presence of one increases the risk of the other. The association between chronic physical illness in children and the emergence of behavioural and emotional disturbance as well as psychiatric disorder has been well documented in research literature and continues to be the focus of increasing concern. Most of these studies have been cross-sectional in design and conducted in clinical samples, although recently several longitudinal studies have attempted to better understand the risk of mental disorder and the underlying mechanisms linking chronic physical illness and mental health conditions (4).

Disorders most likely to be associated with chronic physical illness across childhood include anxiety, depression, post-traumatic stress disorder, adjustment disorder and problem behaviour such as oppositionality (5). Rates of mental disorder may vary over the course of physical illness; some studies highlight the peri-diagnostic period as being a particularly risky time for mental illness, whereas others demonstrate stability of multimorbidity over time. For example, adjustment disorders are more likely to be seen around the time of a diagnosis or change in treatment (starting dialysis), whereas depression has been shown to be strongly related to quality of life in children with chronic kidney disease (6).

Rutter and colleagues' seminal work in 1970 (7) reported that children with a chronic illness affecting the central nervous system are especially at risk of mental health problems, being five times as likely to have a psychiatric disorder as physically healthy children. However, significant behavioural problems and poorer social competence are found in children with any chronic physical ill-health problem, with little difference attributable to other factors such as age or gender (1). The specific condition does not seem to be predictive of child adjustment or emotional health following a physical diagnosis (8).

In addition to any direct effects on brain function, risks of developing a specific mental health problem, such as anxiety or depression, are likely to be mediated by type and speed of admission to hospital, pain and trauma (including those associated with lengthy or unpleasant treatment), effects on family functioning, caregiver health and restriction of social and educational opportunities. If the disease is life-threatening, adjustment is likely to be poorer.

The Intersection between Physical Illness, Educational and Social Opportunities and Mental Health

Childhood and adolescence represent periods of rapid change and development across physical, social and psychological domains, for which educational and social activities are crucial. The presence of chronic physical illness and subsequent treatment is likely to reduce social and educational opportunities, with nearly 30% of young people reporting an impact on these activities. Activity limitation has been linked to higher rates of depression in this patient group and may be particularly relevant during adolescence when peer relationships and personal identity become increasingly important (9).

Difficulties associated with intrinsic disorders (primary psychiatric conditions and neurodevelopmental disorders) also tend to come to the fore during middle childhood, and they are most likely to be noticed in an educational setting or through observation of peer interactions. Limited time in educational and social settings with peers potentially delays diagnosis and treatment. Unrecognised and unmanaged neurodevelopmental disorders such as attention deficit hyperactivity disorder (ADHD), autistic spectrum conditions (ASC) and intellectual disability have the potential to adversely affect care of chronic physical illness. Diabetes represents a salient example, where risky behaviour, poor medication adherence, poor diet, anxiety and attendance at hospital can affect both the physical and mental health of young people. Neurodevelopmental disorders are also associated with an increased prevalence of physical co-morbidities such as epilepsy, migraine and asthma, and they are increasingly recognised as part of the clinical phenotype in genetic disorders and syndromes, for example the association between neurofibromatosis and Tourette syndrome. In some cases, the parents themselves may also be affected which may also have an impact on the care and health of the young person.

Chronic Illness and Adversity

The bio-psycho-social effects of chronic physical illness are multiple and cumulative over time. On an individual level, neurological conditions in particular may impact directly on behaviour and cognition, while stress-related increases in cortisol impact physiology during crucial times of physical development. Systemically, the burden of chronic illness can lead to increased stress in the family and may lead to family discord, parental ill health and parental separation. The competing demands of work and frequent hospital attendances may affect parental employment and contribute to financial difficulties, therefore exposing the child to greater adversity.

Childhood adversity in turn has been linked to mental and physical ill health. It has been hypothesised that childhood adversity and exposure to chronic stress affects the nervous, endocrine and immune systems, leading to impaired psychosocial and cognitive functioning and increasing the risk of both mental and physical ill health. Pilot studies are exploring putative biomarkers of physiological and psychological stress. Urinary F2-isoprostanes are compounds which are formed from the peroxidation of essential fatty acids and are inflammatory mediators that can be used to accurately measure oxidative stress in individuals. Measuring their levels has been used to further our understanding of potential mediating factors of the relationship between adverse childhood experiences (ACEs) and mental illness, raising the possibility that these biomarkers could be used to identify children and young people at high risk and help to tailor interventions (10).

Difficulties with Diagnosis

Diagnostic overshadowing of emotional and intrinsic difficulties can impact access to effective support and treatment. For example, it can be difficult to diagnose depression, the symptoms of which (changes in sleep, appetite, concentration and mood) may be confused with medication side effects (such those from steroids or chemotherapy) or symptoms of physical illness. Anxiety and distress can be normal and appropriate and may even contribute to developing coping mechanisms in children and family systems in the context of a chronic illness or new life-changing diagnosis. The threshold for intervention and treatment of emotional components of presentations therefore can be difficult to establish and is often resource-dependent.

The Need for Paediatric Liaison Services

The previous paragraphs illustrate the complex interplay between physical and mental problems in childhood and their wider implications for long-term well-being, access to education and social opportunities and the bidirectional relationship with adversity.

Despite recognition of the mental health needs of children with chronic physical illness, the provision and composition of mental health services to paediatric units vary greatly from one centre to another (11). Much of the mental health research in children with chronic illness has been diagnosis-specific, focussing on, for example, diabetes or cancer rather than the psychosocial sequelae of chronic illness. This may explain why provision varies not only between paediatric centres but also within centres. Children with chronic illness, regardless of diagnosis, are likely to have much in common such as adjusting to treatment, disruption of education and friendships, change in self-image and frequent hospital attendance or admission. Some centres have a combined self-harm/emergency and psychological/physical illness service. In others, the self-harm and emergency work is carried out by local CAMHs or specialist emergency department-based liaison teams. Funding for mental health services has always trailed behind other provision in the National Health Service (NHS); paediatric liaison more so because it sits outside the tiered model of CAMHs and more modern service describers such as i-Thrive (12).

The paediatric liaison team has distinct features and should complement other CAMHs in terms of skill mix and therapeutic offer:

Improving access and closing care provision gaps. Most cases seen by paediatric liaison services have not been seen by a CAMHs practitioner before, illustrating the difference in thresholds for these teams and emphasising an important function of the liaison team in terms of providing for an unmet need.

System mechanics. Co-located paediatric services and flexibility in working practices are essential characteristics of a paediatric liaison team. Close collaboration with paediatric services provides learning, teaching and training opportunities. Rapid response times and flexible and joint appointments are needed because of the nature of acute ward work and to minimise the number of hospital visits and further educational disruption.

A specialist, holistic approach. Paediatric liaison teams are required to undertake a wide range of work requiring a specific skill set to provide assessment and intervention across a broad range of clinical presentations and psychosocial difficulties. By taking a whole-system-around-the-child approach, they help further the understanding of developmental, educational, emotional, systemic and family factors that contribute to the clinical picture (13). In the absence of mental illness or obvious psychiatric symptoms, psychological factors contributing to the illness presentation and efficacy of treatments may not be apparent to the parents, child or medical team; this is particularly pertinent in cases where there are medically unexplained or functional somatic symptoms.

Risk assessment. Addressing quality-of-life issues and the negative psychological impact of living with a long-term or chronic physical illness is dovetailed with skills in acute and longer-term risk assessment and management; there is an increased risk of suicide in children and young people with serious medical illness (14).

Working with families. The suggestion of mental illness or mention of mental health services can be met with resistance from families. Parity of esteem with physical illness services has not yet been achieved and mental illness may be seen as stigmatising. The paediatric liaison team can help parents understand the many functions of the service and the potential impact of therapeutic work and break down barriers to engagement. This is particularly relevant in the treatment of medically unexplained symptoms where there has usually been a focus by both families and professionals on identifying a physical cause of illness (15). It is thought to be helpful to be able to have paediatric liaison as part of the multidisciplinary team from the beginning of such a journey in paediatric services.

Specialist assessment and interventions. 'Must-see' cases were outlined in Chapter 2 for trainees in liaison psychiatry placements. Paediatric liaison team members also develop a specialist skillset in assessing, managing and providing support for the treating team across a range of clinical scenarios commonly encountered in medical and surgical settings. Specific psychiatric presentations are discussed later in this chapter. In broad brushstrokes, the paediatric liaison skillset includes but is not limited to:

- Management of neuropsychiatric conditions including paediatric delirium, catatonia, altered mental states in encephalitis and other forms of acquired brain injury.
- Review of medications as a potential contributing factor to the clinical presentation, especially on paediatric intensive care wards.
- Assessment and management of chronic somatic symptoms and factitious disorders.
- Specialist contribution to epilepsy surgery, surgical oncology, transplantation or cardiac surgery in tertiary centres.
- Providing informed guidance on management of young people with pre-established mental health conditions on the paediatric wards. This may involve support for multidisciplinary team communication and management of the environment and nursing observations or advice on medication management.
- Advising on medicolegal issues in paediatric settings including consent, competence, the Mental Health Act and complex safeguarding scenarios.
- Assessment and management of young people and families presenting in distress, whether or not an identifiable mental illness is present.
- Identifying and helping to manage psychodynamic processes such as splitting in the team and family and working systemically with the families and wider systems, including in some circumstances containing professionals' anxieties (such as when waiting for an appropriate mental health bed). This underscores the need for teams to be multidisciplinary in their make-up.

Reintegration. The paediatric liaison team proactively contributes to safe and effective discharge planning and plans for children and young people to reintegrate into education and their community of peers after long absences (including contributing to education health and care plans).

Improving short- and long-term outcomes. Service sustainability and further development can be informed by collecting relevant outcome measures. The measured effects on hospital outcomes (such as length of admission/frequency of readmission) are popular and sometimes useful metrics used across different types of liaison mental health services (16). In terms of the longer-term impact of illness and intervention, persistent ill health can lead to poorer psychosocial outcomes in adulthood (17); effects are mediated by the impact on development, schooling and life expectancy, as well as the effects of disease and treatment that directly affect the brain and cognition. It is difficult to accurately ascertain the impact of intervention because of the heterogeneity of disorders in their impact and severity and differential treatment effectiveness.

In summary, the paediatric liaison team offers multidisciplinary assessment, formulation, interventions and proactive collaboration with other services across a range of clinical, psychological, educational, social and medicolegal scenarios with the aim of contributing to integrated, safe and effective care for young people.

Clinical Aspects of Paediatric Liaison Practice

Developmental View of Assessment and Intervention in Paediatric Liaison

Many mental health conditions emerge before the age of 12, with the potential for long-term effects on individuals and their families. There has been a significant focus in recent years on the mental health and wellness of adolescents and adults with physical health conditions, for example cystic fibrosis, but less attention to specifics of depression and anxiety in younger children, or to other common paediatric co-morbidities including traumatic experience, developmental disorders (e.g. ADHD and autism spectrum conditions) and behavioural problems (18).

Children often display anxious and depressive symptoms in response to illness (19). Post-traumatic stress is also evident in children who have been acutely unwell with severe illness and/or have had multiple invasive procedures during the treatment phase. Support from family and classmates is associated with better adjustment to illness and adherence to treatment plans.

Children's adjustment to chronic illness can change with time. For example, the psychosocial adjustment of children with cancer is mediated by other life events unrelated to the cancer (20). Children's understanding of illness is different from adults' and progresses through a number of stages (e.g. from believing that illness comes about through magic, through contamination and contagion theories), to a more adult view of internal as well as external causation. Knowledge of these stages (which mostly relate to Piagetian ideas of cognitive development) is essential if clinicians are to communicate effectively with children; see (21) for a dated but decent review. Those who are unable to express their distress or seek help appropriately for emotional symptoms may have particular adjustment problems, such as those with pre-existing communication difficulties, for example autism spectrum conditions. Asking a child to explain what they think is happening to their body in their own words will often provide useful pointers regarding their current level of ability to conceptualise illness.

Piaget's stages of development and conception of illness (21):

Sensorimotor (0–2 years): Limited verbal ability and therefore no internal narrative or formal reasoning. Experience of illness is based on immediate sensory experience.

Preoperational (2–6 years): Similar experiences to preoperational children but with specific awareness of particular body parts and the basic premise of cause and effect emerges. It is imperfect and illness is mostly attributed to external, sometimes magical causes or entities that are temporally related to the emergence of symptoms ('the sun came out when I coughed; it's caused my cold').

Concrete operational (7–11 years): Logic develops, as does increased factual knowledge about the body, but cause-and-effect reasoning is limited by inability to engage in abstract reasoning, single cause, single affected organ, single or limited number of effects).

Formal operational (11 years and older): Abstract reasoning affords a more holistic, systems-based view of the body and contributing causes to illness.

These life-stage issues are of relevance not just to the time of disease onset and disability but also to the individual psychological development of the child as they age. Disruptions to schooling caused by hospitalisation or treatments may have a social impact, for example loss of friends, as well as the more obvious issues in respect to learning and preparation for examinations, despite the generally much improved provision of schooling in hospitals. Pain, restriction of activity and the necessity of adherence to medication and treatment may all have an impact on children's development, self-esteem and sense of self. Long-term physical effects of some treatments on growth and reproduction may also have negative mental health consequences.

Interviewing Children and Adolescents in Paediatric Settings and Working with Paediatric Teams

The paediatric liaison practitioner will call upon all their generic competencies in interviewing and engaging children and adolescents. General hospital settings provide specific challenges, however, such as the ability to engage children who are in pain, experiencing delirium or receiving invasive medical treatments such as dialysis or chemotherapy or those who have co-existing communication difficulties due to surgical procedures or tracheostomy. This might include adapting clinician's language and/or the environment or frequent, brief visits to enable engagement. There are also skills in being able to carry out such assessments in the context of busy paediatric wards and communicating effectively with the paediatric team. Assessment of seriously disruptive or aggressive children, or those who are at risk of self-harm, is a not an uncommon request and the practitioner should be able to contribute to and, if appropriate, lead the assessment of risk to the patient, other patients and the paediatric environment, and to give advice on the management of such risks.

Engagement of children and parents who reject the relevance of psychological factors can be a challenging task. A joint understanding or formulation of the development of the difficulties and the treatment required among the professionals involved in the patients' care is crucial and should be established early in the referral process to a liaison team, for example by way of an initial professionals' meeting, ensuring a 'same-page' approach.

Tips on interviewing children and adolescents:

- Make time to see the child with parents and also to speak with parents and child separately.
- Adjust your language according to the child's developmental level; try to avoid being patronising, jargonistic or 'cool'.
- Explain confidentiality early in the consultation; be transparent about what can and cannot be kept from others and why (risk). Reassure that you will maintain confidentiality as much as you are reasonably able.
- Be willing to go a little off-piste to build rapport. Asking about school, interests or friends can also highlight potential stressors (bullying, relationship breakdown, family discord), sources of support (face-to-face and online) and contributions to resilience.
- Build collaborative relationships with parents. This offers insight into family dynamics and valuable collateral history and can form the foundations of building a same-page approach when delivering psychological and medical interventions.

Parental Involvement and Working with Families

Parents are profoundly affected by the illness of their children. Much more is known about maternal than paternal coping (22). Studies suggest that the correlates associated with maternal and paternal psychological adjustment to chronic childhood disease differ; for example, maternal coping is often correlated with increased social support whereas paternal coping is not (23). These differences are important to consider when providing care to children with chronic disease and their families.

Parents of children with physical disease are more likely to experience marital distress. There is also evidence of increased risk of behavioural and emotional disturbance in the siblings of children who are chronically ill. The diagnosis of chronic illness in a child has effects which can bring about major changes within individuals and in the relationships between family members (24). Having a child with a chronic illness may also increase a family's economic difficulties as a result of reduced earning capacity, with increased work required at home and increasing costs in caring for children.

Parents, particularly mothers, are often crucial in mediating the patient's treatment, particularly for younger children, for example the child's adherence to management strategies. Sometimes parents do not share a view and additional perspectives from step-parents may also be offered; all of this requires careful navigation, ensuring all perspectives are taken on board while placing the child's well-being at the centre of the dialogue. Through adolescence the patient becomes increasingly autonomous and should develop increasing competence and the ability to make informed decisions about their own treatment. This is, of course, also dependent on the young person's cognitive and social/emotional development, which may mature at different stages, and the parents' ability to recognise and respect this increasing autonomy. Parental expectations may be mismatched with actual competence and this can cause distress and challenges in physical and mental healthcare; for example, high levels of anxiety in parents may reduce access for children and adolescents to required learning opportunities to develop self-care skills and undermine self-efficacy. Conversely, neglectful home environments may impact on robust development of skills needed to manage physical illness, including appropriate care-seeking and self-care.

It is therefore important for both paediatricians and liaison practitioners to take account of family functioning, parental understanding of the diagnosis and likely course, and how the family copes or the style in which they work together to support the young person. Formal systemic work can be useful in certain diagnoses, such as anorexia nervosa (25).

Psychiatric Presentations in Paediatric Settings

Children and young people may find themselves on a paediatric ward for predominantly psychiatric or psychosocial needs in a number of ways. Relevant to all psychiatry but particularly so in child psychiatry is the need to prioritise accurate understanding of presentations and formulation of difficulties over discrete diagnoses.

Those presenting in *mental health crisis* may be admitted for medical treatment of resulting harm but are also admitted to allow for safe and timely psychosocial assessment by mental health teams. Psychiatric involvement and intervention may be needed where complexity warrants or where medication might be appropriate. Such presentations can include mood disorder, emotional dysregulation, attachment difficulties or psychosis. Depending on service configuration, the psychiatrist involved may be part of community CAMHs, crisis CAMHs or paediatric liaison.

Those admitted for predominantly physical health reasons may be referred to liaison psychiatry for a variety of indications, commonly *mental health co-morbidity* and co-existence of intrinsic difficulties. This may be to a lesser or greater extent associated with the physical presentation and on a spectrum of complexity. Paediatricians may need support managing physical health needs in the context of neurodevelopmental conditions such as ASC and ADHD, as well as mental illness such as anxiety disorder or depression or indeed challenging behaviour that may be associated with additional learning needs, attachment difficulties or experience of trauma. Young people may need commencement of or adjustment of treatment for co-existing mental health diagnoses that may be long-term or new. The stresses associated with physical illness and associated admission and treatment may precipitate or exacerbate mental illness and psychiatric symptoms via wide-ranging mechanisms (sleep disturbance, separation from parents and family).

Somatoform disorders are presented in diagnostic manuals such as the *Diagnostic and Statistical Manual of Mental Disorders* (DSM) 5 (26) as discrete disorders, implying that they are easily differentiated from one another. These differentiations in practice are more often than not extremely difficult, and diagnostic attempts by paediatric and associated treating teams can be surprisingly unhelpful. Such attempts contribute to stigmatisation of those young people presenting with somatisation or medically unexplained symptoms. This can result in patients presenting with somatisation feeling disbelieved about all their symptoms or symptoms being dismissed as 'all in my head', which can then cause further distress, symptomatology, loss of function and potentially more exaggeration of symptoms.

It may be helpful to consider various continuums forming complex webs within psychosocial formulations, including greater and lesser degrees of:

- Symptoms that are present but affected by psychological factors versus symptoms fabricated (via normal bodily sensations perceived as abnormal and presented as symptoms)
- Genuine anxiety initiating or escalating physical symptoms versus intentional fabrications or exaggeration of symptoms in the context of feeling disbelieved (medical, parental, social, educational) or symptoms not being enough to assume a sick role, escape a distressing situation or prevent intolerable distress
- Secondary gain (sick role, relief from difficult, intolerable or stressful situation) versus the arguably less socially acceptable primary gain (monetary gain which may or may not be in the context of social and financial deprivation)
- Overt versus covert non-adherence to treatment
- Presentations driven by intrinsic difficulties in the child versus those driven by complexity of family systems and needs. Paediatric systems can also contribute with significant potential for iatrogenic illness and symptomatology.

Somatisation disorders are extremely common on paediatric wards and in outpatient clinic settings and represent a huge resource burden for paediatric services, as well as the young people and families they affect. The prevalence of somatisation in primary care paediatric settings has been estimated to be 25–50% of visits, although data are limited, particularly in non-primary care settings (27). The pathway to diagnosis can be tumultuous for some and patients more severely affected can spend a huge amount of time on wards, out of education and isolated from social networks. In contrast to adults, children rarely worry about 'illness' per se prior to adolescence. The parent's response to symptoms may determine the extent of associated distress as they interpret symptoms and influence time off school and associated medical help-seeking (26). Contained medical responses that address both child and family concerns therefore play an important role.

Factitious disorder is differentiated from the above by the presence of falsification of symptoms (physical or psychological) and identified deception. Factitious disorder is differentiated from malingering by the presence of obvious reward (primary gain).

Children are particularly vulnerable to *factitious disorder imposed by another* from parents and caregivers, so this is an important consideration when managing perplexing presentations in paediatric settings. Early involvement of safeguarding teams is important when considering this as a possibility to support careful consideration of child safety and well-being during investigation. It is important to consider that, while highly dangerous and damaging to children both physically and emotionally, the intention of the perpetrator is rarely singularly malicious. Again, binary categorisation (factitious or not) is often unrepresentative of the continuum of presentations. At one end of the spectrum are wilfully neglectful parents, struggling to respond to obvious need, and at the other end of the spectrum are parents who use their children to fulfil their own significant and complex needs by inducing symptoms of illness. There is a middle ground where there are parents struggling with their own mental health or adversity who cannot consistently act in their children's best interests or highly anxious parents who may find themselves exaggerating symptoms to feel heard and gain perceived appropriate responses from services. Approaching either end of this spectrum, the child is put at escalating harm; in the middle ground, appropriate concern and safe risk-taking are flanked by benign neglect or mild over-responsiveness to physical symptoms.

Perceptions among professionals of self-imposed symptoms or predicaments can heighten stigma (often already an issue for young people presenting with mental health difficulties), so those managing these challenging and complex cases may need support to maintain a compassionate approach in the context of challenging behaviours and presentations.

Neuropsychiatric presentations in children require particular consideration due to their impact on development. Children experiencing acquired brain injuries and associated medical and/or surgical treatment may be left with deficits that continue to have an impact on their developmental trajectory as they move into adulthood. The clinical presentation, including psychiatric symptomatology, is likely to evolve and is dependent upon development of skills. In addition to this, children's experiences influence their family systems in a way which in turn can influence development through altered parenting and systemic functioning. Executive cognitive functions are particularly vulnerable when they are damaged during the course of development and are influenced by the social setting. Younger children are said to suffer the 'double hazard' of loss of skills plus interference with further development. Poor attention, cognitive slowing and mental fatigue will affect school progress while they persist and the impact of behavioural changes on access to education can be significant even when no intellectual loss can be identified. The impact on parent–child relationships as well as sibling and peer relationships can also be substantial, thereby feeding into emotional difficulties. It is also important to understand the resulting difficulties in the context of premorbid psychiatric problems such as ADHD, ASD and intellectual disability. Children with depression and anxiety have often had difficulties with these premorbidly. Psychiatric sequelae, particularly behaviour disturbances, are repeatedly stressed as some of the commonest and most disruptive of the sequelae of traumatic brain injury in children (28). Commonly these include mixed restless overactivity, impulsive disobedience and explosive outbursts of anger and irritability. Less commonly, problems of discipline such as lying, stealing and destructiveness may occur, as well as lethargy or passivity. The impacts of these on socio-emotional development and well-being are legion. Again, the family environment has been highlighted as a predictive factor on long-term outcome for behavioural problems in these cases.

Case Example: Priya

Priya is a 13-year-old girl admitted with weight loss and vomiting. Previous history of chest infection and post-infection fatigue leading to poor school attendance and social withdrawal. Reluctant to eat food as feels nauseated and reports vomiting after eating, resulting in a nasogastric tube being passed to feed. Developmental history includes description of separation anxiety on attending school and some social difficulties on transition to high school. Limited attendance at high school due to physical problems.

Observed enmeshed relationship with mum who has stayed with Priya throughout the admission and is off sick from her employment. Mum is noted to be underweight and appears anxious. She is convinced that there is an underlying physical cause for the symptoms. No physical causes are identified to explain the symptoms. Mum describes a family history of chronic fatigue and fibromyalgia.

Resistance to feeding has been observed, including turning the feed rate down, clamping the feeding tube and pulling the tube out. She is reluctant to engage with the psychologist who has seen her from the liaison service and denies any mental health issues other than feeling worried about the symptoms she has and missing home and her parents when they are away from her.

Liaison role includes supporting discussions about the legal framework, such as what is reasonable for parents to decide and give consent for (zone of parental control) in a child of this age, and when consideration of the Mental Health Act might be indicated due to the resistance to treatment. A comprehensive assessment including identifying any underlying developmental disorder should be undertaken. The intervention should include psychoeducation to both Priya and her family, explaining the psychological and systemic formulation as well as individual intervention with Priya to identify motivators for change and goals of treatment.

Case Example: Josh

Josh is an 11-year-old boy with chronic pain which has been an increasing problem over the past year. This has resulted in reduced mobility and school non-attendance. There have been no medical causes of these symptoms identified. He was admitted to hospital after becoming increasingly challenging at home, refusing to go to school or to leave the house with his physical presentation deteriorating. He has threatened to hurt his mother and has talked about wanting to be dead, expressing thoughts of killing himself by hanging.

Prior to being admitted to hospital he was spending most of his day in bed, watching TV and playing on his Xbox. Since being in hospital he has continued to play video games and to only engage in a very limited way with the medical and nursing team. Since being admitted, he has struggled to walk and the ward have provided him with a wheelchair which his mother pushes him around in. He is observed to look miserable and be withdrawn except when with his mum, with whom he is frequently arguing.

It has been observed that his mother does most of his care, washing him, brushing his teeth and dressing him. He has been seen to be verbally abusive to his mother who appears at the end of her tether. When his mum is not on the ward he will sometimes engage with education and has been seen to walk around his room to collect items he needs.

In this case, the teams worked with a formulation of Josh's difficulties emerging in the context of him struggling at school. The more he missed school, the worse the anxieties about returning became. The avoidance of school therefore led to greater resistance and more illness behaviours, eliciting more care and fewer expectations. His mood and general functioning and behaviour were best when he was allowed to do the things he enjoyed with no pressure, and the relationship with his mother became more enmeshed. His ultimate expression of control was in the context of threatening to harm himself, leaving his mum increasingly anxious about not enabling his behaviours.

The liaison role included support for the medical team in developing a plan to rehabilitate, grading this plan in very small steps while identifying treatment goals and motivators. In addition, psychological therapies were started to address his low mood and anxieties around school. He was very motivated to leave hospital so goals to achieve this were identified. Work was done with his mother about boundary setting and understanding the role of mental health. An alternative school placement was identified where a gradual reintegration to his mainstream school was possible.

Legal Aspects Specific to Children (England and Wales)

There are many challenges to navigating medicolegal aspects of clinical presentations in young people, including the involvement of multiple professionals, some of whom will have limited understanding of the legal frameworks available. There is general reliance on parental responsibility underpinning consent for most interventions, as is the way with most interventions on paediatric wards, with variable understanding of the zone of parental responsibility or where the Mental Health Act might apply when there is significant resistance to treatment.

The zone of parental responsibility refers to the decision that a reasonable parent would normally be expected to make as regards their child. It also references awareness of any indication that a parent might not be acting in the best interests of the child. If there are concerns about either of these considerations, then it is likely that the decision being made falls outside this zone. If this is the case, then an alternative legal framework should be considered including the use of the Mental Health Act. Legal frameworks differ across jurisdictions within the UK and across Europe.

Competence, Capacity and Consent

The competence or capacity of young people to make their own decisions raises many concerns for professionals. It is important to understand these concepts and how they are applied to the treatment and management of children and young people. Pursuant to the Mental Capacity Act 2005, young people aged 16 years and over are presumed to have capacity to consent to or refuse treatment unless there is evidence to suggest otherwise (29). The right of a child under the age of 16 years to consent to their own treatment is proportionate to their perceived level of competence. To be deemed competent, the young person needs to understand the purpose of the treatment and be able to weigh up the benefits and risks, retain the information given and communicate their decision.

Parents can consent on behalf of a young person up to the age of 18 years who lacks competence/capacity. It is considered inadvisable, however, to rely on parental consent for invasive/intrusive treatments against a young person's wishes, particularly 16- and 17-year-olds. If the proposed intervention does not constitute emergency treatment (which may be given without consent under common law, if judged to be lifesaving and required immediately), it should be carefully considered by the multidisciplinary team with parents and may involve discussion with the healthcare provider legal team regarding best interests and appropriate legal frameworks, with consideration of the severity of the impact of the decision. As mentioned earlier, it is important to bear in mind that certain aspects of the Mental Capacity Act (MCA 2005) in England and Wales do apply to 16- and 17-year-olds.

Competence and capacity relate to specific situations and cannot be generalised. Young people may be competent to make some decisions but not others where there is more at stake (higher-order decisions). As the young person develops, decisions may need to be revisited and competence or capacity reassessed. Decision-making in complex cases is often not clear-cut and may involve numerous meetings between professionals and families to aid understanding and to support collaborative treatment efforts.

Safeguarding

Safeguarding issues can occur and raise anxieties about how they can be managed. As stated earlier, there is a need to separate out the impact of parental anxiety and the difficulties for some parents in containing their child's anxiety/distress and the rarer spectre of factitious illness. Parental anxiety due to a perception that a physical cause of their child's symptoms has not been identified can manifest itself as health-seeking behaviours and challenges to the professionals involved in their child's care. This can include discrediting current opinions to gain further assessments or seeking second, third or more opinions, interference with the treatment plan if the belief is that this plan is wrong or causing distress, collusion with their child's resistance to treatment or rejection of a psychological formulation for fear that this will lead to further physical deterioration. Developing a trusting relationship with both parents and the young person is key to making progress. This is greatly enhanced by parents and the young person feeling involved in the treatment decisions as much as is possible and rationale for decisions being carefully explained.

Importantly, while children deserve the same rights of confidentiality as adults, this needs balancing with the need for parents to make informed decisions and exercise their parental responsibility, particularly in decisions involving risk to the child. Consideration also needs to be given to *who* holds parental responsibility. This is laid out in the Children's Act (2004) (30) along with the rights, duties and responsibility of parents. The Children's Act also describes responsibilities of local authorities in relation to under-18-year-olds and situations in which they may share parental responsibility.

Paediatric Liaison Service Development

A Word on Interface Work and the Paediatric Liaison Team

Child mental health services as a whole foster and facilitate multidisciplinary and interagency cooperation to provide holistic care for young people and their families and paediatric liaison teams have a particular role in fostering the link between paediatrics and local CAMHs (31). There are multiple examples of interface work within paediatric liaison psychiatry and consideration of dynamics that can arise from these promotes more effective interfacing in terms of navigating areas of potential duplication and conflict within and between services. There are interfaces within paediatric liaison services themselves, and it is important to establish respective roles within the team while acknowledging an overlap in skills, particularly among doctors, health psychologists and mental health nurses.

The principal 'between-service' interface is with paediatricians and paediatric specialties, advising and supporting as well as skilling up paediatric teams in child mental health. The latter allows early recognition of psychosocial needs and early communication of such needs with children and families. This allows timely intervention in paediatric clinics and ward reviews where required. This usually occurs through referral pathways or is accessed through jointly run services, for example multidisciplinary paediatric diabetes teams. Paediatric liaison psychiatrists also have a role in supporting paediatric services to navigate complex social care and mental health service interfaces. In addition to formulating and then communicating an understanding of mental health and social care needs of young people, they are likely to have accumulated, through experience, in-depth understanding of local services, their thresholds and the capacity for intervention and referral mechanisms to help the young person and family access these as efficiently as possible. Similarly, they may be able to identify requirements for and support access to educational interventions and other external agencies such as alcohol, bereavement and criminal justice services. This in turn is born from effective prior interface work with these agencies and CAMH services.

There is significant interaction with local community and inpatient CAMHs, where the boundaries of each service may overlap significantly or indeed gaps can be identified where needs may not be adequately met through limited inclusion or rigid exclusion criteria in respective services or where skill sets and exposure might vary. Examples of gaps within CAMHs might include children with neuropsychiatric disorders such as tics and Tourette syndrome and mental health presentations with predominantly somatic symptoms. Apparent physical health-related emotional difficulties presenting to paediatric liaison services might be found to have or evolve into presentations with wider psychosocial aetiology and impact, best addressed within community CAMHs where services are more likely to have more disciplines (family therapy, psychotherapy, support worker role), closer community links and more established crisis services. To improve this interface, professional consultation may be needed; opportunities for joint work or clearer routes for access to appropriate assessment and intervention may be needed in paediatric liaison services and vice versa.

Models of Service and Service Development

Successive national guidance for the development of paediatric mental health liaison services has emphasised that all paediatric patients should have access to 'appropriately trained paediatric psychology and CAMH services within nationally defined access standards' (32). Royal College of Psychiatry recommendations advise that such specialist services, co-located and commissioned with paediatrics, are essential to the provision of paediatric care (33). The consensus across a range of guidance for commissioning and service development is that child and adolescent mental healthcare provision should be an integral part of paediatric and emergency services. Integrated provision of paediatric and mental healthcare contributes positively to the experience of children and young people and their families in acute care settings and reduces the duration of inpatient stays (34).

It is acknowledged that the delivery and configuration of paediatric liaison services varies considerably, nationally and worldwide. In general, dedicated paediatric liaison services are part of large children's hospitals, whereas paediatric departments within acute general hospitals rely on local CAMHs provision. The latter ad hoc provision is dependent on local CAMHs capacity and expertise and coordination of such services is often further complicated because CAMHs and paediatric services are not co-located and are often not part of the same host organisation.

Ideally, dedicated paediatric mental health liaison services should be multidisciplinary teams that provide care across the range of paediatric specialties. This is not always the case and individual services vary in their professional make-up, as well as the paediatric specialties they cover. Both these factors are influenced by commissioning arrangements such as standard contracts where mental healthcare provision is integral to the delivery of paediatric service. For example, NHS England's Standard Contract for Paediatric Oncology stipulates that there is ready access to specialist psychology and liaison psychiatry to address complex psychological morbidity associated with cancer and its treatment (34). Paediatric diabetes best practice guidance and tariffs have driven the development of services with a mental healthcare component. Such arrangements can result in uneven paediatric mental health support within hospitals and do not promote the formation of multidisciplinary teams that work for all children presenting with physical and mental health needs.

There are no overarching standards relating to paediatric liaison as a whole which are applicable to children with chronic physical illness more broadly. In particular, where they exist at all, pathways and models of service for functional presentations are wide-ranging, underdeveloped and very much dependent on local expertise and conceptualisation of such complex presentations. Most place emphasis on a multidisciplinary rehabilitative clinical model but the pathways, setting, professional skill mix and therapeutic approaches vary.

Acknowledging the gaps in guidelines, in 2019 Ibeziako et al. (35) described the first attempt to develop a clinical pathway and standardise the care of patients with somatic symptoms and related disorders in paediatric hospital settings by a working group of paediatric consultation-liaison psychiatrists from multiple institutions across North America (36). Early recognition, interdisciplinary assessment, meetings and management during inpatient hospitalisation are key to their approach.

Another international example is Kozlowsi's (36) Mind-Body Services in Australia, which places inpatient multidisciplinary rehabilitative components centrally in their Stress System Approach. In the UK, inpatient settings may be used but with the aim for short timescales, and there is overall emphasis on community and outpatient treatment with a focus on functioning within the young person's systems.

Most agree on the need for collaborative services but there is acknowledgement that there are challenges in achieving this. While on individual levels some have developed ways of working together that make the best use of available resources, this is not easily reproducible across settings. In the absence of a liaison service, paediatricians may find it difficult to articulate to commissioners precisely what it is they require and commissioners may rely on proof of effectiveness and evidence that money might be saved before funding a service (37).

Overarching paediatric liaison is a drive for parity of esteem for mental health with physical health. The Royal College of Psychiatrists produced a document on the long-term plan for NHS services (38), predicting that funding for children and young people's mental health services will grow faster than both overall NHS funding and total mental health spending. While paediatric liaison will gain some benefit from this financial boost, the challenges in establishing structure and frameworks within which to develop services mean that progress may be gradual over time.

Research and Audit

Joint research meetings or seminars are useful ways of educating but are also ideal opportunities to share ideas and improve communication between different disciplines. A liaison service also has many opportunities for collaborative research and joint service improvement projects/audits of practice; again, these should ideally be multidisciplinary. Treatment trials for mental health disorders in children are conducted more rarely than in adults for obvious reasons; evidence is often extrapolated from adult research where it may not be appropriate. Examples of useful research that could be done include replications of treatment trials for depression and anxiety in children with concurrent physical health problems.

References

1. Butler A, Van Lieshout RJ, Lipman EL et al. Mental disorder in children with physical conditions: A pilot study. *BMJ Open.* 2018;**8**(1):e019011.

2. Gortmaker S, Sappenfield W. Chronic childhood disorders: Prevalence and impact. *Pediatric Clinics of North America.* 1984;**31**(1):3–18.

3. van der Lee JH, Mokkink LB, Grootenhuis MA et al. Definitions and measurement of chronic health conditions in childhood: A systematic review. *JAMA.* 2007;**297**(24):2741.

4. Adams JS, Chien AT, Wisk LE. Mental illness among youth with chronic physical conditions. *Pediatrics.* 2019;**144**(1): e20181819.

5. Aarons GA, Monn AR, Leslie LK et al. Association between mental and physical health problems in high-risk adolescents: A longitudinal study. *J Adolesc Health.* 2008;**43**(3):260–7.

6. Kogon AJ, Matheson MB, Flynn JT et al. Depressive symptoms in children with chronic kidney disease. *J Pediatr.* 2016;**168**:164–70.e1.

7. Rutter M, Graham, P, Yule WA. *Neuropsychiatric Study in Childhood.* London; 1970.

8. Koning NR, Büchner FL, Vermeiren RRJM et al. Identification of children at risk for mental health problems in primary care: Development of a prediction model with routine health care data. *EClinicalMedicine.* 2019;**17**(15):89–97.

9. Denny S, de Silva M, Fleming T et al. The prevalence of chronic health conditions impacting on daily functioning and the association with emotional well-being among a national sample of high school students. *J Adolesc Health.* 2014;**54** (4):410–15.

10. Horn SR, Leve LD, Levitt P, Fisher PA. Childhood adversity, mental health, and oxidative stress: A pilot study. *PLoS One.* 2019;**14**(4):e0215085.

11. Cottrell D. Prevention and treatment of psychiatric disorders in children with chronic physical illness. *Arch Dis Child.* 2015;**100**(4):303–4.

12. NHS England. Funding boost for young people's mental health services. 2021. www.england.nhs.uk/2021/06/funding-boost-for-young-peoples-mental-health-services.

13. Shaw L, Moore D, Nunns M et al. Experiences of interventions aiming to improve the mental health and well-being of children and young people with a long-term physical condition: A systematic review and meta-ethnography. *Child Care Health Dev.* 2019;**45**(6):832–49.

14. Iannucci J, Nierenberg B. Suicide and suicidality in children and adolescents with chronic illness: A systematic review. *Aggression and Violent Behavior.* 2021;**64**:101581.

15. Hinton D, Kirk S. Families' and healthcare professionals' perceptions of healthcare services for children and young people with medically unexplained symptoms: A narrative review of the literature. *Health Soc Care Community.* 2016;**24**(1):12–26.

16. Centre for Mental Health. Outcomes and performance in liaison psychiatry. 2014. www.centreformentalhealth.org.uk/publi cations/outcomes-and-performance-liaison-psychiatry.

17. Cohen P, Pine D, Must A et al. Prospective associations between somatic illness and mental illness from childhood to adulthood. *AJE.* 1998;**147** (3):232–9.

18 Georgiopoulos AM, Christon LM, Filigno SS et al. Promoting emotional wellness in children with CF, part II: Mental health assessment and intervention. *Pediatr Pulmonol.* 2021;**56**(suppl. 1):S107–S122.

19. Bursch B, Stuber M. Pediatrics. In Levenson JL (ed.), *Textbook of Psychosomatic Medicine.* Washington, DC; 2011, pp. 828–31.

20. Compas BE, Jaser SS, Dunn MJ et al. Coping with chronic illness in childhood and adolescence. *Annu Rev Clin Psychol.* 2012;**8**:455–80.

21. Rushforth H. Practitioner review: Communicating with hospitalised children – Review and application of research pertaining to children's understanding of health and illness. *JCPP.* 1999;**40**(5):683–91.

22. Shahraki ZE, Efffatpanah M, Serajaddin G et al. A comparative study of psychiatric disorders among mothers of children with chronic diseases and mothers of healthy children. *J App Pharm Sci.* 2017;**7** (12):116–20.

23. Dewey D, Crawford SG. Correlates of maternal and paternal adjustment to chronic childhood disease. *JCPMS.* 2007;**14** (3):219–26.

24. Lumsden MR, Smith DM, Wittowski A. Coping in parents of children with congenital heart disease: A systematic review and meta-synthesis. *JCFS.* 2019;**28**:1736–53.

25. National Institute for Health and Care Excellence. Eating disorders: Recognition and treatment. 2020. www.nice.org.uk/gui dance/ng69.

26. American Psychiatric Association. *Diagnostic and Statistical Manual of Mental Disorders: DSM-5.* 5th ed. Washington, DC; 2013.

27. Malas N, Ortiz-Aguayo R, Giles L et al. Pediatric somatic symptom disorders. *Curr Psychiatry Rep.* 2017;**19**(2):11.

28. Petranovich C, Smith-Paine J, Wade S et al. From early childhood to adolescence: Lessons about traumatic brain injury from the Ohio Head Injury Outcomes Study. *J Head Trauma Rehabil.* 2020;**35** (3):226–39.

29. The Stationery Office. Mental Capacity Act 2005 Code of Practice. 2007. https://assets .publishing.service.gov.uk/government/up loads/system/uploads/attachment_data/fil e/921428/Mental-capacity-act-code-of-practice.pdf.

30. Legislation.gov.uk. Children Act 1989. 2022. www.legislation.gov.uk/ukpga/1989/ 41/section/3.

31. Garralda ME, Slaveska-Hollis K. What is special about a Paediatric Liaison Child and Adolescent Mental Health service? *Child Adolesc Ment Health.* 2016;**21** (2):96–101.

32. NHS Commissioning Board. Specialised services commissioning: Women and children. 2013. www.engage.commissioning board.nhs.uk/consultation/ssc-area-e.

33. Royal College of Psychiatrists. CR182. Building and sustaining specialist CAMHS to improve outcomes for children and young people: Update of guidance on workforce, capacity and functions of CAMHS in the UK. 2013. www.rcpsych.ac.uk/docs/default-source/ improving-care/better-mh-policy/ college-reports/college-report-cr182.pdf? sfvrsn=8662b58f_2.

34. The Royal College of Psychiatrists. CR183 liaison psychiatry for every acute hospital. 2013. www.rcpsych.ac.uk/docs/default-source/members/faculties/liaison-psychiatry/cr183liaisonpsych-every-acute-hospital.pdf?sfvrsn=26c57d4_2.

35. Ibeziako P, Brahmbhatt K, Chapman A et al. Developing a clinical pathway for somatic symptom and related disorders in pediatric hospital settings. *Hosp Pediatr.* 2019;9(3):147–55.

36. Kozlowska K. Functional somatic symptoms in childhood and adolescence. *Curr Opin Psychiatry.* 2013;26(5):485–92.

37. Kraemer S. Liaison and co-operation between paediatrics and mental health. *Paediatrics and Child Health.* 2010;20(8):382–7.

38. Royal College of Psychiatrists. The NHS Long Term Plan in England. 2019. www.rcpsych.ac.uk/docs/default-source/improving-care/better-mh-policy/policy/nhs-long-term-plan-briefing.pdf?sfvrsn=f89935ec_2.

Chapter 15

Psychological Treatment

Elspeth Guthrie

Psychological therapies are used widely in liaison mental health settings to treat individuals with a variety of different mental health problems. The three most common clinical problem areas, however, are persistent physical symptoms (PPS), depression/anxiety associated with physical disease and self-harm. There is a relatively strong evidence base for treatments which target PPS, albeit with certain caveats, whereas the evidence for co-morbid depression/anxiety is quite weak. Psychological treatments for self-harm are discussed in Chapter 5. The most common psychological intervention is cognitive behavioural therapy (CBT), for which there is a large evidence base. There is, however, no clear evidence that CBT is superior to most other bona fide therapies which are currently delivered in a National Health Service (NHS) setting.

Difficulties with Evaluating Psychological Treatments

There are a variety of challenges involved in the evaluation of psychological treatments, some of which are common to most mental health settings and some of which are of particular relevance to liaison mental settings. It is important to understand some of the complexities in conducting psychological treatment research, as this helps the reader to evaluate trials and their relevance to NHS settings. There is *no perfect design* for a trial of psychological therapy. Most psychological treatments are evaluated by randomised controlled trials (RCTs). However, unlike trials of pharmacotherapy, participants and therapists cannot be blind to the treatment they are receiving or delivering and neither can participants in a control group be blind to the fact they are not receiving the therapy under evaluation. This inability to blind results in all trials of psychological treatment being given a low rating of quality (i.e. subject to bias) in systematic reviews.

The majority of trials of psychological treatment use a simple pragmatic design where the therapy plus usual care or some kind of enhanced care is compared with enhanced care or usual care alone. This design is particularly suited to trials of cost-effectiveness where it is important to include a usual care control group to estimate the costs associated with usual care. Such trials, however, cannot evaluate the specific effects of the psychological treatment under evaluation, although they often claim to do so, as they do not control for the non-specific effects of psychotherapy. Non-specific effects include therapist effects such as warmth and empathy, the therapeutic alliance (the bond between the client and therapist) and the number of sessions of therapy.

An alternative design is to compare a psychological treatment with a psychological placebo control condition. There are two difficulties with this approach. First, it is difficult to design a psychological placebo which is inert (like a drug placebo) that people would consider worthwhile and attend sessions on a regular basis. Second, any psychological placebo that was considered worthwhile by clients is likely to have a therapeutic effect. Comparisons with a psychological placebo, however, are helpful in evaluating the specific effects or ingredients of a therapy, as in these studies the non-specific effects of a supportive relationship are controlled for. Psychological placebo designs are much less common than pragmatic studies and they usually report lower effects for the therapy under question than pragmatic designs. Therapeutic interventions which are compared with a control condition with an equivalent number of contacts have a much lower effect size (Cohen's D) than therapies which are compared to wait list or usual care (0.15 vs. 0.47) (1). In a recent review of trials of cognitive therapy for persistent physical symptoms/medically unexplained symptoms (PPS/MUS), higher effect sizes were generally reported in studies where the control condition was either wait list or treatment as usual compared to studies which compared CBT to enhanced care (2).

Dosage of therapy also effects outcome. Evidence suggests patients with mental health problems fall into two groups: rapid responders and gradual responders. Rapid responders show improvement by session 4 (mild depression) and gradual responders by session 26. Gradual responders are more likely to be multi-symptomatic and have quite severe symptoms in comparison with rapid responders. Frequency of therapy is also important in that weekly therapy is better than less frequent sessions. In patients with moderate symptoms, session 8 tends to mark the point at which the bulk of the symptomatic change has occurred (3).

The population of participants included in a trial is another factor to consider in relation to outcome, particularly as there are so many different ways of defining functional somatic symptoms or medically unexplained symptoms, one of the most frequently evaluated conditions in a liaison setting. Table 15.1 shows a list of inclusion criteria for trials of cognitive therapy for medically unexplained symptoms from a recent systematic review (2). Nearly all of the trials included in the review had different entry criteria and therefore involved a different population of patients, ranging in severity from quite moderate to very severe symptoms.

There is also great variability in measures that are used to report outcome in trials of treatments for individuals with persistent PPS/MUS. Over 40 questionnaires have been used

Table 15.1 Inclusion criteria for trials of cognitive therapy in medically unexplained symptoms (2)

18–64 years, single or multiple MUS with moderate intensity on analogue scale

30–60 years, fulfilling definition of functional somatic symptoms by Kellner (51)

16–65 years, ≥ 5 MUS for at least 6 months identified by trained primary care physicians

18–65 years, primary MUS identified by trained physician chart raters

≥ 18 years fulfilling criteria for abridged somatisation by Escobar et al. (52)

≥ 2 MUS in last 6 months identified by physician

16–65 years, ≥ 5 MUS for at least 6 months identified by trained primary care physicians

18–65 years, opined as MUS by treating primary care physician with at least 2 specialist referrals in last 3 years

≥ 18 years; ≥ 2 somatoform symptoms; medical explanation ruled out by physician 18–70 years; physical symptoms for at least 6 months not explained by disease with functional impairment

20–45 years; chronic bodily distress syndrome (≥2 years) of multi-organ type with impairment

to measure PPS/MUS, with the number of items within questionnaires ranging from 5 to 78. Symptoms also vary across questionnaires, with headaches being the most commonly included item (70%) followed by nausea/upset stomach (65%), shortness of breath/breathing trouble (58%), dizziness (55%) and (low) back pain/backaches (55%) (4). Other outcome measures which focus on quality of life or mental health outcomes can also be used to record outcome.

Finally, trials of psychological treatment report general population effects for the participants in the study, within which there will be variability of outcome. Some participants in the therapy arm of a study may respond particularly well to the therapy under evaluation, whereas others may have a muted or negative outcome. These differences are aggregated in the overall trial results. Recent research in the last five years has begun to find ways of identifying the characteristics of participants in studies who do particularly well if matched to a particular therapy and conversely less well if matched to a non-optimal therapy (5). Participants matched to an optimal therapy can potentially have much better outcomes, although the research at present is not sufficiently advanced to use in a clinical setting. This is a developing field but opens the possibility that in future we may be able to achieve much better effect sizes for psychological therapies than are currently reported (6).

In summary, there are many challenges in evaluating psychological treatments in a liaison mental health setting. We still do not know what therapy works for which patient, although there is mounting evidence that some (but not all) patients will have a much better outcome if matched to their optimal treatment (5, 7).

Evidence Base

There are now many trials of psychological treatment for PPS/MUS and co-morbid anxiety and depression in physical organic disease. Trials in PPS/MUS have tended to be split into those that use broad definitions of PPS/MUS and those that focus on a specific functional somatic syndrome such as irritable bowel syndrome (IBS).

Persistent Physical Symptoms/Medically Unexplained Symptoms

Van Dessel and colleagues conducted a Cochrane review of non-pharmacological interventions for somatoform disorders and medically unexplained physical symptoms (MUPS) in adults (8). They identified 21 studies with 2,658 randomised participants of which 14 studies evaluated CBT. Fifteen studies employed a usual care or a waiting list as control condition, five studies compared the intervention to enhanced or structured care and one study compared a therapy with another therapy (CBT vs. behavioural therapy). The mean number of sessions ranged from 1 to 13 over a period of 1 day to 9 months. The duration of follow-up varied between 2 weeks and 24 months. The studies were conducted in a variety of different healthcare settings and the duration of symptoms, reported by nine studies, was at least several years, suggesting that most participants had chronic symptoms at baseline.

There was a small effect for a reduction in symptoms for psychological therapy versus wait list control or usual treatment of the order of −0.34 95% CI−0.53 to −0.16 (10 studies, 1,081 participants). Results comparing CBT with usual care were similar to those in the whole group. There was no clear evidence of a difference at the end of treatment for the five studies (624 participants) which compared psychological therapy with enhanced care.

A recent systematic review and meta-analysis of short-term psychodynamic interventions included 37 studies (15 RCTs and 22 pre-post studies) and showed a moderate to large effect size for brief therapy post-treatment and at follow-up (9). As more RCTs are conducted involving psychodynamic therapy, one would expect the effect sizes to fall somewhat to fall in line with results from CBT trials and other psychological treatments.

Functional Somatic Syndromes

Tables 15.2 to 15.4 summarise the main findings of systematic reviews, meta-analyses or critical reviews of psychological treatment studies for chronic fatigue syndrome (CFS), IBS and functional neurological disorders. On balance, the findings support the evidence for psychological treatments. Effect sizes are small to moderate. Most studies in the reviews used a pragmatic design.

Anxiety/Depression in Physical Disease

This is a large subject area and it is not possible in this brief chapter to cover all individual physical conditions. In general, the evidence suggests that psychological treatments result in improvements in anxiety and depression in physical disease but do not impact on the underlying disease itself. However, the variety of disease types, different types of interventions and complexity of studies make it difficult to evaluate. Cancer is the most studied clinical area and there are many systematic reviews of the effects of psychological treatment on depression and anxiety in cancer dating back to the late 1990s. These studies suggest positive results for psychological interventions compared to controls for anxiety and depression but little effect on disease outcome. Two meta-analyses conducted by Sheard and Maguire in 1999 (one for anxiety and one for depression) (21) showed modest effect sizes of the order of 0.3 for psychological interventions in cancer based upon approximately 20 trials per analysis. The majority of the trials were preventative and selected subjects on the basis of a cancer diagnosis rather than on the presence of a diagnosis of depression or anxiety, so the effect sizes would be expected to be low as not everyone in the studies would necessarily suffer from psychological symptoms.

Table 15.5 summarises findings from recent systematic reviews of psychological treatment interventions in cancer. They generally show favourable results with small to moderate effects, with studies focussed on particular kinds of cancer rather than the more generalised nature of earlier reviews. In addition to targeting anxiety and depression, more recent interventions have also focussed on other aspects of disease, such as fear of recurrence, compliance with treatment, fatigue symptoms or depression and anxiety in partners of cancer sufferers.

Tables 15.6 and 15.7 summarise findings from reviews of psychological treatment in chronic obstructive pulmonary disease (COPD) and diabetes. The reported effect sizes are small for depression and anxiety, with no convincing impact on physical health.

Matching Intensity of Interventions According to Severity and Chronicity of Symptoms

Many people who present with PPS/MUS in primary care are receptive to a psychological understanding of their problems. However, work from Liverpool has shown that many patients perceive primary care physicians' explanations as being at odds with their own thinking (36). Analysis of over 400 taped consultations between doctors and patients revealed that most doctors' explanations are experienced as a rejection of patients' suffering. Consultations that were experienced by patients as empowering were ones in which the

Table 15.2 Recent systematic reviews and meta-analyses of trials of psychological treatment in chronic fatigue syndrome

Authors	Intervention	Type of review	Main findings
Price et al. 2008 (10)	Cognitive behavioural therapy	Meta-analysis 15 RCTs	CBT is effective in reducing the symptoms of fatigue at post-treatment compared with usual care. The evidence base at follow-up is limited to a small group of studies with inconsistent findings.
Castell et al. 2011 (11)	Cognitive behavioural therapy and graded exercise therapy	Meta-analysis 16 RCTs	Overall effect sizes suggested that graded exercise therapy (g = 0.28) and CBT (g = 0.33) were equally efficacious.
Marques et al. 2015 (12)	Behavioural interventions/graded exercise therapy	Meta-analysis 16 RCTs	Significant small to medium effect sizes (Hedge's g = 0.25 to g = 0.66) were found for all outcomes at post-treatment (M = 5.2 months) and follow-up (M = 11.7 months), with the exception of physical activity at post-treatment (g = 0.11).
Kim et al. 2020 (13)	Pharmacological and non-pharmacological	Systematic review 55 RCTs 28 non-pharmacological 25 pharmacological	5 non-pharmacological therapies (cognitive behavioural therapy-related treatments, graded exercise-related therapies, rehabilitation, acupuncture and abdominal Tui Na) showed statistically significant outcome. There was no definitely effective intervention with coherence and reproducibility.
Cochrane et al. 2021 (14)	Interventions subjects to a cost-effectiveness evaluation – five CBT and two graded exercise therapy	Systematic review	Evidence from three trials to support CBT as a cost-effective treatment option for adults; however, findings on CBT were not uniform, suggesting that cost-effectiveness may be context-specific.

Table 15.3 Recent systematic reviews and meta-analyses of trials of psychological treatment in irritable bowel syndrome

Authors	Intervention	Type of review	Main findings
Ford et al. 2019 (15)	Pharmacological and non-pharmacological	Systematic and meta-analysis (53 RCTs – 35 RCTs re. psychological treatment)	The relative risk (RR) of symptoms not improving with psychological therapies was 0.69 (95% CI = 0.62–0.76). Cognitive behavioural therapy, hypnotherapy, multicomponent psychological therapy and dynamic psychotherapy were all beneficial.
Laird et al. 2016 (16)	Long- and short-term effects of psychological therapies	Systematic review and meta-analysis 41 RCTs	Psychological therapies had a medium effect on gastrointestinal symptom severity (d = 0.69) immediately after treatment. After short-term follow-up periods (1–6 months after treatment) and long-term follow-up periods (6–12 months after treatment), this effect remained significant and medium in magnitude.
Black et al. 2020 (17)	Psychological therapies	Systematic review and meta-analysis 41 RCTs	Self-administered or minimal contact cognitive behavioural therapy (RR 0.61; 95% CI 0.45 to 0.83, P score 0.66), face-to-face CBT (RR 0.62; 95% CI 0.48 to 0.80, P score 0.65) and gut-directed hypnotherapy (RR 0.67; 95% CI 0.49 to 0.91, P score 0.57). After completion of therapy, among trials recruiting only patients with refractory symptoms, group CBT and gut-directed hypnotherapy were more efficacious than either education and/or support or routine care, and CBT via the telephone, contingency management, CBT via the internet and dynamic psychotherapy were all superior to routine care.
Krouwel et al. 2021 (18)	Hypnotherapy	Systematic review and meta-analysis 12 RCTs – 7 in meta-analysis	Hypnotherapy did not reduce the risk of global gastrointestinal symptoms (total bowel symptom score) compared with controls, (standardised mean difference 0.24, [–0.06, 0.54], I(2) 66%). Higher frequency of sessions and higher number of sessions were associated with small significant effects.

Table 15.4 Recent systematic reviews and meta-analyses of trials of psychological treatment in functional neurological disorders

Authors	Intervention	Type of review	Main findings
Carlson et al. 2017 (19)	CBT, psychodynamic therapy, paradoxical intention therapy, mindfulness and psychoeducation and eclectic interventions for non-epileptic seizures	Meta-analysis 13 studies (228 participants)	Immediate treatment outcomes – 82% participants experienced reduction of episodes of 50% or more after an intervention; 47% experienced freedom from episodes after an intervention. Limitation – no follow-up data reported.
Gutkin et al. 2020 (20)	CBT and psychodynamic therapy across the functional neurological disorder spectrum	Systematic review 19 studies (11 before-and-after studies and 8 RCTs). 12 CBT; 7 psychodynamic therapy (PDT))	Most CBT studies showed significant benefits on physical symptoms but were inconsistent on measures of mental health, function and quality of life. Median pooled pre-post effect size (Cohen's d) for CBT 0.49 after treatment and 0.33 at final follow-up. For PDT, median pooled pre-post effect size (Cohen's d) 0.69 after treatment and 0.49 at final follow-up.

patient was provided with a tangible mechanism of causation of their symptoms, any sense of blame was removed and there was a strong bond between the doctor and patient. These findings provide the basis for all therapeutic interventions with people who experience PPS/MUS.

People with PPS/MUS know that their symptoms are 'real' and therefore must be caused by something. It is entirely understandable that they should seek a causal explanation. They often feel blamed for their symptoms or believe that doctors think they are making up their symptoms or that it is all in their mind. Providing people with a shared understanding of the nature of their problems which avoids blame and offers an opportunity for resolution or mitigation is a key component of all therapeutic approaches.

In a primary care setting, many patients' symptoms will resolve with a very simple approach which relies upon explanation based upon a shared aetiological model and a trusting doctor–patient relationship. Psychological therapies should be reserved for people whose symptoms fail to resolve with general management. Most trials of psychological treatment in PPS/MUS include people with moderate to severe symptoms; that is, people with persistent symptoms which interfere with function and have been present for around two to five years. Psychological therapies in trials usually consist of one-to-one therapy sessions of between 8 and 16 sessions in duration, although group treatments have also been evaluated in a small number of cases.

Table 15.5 Recent systematic reviews and meta-analyses of trials of psychological treatment in certain types of cancer

Authors	Intervention	Type of review	Main findings
Jassim et al. 2015 (22)	Psychological interventions (non-metastatic breast cancer)	Systematic review and meta-analysis 28 RCTs (24 CBT)	A psychological intervention, namely CBT, produced favourable effects on some psychological outcomes, in particular anxiety, depression and mood disturbance. However, the evidence for survival improvement is still lacking.
Richardson et al. 2019 (23)	Psychological interventions for patients with head and neck cancer	Systematic review and narrative synthesis 21 studies – 10 RCTs	Most studies were underpowered to detect significant effects and did not examine whether improvements in quality of life and psychological well-being were sustained over time.
Cillessen et al. 2019 (24)	Mindfulness interventions for psychological and physical health outcomes in cancer	Systematic review and meta-analysis 29 RCTS	Small effects of mindfulness interventions on combined measures of psychological distress were found at post-intervention (Hedge's g = 0.32; 95% CI: 0.22–0.41; P < .001) and follow-up (g = 0.19; 95% CI: 0.07–0.30; P < .002). Small effects also found at either post-intervention or follow-up for anxiety, depression, fear of cancer recurrence, fatigue, sleep disturbances and pain (g = 0.20 to 0.51; P < .001 to .047).
Guarino et al. 2020 (25)	Psychological Interventions in breast cancer for depression and anxiety	Systematic review and meta-analysis 45 studies	Medium effects compared to controls. NB. High methodological heterogeneity.
Mundle et al. 2021 (26)	Psychological interventions for depression, anxiety and distress (prostate cancer)	Systematic review 22 studies	Greater improvements in depression and anxiety compared to controls.

Table 15.6 Recent systematic reviews and meta-analyses of trials of psychological treatment in chronic obstructive pulmonary disease

Authors	Intervention	Type of review	Main findings
Coventry et al. 2013 (27)	Psychological treatment/lifestyle	Systematic review and meta-analysis 29 RCTs	Overall, psychological and/or lifestyle interventions were associated with small reductions in symptoms of depression (standardised mean difference −0.28, 95% CI −0.41 to −0.14) and anxiety (standardised mean difference −0.23, 95% CI −0.38 to −0.09). Multicomponent exercise training was the only intervention subgroup associated with significant treatment effects for depression (standardised mean difference −0.47, 95% CI −0.66 to −0.28) and for anxiety (standardised mean difference −0.45, 95% CI −0.71 to −0.18).
Vestergaard et al. 2014 (28)	Psychological interventions	Systematic review and meta-analysis 20 studies	Positive effect was found for psychological treatments (Hedges' g = 0.38, 95% CI = 0.19–0.58; P < .001) outcomes.
Zhang et al. 2020 (29)	CBT for anxiety and depression in COPD	Systematic review and meta-analysis 10 studies	CBT can improve depression and anxiety in patients with COPD. Subgroup analysis showed that intervention time >/=8 weeks had significant differences in improving anxiety, while intervention time < 8 weeks had significant differences in improving depression.
Ma et al. 2020 (30)	CBT for COPD	Systematic review and meta-analysis 16 RCTs	There were significant improvements in anxiety (standardised mean difference = −0.23; 95% CI: −0.42 to −0.04; P = 0.02), depression (standardised mean difference = −0.29, 95% CI: −0.40 to −0.19, P < 0.01), quality of life (mean difference = −5.21; 95% CI: −10.25 to −0.17; P = 0.04) and mean visits to emergency departments in the CBT groups.

Table 15.7 Recent systematic reviews and meta-analyses of trials of psychological treatment in diabetes

Authors	Intervention	Type of review	Main findings
Uchendu and Blake 2017 (31)	CBT for glycaemic control	Systematic review and meta-analysis 12 RCTs	CBT is effective in reducing short-term and medium-term glycaemic control, although no significant effect was found for long-term glycaemic control. CBT improved short- and medium-term anxiety and depression and long-term depression.
Li et al. 2017 (32)	CBT for depression and anxiety in diabetes	Systematic review and meta-analysis 10 RCTs	Compared with control groups, the CBT groups had statistically significant, long-term improvements in depression (standardised mean differences = −0.65, 95% CI: −0.98 to −0.31, P = 0.0002), quality of life (standardised mean differences = 0.29, 95% CI: 0.08 to 0.51, P = 0.007), fasting glucose (standardised mean differences = 0.21, 95% CI: 0.04 to 0.37, P = 0.01) and anxiety (standardised mean differences = −0.49, 95% CI −0.88 to −0.10, P = 0.01). No improvements were found in glycaemic control.
Winkley et al. 2020 (33)	Psychological interventions to improve self-management of type 1 and type 2 diabetes	Systematic review and meta-analysis and network meta-analysis 96 studies	Psychological treatments offer minimal clinical benefit in improving glycated haemoglobin levels for adults with type 2 diabetes mellitus and no benefit in type 1.
Berhe et al. 2020 (34)	Motivational interviewing on diabetic control and depression	Systematic review and meta-analysis 8 studies	Motivational interviewing resulted in a significant improvement of mean HgbA1C level in the intervention group when compared with the control group (weighted mean difference, −0.29; 95% CI −0.47 to −0.10; P = 0.003, I2 = 48%). No effect on depression. NB. Before-and-after studies included in analysis.
Ngan et al. 2021 (35)	Mindfulness and acceptance-based interventions	Systematic review and meta-analysis 9 RCTs	Interventions significantly reduced diabetes distress (standardised mean difference = −0.37, 95% CI: −0.63, −0.12; P < 0.01) and HbA1c (mean difference = −0.35, 95% CI: −0.67, −0.04; P = 0.03) up to 1 month post-intervention. However, the underpowered studies may have led to overestimation; the interventions for diabetes distress and HbA1c were heterogeneous.

Individuals with severe and chronic PPS/MUS who have persistent, very disabling symptoms are unlikely to benefit from brief psychological treatments. Such people are often in receipt of social benefits related to their disability and also may be receiving carer time (either from a family member or outside professional). Brief treatment once a week is unlikely to have a significant impact if there are many reinforcers in the person's life which help to maintain the symptoms. Intervention in these cases may involve management strategies to limit further investigation and prevent additional iatrogenic harm.

A small number of national units offer inpatient treatment or day-patient treatment for people with severe and chronic PPS/MUS with multimodal treatment programmes offering behavioural/occupational therapy interventions, family work and other relevant treatment strategies.

Generic Aspects of Therapeutic Approaches to PPS/MUS

Referral

Very little attention is paid to the referral process for people with PPS/MUS and those with long-term conditions (LTCs) and associated psychological difficulties. It is not uncommon for people to present for therapy having no idea why they have been referred and for the referral to not have been discussed with them fully by the referring medical or primary care team. A poor referral process results in many patients simply not attending for therapy. In an ideal world, psychological therapy should be offered either as part of a symptom clinic in primary care or as part of a medical specialty clinic in secondary care. Both options help to remove the stigma of being referred to psychological services and also help to normalise attention to psychological concerns in a medical setting.

Most therapy services, however, operate as separate entities to physical health services and in these circumstances how a person is referred can affect whether they attend for treatment. Although it may not be possible to educate all referrers, if a liaison service works closely with particular services, advice should be given about the referral process. Key points that a referrer should address prior to referral are shown in Box 15.1.

Box 15.1 Key Points to Discuss with a Patient with functional somatic symptoms/MUS or LTCs Prior to Referral for Psychological Therapy

1. Emphasise that the patient's symptoms are real
2. Provide an explanation or model for the patient's symptoms based upon a bio-psycho-social model
3. If stress has been discussed, suggest this is contributing to the symptoms but not the main cause
4. Explain psychological therapies are common in a hospital or medical setting to help patients better manage and cope with all kinds of physical health problems including cancer, pain and heart disease
5. Explain the therapy team are experts at delivering treatments for people with physical health problems
6. Do *not* suggest the therapy will cure the patient's problems
7. Explain other physical treatments or investigations that are not indicated at this stage and are likely to be unhelpful

Engagement

All therapies in a liaison setting emphasise the importance of being able to engage the patient in psychological therapy. Some suggest having a longer than usual first session in order to have time to go through the patient's story of their illness in detail. This may involve listening to a lengthy account of the patient's experiences of their management and the previous investigations and treatments they have received. It is not unusual for people to feel dissatisfied with the care they have received – to feel they have not been understood and to feel angry with certain doctors they have encountered. Listening to the patient's account of their experiences not only helps to start to build a trusting relationship but also provides the therapist with a lot of information about the patient's symptoms and relationships with healthcare providers.

Active Listening

Active listening is not a natural process and it needs to be learnt as part of generic psychotherapy skills. Just as a doctor learns to observe in detail the physical appearance of a patient, psychotherapy involves listening intently to what the patient is saying both physically and verbally.

Empathy

Empathy is the ability to perceive and understand the feelings of the other by 'feeling one's way into the experience of another' (53). Empathy has both a cognitive and an emotional aspect and is a crucial interpersonal vehicle for connecting with another person.

Therapeutic Alliance

One of the best predictors of the outcome of psychological treatment is the alliance or bond created between the therapist and client. This is true for all therapies, regardless of modality. The alliance is built by the therapist working hard to listen and understand the patient's problems or difficulties in a non-judgemental fashion.

Shared Model

Listening to the patient's story often helps the therapist to find an explanatory model of the patient's symptoms that can be shared and owned by the patient. Most models involve a bio-psycho-social understanding of symptoms. Common metaphors that people find helpful for different types of symptoms are shown in Table 15.8 but there are many others that can be used.

Clear Rationale and Expectation of Treatment

Another key predictor of outcome is to develop a clear rationale for treatment with the patient. This involves linking the shared model of the patient's symptoms with the reasons for addressing psychological/cognitive issues.

Expertise/Understanding of Physical Health Problems

Although therapists cannot be experts in physical medicine, it helps if the therapist has detailed knowledge of the physical condition in question, whether it is diabetes or irritable bowel syndrome. Some specialism in a particular physical area is therefore very helpful.

Table 15.8 Examples of metaphors that can be used to develop shared models of illness in PPS/MUS

Type of symptom	Common metaphor
Headache	Tension in muscles around the neck and head area exacerbated by anxiety or stress or difficulty in relaxing
Gastrointestinal symptoms	Spasm in the muscles of the gut wall or problems in coordinating the normal squeezing effects of gut muscles to propel food down the gut. Control of muscle function affected by anxiety and stress and higher brain function
Functional neurological symptoms	Problems with the software of the brain as opposed to the hardwiring. Software malfunction influenced by brain areas that control emotion

Healthy Lifestyle

Most therapies for people with physical health problems will focus at some point at trying to improve or maintain a healthy lifestyle. Areas to address include diet, exercise, weight, sleep, alcohol consumption, illicit drug use and smoking.

Individual Therapeutic Approaches

It is not possible to cover all psychotherapeutic approaches in this chapter but the most common types of therapy employed in a liaison setting will be briefly described and discussed. CBT is the most common form of treatment delivered in an NHS setting and also has the largest evidence base; however, bona fide therapies when compared head-to-head with CBT show very little difference in terms of outcome (37, 38). There is no substantive evidence that CBT is superior to any other bona fide therapy, with the exception perhaps of its superiority to behavioural therapy for certain conditions. In clinical practice CBT has similar outcomes to that of psychodynamic interpersonal therapy (39), cognitive analytic therapy (40) and counselling (41).

As discussed earlier, there is increasing evidence that certain people do better with certain types of psychological treatment, although it is not possible at present to discern what works for whom. It is important, however, that different kinds of therapy are available so that patients have greater choice; if they do not have a successful outcome with a particular kind of therapy, they can be offered an alternative, as they may benefit from a different therapeutic approach.

Cognitive Behavioural Therapy

There are many different forms of CBT that have been developed for use in a liaison setting. Most CBT models have been developed for specific diagnostic conditions, for example CBT for CFS, and all are slightly different. There are some limitations to this kind of approach as many patients have more than one condition and therapists need to be flexible and offer treatment to people with multiple co-existing conditions.

Recently, a transdiagnostic approach to treating PPS/MUS has been developed by Chalder and colleagues (42). The therapy is structured according to four distinct stages: (1) engagement and rationale giving; (2) reducing avoidance by exposure techniques;

(3) dealing with symptom-related cognitions and emotions; and (4) relapse prevention. Overall, the intervention aims to help patients to:

- develop an understanding of the relationship between cognitive, emotional, physiological and behavioural aspects of their problem
- understand factors that may be maintaining symptoms
- learn how to modify behavioural and cognitive responses, which may be maintaining the problem
- engage in avoided activities
- address negative thoughts and illness attributions that are maintaining symptoms
- address emotional dysregulation, anxiety, low mood or low self-esteem, if present
- adopt a healthy sleep routine which often maintains symptoms and disrupts healthy living
- find ways of living with uncertainty.

Psychodynamic Interpersonal Therapy

Psychodynamic interpersonal therapy (PIT) has been used to successfully treat patients at the more severe end of the PPS/MUS spectrum, has been shown to be cost-effective and results in a decrease in healthcare utilisation, and is particularly effective for people with histories of childhood abuse, neglect and loss (43). PIT treats both physical and mental experiences alike and refers to them both as feelings. All feelings are considered to have both a physical and mental component and a set of accompanying mental thoughts, images and memories. Together these components are referred to as 'forms of feeling'. Individuals may be more or less aware of the physical or the mental component of any feeing state. In PIT, people are encouraged to experience feeling states in the session with the therapist. This process triggers a growing awareness of the multifaceted nature of symptoms and in the case of PPS/MUS leads to an exploration of personal function and relationship issues which underpin the maintenance of the symptoms. There is an emphasis on facing warded-off or distressing feelings in the session with the therapist so that longstanding maladaptive patterns of interacting with others can change.

PIT is relatively jargon-free and is much less structured than other approaches. It places great emphasis on developing a strong therapeutic relationship and rationale for treatment.

- Patients are encouraged to tell their story of their symptoms and treatment encounters with health professionals.
- The therapist is expected to listen intently to this story, in an encouraging, supportive and facilitative way. Therapists are encouraged to be fascinated by the client's account.
- The therapist is expected to pick up cues about feelings (which in this model are considered to consist of both a physical and mental element).
- The client is encouraged to stay with feeling states and explore thoughts, images or memories that appear connected to these states. By facing difficult feelings in the 'here and now', previous maladaptive ways of avoiding feelings can be addressed.
- Links to feeling states and key relationships emerge which often produce a focus for the remainder of the therapy.
- A shared explanatory model of the client's symptoms is developed which includes biological, physiological, emotional and relationship processes.

- Practical considerations which improve the client's health and lifestyle are discussed, including sleep, appetite, weight, exercise and experiences which improve social and interpersonal relationships.
- There is a continual process of reformulation as the therapy progresses, expanding upon the initial rudimentary explanatory model and ways in which function and relationships can be improved.
- All sessions are recorded and the client is encouraged to record the sessions themselves and listen to them back either alone or with key others. Discussion of the sessions with key others is actively encouraged if appropriate (i.e. this would not be appropriate if the client was in an abusive relationship).
- As the end of therapy approaches, the client is encouraged to think about how they can consolidate the changes they have made and how they can continue to make changes in the future. Links may be made between the ending of therapy and previous losses in the client's life, if appropriate and thought to be helpful.
- The therapist writes and gives to the client a personal and detailed letter which summarises the areas discussed in therapy, meaningful moments, new insights and positive changes the client has made. The letter is positive, encouraging and warm.

Mindfulness

In recent years, there has been an increased interest in studying the effects of mindfulness-based interventions for people with psychological and physical problems. Mindfulness involves paying attention in a particular way to bodily experience in the present moment. It is basically a meditation technique that can be used in a standalone way to help control the severity of pain or other physical or psychological symptoms or it can be combined with CBT or other therapies such as acceptance commitment therapy (ACT) for a more structured therapeutic approach.

Mindfulness-based relaxation has been found to have positive effects on depression and pain in people with chronic disorders, such as fibromyalgia, coronary artery disease, back pain and arthritis (44, 45).

Acceptance and Commitment Therapy

ACT has developed from CBT. The goal of ACT, however, is not the elimination of negative experiences or thoughts but involves the pursuit of valued life areas such as intimate relationships, meaningful work and personal growth in the face of painful or difficult thoughts (46). In this respect it has aspects in common with both counselling and psychodynamic therapies, although this is rarely acknowledged. The original ACT model postulated that avoidance of difficult feelings or experiences resulted in a short-term gain for the individual by removal of distress but leads to longer-term more entrenched difficulties and a continuation of dysfunctional behaviour. The notion of flexibility has been used to describe the willingness of an individual to experience difficult internal events in pursuit of greater goals and values. This again has many similarities with psychodynamic models, including PIT, where the value of facing warded-off or difficult feelings in the here and now with the therapist is understood as a process that leads to positive change and growth consistent with the person's own long-term wishes and ambitions.

Psychological flexibility is cultivated in ACT by strengthening the following six core skills (46):

- flexibly remaining in the present moment 'here and now' by being mindful of thoughts, feelings, bodily sensations and action potentials, including during distressing experiences (vs. losing contact with the present)
- keeping a balanced and broad perspective on thinking and feeling, such that painful or distressing thoughts and feelings do not automatically trigger maladaptive avoidance behaviours
- clarifying fundamental hopes, values and goals such as being there for one's family, pursuing meaningful work and so on (vs. being disconnected from the things and people that matter most)
- cultivating commitment to doing things in line with identified hopes, values and goals
- willingly accepting the unwanted feelings inevitably elicited by taking difficult actions, particularly those consistent with the patient's hopes, values and goals
- defusing or stepping back from thoughts that interfere with valued actions and seeing them for what they are (vs. seeing thoughts as literal truths).

Key in the ACT model is also workability – helping develop greater awareness of one's behaviours and whether those behaviours are working in terms of effectively solving the problem and moving towards valued ends. Mindfulness techniques are also incorporated into the model to help manage distress in letting go of feelings without avoiding them.

ACT is transdiagnostic so can be delivered with relatively minor adjustments for a variety of different conditions. It has also been delivered in a wide range of different formats from one-day workshops to one-to-one therapies.

Hypnosis

Hypnosis has been shown to be effective in reducing pain (47), symptoms of irritable bowel syndrome (18) and asthma (48). It can be delivered in an individual and group format and may be more acceptable to certain groups of patients who do not want conventional psychological treatments. Hypnosis produces an altered state of consciousness that consists of a heightened focus of attention, decreased awareness or peripheral cues and enhanced responsiveness to social cues or suggestion. It also includes a deep sense of relaxation.

Interpersonal Therapy

Interpersonal therapy (IPT) was initially developed as a form of treatment for depression but has been evaluated in the liaison field in a variety of different conditions including HIV, cancer, rheumatoid arthritis and other chronic conditions (49).

IPT addresses illness-related distress with or without depression. There is a particular focus on interpersonal relationships, including how relationships have changed with loved ones or family members as a consequence of illness and also relationships with healthcare personnel. Both loss and role transitions can be key foci of treatment.

Counselling

Person-centred counselling has been evaluated in several studies in the field of cancer to good effect and has comparative effects to CBT. It is used widely in healthcare settings when individuals may not actually be suffering from mental illness but are struggling to cope with illness or life changes caused by illness. There are three core components: congruence, unconditional positive regard and empathy. Congruence is the willingness of the therapist to relate to the client in an open and transparent manner. Unconditional positive regard refers to a non-judgemental attitude towards anything that the client may bring to therapy and empathy refers to the therapist's ability to understand their client's thoughts and feelings.

Cognitive Analytic Therapy

Cognitive analytic therapy (CAT) has an established, well-developed clinical base in the UK. It has a relatively small evidence base but has shown promising results in small trials and before-and-after studies in diabetes, asthma and chronic pain (50).

The model focusses upon the identification of maladaptive behaviours, particularly regarding interpersonal relationships. In the first phase of therapy the therapist develops in collaboration with the client a reformulation of their problems, attending to patterns in relationships and the influence of early childhood experiences. This is presented to the client in the form of a letter which is agreed and becomes the basis for the focus of the rest of the therapy. The second phase of therapy is called the recognition phase and a diagrammatic formulation of the client's difficulties is developed. In the third phase (revision phase) the client and therapist discuss ways in which maladaptive patterns in relationships can be changed or exited. At the end of therapy, the client and therapist both write each other letters which summarise the main problems or difficulties that have been addressed and changes made, and further work that can continue post-treatment.

Who Should Be Referred for Psychological Treatment?

Participation in psychological treatment of any modality requires certain abilities. The person has to be able to concentrate in the session, remember and understand what has been discussed and attend on a regular basis. Physical illness can adversely affect people's ability to participate in therapy. For instance, people undergoing radiotherapy or chemotherapy may feel too ill or too tired to participate. Concentration and memory can also be severely affected in many physical conditions and some therapies can become so disjointed because of frequent relapses of illness that very little progress is made.

Therapists are in fact not very good at predicting who will benefit from therapy, despite some psychotherapy units offering lengthy assessment sessions to determine suitability. It is also not possible at present to accurately predict whether someone will have a better outcome with one kind of therapy than another. Box 15.2 lists some factors that may help determine suitability for therapy, but each person should be considered on their own merits.

The person either has a history of supportive friendships or relationships or, if not, recognises that this is an issue for them and would like to change or address this. Liaison teams are often asked to help people who do not meet some or any of the criteria in Box 15.2; for instance, someone with poor diabetic control, difficulties trusting staff and a history of poor or unsupportive relationships in their personal life. Such an individual is unlikely to accept referral for a psychological treatment or attend for therapy if referred. In these circumstances, liaison teams can use 'generic aspects of therapy' to try to establish and forge a therapeutic relationship with the patient. A low-key supportive relationship which focusses upon improving the patient's relationship with the diabetic team and compliance with medication, while addressing basic lifestyle issues and support networks, can be just as beneficial as full-blown therapy.

Box 15.2 Factors That May Suggest a Person Could Benefit from Psychological Treatment

- Able to concentrate
- Good working memory
- Physical illness is unlikely to significantly impact ability to participate in therapy
- There is an agreed rationale for referral for therapy
- There is an agreed shared bio-psycho-social model of illness
- The person seems motivated to have psychological treatment
- The person has had a good prior experience of therapy which has resulted in some tangible benefit even if it has worn off

Summary

Psychological therapies play an important role in liaison mental health settings. There is good evidence that they result in improved outcomes in PPS/MUS and in the treatment of anxiety and depression in long-term physical conditions. They do not appear to impact on physical health outcomes in LTCs. A variety of different therapies have been evaluated in the liaison setting including CBT, PIT, IPT, CAT, mindfulness, hypnosis and ACT. The best evidence base is for CBT but bona fide therapies when tested head-to-head have similar outcomes. Brief treatments are best targeted for people with moderate to severe symptoms. To maximise uptake and avoid the stigma associated with mental health problems, psychotherapy services should be ideally located in acute hospital settings alongside relevant medical specialties or via symptom clinics in primary care. People with very severe symptoms and pronounced disability require multimodal treatment approaches from either day-patient or inpatient specialist units.

References

1. Baskin TW, Tierney S, Minami T et al. Establishing specificity in psychotherapy: A meta-analysis of structural equivalence of placebo controls. *J Consult Clin Psychol.* 2003;**71**(6):973–9.

2. Menon V, Rajan T, Kuppili P et al. Cognitive behavior therapy for medically unexplained symptoms: A systematic review and meta-analysis of published controlled trials. *Indian J Psychol Med.* 2017;**39**(4):399–406.

3. Robinson L, Delgadillo J, Kellett S. The dose-response effect in routinely delivered psychological therapies: A systematic review. *Psychother Res.* 2020;**30**(1):79–96.

4. Zijlema WL, Stolk R, Lowe B et al. How to assess common somatic symptoms in large-scale studies: A systematic review of questionnaires. *J Psychosom Res.* 2013;**74**(6):459–68.

5. Huibers MJ, Cohen Z, Lemmens L et al. Predicting optimal outcomes in cognitive therapy or interpersonal psychotherapy for depressed individuals using the personalized advantage index approach. *PLoS One.* 2015;**10**(11):e0140771.

6. Delgadillo J, Gonzalez Salas Duhne,P. Targeted prescription of cognitive-behavioral therapy versus person-centered counseling for depression using a machine learning approach. *J Consult Clin Psychol.* 2020;**88**(1):14–24.

7. Friedl N, Berger T, Krieger T et al. Using the Personalized Advantage Index for individual treatment allocation to cognitive

behavioral therapy (CBT) or a CBT with integrated exposure and emotion-focused elements (CBT-EE). *Psychother Res.* 2020;**30**(6):763–75.

8. van Dessel N, den Boeft M, van der Wouden J et al. Non-pharmacological interventions for somatoform disorders and medically unexplained physical symptoms (MUPS) in adults. *Cochrane Database Syst Rev.* 2014;**11**:CD011142.

9. Abbass A, Lumley M, Town J et al. Short-term psychodynamic psychotherapy for functional somatic disorders: A systematic review and meta-analysis of within-treatment effects. *J Psychosom Res.* 2021:110473.

10. Price JR, Tidy ME, Hunot V. Cognitive behaviour therapy for chronic fatigue syndrome in adults. In *Cochrane Database of Systematic Reviews.* London; 2008.

11. Castell BD, Moss-Morris RE. Cognitive behavioral therapy and graded exercise for chronic fatigue syndrome: A meta-analysis. *Clin Psychol Sci.* 2011;**18**:311–24.

12. Marques MM, de Gucht V, Gouveia M et al. Differential effects of behavioral interventions with a graded physical activity component in patients suffering from chronic fatigue (syndrome): An updated systematic review and meta-analysis. *Clin Psychol Rev.* 2015;**40**:123–37.

13. Kim DY, Lee JS, Park SY et al. Systematic review of randomized controlled trials for chronic fatigue syndrome/myalgic encephalomyelitis (CFS/ME). *J Transl Med.* 2020;**18**(1):7.

14. Cochrane M, Mitchell E, Hollingworth W et al. Cost-effectiveness of interventions for chronic fatigue syndrome or myalgic encephalomyelitis: A systematic review of economic evaluations. *Appl Health Econ Health Policy.* 2021;**19**(4):473–86.

15. Ford AC, Harris LA, Quigley EMM, Moayyed P. Effect of antidepressants and psychological therapies in irritable bowel syndrome: An updated systematic review and meta-analysis. *Am J Gastroenterol.* 2019;**114**:21–39.

16. Laird KT, Tanner-Smith EE, Russell AC et al. Short-term and long-term efficacy of psychological therapies for irritable bowel syndrome: A systematic review and meta-analysis. *Clin Gastroenterol Hepatol.* 2016;**14**(7):937–47, e4.

17. Black CJ, Thakur ER, Houghton LA et al. Efficacy of psychological therapies for irritable bowel syndrome: Systematic review and network meta-analysis. *Gut.* 2020;**69**(8):1441–51.

18. Krouwel M, Farley A, Greenfield S et al. Systematic review, meta-analysis with subgroup analysis of hypnotherapy for irritable bowel syndrome: Effect of intervention characteristics. *Complement Ther Med.* 2021;**57**:102672.

19. Carlson P. Psychological interventions for psychogenic non-epileptic seizures: A meta-analysis. *Seizure.* 2017;**45**:142–50.

20. Gutkin M, Brown R, Kanaan RA. Systematic review of psychotherapy for adults with functional neurological disorder. *J Neurol Neurosurg Psychiatry.* 2020:321926.

21. Sheard T, Maguire P. The effect of psychological interventions on anxiety and depression in cancer patients: Results of two meta-analyses. *Br J Cancer.* 1999;**80**(11):1770–80.

22. Jassim GA, Hickey A, Carter B. Psychological interventions for women with non-metastatic breast cancer. *Cochrane Database of Systematic Reviews.* 2015:CD008729.

23. Richardson AE, Broadbent E, Morton, RP. A systematic review of psychological interventions for patients with head and neck cancer. *Support Care Cancer.* 2019;**27**(6):2007–21.

24. Cillessen L, Johannsen M, Speckens AEM et al. Mindfulness-based interventions for psychological and physical health outcomes in cancer patients and survivors: A systematic review and meta-analysis of randomized controlled trials. *Psychooncology.* 2019;**28**(12):2257–69.

25. Guarino A, Polini C, Forte G et al. The effectiveness of psychological treatments in

women with breast cancer: A systematic review and meta-analysis. *J Clin Med.* 2020;**9**(1).

26. Mundle R, Afenya E, Agarwal N. The effectiveness of psychological intervention for depression, anxiety, and distress in prostate cancer: A systematic review of literature. *Prostate Cancer Prostatic Dis.* 2021; **24**(3):674–87.

27. Coventry PA, Bower P, Keyworth C et al. The effect of complex interventions on depression and anxiety in chronic obstructive pulmonary disease: Systematic review and meta-analysis. *PLoS One.* 2013;**8**(4):e60532.

28. Farver-Vestergaard I, Jacobsen D, Zachariae R. Efficacy of psychosocial interventions on psychological and physical health outcomes in chronic obstructive pulmonary disease: A systematic review and meta-analysis. *Psychother Psychosom.* 2015;**84**(1):37–50.

29. Zhang X, Yin C, Tian W et al. Effects of cognitive behavioral therapy on anxiety and depression in patients with chronic obstructive pulmonary disease: A meta-analysis and systematic review. *Clin Respir J.* 2020;**14**(10):891–900.

30. Ma RC, Chin YY, Wang YQ et al. Effectiveness of cognitive behavioural therapy for chronic obstructive pulmonary disease patients: A systematic review and meta-analysis. *Complement Ther Clin Pract.* 2020;**38**:101071.

31. Uchendu C, Blake H. Effectiveness of cognitive-behavioural therapy on glycaemic control and psychological outcomes in adults with diabetes mellitus: A systematic review and meta-analysis of randomized controlled trials. *Diabet Med.* 2017;**34**(3):328–39.

32. Li C, Xu D, Hu M et al. A systematic review and meta-analysis of randomized controlled trials of cognitive behavior therapy for patients with diabetes and depression. *J Psychosom Res.* 2017;**95**:44–54.

33. Winkley K, Upsher R, Stahl D et al. Psychological interventions to improve self-management of type 1 and type 2 diabetes: A systematic review. *Health Technol Assess.* 2020;**24**(28):1–232.

34. Berhe KK, Gebru HB, Kahsay HB. Effect of motivational interviewing intervention on HgbA1C and depression in people with type 2 diabetes mellitus (systematic review and meta-analysis). *PLoS One.* 2020;**15**(10): e0240839.

35. Ngan HY, Chong YY, Chien WT. Effects of mindfulness- and acceptance-based interventions on diabetes distress and glycaemic level in people with type 2 diabetes: Systematic review and meta-analysis. *Diabet Med.* 2021;**38**(4):e14525.

36. Salmon P, Ring A, Dowrick CF et al. What do general practice patients want when they present medically unexplained symptoms, and why do their doctors feel pressurized? *J Psychosom Res.* 2005;**59** (4):255–60; discussion 261–2.

37. Baardseth TP, Goldberg SB, Pace BT et al. Cognitive-behavioral therapy versus other therapies: Redux. *Clin Psychol Rev.* 2013;**33** (3):395–405.

38. Wampold BE, Minami T, Baskin TW et al. A meta-(re)analysis of the effects of cognitive therapy versus 'other therapies' for depression. *J Affect Disord,* 2002;**68**(2–3):159–65.

39. Paley G, Cahill J, Barkham M et al. The effectiveness of psychodynamic-interpersonal therapy (PIT) in routine clinical practice: A benchmarking comparison. *Psychol Psychother.* 2008;**81**(Pt 2):157–75.

40. Wakefield S, Delgadillo J, Kellett S et al. The effectiveness of brief cognitive analytic therapy for anxiety and depression: A quasi-experimental case-control study. *Br J Clin Psychol.* 2021;**60**(2):194–211.

41. Barkham M, Saxon D. The effectiveness of high-intensity CBT and counselling alone and following low-intensity CBT: A reanalysis of the 2nd UK National Audit of Psychological Therapies data. *BMC Psychiatry.* 2018;**18**(1):321.

42. Chalder T, Patel M, James K et al. Persistent physical symptoms reduction intervention: A system change and evaluation in secondary care (PRINCE secondary) –

A CBT-based transdiagnostic approach: study protocol for a randomised controlled trial. *BMC Psychiatry*. 2019;**19**(1):307.

43. Barkham M, Guthrie E, Hardy G, Margison F. *Psychodynamic-Interpersonal Therapy*. London;2017.

44. Pei JH, Ma T, Nan RL et al. Mindfulness-based cognitive therapy for treating chronic pain: A systematic review and meta-analysis. *Psychol Health Med*. 2021;**26**(3):333–46.

45. Zhou B, Wang G, Hong Y et al. Mindfulness interventions for rheumatoid arthritis: A systematic review and meta-analysis. *Complement Ther Clin Pract*. 2020;**39**:101088.

46. Dindo L, Van Liew JR, Arch JJ. Acceptance and commitment therapy: A transdiagnostic behavioral intervention for mental health and medical conditions. *Neurotherapeutics*. 2017;**14**(3):546–53.

47. Patterson DR, Jensen MP. Hypnosis and clinical pain. *Psychol Bull*. 2003;**129**(4):495–521.

48. Brown D. Evidence-based hypnotherapy for asthma: A critical review. *Int J Clin Exp Hypn*. 2007;**55**(2):220–49.

49. Weissman MM. Interpersonal psychotherapy: History and future. *Am J Psychother*. 2020;**73**(1):3–7.

50. Hallam C, Simmonds-Buckley M, Kellett S et al. The acceptability, effectiveness, and durability of cognitive analytic therapy: Systematic review and meta-analysis. *Psychol Psychother*. 2021;**94**(Suppl. 1):8–35.

51. Kellner R. Functional somatic symptoms and hypochondriasis: A survey of empirical studies. *Arch Gen Psychiatry*. 1985 Aug;**42**(8):821–33. doi: 10.1001/archpsyc.1985.01790310089012. PMID: 2861797.

52. Escobar JI, Waitzkin H, Silver RC, Gara M, Holman A. Abridged somatization: A study in primary care. *Psychosom Med*. 1998;**60**(4):466–72. doi: 10.1097/00006842-199807000-00012. PMID: 9710292.

53. Riess H. The science of empathy. *J Patient Exp*. 2017;**4**(2):74–7. doi: 10.1177/2374373517699267. PMID: 28725865.

Legal and Ethical Issues in Consultation-Liaison Psychiatry

16

Elena Baker-Glenn and Annabel Price

Introduction

Liaison psychiatry practice is built on a foundation of core ethical principles that apply wherever there are people needing mental healthcare (1). In the UK, liaison psychiatry is practised in accordance with the Human Rights Act 1998 (HRA) (2), the articles of the European Convention on Human Rights (ECHR) and the UN Convention on the Rights of Persons with Disabilities (CRPD).

The UK accepted the jurisdiction of the ECHR in 1966 and it was incorporated into UK law in the HRA, which came into force in 2000 and allowed individuals to bring legal actions against the state in UK courts if their individual rights were violated (3). Six articles are key to mental health law: Article 2, the right to life; Article 3, which prohibits torture and inhuman or degrading treatment or punishment; Article 5, the right to liberty and security of person; Article 6, the right to a fair trial; Article 8, the right to respect for private and family life; and Article 14, which prohibits discrimination.

The CRPD was adopted by the United Nations General Assembly in 2006 and ratified by the UK in 2009. Articles 12 and 14 present particular challenges for mental health law (4): Article 12 focusses on equal rights for those with and without disabilities, where 'persons with disabilities enjoy legal capacity on an equal basis with others in all aspects of life', while Article 14 addresses the liberty and security of person. As revisions are made to commonly used legislative frameworks, they will have to ensure compatibility with these laws as far as possible.

This chapter will consider legal frameworks for care of patients in the general hospital. Many people choose to attend hospital for help and understand the treatments offered to them and can make capacitous decisions about them. However, at times, patients may not have capacity to make decisions and their treatment may require a deprivation of liberty. In addition, patients may present to the general hospital with symptoms of a mental illness and consideration may need to be given as to whether the use of mental health legislation is required, either to continue psychiatric treatment there or for admission to a psychiatric unit.

This chapter will cover England and Wales legislation in detail with the Mental Health Act 1983 (amended 2007) (MHA) (5) and the Mental Capacity Act 2005 (MCA) (6), with consideration of the equivalent legal frameworks used in other jurisdictions. It will also consider the interface between the mental health and capacity legislations.

Mental Capacity: From Concept to Practice

The concept of mental capacity, and the associated clinical and legal practice, is central to medical and social care. It is based on the guiding principle that if individuals can act autonomously, they should be allowed and supported to do so.

Depending on the jurisdiction, determination of capacity may be guided by relevant legislation and associated codes of practice. In the UK, the Scottish legislation, the Adults with Incapacity (Scotland) Act 2000 (7), preceded the MCA in England and Wales. The fundamentals of the two Acts (and the tests of capacity) are similar, and both relate to adults over the age of 16. In Northern Ireland, a fusion law yet to be fully enacted will replace the current mental health legislation, with capacity-based legislation that encompasses both physical and mental healthcare decisions.

Internationally, most jurisdictions base their capacity laws on a 'functional' or ability-led approach, which is decision- and time-specific, and capacity is presumed at the outset. Different jurisdictions use different components for capacity determination; for example, in the USA the capacity test is based on national case law and evaluates the abilities of 'understanding', 'appreciation', 'reasoning' and 'expressing' a choice, while in England and Wales the test is based on specific legislation and is based on the ability to 'understand', 'retain', 'use and weigh' and 'communicate a decision'.

While determination of mental capacity is a skill expected of all health and social care professionals, psychiatrists have particular experience in the interface between psychopathology and capacity, and liaison psychiatrists have more specialist experience at the interface between physical and mental illness. In the general hospital setting, liaison psychiatry services are often asked to support the determination of mental capacity for a range of decisions, especially in relation to medical investigations or procedures, care in hospital or discharge planning.

The Mental Capacity Act 2005 (MCA)

The MCA relates to two broad areas:

1. Acts in connection with current care and treatment: this area encompasses determination of capacity and best interests decision-making
2. Decisions about future care and treatment, comprising two elements: donating lasting power of attorney (LPA) and advance decision-making. These decisions are enacted when a person loses capacity to act on their own behalf at a future time and are important in determining the *best interests* of a person lacking capacity in relation to a particular decision.

The MCA is intended as the legal framework for the majority of decisions that a person would need to make, though there are some specific tests of capacity based on case law, such as testamentary capacity (capacity to make a will).

The MCA is based on five key principles (with minor paraphrasing from the wording of the Act):

1. A person must be assumed to have capacity unless it is established that they lack capacity (a presumption of capacity)
2. A person is not to be treated as unable to make a decision unless all practicable steps to help them to do so have been taken without success (therefore we have a duty to support people in making decisions)
3. A person is not to be treated as unable to make a decision merely because they make an unwise decision
4. An act done or decision made, under the Act, for or on behalf of a person who lacks capacity must be done or made in their best interests

5. Before the act is done or the decision made (in a person's best interests), consideration must be made as to whether the purpose for which it is needed can be achieved in a way that is less restrictive of the person's rights and freedom of action.

Determination of capacity under the MCA is a two-step, *connected* process:

1. In relation to a specific decision at a specific time: can the person (with appropriate support) *understand* the relevant information, *retain* it for the duration of time needed to make the decision, *use or weigh* the relevant information and *communicate* the decision once made?
2. If they cannot do one or more of the above, *is it due to an impairment or disturbance of the functioning of the mind or brain*?

The MCA does not specify what would constitute impairment or disturbance, and they could therefore include a wide range of conditions. These include (but are by no means limited to):

- permanent and irreversible conditions, such as dementia, intellectual disability or brain injury
- temporary impairment of cognition in delirium or in the context of a physical illness
- abnormal mood states during relapse of mood disorders such as depression or mania
- an episode of psychotic illness
- an eating disorder such as anorexia nervosa
- acute disturbance of mental state associated with emotionally unstable personality disorder.

This list is not limited to those with a diagnosis of a mental disorder; a person who has no mental disorder may become temporarily unable to make a decision, for example because of an extreme emotional state (e.g. fear, anger) or substance intoxication.

Assessment of Mental Capacity

Most capacity assessments in hospital supported by liaison psychiatry are not done in acute emergencies, and time and care can be taken to optimise the circumstances and quality of the assessment. However, sometimes an assessment of capacity is needed in an emergency and, although the principles are the same, there may not be time to work methodically through the steps detailed below.

The following practical steps would apply to any assessment of capacity but may be particularly helpful to the liaison psychiatry practitioner when a request for assessment is made.

Address the Following Questions Prior to Assessment

1. Is a mental capacity assessment required? (See Box 16.1.) Sometimes, on exploration with the referrer, the situation does not require a capacity assessment but may represent a 'disagreement' on the way forward between treating team and patient, or an impasse of another sort. In this situation the role of the liaison psychiatry team can sometimes be to help to better elucidate the problem and support the relevant teams towards a solution.
2. Why is capacity in doubt? Does the patient have a known condition that is likely to impact on capacity? Has the patient made a decision that has led the treating team to question their capacity? Has someone else raised concerns about capacity?

Box 16.1 Is a Mental Capacity Assessment Required?

Example

A capacity assessment regarding place of care on discharge was requested by the medical team caring for an 85-year-old lady admitted to hospital after a fall. While in hospital she had been evicted from her privately arranged sheltered accommodation as staff there felt unable to meet her needs prior to admission. She was refusing to consider the option of discharge to an interim care home placement while other arrangements were considered, instead insisting that she would stay with her son or friends. She no longer had any acute medical needs that required ongoing inpatient admission. After detailed exploration, no viable alternative arrangements were possible within a reasonable time frame, including staying with friends or family.

After much discussion, it was established that the patient was not being presented with a choice and that the main issue was the uncomfortable situation of potentially having to remove her from hospital to the only viable discharge destination.

Following much negotiation with the patient, her family, the treating team, safeguarding team and hospital discharge planning teams, the patient reluctantly agreed to go to a local care home pending more definite discharge arrangements.

3. Is this the right time to do the capacity assessment? If a person is, for example, acutely delirious or intoxicated, it would be better if the decision could be safely deferred until the person regains capacity or is as close as possible to their cognitive baseline. It might not be possible for urgent assessments to wait if the decision to be made may immediately impact on survival or critical health outcomes.

4. What is the decision that the patient is being asked to make? What options are being presented to the patient? Are the risks and benefits of these options understood?

5. Who is the decision maker? The decision as to whether the patient lacks capacity is the responsibility of the person or persons responsible for implementing the decision.

6. Are there advance directives relevant to the decision or does the person have an LPA in place?

7. Are there concerns that there is undue influence on the person in their decision-making?

Setting Up the Assessment

1. Plan the assessment in advance:

   a. Is there a suitable room or area that provides privacy and quiet and can comfortably accommodate the patient and all of the people who need to be present?

2. Does the set-up optimise autonomous decision-making?

   a. Are sensory impairments optimised? This can range from making sure that the patient is wearing glasses and hearing aids, if needed, to more sophisticated solutions for optimising communication (e.g. alphabet boards or a tablet).

   b. Who else might be able to support the patient? Consider including individuals such as an interpreter, carer, social worker, support worker, member of trusted ward staff or speech and language therapist in the assessment, as appropriate.

   c. Has the patient already had an opportunity to consider their options? Have they been given time to discuss them and any supplementary information given, such as written information about a treatment or procedure?

   d. In accordance with the Equality Act 2010 (England and Wales) there is a legal duty to make 'reasonable adjustments' so that a person with a disability is not disadvantaged by the capacity determination process (8). This will include providing information 'in an accessible format', which may include written, verbal and other media. Many acute hospitals have a learning disabilities service that can provide advice and support when assessing capacity.

3. Before starting the assessment:

   a. Is the patient well rested and not in need of immediate personal/comfort care?

   b. Can an uninterrupted discussion take place?

   c. Can distractions be minimised? Hospital staff become quite good at 'tuning out' myriad distractions, but patients may not have acquired the same ability to ignore them and these may have a negative impact on their ability to manage the conversation.

Conducting the Assessment

1. Introduce yourself, and anyone else with you, with a clear explanation of who you are, why you are there and what the patient can expect from the conversation.
2. Try to use a combination of open questions and more focussed questions (see Example of an MCA Assessment).
3. Try to use language and terminology that is not overly technical and makes use of the patient's own understanding.
4. Take opportunities to check and summarise the conversation as it progresses.
5. If possible, try to end the conversation with a shared understanding of the outcome.

Example of an MCA Assessment

Jim is an 89-year-old man with an established diagnosis of vascular dementia who is admitted to hospital with delirium and a deteriorating ability to care for himself, on a background of critical ischaemia of the toes of his right foot. Two months earlier he had unsuccessful vascular surgery in an attempt to vascularise the foot and was adamant at that time that he did not want to consider amputation. He accepts all care offered in hospital, including antibiotics and analgesia. He lives alone, has no close friends or family and has not donated power of attorney or made any advance decisions. He describes activities he enjoys at home and wishes to get back to his flat, and his delirium is much better after a course of antibiotics. He is referred to liaison psychiatry for an assessment of capacity to refuse amputation. The liaison psychiatrist sees the patient after gaining a detailed understanding of the care plan and options available. After introductions and a general discussion about his care in hospital, the following conversation takes place:

LIAISON PSYCHIATRIST: Can you tell me about the medical problems you have at the moment? *(Open question)*

JIM: I'm alright now I think, I want to get home soon.

LIAISON PSYCHIATRIST: Have you had any problems with your foot? *(Open question)*

JIM: Oh yes, it's been sore but it's drying up nicely now and I can get to the toilet and back by myself if I go slowly.

LIAISON PSYCHIATRIST: Can you tell me what's wrong with your foot? *(Open question but more focussed)*

JIM: The toes have gone black.

LIAISON PSYCHIATRIST: Do you know why? *(Open question but more focussed)*

JIM: No, I can't remember.

LIAISON PSYCHIATRIST: I've heard that the blood supply isn't reaching the toes and the vascular surgeons haven't been able to fix that for you *(Introduction of relevant information for consideration)*

JIM: Oh yes, that's right.

LIAISON PSYCHIATRIST: Have the surgeons offered any other treatment for your foot? *(Open question but more focussed)*

JIM: Oh yes, they want to cut off my foot but I told them 'No chopping!'

LIAISON PSYCHIATRIST: Can I ask you why you said that? *(Open question but more focussed)*

JIM: I just want to keep my leg; I want to be able to walk around my flat.

LIAISON PSYCHIATRIST: Did the surgeon who talked to you about amputating, I mean cutting off the foot [note: liaison psychiatrist realises they have used a technical term without clarifying the meaning], say why they recommended it? *(Open question but more focussed)*

JIM: I don't remember.

LIAISON PSYCHIATRIST: The doctors looking after you think that you have an infection in the foot and it could get worse and make you very ill. It might even make you ill enough to die [note: liaison psychiatrist uses very simple, clear language to communicate risk]. It's already made you ill enough to need a hospital stay and treatment with antibiotics. *(Introduction of relevant information for consideration)*

JIM: I don't think so, it looked a bit better to me when they last changed the dressing.

LIAISON PSYCHIATRIST: I understand that the black area is getting bigger and even with the antibiotics you might get very unwell if you keep the foot. *(Introduction of relevant information for consideration)*

JIM: I told them no chopping and I'm not going to change my mind. I'll be alright when I get home.

LIAISON PSYCHIATRIST: Can I make sure I understand what you've told me? You agreed with me that you have black toes because they are not getting enough blood supply . . . *(Clarification)*

JIM: Yes.

LIAISON PSYCHIATRIST: . . . and you've had treatment to try to help with that but it didn't work? *(Clarification)*

JIM: That's right.

LIAISON PSYCHIATRIST: . . . and you've been offered an amputation . . . *(Clarification)*

JIM: I told them no chopping; my foot will be alright. Tell them I said no chopping. Can you get me home soon?

LIAISON PSYCHIATRIST: Can we talk about what life might be like if you did have the amputation? *(Open question)*

JIM: I don't want to talk about that because it's not happening. I said no chopping and that's that.

LIAISON PSYCHIATRIST: Thank you for being so clear with me. From what we have talked about I understand that you want to keep your foot no matter what happens. Is that still the case even if keeping it makes you more ill or even means you die sooner? *(Clarification and focussed question)*

JIM: I don't think it's going to bother me anymore; I feel fine. Now get me home.

Assessment outcome: While Jim knows when prompted that he has an ischaemic foot, and that the option of amputation has been offered to him after unsuccessful vascular surgery, he does not understand what may happen without amputation. While he is able to communicate the decision that he does not want amputation, he has not shown an ability to weigh his options with an understanding of the likely outcomes of each. Cognitive impairment due to the vascular dementia was impacting on Jim's ability to understand the information relevant to the decision. The conclusion reached after the conversation above was that Jim lacked the capacity to refuse amputation and this outcome was because of cognitive impairment due to vascular dementia. The interview above demonstrates significant impairment of memory and ability to incorporate new information into his ability to make the relevant decision.

Documentation

It is essential that a detailed record is made as soon as possible after a capacity assessment. Capacity determination has important legal ramifications, and relevant documentation may subsequently be scrutinised in court.

Documentation should include:

- the decision being made
- the options available
- key information relevant to the decision
- efforts made to optimise decision-making
- evidence for assessment according to the relevant Act or jurisdiction
- a statement concerning the disorder of the functioning of mind or brain (including whether it is temporary, permanent or fluctuating) and why the person that has been assessed lacked capacity for the decision at the time because of this disorder.

Best Interests

If a person is found to be unable to act or make a decision, it may be necessary to act or make a decision on their behalf, in their *best interests*. The term 'best interests' is not specifically defined in the MCA, but the code of practice sets out a number of factors to take into account when determining best interests:

- avoid discrimination: people who lack capacity should not be treated less favourably because of their lack of capacity
- identify *all relevant* circumstances
- assess whether the person might regain capacity (can the decision or action be deferred?)
- encourage participation
- do not be motivated by a desire to bring about the person's death
- find out the person's views and wishes (from both the person themselves and relevant others)
- consult others (particularly those who hold power of attorney)
- avoid restriction of the person's rights.

A best interests decision takes time and effort and can involve a number of people. Often a meeting involving these people (including the person who the decision is for if possible) can be very helpful. When determining best interests, it is important to check whether the person has made an advance statement or decision or has donated power of attorney.

Lasting Power of Attorney (LPA)

A person with capacity to make the decision can 'donate' decision-making power to another person in the event that they lose capacity to make relevant decisions or *another reason* (if for another reason they lose the ability to act on their own behalf in relation to a decision).

In England and Wales, LPA is administered by the Office of the Public Guardian (9). There are two types of LPA: health and welfare, and finances. LPA for health and welfare can only be enacted if the person loses capacity to make the relevant decision. In this case, the person with power of attorney is able to make the decision on the person's behalf. If the person is able to make their own decision, then the LPA is not relevant.

LPA for finances can be enacted if the person loses capacity to make the relevant decision or decisions, but also in some cases if they retain capacity and are unable to enact the decision for themselves, for example if the person is in hospital and unable to do essential banking.

Advance Decision-Making

This part of the Act aims to ensure that a person's wishes are respected even when they lose capacity. Advance statements can be care preferences or choices of treatment, or refusal of specific treatments. Advance preferences should be taken into account but are not legally binding as it may not be possible to provide the wish or providing the wish may be harmful.

Advance decisions to refuse care are legally binding as long as they are *valid* (made when the person had capacity) and *applicable* (relate specifically to the decision being made). Advance refusals may relate to decisions that do not involve life-sustaining treatment. If that is the case, they do not have to be written down (although it is easier to communicate the decision to relevant people if they are), but they do need to be precise about the treatment being refused and the circumstances in which they would be refused.

Advance decisions related to life-sustaining treatment must be written down and must specify the treatments to be refused and the circumstances in which they would be refused. The refusal should be made by someone who was 18 years or older and had capacity to make the decision at the time of the advance decision. The statement should be signed and witnessed, and a statement that the decision should apply even if the person's life is at risk should be included.

A person wishing to ensure that their advance refusal is considered valid when it is applicable may consider having their written advance decision witnessed and certified by a solicitor, particularly if it relates to withdrawal of life-sustaining treatment, but it is not a legal requirement (Box 16.2).

Box 16.2 Advanced Preference and Refusal

Example of an Advance Preference

I wish to continue living in my own home until the end of my life including dying at home.

Example of an Advance Refusal

I do not wish to receive any ventilatory support if I irreversibly lose the ability to breathe for myself or receive artificial nutrition if I irreversibly lose the ability to swallow. I understand that my life may be at risk if these wishes are carried out.

What Happens If There Is Nobody to Consult When Making a Best Interests Decision?

It is sadly not an uncommon scenario for a person not to have a family member or relevant other to speak with in relation to a best interests decision. Many people do not donate power of attorney or make advance decisions to refuse treatment. In such cases, when the decision relates to a long-term change in accommodation or a serious medical treatment, under the MCA an Independent Mental Capacity Advocate (IMCA) *must* be instructed to support the process of ascertaining the best interests of the person and to represent these interests (Box 16.3).

Box 16.3 Best Interests Decision

Example of a Best Interests Decision

We return to Jim, whose capacity has already been assessed earlier in this chapter, where it was determined that he lacks capacity to refuse limb amputation for critical ischaemia of the foot. An IMCA is consulted who advocates for Jim's wish not to have the amputation, and there follows a professionals' meeting, which includes a renal physician, a vascular surgeon, a liaison psychiatrist, a palliative care physician and a member of the hospital discharge team. The patient is consulted again about his wishes and he reiterates his wish not to have an amputation. Even if it does prolong his life, it is decided that living with the impact of an amputation that he does not want is not in his best interests, and plans are made to try to discharge him home with care.

Unfortunately, his condition deteriorates in hospital. He becomes more distressed by pain and delirium returns despite treatment with antibiotics. Adjustments are made to his analgesia which make him more comfortable, but he deteriorates further and dies peacefully in hospital.

Deprivation of Liberty Safeguards

In England and Wales, Deprivation of Liberty Safeguards (DOLS) exist to ensure that people who lack capacity to consent to the arrangements made for their care have access to a process by which these arrangements can be independently assessed to ensure that they are in that individual's best interests.

Box 16.4 Deprivation of Liberty

Example

A 29-year-old man with cognitive impairment following a brain injury as a teenager is admitted to hospital with abdominal pain. He is diagnosed with a bowel perforation secondary to severe constipation and undergoes emergency surgery in his best interests under the MCA. His post-operative recovery is complex and he remains in hospital for several weeks. During this time, he is often agitated and restraint is occasionally used to facilitate provision of essential care. He has one-to-one observations in place for the majority of his hospital stay. As he recovers and becomes more mobile, he is occasionally prevented from leaving the ward as staff redirect him away from the door.

This annex to the MCA was introduced after it was recognised that there are individuals who lack capacity to consent to their care arrangements, but that there was no legal protection of their rights under the ECHR.

To require DOLS authorisation the person must be:

- 18 or over
- detained in a hospital or care home for care or treatment
- in circumstances that constitute a deprivation of their liberty.

What Constitutes a Deprivation of Liberty?

Following a supreme court judgment in *Cheshire West*, a deprivation of liberty occurs when there is *a lack of capacity to consent to arrangements for care and treatment* and the individual is *subject to continuous control and supervision* and is *not free to leave*. If a deprivation of liberty is suspected, then hospitals can apply for an urgent DOLS authorisation followed by an application for standard authorisation (Box 16.4).

Can Treatment Be Given in Hospital under DOLS?

Medical treatment given to people who lack capacity to consent must be given in their best interests under the MCA. They may also be deprived of their liberty in the course of this treatment and, if so, DOLS may also be necessary. At the time of writing, DOLS are to be superseded by Liberty Protection Safeguards (LPS) when the Mental Capacity Amendment Act comes into force following the publication of the code of practice.

The Mental Health Act (MHA)

The MHA 1983 in England and Wales is legislation covering the assessment, treatment and rights of people with a mental disorder. The MHA 1959 led to significant changes as patients could be compelled to accept treatment for mental disorders. The charity Mind suggested reforms to this Act, and government reviews attempted to reconcile conflicting views, resulting in the MHA 1983. This Act continued to focus on hospital treatment and only patients deemed treatable could be detained. Where people require urgent treatment for their mental illness and there are concerns that they are presenting with risks to themselves or others, this legislation can authorise their admission to hospital against their will, even if the person has capacity to refuse. It also provides patients with a number of rights, such as the right to appeal.

Amendments were made to the MHA 1983 in 2007, which were brought into force in 2008. The essential changes included:

- a single definition of mental disorder
- replacing the treatability test with an appropriate treatment test
- allowing a wider range of professional disciplines to become Approved Mental Health Practitioners (AMHPs), the equivalent role previously being restricted to social workers
- the right for people to apply to have their nearest relative removed
- introduction of community treatment orders (CTOs)
- changes to electroconvulsive therapy (ECT) so that consent is required and advance decisions to refuse ECT can no longer be overridden
- changes to advocacy
- through amending the MCA 2005, the introduction of DOLS.

There is no equivalent to the MHA for those with physical illness, where treatment cannot be given against capacitous patients' wishes unless they meet criteria within the Public Health (Control of Diseases) Act 1984.

Use of the MHA in the General Hospital

In England, hospitals have to be registered with the Care Quality Commission (CQC) in order for patients to be able to be detained to the hospital under the MHA. There should be service-level agreements between acute healthcare providers and mental healthcare providers that outline the local process. If accepting detained patients, hospitals need to identify administrators and hospital managers who have the necessary skills to hear appeals against detention.

The Responsible Clinician (RC) role often rests with the liaison psychiatry consultant and with the on-call psychiatry consultant out of hours. The Sections of the MHA that are more commonly used within liaison psychiatry are detailed next.

Section 136

Section 136 is used by police officers in a public place in order to take a person to a place of safety to await an MHA assessment. The section can last for up to 24 hours and occasionally may be extended by 12 hours. The equivalent in Scotland is Section 297 Mental Health (Care and Treatment) (Scotland) Act 2003 and in Northern Ireland is Article 130 Mental Health (Northern Ireland) Order 1986 (10).

Police cells could previously be used as the main place of safety, but following concerns that patients were being taken to police stations in a mental health crisis, more health-based places of safety were created. When these locations are full, or where there are concerns about a person's physical health, the emergency department (ED) can also be used as the place of safety (11). There are, however, standards from the Royal College of Psychiatrists indicating that EDs should only be used as places of safety when there are concerns that there are medical problems that require urgent assessment and treatment (12). Because of gaps in the current legislation, if a patient tries to leave the ED and is not subject to a legal framework, and the mental capacity legislation does not apply, staff may be able to ask the police to support and to consider a Section 136.

Section 5(2)

Section 5(2) is a doctor's holding power which lasts up to 72 hours while an MHA assessment is arranged. Currently, this section cannot be used in the ED, but it can be applied to patients admitted to hospital where the hospital is registered with CQC to have detained patients. The local policy will determine who is able to use a Section 5(2), but in the general hospital setting it is often the medical or surgical consultant caring for the patient or their nominated deputy. Some areas have agreements that the liaison psychiatrist is able to fulfil that role.

Section 2 and Section 3

For both Section 2 and Section 3, the assessment will be conducted face to face by two registered medical practitioners and an AMHP. At least one of the doctors should be approved under Section 12 of the MHA by the secretary of state as having special experience in diagnosis or treatment of mental disorder, and ideally one doctor should have previous acquaintance with the patient. The doctors complete statutory documentation (medical recommendations), which can be done separately or as a joint recommendation. The AMHP is another healthcare professional with appropriate experience and training; they are approved by a local social services authority to carry out certain duties under the MHA, and if the medical recommendations are completed, they are able to decide to make an application for detention under the MHA. Although rare in practice, a nearest relative is also able to make an application for detention.

Section 2 of the MHA is for compulsory admission of a patient to hospital for assessment, for a period of up to 28 days. The person must be suffering from a mental disorder of a nature or degree that would warrant detention in hospital, and it must be in the interests of their health or safety or to protect others. This section is equivalent to a short-term detention certificate in Scotland (Mental Health (Care and Treatment) (Scotland) Act 2003). Article 4, Mental Health (Northern Ireland) Order 1986, is the closest equivalent in Northern Ireland.

Section 3 of the MHA allows for the compulsory admission of a patient to hospital for treatment and can last for up to six months. For Section 3, the nearest relative as defined in the Act must not object to the application, and appropriate treatment should be available.

Both Section 2 and Section 3 allow for transfer of a patient to a psychiatric hospital, and patients are commonly detained to the psychiatric hospital prior to transfer rather than to the general hospital. There are times, however, when a patient is too physically unwell to be transferred but requires psychiatric treatment; for example, patients not eating and drinking who require ECT, or someone with anorexia who is requiring nasogastric (NG) feeds. These patients may therefore need to be detained to the general hospital.

Patients may also be transferred from the psychiatric hospital to the general hospital if they have a physical health need requiring assessment and possible admission. In this case, they may initially be given Section 17 leave; however, if the stay is prolonged for more than a few days, the RC may request that the section is taken over by the receiving hospital. An agreement to take over the RC role would need to be made by the appropriate clinician, in practice usually a consultant liaison psychiatrist at the admitting hospital. Some hospitals may not be registered to have detained patients, resulting in a legal loophole for people who are not physically well enough to transfer to another setting or need transfer to that hospital for physical healthcare.

Mental Health Act or Mental Capacity Act?

In clinical practice, sometimes it is unclear whether the MHA or MCA-DOLS is the right legislative framework to use in a given situation, as there can be circumstances where either legislation may be applicable and the relevant codes of practice cannot cover every potential scenario. The MHA code of practice acknowledges that sometimes disagreement will arise over which legislation to use and advises above all that if an individual lacks capacity to consent and is deprived of their liberty, then 'they should receive the safeguards afforded' by the MHA, DOLS or Court of Protection.

The MCA aims to protect incapacitous adults, empowering people to make decisions for themselves wherever possible (13), and is focussed on patient autonomy and consideration of best interests (14). It is not specifically related to mental health or its consequences and includes any *disorder of the mind or brain* that may impact on capacity. The MHA is specifically for treatment of mental disorder (and its consequences), with an emphasis on the management of risk.

The MCA can be used concurrently with MHA detention (if the person lacks capacity to consent to non-mental health aspects of their treatment), but the MHA and DOLS cannot be used concurrently. The decision aid in the MHA code of practice (15) centres around three central concepts: *capacity*, *consent* and *objection*.

- Capacity and consent: if the patient has the capacity to consent and does consent, then the treatment/action can proceed.
- Capacity but no consent: if the patient has capacity but does not consent (to mental health treatment) and fulfil criteria for detention under the MHA, then this option is available.
- Lacks capacity and objects: if the patient lacks capacity to consent and objects to mental health treatment, then the MHA is also available as an option if detention criteria are fulfilled.
- Lacks capacity but no objection: if the patient lacks capacity to consent and does not object, then treatment in their best interests under the MCA should be considered and, if they are subject to continuous supervision and control and not free to leave, then a DOLS application should also be made.
- Under the age of 18: if the person lacks capacity and is deprived of their liberty but is under 18 or there is a risk to others, then the MHA would be the appropriate legislation if ongoing detention is required for provision of care and treatment.

If a person is deprived of their liberty, they may be eligible for DOLS unless:

- they are detained under the MHA. This does not take into account deprivation of liberty related to an unrelated physical disorder: here the only lawful authority is the high court
- not in hospital but subject to the MHA (e.g. Section 17 leave) or guardianship
- they could be detained under MHA S2 or S3 and are an 'objecting mental health patient'.

The decision is often most difficult when a person has concurrent mental health and physical health needs. A helpful question here is 'what is the primary reason for confinement?' Are they primarily a 'physical health patient' or a 'mental health patient'? In the general hospital setting, most patients are primarily there in the context of their physical health, including those with dementia. If the individual could lawfully be detained, there may be an option for either legislation; however, it is not always straightforward to determine whether the person is objecting. The objection does not have to be vocal: it may, for example, be trying a door, physical resistance to care or spitting out medications. This point is particularly relevant for people who are unable to vocalise objection, perhaps due to advanced dementia.

Challenging Areas of Practice

Capacity to End One's Own Life

One area of controversy is the question of whether a person can have capacity to end their own life and, if so, whether they should be allowed to. In this circumstance, a person with suicidal intent who is judged to have capacity to end their life might not be prevented from ending their life. Concern has been raised that this might result in vulnerable people not receiving assistance if they are considered to have capacity to make the decision based on the outcome of a capacity assessment.

Clinicians working in liaison psychiatry services will be familiar with capacity assessments relating to refusal of life-sustaining treatment, and the MCA makes specific reference to these types of decisions; however, neither the MCA nor the code of practice make any specific statements regarding capacity to carry out suicide.

The ECHR accepts that a person can have capacity to decide when their life ends and that it is compatible with Article 8 of the Convention (right to a private life), although it may not be compatible with Article 2 (a right to life). In English law, the HRA does not equate Article 2, right to life, with a right to die.

The case of C received a lot of media attention and illustrates the right to die (16): C was described as having a 'sparkly' lifestyle and attempted suicide after treatment for breast cancer but survived and subsequently required renal dialysis. She refused the dialysis and her family supported her decision, but two psychiatrists who examined C felt that she did not have capacity to refuse dialysis. In the subsequent court case, Mr Justice MacDonald noted that

> where a patient refuses lifesaving medical treatment the court is only entitled to intervene in circumstances where the court is satisfied that the patient does not have the mental capacity to decide whether or not to accept or refuse such treatment. Where the court is satisfied, on the balance of probabilities, that the patient lacks capacity in this regard, the court may take the decision as to what course of action is in the patient's best interests.

The judge disagreed, however, with the healthcare provider's view that she lacked capacity to make the decision, and while accepting that her decision might be considered unwise, 'as a capacitous individual C was, in respect of her own body and mind, sovereign'.

In clinical practice, decisions often require consideration of an individual's right to self-determination versus protection of that person from harm. In the circumstance of a person who wishes to end their life, these two rights may not be compatible. When decision makers do not consider a range of possible options, opportunities can be missed to provide care. Having mental capacity for the decision, as determined by the steps of the MCA test of capacity, is not the only consideration when responding to a person who is distressed enough to wish to die, nor is the MCA the only legislative framework that should be considered when there is risk of harm.

The case of Kerrie Wooltorton, a 26-year-old who died following antifreeze poisoning after presenting to the ED and refusing medical treatment, illustrates some of the challenges.

Kerrie had been self-harming since she was 15 years old, had been given a diagnosis of emotionally unstable personality disorder and had been subject to multiple psychiatric admissions. On her final presentation, she produced a document that stated that she did not want lifesaving treatment but only treatment to relieve her discomfort. On assessment, it was found that she had the capacity to decide about her treatment, meaning that she had the right to refuse any lifesaving treatment; it was thought that treating her against a previously stated wish could be an assault. An alternative option that could have been considered in this case would have been to use the MHA to provide the required treatment (7). The MHA can be used to provide treatment for the consequence of a mental disorder, such as treatment of self-harm, as well as treatment for the disorder itself.

Eating Disorders

Eating disorders present one of the few situations where physical health treatment, such as force-feeding, can be authorised as a treatment for the disorder using the MHA. Recent case law in eating disorders emphasises the importance of patient choice and wishes in making best interests decisions when patients no longer have capacity. There have been several cases involving patients with anorexia nervosa who lacked capacity to make decisions about treatment, with the cases being heard in the Court of Protection. In some cases, the patient was allowed to stop treatment, even though the likely outcome was death (18, 19, 20).

One such case was Z, which involved a 46-year-old with anorexia nervosa who had required multiple admissions without recovery. She experienced significant physical health complications and was detained under Section 3 of the MHA for treatment. The treating healthcare provider brought the case to court with three options: (1) continue treatment under the MHA with NG feeding under physical restraint, (2) NG feed using chemical restraint or (3) discharge from the MHA and treat on a voluntary basis as far as possible (17). The judge believed that the patient in this case should be discharged from detention, which mirrored similar decisions made in the cases of X and W not to force treatment (18, 19).

Despite lacking capacity, these patients were allowed to die, and it was argued that the decisions were in their best interests. Treatment for severe anorexia nervosa is intrusive and often requires restraint, causing distress for patients, families and staff. There are risks of treatment, which may cause suffering and be in breach of the ECHR. Referral to the Court of Protection for opinions relating to ongoing invasive treatment may be appropriate, particularly where there are strong objections made.

However, not all eating disorder cases that go to the Court of Protection result in patients being permitted to refuse treatment, and every case has to be judged on its own unique set of circumstances. E was a 32-year-old woman who suffered from severe anorexia nervosa and emotionally unstable borderline personality disorder, as well as alcohol and opiate dependence, and she was being cared for under a palliative care regime when her case was referred to the Court of Protection. Despite twice attempting to make an advanced decision preventing treatment, after carefully weighing the different factors in the case, the judgment of the court was that it was in the patient's best interests to receive treatment (21).

Future Legislative Changes

The Mental Capacity Act Amendment Act (22) was due to come into force in 2022 but was delayed by the coronavirus pandemic. At the time of writing (2023), this amendment is yet to come into force. This Act will introduce Schedule AA1 LPS, which will replace DOLS.

For liaison psychiatrists working in general hospital settings, the key change that this Act will bring is the introduction of statutory authority to deprive a person of their liberty temporarily in urgent situations to (a) enable life-sustaining treatment or (b) prevent serious deterioration in health (a vital act).

In 2018, there was an Independent Review of the Mental Health Act (23) and a number of reforms were proposed in the White Paper 'Reforming the Mental Health Act', emphasising more choice and autonomy and ensuring that least restrictive options are used and therapeutic benefit is achieved. It also aims to address the racial inequality that currently exists within mental health service provision.

At present, there is a gap in the law for patients in the ED setting, and liaison psychiatrists are often asked for support in such cases. Patients in the ED with a mental health crisis sometimes wish to leave the hospital, but there may be concerns about risk if they do leave. Emergency holding powers under the MHA do not currently apply in the ED, and there is a debate about whether Section 5 MHA powers should be extended to hold someone either in the ED or in another appropriate location while they have a further assessment of their mental health, or if the LPS could and should be used to hold such patients pending further assessment.

Summary

1. Liaison psychiatry practice is built on a foundation of core ethical and legal principles that apply wherever there are people needing mental healthcare.
2. Expertise in mental health and mental capacity law is essential to liaison psychiatry knowledge and practice.
3. Developments in mental health and mental capacity law will impact on liaison psychiatry practice in the coming years with amendments to both the Mental Health Act and Mental Capacity Act in England and Wales and a fusion law in Northern Ireland.

References

1. Royal College of Psychiatrists. Good psychiatric practice. Code of ethics. CR186. www.rcpsych.ac.uk/docs/default-source/improving-care/better-mh-policy/college-reports/college-report-cr186.pdf?sfvrsn=15f49e84_2.

2. Human Rights Act 1988. www.legislation.gov.uk/ukpga/1998/42/contents.

3. Convention for the Protection of Human Rights and Fundamental Freedoms (adopted 4 November 1950, entered into force 3 September 1953). 213 UNTS 221.

4. Convention on the Rights of Persons with Disabilities (adopted 13 December 2006, entered into force 3 May 2008). 2515 UNTS 3.

5. Mental Health Act 1983. www.legislation.gov.uk/ukpga/1983/20/contents.

6. Mental Capacity Act 2005. www.legislation.gov.uk/ukpga/2005/9/contents.

7. Adults with Incapacity (Scotland) Act 2000. www.legislation.gov.uk/asp/2000/4/contents.

8. Equality Act 2010. www.legislation.gov.uk/ukpga/2010/15/contents.

9. Office of the Public Guardian. www.gov.uk/government/organisations/office-of-the-public-guardian.

10. The Mental Health (Northern Ireland) Order 1986. www.legislation.gov.uk/nisi/1986/595/article/130.

11. Care Quality Commission. A safer place to be. 20141021. www.cqc.org.uk/sites/default/files/20141021%20CQC_SaferPlace_2014_07_FINAL%20for%20WEB.pdf.

12. Royal College of Psychiatrists. Guidance for commissioners: Service provision for Section 136 of the Mental Health Act 1983. Position statement PS2/2013. www.rcpsych.ac.uk/pdf/PS02_2013.pdf.

13. Khalique N. Deprivation of liberty: The overlap between the Mental Health Act 1983 and the Mental Capacity Act 2005 (No. 5 Barristers Chambers 2011). www.no5.com/news-and-publications/publications/74-deprivation-of-liberty-the-overlap-between-the-mental-health-act-1983-and-the-mental-capacity-act-2005.

14. Cairns R, Richardson G, Hotopf M. Deprivation of liberty: Mental Capacity Act safeguards versus the Mental Health Act. *The Psychiatrist*. 2010;246.

15. Code of Practice Mental Health Act 1983. www.rcpsych.ac.uk/pdf/PS02_2013.pdf.

16. *Kings College Hospital NHS Foundation Trust v C & Anor* (2015) EWCOP 80. www.bailii.org/ew/cases/EWCOP/2015/80.html.

17. David AS, Hotopf M, Moran P et al. Mentally disordered or lacking capacity? Lessons for management of serious deliberate self-harm. *BMJ*. 2010;341:c4489. doi: 10.1136/bmj.c4489.

18. *Cheshire & Wirral Partnership NHS Foundation Trust v Z* (2016) EWCOP 50. www.bailii.org/ew/cases/EWCOP/2016/56.html.

19. *A NHS Foundation Trust v Ms X* (2014) EWCOP 35 (2015) 2 FCR 418 (2015) COPLR 11. www.bailii.org/ew/cases/EWCOP/2014/35.html.

20. *Betsi Cadwaladr University Local Health Board v Miss W (by her litigation friend, the Official Solicitor)* (2016) EWCOP 13. www.bailii.org/ew/cases/EWCOP/2016/13.html.

21. *Local Authority v E* (2012) EWHC 1639 (COP). www.bailii.org/ew/cases/EWHC/COP/2012/1639.html.

22. Mental Capacity Act (Amendment) Act 2019. www.legislation.gov.uk/ukpga/2019/18/enacted.

23. Modernising the Mental Health Act: Increasing choice, reducing compulsion. Final report of the Independent Review of the Mental Health Act 1983. 2018. https://assets.publishing.service.gov.uk/government/uploads/system/uploads/attachment_data/file/778897/Modernising_the_Mental_Health_Act_-_increasing_choice__reducing_compulsion.pdf.

Further Reading

Jacob R, Gunn M, Holland A. *Mental Capacity Legislation: Principles and Practice*, 2nd ed. Cambridge; 2019.

Essex Chambers. www.39essex.com.
Mental Capacity Law and Policy. www.mentalcapacitylawandpolicy.org.uk.

Social Aspects of Consultation-Liaison Psychiatry

Max Henderson

Taking a history is an essential part of patient care for all clinicians but there can be a tendency for the social history to be brief, formulaic or even absent. The possible reasons for this and how liaison psychiatry might respond, given that history-taking skills are highly developed in the specialty, are described. The individual in the wider multidisciplinary team who is best placed to take a social history from a patient is considered, reviewing the attitudes of both doctors and nurses alongside evidence from studies where frameworks have been established to take the social history from all patients. The sources of information other than the patient that might be considered are described. Several key aspects of the social history are explored in detail – debt, employment, housing and social isolation. The evidence of impact on physical health and mental health is detailed for each, together with a summary of the evidence of benefit for interventions. Finally, the issue of how the information obtained should be shared and with whom and what can be done to improve patient outcomes is discussed.

What Are the Social Aspects of Liaison Psychiatry?

The social aspects of liaison psychiatry are the same social aspects as in other psychiatric subspecialties which really should be the same as the social aspects of all medicine. This is not always the case and some possible reasons for this are explored in what follows. History-taking is an art and a skill that can be constantly improved even over a long career. Buried within the history and the discussion with the patient that is required to obtain it are often gems, the importance of which may only be apparent to liaison psychiatry practitioners who need to hold a physical medicine paradigm and a psychological medicine paradigm in their heads at the same time.

The social aspects are the context in which the patient's presenting symptoms have emerged. They include the patient's key relationships – partner, children, family, friends, where (and how) they live, what job if any they do and how they spend their time. It is in this space that clues may emerge about diagnosis and causation and it is the impact on these elements that frames concepts such as severity and disability. Only by understanding the social aspects can safe and effective planning of future care take place.

The Place of the Social History in an Assessment

Liaison psychiatry exists at the interface between physical and mental health. Given how medicine, organisations and society are structured, this interface can be seen and understood in a number of different ways. It is also the interface between psychiatry and other medical disciplines. It is often, regrettably, the interface between different healthcare providers – medical and psychiatric. On occasions it is also the interface between two different and not always complementary mindsets. On one side the focus is often the problem or the diagnosis or the lesion, whereas on the other there may be less emphasis on diagnosis and less clarity about the lesion. On one side the whole person, their family and their community can appear to be of somewhat lesser importance, but on the other there is more commonly a greater emphasis on the understanding of these wider determinants of health.

Interfaces can be sources of friction. It is here that wear and tear occurs. Misalignment can produce a jolty, uneven engagement. It is often in these spaces, however, that new insight and new learning can occur. Creative tension cannot exist in only one party. Tension exists between two or more parties. At an interface it is possible to face in, to the safe and to the familiar, to concentrate on one's own interests. Alternatively, it is possible to face out, across to the less familiar and potentially challenging other. This is a choice.

The social aspects of liaison psychiatry are fundamentally important to the way liaison psychiatry is practised and how we are seen by our patients and by those who ask us to see their patients. Few aspects of liaison psychiatry illuminate the tensions, challenges and opportunities of interface working better than this. Liaison psychiatry practitioners are only rarely referred patients on the basis of an aspect of their social difficulties, but most liaison psychiatry practitioners would struggle to provide valid and meaningful input to a patient's care in the absence of an understanding of the patient's social situation. This potential disjunct between what has been asked for and what might be offered or provided goes to the heart of what medicine (broadly defined) is for and how the constituents of different multidisciplinary teams work together in the patient's interests.

Modern Western medicine has become increasingly specialised. As knowledge accumulates, one person and one team can only know so much – they can only be truly expert in a certain proportion. This can lead to great benefits for many patients. If you need a surgical procedure carried out, knowing your surgeon does several hundred such procedures each year is very reassuring. If your long-term condition is complex or proving resistant to treatment, you are not concerned that your physician knows much less about another long-term condition. You want their focussed expertise on yours. However, a narrow focus on one aspect of a patient infers that other aspects of the patient's care are to be carried out by someone else. If, for example, care is provided by a multidisciplinary team and each member is clear about their role, then this should not be a problem. In healthcare systems where primary care is strong, much of the generalist care is delivered by the primary care physician. As long as there are good lines of communication between members of this wider multidisciplinary team, then no difficulties should arise.

In reality, systems and teams are only as good as their weakest component. Often in medicine the weak link *is* the link, the communication, the transfer of relevant information from the party that has that information to the party that requires it. In a system of specialists, each team member can be so focussed on their own role that they lose touch with the wider aspects of a patient's care. How do individual clinicians decide which areas to focus on? Commonly, it will be those aspects that the clinician feels are important for the patient to get the best outcome. However, another factor that clinicians perhaps unconsciously consider is 'Can I make a difference?'. Clinicians like *doing*, and they like impact. Doing without impact raises uncomfortable questions about competence and efficacy – 'Why is the patient not getting better?'. It is possible that some of the reluctance to open up a discussion about social circumstances stems from an anxiety that, while they are empathetic with the patient's suffering, there is nothing the clinician feels able to do about it.

As will be explored in what follows, there are legitimate debates within medicine about whether the wider social aspects of a patient's life should be explored, to what extent, with what aim and by whom. Liaison psychiatry should be a vocal contributor to these discussions. There is a risk in such a situation that liaison psychiatry's powerful advocacy for the importance of understanding the patient's social situation can lead to the conclusion that taking a social history is only liaison psychiatry's job. Many liaison psychiatry clinicians will be familiar with referrals where in essence the taking of a good history has been 'outsourced' to them. This is good for neither the patient nor liaison psychiatry. While the history-taking skills of liaison psychiatry practitioners are often highly developed, that is not a reason for this to become exclusively their role. Advice can be provided and support given for more difficult or complex areas. But in the same way that liaison psychiatry would encourage all health professionals to be able to make basic assessments of a patient's mental state or suicide risk, liaison psychiatry should support the premise that a good assessment of a patient's social situation is an essential part of every examination.

Who Should Ask?

The evidence that social factors influence clinical outcomes is overwhelming and largely uncontested. The British Medical Association (1) has suggested that doctors should assess patients in the context of social factors. The US National Academy of Medicine (2) has gone further and recommended specifically which social determinants should be measured and how. In most settings, whether to capture information about social factors is down to individual preference. Is the issue with clinical staff, doctors and nurses asking the patient, or with the patient not wishing to be asked?

Nurses are the members of the multidisciplinary team who spend the greatest time with patients. Are they best placed to identify and respond to the patient's social needs? This could be liaison psychiatry nurses or general hospital nurses supported by the liaison psychiatry team. Brooks Carthon examined just this possibility (3). A number of important themes emerged from this qualitative study. While nurses can and often do identify specific social issues, their need to prioritise sometimes more pressing medical issues can make this difficult and make it hard to address those needs. A combined approach between psychiatric and general hospital staff would therefore seem ideal. Some less helpful findings were also identified, however. Some nurses reported that organisational factors – staff numbers, information technology and managerial attitudes could impact on their ability to spend the requisite time with patients. Other studies have highlighted that staff may lack the confidence or the skills to begin discussing wider social issues (4). Others described a reluctance to explore social aspects for fear of labelling patients. Liaison psychiatry would seem to have a key role training and supporting general hospital nursing staff in developing the confidence to open up such a discussion with general hospital patients.

A number of studies have examined the attitudes of doctors to identifying and managing social aspects of a patient's presentation (5). Some believe it to be outside their remit, simply not their job (6). Others have voiced concerns about patient privacy (5). It has been argued that doctors do not have the time (7). A study of 1,000 doctors in 2011 underlined the similarities in positions between doctors and nurses (8). While 85% of doctors agreed that unmet social needs led to poor health, only 15% were confident in addressing these. In a more recent survey, 66% of doctors stated that their patients would benefit from transport assistance, yet 69% felt it was not part of their job.

Virchow famously stated, 'The physicians are the natural attorneys of the poor, and social problems fall to a large extent within their jurisdiction' in the first edition of *Die medizinische Reform* in 1948 (48). At times it feels that while the science of medicine has accelerated forward, the soul of medicine may have shrunk back. Do the junior doctors and medical students of today understand and accept the position so powerfully advocated by Virchow? There is some evidence emerging that frameworks can be put in place to collect data on patients' social situations in a way that is constructive and meaningful. In 2010 a group of health organisations in Toronto came together to develop an evidence-based approach to collecting patient data. Patient participation was 85%, demonstrating this could be done, although appropriate training of those collecting the data was essential. The success of the project led to a directive that all hospitals in Toronto collect social data on patients across eight separate domains (9). A study of over 1,000 patients across community health clinics in Oregon also showed such routine data collection is possible, though the same emphasis was placed on training those professionals who collect the data (10).

Turf wars about particular aspects of an assessment are unhelpful and unbecoming. Most important is that the liaison psychiatrist recognises and appreciates the central role of the social environment in every patient's presentation and journey in hospital or out-patients. They may need to take responsibility for ensuring that a suitably detailed and helpful account is taken from the patient. How that task is divided up is likely to vary between patients and teams. Often liaison psychiatry clinicians have the benefit of time that is not always available to our general hospital colleagues. Engaging the patient sufficiently to generate a good enough rapport takes time. Social histories cannot be obtained by stethoscope. Several visits may be required for the full picture to emerge.

The social history will be important for almost all patients, however, not just those referred to liaison psychiatry. So, liaison psychiatry has a wider role, beyond the patients they see, in encouraging and facilitating this aspect of the assessment. In part this can come from modelling – general hospital teams who see the benefits of a full social history in patients shared with liaison psychiatry are more likely to pursue these areas in their other patients. Sometimes, unavoidably, specific training will be needed to upskill colleagues in asking some of the more difficult questions, akin to the training that many liaison psychiatry teams deliver on the assessment of suicide risk. It is notable that the American and Canadian studies that examined a population-based approach to obtaining more detailed social histories each independently emphasised the need for specific training to be delivered to whoever discusses these sensitive matters with patients. Who better than liaison psychiatry practitioners to deliver this?

What Should Be Asked?

The social history in many assessments is minimised or left until the end, treated as an 'optional extra'. Authors have referred to 'TED' – tobacco, ethanol, drugs (11) or 'Do you work? Are you married? Do you smoke or drink?' (12). The closed questions speak volumes. Many liaison psychiatrists will be familiar with the one-word entry in the social history section of some referrals – perhaps 'divorced' or 'unemployed'. Yet a properly detailed social history is essential to place the patient in their wider context. This allows a far greater and nuanced understanding of the patient's current presentation by way, for example, of their ability to access effective healthcare and how they are managing in hospital. Some have advocated starting an assessment with the social history (13). Just as important, these factors impact on what health services aim to improve – outcomes. Marmot's often-cited question 'What good does it do to treat people and send them back to the conditions that made them sick?' (49) requires knowledge of those conditions if we wish to avoid the patient returning with the same condition at a later stage. A cycle of poor outcomes, unnecessary expenditure and low patient satisfaction should be avoided wherever possible.

The exact list of topics to be covered, in what detail, must remain a matter for individual clinical judgement. Some issues such as age, ethnicity or preferred language, all of which were included in the Toronto dataset (9), might be seen less as aspects of a social history and more of an administrative dataset. Certainly, these elements are likely to change little over the life course and to be unimpacted by changes in a patient's health. What follows is a more detailed exploration of four particular areas of the social history. These have been selected on the basis that they have strong associations with physical ill health and are therefore likely to be of relevance to patients seen in the general hospital or in outpatients, have strong associations with mental ill health and are therefore likely to sit at least in part within the remit of the liaison psychiatrist, and are areas where interventions might be possible, and these interventions in turn may lead to positive health outcomes. The list is not exhaustive – others may have included sexual orientation or religious and spiritual needs here.

1. Debt

Questions about a patient's financial position or their experiences of debt rarely form part of a standard assessment for patients seen in a publicly funded healthcare system such as the UK National Health Service (NHS). Such services are free at the point of need – no evidence of a means of payment is required. This may be at least subtly different in settings where part or full payment is required. It is likely also to be different in cultures where discussions about money are less awkward than in the UK. Understanding finance poverty and debt is, though, a regular part of primary care as primary care physicians get to know the patient across their life, and also their family, all within the context of their community.

Psychiatrists too are more likely to see debt as part of a standard assessment, though this is likely to be because such a large proportion of any psychiatric caseload is detached from the labour market and often in debt. All members of mental health multidisciplinary teams are familiar with supporting patients with benefit claims and almost as often appeals against such claims being rejected. Debt and poverty are areas where liaison psychiatry needs to draw on its roots in general psychiatry and increase the awareness in general hospital settings of the malign role of debt and poverty in patient outcomes.

There is a strong relationship between poor mental health and debt, poverty and low socio-economic status. Jenkins et al., using data from the UK Psychiatric Comorbidity study, showed that while around 8% of participants without debt had a mental disorder, the figure was 25% for those participants in debt (14). The global economic crisis impacted most of those already disadvantaged, including those in debt and those with psychiatric illness

(15). The relationship between poverty and mental disorder works both ways. Patients with psychiatric illness are less likely to be employed and if employed more likely to be in lowly paid or precarious employment. Poverty, secondary, for example, to loss of employment, is associated with greater risk of mental disorder (16).

The relationship between poverty and poor physical health is also strong. Patients from lower economic groups have worse physical health, mental health and risk of death (17). One example is diabetes; Tanaka et al. showed that the poorest quintiles of society had higher levels of both prevalent and incident diabetes, underscoring the bidirectional relationship (18).

One particularly pernicious aspect of a patient's socio-economic situation that can be included in a liaison psychiatry assessment is debt. Personal debt has been growing in many Western countries in the last 20 years. Indebtedness remains a source of significant social stigma (19) but may nonetheless be more straightforwardly asked about than income, and there is evidence debt may be a better indicator of health outcomes than a crude measure such as income (20). Numerous studies have reported an association between personal debt and both psychological distress and mental disorders such as depression. Several explanations have been suggested. Beyond the simple anxiety about whether repayments can be made, 'debt stress' can lead to unhealthy coping behaviours which in turn lead to poor health (21). As with other aspects of poverty, debt impacts on physical health. Bridges and Disney describe a vicious cycle of poor health leading to reduced work capacity or job loss, which results in personal and household debt, which in turn further reduces health and quality of life (22).

Several studies highlight that it is the unmanageability of personal debt that is the key issue; mortgage debt is much less of an issue than (unsecured) consumer credit (23). It is in this space that the clinician can open up a conversation. While a simple question such as 'Are you in debt?' rarely seems to cause offence or irritation, gentler strategies are perhaps more advisable. Butterworth has reported on an elegant study following up participants of birth cohort studies. This showed a clear relationship between financial hardship and depression four years later after adjustment for baseline depression and a range of socio-economic characteristics. The participants were asked whether they had had to go without things they really needed in the previous year because they were short of money – a simple but potentially revealing question and one the author has used successfully (50).

Liaison psychiatry cannot increase patients' incomes. However, for patients in whom financial hardship is identified, signposting or referring to social work services or other, possibly third-sector support in this area could be a crucial intervention. Given the stigma involved, the assessing clinician may have been the first to identify the issue or link it with the patient's physical or mental health. Furthermore, Hojman has shown that the impact of debt on depression declines when individuals are better able to manage their debt and personal finance (24).

2. Housing

Almost all general hospital inpatients seen by liaison psychiatry services will go home when discharged. Home is the next step on the journey to recovery, yet may also be part of the reason the person became ill. In returning them there, the wider multidisciplinary team needs to understand the impact housing may have had on the patient becoming ill, and also in sustaining their recovery following discharge.

Housing is a cultural issue. The nature of the accommodation, whether it is owned or rented, its condition and with how many others it is shared vary across regions, countries, eras and ages. Within Europe, roughly two-thirds of the population are owner-occupiers, the other third in rented accommodation, although there are wide variations between countries. In Switzerland, for example, 57% of people live in rented property.

The quality of housing varies greatly. In England in 2019, 17% of homes failed to meet the standard of 'decency' set out by the government (25), although this represents an improvement from 30% a decade earlier. Non-decent homes have issues with hazards, damp, poor thermal efficiency or a lack of 'reasonably modern facilities'. Most non-decent homes are in the privately rented sector.

There is a well-recognised association between dampness as a housing problem and a number of respiratory problems but wider associations between poor housing and poor health are also described (26). In 2010, the estimated cost to the NHS of conditions related to poor housing was £2.5 billion (27). The health risks of substandard housing extend beyond damp-related infectious disease and cardiovascular complications of cold. Falls are more likely in poorly maintained properties. Less than half of homes in England have a carbon monoxide alarm, and one in seven privately rented properties do not have a working smoke alarm. Poor-quality housing negatively impacts mental health too. A range of factors contribute. They include the financial strain of poor affordability and the psychological impact of physical ill health, but most obviously overcrowding. There is a steep social gradient in overcrowding, with the less well-off very much more likely to live in over-crowded conditions. In the UK overall around 4% of homes are regarded as overcrowded, still just under 1 million. Behind these data, however, there are wide discrepancies – only about 1% of owner-occupied homes are overcrowded compared to 9% of those in the socially rented sector (27).

Can improving housing improve health, or just provide a nicer environment in which to be ill? Thomson et al. have carried out a systematic review and their findings are encouraging (28). They found evidence suggesting that overall health, respiratory health and mental health could all be improved by making homes warmer and more energy-efficient. A study from Glasgow looked at the physical and mental health implications of four specific types of housing improvement. Mental health benefits were shown for fabric works such as insulation, improving kitchens and bathrooms, and providing secure front doors (29).

It is good medical practice, and therefore good psychiatric practice, to assess the patient in the context of their wider environment. Understanding the many factors which have contributed to a patient becoming ill, and possibly admitted to hospital, is a core aspect of liaison psychiatry, as is thinking about how the clinical recovery initiated in hospital can be sustained and translated into functional recovery. This cannot really be done without asking about home, and even small pieces of information can assist in understanding the patient's life and how they relate to their family, their community and the wider world. Evidence that improvements in housing can make a real difference to a patient's mental health should make it even more relevant for this to be part of a liaison psychiatry assessment.

3. Employment

In contrast to housing and debt, at least Srivastava (12) was taught to ask 'Do you work?'. The question is a closed one and it is unusual to see much beyond a single-word statement of the patient's employment status in the medical notes. That this single word is most commonly 'unemployed' tells an important story, the relevance of which is frequently missed. However, the close and sometimes complex relationship between employment and health is slowly being rediscovered, and policymakers too increasingly recognise the relevance of each to the other (30).

The 'Are you in work?' question is a good start, especially if the answer is 'No'. Unemployment is associated with poor physical health. Those out of work use more primary care services and have more emergency admissions to hospital, increased inflammatory markers and greater overall mortality. There are multiple possible explanations for these associations. Bartley has outlined four possible candidates (31). First, unemployment, especially the transition into unemployment, is a threat and a stressor, akin to bereavement. This stress may act in part via anxiety to produce negative health outcomes. The second is poverty – being out of work will often lead to substantially lower incomes which are strongly associated with poor health outcomes. Third, unemployment is associated with an increase in unhealthy behaviours such as smoking and drinking. Finally, Bartley suggests that the adverse health consequences of unemployment are related to the longer-term impacts, often via continued employment difficulties. A period of unemployment makes a further period more likely. The majority of unemployment episodes are experienced by a small minority of people.

It is rarely the role of the liaison psychiatrist to specify which of Bartley's potential explanations provided the best fit, but being aware of these possibilities can help the clinician generate a more thoughtful and detailed approach than just 'Are you in work?'. In doing so the clinician should also be aware that poor health and unemployment have a bidirectional relationship – poor health leads to unemployment just as unemployment can lead to poor health (32). In doing so, however, they should not make the assumption that all work is good. Precarious employment, which is poorly paid, insecure and sometimes dangerous, is increasingly common. It is associated with poor health outcomes. It is also important to sensitively enquire about the possibility of exploitation.

The liaison psychiatrist should be aware that there is an especially close relationship between employment and mental health (33). There is a wealth of evidence linking job loss and subsequent debt and financial difficulties with worse mental health (34). This has been well established but became especially clear following the financial crash of 2008, when depression, self-harm and suicide were seen to increase (35). On the flip side, there is good evidence too that good work is good for mental health (36). This is about very much more than income – employment can provide a structure for the day, engagement with others and a sense of achievement. There is, however, a particular emphasis on the 'good'; sometimes no job is better than a bad job (37).

4. Social Isolation

Social isolation refers to the lack of contact or interactions with friends, family and society more widely. It is about being cut-off from a social network, or not having a network at all. It is a much more objective phenomenon than loneliness which describes the feeling of a gap between the level of contact an individual wishes to have with other people and the actual degree of contact they have. Not all isolated people are lonely. Some choose to be isolated, but loneliness is a negative state that is never chosen. The feeling of loneliness can be influenced by the perception of the individual state by, for example, a mood disorder. A person might have contact with many people but still feel lonely.

Social isolation is less well described and researched than loneliness but is associated with a number of poor physical health outcomes. Several meta-analyses have shown it to be an independent risk factor for death, whatever the underlying illness (38). It is best described in cardiovascular disease; for example, it is strongly linked to hospital readmissions in patients with heart failure and death post-myocardial infarction. It is common in patients with arthritis and is associated with treatment non-adherence in renal transplant patients, increased mortality in cancer patients and more sickness absence in back-pain patients. Social isolation is especially relevant to liaison psychiatry – even after adjusting for demographic and clinical factors, and prior healthcare utilisation, a single question about social isolation was associated with a greater risk of emergency department visits and hospital readmission (39).

Social isolation is strongly linked with both common mental disorders and psychotic illness. In depression there is a two-way relationship – depression is more common in isolated people, and depressed people can become isolated, which in turn perpetuates their illness (40). The association between social isolation and reduced physical activity in people with psychotic illnesses is one mechanism that may drive poor physical health outcomes in these populations. There is some evidence that patients with substance misuse disorders have different issues to those with common mental disorders with regard to social networks. Depressed and anxious patients have infrequent close contact with friends, distinct from patients with substance misuse disorders. Smyth, studying patients in south London, also showed that a high level of emotional support was associated with reduced odds of experiencing a common mental disorder, while finding no association between any measure of social network or support and hazardous use of alcohol (41).

From Whom Should the Social History Be Taken?

It is often suggested that patients do not wish to discuss their social circumstances. However, studies that have specifically investigated the patient perspective have found positive results (42) supporting those authors who suggest that bringing up issues of social and economic difficulty can enhance the quality of communication between clinician and patient. In the UK, midwives routinely ask expectant mothers about a wide range of social issues without apparent difficulty. By and large with a sensitive approach, appropriate timing and sufficient explanation, most patients will engage in a discussion about their social circumstances.

Other sources of information are potentially available too. Teams with local knowledge may recognise a patient's postcode as indicating a 'deprived area'. However, great care should be exercised before drawing the conclusion that only 'deprived' patients live in 'deprived areas'. In reality, certainly in most UK towns and cities, there is substantial variation within even small geographical areas, and the front door of a house or flat is a poor indicator of what sits behind it. Many, though by no means all, patients have partners, children or families. Engaging a family member in a discussion about social issues can be of great benefit, with of course appropriate consent from the patient. Those close to the patient can often provide a useful context to matters brought up with the patient, especially regarding how things have changed over time. Finally, the patient's primary care physician, where available, will often be a source of vital information about a patient's situation and how this may have impacted their presentation and their health more generally. Primary care physicians spend one-fifth of their time with patients on non-health matters (43) and will frequently know about a patient's home, their family and their work.

What is not yet clear is which patients find which aspects the most comfortable or uncomfortable to discuss with their clinical team. This is an under-explored area of research. Understanding how best to engage patients in these discussions will enhance the quality of information available and therefore the ability of the multidisciplinary team to provide optimum care. We do, however, know that a number of patients who initially answer these questions subsequently decline assistance with the very issues identified (44). Here too the reasons are not clear. They may relate to concerns about stigma or an understandable wish on the part of the patient to keep 'health' and 'non-health' matters separate. If what occurs as a result is that the patient with fewer needs receives assistance but those with greater needs do not get help, there is a risk that pre-existing health inequalities are widened. More research is needed to help guard against this unintended consequence.

What Should Be Done with the Information Gathered in a Social History?

The social history is not an end in itself. It is not a box-ticking exercise. Information gathered as part of a social history is to be used to produce better outcomes for the patient than would be achieved had the information not been gathered. To be useful, it needs to be appropriately shared. If, as described by Moskowitz (45), knowledge of the patient's social circumstances improves engagement and communication, then it needs to form part of a dialogue with patients themselves. The team can acknowledge where things have been hard and begin to develop collaborative approaches to improving the situation. While the flow of helpful information about the patient's social difficulties is mostly from the patient's primary care physician to the liaison psychiatry and general hospital teams, there may be great benefit in communicating new insights back to the primary care physician either directly or in any discharge communication. It may be helpful for the primary care physician themselves, or even a team such as yours in the future asking the primary care physician for help and advice!

Social information should also be shared with the treating team (for inpatients). Most liaison psychiatry services share medical records with their general hospital colleagues but should not assume they are always read and understood. Important and relevant information that may impact on diagnosis or on future care planning including around discharge needs to be shared proactively with the multidisciplinary team. It is in these patient-focussed discussions that members of the liaison psychiatry team can model the bio-psycho-social approach for the general hospital team. Clear thinking, clearly delivered almost always makes a difference. One potential unintended consequence must be carefully guarded against, however.

Most liaison psychiatry clinicians will be aware that on occasions general hospital patients feel stigmatised on the basis of any psychiatric history they may have (46) and that as a result, one of the roles of the liaison psychiatry team is to advocate for their patients. The contents of a good social history may also contain elements that on occasion generate views from colleagues that patients may perceive as stigmatising. Examples include being out of work and being in debt. Opinions about the role of individual agency regarding being unemployed or alcohol-dependent, for example, are commonplace in wider society and it should be no surprise that some health professionals share these views. In exposing the patient's social difficulties to the wider multidisciplinary team, care needs to be taken not to allow patient-blaming to occur. Explanation, education and gentle contextualising are sometimes needed in addition to facts.

Sharing is necessary but often insufficient. Action is needed too. Liaison psychiatry cannot lift a patient out of debt, rehouse them, employ them or generate a social network. But liaison psychiatry can persuade the wider multidisciplinary team that these aspects are relevant either as predisposing, precipitating or maintaining factors. They can advocate that to achieve the best outcome for the patient, which must always extend beyond the simple biomedical, these aspects need to be addressed. In conjunction with allied health professionals such as occupational therapists, social workers, the patient's family where appropriate and the primary care physician, the liaison psychiatry team can link, signpost or refer the patient to resources that can begin to address these aspects of the patient's difficulties. This may involve social prescribing (47), which is aimed in particular at the socially isolated and those with co-morbid physical and mental health problems. Although the evidence for effectiveness is currently limited, this is in part due to a paucity of high-quality studies in an area where it can be hard to account for all the possible influences on health outcomes. Nevertheless, it is being rolled out in the UK NHS.

Taking a good social history is an unsung and under-recognised skill in medicine. As a skill, it is often most highly developed with liaison psychiatry teams – it is an essential part of high-quality liaison psychiatry practice. Championing it, teaching it, doing it and interpreting it can all fall within the remit of the liaison psychiatry team. In doing so, liaison psychiatry practitioners can directly improve the patient experience in the hospital or the clinic, can enhance the work of general hospital team in caring for that patient and potentially others not referred, and can help the patient make the most of that care once discharged, thereby reducing the possibility of adverse longer-term outcomes.

References

1. Medical Association B. *Social Determinants of Health: What Doctors Can Do*. London; 2011.

2. Committee on the Recommended Social and Behavioral Domains and Measures for Electronic Health Records, Board on Population Health and Public Health Practice, Institute of Medicine. *Capturing Social and Behavioral Domains in Electronic Health Records: Phase 1*. Washington, DC; 2014.

3. Brooks Carthon JM, Hedgeland T, Brom H, Hounshell D, Cacchione PZ. 'You only have time for so much in 12 hours' unmet social needs of hospitalised patients': A qualitative study of acute care nurses. *J Clin Nurs*. 2019;28(19–20):3529–37.

4. Henize AW, Beck AF, Klein MD, Adams M, Kahn RS. A road map to address the social determinants of health through community collaboration. *Pediatrics*. 2015;136(4):e993–1001.

5. Moscrop A, Ziebland S, Roberts N, Papanikitas A. A systematic review of reasons for and against asking patients about their socioeconomic contexts. *Int J Equity Health*. 2019;18(1):112.

6. Solberg LI. Theory vs practice: Should primary care practice take on social determinants of health now? No. *Ann Fam Med*. 2016;14(2):102–3.

7. Darvill D. Tackling health inequalities in primary care. Doctors in less affluent areas don't have the time to collect more data. *BMJ*. 1999;319(7207):454.

8. Goldstein D. Physicians daily life report. Robert Wood Johnson Foundation. 2011. www.rwjf.org/content/dam/farm/reports/

surveys_and_polls/2011/rwjf71795/subas
sets/rwjf71795_1.

9. Wray R, Agic B, Bennett-AbuAyyash C et al. We ask because we care: The Tri-Hospital + TPH health equity data collection research project: Summary Report; 2013.

10. Gold R, Bunce A, Cowburn S et al. Adoption of social determinants of health EHR tools by community health centers. *Ann Fam Med.* 2018;**16**(5):399–407.

11. Behforouz HL, Drain PK, Rhatigan JJ. Rethinking the social history. *N Engl J Med.* 2014;**371**(14):1277–9.

12. Srivastava R. Complicated lives: Taking the social history. *N Engl J Med.* 2011;**365** (7):587–9.

13. Wu BJ. History taking in reverse: Beginning with social history. *Consultant.* 2013;**53**(1):34–6.

14. Jenkins R, Bhugra D, Bebbington P et al. Debt, income and mental disorder in the general population. *Psychol Med.* 2008;**38** (10):1485–93.

15. Stuckler D, Reeves A, Loopstra R, Karanikolos M, McKee M. Austerity and health: The impact in the UK and Europe. *Eur J Public Health.* 2017;**27**(suppl. 4):18–21.

16. Moore THM, Kapur N, Hawton K, Richards A, Metcalfe C, Gunnell D. Interventions to reduce the impact of unemployment and economic hardship on mental health in the general population: A systematic review. *Psychol Med.* 2017;**47** (6):1062–84.

17. Bosma H, Schrijvers C, Mackenbach JP. Socioeconomic inequalities in mortality and importance of perceived control: Cohort study. *BMJ.* 1999;**319** (7223):1469–70.

18. Tanaka T, Gjonça E, Gulliford MC. Income, wealth and risk of diabetes among older adults: Cohort study using the English longitudinal study of ageing. *Eur J Public Health.* 2012;**22**(3):310–17.

19. Dossey L. Debt and health. *Explore.* 2007;**3** (2):83–90.

20. Drentea P, Lavrakas PJ. Over the limit: The association among health, race and debt. *Soc Sci Med.* 2000;**50**(4):517–29.

21. Gathergood J. Debt and depression: Causal links and social norm effects. *Econ J.* 2012;**122**(563):1094–114.

22. Bridges S, Disney R. Debt and depression. *J Health Econ.* 2010;**29** (3):388–403.

23. Hiilamo A. Debt matters? Mental wellbeing of older adults with household debt in England. *SSM Popul Health.* 2020;**12**:100658.

24. Hojman DA, Miranda Á, Ruiz-Tagle J. Debt trajectories and mental health. *Soc Sci Med.* 2016;**167**:54–62.

25. English Housing Survey: Headline Report 2019 to 2020. Ministry of Housing, Communities & Local Government; 2020. www.gov.uk/government/statistics /english-housing-survey-2019-to-2020-headline-report.

26. Marmot M. Fair society, healthy lives: The Marmot Review. Institute for Health Equity; 2010.

27. Nicol S, Roys M, Garrett H. The cost of poor housing to the NHS. The Building Research Establishment. 2015. https://files .bregroup.com/bre-co-uk-file-library-copy /filelibrary/pdf/87741-Cost-of-Poor-Housing-Briefing-Paper-v3.pdf.

28. Thomson H, Thomas S, Sellstrom E, Petticrew M. Housing improvements for health and associated socio-economic outcomes. *Cochrane Database Syst Rev.* 2013; **28**(2):CD008657.

29. Curl A, Kearns A, Mason P, Egan M, Tannahill C, Ellaway A. Physical and mental health outcomes following housing improvements: evidence from the GoWell study. *J Epidemiol Community Health.* 2015;**69**(1):12–19.

30. Davies SC. Annual report of the chief medical officer: Public mental health priorities – Investing in the evidence. Department of Health; 2014. www.gov.uk/ government/publications/chief-medical-officer-cmo-annual-report-public-mental-health.

31. Bartley M. Unemployment and ill health: Understanding the relationship. *J Epidemiol Community Health.* 1994;**48** (4):333–7.

32. van Rijn RM, Robroek SJW, Brouwer S, Burdorf A. Influence of poor health on exit from paid employment: A systematic review. *Occup Environ Med.* 2014;**71**(4):295–301.

33. Henderson M, Harvey SB, Overland S, Mykletun A, Hotopf M. Work and common psychiatric disorders. *J R Soc Med.* 2011;**104**(5):198–207.

34. Fitch C, Hamilton S, Bassett P, Davey R. The relationship between personal debt and mental health: A systematic review. *Mental Health Review Journal.* 2011;**39**:88.

35. Stuckler D, Basu S, Suhrcke M, Coutts A, McKee M. The public health effect of economic crises and alternative policy responses in Europe: An empirical analysis. *Lancet.* 2009;**374**(9686):315–23.

36. Modini M, Joyce S, Mykletun A et al. The mental health benefits of employment: Results of a systematic meta-review. *Australas Psychiatry.* 2016;**24**(4):331–6.

37. Butterworth P, Leach LS, McManus S, Stansfeld SA. Common mental disorders, unemployment and psychosocial job quality: Is a poor job better than no job at all? *Psychol Med.* 2013;**43**(8):1763–72.

38. Holt-Lunstad J, Smith T, Layton J. Social relationships and mortality risk: A meta-analytic review. *SciVee.* 2010; http://dx.doi.org/10.4016/19865.01.

39. Mosen DM, Banegas MP, Tucker-Seeley RD et al. Social isolation associated with future health care utilization. *Popul Health Manag.* 2020; http://dx.doi.org/10.1089/pop.2020.0106.

40. Santini ZI, Koyanagi A, Tyrovolas S, Mason C, Haro JM. The association between social relationships and depression: A systematic review. *J Affect Disord.* 2015;**175**:53–65.

41. Smyth N, Siriwardhana C, Hotopf M, Hatch SL. Social networks, social support and psychiatric symptoms: Social determinants and associations within a multicultural community population. *Soc Psychiatry Psychiatr Epidemiol.* 2015;**50**(7):1111–20.

42. Brcic V, Eberdt C, Kaczorowski J. Development of a tool to identify poverty in a family practice setting: A pilot study. *Int J Family Med.* 2011;**26**:812182.

43. Caper K, Plunkett J. A very general practice: How much time do GPs spend on issues other than health? Citizens Advice; 2015.

44. Tong ST, Liaw WR, Kashiri PL et al. Clinician experiences with screening for social needs in primary care. *J Am Board Fam Med.* 2018;**31**(3):351–63.

45. Moskowitz D, Lyles CR, Karter AJ, Adler N, Moffet HH, Schillinger D. Patient reported interpersonal processes of care and perceived social position: The Diabetes Study of Northern California (DISTANCE). *Patient Educ Couns.* 2013;**90**(3):392–8.

46. Liggins J, Hatcher S. Stigma toward the mentally ill in the general hospital: A qualitative study. *Gen Hosp Psychiatry.* 2005;**27**(5):359–64.

47. Drinkwater C, Wildman J, Moffatt S. Social prescribing. *BMJ.* 2019; **28**(364):l1285.

48. Virchow R. Der Armenarzt. *Die medicinische Reform.* 1948(18):124–7.

49. Marmot M. *The Health Gap: The Challenge of an Unequal World.* London; 2015, p. 1.

50. Butterworth P, Rodgers B, Windsor TD. Financial hardship, socio-economic position and depression: Results from the PATH Through Life Survey. *Soc Sci Med.* 2009;**69**(2):229–37. doi: 10.1016/j.socscimed.2009.05.008. PMID: 19501441.

Chapter 18

Education for Acute Hospital Staff

Mathew Harrison and Max Henderson

The Case for Teaching

Liaison psychiatry operates across psychiatry, medical and surgical settings and, in some departments, primary care. There are a myriad of interfaces and interactions on an almost daily basis with others who potentially know little about the interesting and stimulating academic areas within it and its potential benefits to patients and staff.

The interface between mental and physical health is all too frequently one of 'oil and water' and perhaps one function of the liaison psychiatrist can be seen as acting as the emulsifier between these two substances. The emulsifying agent proposed here is that of education and training. The skills of a liaison psychiatrist – being able to synthesise and communicate complex information in a jargon-free and accessible way, being adaptable and flexible and thinking critically – overlap with the skills of medical educators (1). A liaison psychiatrist is often educating informally, sometimes unknowingly, in the process of consultation with other healthcare professionals. Many departments may already be engaged in more formal education and training within the general hospital. Expanding this education or establishing teaching where it does not yet exist can benefit liaison psychiatry, other healthcare professionals and, most importantly, patients admitted to medical and surgical wards.

Psychiatric disorders are prevalent both in general hospital wards and in medical and surgical outpatient departments (2). Recognition rates of mental illness by non-psychiatric healthcare professionals remain poor, however (3), suggesting that there are a proportion of patients whose illness remains unidentified in the general hospital and hence who are denied the help that psychiatry might be able to offer them. Education around this group of patients cannot be delivered through consultation as this requires their treating team to identify them and seek consultation. Teaching as part of a broader general hospital programme, such as 'grand-rounds', has been shown to improve recognition of disorders by general hospital physicians (4) and by undergraduate students in primary care (5). A liaison psychiatry teaching programme can positively influence the attitudes of junior medical staff towards the importance and benefits of psychiatric consultation, and may contribute to greater concern with psychosocial issues in caring for their patients (6). Engagement in teaching within the general hospital enables the liaison psychiatry team to help general hospital staff improve their awareness and assessment of mental health issues and to improve the confidence and skills in addressing psychosocial issues.

Working across a range of medical and surgical specialties gives the liaison psychiatrist a privileged perspective on the general hospital. The position of the liaison psychiatrist as a generalist and an associated ability to gather and integrate broad sets of data in the service of patient care has long been noted and advocated as a skill that can be brought to bear in the education of other clinicians (7).

Although liaison psychiatrists may view their position as generalists, sometimes they are seen by general hospital staff as occupying a distant and unique niche. The mystification of mental disorder and perception of those who suffer from it (and doctors that treat it) as 'other' and somehow separate from society has contributed to stigma and disparity over many years. Fears resulting from this 'otherness', such as assuming patients with mental disorders are 'unpredictable', 'emotional' or 'dangerous', are present in studies of medical and surgical nursing staff and lead to barriers in care (8, 9). Reducing this sense of otherness has the potential to improve the relationship between liaison psychiatry and the rest of the hospital but also to improve the relationship between general hospital staff and the patients they care for. The task of making mental illness not alien but human has recently gained increased exposure in the media. It is a task in which education plays a pivotal role. In their interface with other areas of healthcare, liaison psychiatrists not only have greater opportunity than our general psychiatry colleagues to take up this task but also, perhaps, a moral obligation to do so.

Teaching in the general hospital is not without its challenges. Potential learners must be curious and motivated, something that cannot be guaranteed. A positive working relationship with educators in the general hospital is important; this helps find audiences, venues and topics for potential training. This may be easier for a service that is geographically located within the general hospital itself than a 'visiting' service.

A greater awareness of liaison psychiatry, which might result from teaching, can result in an increase in referrals to the liaison psychiatry service. Some of these referrals will be for those who would benefit from liaison psychiatry. Others may be an attempt to evacuate the newly identified mentally unwell into another service, without thought about whether it might be of use to them. A liaison psychiatrist might need to think about how these consequences might be managed both within the training itself and within their own department.

In addition to these potential challenges, teaching requires resources in terms of both staff time and skills. However, we would argue it is a sure investment, given the potential benefits.

In this chapter we will discuss potential audiences for liaison psychiatry teaching in the general hospital, topics and learning environments, with the hope that it provides ideas and inspiration for others to develop their role in education.

Audiences

Medical Staff

Medical staff probably form the traditional audience for teaching in liaison psychiatry, perhaps because it was the attending physician who often acted as 'customer' for liaison psychiatry services. Medical and surgical departments often have established educational programmes into which a session from liaison psychiatry could easily fit. Offers to deliver part of a programme are often gratefully received by its organisers. The fact that there is an established teaching structure and identified audience for these programmes means that they require less investment, in terms of resource, from liaison psychiatry rather than establishing a programme *de novo*, and hence they are the usual starting place for liaison psychiatry teaching. An additional feature of these programmes is that there tends to be a range of grades of medical staff in attendance, which helps teaching to reach consultants and non-training grade doctors, who might be harder to reach by other means.

Doctors in training also tend to have specific educational programmes, which in some cases are delivered regionally. The mental and physical health interface forms an aspect of many medical training programmes and is part of the curriculum for the UK Foundation Programme, Core Medical Training and Core Surgical Training. These aspects of the respective curricula would seem to be primed for input from liaison psychiatry and provide the opportunity to deliver a relevant and accessible message to a large audience.

Historically, liaison psychiatrists have been involved in the teaching of medical students. Despite this, liaison psychiatry is seldom integrated into other areas of the medical curriculum with, for example, the teaching of medically unexplained symptoms (MUS) in UK medical schools has been found to be highly variable (10). The exposure of medical students to liaison psychiatry within their general medical placements has the potential to demystify mental health at an early stage of training and address the development of barriers between mental and physical health. Liaison psychiatrists may demonstrate the application of psychiatric knowledge to other areas of medicine in a way that could make mental health more accessible to future doctors, opening doors into psychiatry. Medical student education within the general hospital offers exciting possibilities for integration of medical training. Currently, most medical students must wait until the psychiatric component of their training to meet a liaison psychiatrist, which results in missed opportunities earlier in training.

One of the benefits of teaching medical staff, from the point of view of the liaison psychiatrist, is that they share an educational background. This may help to provide a context and framework for teaching and helps make the educator relatable to the audience; we will discuss later how these factors are important for an effective learning experience. Teaching non-medical staff, or involving the multidisciplinary team in teaching activities, can bring alternative perspectives and challenges as well as new potential audiences.

Nursing Staff and Allied Health Professionals

Many liaison psychiatry services in the UK are multidisciplinary and have mental health nurses working within them. These nurses usually have a key role in the education of their general hospital colleagues, alongside the multidisciplinary team, in the process of consultation (11). When compared to literature focussing on medical education, there is relatively little published with regards to teaching liaison psychiatry to general hospital nursing staff. This is doubly surprising given that general hospital nurses may, in the process of their work, come to know their patients in a way that is different to medical staff and from this position could be more equipped to recognise psychiatric or psychological distress. Developing teaching opportunities with general hospital nurses requires positive links with nursing as well as medical leaders but is a fertile area for growth. In our own department, liaison psychiatry nurses deliver teaching to their general hospital colleagues as part of a rolling educational programme and recently nurses recruited to acute medicine have received mental health training, delivered by liaison psychiatry, as part of their induction programme.

Allied health professionals – psychologists, healthcare assistants, physiotherapists, dieticians, occupational therapists, radiographers and others too numerous to list here – each have a different and valuable relationship with their patients. This relationship comes with opportunities to identify mental illness, make interventions and alongside this the potential to enrich these opportunities by training from liaison psychiatry. Allied health professionals are even more neglected in the literature than general hospital nursing staff. The published literature often refers to mental health work in these professions as a discrete subspeciality; for example, dieticians specialising in eating disorder (12) or mental health physiotherapy (13) rather than being integrated into general hospital practice.

A notable international exception to this is physiotherapy training in Scandinavia, which traditionally is more integrated into psychology, particularly behavioural psychology (14). There is evidence that musculoskeletal physiotherapists are more widely are aware of the benefits of psychological interventions but do not feel sufficiently trained to implement them in their practice (15). This suggests that there is not only an appetite for training in this professional group but also that a bio-psycho-social model of working alongside mental health professionals is eminently possible.

Much of the work concerning mental health training of healthcare assistants has focussed on education around dementia and advanced disease in the residential or nursing home setting (16, 17). These studies have included programmes teaching dementia-specific communication skills, which were shown to improve healthcare assistants' caregiving responses and reduce staff turnover without increasing the amount of time required to deliver care interventions. The application of these models to the general hospital setting is an area where education delivered by liaison psychiatry has the potential to result in a significant positive impact.

Although evidence is sparse when considering liaison psychiatry teaching for nursing staff and allied health professionals, the foregoing discussion suggests that training is possible and can lead to improved patient outcomes. Keeping these staff groups in mind when planning teaching could result in many new and interesting avenues for training being opened up and a richer, more holistic experience for patients in the general hospital.

What to Teach

Determining the content of any teaching delivered in the general hospital can be difficult. It is important to put careful thought into the needs of the audience when planning any teaching session. Some of these needs may be explicitly determined by the audience as part of a teaching programme, for instance curriculum objectives for doctors in training. Other needs are not known by the audience, because they are not aware either of gaps in their knowledge or, indeed, that particular topics exist as areas of interest within psychiatry. Teaching that might meet needs unknown to the audience requires liaison psychiatrists to be actively involved not only in delivery but also in planning. Liaison psychiatrists have the potential to drive teaching in important but neglected areas. Teaching MUS is an example of one such area and is discussed further later.

One of the cornerstones of liaison psychiatry is ameliorating the barriers that result from mental ill health, which can prevent individuals making the best use of medical care. Keeping this mission in mind can be helpful in planning teaching topics. Teaching the neurophysiology of psychosis, though academically interesting, is unlikely to be of help to the physician struggling to offer diabetic care to an individual with schizophrenia. Nevertheless, the physician may derive great benefit from teaching in understanding symptoms of psychosis.

In the following sections we do not intend to provide an exhaustive list of teaching topics but rather a menu of possibilities. Broadly potential topics fall into three main areas: general psychiatry as applied to the general hospital, liaison psychiatry-specific topics and mental health law. The detailed content that might be imparted about a particular topic, including epidemiology, identification, metapsychology and management, can be found elsewhere.

General Psychiatry

The bio-psycho-social model of psychiatry, which prompts the understanding of the patient in the context of their life, relationships, society and environment, can shed light on difficulties that are hard to understand through biology alone. It is a relatively easy-to-understand framework that can be used to build training in general psychiatry and can be applied to liaison psychiatry-specific issues, such as long-term conditions.

Common Mental Health Disorders

The assessment and management of anxiety and depression may not always be the role of the liaison psychiatrist; these conditions are prevalent in the general hospital population and are perhaps more likely to be seen by other doctors. General hospital staff have an opportunity to identify these disorders, signpost their patients to appropriate management and refer them on if necessary. These factors mean that training in this area is potentially important. In addition, a basic understanding of anxiety and depression can be used as a foundation on which to build more liaison psychiatry-specific knowledge, for example the complexities of depression and anxiety in advanced physical disease.

A significant proportion of older adults admitted to the general hospital suffer cognitive impairment (18). Again, although cognitive impairment is not an area of mental healthcare specific to liaison psychiatry, teaching the basics of dementia and its behavioural and psychological symptoms may help hospital staff in their work with this patient group.

Although common in the psychiatric population, psychosis and bipolar disorder are relatively rare in the general hospital population but can pose complex issues when they do arise. Because of this, detailed training in these areas may be less relevant to general hospital staff. There are rare but important conditions, however, which do represent important opportunities for teaching. A key example is training in perinatal psychosis for midwives and obstetricians.

Risk Assessment and Self-Harm

The assessment of risk for suicide and self-harm is a common task in general psychiatry, though it is not a task reserved for the specialty. Current National Institute for Health and Care Excellence (NICE) guidance suggests that initial psychosocial assessment, including risk assessment, in those presenting with self-harm should be completed by emergency department staff. Emergency department clinicians may not feel confident that they have sufficient skills or knowledge in this area (19). Furthermore, suicide prevention training has been shown to generate positive attitudinal changes in non-mental health staff which were maintained at a six-month follow-up (20).

These factors open up a potential space for teaching and training which liaison psychiatry seems well placed to occupy. The fact that many patients presenting with self-harm are referred to liaison psychiatry means that a dialogue likely already exists between educator and potential audience. A teaching programme in this area might therefore be relatively easy to introduce. Teaching about risk assessment for suicide and self-harm has a mix of knowledge and skill-based components and hence can be suitable for a variety of teaching settings. Knowledge-based aspects include the epidemiology of suicide and awareness of risks factors for repeated self-harm (see Chapter 5 for further detail). Skill-development components might include talking to patients about suicidal ideation and effective non-judgemental communication in those presenting in a state of distress or refusing care.

History-Taking and Communication Skills

The ability to gather a careful and thorough account of a patient's distress is a cornerstone of medicine. Perhaps because psychiatrists have few other investigations available, the ability to sensitively gather detailed history, while picking up on emotions and non-verbal cues, is particularly emphasised in psychiatric training. Psychiatrists also bring to history-taking a particular attention to the patient's life beyond their presenting problem, in terms of their history, family and the environment and society in which they live. It has been suggested that psychiatrists can teach these skills to specialties who may also need to explore complex interpersonal topics, for example in sexual health (21).

Good interpersonal communication skills often go hand in hand with good history-taking and are part of the psychiatrist's toolkit. Liaison psychiatry in particular may have something to offer communication skills training given that liaison psychiatrists spend much of their time communicating complex and sometimes unfamiliar concepts to non-mental health professionals. Communication skills training is now mandatory in all UK medical schools, meaning that UK graduates will hopefully have an awareness of the basics of what comprises good communication with patients and colleagues. Although there is a case for liaison psychiatry to be involved in communication skills training at all stages, the foundation which has hopefully been laid down in medical school can act as the ground-work for liaison psychiatrists to teach more advanced communication skills topics, such as communication in dementia or in those with a history of childhood trauma.

Teaching history-taking and communication skills is not without its challenges and there is variety in the literature as to what is delivered and how. Skill development is difficult to achieve through established lecture-based teaching programmes and is likely to require small-group work, simulation or supervision. The ability to gather an account of a patient and their life and establish meaningful communication with them is a complex skill that psychiatrists and other mental health workers spend many years honing. There are several frameworks for the teaching and assessing of communication skills which have been demonstrated to be effective. These might form a helpful starting point for a teaching programme; they include SEGUE (22), 'Four Habits' (23) and SPIKES (24).

Psychotherapeutic Interventions

There is evidence that non-mental health practitioners can be trained to deliver psycho-therapeutic interventions; however, more research in this area is required. Moorey et al. (25) found positive results when training general hospital staff to use cognitive behavioural therapy and behavioural activation, whereas as a recent study examining training in motivational interviewing (26) did not demonstrate such an outcome.

The teaching of psychotherapy usually requires both workshops and ongoing supervision. Such a model has been employed in liaison psychiatry services and although teaching in psychotherapy might require a commitment of resource, both in terms of time and expertise, it is an area for potentially exciting development.

Psychopharmacology

Psychopharmacology is a broad area which may have limited relevance to general hospital staff. There are, however, psychiatric medications which have potential medical sequelae or risk of adverse events if not attended to in the general hospital, for example lithium and clozapine. Equally, there are commonly prescribed psychiatric medications which general hospital staff may come across but have limited knowledge about, such as antidepressants. The 'need-to-know' information for general hospital staff about these medications is limited and hard to remember if not frequently refreshed. Because of this, they may not be suitable topics as part of a teaching programme with a limited amount of time, but they can lend themselves as topics for educational bulletins and digital or social media content.

Liaison psychiatrists may also be called upon to deliver teaching in areas of pharmacology where psychiatrists have particular expertise, such as the management of disturbed behaviour or, in some areas, withdrawal from drugs and alcohol.

Liaison Psychiatry-Specific Teaching

Mental and Physical Health Co-morbidity

The interface between mental and physical health has many facets and many opportunities for teaching. Although there is very limited literature looking at teaching in this particular area, Cushing and Evans (27) have written a recent review. The areas for teaching in this area are mental health sequelae of physical disease, the interrelatedness of long-term physical health conditions and mental health, and physical healthcare in those with severe mental illness. The first two areas are likely to be of greatest interest to hospital staff given the relatively rarity of severe mental illness in the general hospital.

Teaching about mental health sequelae of physical disease can be delivered in terms of broad concepts but can also be tailored to focus on specific conditions in certain groups, for example mental health impacts of HIV delivered to infectious disease specialists, anxiety in breathlessness delivered to respiratory physicians or post-operative delirium delivered to surgeons and anaesthetists. There is potential for imparting knowledge and skill-development training. Skill-development projects might include training cardiac care staff in the assessment of depression.

Knowledge about mental illness in long-term conditions is useful to general hospital staff in terms of recognition but might also offer opportunities for teaching in medical outpatients. General hospitals generally have clinics for patients with individual long-term conditions, such as a diabetic clinic or chronic respiratory disease clinic. The staff in these clinics would seem to be an ideal audience for training around recognition, assessment and basic management of mental disorders.

Medically Unexplained Symptoms (MUS)

Training on medically unexplained symptoms has been identified as a significant gap in UK postgraduate medical education, with only 6 out of 53 foundation schools reporting delivering any form of formal training in MUS (28). This issue is not just reserved for foundation training; surveys of senior physicians also report little to no formal training in this area (29). MUS has also been noted to be an area neglected in emergency medicine training, despite patients with MUS commonly presenting to the emergency department (30). Junior doctors report poor awareness of MUS and few role models for its management among senior medical staff, with resulting fear, frustration and desire to 'over-investigate' this group of patients (31).

A recent study looking at the barriers to training in MUS revealed that educators in UK medical schools held their own negative views about patients with MUS and felt it to be a complex area of low clinical priority. Educators also thought MUS were so ubiquitous that someone must be teaching medical students about them, without checking that this assumption was incorrect (32).

Despite this clear gap in training, there is a dearth of literature focussed on specific training interventions around MUS. Weiland et al. (33) report on the development of an experiential skill-development programme for medical specialists in the Netherlands, which could be applied to education in the UK. Training in MUS is an area that requires significant development and is an area of growth potential in liaison psychiatry teaching.

Mental Health Law and Ethics

Liaison psychiatrists are often some of the only clinicians in the general hospital with formal training and practical knowledge of mental health law (see Chapter 16 for further detail). Errors in the application and use of the Mental Health Act are more common in the general hospital when a psychiatrist is not involved (34). This is perhaps unsurprising given the interface between the Mental Health Act, Mental Capacity Act, Deprivation of Liberty Safeguards in England and Wales and equivalent legislation in Scotland is a complex area. Training interventions have been shown to increase the confidence and knowledge of general hospital doctors in the use of the Mental Health Act and Mental Capacity Act (35). The low level of baseline knowledge and potential improvements to patient care suggest that mental health law offers a rich seam of potential teaching opportunities. Mental health law is a largely knowledge-based area and so readily lends itself to lecture or small-group-based teaching as part of a teaching programme; equally, there is likely to be opportunity for informal teaching around individual cases during consultations.

It has been argued that liaison psychiatry is ideally placed to contribute to teaching medical ethics. Although many liaison psychiatrists may not see this as their role, they are often involved in cases where complex ethical decisions are under consideration and can bring an understanding of psychosocial factors and a perspective on the doctor–patient relationship (36).

How to Teach

There are many theories of adult learning and a review of these is beyond the scope of this chapter. We will focus on the practical aspects of teaching. For those interested in the theoretical aspects of adult learning in the context of medical education more broadly, there are relevant reviews in the literature (37, 38).

Bird et al. (39) offer a comprehensive review of the application of educational methodology to the teaching of psychiatry to non-psychiatrists. They suggest that teaching 'procedures' may have one of three primary aims, with the caveat that teaching may impact other areas even if it is not its primary aim. The aims of these three teaching procedures are 'knowledge-imparting', 'attitude change' and 'skill development'. Each procedure calls for different means of teaching. For example, in traditional medical education, a knowledge-imparting procedure might be a lecture delivered to a large audience, whereas a skill-development procedure might be the 'see one, do one, teach one' approach of medical apprenticeships. Thinking about which procedure one is aiming to carry out can be useful in planning the most effective teaching. This will invariably mean weighing up effectiveness and efficiency. Attempting to develop a skill by means of a lecture is likely to be ineffective, but imparting knowledge by means of one-to-one supervision, though effective, is inefficient. Before moving on to discuss specific teaching environments, it is worth reviewing the qualities of effective teaching in these areas as outlined by Bird et al. and others.

Cognitive psychology has demonstrated that knowledge is assimilated and retained if presented within a clear conceptual framework. The bio-psycho-social model is one example of this. The following steps in any knowledge-imparting teaching have been shown to improve registration and recall:

- Set the scene for the teaching with clear orientation, reference to existing conceptual framework and objectives.
- Deliver the teaching.
- Use short, easily digestible sentences and cluster information into clearly labelled sections.
- Present key information first and last and repeat in several forms.
- Link to the audience's existing knowledge base.
- Provide specific concrete examples such as clinical cases.
- Summarise what has been said, referencing key information.
- Provide opportunity for questions and discussion.

The steps for skill-development training follows a similar structure:

- Set the scene, referencing conceptual framework and links between the skill and existing knowledge.
- Brief description of the theoretical basis of the skill and steps that are going to be taught.
- Demonstration of the skill with commentary and observations.
- Rehearsal of the skill by the trainee through simulation. Complex skills should be broken down into stages which can be rehearsed individually before being incorporated to form the whole.
- Feedback and reflection from both trainee and trainer. This should be frequent, concrete, specific and structured with opportunity for questions and discussion.
- The trainee practises the skill in increasingly natural settings with supervision as needed.

We do not intend to discuss 'attitude-change' procedures as described by Bird et al. in detail here because attitude change is seldom the primary objective of a teaching intervention and, as the authors point out, there are ethical considerations in using the procedure as originally outlined. Attitude change may come about as a result of a teaching intervention, for example in suicide awareness, as mentioned earlier. It may be that teachers are exemplifying the qualities of 'attitude-change' procedures such as presenting as an 'attractive expert', using balanced argument or rewarding positive attitudes, without being consciously aware of this.

Before planning teaching, it is important to know your own objectives and the objectives of those 'commissioning' the training. It is also important to have an idea of the audience size and composition. This will help determine your tasks as the educator and what teaching environment might be best suited to help you achieve these.

Teaching Environments

Lectures

Lecture theatres have long been used in medical education and lectures, of one form or another, remain the mainstay of postgraduate education. They are useful in imparting knowledge to a large audience in an efficient manner but are less suited to skill development. It has been argued that they are better at imparting knowledge than written material as they exploit a human tendency to attend to verbal information.

Lectures can also lend themselves to being recorded for transmission or for rewatching at a later date. Some organisations produce a library of content for students to access 'on demand'. Producing a lecture for recording requires the lecturer to attend to the fact that students may be watching at a future time, which might require additional clarification of context or summarising of discussions which can be lost in transcription from the live environment to tape.

One of the main challenges of lectures is being able to engage the audience in dynamic discussion. This is a task which is almost impossible for large groups. One way of addressing this is providing a forum outside the lecture for students; this might be via message boards or, less usefully, individual email communication. Some technologies do aid interaction between lecturer and audience; for example, there are applications which permit real-time audience polls or question-and-answer feeds, but one should be practised in the use of these before attempting to deploy them 'live'.

Lectures almost always include some sort of audio-visual aid. These should be carefully constructed using the principles of knowledge-imparting teaching described earlier. We have all been the victim of audio-visual aids which have impeded rather than augmented an educational experience. Delivering lectures to smaller groups can help in balancing the transmission of information with audience participation and discussion.

Small-Group Teaching

It is perhaps useful to consider briefly what constitutes a 'small' group. The lower end of the range is easy to determine, being more than one participant, though a group of three or more is useful in promoting discussion between group members. The upper end of the range is less easy to define and is probably determined by individual confidence in running groups and the dynamics of the group itself. Our experience is that groups tend to become unwieldy at around 16 people and certainly groups of more than 20 people are much more easily catered for by a lecture.

Learning Groups

Learning groups in the general hospital take several forms. Many departments retain journal clubs, where individuals come together to discuss academic papers, or case discussion groups, where noteworthy clinical cases are discussed for the purposes of collective learning. In addition, some smaller departments may have an educational programme composed entirely of small-group discussion, often with members taking turns to present a topic. There may be opportunity for liaison psychiatry to contribute to these groups, particularly if they have been involved in a case through the process of consultation.

Sometimes learning groups are arranged around a condition rather than a department. These allow interested clinicians from several departments to come together for the purpose of education. Liaison psychiatry conditions, by their nature, overlap several departments and lend themselves to the establishment of such groups. For example, there are regional learning groups for functional neurological disease, which include liaison psychiatrists, neurologists, specialist nurses, physiotherapists and psychologists.

Clinical Supervision Groups

Providing psychiatric supervision to members of general hospital staff usually involves them presenting a clinical case which is then discussed with the aim of helping the group come to an understanding of the difficulty. The liaison psychiatrist can then suggest management options, which can be explored further within the group. Supervision groups of this nature naturally fulfil many of the steps known to improve registration and recall listed earlier. The contextual framework for the learning is provided by the group who brings the case already linked to their own knowledge; the case also acts as a concrete example to deliver teaching around. If the group is sufficiently small, it can also be used flexibly for skill development or simulation.

The disadvantage of such groups is that while they may achieve a greater depth of understanding than might be achieved in a lecture, they cannot deliver the same breadth of information. Depending on the size of the group, only one or two cases can be discussed in an hour. Another potential disadvantage of groups run in this way from the educator's point of view is that the topic is seldom known before the group meets, as this is determined by the case. This requires the liaison psychiatrist to be able to call upon their expert knowledge and quickly integrate it into the case; this can be both daunting and stimulating.

Supervision groups can be arranged around topics rather than cases, which allows pre-planning to some degree. This in itself can pose problems. If there is no clinical case at all, then the group is probably acting as a learning group rather than clinical supervision. If a case is pre-planned, then it is hard to attend to ones that might be more pressing on the day and supervisees may not feel they can affect the 'agenda' of the supervision session.

Despite the ubiquitous use of clinical supervision in medical training, there is very little theoretical or empirical research around the process. It has been suggested that it is the relationship between supervisor and supervisees that is the single most important factor in the effectiveness of clinical supervision, with other factors being the supervisees' ability to input into the process and finding protected time for supervision (40). The importance of the relationship suggests that supervision groups might be most helpful if delivered as part of an ongoing programme or if they take place in a department where the liaison psychiatrist already has a relationship with the staff.

Reflective Practice Groups

Reflective practice groups have similarities with clinical supervision groups in that they usually involve a group discussing a clinical case, though they can also be applied to organisational issues. They differ from supervision groups in that their aim is not to 'formulate' the case or provide a management plan but to help staff explore the emotional component of their relationship with the patient or system under discussion.

Reflective practice groups delivered by liaison psychiatry nurses have been shown to have a positive impact on clinical care, self-awareness and resilience among general hospital nurses and midwives (41). Facilitating reflective practice groups requires skills in attending to the emotional content of dialogue and containing what can be uncomfortable experiences for the group members. It is important that they have regularity and that facilitators have access to specialist supervision (42). Because of this, they may require a significant commitment of resources.

Teaching Rounds

In 'ombudsman' rounds, the liaison psychiatrist attends a modified ward round with the treating clinical team. There is opportunity for discussion, the patient is reviewed along with the treating team and then there is further space for discussion and teaching. Despite reports that these rounds favourably impact attitudes of medical staff and improve patient care and relationships within the attending teams, they seem to have fallen out of favour in the literature (43). This may reflect changing working practices; a consultant followed by a large entourage of an extended clinical team is a less common sight in the general hospital nowadays, and there may be less opportunity for a liaison psychiatrist to join 'the round' in the traditional sense. Joint patient reviews by liaison psychiatrist and treating teams do occur in the process of consultation and there might be the opportunity to follow a review with some teaching around a topic relevant to the case, forming an opportunistic teaching round.

A modern iteration of the teaching round might be the teaching 'board round', where a liaison psychiatrist attends a multidisciplinary team meeting in the general hospital. Cases with mental health issues are discussed and the psychiatrist delivers ad hoc teaching in discussion around the case.

Simulation

The word simulation evokes many associations; here we are referring to real-world simulations or role play. Modern technology can produce detailed virtual or augmented reality, but this is yet to be widely applied to psychiatric training and further research in this area is required (44). Simulation has been found to be effective in training medical doctors (45) and nursing students in psychiatry (46). It is ideal for skill development, allowing trainees to rehearse scenarios in a controlled environment. Simulations vary from role play in a small-group setting to the use of advanced simulation centres which contain mock hospital environments with the opportunity for groups to observe their colleagues or look back at their own practice through digital recording. An example of the use of simulation-based training in psychiatry includes the management of agitated patients, where simulation was demonstrated to improve knowledge and performance in psychiatric trainees (47).

Simulation is not only reserved for direct patient experiences. Handovers and other forms of communication between professionals can be simulated with trainees, for example letter writing with a simulated writer and receiver (48). Applications of this to liaison psychiatry might include writing a referral following a review of a simulated patient.

Digital Content and Social Media

Many general hospitals have some form of intranet which is accessible by staff. Provided that it is sufficiently well designed and navigable, it can be a useful resource for general hospital staff and a place where liaison psychiatry can contribute to educational content.

Often this content will consist of written clinical guidelines and reference guides. If used thoughtfully, a liaison psychiatry intranet page can be used to augment teaching delivered by the department. A page might contain quick-reference guides to mental health law or psychotropic medications which can be signposted to during teaching. Depending on the technology available, it is possible for such a site to contain educational videos or links to podcasts relevant to liaison psychiatry. The disadvantage of intranet sites is that they require a degree of maintenance; a page can contain too much information as well as too little and needs to be pruned as well as grown. A disadvantage of the hospital intranet is that it seldom has the ease of use and accessibility of internet sites which are available at the touch of a button on most mobile devices.

Many healthcare professionals use social media in one form or another, but most studies have looked at the risk of social media in psychiatric education without considering the potential benefits (44). There have, however, been interesting developments in this field, for instance with departments using Twitter to signpost trainees to educational material or journal articles (49) or podcasts where trainees in psychiatry discuss a condition with an expert. Although these studies concern general psychiatry training, these methods of engagement and education could be easily applied to liaison psychiatry in the general hospital.

Video Conference versus Face-to-Face Teaching

At the time of writing there has recently been a rapid transition from teaching being mainly delivered face-to-face to being delivered via video-conferencing platforms. This transition brings its own challenges and benefits.

The benefits of training via video conference include its relative accessibility; staff can attend from wherever they happen to be so long as they have access to a smartphone or computer. Teaching sessions can be streamed to areas of wards, allowing staff to attend much more easily. Without the physical constraints of a room, theoretically a much larger group of people can attend from a wider geographical area. This can be particularly helpful for organisations which operate over several sites that have staff who might have been excluded from teaching in the past by means of their location.

However, we must also recognise that video conferencing has challenges which might require us to adapt our teaching methods. As with face-to-face lectures, audience discussion can be very difficult. There are inventive ways to overcome this; most video-conferencing platforms have a 'chat' function which allows a discussion to occur parallel to the lecture. Small-group discussions can still occur; however, our experience is that the group becomes too 'big' at a much smaller number of participants. Attempting to facilitate a discussion between eight or more people via video conference is potentially challenging. Facilitators of reflective practice groups may need to attend to confidentiality and boundaries in a much more explicit way when compared to meeting face-to-face in a room.

An unforeseen challenge of teaching over video conferencing is maintaining concentration, a phenomenon which has become known as 'Zoom fatigue'. It has been theorised that this is due to the facial expressions and body language humans use in reciprocal communication to unconsciously monitor that they are being attended to either being absent or slightly out of synchrony. The extra effort to 'correct' this can make a one-hour video conference an exhausting experience (50). This might be addressed by incorporating more breaks in a teaching programme or modifying the content of the teaching so that it can be delivered over a shorter period of time. These shorter sessions could be offset by more frequent sessions, taking advantage of the increased accessibility offered by video conferencing. For example, the general psychiatry teaching programme in our local mental health-care provider has been changed from three 45-minute sessions, which took place fortnightly, to two 20-minute sessions, which now take place weekly.

Gathering Feedback

Evaluating teaching is an important aspect of the process and helps to guide the development of further teaching and assess the efficacy of the teaching delivered (39). The efficacy of a teaching programme can be assessed through research looking at the outcomes of the teaching, which are determined by the aims and objectives of the programme. It is not practical to undertake such research for every piece of teaching that is delivered and feedback more frequently takes the form of assessing acceptability and feasibility of the teaching to students.

Self-administered questionnaires are an inexpensive, straightforward and commonly used means of gathering data on acceptability and feasibility. Students can be asked to rate the objectives and effectiveness of the teaching and be invited to offer 'free text' suggestions for further improvement. Questionnaires themselves must be easy to complete and accessible and there is a balance to be struck between gathering the data required and not burdening hospital staff.

Timing must be considered when gathering feedback. Questionnaires delivered even a short time after a teaching session are easily forgotten and it is a good idea to allow some time at the end of a session to allow students to complete feedback there and then. Online forms ease the collation of data but often require students to make time outside the teaching session to complete these, something that can be difficult given the work pressures of the general hospital. Relatively frequent training, such as clinical supervision groups, need not be evaluated after every group as this has the potential to become onerous to the group members without providing additional useful data. The final stage of feedback is acting on it: thinking about one's own practice in response to the input of students and using this to further develop one's skills and the department's teaching programme.

Summary

Education has long been part of the role of the liaison psychiatrist; the juxtaposition of the specialty with medicine and the skills associated with liaison psychiatrists ideally places these clinicians as educators. Training and education in the general hospital can improve recognition and confidence among general hospital staff around mental health issues and has the potential to improve the relationship between psychiatry and the rest of medicine for the benefit of both its staff and its patients. Teaching in the general hospital has challenges but there are a wide variety of audiences, topics and environments in which teaching can be established and grow. We wish you luck in this endeavour.

References

1. Hatem CJ, Searle NS, Gunderman R et al. The educational attributes and responsibilities of effective medical educators. *Acad Med*. 2011;**86**:474–80.

https://doi.org/10.1097/ACM
.0b013e31820cb28a.

2. Mayou R, Hawton K. Psychiatric disorder in the general hospital. *Br J Psychiatry*. 1986;**149**:172–90. https://doi.org/10.1192/bjp.149.2.172.

3. Mansour H, Mueller C, Davis KAS et al. Severe mental illness diagnosis in English general hospitals 2006–2017: A registry linkage study. *PLOS Med*. 2020;**17**: e1003306. https://doi.org/10.1371/journal.pmed.1003306.

4. Rockwood K, Cosway S, Stolee P et al. Increasing the recognition of delirium in elderly patients. *J Am Geriat Soc*. 1994;**42**:252–6. https://doi.org/10.1111/j.1532-5415.1994.tb01747.x.

5. Walters K, Raven P, Rosenthal J, Russell J, Humphrey C, Buszewicz M. Teaching undergraduate psychiatry in primary care: The impact on student learning and attitudes. *Med Educ*. 2007;**41**:100–8. https://doi.org/10.1111/j.1365-2929.2006.02653.x.

6. Hales R, Borus J. Teaching psychosocial issues to medical house staff: A liaison program on an oncology service. *Gen Hosp Psychiatry*. 1982;**4**:1–6.

7. Lipowski ZJ. Consultation-liaison psychiatry: An overview. *Am J Psychiatry*. 1974;**131**:623–30. https://doi.org/10.1176/ajp.131.6.623.

8. Brinn F. Patients with mental illness: General nurses' attitudes and expectations. *Nurs Stand*. 2000;**14**:32–6.

9. Brunero S, Buus N, West S. Categorising patients' mental illness by medical surgical nurses in the general hospital ward: A focus group study. *Arch Psychiatr Nurs*. 2017; **31**:614–23. https://doi.org/10.1016/j.apnu.2017.09.003.

10. Howman M, Walters K, Rosenthal J, Good M, Buszewicz M. Teaching about medically unexplained symptoms at medical schools in the United Kingdom. *Med Teach*. 2012;**34**:327–9. https://doi.org/10.3109/0142159X.2012.660219.

11. Sharrock J, Happell B. The psychiatric consultation-liaison nurse: Thriving in a general hospital setting. *Int J Ment Health Nurs*. 2002;**11**:24–33. https://doi.org/10.1046/j.1440-0979.2002.00205.x.

12. Reiter CS, Graves L. Nutrition therapy for eating disorders. *Nutr Clin Pract*. 2010;**25**:122–36. https://doi.org/10.1177/0884533610361606.

13. Probst M, Skjaerven LH. *Physiotherapy in Mental Health and Psychiatry E-Book: A Scientific and Clinical Based Approach*. New York; 2017.

14. Sandborgh M, Dean E, Denison E et al. Integration of behavioral medicine competencies into physiotherapy curriculum in an exemplary Swedish program: Rationale, process, and review. *Physiother Theory Pract*. 2020;**36**:365–77. https://doi.org/10.1080/09593985.2018.1488192.

15. Alexanders J, Anderson A, Henderson S. Musculoskeletal physiotherapists' use of psychological interventions: A systematic review of therapists' perceptions and practice. *Physiotherapy*. 2015;**101**:95–102. https://doi.org/10.1016/j.physio.2014.03.008.

16. Kramer NA, Smith MC. *Training Nursing Assistants to Care for Nursing Home Residents with Dementia*. New York; 2000, pp. 227–56.

17. Burgio LD, Allen-Burge R, Roth DL et al. Come talk with me: Improving communication between nursing assistants and nursing home residents during care routines. *The Gerontologist*. 2001;**41**:449–60. https://doi.org/10.1093/geront/41.4.449.

18. Goldberg SE, Whittamore KH, Harwood RH et al. The prevalence of mental health problems among older adults admitted as an emergency to a general hospital. *Age Ageing*. 2012;**41**:80–6. https://doi.org/10.1093/ageing/afr106.

19. Gordon JT. Emergency department junior medical staff's knowledge, skills and confidence with psychiatric patients: A survey. *The Psychiatrist*. 2012;**36**:186–8. https://doi.org/10.1192/pb.bp.111.035188.

20. Botega NJ, Silva SV, Reginato DG et al. Maintained attitudinal changes in nursing

personnel after a brief training on suicide prevention. *Suicide Life Threat Behav.* 2007;**37**:145–53. https://doi.org/10.1521/s uli.2007.37.2.145.

21. Dunn ME, Abulu J. Psychiatrists' role in teaching human sexuality to other medical specialties. *Acad Psychiatry.* 2010;**34**:381–5. https://doi.org/10.1176/appi.ap.34.5.381.

22. Makoul G. The SEGUE Framework for teaching and assessing communication skills. *Patient Educ Couns.* 2001;**45**:23–34. https://doi.org/10.1016/S0738-399101 .00136-7.

23. Fossli Jensen B, Gulbrandsen P, Dahl FA, Krupat E, Frankel RM, Finset A. Effectiveness of a short course in clinical communication skills for hospital doctors: Results of a crossover randomized controlled trial ISRCTN22153332. *Patient Educ Couns.* 2011;**84**:163–9. https://doi.org/ 10.1016/j.pec.2010.08.028.

24. Baile WF, Blatner A. Teaching communication skills: Using action methods to enhance role-play in problem-based learning. *Simul Healthc.* 2014;**9**:220–7. https://doi.org/10.1097/SIH .0000000000000019.

25. Moorey S, Cort E, Kapari M et al. A cluster randomized controlled trial of cognitive behaviour therapy for common mental disorders in patients with advanced cancer. *Psychol Med.* 2009;**39**:713–23. https://doi .org/10.1017/S0033291708004169.

26. Martino S, Zimbrean P, Forray A et al. Implementing motivational interviewing for substance misuse on medical inpatient units: A randomized controlled trial. *J Gen Intern Med.* 2019;**34**:2520–9. https://doi .org/10.1007/s11606-019-05257-3.

27. Cushing A, Evans S. Training physicians at undergraduate and postgraduate levels about comorbidity. *Comorbidity Ment Phys Disord.* 2015;**179**:137.

28. Yon K, Habermann S, Rosenthal J et al. Improving teaching about medically unexplained symptoms for newly qualified doctors in the UK: Findings from a questionnaire survey and expert workshop. *BMJ Open.* 2017;**7**: e014720.

https://doi.org/10.1136/bmjopen-2016-014720.

29. Warner A, Walters K, Lamahewa K, Buszewicz M. How do hospital doctors manage patients with medically unexplained symptoms? A qualitative study of physicians. *J R Soc Med.* 2017;**110**:65–72. https://doi.org/10.1177/0141076816686348.

30. Stephenson DT, Price JR. Medically unexplained physical symptoms in emergency medicine. *Emerg Med J.* 2006;**23**:595–600. https://doi.org/10.1136/ emj.2005.032854.

31. Yon K, Nettleton S, Walters K, Lamahewa K, Buszewicz M. Junior doctors' experiences of managing patients with medically unexplained symptoms: A qualitative study. *BMJ Open.* 2015;**5**: e009593. https://doi.org/10.1136/bmjo pen-2015-009593.

32. Joyce E, Cowing J, Lazarus C, Smith C, Zenzuck V, Peters S. Training tomorrow's doctors to explain 'medically unexplained' physical symptoms: An examination of UK medical educators' views of barriers and solutions. *Patient Educ Couns.* 2018; **101**:878–84. https://doi.org/10.1016/j .pec.2017.11.020.

33. Weiland A, Blankenstein AH, Willems MHA et al. Post-graduate education for medical specialists focused on patients with medically unexplained physical symptoms: Development of a communication skills training programme. *Patient Educ Couns.* 2013;**92**:355–60. https://doi.org/10.1016/j .pec.2013.06.027.

34. Smith M, O'Regan R, Goldbeck R. Detaining patients in the general hospital: Current practice and pitfalls. *Scott Med J.* 2019;**64**:91–6. https://doi.org/10.1177/ 0036933019836054.

35. Richards F, Dale J. The Mental Health Act 1983 and incapacity: What general hospital doctors know. *Psychiatr Bull.* 2009;**33**:176–8. https://doi.org/10.1192/pb .bp.108.020537.

36. McCartney J. Consultation-liaison psychiatry and the teaching of ethics. *Gen Hosp Psychiatry.* 1986;**8**:411–14.

37. Taylor DCM, Hamdy H. Adult learning theories: Implications for learning and teaching in medical education: AMEE Guide No. 83. *Med Teach*. 2013;35:e1561–72. https://doi.org/10.3109/0142159X.2013.828153.

38. Mukhalalati BA, Taylor A. Adult learning theories in context: A quick guide for healthcare professional educators. *J Med Educ Curric Dev*. 2019;6:2382120519840332. https://doi.org/10.1177/2382120519840332.

39. Bird J, Cohen-Cole S, Boker J, Freeman A. Teaching psychiatry to non-psychiatrists: I. The application of educational methodology. *Gen Hosp Psychiatry*. 1983;5:247–53.

40. Kilminster SM, Jolly BC. Effective supervision in clinical practice settings: A literature review. *Med Educ*. 2000;34:827–40. https://doi.org/10.1046/j.1365-2923.2000.00758.x.

41. Dawber C. Reflective practice groups for nurses: A consultation liaison psychiatry nursing initiative. Part 2 – The evaluation. *Int J Ment Health Nurs*. 2013;22:241–8. https://doi.org/10.1111/j.1447-0349.2012.00841.x.

42. Johnston J, Paley G. Mirror mirror on the ward: Who is the unfairest of them all? Reflections on reflective practice groups in acute psychiatric settings. *Psychoanal Psychother*. 2013;27:170–86. https://doi.org/10.1080/02668734.2013.772535.

43. Spikes J, Gadlin W. Ombudsman rounds revisited: A controlled study of attitudinal change in response to liaison psychiatry teaching. *Gen Hosp Psychiatry*. 1986;8:273–8. https://doi.org/10.1016/0163-834386.90009-5.

44. Ho PA, Girgis C, Rustad JK, Noorday D, Stern T. Advancing the mission of consultation-liaison psychiatry through innovation in teaching. *Psychosomatics*. 2019;60:539–48.

45. Piot M-A, Dechartres A, Attoe C et al. Simulation in psychiatry for medical doctors: A systematic review and meta-analysis. *Med Educ*. 2020;54:696–708. https://doi.org/10.1111/medu.14166.

46. Vandyk AD, Lalonde M, Merali S, Wright E, Bajnok I, Davies B. The use of psychiatry-focused simulation in undergraduate nursing education: A systematic search and review. *Int J Ment Health Nurs*. 2018;27:514–35. https://doi.org/10.1111/inm.12419.

47. Vestal HS, Sowden G, Nejad S et al. Simulation-based training for residents in the management of acute agitation: A cluster randomized controlled trial. *Acad Psychiatry*. 2017;41:62–7. https://doi.org/10.1007/s40596-016-0559-2.

48. Castle D, Sanci L, Hamilton B, Couper J. Teaching psychiatry to undergraduates: Peer-peer learning using a 'GP letter'. *Acad Psychiatry*. 2014;38:433–7. https://doi.org/10.1007/s40596-014-0088-9.

49. Walsh AL, Peters ME, Saralkar RL, Chisolm MS. Psychiatry residents integrating social media PRISM: Using Twitter in graduate medical education. *Acad Psychiatry*. 2019;43:319–23. https://doi.org/10.1007/s40596-018-1017-0.

50. Wiederhold BK. Connecting through technology during the coronavirus disease 2019 pandemic: Avoiding 'Zoom fatigue'. *Cyberpsychology Behav Soc Netw*. 2020;23:437–8.

Considerations in the Planning and Delivery of Consultation-Liaison Psychiatry Services

19

Allan House

Introduction

The planning and delivery of liaison psychiatry services requires many decisions regarding, for example, staffing profile; the type of work to be undertaken and by which members of the team; the relation between the team's work and the work of other parts of the local mental health services; and how outcomes will be measured. Putting all these decisions together with the rationale for them amounts to what is sometimes called a *programme theory* or *logic model* for the service – outlining what is expected to work for whom and under what circumstances. These decisions are not made in isolation: key influences on the final shape of a service will depend upon the views (and financial support!) of service commissioners, which are in turn influenced by national policy. Even a carefully worked-out configuration for a liaison service is unlikely to be realised exactly as planned – implementation (delivery) will be influenced by the practical limitations experienced by staff in day-to-day work, and by the views of patients and of the health professionals who do (or do not) refer to the service.

With all this in mind, it may help to think of four stages in planning a service:

1. Taking stock – of existing staff, what clinical problems are seen by whom and where, what other work is undertaken.
2. Seeking the views of the main interested parties.
3. Outlining an ideal, or desired, service configuration.
4. Developing an implementation plan.

Taking Stock: How Do Services Currently Work?

The Current Picture: Is There a Typical Liaison Psychiatry Service?

In the context of these multiple influences on service design and operation, it is not surprising that national and international surveys reveal a great deal of variability in the structures and functions of liaison services – an inevitable consequence of setting priorities and making compromises and trade-offs in varied working circumstances.

A series of national surveys (1) starting in 2015 in England has painted a picture similar to that in most countries where liaison services are reasonably developed. The great majority of services are multidisciplinary, employing at the least psychiatrists and psychiatric nurses and often also staff from a rehabilitation or social work background. One of the striking features of the UK scene is that only in a minority of services is clinical psychology also part of the team, for historical and organisational reasons that do not stand up to logical scrutiny.

There are several advantages to this multidisciplinary style (2–4), which is a feature of many medical services now and is widely accepted to improve outcomes in fields as diverse as cancer, stroke and chronic pain.

- Diversity in the team makes it easier to match clinical problems to somebody with the right skills.
- There are improved care outcomes from the sharing of knowledge and skills that is possible between team members from different backgrounds.
- Team-working allows sharing of dilemmas in decision-making.
- Multidisciplinary teams are likely to generate not more but higher-quality innovations in practice.

The size of these teams is influenced mainly by the throughput of the hospital (admission and discharge rates) rather than, for example, number of beds, and also by history – all teams grow incrementally and larger teams tend to be those that have been established longest.

Although there is considerable overlap in the functions of team members from different disciplines, there are also differences (5). Doctors are more likely to be involved in cases that require complex diagnostic formulation, where medication management is an issue and when there is behavioural disturbance requiring urgent intervention – including the possibility of use of powers covered by the Mental Health Act. Nurses are more often involved in assessment and formulation where the problems are typically psychosocial, for example following self-harm or mental health presentations related to alcohol or substance misuse. They are more likely to see referrals in the emergency department (ED) but may offer advice on inpatient wards about nursing management. In both settings they are more likely to receive referrals from general medical nurses than are doctors on the liaison team – a practice that can usefully facilitate access to the liaison service (6).

Rehabilitation therapists have, as a primary aim, the improvement of abilities in activities of daily living and support for active participation in the world and interaction with others. Their input is invaluable in the management of long-term conditions, whether functional or due to established bodily disease.

Even in a busy service with a large number of acute referrals, not all consultations need to be made by a consultant psychiatrist – anything from a third to a half can be made first by a non-consultant member of the team. Widely different practice in this respect suggests that there is no standardised approach in these matters, with local custom being an important determinant of practice.

Hours of cover are very variable. Nearly all services in the UK now work at least office hours and many work some of the weekend, but it is still only a minority that provide 24/7 cover for the hospital. It has become common for services to work to nominated response times – that is, to undertake to see a referred patient within a specified time since referral – and increasingly there has been a move from these times being self-defined to their being mandated. A one-hour wait for referrals from ED would be typical, with ward referrals being seen within a working day.

The other source of variability is the degree to which the liaison service consists of more or less separate sub-teams offering specialist age-related services. In recent years this has become a much commoner part of older people's care – about a third of UK services now provide at least a degree of specialist input from old-age liaison psychiatry – the rationale being the high proportion of older people in the inpatient population, their high rates of psychopathology and the need for good links to community services for older people. The counter-argument is that so much hospital care now involves older people that it is everybody's job and can therefore be managed within a generic liaison team. There is more uniformity about child and adolescent liaison – the profile of disorders and treatments is different, the young person's developmental trajectory is central to the formulation and links to services outside healthcare, especially in social care and education, are key to longer-term management. Liaison psychiatry of children and adolescents is less well developed than that for adults, and where it exists it is almost universally managed separately from the adult service.

The Current Picture: Is There a Typical Pattern of Liaison Psychiatry Activity?

Typically, much of the work in liaison psychiatry is short-order – referral comes from clinicians seeking help with diagnosis and formulation of what looks like a mental health problem, advice about immediate management and arrangement of follow-up plans which more often than not involve referral to other agencies (7). The commonest clinical problems seen in this mode are as follows:

- co-morbidity – usually mood disorder (depression, anxiety, other adjustment disorders) associated with and influencing the management of physical illness
- cognitive impairment – especially delirium and dementia in older people
- self-harm and suicidal thinking – which typically presents first in the ED
- substance misuse – atypical intoxication, withdrawal states, physical disorder that is substance-related
- emergencies – such as aggression, wandering or attempting to leave when too ill to do so.

Although this acute aspect of liaison work has come to dominate current practice – at least in part due to a need to respond to pressures not met by community services – there is another important aspect of liaison work, which is involvement in the longer-term management of chronic and complex cases. Typically, these are of two sorts: medically unexplained syndromes (also known as functional disorders or somatoform disorders) and chronic or disabling physical illness complicated by mental co-morbidity or difficulties with adjustment.

This longer-term work takes place in two settings. Outpatient clinics, which currently operate in about a quarter of UK services, can follow up patients seen initially during an inpatient episode or see patients referred directly as outpatients from other clinicians in the hospital or from primary care. Second, there are more formal specialist services where shared care can form part of the management plan for some patients or for the whole service. Most commonly, such joint working arrangements exist with neurology, cancer and palliative care, gastroenterology and transplant services. In one recent survey, more than 30 clinical specialties were nominated by responding liaison services as having such links. No doubt the specifics of service configuration depend upon a whole range of factors (8), including local interest, personal relationships funding arrangements and existing service provision (Table 19.1). Dedicated psycho-oncology and neuropsychiatry services are often present in tertiary specialist centres.

Table 19.1 Factors to consider during service planning

Level	Broad themes	Specific themes
National	Guidelines	National service frameworks
	National reports	
	National professional associations	Training requirements
		Recognition of the specialty as important
	Government policy	
	User lobbying	
	Political understanding of evidence	How politicians prioritise evidence
	Shortage of doctors	
Service	Internal factors	Proximity of the service to the general hospital
		Stability of the service in terms of structure, function and management
		Staffing levels, inappropriate staffing, high staff turnover
		Whether the service is managed by the general hospital trust or the mental health trust
		The funding and resources that the service receives
	External factors	Links (both formal and informal) to psychiatry and psychology
		Other liaison psychiatry service providers working in the same general hospital
		The need of general hospital patients to receive mental health input
		Training of professionals in the general hospital to recognise mental health problems and refer
	Reputation factors	Complaints and untoward incidents
		Data collection and evidence of effectiveness of interventions
		Feeling ashamed at the poor quality of psychiatric service provided to the general hospital
		Interpersonal relationships between members of the liaison psychiatry team and individuals in the general hospital trust
		Level of demand of mental health input from general hospital services
		Promotion and marketing of the service

Table 19.1 (cont.)

Level	Broad themes	Specific themes
		Quality of service including response times, clarity of advice, being available, good communication
		Significant individuals with specific skills, interests or links to general hospital departments
		Promotion and marketing of the service
		Understanding and interest of general hospital staff

There is another strand of non-clinical work to be considered – education and staff training; that is, advice to staff couched in more general terms than advice about management of single patients. Such educational activity takes time to prepare, is difficult to deliver because of staff availability and needs frequent repetition because of staff turnover. It is unfortunate, therefore, that it is rarely built into formal planning of services – for example, there are no norms for proportion of clinicians' time spent on such activities.

Seeking the Views of Key Interested Parties

The Role of Commissioners and Senior Managers

Decisions about service configuration cannot be made by clinicians in isolation. Clearly, those who commission and pay for services are important players and it is unfortunate therefore that the two parties (clinicians, commissioners) do not always feel that they have a good working relationship. One reason may be that the relationship is often mediated by third parties – managers or senior clinicians in the wider mental health service locally, who may themselves have little grasp of exactly what liaison psychiatry entails and whose own priorities may lie elsewhere. It is worth making the effort to engage in direct discussion, however – commissioners (notwithstanding their reputation) generally prefer the idea of co-production in service specifications; they are challenged by (and need expert guidance on) the idea of different services and pathways that seem to meet overlapping patient needs; and, of course, they rarely have personal experience of the nature of liaison services upon which to draw. Commissioners themselves have multiple influences on their decision-making (9). The most important are the need to enact national policies and the need to manage an economically sustainable local health service as well as a clinically effective one.

It is not unduly cynical to say that some *national policy* statements carry little weight when it comes to influencing local spending. For example, a claim to value mental and physical healthcare equally (see, e.g. www.gov.uk/government/speeches/achieving-parity-of-esteem-between-mental-and-physical-health) has not stood up well to the pressure coming from the costs of acute hospital care. Some policies do have salience in planning, even when they are not backed by substantial ear-marked funding – the national suicide prevention strategy, for example, assumes its importance because suicide is always newsworthy in a way that underfunded mental health services generally are not.

The national policies with most leverage are those that come with designated funding and a central mandate for delivery. Some are relatively transient – such as dealing with the challenge of unwarranted frequent attendance in ED, or winter bed pressures – while others can lead to more sustained change. Examples include the policy expectation that all acute hospitals have access to a learning disability specialist for liaison about inpatients, and the current National Health Service (NHS) England policy of investment to enable 24/7 coverage for urgent referrals, so-called CORE-24 funding (10). Even here, it is worth noting that commissioners have expressed some frustration at the inflexibility of the CORE-24 formulation and the degree of its exclusive focus on the acute care side of liaison work.

The Economic Arguments for Service Delivery

Recent discussions about the value of liaison psychiatry services have been dominated by arguments about the cost savings they may generate, but in reality many local commissioners are (rightly) sceptical about promises of huge financial benefits. Instead, a discussion could be couched in more general terms about value for money: how can that be judged for liaison psychiatry services?

In much medical practice, cost-effectiveness is a very important indicator and is used, for example, by the National Institute for Health and Care Excellence (NICE) in decisions about specific treatments. The ability to compare one treatment to another depends upon there being good-quality economic data on both – so that we can say that it is more cost-effective to offer Treatment A to patient group X than it is to offer Treatment B to that group, or indeed to another group. However, the concept transfers poorly into decisions about liaison psychiatry services. Suppose it is shown that, for example, giving cognitive behavioural therapy to somebody with cancer and moderate depression is more cost-effective than offering no psychological help. If we then decide that our service should offer this therapy to this group, then the therapists have to stop doing something else (there just aren't lots of therapists doing nothing, waiting to be deployed) or they have to be employed *de novo*. Both these options involve costs – the former opportunity costs, the latter direct costs – that will not have been considered in the original research.

The result is that the decision resolves to one not of economic benefit but of social and personal values. To inform that decision, the commissioner needs to have an understanding of the types of problem being seen by the liaison service, especially in terms of severity, complexity and known costs to the health service, the scale of the problem in terms of numbers of patients and of clinical contacts, and the potential clinical benefits that can accrue from effective intervention. This acknowledgement of the value of intervention is a good starting point from which to build agreement about the shape and scale of investment in liaison psychiatry.

The Clinician's Perspective

When we speak to clinicians working in a busy liaison psychiatry service, or talk with colleagues informally, a number of common influences on practice emerge (11).

- A recurring theme is the importance of strong functional links to other services. Most commonly mentioned are old-age community services, especially critical when it comes to tackling unnecessary or prolonged hospital admission, community mental health services, where it is important to establish referral criteria that do not leave patients falling between service gaps, drug and alcohol services because of the frequency of substance misuse problems in liaison practice, and the local mental health services when out-of-hours or on-call arrangements need to be negotiated.

- Clinical health psychology and Improving Access to Psychological Therapies (IAPT) services see an overlapping population with chronic health problems, co-morbidity or medically unexplained symptoms – typically rather less severe and complex than those seen in liaison psychiatry. Coordination of referral criteria and possibilities of joint working are desirable but surprisingly rarely in place.
- The influence of information systems is not always positive. Even in the current era, time taken in data entry is a burden and accessing digital records is not always easy, especially across organisations; confidentiality concerns persist and data entry can militate against in-depth writing and therefore inter-disciplinary communication.

The Patient's Perspective

Feedback from patients and those close to them is consistent. Valued experiences include a rapid response to referral, a therapeutic, helpful first contact that involves more than assessment and includes a person or problem-focussed discussion of current issues, and follow-up arrangements that are perceived as relevant and not over-reliant on the patient's resources.

On the other hand, common causes for concern include long waits to be seen, especially when these follow presentation in the ED; perfunctory assessment that appears preoccupied with risk; intolerant attitudes, which are experienced especially by those with a history of frequent attendance or repeated self-harm; and follow-up suggestions that are perceived as inadequate ('make an appointment with your primary care physician'; 'call this helpline') or involve re-referral to agencies that have had previous unrewarding involvement.

All this feedback suggests that when things go badly, the issue is an over-emphasis on short-order referral with rapid assessment and discharge, taking place in a setting where links to other services are poor so that appropriate follow-up is difficult. By contrast, services that work well include an aim to make every contact therapeutic, communicate effectively across service boundaries and either have good contacts with other services or the ability to arrange follow-up in their own clinics.

Outlining a Model or Desired Service Configuration

Starting from the current position in a particular liaison service, often arrived at based on incremental change and influenced by a variety of local contingencies rather than just rational planning, what are the common considerations in deciding how the service should be delivered? The two key clusters of decisions often involve trade-offs between competing demands and interests (12).

There are a number of questions related to the balance between two broad types of care offered by the service – how much the focus is on acute care versus the non-acute and, linked to this question, the amount of resource that is invested in short-order contact in the ED or on the wards, rather than longer-term treatment of chronic and complex problems in the outpatient clinic or special units.

A second, and not unrelated, cluster of questions relates to the skill-mix and experience in the team: the degree to which there is specialisation (in particular, therapeutic approaches or clinical areas) as opposed to the provision of generic service across the hospital.

Specialisation often involves liaison and not just consultation work, organisational or systemic thinking and not just an individual clinical focus, and a sustained element of education and supervision in the primary clinical team.

It is not possible to determine the configuration of a service based on a one-off decision. The balance of competing demands can change over time in multicomponent services: challenges in delivery, or unintended consequences of a particular initiative, can lead to a need for adjustment to original plans. For example, employing more staff and introducing a rapid-response model may not yield the cost savings originally hoped for, referrals may increase in response to the greater accessibility of service, less time can be spent at each contact, each contact is less conclusive and the result is increased re-presentations. If this happens, then a rethink may be needed with a shift to provision of more definitive follow-up services and a different way of delivering assessment for non-urgent referrals.

In coming to a decision about how these competing priorities can be resolved into an acceptable service configuration, it is desirable to involve all interested parties in the discussion. However, in contrast to many accounts of so-called co-creation or co-production, it is rarely possible to get the key players together for planning meetings, so the best that can be achieved is a sequence of discussions at which ideas are shared and refined. This process is easier if a framework can be agreed for describing the service. The metaphor of a care pathway will not do for a multicomponent service working with people, many of whom have multi-morbidities. It can be useful instead to develop a simple matrix along the lines shown in Table 19.2. In each cell a brief vignette describes a typical scenario, both in terms of the clinical problem and the staff involved.

Typical scenarios can readily be provided from the clinical experience of staff members. These descriptions of the service will be essentially qualitative and need supplementing with two pieces of quantitative information:

- The scale of the problem – identified through an audit of service activity, which need not be too onerous if undertaken over a typical one to two weeks; that is, the typical number

Table 19.2 Framework for providing a basic service description

Location of contact	Main clinical problem	Staff involvement
Emergency department	Self-harm	Liaison nurse specialist
	Behaviour disturbance with hallucinations	
	Recurrent functional symptoms	
Inpatient ward	Repeat admission with uncontrolled asthma or diabetes	
	Non-resolving delirium	Old-age liaison team
Liaison outpatient clinic	Persistent pain	
Specialist unit	Functional disorders	
Educational forum	Unwillingness to accept treatment	

of cases seen and by whom and the number that could be seen in a model or desirable service.

- The preferred measures of process and outcomes by which this aspect of service can be evaluated (see Chapter 20).

Developing an Implementation Plan

With an ideal service in mind, all that remains to be done is to develop a plan of action to develop the new service. This is often undertaken piecemeal in collaboration with a local manager and may take advantage of opportunities created by the emergence of new or unexpected demands such as those created by the beginnings of the AIDS epidemic or the COVID-19 pandemic. Opportunism is not to be sneered at and useful developments can arise from it, but it is best for it not to be the sole motivator of change. More formal approaches to planning and implementing desired service changes are available – typically involving two key processes – deciding on the necessary order if change (based upon importance and upon which actions need to proceed before others can be implemented) and deciding on who to involve and how to involve them in the desired activities. It is beyond the scope of his chapter to review such approaches; simply, it is worth being familiar with the outlines of at least one such approach.

The Theory of Change is a practical framework for service development, the origins of which in global health work (13) mean that it is suited especially in settings where financial support for change is limited. See, for example, https://knowhow.ncvo.org.uk/how-to/how-to-build-a-theory-of-change. One of the most useful strategies from this way of thinking is 'working backwards' from the desired outcome. For example, suppose you decide there are five elements to your new service; looking at the first, you think there are three conditions that need to be met (X, Y and Z) before it will come into being; looking at X, you see that two steps need to be taken (A, B) before it can be realised. And so on. In this way you build up a sequence of actions. Perhaps they will not all be in your control but some will, and making these changes will inevitably shift the balances in an otherwise static system and that will make further change possible.

Conclusion

The main enemy of service planning and delivery in liaison psychiatry is the apparently relentless nature of the short-order acute work entailed, which can come to seem like the raison d'être of the service, especially when changing service configuration can seem so slow to achieve in the face of organisational and financial barriers. However, a clear longer-term vision and an associated implementation plan will almost always support change, not least because it attracts allies more readily than repeated requests for more resources without an accompanying plan that has been thought out and discussed with others.

References

1. Walker A, Barrett JR, Lee W et al. Organisation and delivery of liaison psychiatry services in general hospitals in England: Results of a national survey. *BMJ Open*. 2018;**8**(8):e023091.

2. Fay D, Borrill C, Amir Z, Haward R, West MA. Getting the most out of multidisciplinary teams: A multi-sample study of team innovation in health care. *J Occup Organ Psychol*. 2006;**79**(4):553–67.

3. Baxter SK, Brumfitt SM. Benefits and losses: A qualitative study exploring healthcare staff perceptions of teamworking. *BMJ Qual Saf.* 2008;**17**(2):127–30.

4. Mickan SM. Evaluating the effectiveness of health care teams. *Austral Health Rev.* 2005;**29**(2):211–17.

5. Guthrie EA, McMeekin AT, Khan S, Makin S, Shaw B, Longson D. An analysis of whether a working-age ward-based liaison psychiatry service requires the input of a liaison psychiatrist. *BJPsych Bull.* 2017;**41**(3):151–5.

6. Solomons LC, Thachil A, Burgess C et al. Quality of psychiatric care in the general hospital: Referrer perceptions of an inpatient liaison psychiatry service. *Gen Hosp Psychiatry.* 2011;**33**(3):260–6.

7. Saraiva S, Guthrie E, Walker A et al. The nature and activity of liaison mental services in acute hospital settings: A multi-site cross sectional study. *BMC Health Serv Res.* 2020;**20**(1):308.

8. Ruddy R, House A. Is clinical service development simply applied evidence-based medicine? A focus group study. *Psychiatric Bull.* 2005;**29**(7):259–61.

9. Fossey M, Godier-McBard L, Guthrie EA et al. Understanding liaison psychiatry commissioning: An observational study. *Ment Health Rev J.* 2020;**25**(4):301–16.

10. NHS England. *Implementing the Five-Year Forward View for Mental Health.* London; 2016.

11. Jasmin K, Walker A, Guthrie E et al. Integrated liaison psychiatry services in England: A qualitative study of the views of liaison practitioners and acute hospital staffs from four distinctly different kinds of liaison service. *BMC Health Serv Res.* 2019;**19**(1):522.

12. House A, Guthrie E, Walker A et al. A programme theory for liaison mental health services in England. *BMC Health Serv Res.* 2018;**18**(1):742.

13. Breuer E, De Silva MJ, Shidaye R et al. Planning and evaluating mental health services in low-and middle-income countries using theory of change. *BJPsych.* 2016;**208**(s56):s55–62.

Chapter 20

Outcome Measurement in Consultation-Liaison Psychiatry

Allan House

Placing Outcome Measurement in Context

The purpose of outcome measurement in healthcare is to establish the effect of a clinical or organisational activity. A useful initial step is therefore to clarify not just what outcome is being assessed but also what activity is being evaluated by measuring that outcome. In terms of describing the activity of liaison psychiatry, the service can be understood as a complex intervention in healthcare. That is, it has multiple components, each with its own mechanism of action and possible effects. This raises a fundamental question about outcome measurement – what part of this complex system is being evaluated? Before considering the particulars of outcome measurement, we therefore need to have a way of characterising liaison services and how they might work.

One of the longest-established ways of thinking about health services is Donabedian's (1) distinction between *structures, processes* and *outcomes*. In this context structure refers mainly to staffing levels and the facilities and resources available to them. Processes are the activities – clinical and organisational – delivered by the service's establishment.

Occasionally knowing about structure or process is in itself important because either may be linked to outcomes even when we do not quite know why. For example, in 1997 it was shown that people who were admitted to hospital after stroke had better outcomes if they were admitted to a specialist stroke unit (defined by their structures) than they did if they were admitted to a general ward (2). Research only came later to explore what processes in specialist units explained this finding. National Institute for Health and Care Excellence (NICE) Quality Standards are often related to organisational processes: to take another example from stroke, one of the standards for stroke care in adults is: 'adults who have had a stroke have their rehabilitation goals reviewed at regular intervals'. The UK's Psychiatric Liaison Accreditation Network has developed Quality Standards for Liaison Psychiatry Services (3), many of which are related to processes of care (see Chapter 24).

For the most part, however, it is helpful if all three elements of service are taken into account so that outcomes can be logically linked to both structures *and* processes. To give two examples: National Health Service (NHS) England has recently adopted a policy of investment in liaison psychiatry services in England, aimed at ensuring there are enough staff (usually nursing and medical) to allow for 24/7 cover of all acute hospitals (4). This structural change is designed to enable a change in processes so that rapid specialist assessment can be arranged at any time of day. The expected outcome is a reduction in acute inpatient admission for those seen in the emergency department, or perhaps a reduction in inpatient lengths of stay for those seen during a current inpatient spell. It can readily be seen that an understanding of the success or otherwise of this investment, as judged by how well it achieves these outcomes, will depend upon an exact understanding of the numbers and skills of those employed under the policy, and also of how the new staff are working in practice in the expanded service.

The second example starts not with a prescribed structure but with a desired process or set of processes – variously known as continuity of care, seamless care or integrated care (5). The processes with these labels are designed to ensure that patients do not fall into gaps between services, such gaps being typically created by inadequate mechanisms for referral or transfer of care. One structural solution to this challenge is to have good-quality shared health records, based upon information technology systems. The resulting sharing of data can achieve what has been called *informational continuity of care*, which is aimed at improving clinical outcomes by ensuring that all relevant health information is available to the clinical team even when, as often happens, a patient with complex needs moves between services.

A more detailed approach to describing complex interventions is the *logic model* (6). In this approach there is more elaboration of the structure + process = outcome formula: On the 'input' side, consideration is given not just to the resources available and how they might work in a complex system but also to the context in which the service operates; on the 'consequences' side, there is recognition that interim effects (outputs) are likely to be required as a step on the path to achieving final outcomes.

A related idea is the *programme theory* (7, 8), which poses the question slightly differently – not just what works, but what works for whom and under what circumstances? This way of thinking arose from the observation that apparently similar programmes of activity have very different effects in different places. Great emphasis is therefore placed upon understanding the specifics of local action – exactly who is doing what, with whom and influenced by what local circumstances? For example, it is almost impossible to understand the impact of old-age liaison services on discharge and admission practices without information about the structure and function of local community services for older people, and especially those related to dementia and physical disability. Inquiry into these questions can produce rich and meaningful accounts of a how a service works and can explain variation in outcomes between services.

One practical tool for capturing these ideas is the TIDiER (Template for Intervention Description and Replication) framework (9). It was originally developed to aid researchers in standardising the description of complex interventions but it can have a wider application to support the planning and evaluation of liaison services in routine practice, providing as it does a framework for thinking about a whole service or parts of a service and how outcomes are generated (see Box 20.1).

Outcomes Can Be Measured at Different Levels of Service Activity

Clinicians are naturally inclined to think of outcomes in terms of the response of an individual patient to treatment. Evaluation of the whole or part of a service can, however, involve a higher level of aggregation and can include groups other than patients.

Much work in this area has been based on services in acute hospitals because that is where most liaison psychiatry services have developed, even in countries like the UK with strong primary care services. The principles of evaluation are, however, the same for services based in primary care, although the emphasis may differ.

Box 20.1 Items Included in the Template for Intervention Description and Replication

Brief name

1   Provide the name or a phrase that describes the intervention

Why

2   Describe any rationale, theory or goal of the elements essential to the intervention

What

3   Materials: describe any physical or informational materials used in the intervention, including those provided to participants or used in intervention delivery or in training of intervention providers. Provide information on where the materials can be accessed (such as online appendix, URL)

4   Procedures: describe each of the procedures, activities, and/or processes used in the intervention, including any enabling or support activities

Who provided

5   For each category of intervention provider (such as psychologist, nursing assistant), describe their expertise, background and any specific training given

How

6   Describe the modes of delivery (such as face-to-face or by some other mechanism, such as internet or telephone) of the intervention and whether it was provided individually or in a group

Where

7   Describe the type(s) of location(s) where the intervention occurred, including any necessary infrastructure or relevant features

When and how much

8   Describe the number of times the intervention was delivered and over what period of time, including the number of sessions, their schedule and their duration, intensity or dose

Organisational Outcomes

A liaison psychiatry service may be evaluated by measurable outcomes at the level of the hospital or hospital department to which it provides service rather than at the patient level.

Inpatient Length of Stay

It has been suggested for some time that early psychiatric intervention might reduce lengths of hospital stays for complex cases – perhaps with sufficient impact in enough cases that the whole service could be paid for from the resultant savings, the so-called cost-offset effect. At hospital or department level this question can be surprisingly difficult to answer: length-of-stay data are skewed in distribution with a high initial peak due to day cases or single overnight stays and a long tail due to hard-to-discharge patients; readmission to hospital within a 6- or 12-month period is common, leading to clustering of inpatient spells within patient; the more complex inpatient spells are often marked by multiple consultant episodes as care is transferred between or shared by teams, so that length of inpatient stay for the total spell may not be a good indicator of the effect of particular consultant episodes.

All these complexities in the data mean that an apparently simple statistic like mean length of stay can be extremely misleading. It is a drawback that expert statistical analysis is required for evaluating length-of-stay data, making them of limited use for routine measurement of service outcomes.

Early Readmission Rates

Unscheduled readmission is recognised as undesirable, although it is not always unavoidable. A common metric for hospital performance is the proportion of readmissions with 28 days of a discharge from hospital. This may be related to other indicators because when there is pressure to reduce inpatient lengths of stay, there is a risk that increasing early discharge comes with an increase in early readmission.

Specialist Referral Rates

One marker of complexity of care is the number of specialists who become involved in care. The additional contacts can add complexity and costs, not least because of the additional investigation that such referral often engenders (see Figure 20.1). See Chapter 22 for further detail.

Waiting Times (e.g. in the Emergency Department)

A common focus of concern in health services is the crowded emergency department or over-busy ward, in which patients wait too long for a specialist assessment before appropriate action is taken. In the emergency department it is a relatively simple matter to find out (because it is part of the routine record) the time from admission to discharge from the department, which may be a reasonable measure for those patients referred to the liaison psychiatry service – although it does not take into account time to referral to psychiatry, it has the advantage of ease of collection. For ward referrals, the appropriate measure is time for referral to time of first contact – the disadvantage of which is the opportunity it offers for gaming if the first contact is not a clinically meaningful one.

Untoward and Serious Incidents

Patients with psychiatric problems can generate untoward incidents – people with delirium or dementia can abscond or assault another patient or member of staff; drug intoxication or withdrawal can cause serious behavioural problems in the emergency department; suicide or attempted suicide occasionally happen on medical wards. Such incidents cause understandable distress and can have organisational consequences – for example, in the elderly with dementia a record of aggressive episodes can lead to delayed discharge to residential care if the receiving organisation is reluctant to deal with potential disturbance.

If such incidents are to be recorded as part of evaluation of a liaison service, then it is important to ensure that records are also kept of aspects of care that make it reasonable to attribute the outcome to the liaison service: examples might be time from referral to first contact for somebody with dementia, or rates of initiation and completion of Mental Health Act assessments.

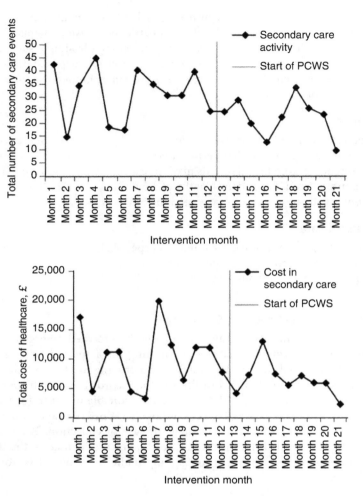

Figure 20.1 Contacts in secondary care, and cost of healthcare, in the months before and after development of a primary care liaison service (10).

Patient Complaints and Patient Satisfaction

Many of us, if we have had NHS treatment in recent years, will have been asked to complete the NHS Friends and Family Test (11). It asks only one question – 'How likely are you to recommend the service to friends and family if they needed similar care and treatment?' – with a five-point Likert scale response from extremely likely to extremely unlikely. It has the advantage of brevity, simplicity and familiarity. Its main disadvantage is the lack of explanation it offers for the result – free-text explanations are solicited but rarely completed. We know that patients distinguish, in their satisfaction ratings, between the emotional or interpersonal aspects of care and the technical aspects. It is probably safe to assume that it is the former that has the greater influence on scores on the Friends and Family Test. One reason for this is that patient complaints are very frequently about the personal side of care – being kept waiting, perceived rudeness, poor communication.

Organisation-Level Outcomes Have Limitations

A challenge in using any of these organisational outcomes is the question of attribution. Liaison psychiatry services typically see only a small proportion (up to about 5%) of all cases treated in the acute hospital (12) and it can be difficult to pick out the service's influence against the background of change in the wider organisation.

A second problem is that not all systems capture liaison psychiatry contact in the main clinical record, and an effort at cross-checking between medical and psychiatric records may be required. In reality, it is therefore unlikely that a liaison service can effect significant change in a hospital-wide measure but it may be able to influence the outcome in particular groups such as those with badly controlled type 1 diabetes or asthma.

Population-Level Clinical Outcomes

Well-staffed services have the opportunity to work closely with single departments or groups of patients. Top of the list is of course the emergency department; in one survey in the UK (13), the commonest such arrangements with other parts of the hospital were in cancer, gastroenterology, palliative care and neurology. For reasons noted earlier, it is likely to be more productive to measure outcomes in such selected sub-groups of the hospital population.

Frequent Attendance

In the emergency department, a group of patients who are often a focus of attention is those who attend frequently. The reasons for frequent attendance are complicated and include social as well as clinical factors, and many people in this group have mental health problems. Frequent attendance is usually an episodic phenomenon – people go through spells in life when it becomes a way of help-seeking and then circumstances change and the frequent attendance stops, or at least remits for a while. Since intervention is likely to be sought at a time of high attendance, reduction is likely as part of the natural course of events; the implication is that care should be taken when considering whether to commit long-term resources based on an apparent effect on the outcome, unless sustained benefit can be demonstrated.

Condition-Specific Measures for Particular Services

One model for outcome measurement in particular clinical populations is the UK's Quality Outcomes Framework (QOF) in primary care. Standards are set in the QOF system (14), with financial incentives for the primary care team to meet the prescribed targets. The team is required to keep a register of all patients with each of the conditions specified in the QOF, and that forms the basis for self-evaluation against the standards. Some of the standards relate to process – for example, 'the percentage of patients aged 8 or over with asthma (diagnosed on or after 1 April 2006), on the register, with measures of variability or reversibility recorded between 3 months before or any time after diagnosis'. Other targets relate to outcomes. For example, 'the percentage of patients with diabetes, on the register, in whom the last IFCC-HbA1c is 64 mmol/mol or less in the preceding 12 months'.

These physical outcomes are worth noting for two reasons. First, they give an idea of case mix – indicating the complexity or severity of illness being seen by the liaison service. Second, improvements are an important aim of the liaison service, which should not concern itself solely with mental health outcomes. This is an important point – if psychiatric treatment is to be effective at improving a patient's quality of life and function, then it must aim at improving all aspects of health, mental and physical.

As suggested by the QOF example, these population-level clinical outcomes are likely to be aggregates of individual-level outcomes. The choice of outcome and the results deemed desirable or acceptable are likely to have been agreed by an external organisation such as NICE or professional bodies.

Clinical Population-Level Outcomes Have Limitations

A challenge for liaison services is that, in primary and secondary physical healthcare, mental health outcomes are rarely, if ever, collected routinely in the same way as physical outcomes are. The liaison service then has to rely on mental health outcome data only for those patients seen in the service.

Individual-Level Clinical Outcomes

For many purposes, it is patient outcomes following clinical contact that are of most interest to the service – if not always to its managers. The diversity of clinical work in a typical service means that it is not possible to measure every possible outcome in every patient: for example, a recent summary of possible clinical factors in case management (15) suggested at least 21 items in 7 domains (see Table 20.1).

Table 20.1 Possible clinical outcomes to measure following liaison psychiatry contact

Domain	Items
Mood	Low mood
	Suicidal ideation or self-harm
	Psychological adjustment to physical illness
Psychosis	Perceptual disturbances
	Abnormal thought content
	Abnormal mood (excluding depression)
Cognition	Problems with orientation
	Problems with concentration
	Problems with memory
Substance misuse	Alcohol-related problems
	Illicit-drug-related problems
	Proprietary medication problems
	Acute alcohol or drug withdrawal
Mind and body	Disproportionate disability
	Excessive or major worry about physical health
	Pain
	Disproportionate treatment-seeking behaviour
Disturbed behaviour	Agitation or aggressive behaviour
	Non-compliance with treatment
	Consciousness and hypoactivity
Additional items	Side effects of psychotropic medication
	Problems with capacity to consent to medical/surgical treatment

In deciding how to target outcome measurement in this context, it is worth thinking of clinical outcomes at three levels of specificity: *generic measures* apply to everybody in the clinical population, *domain-specific measures* apply to those with particular problems and *condition-specific measures* apply only to those with particular diagnoses. In each of these categories there will be measures that are completed by a clinician and some that will be completed by the patient themselves – or a proxy if the patient cannot complete for some reason such as sensory impairment or weakness – so-called PROMS (Patient Reported Outcome Measures).

Generic measures cover areas like health-related quality of life, physical function or activities of daily living, and social function. Examples include the clinician-rated Clinical Global Impression scale, CGI (16); the Recovery Quality of Life (ReQoL) questionnaire (17), which is patient-rated; and all the common measures of emotional distress or well-being. Social participation measures are important for older people living in the community (18) and therefore may be useful for evaluating outpatient interventions but are not useful for evaluating inpatient work.

Domain-specific measures include common problems like pain, fatigue, sleep disturbance or daytime sleepiness, mood disorder or physical symptom burden. *Condition-specific measures* are typically either physiological, such as $HbA1_c$ PEFR; related to function such as cognitive function or delirium; or symptom-related measures that are specific to the condition under consideration.

Choosing a Clinical Outcome Measure: Some General Considerations

It is not the purpose of this chapter to present a list of recommended 'best' clinical outcome measures for use in liaison psychiatry – the circumstances calling for outcome measurement are too various and new measures continue to appear, rapidly making such lists redundant. Instead, it is worth outlining the main considerations for the clinician in choosing a measure for a particular project.

- Choose a measure that is already widely used – its popularity suggests it has desirable characteristics, and comparison of the results with those already available will be easier. Many services in secondary and primary care are expected to record outcomes and it is worth considering use of the same measures. In the UK this includes information collected by the Improving Access to Psychological Therapies (IAPT) programme (19) and by mental healthcare providers for the mental health minimum dataset.

- Check which measures are commonly used by researchers: identify a recent literature review from NICE, the Cochrane Library or a quick search of easily accessible resources like PubMed and Google Scholar. The aim is not to review the evidence but to identify the most widely used measure in research in your area of interest.

- Identify the main target audience for your results and ask its members what they want. Patient groups, service managers and healthcare commissioners do not necessarily share the same priorities as clinicians and your findings will have more impact if they meet the needs of the decision makers with whom they are shared.

- Ensure that your chosen measure is likely to be sensitive to your intervention. For example, reduction in use of analgesia, increase in measures of social function or improvement in distress may respond more quickly to intervention than change in self-reported chronic unexplained pain.

- Pick a measure that is brief and simple to complete – high rates of non-completion undermine any study. Measures are most likely to be completed if they are clinician-rated by a member of the liaison team when the whole team is engaged with the evaluation.
- Remember, some properties of a test are more important than others. 'Validity' is often reported for a test but may have been assessed as construct validity using factor analysis, which is a feature of limited use in practice. Repeatability and sensitivity to change are more important for most uses. For example, although the quality-of-life measure EQ5D (https://euroqol.org) has been more widely used than any other and it might be tempting to use it, it is not very sensitive to change in mental disorder and an alternative will be preferable if the main intervention is aimed at improving mental state.
- Consider using more than one outcome measure. We cannot always be sure which of a number of facets of somebody's health might improve when we intervene. Symptoms may improve without any great improvement in function – a common outcome after treatment for depression in disabling physical illness. On the other hand, function may improve when certain core symptoms do not, or at least not to the same extent – a fairly common observation in chronic pain management.
- Where several outcomes are under consideration, it is tempting to combine these outcomes. For example, in self-harm work, suicidality is often used as an umbrella term for suicidal thinking, non-fatal acts of self-harm and actual suicide. Delirium and dementia might be combined into a measure of cognitive dysfunction. However, a composite measure should include only items that can be shown to have similar associations and to move in similar ways, justifying their aggregation. It is often better simply to record more than one outcome, kept separately.

This illustrates some of the difficulties in measuring outcome in liaison psychiatry, and there is no recognised standardised measure or set of measures to guide clinicians. A scorecard approach can be used in which individual symptom-specific measures are employed for individual patients depending upon the nature of their problems (e.g. an alcohol measure for a patient with alcohol problems and a cognition scale for a patient with dementia); however, this is difficult to implement fully in practice. The Royal College of Psychiatrists, Liaison Faculty has recently developed a framework (FROM-LP) for the clinical evaluation of liaison psychiatry services (20). This includes recommendations to use a simple set of measures to assess outcome and a typology to describe different forms of clinical interventions employed by liaison psychiatry services; the Identify and Rate the Aim of the Contact (IRAC) scale (20). The IRAC has shown good clinical utility in correctly identifying the type of interventions implemented by liaison psychiatry teams (21). The Royal College of Psychiatrists recommends that all liaison psychiatry services use the framework to improve the recording of clinical data.

A new liaison outcome measure has also been developed which has been specifically designed to take account of the complexity and diversity of patients seen in a liaison setting (15). The items in the Clinician-Rated Outcome Measure (CROM-LP) are listed in Figure 20.2 and cover mood, psychotic experiences, cognitive function, substance misuse, disturbed behaviour, side effects of medication and capacity. A further subscale of contextual factors is optional and includes degree of physical disease, intellectual difficulties, psychosocial stress, enduring mental health problems, social function and activities of daily living. The measure is acceptable to use by staff and shows good reliability and

Items to be rated over the previous 7 days according to the most severe during that period (a)

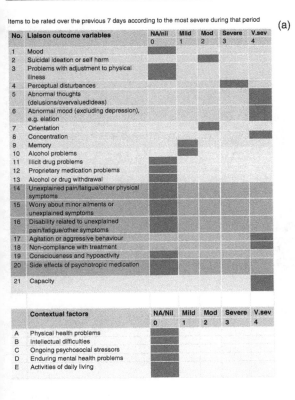

Baseline assessment
Patient A
Total score 41
Admitted with
confusion but
hypomanic and
diagnosis was bipolar
Detained under MHA,
started on
antipsychotics

Items to be rated over the previous 7 days according to the most severe during that period (b)

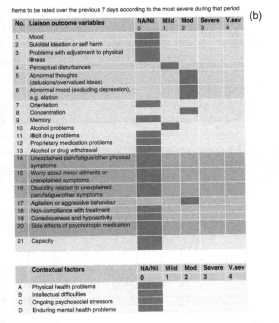

Patient A
Week 1 assessment
Total score =10
Mildly elated and
concentration still
poor

Figure 20.2 (a) Baseline scores on CROM-LP over a three-week period for a patient with confusion and hypomania; (b) Week 1 scores on CROM-LP for the same patient; (c) Week 3 scores on CROM-LP for the same patient.

Items to be rated over the previous 7 days according to the most severe during that period

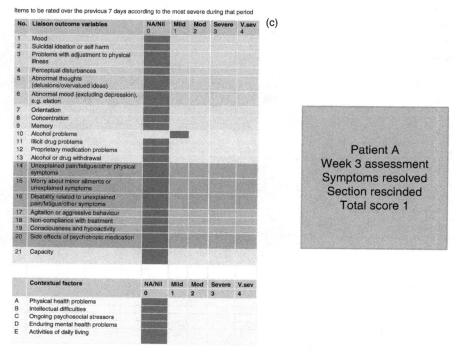

No.	Liaison outcome variables	NA/Nil 0	Mild 1	Mod 2	Severe 3	V.sev 4
1	Mood					
2	Suicidal ideation or self harm					
3	Problems with adjustment to physical illness					
4	Perceptual disturbances					
5	Abnormal thoughts (delusions/overvalued ideas)					
6	Abnormal mood (excluding depression), e.g. elation					
7	Orientation					
8	Concentration					
9	Memory					
10	Alcohol problems					
11	Illicit drug problems					
12	Proprietary medication problems					
13	Alcohol or drug withdrawal					
14	Unexplained pain/fatigue/other physical symptoms					
15	Worry about minor ailments or unexplained symptoms					
16	Disability related to unexplained pain/fatigue/other symptoms					
17	Agitation or aggressive behaviour					
18	Non-compliance with treatment					
19	Consciousness and hypoactivity					
20	Side effects of psychotropic medication					
21	Capacity					

	Contextual factors	NA/Nil 0	Mild 1	Mod 2	Severe 3	V.sev 4
A	Physical health problems					
B	Intellectual difficulties					
C	Ongoing psychosocial stressors					
D	Enduring mental health problems					
E	Activities of daily living					

(c)

Patient A
Week 3 assessment
Symptoms resolved
Section rescinded
Total score 1

Figure 20.2 (cont.)

sensitivity to change. A clinician-rated measure is necessary in liaison settings as many patients are unable to complete patient-rated outcome measures due to poor physical health or cognitive impairment.

Figure 20.2 is an example of how the CROM-LP measure is used in practice. Figure 20.2a shows the scores of a female patient who was admitted to a medical ward with delirium. She also showed symptoms of hypomania and was dancing and taking her clothes off on the ward. Her initial score was 41, with high scores on the psychosis subscale (perceptual disturbances, abnormal thoughts and abnormal mood) and high scores on problems with concentration, agitation, non-compliance with treatment and capacity. Over two weeks, her symptoms gradually resolved with treatment and she could be discharged before a mental health bed became available.

Non-psychiatric Staff Responses

Patients are not the only recipients of liaison psychiatry services. The referring clinician should be taken into consideration. A simple way to do this is to apply the Staff Friends and Family Test, but there are other simple measures of satisfaction with the service. An interesting indirect way of assessing what referring clinicians make of the service is to assess concordance with recommendations following consultation.

In certain special circumstances it may be worth considering other staff outcomes. For example, in services where mental co-morbidity is common, it may be useful to evaluate medical or nursing knowledge of the common problems, their skills in identification or their knowledge about possible treatments. Such an evaluation is likely to be most useful if it follows an educational intervention when assessment can reinforce learning goals.

In services where the work is especially stressful, staff levels of work satisfaction or emotional problems may be affected by the liaison service. This issue was raised during the recent COVID-19 pandemic, in which hospitals experienced major service disruptions, high patient fatality rates and threat from potentially fatal infection in healthcare staff. Caution needs to be exercised, however – there is little evidence that early active psychological intervention is what is required as opposed to supportive and well-organised clinical services.

Evaluation Design: The Framework within which Outcome Measures Are Used

It is a truism that the randomised controlled trial is the best design for an evaluation study, but of course it is not feasible as an approach to routine service evaluation. What other options are there?

Case series simply measuring outcomes in a consecutive series of patients can be useful: for example, the proportion who are depressed, or who have cognitive problems that meet a certain criterion, at discharge. These results tell you about the complexity of the case mix (see later) and also how many patients are meeting standards of recovery at the end of treatment.

Before-and-after studies – this is a weak design and it is difficult to attribute change to the service; intervention tends to occur at peak difficulty and natural recovery is therefore to be expected. However, the baseline measures tell you about case mix and this approach gives an idea of the proportion who improve: you can relate results to expected outcomes either from research interventions or published findings from other services such as IAPT. Bear in mind that results from either of these sources are often based upon selected samples; most research studies include less than 50% of the target population.

Interrupted time series (22) – this is a stronger design than a simple before-and-after study because it allows you to take account of trends over time, and also includes multiple data points which increases power. Its disadvantages are that it requires lots of data points; it is not always easy to place where the 'interruption' is especially for service changes where implementation takes time; it is not always apparent how to set the 'pre-interruption' time period; and analysis is complex. The visual presentation can be effective, though, even with simple statistics.

Figure 20.3 is an example of a study using interrupted time series to test a finding reported from a before-and-after study (12). The original study reported a marked drop in hospital lengths of stay following introduction of a liaison service; the time series study suggested that the identified fall was part of a longer-standing reduction in length of stay that was apparent before the new service was introduced. One explanation might be that the original study misinterpreted the meaning of its results by not taking the longer view; alternatively, the new service could have continued a trend that would otherwise have reached a plateau. Either way, the evaluation design allows for a more nuanced discussion of the meaning of the results than is possible from studying simple before-and-after findings.

Single-case designs can be an interesting way to demonstrate effectiveness, especially for intervention in extreme cases. Repeated measures can track change over time – for example, in self-reported symptoms, use of medication or unscheduled presentations. Visual

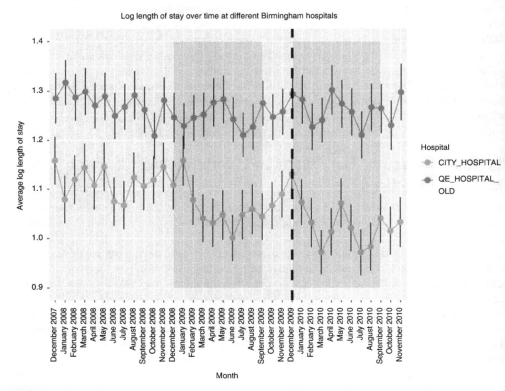

Figure 20.3 Interrupted time series showing length of stay in two hospitals. The dotted line marks introduction of liaison psychiatry service in one of those hospitals.

representation of the results from a single patient can look very like the results from an interrupted time series study and can be used in the same way.

Qualitative designs have not conventionally been a part of outcomes research but they are a useful way of obtaining information to help think about what might be the important elements of an intervention. In a research context, so-called *process evaluation* (23) is often used in parallel with a randomised trial to explore what happens in treatment and control arms and to try and explain the findings. For example, rather than administering (often poorly completed) patient satisfaction questionnaires, interviewing a small number of patients about their experience of treatment or of service processes can be an illuminating way of exploring what quality improvements are needed in a particular service.

Recording Case Mix: The Context within which Outcome Measures Are Used

Whatever design is adopted, an important and often overlooked consideration is the measurement of case mix. It is impossible to interpret outcomes in any clinical service if you do not know the nature of the clinical cases being treated. Important features are

---

Box 20.2 Indications of Complexity in Case Mix of Liaison Psychiatry Referrals

1. **Diagnostic complexity (physical health)**

   a. Multiple or persistent severe symptoms that do not fit standard diagnostic categories or encompass multiple diagnostic categories

   b. Multiple drug treatments including opioid or equivalent analgesia

   c. Multiple physical diagnoses

   d. Erroneous physical diagnosis assigned in past or by third parties

   e. Disability out of proportion to physical disease severity

   f. Major non-adherence or misuse of therapeutic regime, including induced illness

2. **Diagnostic complexity (mental health)**

   a. Illness conviction – can sometimes have a delusional quality, sometimes shared by close others

   b. Suicidal and related thinking, self-harm history or current risk

3. **Organisational complexity (healthcare)**

   a. Frequent unscheduled attendance – primary care physician surgery; emergency department; other healthcare

   b. Recurrent unscheduled acute admission

   c. Recurrent unwarranted physical investigation

   d. Multiple healthcare providers

   e. Drop-out from or failure to respond to first-line treatment, with persistent problems

4. **Organisational complexity (social care)**

---

severity, *chronicity* and *complexity*. The first of these is typically captured by standard outcome measures and the second is easily asked about.

Because there are numerous contributions to complexity of care (see Box 20.2), there is no widely used standard measure. It is, however, well worth noting these features since they distinguish the practice of specialist services in a way that diagnostic statements or symptom severity levels do not. One simple approach would be to develop a checklist based upon these items and use it to derive a three- or five-point scale of complexity.

Conclusion

All service evaluations involve collecting, collating and analysing significant amounts of data, and it is worth some exploration before starting to decide where the data might come from. Routine data collection at every clinical contact (based typically upon the idea of collecting a minimum dataset) often seems desirable in theory but in practice it is difficult to implement: a recent survey in England showed that only a minority of liaison psychiatry services routinely used standardised measures at clinical contact, and although a minimum dataset for liaison psychiatry services has been proposed (20), it has yet to be implemented in the face of challenging levels of workload and instability in the service staffing.

Routinely collected data may be useful, especially for organisational outcomes such as length of stay. Both service commissioners and providers collect data routinely, and they are usually willing to allow access for the purposes of service improvement.

For most projects, however, one-off (ad hoc) data collection by the service, such as might be collected for an audit project, is the best possible approach. Disadvantages are that it is time-consuming and easily forgotten in the hurly-burly of practice, so missing data are common. It is likely to be most effective, therefore, to adopt a rolling programme of evaluation – picking a topic, using the framework outlined in this chapter (see Table 20.2) to design a project plan and choose desired outcome measures, and concentrating on engaging the team in a sequence of fixed-term 'task-and-finish' efforts, rather than hoping for an open-ended commitment to collecting outcomes.

Table 20.2 Planning to use outcome measures: a checklist

What do I want to evaluate?		
	The whole service or a service component	TIDiER framework may be a useful starting place
	A specified group of patients	Including not just diagnosis but also measures of complexity, severity and chronicity
	An individual patient	
What outcomes am I interested in?		
	Organisational	
	Physical health	
	Mental health	
	Generic	
	Domain-specific	
	Condition-specific	
What evaluation design will I use?	Case series	
	Before-and-after	
	Interrupted time series	
	Single-case design	
	Qualitative study	
What measures of case mix will I record?		
	Severity	
	Chronicity	
	Complexity	

Table 20.2 (cont.)

What sources of information will I use?	
	Service collects data (routine or one-off)
	Routine hospital data
	Other sources, e.g. integrated care board
How will I present findings?	
	Narrative
	Graphics
	Statistics
Have I got a project plan?	
	Staff and other resources
	Numbers to include
	Timetable
	Reporting plan

References

1. Donabedian A. Evaluating the quality of medical care. *Milbank Quart*. 2005;**83**(4):691–729.

2. Stroke Unit Trialists' Collaboration, Collaborative systematic review of the randomised trials of organised inpatient (stroke unit) care after stroke. *BMJ*. 1997;**314**(7088):1151–9.

3. Brightey-Gibbons F, Patterson E, Rhodes E, Ryley A, Hodge S (eds.). *Quality Standards for Liaison Psychiatry Services*, 5th ed. London; 2017.

4. NHS England. *Guidance for Commissioning Liaison Psychiatry Services*. London; 2014.

5. Haggerty JL, Reid RJ, Freeman GK, Starfield BH, Adair CE, McKendry R. Continuity of care: A multidisciplinary review. *BMJ*. 2003;**327**(7425):1219–21.

6. McLaughlin JA, Jordan GB. Logic models: A tool for telling your programs performance story. *Eval Prog Plan*. 1999;**22**(1):65–72.

7. Pawson R, Tilley N. *Realistic Evaluation*. London; 1997.

8. House A, Guthrie E, Walker A et al. A programme theory for liaison mental health services in England. *BMC Health Serv Res*. 2018;**18**(1):742.

9. Hoffmann TC, Glasziou PP, Boutron I et al. Better reporting of interventions: Template for intervention description and replication (TIDieR) checklist and guide. *BMJ*. 2014;**348**:g1687.

10. Bestall J, Siddiqi N, Heywood-Everett S et al. New models of care: A liaison psychiatry service for medically unexplained symptoms and frequent attenders in primary care. *BJPsych Bull*. 2017;**41**(6):340–4.

11. NHS Friends and Family Test. www.nhs.uk/using-the-nhs/about-the-nhs/friends-and-family-test-fft.

12. House A, West R, Smith C, Tubeuf S, Guthrie E, Trigwell P. The effect of a hospital liaison psychiatry service on inpatient lengths of stay: Interrupted time series analysis using routinely collected NHS hospital episode statistics. *BMC Psychiatry*. 2020;**20**(1):27.

13. Walker A, Barrett JR, Lee W et al. Organisation and delivery of liaison psychiatry services in general hospitals in England: Results of a national survey. *BMJ Open.* 2018;**8**(8):e023091.

14. National Institute for Health and Care Excellence Quality and Outcomes Framework Indicator. www.nice.org.uk/standards-and-indicators/qofindicators.

15. Guthrie E, Harrison M, Brown R et al. The development of an outcome measure for liaison mental health services. *BJPsych Bull.* 2018;**42**(3):109–14.

16. Busner J, Targum SD. The clinical global impressions scale: Applying a research tool in clinical practice. *Psychiatry.* 2007;**4**(7):28.

17. Keetharuth AD, Brazier J, Connell J et al. Recovering Quality of Life (ReQoL): A new generic self-reported outcome measure for use with people experiencing mental health difficulties. *Br J Psychiatry.* 2018;**212**(1):42–9.

18. Dickens AP, Richards SH, Greaves CJ, Campbell JL. Interventions targeting social isolation in older people: A systematic review. *BMC Public Health.* 2011;**11**(1):647.

19. NHS England. *Implementing the Five Year Forward View for Mental Health.* London; 2014.

20. Trigwell P, Kustow J. A multidimensional Framework for Routine Outcome Measurement in Liaison Psychiatry (FROM-LP). *BJPsych Bull.* 2016;**40**(4):192–4.

21. Guest C, Crockett S, Little P, Patel A. The clinical utility of the IRAC component of the Framework for Routine Outcome Measurement in Liaison Psychiatry (FROM-LP). *BJPsych Bull.* 2018;**42**(4):152–6.

22. Ramsay CR, Matowe L, Grilli R, Grimshaw JM, Thomas RE. Interrupted time series designs in health technology assessment: Lessons from two systematic reviews of behavior change strategies. *IJTAHC.* 2003;**19**(4):613–23.

23. Moore GF, Audrey S, Barker M et al. Process evaluation of complex interventions: Medical Research Council guidance. *BMJ.* 2015;**350**:h1258.

The Evidence Base for Consultation-Liaison Psychiatry

Elspeth Guthrie

Introduction

This chapter will focus on the evaluation of liaison services, including the evidence regarding what liaison services actually do (activity), the types of clinical problems they manage and how they effect change and service outcomes. Liaison services in different settings, including the acute hospital, emergency department (ED) and primary care, will be discussed. Individual psychological or pharmacological treatments for specific conditions are covered elsewhere in this book. Interventions for self-harm are discussed in Chapter 5 and psychological treatments for persistent physical symptoms and co-morbid depression and physical disease are discussed in Chapter 15. The challenges and complexities involved in the assessment of liaison services are explained in Chapter 20.

There is robust evidence that certain specific liaison mental health interventions such as for the treatment and management of self-harm and the treatment of persistent physical symptoms are effective and may be cost-effective in some service configurations. The effectiveness and cost-effectiveness, however, of whole liaison mental health teams who treat a wide variety of different clinical problems is much more challenging to evaluate than a single intervention for a specific condition. The evidence discussed in this chapter is therefore not as compelling as that for single-intervention, single-condition trials but nevertheless helps to build a case for the value of liaison services and the particular skills of practitioners who work within them.

Activity of Liaison Services

Most liaison services in the UK and those around the world assess and treat only a small proportion of the overall population of people in acute hospital settings with co-morbid physical and mental health problems. The largest study in this field, the European Consultation-Liaison Workgroup (ECLW) Collaborative Study, collected data from 56 different liaison services in 11 European countries, included 10,560 patients and reported a mean consultation rate of 1.4% of all inpatient admissions (1).

More recently, a UK study involving 18 hospitals with differing types of liaison services estimated that the ward consultation rate (number of referrals divided by average weekly hospital admissions) ranged from 0.7% to 6.0% (mean 2.2%), and the estimated ED consultation rate (number of weekly referrals divided by average weekly attendance) ranged from 0.5% to 3.4% (mean 1.5%) (2). Just over half the contacts were initial assessments and the remaining were follow-up assessments. Approximately 60% of patients were seen by a mental health nurse, 30% by a doctor and the remaining 10% by other members of the liaison team such as a psychologist or social worker.

The consultation rates recorded by the above study for hospital inpatients accord with those reported by other non-UK studies (1, 3, 4) and represent a tiny proportion of the 25% of adults of working age and the 60% of older people in the general hospital who are known to have mental health problems. The coverage is better in the ED setting. Approximately 4% of people who attend EDs in the UK have recognised mental health problems, of which roughly over one-third will be referred to liaison services. Liaison mental health services only see a small proportion of people admitted to the acute hospital who could potentially benefit from their input.

The same study (2) also showed that the activity of liaison services was correlated with the number of ED attendances and hospital admissions in an acute hospital, but not the number of its beds, so liaison psychiatry activity is related to the throughput of patients rather than a hospital's actual size. Planning of service resources for liaison services, therefore, needs to be based on the throughput of hospital services, not on the size of the hospital in terms of beds. Liaison activity is related to the flow of patients through acute hospital (both ward admissions and ED attendances) rather than the size of the hospital in terms of number of beds.

Common Clinical Problem Scenarios

The most common problems referred to liaison mental health services are shown in Table 21.1 (2). In the ED, acute presentations of psychiatric symptoms (depression or schizophrenia), self-harm and alcohol problems predominate, whereas in the inpatient setting, patients are most commonly referred if they have co-morbid physical and mental health problems, cognitive impairment and to a lesser extent self-harm (2).

Interviews with liaison staff also suggest that vulnerable groups, including homeless people and those who experience domestic abuse, are particularly likely to be referred to liaison teams, and hospitals which serve particularly large ageing or student populations experience more referrals from these groups.

Table 21.1. Main types of clinical problems referred to liaison mental health services in emergency department and inpatient settings (ranked in order of frequency) (2)

Main clinical problems assessed in the emergency department	Main clinical problems assessed on acute hospital wards
Psychiatric symptoms	Co-morbid psychiatric symptoms
Self-harm	Cognitive impairment
Alcohol and/or drugs	Self-harm
Acute behaviour disturbance	Acute behavioural disturbance
Cognitive impairment	Psychological adjustment to physical illness
Psychological adjustment to physical illness	Alcohol and/or drugs
Medically unexplained symptoms	Medically unexplained symptoms
Other	Other

How Do Liaison Services Effect Change?

Although it may seem obvious to liaison psychiatrists how they bring about change, it is not obvious to commissioners or other key acute hospital staff what liaison services provide and what they actually do. Several studies have helped to map and describe the characteristic work that liaison services undertake (2, 5–7).

The most important vehicle for bringing about change is the assessment. This is described by liaison team members as an interactive, patient-focussed approach which involves a detailed dynamic formulation of the patient's physical and mental problems. After the assessment, the liaison practitioner discusses a plan with the patient and their hospital team. The plan could involve taking over the patient's care and recommending transfer to a mental health bed, providing shared care with the medical/surgical team while the patient is in hospital or providing advice to the medical team with signposting or referral to a community service post-discharge.

Another way liaison staff believe they effect change is by risk assessment and preventing suicide for people who present in suicidal crisis. Staff strongly value this aspect of their role and believe it is important to help people when they are at their most vulnerable. They believe that assessment, careful management of risk, safety planning and organised aftercare mean these patients can be discharged safely or, if required, admitted to an inpatient facility. The most important aspect of the intervention is that it is therapeutic in nature and not just a tick-box exercise as some risk assessments are criticised for being.

Other mechanisms for achieving change are medical advice and/or co-management – for example, management of agitated delirium, drug treatment for psychosis, restarting psychotropic medication which has been stopped and alcohol or drug withdrawal. Liaison teams that have psychologists, therapists or mental health nurses trained in specific interventions (like cognitive behavioural therapy) offer brief interventions while patients are hospital inpatients or follow-up after they have been discharged.

The most common types of liaison interventions are shown in Table 21.2 (8). In addition to the interventions discussed earlier, liaison teams also use powers under the Mental Health Act (MHA) to detain patients when appropriate and retain responsibility for them until they are transferred to a psychiatric unit or discharged from the Act. The consultant-liaison psychiatrist usually assumes 'Responsible Officer Status' for the patient while they remain in an acute hospital setting. Patients detained under the MHA in a hospital setting require regular review to ensure they are being safely managed in the busy and chaotic environment

Table 21.2 Main types of intervention in liaison psychiatry services

Assessment, diagnosis, formulation

Assessment and management of risk

Medication management

Treatment

Providing advice/signposting

Mental Health Act assessment

Assessment of mental capacity

Management of disturbed behaviour

of an acute hospital ward. Liaison teams also provide expert advice on complex cases requiring assessment under the Mental Capacity Act. Such cases often involve judgements as to whether mental health issues are impeding a person's ability to weigh in the balance the decision they are making about medical treatment. Decisions as to whether people can understand and retain information are usually more straightforward and can be made by most medical staff without the advice of a psychiatrist.

Other ways staff believe they effect change are by: supporting physical recovery through addressing a new or historic mental health problem (e.g., depression following a stroke); helping those with co-morbid physical and mental health problems with poor adherence to medication to improve their adherence; improving the quality of life and daily function of people with complex, unexplained or long-term mental health problems; reducing length of stay in acute hospitals and limiting the amount of time a patient is in the ED; helping patients better control their physical conditions (e.g., poorly controlled diabetes) to prevent longer-term complications or frequent presentations at hospital; and ensuring patients with severe mental illness admitted to acute hospital receive high-quality mental healthcare so their mental health condition does not deteriorate while being a hospital inpatient.

In addition to direct interventions with patients, change can also occur through collaborative work with acute hospital teams. This may be via shared care of a patient or via advice or be more of an iterative process over time where hospital staff become more confident and familiar with managing patients with mental health problems because of ongoing support and education from the liaison team.

The vast majority of interventions in the liaison setting are delivered by liaison mental health nurses as part of a team of mental health professionals including a consultant psychiatrist, although there are also nurse-led liaison services. It has been estimated that approximately 60–70% of ward referrals to working-age liaison services require the involvement of a psychiatrist because of the complexity of the work (9), whereas this figure is much smaller for older adult liaison services and liaison services to the ED.

Evaluations of Liaison Services

The design of evaluations of liaison services can be split broadly into two types: randomised controlled trials (RCTs) and before-and-after evaluations. There are many challenges in conducting RCTs to evaluate liaison services as there are many different components to service delivery which are difficult to define and most services cater for people with a wide variety of clinical problems. Even if trials of whole services produce positive outcomes, it is difficult to determine which aspects of a service have been effective and for whom, and whether the results can be generalised to other liaison services with different types of service configuration. In an attempt to simplify trial design, most RCTs in the liaison setting focus on relatively discreet interventions for particular patient sub-groups (such as a liaison nurse intervention for elderly hospitalised inpatients with mental health problems), so are often not generalisable to mainstream liaison work.

Before-and-after evaluations usually involve a comparison of outcomes of a service for the year prior to and following its inception. These types of studies, however, are subject to a wide variety of biases (some known and some unknown) which cannot be controlled for, and therefore the quality of the evidence from such studies is generally considered to be weak. Rudimentary before-and-after studies cannot account for other changes in the hospital system that may have coincided with the onset of the service under study, and they rarely take account of underlying trends (such as a general decline in hospital admissions year on year) which may have preceded the onset of the service. There are more sophisticated types of before-and-after evaluations which involve time-series analyses, comparing several points in time prior to and after the development of a series of services over several years, so that wider underlying trends in outcomes can be accounted for and the timing of changes can be more confidently linked to service development. These types of robust evaluation, however, are quite rare.

The quality of the evidence from a study does not necessarily equate with the impact of its results on the commissioning or funding of services. It is not uncommon for local commissioners to give greater credence to small, locally conducted, relatively crude evaluations of services that purport to save large amounts of money than larger, well-conducted trials that report less impressive results.

Liaison Psychiatric Services for Hospital Inpatients

In the last 5–10 years, UK evaluations of the implementation or extension of liaison services in Birmingham (10), London (11) and Sheffield (12) have suggested that they may produce large cost savings (estimated between £1 million and £3 million per year per site), primarily as a result of reductions in hospital length of stay in elderly patients with dementia. However, the methods employed by these studies mainly involved comparisons of retrospective data before and after the introduction of the service over relatively short periods of time. Costing in the studies was rudimentary and limited to the use of one or two national average costs which were simply multiplied by volume, then compared before and after. None of the studies evaluated: the wider National Health Service (NHS) impact; other changes, independent of the liaison services, which may have affected outcomes; cost displacements in other areas of acute services; trends in performance of key parameters over longer periods of time prior to service development; and changes in recording of mental health diagnoses.

A recent robust time-series evaluation of the implementation of a liaison service in Birmingham, which had previously been reported to save hospital costs of several million pounds per annum, found little evidence of any likely cost savings (14). In the initial evaluation, cost savings were attributed to the indirect effects of the service on a small number of elderly patients with dementia and extrapolated by the investigators to estimate cost savings for the whole hospital population for an entire year. In the more robust time-series evaluation, length of stay was examined for the entire hospital population over several years prior to and following implementation of the service. Little discernible impact of the liaison service could be found on a general trend in the fall in length of stay over several years prior to the establishment of the liaison service (14).

A systematic review of the effectiveness and cost-effectiveness of liaison services included 40 studies of varying design (15). Most of the studies involved simple before-and-after designs and were methodologically weak. The studies were grouped by the reviewers according to five measurements of effectiveness: cost-effectiveness, length of stay, concordance (whether hospital staff implemented advice given by liaison teams), staff and patient experience, and follow-up outcomes. The reviewers concluded that there was some evidence that liaison services were cost-effective and may reduce length of hospital stay if involved early in a patient's care and if hospital staff followed key recommendations from the liaison team. However, many of the studies were methodologically flawed and there were disparate and inconsistent findings across the studies as a whole.

The National Institute for Health and Care Excellence (NICE) recently undertook a systematic review to determine whether 'acute psychiatric services improved outcomes for patients with mental health disturbance presenting with an acute medical emergency' (16). The review largely focussed on liaison psychiatric services and only included studies which had employed a randomised controlled design. Seven studies were included in the review, comprising 1,738 people (17–23), five of which focussed on interventions for older adults in the acute medical setting (18–22). Four of the studies were published over 25 years ago (17, 18, 22, 23). The quality of evidence ranged from very low to moderate. The recommendation of the review was that liaison services may provide a benefit in reduced length of stay and improved patient care and or carer satisfaction, but further, more robust evaluation was required. Of some concern, the NICE reviewers found increased mortality associated with liaison mental health intervention which they could not logically explain and attributed to an anomalous finding, most likely the result of the poor quality of the included studies resulting in unidentified confounding. A systematic review published in 2021 which included eight RCTs (most of which were included in the NICE review) came to similar conclusions to the NICE reviewers (24). Taking all the above evidence into consideration, there remains considerable uncertainty as to whether hospital inpatient liaison services are effective and actually produce significant cost savings.

Liaison Psychiatry Services in an Emergency Department Setting

A recent systematic review of different models of liaison mental health services in the ED setting identified 17 separate studies of 15 different services (25). Of the studies included in the review, eight used before-and-after designs, six used uncontrolled cohort designs, one involved a matched cohort design, one was a natural experiment, one involved a cross-over design and one reported uncontrolled descriptive statistics. Studies were identified from Australia, Canada, the UK and the USA. Sample sizes ranged from 100 to 2,715 patients and study durations ranged from 30 days to 6 years. Only one study was rated by the review team as being of good quality (26).

Four different models of liaison service were identified: those with liaison staff which were integrated into the ED; those with liaison staff which were co-located in the ED; those with liaison staff based in the hospital but not specifically ED; and those where ED staff referred patients to external mental health units. Outcomes measured included waiting times, patient satisfaction, treatments used, costs, onward destinations for patients and number of attendances for mental health reasons.

Eight studies evaluated services with integrated ED staff. These were staff who were considered to be part of the ED team but had specialist skills in mental health assessment and most were qualified mental health nurses. At times, however, when they were not undertaking mental health assessments, they helped with the routine ED work and some also participated in triage. Most of these eight studies reported reductions in waiting times after introduction of the mental health nurses, with two describing large effects; an average reduction in wait time of 9.5 hours per patient (27); and a reduction of 3.3 hours per patient (28). Of note, the study which was rated as high quality by the reviewers was the only study not to report a significant impact on waiting times (16). Most of the studies reported high rates of satisfaction with the integrated mental health nurses by both patients and ED staff, except for the 'high-quality' study, which reported no change in satisfaction before and after service development.

Three studies described mental health teams that were co-located in ED but were not part of the ED team. One reported an average reduction in wait time of just under 2 hours (29). The other two did not provide sufficient data for this outcome to be assessed. Patient or staff satisfaction was not assessed.

Three services described hospital-based liaison teams which were not based in the ED. These did not impact on length of stay in the ED and waiting times were not specifically assessed. Patient or staff satisfaction was not assessed.

Three studies described evaluations of services providing external mental health assessment. In these services, there was no on-site mental health provision and all patients who required mental health assessment had to be transported from the ED to a specialist psychiatric facility by ambulance. The specialist psychiatric facility often served several EDs in a regional area. All three studies with this type of liaison model were North American. Two of the studies reported the evaluation of a psychiatric emergency service model introduced at the same centre in North America and the third study described a Crisis and Assessment Linkage and Management (CALM) model which involved a psychiatric multidisciplinary team who were based outside of the ED (30). All three studies suggested that the externally located models improved care for patients in a variety of ways, including reduced ED length of stay, less seclusion and restraint and less emergency psychiatric medication, but as with most of the studies in the review, there were methodological weaknesses in study design and execution. It is difficult to transpose these models of care to a UK setting, as it would not be feasible to transfer all patients who presented to ED with acute mental health problems to a separate psychiatric facility by ambulance. It is also extremely unlikely in the UK that such services would reduce wait times or length of stay in ED, as there has been an enormous focus on these particular outcomes in the last 10 years, with major reductions in both.

Of note, several studies, evaluating different models of care, reported reductions in the number of people with mental health problems leaving the ED prior to assessment and care for mental health patients was found to be safer and more appropriate when a psychiatrist was involved, regardless of type of service or venue. The reviewers concluded that there was insufficient evidence to support any particular model of psychiatric liaison to the ED due to the disparate findings and methodological weaknesses of most of the studies. Services in the UK generally resemble the second model, with a psychiatric liaison team co-located in the ED but not actually part of the ED team itself. Overall, there was sufficient evidence to suggest that liaison services help to reduce wait times and time spent in the ED and patients and staff report high levels of satisfaction.

Frequent Attender Services in the Emergency Department

Specific services to help patients who frequently attend EDs have been developed in recent years. Most of these services are based in EDs and are most frequently staffed by liaison mental health practitioners, but some services are run and staffed by ED personnel and a small number are based in the community, often run by third-sector organisations. Frequent attendance at the ED is often a symptom or sign of severe distress and unmet need (31), and high rates of ED attendance are associated with mental health problems, including depression, unexplained physical symptoms, alcohol and drug abuse and social difficulties such as homelessness or social isolation.

Several rudimentary evaluations of services for frequent attenders have shown reductions in ED use with estimations of large cost savings to the NHS (32–35). However, there is a high degree of natural attrition (36), with less than one-half of frequent attenders persisting in their use for longer than 12 months (37, 38), so uncontrolled evaluations are likely to result in overestimates of service impact. Up to 25% of frequent users are multisite users (39, 40), and these people are more likely to have mental health problems than single-site users.

Two systematic reviews examined the effectiveness of interventions to decrease ED visits by adult frequent attenders (41, 42). All reported similar findings: there is evidence for reductions in ED use from uncontrolled designs but very weak evidence from a small number of RCTs (n = 6). More robust evaluations of services for frequent attenders are required before their effectiveness can be established.

Liaison Psychiatry in Specialist Clinics

Some treatments offered by liaison psychiatry services are necessarily confined to the hospital episode in which referral is made, for example safety planning after self-harm, rapid sedation for acute behavioural disturbance and management of alcohol withdrawal syndromes. However, some treatments require longer-term contact with the patients and in these situations acute hospital lengths of stay are typically so short that outpatient follow-up is required.

Around a quarter of liaison psychiatry services in England and Wales provide outpatient clinics, which take one of two forms. First, it is quite common for patients to be followed up for a short time after discharge, to ensure resolution of an acute episode. Second, some services offer longer-term follow-up so they can provide therapy for more persistent problems – most usually psychiatric co-morbidity or problems with adjustment to severe chronic illness, or somatoform disorders. No substantial research studies have evaluated such clinics at the service level, and evidence for the individual therapies in them is discussed in other chapters in this volume.

Liaison Psychiatry in Primary Care

There has been growing interest in developing liaison mental health services to support primary care teams to manage patients with complex physical and mental health problems (Chapter 22 offers further detail). Liaison teams have the necessary skill and expertise to treat these kinds of clinical problems, which are challenging for primary care teams or community-based psychological services such as the Improving Access to Psychological Treatment (IAPT) services (a UK-based psychological service offering brief treatment).

Evidence for effectiveness and cost-effectiveness comes largely from trials of psychological treatment for medically unexplained symptoms (MUS) and long-term conditions (LTCs). A report from the Liaison Faculty of the Royal College of Psychiatrists in 2012 (43) set out the potential cost savings to the NHS were patients with MUS and LTCs to receive appropriate treatment. Since then, several local evaluations of primary care liaison services have established that it is feasible to set up such services and they result in high levels of patient and staff satisfactions and reductions in the utilisation of primary and secondary healthcare, with associated cost savings (see Chapter 22). Further, more robust evaluations are awaited.

Gillies and colleagues (44) undertook a systematic review and meta-analysis of consultation-liaison services in a primary care setting. They identified 12 RCTs, 11 of which compared consultation-liaison psychiatry to standard care and one of which compared consultation-liaison psychiatry to collaborative care. Eight of the trials focussed on the management of depression, with the other four including patients with a variety of different disorders including depression, anxiety, MUS and alcohol-related problems. Most of these trials did not involve patients with complex problems or those with co-morbid physical and mental health problems. The 'consultation-liaison' term used by the reviewers refers to the model of service (i.e. psychiatric assessment and advice) rather than the type of clinical problem addressed. The quality of the trials was generally low, with many trials rated by the reviewers as being at high risk of bias. None of the studies focussed upon the kinds of clinical problems that liaison primary care teams usually manage in the UK.

The reviewers concluded there was some evidence that consultation-liaison improved mental health up to 3 months following the start of treatment but there was no evidence of its effectiveness between 3 and 12 months. Consultation-liaison also appeared to improve consumer satisfaction and adherence up to 12 months.

Summary

In summary, liaison mental health teams see a wide variety of different clinical problems in the inpatient, ED and primary care setting and undertake a wide variety of different mental health interventions. Only a very small proportion of hospital inpatients who have mental health problems are actually referred to liaison services. There are many local evaluations which suggest liaison mental services result in improved outcomes and reduce costs, but more robust studies are required.

References

1. Huyse FJ, Herzog T, Lobo A et al. European consultation-liaison psychiatric services: The ECLW collaborative study. *Acta Psychiatr Scand.* 2000;**101**(5):360–6.

2. Saraiva S, Guthrie E, Walker A et al. The nature and activity of liaison mental services in acute hospital settings: A multi-site cross sectional study. *BMC Health Serv Res.* 2020;**20**(1):308.

3. Diefenbacher A. Implementation of a psychiatric consultation service: A single-site observational study over a 1-year-period. *Psychosomatics.* 2001;**42**(5):404–10.

4. Christodoulou C, Fineti K, Douzenis A, Moussas G, Michopoulos I, Lykouras L. Transfers to psychiatry through the consultation-liaison psychiatry service: 11 years of experience. *Ann Gen Psychiatry.* 2008;7:10.

5. House A, Guthrie E, Walker A et al. A programme theory for liaison mental health services in England. *BMC Health Serv Res.* 2018;**18**(1):742.

6. Walker A, Barrett JR, Lee W et al. Organisation and delivery of liaison psychiatry services in general hospitals in England: Results of a national survey. *BMJ Open.* 2018;**8**(8):e023091.

7. Jasmin K, Walker A, Guthrie E et al. Integrated liaison psychiatry services in England: A qualitative study of the views of liaison practitioners and acute hospital staffs from four distinctly different kinds of liaison service. *BMC Health Serv Res.* 2019;**19**(1):522.

8. Guthrie E, McMeekin A, Thomasson R et al. Opening the 'black box': Liaison psychiatry services and what they actually do. *BJPsych Bull.* 2016;**40**(4):175–80.

9. Guthrie EA, McMeekin AT, Khan S, Makin S, Shaw B, Longson D. An analysis of whether a working-age ward-based liaison psychiatry service requires the input of a liaison psychiatrist. *BJPsych Bull.* 2017;**41**(3):151–5.

10. Tadros GSRKP, Mustafa N, Johnson E, Pannell R, Hashmi M. Impact of an integrated rapid response psychiatric liaison team on quality improvement and cost savings: The Birmingham RAID model. *Psychiatrist.* 2013;**37**:4–10.

11. Becker LSR, Hardy R, Pilling S. *The RAID Model of Liaison Psychiatry: Report on the Evaluation of Four Pilot Services in East London.* London; 2016.

12. Breckon JKS, McClimnes A, Mubarak I, Burley K. *Adult Mental Health Hospital Liaison Service Evaluation.* Sheffield; 2016.

13. Durham and Darlington Liaison Service Evaluation Report. 2013.

14. House A, West R, Smith C, Tubeuf S, Guthrie E, Trigwell P. The effect of a hospital liaison psychiatry service on inpatient lengths of stay: Interrupted time series analysis using routinely collected NHS hospital episode statistics. *BMC Psychiatry.* 2020;**20**(1):27.

15. Wood R, Wand AP. The effectiveness of consultation-liaison psychiatry in the general hospital setting: A systematic review. *J Psychosom Res.* 2014;**76**(3):175–92.

16. National Institute for Health and Care Excellence. *Emergency and Acute Medical Care in Over 16s: Service Delivery and Organisation.* London; 2018.

17. Levenson JL, Hamer RM, Rossiter LF. A randomized controlled study of psychiatric consultation guided by screening in general medical inpatients. *Am J Psychiatry.* 1992;**149**(5):631–7.

18. Cole MG, Fenton FR, Engelsmann F, Mansouri I. Effectiveness of geriatric psychiatry consultation in an acute care hospital: A randomized clinical trial. *J Am Geriatr Soc.* 1991;**39**(12):1183–8.

19. Cole MG, McCusker J, Bellavance F et al. Systematic detection and multidisciplinary care of delirium in older medical inpatients: A randomized trial. *CMAJ.* 2002;**167**(7):753–9.

20. Cullum S, Tucker S, Todd C, Brayne C. Effectiveness of liaison psychiatric nursing in older medical inpatients with depression: A randomised controlled trial. *Age Ageing.* 2007;**36**(4):436–42.

21. Baldwin R, Pratt H, Goring H, Marriott A, Roberts C. Does a nurse-led mental health liaison service for older people reduce psychiatric morbidity in acute general medical wards? A randomised controlled trial. *Age Ageing.* 2004;**33**(5):472–8.

22. Slaets JP, Kauffmann RH, Duivenvoorden HJ, Pelemans W, Schudel WJ. A randomized trial of geriatric liaison intervention in elderly medical inpatients. *Psychosom Med.* 1997;**59**(6):585–91.

23. Talley S, Davis DS, Goicoechea N, Brown L, Barber LL. Effect of psychiatric liaison nurse specialist consultation on the care of medical-surgical patients with sitters. *Arch Psychiatr Nurs.* 1990;**4**(2):114–23.

24. Toynbee M, Walker J, Clay F et al. The effectiveness of inpatient consultation-liaison psychiatry service models: A systematic review of randomized trials. *Gen Hosp Psychiatry.* 2021;**71**:11–19.

25. Evans R, Connell J, Ablard S, Rimmer M, O'Keeffe C, Mason S. The impact of different liaison psychiatry models on the emergency department: A systematic review of the international evidence. *J Psychosom Res.* 2019;**119**:53–64.

26. Sinclair LHRHS, Nelson D, Hunt J. How effective are mental health nurses in A&E departments? *Emerg Med.* 2005;**23**:687–92.

27. Ngo DA, Ait-Daoud N, Rege SV et al. Differentials and trends in emergency department visits due to alcohol intoxication and co-occurring conditions among students in a U.S. public university. *Drug Alcohol Depend.* 2018;**183**:89–95.

28. McDonough S, Wynaden D, Finn M et al. Emergency department mental health triage consultancy service: An evaluation of

the first year of the service. *Accident & Emergency Nursing*. 2004;**12**:31–8.

29. Nielsen D, Klein EA. The care of mental health patients in the emergency department: One rural hospital's approach. *J Emerg Med*. 2009;**37**(4):430–2.

30. Lester NA, Thompson LR, Herget K et al. CALM interventions: Behavioural health crisis assessment, linkage, and management improve patient care. *Am J Med Qual*. 2018;**33**(1):65–71.

31. Mason SM. Frequent attendance at the emergency department is a symptom but not a disease. *Emerg Med J*. 2014;**31**:524–5.

32. NHS England. *Mental Health and A&E Pressures: Further Examples of Mental Health Schemes That Help Alleviate Operational A&E Pressures*. London; 2018.

33. Sousa S Hilder T, Burdess C et al. 2.5 years on: What are the effects of a 'frequent attenders' service in the Emergency Department? *BJPsych Bull*. 2019;**43**(3):112–16.

34. Ng A, Nadarajan V, McIver S et al. Frequent attendances to a London emergency department. *J Primary Care*. 2015;**7**:70–7.

35. Kontogeorgis D, Masoura C, Mhlanga Y. *Frequent Attenders Initiative*. Oxford Academic Health Science Network. Oxford; 2018.

36. Peddie S, Richardson S, Salt L, Ardagh M. Frequent attenders at emergency departments: Research regarding the utility of management plans fails to take into account the natural attrition of attendance. *N Z Med J*. 2011;**124**(1331):61–6.

37. LaCalle ERE. Frequent users of emergency departments: The myths, the data and the policy implications. *Ann Emerg Med*. 2009;**56**:42–8.

38. Colligan EM, Pines JM, Colantuoni E, Howell B, Wolff JL. Risk factors for persistent frequent emergency department use in Medicare beneficiaries. *Ann Emerg Med*. 2016;**67**(6):721–9.

39. Giannouchos TV, Washburn DJ, Kum HC, Sage WM, Ohsfeldt RL. Predictors of multiple emergency department utilization among frequent emergency department users in 3 states. *Med Care*. 2020;**58**(2):137–45.

40. Maruster L, van der Zee DJ, Hatenboer J, Buskens E. Tracing frequent users of regional care services using emergency medical services data: A networked approach. *BMJ Open*. 2020;**10**(5):e036139.

41. Althaus F, Paroz S, Hugli O et al. Effectiveness of interventions targeting frequent users of emergency departments: A systematic review. *Ann Emerg Med*. 2011;**58**(1):41–52, e42.

42. Soril LJ, Leggett LE, Lorenzetti DL, Noseworthy TW, Clement FM. Reducing frequent visits to the emergency department: A systematic review of interventions. *PLoS One*. 2015;**10**(4):e0123660.

43. Psychiatry RCoPFoL. *Liaison Psychiatry and the Management of Long-Term Conditions and Medically Unexplained Symptoms*. London; 2012.

44. Gillies D, Buykx P, Parker AG, Hetrick SE. Consultation liaison in primary care for people with mental disorders. *Cochrane Database Syst Rev*. 2015;**9**:CD007193.

Primary Care Consultation-Liaison Services

22

Chris Schofield and Philippa Bolton

Summary

This chapter aims to outline a model of how consultation-liaison teams can work as an effective service in primary care for complex patients with persistent physical symptoms. We will outline the patients who might be seen, the problems they may present with, the type of interventions that a primary care liaison team may provide and the type of staff mix you might need to provide those interventions. We will also look at how the team can influence healthcare across the primary care setting to improve outcomes both for patients and healthcare.

Definitions

For the purposes of this chapter, we will use the term 'functional disorders' to encompass disorders that have no specific organic disease correlates. A variety of diagnostic labels have been used previously to encompass these conditions but in the light of recent research, preference appears to trend towards functional disorders.

Case Examples

Case Vignette 1

Carol is a 54-year-old lady who has a history of complex physical symptoms spanning the last 15 years. This started with a fall that caused chronic back pain; she has subsequently developed problems with her bowel, which is thought to be irritable bowel syndrome (IBS), urinary retention for which she self-catheterises, nausea, problems with swallowing, headaches, palpitations and intermittent dizziness, high blood pressure, stress-induced asthma, obesity, and type 2 diabetes. She attends her primary care physician surgery on average every two weeks asking for help with her symptoms. She is open to cardiology for falls and syncope, the pain clinic, gastroenterology, urology and otorhinolaryngology. She does not want a referral to mental health as she says it is not 'all in my head'.

Case Vignette 2

Isaac is a 20-year-old geography student who has just received a diagnosis of non-epileptic attack disorder and functional weakness on his right side. He has been referred for treatment to your service.

Case Vignette 3

Neil is 34 and has chronic back pain. He is unemployed and stays in the house all day as he has agoraphobia and depression. He self-medicates his pain with cannabis and drinks four cans of lager every night to get to sleep. He has been referred to the pain service in the past but finds it difficult to attend appointments because of his anxiety, so often ends up discharged due to not attending. He is on 80 mg of morphine equivalent a day and the primary care physician wants to reduce and stop this, but Neil feels that he cannot cope without the medication and that he needs more.

Introduction

Patients like Carol, Neil and Isaac make up about 20% of a primary care physician's caseload but are not getting helpful treatments in the National Health Service (NHS) as it is set up at present. Prevalence data are similar in the USA (1). Most healthcare providers do not have services for patients with functional disorders; many find it difficult to engage people with long-term physical health conditions who have co-morbid mental health issues and who may need adaptations and support. Mental health services struggle with physical health conditions and siloed working between physical and mental health services means that there is often poor communication between services regarding how to manage patients with both physical and mental health disorders.

There are several intersecting issues within the NHS that adversely affect patients with functional symptoms. For example, there are issues of ownership: there can be reluctance to say 'this is our patient'. Mental health services focus on the physical symptoms and refer to acute services/primary care, just as acute services/primary care focus on mental health issues in these patients and refer to mental health services. Mental health services are often not directly impacted by patients with functional symptoms in the way that primary care and acute hospitals are affected (repeat attendance, resource-intensive); as such, there is less impetus for mental health services to implement assessment and treatment pathways for this patient group. Mental health services may not have access to data to prove cost-effectiveness in design and delivery of these pathways.

Acute services do not routinely integrate liaison mental services health or clinical health psychology into outpatient services. This leads to patchy provision across regions, and health practitioners in acute services do not have sufficient training and skills in mental health to treat these patients. Mental and physical healthcare for these patients is also often fragmented. As well as a lack of integration across professional disciplines, there is a lack of education within both mental health and physical health services about managing patients with functional symptoms and co-morbid physical and mental health conditions. Very few healthcare providers have mandatory training on these topics.

Logistical issues such as separate information technology systems with separate patient notes, information governance issues around notes and data-sharing and different ways of working cause significant issues with integrated care. It is extremely difficult to set up joint communication between primary care, mental health services and acute physicians to construct integrated care plans for patients.

Although therapists within Improving Access to Psychological Therapies (IAPT) could theoretically integrate into primary care and outpatient clinics for patients with long-term

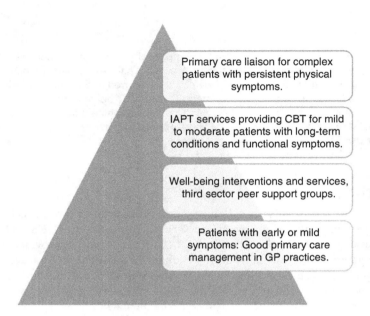

Figure 22.1 Tiered system for patients with functional disorders.

conditions, there are barriers to this prospect. These include agreed tariffs, which do not account for supervision or joint meetings with professionals, joint consultations with professionals or other aspects of integrated care. Services are only paid for individual contact with patients.

Most services are set up to treat 'disease' but most patients are struggling with symptoms, not diseases. There is a major gap in services for many patients and this is where a primary care consultation-liaison service can be instrumental in improving care for patients. These patients tend to fall between services as their symptom needs are so varied that they never get into a service that works for them. Primary care liaison is not the only service that might see these patients and it is helpful to think of a team in terms of being a 'step up' for complex patients that other services cannot manage. It can be positioned in the primary care setting as in Figure 22.1.

The step up is necessary. The therapists operating within IAPT can provide evidence-based cognitive behavioural therapy (CBT) for depression and anxiety in long-term conditions, including health anxiety, but as outlined earlier, they often have significant difficulty integrating into other services due to their strict commissioning arrangements. Patients with symptoms that require support from other Allied Health Practitioners, such as physiotherapy for functional neurological disorder, are not able to be treated in IAPT services, and IAPT do not provide more complex rehabilitation services for those patients who are significantly disabled by their physical symptoms.

Obviously, this is an oversimplified model and each area will have different services available for different conditions, for example a pain service, an IBS service, a chronic fatigue service. In essence, this is the problem – there is always a gap as there is no uniform commissioning and almost none of those services treat more than one condition, which is what patients often have.

So What Is the Function of a Primary Care Consultation-Liaison Service?

In summary, a primary care consultation-liaison service will see patients who are too complex psychiatrically for physical health services and too complex physically for mental health services to manage with one or more of the following:

- complex long-term conditions and functional conditions
- multiple symptoms
- multiple organs involved
- co-morbid mental health conditions
- no current defined service for their needs.

Symptoms: The Basic Sciences behind the Explanation

Before going further, it is important to understand that this is an area which encompasses a rapidly increasing field of research focused on how symptoms themselves are generated and maintained, and whether they are linked to disease. Historically, medical schools taught that physical symptoms and signs were simply correlates of organic disease, but we are becoming increasingly aware of a more complex, multifaceted relationship. This is illustrated in Table 22.1.

It is beyond the scope of this chapter to talk in depth about symptom mechanisms, but the authors would encourage further reading on this topic to gain a fuller understanding. In essence, symptoms are not 'medically unexplained'; they are 'medically starting to become understood'. Tangible, body-based explanations are most helpful for patients, so understanding symptom mechanisms is a vital basis for patient explanation (2). Reattributing symptoms to life events or 'stress' has not been shown to be effective and if the clinician

Table 22.1 Correlations between symptoms and disease

Symptoms that may have little or no disease correlation	Symptoms and disease correlate well	Symptoms and disease correlate poorly	Disease with little or no symptom correlation
Chronic pain	Sore throat and tonsilitis	Chronic obstructive pulmonary disease and breathlessness	Asymptomatic covid
Weakness, seizures, dizziness, etc. due to functional neurological disorders	Fever and sepsis	Chest pain post-heart attack	Hypertension
Bowel problems due to IBS	Pain and broken leg	Osteoarthritis and back pain	Mild type 2 diabetes
Fibromyalgia	Weight loss, polyuria, polydipsia and type 1 diabetes	Endometriosis and pain	Early ovarian cancer

leads with this, the patient is likely to develop the idea that the clinician thinks 'it is all in my head'. While a history of adverse childhood events (ACEs) represents a risk factor for persistent symptoms and other long-term conditions, and while stress can make many symptoms worse, this is not true for all patients, so an individual approach is necessary. Even though ACEs and stress can make things worse, it is still important to relate explanations to what is happening in the body. Examples from recent research are outlined next. They are also mapped to our case vignettes at the start of the chapter.

Changes in Neurological Function

Functional neurological disorder is a rapidly expanding area of research and changes in the way the brain communicates within itself and with the body are the basis for understanding how such symptoms are produced. This is a huge area but below are two examples of how this might work using functional dizziness and non-epileptic attack disorder.

A recently proposed mechanism for functional dizziness suggests that previous trauma to the vestibular system (e.g., an infection, a fall, etc.) results in the brain 'losing confidence' in that system and so it 'switches it off', choosing to rely on visual cues for balance. The visual system usually works in tandem with the vestibular system to help compute one's body position in space and is not good at this by itself. As such, patients will describe feeling seasick and the floor feeling unsteady, which is worse when tired or at night. The visual system is overworked in these patients, which leads to high levels of fatigue and difficulties with concentration on other tasks. To retrain the brain to have confidence in the vestibular system, CBT-informed physiotherapy is the treatment of choice, although the prognosis worsens after one year of untreated disease so early diagnosis is important.

Evidence is accumulating regarding the underlying mechanisms of non-epileptic attack disorder, but in relation to treatment, an interesting suggestion information is that attentional focus is locked internally during attacks. This may well explain why strong grounding techniques during the prodrome to an attack can work effectively to stop attacks occurring. So, when talking to Isaac, this information will help him understand the rationale for utilising these techniques (some of which, like the use of smelling salts as a very strong grounding technique, may seem a little strange at first!).

Body Changes: The Autonomic Nervous System, Hormones and Muscles

In patients with diffuse symptoms, such as Carol, it can be the case that their bodies have entered a chronic stress state which generates and maintains a wide range of unpleasant physical symptoms. In these patients, the parasympathetic nervous system is downregulated and the sympathetic nervous system is upregulated. If you think about the broad remit of the vagal nerve (the main representative of the parasympathetic system), you can see that the effects on the organs of the body can be substantial. If the vagal tone is reduced in the context of relative sympathetic overdrive, then patients can experience a complex range of symptoms: muscles around the throat tightening (globus pharyngeus), faster heart rate (including palpitations), shortness of breath, nausea, exacerbations of IBS and urinary voiding issues. Hormone changes, including cortisol, can cause issues with fatigue, increased pain sensitivity, reduced glycaemic control, high blood pressure, memory impairment and other difficulties. Chronic muscle tension and soreness leads to pain, fatigue, joint pain and headaches.

Understanding these mechanisms can help people understand why their bodies are producing symptoms and also provide a rationale for treatment. Demonstrating that someone's shoulders are tense and elevated and using this as an example of why they might get headaches can then lead to better understanding of why you might prescribe exercises like Pilates, yoga and tai chi, all of which are good for stretching out muscles, retraining breathing and improving vagal nerve function. Patients like Carol often end up with multiple specialities looking at individual parts; consultation-liaison input involves taking a step back and seeing how all the symptoms might have a common denominator which, if, addressed, might lead to a global improvement.

Chronic Pain

The field of pain science is helping us to understand that pain is a protective mechanism, not a sensory mechanism; it will produce pain as an alarm to elicit help-seeking behaviour (e.g. abdominal pain in appendicitis) or to stop you moving a broken or injured limb which might make it worse. But there are very poor correlates between pain and tissue damage, and the production of pain (and other symptoms) is hugely influenced by memory, emotion, attention, agency and circumstance. There are also mechanisms which attenuate pain, the significance of which are only starting to be understood.

Take Neil – he might have had an MRI which showed some degenerative (osteoarthritic) changes. Given that 50% of 50-year-olds who are asymptomatic have similar positive findings on MRI, such as osteoarthritic changes and disc bulges, is this really the principal driver of his pain? In chronic pain, the tissue damage has healed but the pain continues because the brain has trained itself to produce pain with movement as it believes it is protecting the body while it is healing but has not then 'switched off' this pain response after the healing process has completed. Pain becomes a conditioned response to movement rather than tissue damage.

We would recommend watching Lorimer Mosely's 'The Pain Revolution' (3) and 'Understanding Pain in Less Than 5 Minutes' (4) as a starting point to understand this further – these are great videos for patients to watch and can help with a shared understanding.

Going back to Neil, let's say he has been told he has osteoarthritis; this may lead to a belief that he will have long-term pain and that it will get worse. He believes he has no agency in managing his pain; he is depressed and feels hopeless about his pain. He is in the house all day with nothing to do apart from think about his pain. These factors coalesce and act as a volume dial to turn up his pain. Treatment would centre on education around pain and work to address the above issues to 'turn the volume dial down' on pain. Retraining the brain takes time – in the above case, you might work to increase agency through education and CBT, giving Neil tools that he can use to influence his pain. You might use eye movement desensitisation and reprocessing (EMDR) for the memory component of pain, graded exercise to overcome the conditioned responses that link movement with pain and antidepressants to improve mood and anxiety, which increase pain.

What Is the Team Makeup?

In order to help people like Carol, Neil and Isaac, a multidisciplinary team (MDT) is necessary as their needs are physical, psychiatric, psychological and social. Having a team that can have these elements covered while working in primary care is important.

The Durham and Nottinghamshire teams are both based on the MDT model and both have (with some slight differences) the following disciplines, the roles and remit of each will be discussed later in this chapter. Members of the MDT include mental health liaison nurses, physiotherapists, occupational therapists, psychologists, liaison psychiatrists, data analysts and admin staff.

Where Are Patients Seen?

Seeing the patient in the community, especially in their home, is a very valuable means of understanding their whole situation. The Nottinghamshire team see patients only in the person's home or in a primary care physician practice. This has opened up the assessment process in two ways. Understanding the situation that the patient finds themselves in day to day is very valuable. Having an MDT that can go into the home and assess from a medical, psychiatric, psychological, occupation therapy, physiotherapy and social care view enables fully integrated and holistic care planning. Also, patients that might be reluctant to attend hospital outpatient or community mental health team settings may be willing to attend their primary care physician surgery or accept home visits. This is particularly valuable for patients that are effectively housebound at the point of consultation.

Team flexibility enables patient contact to be tailored according to patient needs and progress. Visits may entail meeting outside for a walk in the park, or over a coffee, or taking them to a community group. Offering coping strategies, CBT and symptom management while helping a patient to get out of the house can be highly effective according to patient feedback. Feeling listened to and being treated as a whole person rather than disparate segments are also common areas of positive feedback for our primary care liaison service.

Team Meetings

Bringing a whole-person bio-psycho-social perspective and engaging a broad MDT for complex cases in team meetings is very important. It facilitates internal discussion within the team, in addition to informing wider consultation with other professionals involved in the patient's care. This often includes many hospital teams, but also community teams and general practice. Primary care liaison teams have a key role to play in terms of encouraging crosstalk between healthcare professionals such that mental and physical healthcare needs for individual patients are integrated and tackled using a 'same-page' approach. Education forms part of this role, with regular training session being offered to varied disciplines and settings.

Tips for Primary Care Physician and Juniors

Let's Think about One of Our Case Vignettes for a Moment

At the primary care physician complex-case MDT, which happens monthly, Carol is discussed. The primary care physicians do not know how to take things forward; she keeps presenting with symptoms and nothing is making them better. She will not engage with mental health services or with primary care liaison psychiatry. Consultation with the practice is vital in a case like this so that shared perspective-taking can take place with a mutually agreed plan as to how best to take things forward for Carol. Below is a list of do's and don'ts to help the practice understand how they can best help Carol.

Do

Wherever possible, see one primary care physician only, with a named alternative to cover. Consistency is key in Carol's situation. Although service constraints within the practice might pose barriers to this, shared medium- to long-term goal-setting such as reducing the number of consultations can result in a degree of flexibility to accommodate this critically important step. It should be noted that the patient will likely test the system in the early stages to see if it works. This is part of what should be expected.

See Carol for regular set appointments. Agree with the practice and Carol that if she feels that she needs to be seen out of those times, this should only be for new or dramatically worsened symptoms. If she requests a consultation regarding her usual symptom profile, she will be asked to discuss them at the next scheduled appointment.

Believe, clarify and understand Carol's symptoms with compassion and obtain relevant medical detail throughout. This is a vital part of treatment. When discussing pain, for example, what type, locations, how often, what does it feel like, when does it happen . . .?

If possible, have a one-off, longer appointment to map out a symptom timeline, go through what has and has not already been done in terms of referrals, tests and investigations, and define any areas that are still outstanding. Explain how tests can only show damage, so can rule out serious disease, but cannot show how the body is functioning and communicating with itself, so cannot tell Carol helpful information about why she is getting symptoms.

Agree that further tests will only be done if symptoms dramatically change or new symptoms arise. The testing process is not necessarily benign and can cause distress. Remember the 5% rule: 5% of tests come back with an abnormal result. The more you test unnecessarily, the more you will get unnecessary abnormal results which may be incidental and have no bearing on the current symptom profile.

It should be noted that having functional symptoms does not safeguard from future illness or disease. Therefore, in a patient with IBS, for example, if the new symptoms sound like cholecystitis, then test appropriately for cholecystitis. Do not just jump to 'it's your IBS'; listen well to the change of symptoms.

Review medication and rationalise as appropriate – many in this patient group are on multiple medications, some of which may be perpetuating or exacerbating some of their symptoms. Also find out what has and has not worked in the past in terms of medication, talking therapies and other treatments.

Work with Carol to provide helpful explanations in relation to her symptoms and point to relevant information, for example the pain toolkit (5). The consultation-liaison team can have a vital role in training primary care physicians how to do this. Screen for and treat any underlying anxiety and depression using helpful explanations, such as 'living with these kinds of symptoms can be really tough – I wonder how you have been coping?'; 'it sounds like your mood has become low, which can make living with these symptoms even harder. It might be worth considering an antidepressant to help support you with this'.

Work collaboratively with Carol to understand what makes things better and worse. Primary care physicians can be supervised to do basic symptom/activity diaries with her to explore this. Start giving Carol some basic tools to manage her symptoms, such as pacing and graded activity, relaxation exercises, education about exercise and so on. One of the key points of feedback we have had from primary care physicians is that with a care plan from the liaison team, they feel better able to manage the situation positively and proactively rather than feeling at a loss as to what to do next.

Don't

- Let Carol see lots of different primary care physicians. Different styles and messages may confuse things.
- Do more tests than necessary or repeat tests 'just in case'. This increases focus on symptoms and worry. People with acute back pain are more likely to develop chronic back pain if they are given an MRI as this reduces agency, increases attention and increases worry and belief that it is 'something serious', and so is more likely to dial up the pain response as the perceived level of threat has increased. Another key issue here is that tests will produce only short-term reassurance. Patients describe increasing anxiety leading up to a test and a sharp decrease when tests are negative but then, as symptoms persist, an increase back to the previous level until another test is done. This cycle continues and worsens over time – patients can end up despairing and fed up. Women with chronic pelvic pain spend on average eight years going round a cycle of tests until they 'drop out' of the NHS feeling demoralised and hopeless.
- Tell Carol that her tests are all normal so there is *nothing wrong with her*. This is not true and does not help Carol understand and manage her symptoms.
- Tell Carol that the symptoms are likely to be due to stress. Stress may or may not be a factor, but Carol needs to work with her primary care physician to discover this for herself or she is likely to think that you do not believe her.
- Tell Carol there is nothing more that anyone can do. Carol has symptoms she is struggling with; she needs the right support. Regular, therapeutic appointments with a primary care physician are extremely helpful in establishing a good starting point for gaining a better understanding of and managing symptoms.

Care Pathway; Initial Assessment and Psychoeducation

Patients are offered an initial assessment appointment, which is frequently undertaken by the team psychiatrist. This model is used in Durham as patients prefer seeing a psychiatrist initially and we observed much better attendance when this was introduced. The reason for this is that psychiatrists, being medical doctors, offer face validity to patients regarding the physical aspect of their presentation and are better placed to utilise a medical model in initial psychoeducation that combines a mind/body approach. Research from the North East Academic Health Sciences network has demonstrated that this is the most helpful way of engaging patients from a patient perspective. Interestingly, in Nottinghamshire, this model was used in the early stages of service delivery, but now the service is more firmly embedded. Nursing colleagues undertake a large proportion of initial assessments. This prevents bottlenecking of referrals around one individual and faster dissemination into the MDT for care planning. It should be highlighted that having a consultant psychiatrist dedicated to the team is an integral part of the patient care pathway. The psychiatrist is involved at some point in almost all the cases, though they may not be the initial point of contact.

The initial assessment involves understanding existing medical conditions, looking at co-morbid psychiatric conditions, initiating, reviewing and rationalising medication as appropriate, and offering initial psychoeducation. At this point, a small number of referrals are redirected to other mental health services as patients have been found to have other significant problems such as psychosis or risk issues that require input from an appropriate service.

Brief Psychological Intervention or Support Worker, Occupational Therapist or Physiotherapy Intervention

A CBT-informed approach will often be considered and is delivered by the liaison nurse, occupational therapist, physiotherapist or psychiatrist. Additional input is sometimes required from support workers to help the patient to improve levels of functioning, for example improving their range of activities, returning to independent travel and increasing confidence. This work is also based on a CBT model or uses behavioural activation approaches as an augmenting strategy. Some patients will leave the service following this intervention. For others, this intervention is a necessary step before embarking on more specific psychological interventions and is used to provide stability and scaffold so that they are able to engage in more in-depth psychological interventions safely.

Physiotherapy

The team physiotherapist will commonly see the following patients:

(1) Psychologically informed physiotherapy is a first-line, evidence-based treatment for functional motor disorders (e.g. tremor, gait disorders, paralysis, dystonia and sensory disturbance affecting mobility or coordination), so all these patients are seen early on in their treatment pathway. This is highly specialist work and few centres offer this type of intervention.

(2) Headache by reduction of muscle tension in the neck.

(3) Dizziness with vestibular retraining therapy.

(4) Functional breathing disorders using breathing retraining.

(5) Treatment for medically unexplained pain, with exercise and graded, paced, prescribed movement.

(6) Assessment and management of risk such as from falls.

All of the above conditions have evidence-based recommendations for physiotherapy as a treatment approach (6). We observe that our patients find a physiotherapy-based approach very helpful; they progress faster through treatment and have better functional outcomes.

Occupational Therapy

The occupational therapist plays a key role in the following scenarios:

(1) Assessment and management of risk – falls, domestic risk (cooking, managing stairs, accessing washing facilities, etc.) – and allowing a positive risk-taking approach to be used with patients: physical risk can only be managed to a certain point, and then the risks of avoiding activities are outweighed by the potential benefits of engaging with work, leisure and independence.

(2) Utilising appropriate short-term aids and adaptations in specialised way – aids and adaptations can exacerbate functional disorders and as such they require specialist consideration to mitigate against this. An example is the use of wheelchairs – patients are often put in wheelchairs because of fall risks. However, in functional disorders, wheelchairs reduce opportunities for normal movement, and the further patients move from independence, the less likely they are to recover.

(3) Improving patient functioning and independence by assessing patients and working with them to define goals and then breaking these into manageable and achievable 'mini goals', taking into account physical impairment and risks. An example might be, in non-epileptic attack disorder, working with the patient and family to tolerate a degree of 'risk' regarding seizures such as injury from falls, to allow independence, grading independence goals such as walking outside, going on a bus, going to a shop and so on, and then looking at realistic goals to get back to work. Someone with non-epileptic attacks may not be able to work in a building site on scaffolding but can work in an office. Supporting that person back to work by taking symptoms into account is extremely important.

(4) Working with patients in a graded and paced way to encourage helpful activities such as social groups and exercise, as well as work.

(5) Supervising and working with the support workers to put action plans in place which can then be reviewed.

As with physiotherapy, our occupational therapist can work with patients to significantly improve functioning and independence using skills specific to that profession. As a dual-trained professional (i.e. occupational therapists are trained in physical and mental health), they are well placed to deliver care for patients with physical and psychological symptoms.

For both physiotherapy and occupational therapy, appropriate skillsets have to be developed to enable successful interventional work with patients that have functional disorders. When working with this patient group, feedback from community physiotherapists and occupational therapists without specific training included:

(1) The patient cohort was too complex.

(2) Staff had no prior experience of patients with functional disorders and did not know how to move forwards with these cases.

(3) Staff did not liaise with the primary care consultation-liaison team, so an integrated approach was not implemented, to the detriment of the patient.

(4) The interventions that were delivered were too short to create sustained improvements. Many of these patients require more sessional time than these services are commissioned to provide.

(5) The interventions that were delivered were not always appropriate for patients with functional disorders and increased the risk of symptom exacerbation/perpetuation (e.g. putting in lots of aids and adaptations at an early stage such as a wheelchair).

Support Workers

Support workers are able to facilitate the work of the occupational therapist and physiotherapist by seeing patients in between sessions to practically support them with implementing the care plan. This may involve supporting the patient to engage in specific occupational activities, role-related actions, independence-related activities and physiotherapy exercises. This works especially well early on when gathering motivation and energy can be difficult for the patient.

Support workers can also be trained in delivering the pain toolkit (5). This is a guided self-help booklet for people who live with persistent pain, written by a pain rehabilitation specialist and an expert by experience. For patients with chronic pain, support staff work through the booklet with them, looking at a range of skills to manage chronic pain. This includes acceptance that the pain is present, grading and pacing activity and setting goals, plus stretching and relaxation skills.

The Data Analyst as a Team Member

Having some data analyst time dedicated to the service helps with generating outcome measures, and system metrics is very useful to show the impact of the service on patients and wider system demands. It also helps with integrating databases across healthcare systems to better integrate care.

Specific Psychological Input

Psychological input includes CBT for symptom management, health anxiety and low mood. It is most helpful if symptoms and mood/anxiety are managed together. An example would include graded exercise, mindfulness and meaningful activity as helpful interventions for both depression and pain management. Integrating mental and physical health issues in therapy is considered to be a better way forward. In terms of trauma-based therapies, approximately one-third of patients have symptoms directly related to trauma; a further third have had ACEs or trauma conferring increased risk of developing symptoms such as chronic pain; and the remaining third have no evidence of ACEs or trauma. EMDR can be used for trauma-based symptoms; over the last few years, EMDR specifically targeting symptoms is being increasingly used. In this therapeutic modality, the target is the symptom, not the trauma. Compassion-focussed therapy (CFT) can be helpful for some patients as there is a specific cohort that find pacing and grading of activity very difficult as they often are in caring/parental roles and struggle to validate and prioritise their own health needs. CFT can help them identify the flaws in this thinking and allow those patients to take time out to recharge.

Systemic Approaches

Some of our complex patients are frequent attenders at the primary care physician surgery, secondary care and/or emergency department. Systemic approaches across healthcare are necessary for these patients to prevent repeated, unnecessary investigations and treatments. Liaising with professionals who are recurrently involved to inform and encourage a 'same-page' approach is a critically important role of a consultation-liaison psychiatry service in the community.

Diagnosis and Medication

The consultation-liaison psychiatrist has specialist training in working with co-morbid physical and psychiatric illness and is well placed to consider an often complex list of diagnoses and medications. The liaison psychiatrist is well placed to provide a three-dimensional overview of the patient's medical and psychiatric diagnoses and how these may intersect. The psychiatric diagnostic formulation can also be appraised and reworked as appropriate. Over or underdiagnosis is not helpful. Although problem lists are very valuable and used regularly for all patients, diagnoses can help to unlock resources for patients where problem lists do not.

In terms of specialist prescribing skills, this often includes appraising the utility of polypharmacy and streamlining where appropriate, as both medications and side effects can accumulate. Pain or sleep medications are often prescribed but may be seldom reviewed. National Institute for Health and Care Excellence (NICE) guidelines for chronic pain recommend antidepressants as opposed to analgesia as first-line medication, yet patients are commonly prescribed analgesics and are not counselled regarding overuse syndromes. Assisting the primary care physician with specialist pain, sleep and psychotropic medication reviews can significantly reduce propensity for addictive and, when taken long term, unhelpful medication regimens. The teams in Durham and Nottinghamshire have observed dramatic reductions in opioid use and improvements in pain management.

Assessment and prescribing for co-morbid mental health are helpful as long as there is a clear rationale for both specialist review and a pharmacological approach, and the symptoms are monitored to assess efficacy. Prescribing can be complex as there is often polypharmacy. In our experience, many patients are very sensitive to medications. We use a graded approach to prescribing, using small doses and titrating upwards slowly, sometimes using liquid preparations in order to be able to effect this. Thoughtful prescribing with the patient fully aware of the rationale works best. Some primary care physician colleagues are understandably concerned that highly anxious patients with possible health anxiety could be made worse by having a detailed conversation about indications, interactions, time course and side effects. We find, however, that once patients are aware of our MDT approach and that medication is one part of a holistic treatment package, fruitful and meaningful conversations about medication can happen even with the most anxious patients.

The consultation-liaison psychiatrist prescribing toolkit also includes tailoring medication routes (oral, tablet liquid, sublingual), timings and dose variations (allowing patients to manage doses according to symptoms), such that prescribing becomes more collaborative and patient-centred, thus potentially improving concordance. Looking at the above approaches, how do they work for our patients Isaac and Neil?

Isaac

Isaac comes in for initial assessment with a psychiatrist. The psychiatrist has been able to read all the information from neurology. A full history is taken, which establishes he is experiencing dissociative seizures and functional left-sided weakness, which happened suddenly when he had been called to his head of faculty as he was behind on assignments. Isaac has always struggled with stress and emotional regulation and still has flashbacks and nightmares from his childhood trauma. He screens positive for moderate depression. His left-sided weakness has left him walking with a crutch and he is worried about going out alone because of seizures.

Plan

- Psychoeducation regarding his functional neurological disorders. This might include explaining that for the left-sided weakness, there is no damage in the body, but there is a problem with communication between the brain and the left side which is causing the weakness and this needs retraining.
- Explain that the retraining of the left side will need physiotherapy as a first step, and occupational therapy to support Isaac to use and not neglect the left side.
- Start with basic CBT for non-epileptic attack disorder.
- Treat depression with antidepressants.

- Build confidence to go out independently with the support worker in the team.
- Once these things are in place and Isaac's symptoms and functioning are stabilised, then consider EMDR for the post-traumatic stress disorder which will be a vulnerability factor for maintenance of symptoms and relapse.

Neil

Following assessment of Neil's pain, a comprehensive explanation of chronic pain is given. Neil does not have to believe it at first, but explain that as nothing else has worked, it is worth giving a new approach a try. The key shared goal would be to improve quality of life, not reduce pain (although this may well happen, it should *not* be the primary goal in terms of reframing expectations). As Neil finds it really difficult to get to appointments, initial appointments can be at home.

Plan

- Review medication and treat underlying depression and anxiety.
- A proportion of patients with chronic pain are tempted to trial cannabis, opiates and alcohol. In our experience, patients like Neil need to gain trust in the team and gain confidence in the therapeutic process before looking at reductions in those areas. Start with some small goal-setting with support worker help – for example, making sure Neil gets up, washed and dressed every day.
- Start with some basic and gentle physiotherapy to integrate with the chronic pain model that was explained to him and start some very gentle exercise. Gradually build up what Neil can do; start getting him out and about; accompany him to groups that can be supportive and build confidence. This would utilise a behavioural activation model of intervention. Start reducing cannabis, opiates and alcohol.
- Start using a CBT model to understand more about what is influencing his pain.
- Continue to increase activity until Neil feels that he has regained some quality of life and can independently manage his pain.

Always remember the route to better health is via wobbly lines! By this we mean most of us want each day to be an improvement on the last one. However, that is not how people get better. Some periods of time are hallmarked by improvement, yet at other times there is a dip. Just like walking up a mountain is not always in a linear, upwards direction, so walking to better health is not either. Sharing this metaphor early on can be helpful for patients beginning their therapeutic journey.

Useful Facts and Figures from Primary Care Consultation-Liaison Teams in Nottinghamshire

Case Mix

Demographics – patients seen the primary care liaison services:

2:1 female to male ratio

Average age 51

Regarding health inequalities at baseline measure:

> According to the index of multiple deprivation (IMD), our patients scored 21% lower than expected for their area
>
> The proportion of patients in Black, Asian and Minority-Ethnic groups is double that of the general population of Nottinghamshire (13% vs. 5.9%)
>
> Unemployment is double that of the general population of Nottinghamshire (25% vs. 49.9%)

Patient-Rated Outcome Measures (PROMS)

Both the Durham and Nottinghamshire teams collect the following PROMS.

PHQ-15 – Somatic Symptoms

We have found that the average patient is on the 96th centile for somatic symptoms scores. We suspect this is significantly above measures commonly encountered by community-based psychological therapy services for long-term conditions (IAPT-LTC).

Both teams have seen statistically significant reductions in PHQ-15 scores after six months, with patients generally transitioning from severe scores to moderate or mild scores.

PHQ-9 – Depression

Both services have shown statistically significant improvements, with patients generally transitioning from severe/moderate to mild scores.

GAD-7 – Anxiety

Both services have shown statistically significant improvements, with patients generally transitioning from severe/moderate to moderate/mild scores.

EQ-5D-5L – Whole-Health System Score

Both services have shown statistically significant improvements. Data from the Nottinghamshire team illustrate that at baseline, patients were leaving the house 2.5 times per week and after 6 months they were leaving 5.5 times per week (of note is that this data collection period included the COVID-19 period, March to October 2020).

In summary, the following transition is feasible according to our PROMS data collected thus far:

Baseline:

- Severe somatic symptoms
- Severe/moderate depression
- Severe anxiety
- Severe whole system
- Leaving house 2.5 days per week

After six months they have improved to:

- Mild/moderate somatic symptoms
- Mild depression
- Mild/moderate anxiety
- Moderate whole system
- Leaving house 5.5 days per week

It is important to note that the people that we see have high scores in multiple areas, which is why services with less of a multidisciplinary resource and/or holistic focus struggle to serve their needs. This is why a fully functional MDT in the community is required to look together at all the facets of the patient's condition. Coming together and working with the patient to facilitate understanding of their symptoms and the impact this has on them, and liaising with other services involved in their care, has a significant impact on a patient group that otherwise struggles to receive appropriate care.

Healthcare Utilisation Impact

The Nottinghamshire team undertook analysis of the premise that once people feel better, they tend to come and see health services less. We have been able to show that once patients' symptoms improve, their healthcare utilisation reduces and, as such, this bolsters the economic argument for services directly contributing to reduced healthcare utilisation (7, 8). Patients recurrently utilise healthcare services because their suffering continues and they have not yet received the help and support they need. Once this is delivered, they are able to lead more independent lives; many who were essentially housebound are then able to get out in their local area and a large proportion return to some form of paid work.

Using Clinical Commissioning Group (CCG) patient-level data, we have been able to show that patients had consistently high rates of healthcare utilisation in the 3.5 years prior to engaging with primary care liaison services, with significant reduction after eight months in the service. These improvements were maintained at least 18 months after discharge from the service. These timeframes support the argument that patients are not merely demonstrating regression to the mean after engaging with the liaison service for a period of time.

Acute Healthcare Provider Admissions after Eight Months in the Service

- Numbers of admissions −33%
- Emergency admissions −39%
- Length of stay −16%
- Admission CCG tariff costs −74%
- Emergency department attendance −32%

Outpatient appointments −32%

Primary Care

- Contacts −2%
- Referrals −20%
- Investigations −3%
- Acute appointments +30%
- Sick notes −31%

Ambulance usage −71%

Economic Impact

The Centre for Mental Health analysis shows that for each patient seen by a primary care liaison team, £524 is saved per year (7). Given that a three-year post-discharge effect is also observed, the service can reasonably claim four years' savings (approximately £2,000) per case (one year in service and three years after service). If, on average, 200 patients are seen every year, that equates to approximately £400,000 in savings. These metrics have shown that the Nottinghamshire service was cost-neutral after 15 months and cost-saving thereafter. As such, a holistic MDT approach involving collaboration between consultation-liaison mental health and primary care reduces symptom burden, resulting healthcare needs and healthcare costs. These findings could potentially facilitate dialogue with commissioning groups for those thinking of setting up similar services. This model of care has been of national interest and is published in the Kings Fund (8).

References

1. Hubley S, Uebelacker L, Eaton C. Managing medically unexplained symptoms in primary care: A narrative review and treatment recommendations. *Am J Lifestyle Med*. 2014;**10**(2):109–19.

2. Van der Kolk B. *The Body Keeps the Score*. London; 2015.

3. People in Pain Network. Professor Lorimer Mosley: The pain revolution (video). 2017. www.youtube.com/watch?v=nifGFIuVkUk.

4. Live Active Chiropractic. Understanding pain in less than 5 minutes, and what to do about it (video). 2013. www.youtube.com/watch?v=C_3phB93rvI.

5. Moore P. The pain toolkit. 2023. www.paintoolkit.org.

6. Nielsen G, Stone J, Matthews A et al. Physiotherapy for functional motor disorders: A consensus recommendation. *J Neurol Neurosurg Psychiatry*. 2015;**86**(10):1113–19.

7. O'Shea N. Centre for Mental Health. A new approach: Primary care psychological medicine first year evaluation. 2019. www.centreformentalhealth.org.uk/sites/default/files/2019-09/CentreforMH_A_New_Approach_To_Complex_Needs_0.pdf.

8. Naylor C, Taggart H, Charles A. The Kings Fund. Mental health and new models of care: Lessons from the vanguards. 2017. www.kingsfund.org.uk/sites/default/files/field/field_publication_file/MH_new_models_care_Kings_Fund_May_2017_0.pdf.

Emergency Department Psychiatry

Alex Thomson and Rikke Albert

Introduction

The emergency department (ED) is at the heart of the health system for responding to urgent health needs. In addition to patients with psychiatric emergencies, many patients attending ED with medical emergencies have concurrent mental health needs. Given the urgency, variety and need for clinical skills and systems leadership in a fast-paced environment, this area of liaison psychiatry is both challenging and rewarding as a field in which to develop specialist expertise.

Principles of Emergency Department Care

Triage and Side-by-Side Working

While the first clinical encounter in the ED is typically a triage assessment, an important principle of effective liaison psychiatry is to provide timely mental health assistance concurrently and in collaboration with emergency medicine colleagues. Triage should consider immediate medical needs, mental state and self-harm or suicide risk, with early involvement of liaison psychiatry (1). The focus should be on assistance: helping the patient access emergency medical care, advising referrers on investigation and treatment, advocating where necessary and arranging aftercare. Where patients have both physical and mental health needs, emergency medicine and liaison psychiatry should see and treat a patient concurrently (2). 'Assessment' is an ongoing process of history-taking, examination and therapeutic engagement rather than a discrete event to be conducted only once all medical care has been concluded. The advantages of a collaborative approach include:

- early recognition of needs and risk
- early alleviation of distress
- reduced rates of patients leaving before assessment and treatment is complete
- improved patient experience
- reduction in reported experiences of mental health stigma and discrimination.

The use of a screening checklist can safely identify patients who can be referred directly to liaison psychiatry without extensive medical assessment (3). Good working relationships between the ED and liaison psychiatry, with clear pathways and principles, can support effective side-by-side working and ultimately lead to better patient experience and outcomes (4, 5).

Diagnostic Overshadowing

Where a patient is identified as having an existing mental disorder, intellectual disability or cognitive dysfunction, diagnostic overshadowing refers to the cognitive error of attributing new medical symptoms to the existing condition (6, 7). Safeguards to mitigate the risk of diagnostic overshadowing include awareness of the concept, careful history-taking, availability of a 24/7 liaison psychiatry team that works collaboratively rather than waiting for 'medical clearance' and regular meetings between liaison psychiatry and ED staff (8). Participation in reflective practice and case reviews of missed diagnoses may help.

Patient Experience and Responding to Distress

While good clinical knowledge of the wide range of mental disorders and needs encountered in the ED is essential, the ability to relate to patients and carers is equally so. This requires listening, collaboration and supporting the patient during their time in ED and beyond. The role of a good liaison psychiatry service is far broader than conducting a discrete assessment to determine whether a patient needs admission or any follow-up, and includes optimising patients' experience of care during their stay in the department.

The nature of a mental health crisis, the physical environment, interpersonal relationships and the manner of staff can all alleviate or worsen a patient's distress (4, 9). Teams who have awareness of these factors, and leadership who support staff to be creative in their response, do better in supporting the patient (10). Appreciation of the principles of trauma-informed care and how previous experiences, both in health-care and beyond, may lead to a patient feeling unsafe can help alleviate a patient's distress.

De-escalation

The principle of de-escalation is to work with a patient who is distressed, agitated or aroused to explore and address what is causing the distress (see also Chapter 11 for further detail). Expression of distress may be directed towards the patient themselves or towards others and can be verbal or physical in nature. Agitation may stem from feelings of fear, stress or pain. Therefore, it is important to consider and recognise these drivers as a first step in responding to a patient. As well as preventing escalation in patients' distress, the aim should be to avoid an escalation of staff response, with a focus on minimising the use of restriction or coercion (10).

- Consider the environment: invite the patient to move to a quieter area; consider sitting down alongside them rather than opposite.
- Consider who is with the patient: uniformed staff such as security guards or police officers can be intimidating and aggravate a situation – unless absolutely necessary, try to keep uniformed staff out of sight or at a distance. Consider having carers or friends present to support the patient.
- Consider the patient's needs: try and find out why they are distressed – for example pain, hunger, thirst, fear, stress, frustration with waiting – and try to alleviate these.
- Address communication needs: lack of information from staff or difficulty with communication or understanding can increase frustration.

Rapid Tranquillisation

Where a patient is visibly very distressed, agitated or aggressive to others and is not responding to verbal or environmental approaches, the priority must be to alleviate their distress and ensure safety. This may require the use of sedating or tranquillising drugs (see Chapter 11). Prolonged distress or insomnia prior to arrival in the ED may worsen agitation, so helping the patient to rest may allow recovery, with ongoing assessment and development of a treatment plan once they are more alert. It is never appropriate to withhold treatment that might alleviate distress for fear that rapid tranquillisation might prolong a patient's time in the ED or delay statutory assessments under mental health law. The choice of medicines for rapid tranquillisation may depend on what is available as stock in the ED and a patient's concurrent medical needs, such as cardiovascular or respiratory disease (11).

Ending Mechanical Restraint

Police officers may use handcuffs and leg restraints to facilitate conveyance, and patients in the ED may still be mechanically restrained. Beyond the obvious issues related to dignity and emotional trauma, restraint is a clinical emergency, associated with risk of injury and death (12). The pain and restriction caused by mechanical restraint worsen agitation, which can be misinterpreted as justifying the need to continue restraint. Urgent assistance from liaison psychiatry is needed alongside emergency medicine and police to end the restraint as soon as possible. Regular communication and negotiation between all parties – including the patient and any carers – is essential. The first step is to consider simply removing the restraints: they may not have been applied because of violence or dangerousness but merely to facilitate conveyance. Where a patient appears too restless to completely remove restraints, consider verbal de-escalation, environmental measures, one-to-one nursing observation and a gradual stepping down of the level of restraint, for example moving hands from behind the back to in front of the patient, or from cuffing to trolley rails to hands cuffed together. Evaluation of response to the change may allow a decision about removal. The next stage is to consider rapid tranquillisation, with removal of mechanical restraint as soon as possible.

Frequent Attendance

Patients attend the ED at varying rates, from occasional or no visits to very frequent visits. There is little consensus on what rate of attendance is considered 'frequent', and various values have been proposed. A statistical analysis of one UK ED population found that five or more ED attendances in 12 months is unlikely to be attributable to chance (13). Frequent attendance is a characteristic of clinical systems rather than individual patients: a state-wide USA study found that 71.2% of patients who attended frequently in one year did not do so the following year, and a longitudinal UK study found similar year-on-year variation in patients' attendance patterns (14, 15). There has been longstanding stigma towards this group of patients with an added risk of diagnostic overshadowing by staff becoming complacent about the patient's needs (16, 17).

Risk factors for frequent ED attendance include long-term conditions such as medical illnesses, mental disorders and addictions, deprivation, and social adversity such as domestic violence or homelessness (see Chapter 17) (18). Frequent ED attendance is therefore dependent on local context and service availability, and should be seen as a red flag for vulnerability and unmet needs. Some services have trialled the use of behavioural interventions for frequent attendance, including anticipatory care plans which pre-emptively exclude patients from mental healthcare, and criminal sanctions such as prosecution, imprisonment or community orders for alleged offences associated with self-harm or suicidality (19–21). Such approaches raise serious ethical and safety concerns and there is no evidence to support their effectiveness (22–24). Identifying factors associated with frequent ED attendances can help improve care for individual patients and inform improvements in the wider health and social care system. Additionally, there is some evidence that case management and advance care planning can improve outcomes (25). A combination of a person-centred approach to preventative care planning, good relations with community health and social care services and a systems-focussed approach to identifying and addressing gaps or access barriers may reduce the likelihood of emergencies arising or care defaulting to the ED.

Stigma, Discrimination and Abuse

Antipathy and prejudice towards people with mental disorders persist in wider society and in healthcare services (26, 27). While overt physical or sexual abuse is thankfully rare, there is contemporary evidence that less visible forms of abuse and discriminatory staff behaviour remain unacceptably prevalent (4, 28–31). Microaggressions are defined as brief derogatory slights or insults, communicated verbally, behaviourally or environmentally, for example telling a patient that they are inappropriately taking up space in the ED during a psychiatric emergency (32). Structural discrimination includes removing the trolley from a cubicle so the patient has nowhere to lie down, routine use of security guards or police officers for one-to-one care more appropriately performed by a nurse and routine use of cage vehicles for transport of non-violent patients.

More overt abuse includes verbal and emotional abuse, physical abuse such as intentionally inflicting pain by suturing or debriding injuries without anaesthetic and vexatious exclusion from emergency treatment (33–35). These are rarely done in sight of staff who may challenge them, and the latter may be particularly challenging to differentiate from poor practice: despite UK-wide standards recommending that patients who have self-harmed receive a psychosocial assessment of needs and risk from a suitably skilled practitioner on every occasion, in practice this only happens on 53.2% of ED attendances (23, 36, 37). Behaviour modification approaches involving punishment or non-attention are outdated and unacceptable in contemporary clinical practice, though they may linger behind such pejorative terms as 'attention-seeking' and 'manipulative' and behind such practices as pre-emptive exclusionary care plans or misuse of 'capacity' as a justification for refusing referrals (38).

Addressing stigma, discrimination and abuse requires a combination of preventative and reactive measures focussed on staff culture and behaviour. There is little evidence to guide anti-stigma interventions in healthcare settings (39, 40). Externally facilitated reflective practice can help to prevent groupthink and closed cultures, as can membership of a peer accreditation network (41). Inspectorates have an important role in addressing closed cultures (42). Active bystander interventions have been developed to address problematic cultures in other spheres and may have value in addressing derogatory comments or behaviour in the moment (43). Overall, both bottom-up and top-down approaches are necessary, including the development of consensus among leaders that such conduct is unacceptable, strong emphasis on preventative measures and the use of zero-tolerance approaches where appropriate.

Consent, Capacity and Leaving the Department

Colleagues in the ED may need assistance with the assessment of capacity in relation to decisions about medical care or leaving the department (see also Chapter 16). While the process of seeking informed consent and assessing capacity should be done by the clinician who is providing the specific care, they may need specialist guidance and joint assessment by liaison psychiatry, following the principle of side-by-side working.

Although most patients who leave before assessment and treatment is complete are 'low acuity', rates of adverse outcomes are higher (44). The initial assessments from ED and liaison psychiatry should consider how to support patients to stay until assessment and treatment is complete. The most consistent factor associated with leaving before treatment is complete is long waiting times (45). There may be other reasons related to experience and environment rather than patient characteristics, for example apprehension based on previous aversive experiences, an unwelcoming environment, being supervised by security guards, stigmatising staff responses and fear of being detained.

The rate of patients leaving can be minimised by addressing these factors: improving the environment; fostering a respectful, caring culture towards patients with mental health needs; providing written information as well as regular updates on progress; and stopping the use of security guards for one-to-one nursing observations. Delays should be minimised by appropriate triaging, eradicating delays caused by waits for 'medical clearance' and improving efficiency of emergency mental health pathways beyond the liaison psychiatry response (2, 23).

Where a patient is refusing treatment or wanting to leave before treatment is complete, any action to override their wishes must be a last resort after attempts at negotiation and compromise, authorised by mental health or capacity law, compatible with their best interests, and represent the least restrictive course of action. Response should be proportionate and based on clinical judgement, including attempts to contact the patient or carers and handover to community mental health services to follow-up or visit at home. Routinely calling police for 'welfare checks' can expose patients to risk of physical violence and criminalisation, and should only be a last resort where there is an imminent and high probability of serious harm (46, 47).

Specific Conditions

Mania and Psychosis

Patients may attend the ED with hallucinations, delusions, elevated mood and associated distress or dysfunction. It is necessary to determine who may need investigation for organic causes of psychosis (48). Refer to Chapters 10 and 12 for further detail. Close collaboration with the treating team is essential and, where available, liaison with colleagues in neurosciences (neurology, neuropsychiatry, neuropsychology) can further diagnostic pursuit and treatment options.

Where a patient is distressed or agitated, address interpersonal and environmental factors which may lead to overstimulation by ensuring access to a calm, quiet space. Offer the patient their regular medicines and consider offering a sedative or hypnotic; insomnia is a significant exacerbating factor and allowing a patient to sleep or rest while consulting family or carers can help address immediate distress or safety concerns and assist with determining whether hospital admission is warranted. If there is concern about self-neglect, consider assessing nutrition and hydration and checking for injuries, and consider the management of any concurrent medical conditions.

People with long-term mental disorders may attend the ED with emergency medical needs. In such situations, the liaison psychiatry team plays a role in helping to advise referrers and supporting and advocating for the patient to engage in and receive appropriate medical care.

Delirium

Delirium is a medical emergency, associated with increased six-month mortality (49). The standard of care for delirium should therefore be primary management by acute and emergency medicine or geriatrics, with advice and support from liaison psychiatry where necessary. Indications for referral and joint management include assisting with making the diagnosis, advising on investigation and management, supporting a fearful or distressed patient, training and advising colleagues, and advising on mental health and capacity law. There are comprehensive clinical guidelines focussed on assessment and management of delirium, including those published by Healthcare Improvement Scotland (50).

Delirium describes acute clouding of consciousness secondary to physiological disturbance. It is a clinical diagnosis based on acuity of onset, fluctuating course and impaired attention. Risk factors for delirium in ED include nursing home residence, cognitive impairment, hearing impairment and a history of stroke (51). Although differential diagnoses include severe depression and progression of existing dementia, these conditions are risk factors for delirium, which may occur without significant physiological insult. Careful history-taking from an informant of the onset and course, along with the use of brief standardised tools, are the keys to diagnosis. Newly detected dementia is less likely; where this is suspected, more detailed cognitive assessment should be deferred until follow-up, when a patient is optimised and in a familiar environment (52). Brain imaging is indicated with neurological abnormalities, head trauma or falls, though is not useful routinely for delirium (50). Clinical investigations can identify the cause but normal investigations cannot 'rule out' delirium. It is possible that basic screening has not identified the cause, or that a transient self-limiting illness has precipitated an episode of delirium that may take longer to fully remit.

Management should focus on correcting any identified medical conditions, alleviating pain and attention to nutrition, hydration and environment, with regular orientation to time and place, facilitating visits by familiar people and early supported discharge to a familiar environment. There is little evidence for pharmacological interventions. Antipsychotics do not reduce the duration or severity of delirium, though empirical use of analgesia for unidentified pain should be considered (51, 53). Rapid tranquillisation should only be considered as a last resort for extreme agitation or distress, and in low doses with caution to not exacerbate confusion.

Anxiety Disorders

People with generalised anxiety disorder, post-traumatic stress disorder, obsessive-compulsive disorder and related conditions may attend the ED acutely with overwhelming distress, self-harm or suicide attempts or in crisis (54). Liaison psychiatry staff can assist with reassurance, support to engage with medical care, assessment of immediate needs and referral for aftercare and treatment (55). People may also attend with physical symptoms or health anxiety. The balance between diagnostic overshadowing and over-investigation is challenging. Ideally, the ED should be planned in collaboration with appropriate outpatient treatment, which may involve the development of care plans for future ED attendance, with the consent of the patient.

Intellectual Disability

People with intellectual disabilities attend the ED with both medical and mental health needs, requiring either assistance and advocacy to facilitate medical assessment or a mental health assessment. Caution must be taken to avoid diagnostic overshadowing, for example if agitation or a change in behaviour arises from pain. The skills which the teams have around communication and engagement are transferable to patients with intellectual disabilities. Family members and carers should be contacted, consulted and involved in care. Patients with intellectual disabilities have higher rates of self-harm and suicide (56). The assessment may need to be adapted to ensure the patient is able to engage with the assessment but the principle of engagement and joint decisions is as relevant to this group of patients as others.

Suicidality and Self-Harm

As well as attending the ED following self-harm or a suicide attempt, people may seek help with thoughts of suicide prior to an attempt. It is preferable to deliver care which may prevent self-harm rather than to respond after the event. The principles of prompt, side-by-side response, including seeing and speaking to the patient on every occasion, should be applied to suicidality in the same way as to self-harm (23, 37). Ascertain whether someone disclosing suicidality has already harmed themselves. As far as possible, response, treatment and psychosocial interventions for self-harm should be condition-specific and needs-specific, following a diagnostic assessment, formulation and assessment of needs (see Chapter 5 for further detail).

Liaison psychiatry has an important role in addressing the stigma and discrimination associated with self-harm in the ED setting. Teaching and role-modelling in responses to the patient is essential. For emergency medicine colleagues, suicide risk assessment is a source of anxiety which may influence their response to the patient. Understanding this dynamic is important when role-modelling communication and care to ED colleagues. Regular teaching focussing on communication with patients attending the ED with mental health needs is useful. See Chapter 18.

Alcohol and Other Drugs

Around 70% of ED attendances are alcohol- and drug-related. Understanding how drugs and alcohol impact on the patient's mental health or manifest as a mental illness is important in supporting patients. Although attendances of patients with apparently avoidable intoxication-related injuries may cause frustration to emergency medicine staff, it is important to ensure that patients with addiction-related needs are able to access emergency care without encountering judgemental responses (57).

Although most patients attending the ED while intoxicated do not need the attention of mental health services, liaison psychiatry has important roles in collaborative care with emergency and acute medicine, including assisting with diagnosis, advising on immediate management of emergencies associated with both intoxication and withdrawal states, advocacy and support to facilitate medical care, and arranging onward care. Hallucinations, delusions and agitation may arise from intoxication with stimulants, hallucinogens and novel psychoactive substances, particularly synthetic cannabinoids and cathinones. Neuropsychiatric emergencies leading to altered consciousness include delirium tremens, Wernicke's encephalopathy and gamma-butyrolactone (GBL) withdrawal delirium; such patients will usually need medical admission with joint liaison psychiatry care. Alcohol and other drug use is covered in Chapters 8 and 9.

Factitious Disorder and Malingering

Intentional feigning of symptoms or signs is rare. A far bigger problem is the incorrect assumption that a patient is feigning when they are not (58). Self-harm by swallowing objects or insertion in body cavities is not factitious disorder unless there is evidence of intent to deceive and should be approached as other forms of self-harm. Diagnosis of factitious disorder is a subspecialist area: although making a diagnosis may be necessary to minimise harm from non-indicated investigations or treatments, it exposes a patient to considerable risk of other harms, including exclusion from medical and psychiatric treatment and punitive treatment by staff who may react angrily to the suggestion that they have been deceived. The diagnosis should never be made during an emergency situation and only after subspecialist assessment and consultation with colleagues in the specialties associated with the suspected feigning (59).

People who have factitious disorder deserve respect, compassion and dignity, and may need longer-term psychotherapy. The role of liaison psychiatry in the ED is to educate staff, to advocate and to safeguard against derogatory treatment. The diagnosis and its implication for investigation and treatment must be explained openly to the patient. Where a patient has a combination of recognised medical or psychiatric conditions alongside symptoms believed to be feigned, inter-specialty collaboration and open discussion with the patient are necessary to develop an approach to investigation and treatment.

Adversity and Crisis

Safeguarding and Protection

All hospital staff are responsible for identifying safeguarding and protection concerns. Domestic violence and abuse, violent crime and other forms of abuse are perpetrated against people with mental disorders at higher rates (60, 61). Routine enquiry for domestic violence and other types of abuse is recommended as part of mental health assessment, particularly where other risk factors exist, for example ethnic minority, marginalised sexual orientation or gender, self-harm, pregnancy, unexplained injury or frequent ED attendance (35, 62).

Patients may have responsibilities as parents or carers. Considering how mental health affects caring responsibilities and support needs should be a core aspect of assessment. Many patients describe fears of being judged as an unfit parent or carer and this is a factor in people not seeking help. Any discussion around safeguarding or support should be done sensitively, taking this fear into account (63).

Homelessness

Homelessness, including rough sleeping, sofa surfing, temporary accommodation and hostels, has a considerable adverse impact on mental health. Homelessness can be a considerable barrier to accessing non-emergency care, which may lead to the ED becoming the default point of access. Mental disorders are prevalent in homeless people. In a recent UK homeless health needs audit, 86% of respondents reported having a diagnosed or undiagnosed mental health issue, with 44% reporting a diagnosed mental disorder, most commonly depression in 34% (64). Mental disorders, social deprivation and harmful drug or alcohol use are all associated with higher suicide rates. However, people with a combination of alcohol- or other drug-related needs and mental health needs may be mistakenly judged as 'low risk' (65). Homelessness may also be a symptom of reduced functioning as a result of the mental illness. Healthcare staff have an ethical duty, and in some countries a legal duty, to refer homeless patients to statutory housing services. It is important to be familiar with local services and ensure that homeless patients are offered referral to local services, key working and legal advice (66–68).

Refugees and Asylum Seekers

Refugees, asylum seekers and people with immigration-related issues face barriers to accessing healthcare, which may lead to higher rates of emergencies as well as non-emergency care defaulting to the ED. Prolonged insecurity and uncertainty during the asylum application process may exacerbate any existing mental disorders. Refusal of asylum claims may be associated with decompensation due to the experience of not being believed, threat of return to a dangerous place and loss of financial support, accommodation and entitlement to free healthcare. In addition to assessment for mental disorders and treatment planning, it is important to be aware of how to access legal support, financial assistance, accommodation and specialist support for survivors of torture (69).

Service Configuration

Integration with Mental Health Services

Within the acute hospital, attention needs to be given to fostering collaborative working between mental health staff and services with different areas of focus, addiction specialists, intellectual disability, neuropsychiatry and perinatal psychiatry. This includes agreeing joint working arrangements, referral processes and lines of responsibility both in and out of hours, and collaborating on anticipatory care plans or 'hospital passports'. Providing paediatric, adult and old-age liaison psychiatry may involve a combination of collaborative working and access to age-appropriate expertise (70, 71).

Governance

Shared regular meetings between the liaison psychiatry team and ED is important to share learning from an incident. It also fosters a culture of integrated working and can add to a positive mental health culture in the department. Some EDs have 'Morbidity and Mortality' reviews where the clinical teams jointly review specific patient care; this is another example of sharing learning and improve working relationships (72). Relationships should be maintained with local police, with clear agreements for prompt response to patients conveyed to hospital under police powers for statutory mental health assessment.

Staffing

Staffing requirements depend on the local needs and activity. Sufficient staff are needed on site to ensure prompt response to referrals, with access to senior decision-making, leadership and treatment advice both in and out of hours. This includes psychiatric liaison nurses, junior doctors, consultant liaison psychiatrists or on-call consultants, and allied health professionals including psychologists, occupational therapists, pharmacists and social workers. Guidelines and staffing models have been developed (73). Where one-to-one observation is required, EDs must have arrangements for staffing that avoid the use of security guards (23).

Facilities in the Emergency Department

Given that mental health emergency response is a core responsibility of EDs, facilities must be designed to meet patients' needs. Good ED design and facilities will also meet the needs of a broader range of patients, including patients with dementia, victims of sexual assault and bereaved or concerned family members. Standards for mental health facilities in the ED include ensuring adequate privacy, lines of sight, appropriate décor, access to alarms, reduced ligature points and appropriate exit doors (70). Patients need access to food, drink, regular medicines and appropriate comfort such as blankets and a place to lie down; having basic needs met can help reduce some distress. The liaison psychiatry team base should ideally be located close to the ED.

Mental Health Emergency Centres/Psychiatric Decision Units

The coronavirus pandemic has accelerated the development of areas designed for immediate assessment and treatment of psychiatric emergencies, variously known as mental health emergency centres, psychiatric decision units or assessment hubs. Models include integrated centres as part of the ED, co-located centres on the same hospital site as ED and fully segregated centres on a different site. Systematic evaluation of the pros and cons has not kept pace with the rate of change, and there is so far little research evidence on which to base recommendations. The following principles should be considered (74):

- Most patients referred to liaison psychiatry in the ED have concurrent medical needs and so cannot be 'diverted' to a segregated centre.
- Where areas do not yet have a fully resourced liaison psychiatry team, the focus of investment should be establishing already-evaluated models of care.
- Segregated centres on different sites risk reinforcing structural discrimination and prejudices that people with mental health needs do not 'belong' in the ED.
- It is important that they do not become merely holding spaces that subject patients to repeated reassessments or hide delays in admissions to wards.
- Integrated or co-located centres may add considerable value if they facilitate access to social interventions, early prescribing reviews and access to psychological therapies.

Follow-Up Clinics

Follow-up clinics can target specific types of presentations to the ED such as self-harm, frequent attending, drugs and alcohol, and medically unexplained symptoms. Clinic can be a supportive way to provide follow-up and reflection on the crisis that led to the attendance and a check-in point to see if the crisis plan is working. For patients who have attended with medically unexplained symptoms or health anxieties, meeting with liaison psychiatry staff who specialise in the interface between physical and mental health is helpful.

Training

Training focussing on communication, person-centred care and the challenges of stigma and recognising bias should be an important part of education for ED staff. Regular discussions and training around assessments of mental health needs can help improve the confidence of staff working in the ED. It is not only a good thing to do – it can also help reduce the rates of burn-out in ED staff. Training and reflection on the challenges of working in the ED setting can improve care for patients with mental illnesses as well as staff stress. Equally, all new staff, whether trainees, locum or permanent staff, should receive regular training on working with patients in a mental health crisis, including assessment of suicidality and formulating a person-centred care plan (75).

Regular teaching sessions by the liaison psychiatry team can increase ED staff understanding of the experiences of crisis. They should include the importance of good communication skills, calm environments and the attitude of staff.

Outcome Measurement

The sheer variety of conditions and interventions seen in the ED, along with the brief time of contact, makes routine outcome measurement challenging and results in a focus on process measures such as referral numbers, response times and time in department. Although these measures are important – it is not possible to deliver high-quality care if it involves lengthy delays – there is a risk of unintended consequences: it is certainly possible to deliver very quick, though not necessarily helpful responses. The balanced scorecard approach of the Framework for Routine Outcome Measurement in Liaison Psychiatry, which includes clinician-rated outcomes, patient experience and referrer experience, is therefore recommended for benchmarking and service improvement (76). In the ED, patient and carer experience should be viewed as an important reflection of high-quality care and more detailed measures considered (77).

The brevity and acuity of ED attendances present challenges in routine outcome measurement. Multiple approaches to collecting outcomes and feedback may be needed, including asking in the department, follow-up after discharge, paper forms, online surveys and approaches through service user groups. The most important aspect is to ensure that outcomes are collected for a clear purpose, including regular feedback to staff, and guiding service improvement.

Onward Care

Where patients are being discharged home, arranging a taxi or transport should be considered in discharge planning. Patients brought to the ED by ambulance or police may not have brought money, may not be wearing suitable clothing and may not be in an appropriate frame of mind to negotiate public transport. A patient in distress leaving hospital is at risk of being targeted or assaulted, particularly overnight. Where discharge is proposed, it is never appropriate to use security or police to eject a non-violent patient who does not feel safe to leave hospital. Rather, the patient should be allowed a little more time to gather themselves and consider their options. If they are completely unable to leave the department, it will be necessary to revisit the management plan in collaboration with the patient, their carers and family, and any regular services involved in their care.

For all the challenges inherent in the integration of mental health services into acute and emergency medicine, it can be a challenge of equal magnitude to ensure liaison psychiatry is seamlessly integrated with other parts of the mental healthcare system. Beyond the acute hospital, integration is needed with inpatient, crisis and community mental health services. These need to consider arrangements for prompt statutory assessment under mental health law, for medical assessment and medical handover prior to transfer to inpatient psychiatric wards, and for minimising repeated reassessment prior to giving support and treatment (78). Awareness of other local community services is important, for example social prescribing, day centres and support groups.

References

1. Sands N, Elsom S, Colgate R, Haylor H, Prematunga R. Development and interrater reliability of the UK Mental Health Triage Scale. *Int J Ment Health Nurs*. 2016;**25**(4):330–6.

2. Brown S, Eales S, Hayhurst C et al. Side by side: A UK-wide consensus statement on working together to help patients with mental health needs in acute hospitals. The Royal College of Psychiatrists, The Royal College of Nursing, The Royal College of Emergency Medicine and The Royal College of Physicians. 2020, p. 8. www.rcpsych.ac.uk/docs/default-source/members/faculties/liaison-psychiatry/liaison-sidebyside.pdf.

3. Shah SJ, Fiorito M, McNamara RM. A screening tool to medically clear psychiatric patients in the emergency department. *J Emerg Med*. 2012;**43**(5):871–5.

4. Carstensen K, Lou S, Groth Jensen L et al. Psychiatric service users' experiences of emergency departments: A CERQual review of qualitative studies. *Nord J Psychiatry*. 2017;**71**(4):315–23.

5. The National Confidential Enquiry into Patient Outcome and Death. Treat as one. London; 2017.

6. Happell B, Ewart SB, Bocking J, Platania-Phung C, Stanton R. 'That red flag on your file': Misinterpreting physical symptoms as mental illness. *J Clin Nurs*. 2016;**25**(19–20):2933–42.

7. Thornicroft G, Rose D, Kassam A. Discrimination in health care against people with mental illness. *Int Rev Psychiatry*. 2007;**19**(2):113–22.

8. Shefer G, Cross S, Howard LM, Murray J, Thornicroft G, Henderson C. Improving the diagnosis of physical illness in patients with mental illness who present in emergency departments: Consensus study. *J Psychosom Res*. 2015;**78**(4):346–51.

9. Quinlivan LM, Gorman L, Littlewood DL et al. 'Relieved to be seen': Patient and carer experiences of psychosocial assessment in the emergency department following self-harm – Qualitative analysis of 102 free-text survey responses. *BMJ Open*. 2021;**11**(5):e044434.

10. NHS Protect. Meeting needs and reducing distress: Guidance on the prevention and management of clinically related challenging behaviour in NHS settings . London; 2013. www.crisisprevention.com/CPI/media/Media/Blogs/Meeting-needs-and-reducing-distress-NHS-Protect-CB.pdf.

11. National Institute for Health and Care Excellence. Violence and aggression: Short-term management in mental health, health and community settings . London; 2015. Report no. NG10. www.nice.org.uk/guidance/NG10.

12. Strömmer EMF, Leith W, Zeegers MP, Freeman MD. The role of restraint in fatal excited delirium: A research synthesis and

pooled analysis. *Forensic Sci Med Pathol.* 2020;**16**(4):680–92.

13. Locker TE, Baston S, Mason SM, Nicholl J. Defining frequent use of an urban emergency department. *Emerg Med.* 2007;**24**(6):398–401.

14. Burton C, Stone T, Oliver P, Dickson JM, Lewis J, Mason SM. Frequent attendance at the emergency department shows typical features of complex systems: Analysis of multicentre linked data. *Emerg Med.* 2022;**39**(1):3–9.

15. Fuda KK, Immekus R. Frequent users of Massachusetts emergency departments: A statewide analysis. *Ann Emerg Med.* 2006;**48**(1):9–16.

16. Shefer G, Henderson C, Howard LM, Murray J, Thornicroft G. Diagnostic overshadowing and other challenges involved in the diagnostic process of patients with mental illness who present in emergency departments with physical symptoms: A qualitative study. Dekel S, editor. *PLoS ONE.* 2014;**9**(11):e111682.

17. Thomson AB, McAllister E, Veale D. Frequent attendance with self-harm: What might you be missing? *Emerg Med.* 2020;**37**(6):331–44.

18. Pines JM, Asplin BR, Kaji AH et al. Frequent users of emergency department services: Gaps in knowledge and a proposed research agenda. *Acad Emerg Med.* 2011;**18**(6):e64–9.

19. Anonymous. The crime of wanting to die: My story from Scotland. Recovery in the Bin. 2020. https://recoveryinthebin.org/2020/10/09/the-crime-of-wanting-to-die-my-story-from-scotland.

20. NHS Improvement Scotland. Patient experience Anticipatory Care Planning Team (PACT): Scalability assessment. Edinburgh; 2019. https://ihub.scot/media/6477/lwic-pact-report.pdf.

21. The StopSIM Coalition. StopSIM Coalition consensus statement. 2021. https://stopsim.co.uk/2021/04/21/stopsim-coalition-consensus-statement.

22. Eales S, Molodynski A, McAllister E, Thomson AB. Responsibility, judgement and ethics: Suicide and criminal justice. Edinburgh; 2022. www.rcpsych.ac.uk/events/congress.

23. National Institute for Health and Care Excellence. Self-harm: Assessment, management and preventing recurrence. London; 2022. www.nice.org.uk/guidance/indevelopment/gid-ng10148/documents.

24. Thomson AB, Eales S, McAllister E, Molodynski A. Criminal sanctions for suicidality in the 21st century UK. *BJPsych.* 2022;**221**(5):653–4.

25. Soril LJJ, Leggett LE, Lorenzetti DL, Noseworthy TW, Clement FM. Reducing frequent visits to the emergency department: A systematic review of interventions. Gupta V, editor. *PLoS ONE.* 2015;**10**(4):e0123660.

26. Chandler A. *Self-Injury, Medicine and Society: Authentic Bodies.* London; 2016.

27. Sullivan P. Epistemic injustice and self-injury: A concept with clinical implications. *Philos Psychiatr Psychol.* 2019;**26**(4):349–62.

28. BBC News. Nurse jailed for raping patient at east London hospital. 2018. www.bbc.com/news/uk-england-london-44730147.

29. Care Quality Commission. *Right Here Right Now: People's Experiences of Help, Care and Support during a Mental Health Crisis.* London; 2015.

30. DrEm_79. Self harm and the emergency department. *BMJ.* 2016;**353**:i1150.

31. McDonald V. Hospital security staff 'abused' vulnerable patients. Channel 4 News. 2021. www.channel4.com/news/hospital-security-staff-abused-vulnerable-patients.

32. Barber S, Gronholm PC, Ahuja S, Rüsch N, Thornicroft G. Microaggressions towards people affected by mental health problems: A scoping review. *Epidemiol Psychiatr Sci.* 2019;**29**:e82.

33. Anonymous. I am more than a body to stitch up and label. *BMJ.* 2021;n1003.

34. Thomson AB. Testimonial and hermeneutical injustices in adult protection and patient safety: Practical

lessons for psychiatrists. In Philosophy Special Interest Group Biennial Conference. London; 2021.

35. Thomson AB, Nyein C, Clarke M. Protection and safeguarding of vulnerable adults and children from violence. In Tyrer P, Khwaja M (eds.), *Prevention and Management of Violence: Guidance for Mental Healthcare Professionals*, 2nd ed. Cambridge; 2021.

36. Geulayov G, Kapur N, Turnbull P et al. Epidemiology and trends in non-fatal self-harm in three centres in England, 2000–2012: Findings from the Multicentre Study of Self-harm in England. *BMJ Open.* 2016;**6**(4):e010538.

37. Stone H, Barrett K, Beales D et al. Self-harm and suicide in adults: Final report of the Patient Safety Group. London; 2020. Report no. CR229. www.rcpsych.ac.uk/improving-care/campaigning-for-better-mental-health-policy/college-reports/2020-college-reports/cr229.

38. Beale C. Magical thinking and moral injury: Exclusion culture in psychiatry. *BJPsych Bulletin.* 2021;**14**:1–4.

39. Department of Health. No health without mental health: A cross-government outcomes strategy. London; 2011. www.gov.uk/government/publications/no-health-without-mental-health-a-cross-government-outcomes-strategy.

40. Walsh DAB, Foster JLH. A call to action: A critical review of mental health related anti-stigma campaigns. *Public Health Front.* 2021;**8**. www.frontiersin.org/article/10.3389/fpubh.2020.569539.

41. Gask L, Thomson AB. Suicide prevention in clinical practice. In Khan M, Poole R, Robinson C (eds.), *Preventing Suicide: An Evidence Based Approach*, 1st ed. Cambridge; in press.

42. Care Quality Commission. How CQC identifies and responds to closed cultures. 2021. www.cqc.org.uk/guidance-providers/all-services/how-cqc-identifies-responds-closed-cultures.

43. Mujal GN, Taylor ME, Fry JL, Gochez-Kerr TH, Weaver NL. A systematic review of bystander interventions for the prevention of sexual violence. *Trauma Violence Abuse.* 2021;**22**(2):381–96.

44. Rowe BH, Channan P, Bullard M et al. Characteristics of patients who leave emergency departments without being seen. *Acad Emerg Med.* 2006;**13**(8):848–52.

45. Rathlev NK, Visintainer P, Schmidt J, Hettler J, Albert V, Li H. Patient characteristics and clinical process predictors of patients leaving without being seen from the emergency department. *West J Emerg Med.* 2020;**21**(5):1218–26.

46. DrEm_79. Commentary: 'I've lost count of the times my door has been broken by the police'. *BMJ.* 2017;**356**. www.bmj.com/content/356/bmj.j1165.

47. Hallett N, Duxbury J, McKee T et al. Taser use on individuals experiencing mental distress: An integrative literature review. *J Psychiatr Ment Health Nurs.* 2021;**28**(1):56–71.

48. Cardinal RN, Bullmore E, Bullmore ET. *The Diagnosis of Psychosis.* Cambridge; 2011.

49. Han JH, Shintani A, Eden S et al. Delirium in the emergency department: An independent predictor of death within 6 months. *Ann Emerg Med.* 2010;**56**(3):244–52.e1.

50. Healthcare Improvement Scotland. SIGN 157. Risk reduction and management of delirium: A national clinical guideline. 2019. www.sign.ac.uk/media/1423/sign157.pdf.

51. Oliveira JE, Silva L, Berning MJ et al. Risk factors for delirium in older adults in the emergency department: A systematic review and meta-analysis. *Ann Emerg Med.* 2021;**78**(4):549–65.

52. National Institute for Health and Care Excellence. Dementia: Assessment, management and support for people living with dementia and their carers. London; 2018. www.nice.org.uk/guidance/ng97.

53. Burry L, Mehta S, Perreault MM et al. Antipsychotics for treatment of delirium in hospitalised non-ICU patients. *Cochrane Database of Systematic Reviews.* 2018;**6**. www.cochranelibrary.com/cdsr/doi/10.1002/14651858.CD005594.pub3/full.

54. Dark T, Flynn HA, Rust G, Kinsell H, Harman JS. Epidemiology of emergency department visits for anxiety in the United States: 2009–2011. *Psychiatr Serv.* 2017;**68** (3):238–44.

55. Palombini E, Richardson J, McAllister E, Veale D, Thomson AB. When self-harm is about preventing harm: Emergency management of obsessive-compulsive disorder and associated self-harm. *BJPsych Bulletin.* 2021;**45**(2):109–14.

56. Fuller-Thomson E, Carroll SZ, Yang W. Suicide attempts among individuals with specific learning disorders: An under-recognized issue. *J Learn Disabil.* 2018;**51** (3):283–92.

57. Neale J, Parkman T, Day E, Drummond C. Socio-demographic characteristics and stereotyping of people who frequently attend accident and emergency departments for alcohol-related reasons: Qualitative study. *Drugs Educ Prev Policy.* 2017;**24**(1):67–74.

58. Freeman L, Stewart H. Epistemic microaggressions and epistemic injustices in clinical medicine. In Sherman BR, Goguen S (eds.), *Overcoming Epistemic Injustice: Social and Psychological Perspectives.* London; 2019.

59. Tracy DK, Rix KJB. Malingering mental disorders: Clinical assessment. *BJPsych Adv.* 2017;**23**(1):27–35.

60. Khalifeh H, Johnson S, Howard LM et al. Violent and non-violent crime against adults with severe mental illness. *BJPsych.* 2015;**206**(4):275–82.

61. Khalifeh H, Moran P, Borschmann R et al. Domestic and sexual violence against patients with severe mental illness. *Psychol Med.* 2015;**45**(4):875–86.

62. National Institute for Health and Care Excellence. Domestic violence and abuse. London; 2016. Report no. QS116. www .nice.org.uk/guidance/qs116.

63. Royal College of Psychiatrists. Parents as patients: Supporting the needs of patients who are parents and their children . London; 2011. Report no. CR164. www .rcpsych.ac.uk/improving-care/campaign ing-for-better-mental-health-policy/col lege-reports/2011-2013-college-reports.

64. Homeless Link. Homeless health needs audit. www.homeless.org.uk/our-work/res ources/homeless-health-needs-audit.

65. Rahman MS, Kapur N. Quality of risk assessment prior to suicide and homicide. *Psychiatr Bull.* 2014;**38**(1):46–7.

66. Dorney-Smith S, Schneller K, Swift A, Phelan H, Khan Z. Meeting the needs of homeless people attending the emergency department. *Emerg Nurse.* 2020;**28** (4):31–9.

67. Pathway. Providing legal advice to destitute homeless patients in London: Evaluation report. London; 2019. www .pathway.org.uk/publication/providing-legal-advice-to-destitute-homeless-patients-in-london-evaluation-report.

68. Timms P, Drife J. Mental health services for single homeless people. *BJPsych Adv.* 2021;**27**(2):104–14.

69. Waterman LZ, Katona C, Katona C. Assessing asylum seekers, refugees and undocumented migrants. *BJPsych Bull.* 2020;**44**(2):75–80.

70. Baugh C, Blanchard E, Hopkins I (eds.). *Quality Standards for Liaison Psychiatry Services*, 6th ed. London; 2020. www .rcpsych.ac.uk/improving-care/ccqi/qual ity-networks-accreditation/psychiatric-liaison-accreditation-network-plan/plan-standards.

71. Tadros G, Salama RA, Kingston P et al. Impact of an integrated rapid response psychiatric liaison team on quality improvement and cost savings: The Birmingham RAID model. *Psychiatrist.* 2013;**37**(1):4–10.

72. Care Quality Commission. Assessment of mental health services in acute trusts. London; 2020. www.cqc.org.uk/publica tions/themed-work/assessment-mental-health-services-acute-trusts.

73. Aitken P, Robens S, Emmens T. Liaison psychiatry services: Guidance. Strategic Clinical Network for Mental Health, Dementia and Neurological Conditions South West. 2014. https://mentalhealth

partnerships.com/category/innovation/sev
ere-mental-illness/liaison-psychiatry-
services.

74. Parmar N, Bolton J. Alternatives to
emergency departments for mental health
assessments during the COVID-19
pandemic. London; 2020. www
.rcpsych.ac.uk/docs/default-source/mem
bers/faculties/liaison-psychiatry/alterna
tives-to-eds-for-mental-health-
assessments-august-2020.pdf?
sfvrsn=679256a_2.

75. NHS Health Education England,
University College London, National
Collaborating Centre for Mental Health.
Self-harm and suicide prevention
competence framework: Adults and older
adults. London; 2018. www.hee.nhs.uk/ou
r-work/mental-health/self-harm-suicide-
prevention.

76. Trigwell P, Kustow J, Santhouse A et al.
Framework for routine outcome
measurement in liaison psychiatry

(FROM-LP). London; 2015. Report no. FR/
LP/02.

77. NHS England, National Collaborating
Centre for Mental Health, National Institute
for Health and Care Excellence. Achieving
better access to 24/7 urgent and emergency
mental health care – part 2: Implementing
the evidence-based treatment pathway for
urgent and emergency liaison mental health
services for adults and older adults –
Guidance. London; 2016. www
.england.nhs.uk/publication/achieving-
better-access-to-247-urgent-and-
emergency-mental-health-care-part-2-impl
ementing-the-evidence-based-treatment-
pathway-for-urgent-and-emergency-
liaison-mental-health-services-for–2.

78. National Institute for Health and Care
Excellence. Service user experience in adult
mental health: Improving the experience of
care for people using adult NHS mental
health services. London; 2011. Report no.
CG136. www.nice.org.uk/guidance/cg136.

Setting Standards for Consultation-Liaison Psychiatry Services

24

Jim Bolton

Introduction

This chapter addresses the question of what constitutes a good liaison psychiatry service. It briefly considers two national initiatives that have addressed the quality of mental health-care in general hospitals – the Care Quality Commission (CQC) acute hospital inspection programme and two National Confidential Enquiry into Patient Outcome and Death (NCEPOD) reports. However, the chapter primarily focusses on the setting and measurement of standards for liaison psychiatry services by the UK Psychiatric Liaison Accreditation Network (PLAN).

The chapter discusses the development and revision of the PLAN standards and describes how they are applied. Advice is given for liaison psychiatry services that are undergoing the accreditation process. The chapter also discusses what has been learned from the application of PLAN standards since their introduction and considers the evidence for their enhancement of the quality of care delivered by liaison psychiatry services. The measurement of outcome data is discussed in Chapter 20.

What Makes a Good Liaison Psychiatry Service? What Standards Should It Achieve to be Judged as Good, or Simply Good Enough?

Over recent years UK policy has emphasised the need for health services to reduce variations in the quality of care and to provide evidence of their effectiveness by reporting on their outcomes and performance (1). For individual liaison psychiatry services this raises two questions:

- What standards should services achieve?
- What outcome data should they collect?

One of the main challenges in setting standards for liaison psychiatry services is the fact there are many aspects to the quality of care. Some of these are straightforward to demonstrate, while others are harder to measure. They include:

- the staffing of the service, for example the number of staff employed, their expertise and the support and supervision they receive
- the available facilities, for example adequate office space for the team to operate, information technology systems and areas to conduct safe and private patient assessment

- the operation of the service, for example inclusion and exclusion criteria for referrals, the hours of work, response times to referrals
- how well the service performs, for example the quality of clinical care and teaching provided, the degree of integration into the hospital and the delivery of compassionate care.

This is, of course, not an exhaustive list.

The Care Quality Commission Hospital Inspection Programme

The CQC is the independent regulator of health and social care in England (2). Its roles include the monitoring, inspecting and rating of services. It sets out what it considers to be good and outstanding care and seeks to ensure that services meet fundamental standards below which care must not fall. Fundamental standards that all patients should expect include the provision of person-centred care, being treated with dignity and respect and being safeguarded from abuse and improper treatment.

When inspecting acute hospitals, the CQC focusses on eight core services, such as urgent and emergency, medical and surgical care. Each of these core services has an inspection framework that is regularly updated. Within these frameworks are specific prompts to inspectors to enquire about the provision of liaison psychiatry services and appropriate facilities for the assessment of patients with mental health problems in the acute hospital setting.

'Treat As One'

The UK's NCEPOD aims to support improvements in the standards of care by a number of means, including undertaking confidential surveys and research. It recognised that there are many potential barriers to the delivery of mental healthcare in general hospitals. NCEPOD sought to identify and explore remediable factors in the quality of healthcare provided to patients with mental health problems in UK general hospitals. The findings were published in the reports 'Treat As One' (3) and 'Mental Healthcare of Young People and Young Adults' (4).

Data were collected for these studies from hospitals across the UK pertaining to patient care at both an organisational and individual level. The 'Treat As One' study focussed on patients with co-morbid physical and mental illness. The 'Mental Healthcare of Young People and Young Adults' study included data on young people admitted to general hospitals with primary mental health problems. Questionnaires regarding their care were sent to general hospital and liaison psychiatry clinicians. In addition, the patients' case notes were subject to multidisciplinary peer review.

The reports made a number of recommendations to help bridge the divide between mental and physical healthcare. Many of the recommendations were directly or indirectly relevant to liaison psychiatry services. These include:

- timely assessment by a staff member with sufficient expertise
- clear and concise documentation of assessments, diagnoses and management plans
- integration of data from mental health service providers and general hospitals.

The 'Treat As One' report made reference to the PLAN standards and noted that the presence of an accredited liaison psychiatry team in a hospital was associated with a higher quality of care.

The Psychiatric Liaison Accreditation Network

PLAN is an affiliation of UK liaison psychiatry services run by a central project team within the Royal College of Psychiatrists' (RCPsych's) Centre for Quality Improvement (5). PLAN was developed and is overseen by representatives from the Royal Colleges of Psychiatrists, Emergency Medicine, Physicians and Nursing, and the mental health charity Mind, as well as patient and carer representatives.

PLAN is open to all liaison psychiatry services working with adults and older adults in the UK and Ireland. It aims to facilitate quality improvement and development of its member services through a supportive peer-review network. Services are assessed against a range of quality standards (5). By meeting a required number of standards, services achieve accreditation for three years. The PLAN network also enables communication between its services, encouraging the sharing of best practice, advice and support.

By applying standards, PLAN:

- recognises achievement and identifies areas for improvement
- raises awareness of the value of liaison services
- encourages services to constantly strive for improvement
- provides funders with the confidence to invest in accredited services.

The Development of PLAN Standards

The PLAN standards, against which services are audited, were initially developed from recommendations in key literature and in consultation with a range of stakeholders. Existing standards and health service policy and guidance provided the basis for some standards. For example, established RCPsych guidance on the provision of safe and private emergency department assessment facilities, and recommendations for facilities for patients detained under Section 136 of the Mental Health Act for England and Wales (6), were used to compile the first iteration of the standard described next.

PLAN Standard and Guidance for the Emergency Department High-Risk Assessment Room (5)

Standard

The liaison team has access to assessment rooms suitable for conducting high-risk assessments.

Accompanying Guidance

Facilities should:

- be located within the main emergency department
- have at least two doors which open outwards and are not lockable from the inside
- have an observation panel or window which allows staff from outside the room to check on the patient or staff member but which still provides a sufficient degree of privacy
- have a panic button or alarm system (unless staff carry alarms at all times)
- only include furniture, fittings and equipment which are unlikely to be used to cause harm or injury to the patient or staff member. For example, sinks, sharp-edged furniture,

lightweight chairs, tables, cables, televisions or anything else that could be used to cause harm or as a missile are not permitted
- be appropriately decorated to provide a sense of calm
- have a ceiling which has been risk-assessed
- not have any ligature points
- sharp corners should be covered
- if there is a bed, it should be weighted with no ligature risks
- there should be a process in place to ensure the patient is monitored while in the room
- there should be a process in place to ensure patients are supported to access ligature-free toilet facilities or, at minimum, toilets with thumb-turn locks.

Throughout the process of creating and revising the standards, the views of a wide range of stakeholders have been taken into account. These have included the perspectives of researchers, policy-makers, staff working in liaison psychiatry services, experts from voluntary organisations, healthcare professionals from general hospitals and people who have received care from services and their family and carers.

The standards are revised every three years. They are updated and amended in the light of the experience of their implementation and evolving evidence, policy and guidance. For example, it became apparent that suspended ceilings in emergency department assessment rooms might pose a ligature risk. Hence from the fifth revision of the standards onwards, there has been a requirement that liaison psychiatry services ensure that a risk assessment for the ceiling has been undertaken that judges it to be sufficiently safe.

It is recognised that liaison psychiatry services differ widely in their function, organisation, funding, staffing and levels of service. Hence, PLAN standards focus on function rather than any specific model of service delivery. They are primarily intended for liaison psychiatry services rather than the wider provision of mental healthcare within a general hospital. However, meeting specific standards will often require close collaboration between liaison psychiatry and general hospital staff, for example to establish and equip an emergency department assessment room.

Although the standards were originally developed for established services that are seeking accreditation, they can also be used as a guide for new or developing services. Indeed, PLAN supports developing services to prepare for accreditation without having to commit to the full process.

The PLAN standards are a guide to best practice and do not override the individual responsibility of a professional to make appropriate decisions about an individual case. A healthcare professional in a service applying for or having achieved accreditation should continue to adhere to the code of conduct established by their own governing professional body.

The Categorisation of PLAN Standards

The PLAN standards are categorised in a number of domains that reflect the different functions of liaison psychiatry services. A service seeking accreditation is required to indicate which services it provides; for example, whether it delivers psychological therapies. The service is then assessed against the relevant domains and is exempt from those which do not apply. The accreditation record for the service records which domains it has been measured against. PLAN accreditation is only valid for the service assessed and does not apply to any other affiliated services, for example a separate out-of-hours service that is not staffed by the liaison psychiatry team.

(5) Core Standards for All Liaison Psychiatry Services

Assessment, care planning and treatment

Patient and carer experience

Collaborative working

Workforce

Quality, audit and governance

Children and young people

Although the PLAN standards are intended for services that assess and manage adult patients of 18 years of age and older, it is recognised that some services may also assess patients of 16 and 17 years of age. Hence, the PLAN standards include a domain pertaining to the management of this age group. At time of writing, there is no established accreditation scheme for paediatric liaison psychiatry services, although this may be developed in view of the expansion of such services in the UK.

Each standard is categorised as being one of three types:

- Type 1: failure to meet these standards would result in a significant threat to patient safety, rights or dignity and/or would breach the law. These standards also include the fundamentals of care, including the provision of evidence-based care and treatment.
- Type 2: standards that a service would be expected to meet.
- Type 3: standards that are desirable for a service to meet, or standards that are not the direct responsibility of the service.

Examples of standards of the three types are given next.

Standard No. 16 (Type 1 Standard)

Assessments of patients' capacity (and competency for patients under the age of 16) to consent to care and treatment in the hospital are performed in accordance with current legislation.

Standard No. 66 (Type 2 Standard)

The liaison team comprises a number of staff proportional to national best practice guidance. In the appendices to the Standards, there is a summary of best practice guidance with examples of liaison psychiatry staffing levels.

Standard No. 81 (Type 3 Standard)

Staff members are able to access reflective practice groups at least every six weeks where teams can meet to think about team dynamics and develop their clinical practice. The full set of standards is aspirational and it is unlikely that any service would meet them all. In order to achieve accreditation, a service must meet 100% of type 1 standards, at least 80% of type 2 standards and 60% of type 3 standards.

The Accreditation Process

The key stages of the PLAN accreditation process are listed next. There is also a helpful guidebook available on the RCPsych website (7).

The Key Stages of the PLAN Accreditation Process

1. Service self-review against standards:

    Team joint self-assessment
    Individual assessments by team members
    Case-note audit

2. Collection of feedback:

    General hospital colleagues who refer patients to the service
    Patients treated by the team and their carers

3. Compilation of initial report by PLAN project team

4. Peer-review one-day visit:

    Discussion with team members
    Review of case records
    Review of facilities
    Interviews with patients and carers
    Meeting with general hospital staff
    Verbal feedback to service

5. Revision of report

6. Opportunity for service to meet outstanding standards

7. Final report submitted to Accreditation Committee

Self-Review against the Standards

Team members jointly complete a self-assessment form, noting whether their service meets specific standards and providing further information or evidence of completion. In addition, individual team members complete separate forms to indicate whether they judge specific standards to be met. Such standards include whether a team member receives regular supervision and if they have undertaken training on specific topics.

Team members audit a semi-randomised sample of case records of patients that have recently received care by the service. The selected cases reflect the range of assessments conducted by the team, including patients from across the age span of those treated and assessments of different urgency.

Collection of Feedback

The service being accredited is required to seek feedback from patients treated by the team and their carers. Feedback is collected using a structured form that is based on relevant standards. The form also allows respondents to provide general comments. It can be completed on paper or online. The form identifies the specific liaison psychiatry service but does not collect any information that could be used to identify respondents. Services are required to collect a minimum number of forms.

Services also seek structured written feedback from hospital colleagues who regularly refer patients. Again, the form is based upon the relevant PLAN standards. It seeks respondents' opinions of both the clinical service and training provided. Again, services undergoing accreditation must ensure that a minimum number of forms are completed.

Compilation of the Initial Report

The PLAN central project team compiles an initial report based upon the information collected in the stages above. This report provisionally rates the service against the PLAN standards and summarises the general feedback submitted by patients, carers and hospital colleagues.

Peer-Review Visit

Following compilation of the initial report, each service is visited by a team composed of a member of the PLAN central project team, at least one patient or carer representative and several team members from other liaison psychiatry services who are members of PLAN. All those who take part in these peer-review visits undergo specific training for the role.

During the one-day visit, members of the visiting team meet with both senior clinical and managerial staff from the liaison psychiatry service, as well as the other team members. These meetings provide an opportunity to review the initial report and discuss whether specific standards have been met, particularly the type 1 standards, and those where there is uncertainty.

The visiting team also reviews a number of case notes, which enables further assessment against the relevant standards and corroboration of the data collected in the case-note audit.

The visitors also speak, either in person or by phone, to a small number of patients and carers who have had recent contact with the service. Again, this allows corroboration of the findings from the feedback forms.

A meeting is held between the peer-review team and members of the general hospital staff without the liaison psychiatry team being present. This allows hospital colleagues to provide verbal feedback about the service.

At the end of the day, the visitors provide initial verbal feedback to the service. Such feedback will usually include a summary of key achievements and areas of positive practice, as well as initial suggestions for improving the service or achieving unmet standards.

Revision of the Report

Following the peer-review visit, the service report is revised to indicate which standards have been met. This report is submitted to the service, which then has a brief period of time in which to provide evidence that it is now meeting standards that were previously not achieved, or where more information is required for a decision to be made.

The Accreditation Committee

The PLAN Accreditation Committee meets every few months. It discusses services that have recently undergone the accreditation process to confirm whether they have achieved the required number of standards for accreditation to be awarded.

Where a service has not achieved sufficient standards to be accredited, but it is judged that it may be able to in the near future, accreditation may be deferred. In this instance the service will be given a specific time limit within which to submit evidence that the necessary standards have been met. Where a service is not able to meet the necessary standards, with or without a period of deferral, it will be judged to be 'not accredited'.

A service will occasionally undertake the accreditation process knowing that it is unlikely that it will be successful. This is to enable it to determine what it needs to do, or to provide evidence to managers and commissioners about what resources are required, to achieve accreditation.

Achieving Accreditation

Achieving accreditation can be challenging, especially for services that are embarking on the process for the first time. The following advice is based upon the experience of the author and staff from other liaison psychiatry services that have been accredited.

Preliminary Review of the Standards

Before embarking on the accreditation process, services are advised to review the PLAN standards. This is to determine which standards are currently met and which require action to achieve compliance. This is particularly important for type 1 standards, as a service cannot be accredited without meeting all of these.

Some unmet standards may be straightforward to achieve, for example compiling a brief protocol describing an aspect of service delivery or ensuring that team members have received training in a particular area. Other standards may be more challenging and require time to achieve, hence it is worth starting work on these as soon as possible.

Services may also be asked to provide evidence that they meet specific standards, such as records of attendance at training provided to hospital staff. This can be collated in preparation for the submission of the self-assessment or the peer-review visit.

Team Involvement

Generally, services will appoint a member of their team to coordinate their accreditation and to be the main link with the central PLAN project team. However, it is important to engage and enthuse the other team members, and to delegate tasks. The accreditation process provides opportunities for service improvement projects and audits, which may be valuable training experiences for some team members.

Policies and Protocols

The PLAN standards require services to have written protocols and procedures on aspects of service delivery, such as risk assessment, prescribing and copying correspondence to patients. Services may find it helpful to gather these together as part of their overall operational policy.

Collecting Feedback

Accreditation requires a minimum number of feedback forms to be completed by patients, carers and acute hospital colleagues. The overall experience of liaison psychiatry services is that collecting feedback from patients is challenging. It is often not appropriate to seek feedback when patients are acutely unwell or distressed. Seeking feedback in retrospect can also be difficult as patients may not be able to distinguish the care delivered by the liaison psychiatry service from other aspects of hospital care. In addition, the response rate to postal requests for feedback is often very low.

The author's service has generally sought feedback from patients and carers by a face-to-face request, usually approaching patients towards the end of their inpatient admission, outpatients at the time of their appointment and patients assessed in the emergency department whose mental health problems do not preclude them giving feedback. The staff member explains the purpose of the feedback and outlines which aspects of care it relates to. The patient is then given a few minutes to complete the form and to place it in a sealed envelope to preserve confidentiality. The form is then collected by the staff member.

A personal approach is often of benefit when seeking feedback from hospital colleagues. If an individual member of staff has made a referral to liaison psychiatry, they can be asked to provide feedback once the patient's care has been completed. Individual liaison psychiatry team members often have good working relationships with specific acute hospital staff, from whom they can seek feedback. Teaching sessions provided by the liaison psychiatry team also provide an opportunity to approach a 'captive audience' of potential respondents.

The Peer-Review Visit

Clinical team members of services that are members of PLAN can undertake training to enable them to participate in the reviews of other services. This is a way for staff to familiarise themselves with the standards and the process of accreditation, which may be of benefit when their own service is assessed. In addition, peer reviewers have the opportunity to meet with colleagues in other services and to share areas of good practice. It may also be helpful to discover that services generally face similar pressures and to understand how colleagues in other teams have managed these.

A liaison psychiatry service can use the peer-review visit as an opportunity to engage hospital staff and management and to raise the profile of the service. This can facilitate the cooperation of management colleagues in any changes that need to be made to meet the PLAN standards. Although the visit is not an 'inspection', as may be conducted by other external bodies, the prospect of an external review often galvanises managers into supporting a service to achieve accreditation in order to enhance the reputation of the wider organisation.

The Emergency Department Assessment Room

One of the commonest reasons why a liaison psychiatry service may struggle to achieve accreditation is the lack of a sufficiently safe and private emergency department assessment room. The type 1 PLAN standard for such a room, plus the accompanying guidance, has been described earlier in this chapter.

In 2013, a survey of UK assessment rooms found that, of the 60 emergency departments included in the study, only 23% had a psychiatric assessment room that met all of the PLAN criteria and was judged to be sufficiently safe and private (8). The findings concurred with the perception of PLAN that many liaison psychiatry services were working in departments with inadequate facilities.

A problem frequently cited by respondents to the survey was their perceived lack of influence with acute hospital management in creating an appropriate facility. Liaison psychiatry services are integral to the functioning of an emergency department. PLAN recommends that clinical staff and management from both the emergency department and liaison psychiatry service meet regularly to discuss common issues, such as the need for an assessment room. Regular meetings can enhance the sense of shared responsibility for providing such a facility.

In English hospitals, the case for such a room can be supported by making the hospital managers aware that the CQC may enquire about the provision of an adequate facility during an inspection visit. In addition, the PLAN standard is endorsed by the Royal College of Emergency Medicine, which is a collaborator in PLAN, and which includes the requirement for a room in its own guidance to emergency departments on the management of mental health problems (9).

Publicising Accreditation

Achieving accreditation is a significant achievement and provides an opportunity to enhance the reputation of a liaison psychiatry service and its hospital. Services often find it worthwhile to disseminate the news of accreditation to their management and colleagues, and sometimes to the local press. Being accredited, and any favourable publicity this brings, can boost the morale of liaison psychiatry team members.

Learning from PLAN

In 2023, PLAN had 85 member services, which represented approximately one-third of the UK's general hospitals. Of these services, 34 were accredited and the majority of the rest were undergoing the accreditation process.

In 2016, PLAN published a report that summarised the learning from the application of PLAN standards by member services over the previous four years (10). This review identified areas of notable practice as well as potential improvements.

PLAN found that services frequently received positive feedback from hospital colleagues, patients and carers. Over 90% of general hospital staff who gave feedback agreed that their liaison psychiatry service improved patient outcomes, and two-thirds of respondents were satisfied with the amount of training that their service provided. Almost all of the patients who responded said that they had benefited from seeing the liaison psychiatry service and would recommend it to others with similar needs.

Most liaison psychiatry staff in PLAN services were extremely positive about working in the specialty and were satisfied with the amount of supervision and support they received. PLAN also identified a strong culture of audit, research, service evaluation and learning from feedback among services.

Areas of potential improvement included a need for increased liaison psychiatry staffing, with a quarter of services reporting that they struggled to achieve their core functions at times. PLAN found that over time an increasing number of liaison psychiatry services were providing care for older adults, but that their staff would benefit from additional training and a higher level of expertise to meet the specific needs of older patients. Other areas of staff training that generally required improvement included alcohol and substance misuse, managing challenging behaviour and meeting the needs of patients with learning disability. It was also recommended that liaison psychiatry and acute hospital staff discuss ways to improve joint working, communication and collaborative care.

Evidence for the effectiveness of PLAN in improving the quality of mental health care in general hospitals was provided by the NCEPOD 'Treat As One' report (3). This found that good practice and high-quality mental healthcare were more likely in hospitals that had a PLAN-accredited liaison psychiatry service.

Conclusions

Evidence of the clinical and economic benefits of liaison psychiatry has led to an expansion in services across the UK. Additional investment in the specialty, as well as an increasing emphasis on measuring and reporting on outcomes and performance by health services, have brought a greater focus on setting standards for liaison psychiatry services.

The need to consider both mental and physical health issues in patient care, and to give them equal weight, is fundamental to liaison psychiatry (10). It is also reflected in the standards set by the CQC in its inspections and those applied by NCEPOD in its survey of mental healthcare in UK general hospitals (2–4).

Specific standards for liaison psychiatry services are described by PLAN, which aims to facilitate quality improvement and service development through a peer-review network. Undertaking PLAN accreditation requires time and commitment by liaison psychiatry services. However, it has been shown to improve the quality of the care provided and presents opportunities for enhancing team working, sharing good practice between services and raising the profile of both individual services and liaison psychiatry generally.

What makes a good liaison psychiatry service? Although there are many potential factors, the experience of PLAN is that:

A good liaison service is able to respond to each patient in a prompt, competent and compassionate manner. [It] is well staffed by caring individuals who are knowledgeable, flexible, committed, supported and well led. A good liaison team is integrated into the hospital, where liaison staff can advise and influence acute colleagues, fostering good relations and helping to create a culture where mental health is everyone's business.   (10)

References

1. Department of Health. Operating framework for NHS England. 2022. www.england.nhs.uk/wp-content/uploads/2022/10/B2068-NHS-England-Operating-Framework.pdf

2. Care Quality Commission. How CQC monitors, inspects and regulates NHS trusts. 2021. www.cqc.org.uk/sites/default/files/20210809-how-cqc-regulates-nhs-trusts-august-2021.pdf.

3. National Confidential Enquiry into Patient Outcome and Death. Treat as one: Bridging the gap between mental and physical healthcare in general hospitals. 2017. www.ncepod.org.uk/2017report1/downloads/TreatAsOne_FullReport.pdf.

4. National Confidential Enquiry into Patient Outcome and Death. Mental healthcare in young people and young adults. 2019. www.ncepod.org.uk/2019ypmh.html.

5. Baugh C, Talwar K. Royal College of Psychiatrists. Psychiatric Liaison Accreditation Network (PLAN). Quality standards for liaison psychiatry services, 7th ed. 2022. www.rcpsych.ac.uk/docs/default-source/improving-care/ccqi/quality-networks/psychiatric-liaison-services-plan/plan-7th-edition-standards.pdf?sfvrsn=2f0be3e3_2.

6. Royal College of Psychiatrists. Standards on the use of Section 136 of the Mental Health Act 1983 (England and Wales) CR159. 2011.

www.rcpsych.ac.uk/docs/default-source/improving-care/better-mh-policy/college-reports/college-report-cr159.pdf?sfvrsn=fea0f2a_2.

7. Royal College of Psychiatrists. Psychiatric Liaison Accreditation Network (PLAN). PLAN developmental cycle guidebook. 2019. www.rcpsych.ac.uk/docs/default-source/improving-care/ccqi/quality-networks/psychiatric-liaison-services-plan/plan-developmental-guidebook-v1.pdf?sfvrsn=26153c53_2.

8. Bolton J, Palmer L, Cawdron R. Survey of psychiatric assessment rooms in UK emergency departments. *BJPsych Bull.* 2016;40(2):64–7.

9. Royal College of Emergency Medicine. Mental health in emergency departments: A toolkit for improving care. 2021. https://rcem.ac.uk/wp-content/uploads/2021/10/Mental_Health_Toolkit_June21.pdf.

10. Palmer L, Hodge S, Ryley A et al. Psychiatric Liaison Accreditation Network (PLAN) national report 2012–2015. 2016. www.rcpsych.ac.uk/docs/default-source/improving-care/ccqi/quality-networks/psychiatric-liaison-services-plan/plan-publications-and-links-national-report-2012-15.pdf?sfvrsn=3814f12_2.

Chapter 25

Policy to Practice
Developing Consultation–Liaison Psychiatry Services

Peter Aitken and William Lee

Introduction

For the last decade of the twentieth and first decade of the twenty-first century, UK liaison psychiatry grew incrementally but patchily. By the time of the first full English national survey in 2014 (1), over 90% of acute hospitals were able to report some form of a consultation-liaison service; the specialty was recognised by the Royal College of Psychiatrists with its own faculty and representation in the postgraduate curriculum. The nature of services varied from rudimentary to highly developed: part-time sessions from a few doctors and nurses to teams with multiple members and functions, and specialist clinics. The biggest services tended to be found in teaching hospitals linked to medical schools. Although it was not being formally monitored, there was a general sense that growth had by this time stalled – not least because government funding cuts had affected mental health and community services, with knock-on effects.

This chapter outlines approaches to advocating for new models of care, new interventions and resources. Examples are used to illustrate how this has led to changes in consultation-liaison services.

Bridging the Gulf between Evidence and Practice

It has long been recognised that the timespan between accumulation of research findings and translation into practice is too long. The traditional way of dealing with this problem in the health service has been through active promotion of research and its findings, relying, for example, on the insights obtained from implementation science. The Cooksey report (2) provided impetus for closer alignment between major public funding bodies (the Medical Research Council and the National Institute for Health Research) and additional funding streams focussed on translational research (3). Subsequent applied health research initiatives centred on developing regional partnerships between the National Health Service (NHS) and academic institutions. Examples include the Collaboration for Leadership in Applied Health Research (CLARHC), Academic Health Sciences Centres and Academic Health Sciences Networks. A central focus within these constructs is aligning health services research with regional and national development priorities of the NHS. Mental health issues such as psychosis, self-harm, dementia, eating disorders and alcohol misuse are some of the priority areas highlighted within these organisations (4, 5).

This evidence-practice problem is not exclusive to public sector services. Both the pharmaceutical and device manufacturing sectors have also struggled with long lead times in bringing new medicines and devices to patients. An alternative approach to the above in terms of bridging the translation gap is strategic marketing functions (6).

Strategic Marketing: Principles and Practice

The basic premise of marketing is to find the opportunity for the sale needed to generate return on investment and make some profit. Put simply, who will buy the product or service and how will the buyer know that the offer is there and at a price they can afford? Strategic marketing encompasses everything from research to developing the brand, the messages, message carriers, media and influencers that make sure everyone in the marketplace has the optimal opportunity to buy the product. The same principles of approach apply in health services development. For something as large as a new model of care for the health service, this is quite an undertaking.

The proposition must be very clear. It has to be simple and everyone who can influence its success has to be aligned to the effort.

From implementation science we have learned much about how the process of adoption of new ideas works. In summary, for any given product, service or technology, adoption curves can help characterise stakeholder groups by their readiness to adopt and try new things. Catalysing early adopters is a skill in itself. New things can seem strange and irrelevant, even off-putting. Identifying and engaging with likely early adopters and letting them try out the idea, test it, research it and write about it all helps them talk about it with their peers. Mid-adopters often look to early adopters before they too get involved. Late adopters are often sceptical with a different risk appetite and will wait and see before joining in a hurry, when they judge it more anxiety-provoking to be 'left out'.

Peer-to-peer influencers are key and some have more influence than others. These 'thought leaders' become the go-to people for the marketer. Credible 'thought leaders' are equipped with the proposition, the data supporting it and the key messages about its value, with a view to accelerating adoption.

Also important are the equally influential people who appear reluctant to come aboard. Initially, marketers avoided this group until it became clear that within this cohort were well-respected, highly experienced people with very valid criticisms of the proposal. If these individuals spoke negatively about the innovation, it could deter late and some mid-adopters.

Working with resistors or influencers with or without an interest in the status quo or some alternative to your proposition is important. They may already be working in a more innovative way or have made their reputation on a previous model. Engaging them in research and clinical audit and providing them with protected innovation status will help them feel valued and add value by evidencing their argument. Sometimes they are right! They are to be listened to carefully (see Box 25.1).

Box 25.1 Summary Learning Points: Adoption and Implementation

- Implementation of an idea is not easy and takes time and work.
- A proposition has to be clear, simple and easy for people to align to.
- It needs to fill a 'need state' in the stakeholder and add value to their work.
- Getting people to adopt the idea is work in itself.
- Influencers can accelerate or decelerate adoption.
- Relationships are key.

Relationships Are Key

On 15 July 2018, Billie Jean King, a tennis star of the 1970s and 1980s and a campaigner for gender equality and social justice, summarised three quick things she says to students (7, 8):

(1) Relationships are everything.
(2) Keep learning and keep learning how to learn.
(3) Be a problem-solver.

Stakeholders and Thought Leader Development

For any given programme of change it is necessary to consider its impact on the people involved at every level. This has been described as influencing 'from bench to bedside' or alternatively from the 'politician to the pen'.

The commercial sector has long understood the value of developing relationships with people who carry influence with their peers. In the way that doctors are often more easily persuaded by other doctors, so too accountants by accountants and politicians by politicians. It is useful therefore for any producer of a product or service who wants it bought and paid for to build relationships with influential stakeholders from different backgrounds who can bring others 'like them' to the effort.

Stakeholder mapping is a process whereby everyone likely to be impacted by the proposition can be ascertained and their relationship to one and other described. Positioning is a process by which all the most influential stakeholders can be grouped into their likely places on an adoption curve and plans made to help move them in a direction favourable to implementation of the proposition. Thought leaders are stakeholders who have influence over the position that others hold. They are the people others look to for guidance.

Long-Term Relationships Are Important

Occasionally, influencer or 'thought leader' relationships span many years. Some people who reach national-level business, administration and politics have known each other since university. Many will have had experience of working together throughout their careers. Some will have met at the 'school gate' or in clubs and societies. It is important when working with influencers to have the whole breadth of their social connection in mind.

Finding Common Purpose

Another important accelerant of adoption is to follow a pre-made trail. It is often easier to implement an improvement to an already accepted idea than to be the first to offer the new idea.

In addition, you may have enough in common with a service developed by another such that joining forces is attractive. Sometimes this can be planned in advance. Co-produced ideas from the outset have the advantage of the prospect of delivering to both parties what they need. However, some parties may give away too much of what they need in order to progress. Both processes inevitably mean some adjustment and if made carefully can be mutually beneficial.

So how do the above theoretical principles translate into action with respect to the implementation of consultation-liaison psychiatry services?

Matching the Case to Political Priorities

There is only rarely new policy without political imperative. In other language, a metaphorical and rhetorical 'burning (oil) platform' demands action. This has to be carefully crafted with due consideration to balancing imperatives in the ministerial portfolio. Timing is often everything. Mobilising the media, general public, campaigns to raise awareness, petitions and even giving evidence to parliamentary select committees (9) are commonly used to create an imperative.

For liaison psychiatry, the tension was to create a sense of urgency in the political mindset based on the poorer clinical outcomes associated with the lack of mental health services in general hospitals, in particular emergency departments. This would have to be achieved without aggravating relationships with senior government officials and NHS chief executives as collaboration would be necessary for implementation. Care had to be taken regarding criticism of the care these officials and executives were commissioning and providing.

Since the 1960s, governments have sought to reorganise mental health services in favour of a community-based model (10). Perhaps because of the imperative to address historic underinvestment in community services, the National Service Framework (NSF) for mental health (2000–10) did not address the psychological care of medical patients. The unintended consequence of this was to put pressure on existing liaison psychiatry services.

The Royal College of Psychiatrists' campaigns on 'Parity of Esteem' for people with mental illness and learning disability, and 'No Health without Mental Health', enjoyed almost universal support from charities, third-sector organisations, patients and carers. These began to illuminate the often poor experience of people with mental illness and learning disability attending emergency departments and the lack of access to mental health expertise there. The UK government's 2011 cross-governmental mental health outcomes strategy set out the expectation that there should parity of esteem between mental and physical health services. This was embedded in the NHS constitution in 2013 and successive NHS mandates have set goals for achieving parity. These goals were juxtaposed with existing political pressure placed on the UK NHS in 2010 to see, treat or admit people attending emergency departments within four hours.

How to reconcile goals embedded within parity-of-esteem campaigns with the drive towards more efficient assessment and treatment pathways within emergency departments? For patients with mental health, addiction or behavioural and social problems, there was clearly a need to develop adequate facility, clinical skill and/or onward pathways. Policy-makers, commissioners and other professional groups were also made aware of people who were attending the emergency department and other general health services more frequently than expected, many of whom had complex health and social care problems with associated anxiety and depression.

In response, a policy imperative known as the Crisis Care Concordat was championed by the then minister of state for care and support, Norman Lamb, in 2014 (11). At the same time, the number of people with mental health problems in police custody was causing concern in the Home Office, so a cross-department initiative was created largely to place people detained under the Mental Health Act in designated 'places of safety'. Leaders in the Department of Health were concerned that the new places of safety would not be emergency departments. Psychiatry had a senior seat at that table in the form of the national clinical director for mental health, Dr Geraldine Strathdee. She saw the opportunity to escalate the implementation of the acute accident and emergency element of consultation-liaison psychiatry as part of improving this 'crisis' response from mental health providers.

Once work is agreed to be important, there arises a need to work at the pace of the civil service team charged with bringing forward the policy. There are parliamentary timetables, green papers, white papers, Acts of Parliament, budgets and actions required of departments of state. Ministerial teams and committees need accurate advice and reports at relatively short notice and in language that is accessible to them. It is essential that the policy requirement is articulated clearly and simply and within a performance framework so that the process and outcome of its implementation can be measured and managed. The Department of Health, now the Department of Health and Social Care, makes policy, which it then requires NHS England to deliver. This takes the form of a 'Mandate'. To make sure that something is done by NHS England, first the commitment has to be made in a Mandate.

Policy-Making: Co-production and Partnerships

A notable development based on the initiatives described above was when the national clinical director for mental health established in the Mandate in 2016 the requirement that the NHS deliver liaison psychiatry services in English hospitals (12). To do this, they needed a clear, simple, easy-to-understand proposition that all liaison psychiatrists could support. This was Core24 liaison psychiatry.

An Influential Case Study

The widely discussed consultation-liaison psychiatry service at the City Hospital in Birmingham had drawn political and health professional attention to the importance of getting mental healthcare right in general health pathways. It provided health economic evidence that investing in these kinds of services might unlock money for reinvestment elsewhere, solve the emergency department waiting time problem and save lives. In many ways this model was analogous with the 'first to market' situation. It was originally branded as the Rapid Assessment Interface and Discharge service (RAID) but the acronym was withdrawn due to an intellectual property dispute (13). It had, however, three problems. First, the model was highly contextual to Birmingham. Second, the strength of the evidence on which it was commissioned became a matter of academic debate (14). Third, it was too easy for commissioners around the country to rebadge existing or rudimentary self-harm services as akin to this model without honouring the delivery specification of the original service that showed the benefit. Finally, a similar service piloted across several West London hospitals had also shown promising data and in a different context.

The challenge was to create the clear, simple proposition all could align to without harming advances already made or detracting from around a dozen centres that already had more comprehensive liaison psychiatry and psychological services. Equally, the proposition could not label the less than optimal as ineffective or unsafe without risking them being suspended or closed.

With the help of providers, commissioners, experts by experience and clinicians over a series of workshops at NHS headquarters, a tiered model (Core, Core24, Core24 Enhanced, Comprehensive) was drafted (12). Model services were described within the principles of Core24, a 24-hour, 7-day version of Core and Core24 Enhanced, capable of returning more than its investment and able to address the four-hour wait. Finally, descriptors were added to illustrate fully 'Comprehensive' services and then exemplars were found for each and published. With an eye on propelling all services quickly to Core, anything less than Core was termed 'inadequate', a term useful in policy but perhaps less so for those working in those services.

Whatever was made needed an accompanying clinical outcome programme to ensure model fidelity and to align within a national quality improvement programme. Any research associated with it would need to carry the National Institute for Health and Care Research brand and most importantly there needed to be an agreed funding model with some kind of ringfencing to ensure that when the investments were parcelled out, they were spent as intended.

Finding Common Purpose: Linking to Other Developments in Acute Care

Having stressed the importance of model fidelity and the need to protect the product or service that delivers the promise, it is nevertheless sometimes important to join forces with other powerful influencers who may already be present in decision forums that would be otherwise inaccessible.

In the context of the Five-Year Forward View, in addition to creating an awareness of the lack of mental health services in NHS general or acute hospitals, there was political anxiety about the poor quality of care in police custody, emergency departments and so-called alternative places of safety, which were often acute psychiatric wards and psychiatric intensive care units. None of these environments were well positioned to assess the complex combinations of injury, illness, alcohol and drug misuse and mental illness underpinning many acute presentations. As part of the push for investment, liaison psychiatry was proposed as a solution.

Policy into Practice: Commissioning and Provision

A Framework for Commissioning

In 2013, 'Bridging the Gap' from the Royal College of Psychiatrists and the Centre for Mental Health in the UK set out the economic case for closer integration between physical and mental healthcare systems. Some £3.5 billion was estimated as being spent on the wrong care for people with symptoms unexplained by organic pathology and as much as £14 billion in additional costs in failing to address anxiety and depression complicating long-term health conditions. The Birmingham model offered the prospect of £4 return in bed-day usage reduction for every £1 invested. The next step was for the Collaborating Centre for Mental Health as the established authority to publish guidance for the NHS commissioners of liaison psychiatry services (12).

Historically, these documents operated at the level of principle rather than practice. The national clinical director for mental health subsequently commissioned a group in the southwest of England to produce detailed service descriptors. These took the form of guidance to commissioners and set out minimum requirements from Core to Comprehensive services, drawing from existing model services across the UK.

NHS England was persuaded of the value of a national survey, at census level, to return data on the success of the implementation. The national clinical director for mental health in England requested and later commissioned approximately annual surveys of all hospitals in England with type 1 (consultant-led, 24/7, equipped for major emergency) accident and emergency services, looking at what existed against the test of 'adequacy' based on the description of a Core service.

Patient Advocates and the Critical Importance of Expertise by Experience

Possibly the most significant moment in the evolution of Core24 liaison psychiatry came from a patient experience story being retold by the civil service chair of a Department of Health strategy working group. The chair of the faculty of liaison psychiatry had a place on the group alongside many other leaders from health and social care in an effort to help policy-makers shape their thinking, in this case around the Five-Year Forward View for Mental Health. These were highly competitive meetings which challenged members to pitch their ideas as precisely and concisely as possible in a way that was persuasive both clinically and financially.

Liaison psychiatry services had found this tricky because the cost and quality benefit did not fall neatly within the traditional and separate mental health envelopes. Financially speaking, they largely benefited the acute hospital system in which the service operated. Much work had gone into simplifying the message to a benefit for the system of £4 back for every £1 put in, which had persuaded many, but how best to explain what it takes?

In the end it was a patient, a personal friend of the civil service chair, who had broken a limb and been admitted to a London teaching hospital orthopaedic and trauma ward somewhat depressed and who had been assessed by a consultant liaison psychiatrist, who convinced her of the value. What became clear from that story was not only was the patient a life-long appreciator of liaison psychiatry but so too their friend, the chair of an influential civil service committee in the Department of Health. It is therefore important in any stakeholder assessment to include people who are expert by experience, by being patients, carers or interested parties, and equipping them with messages and media to help them advocate for the service in their locality, region or nationally.

We are now much more aware of how celebrity influencers can help in this space, so seeking celebrity thought leaders and using their share of voice in mainstream and social media can help simplify and clarify the message to politicians, policy-makers, commissioners and professionals of all kinds as to the value of the proposal on the table.

Moving to Implementation

Once the Department of Health has tasked the NHS in its Mandate and made the funds available, it is then down to the NHS to demonstrate that it can deliver the plan. Since the Lansley reforms and the Health and Social Care Act 2012, this is done through agencies such as Monitor, NHS Improvement, the Care Quality Commission and NHS England. The Care Quality Commission has developed standards for inspecting the provision of liaison psychiatry services in the emergency and urgent care pathway (15) and published recommendations for improving mental health service provision in general hospitals (16). Developing the workforce is the preserve of agencies such as Health Education England. Finally, research is commissioned by and managed through the National Institute for Health Research.

All these agencies were key stakeholders in the Core24 programme. For successful implementation, everyone needed to know about the new service and what their part might be in its commissioning, provision and regulation.

Ensuring Quality

One of the critical success factors in developing and delivering Core24 liaison psychiatry for English acute hospitals with emergency departments was to develop in parallel all the necessary quality and effectiveness components for what had been a missing system of care.

The Royal College of Psychiatrists' Psychiatric Liaison Accreditation Network (PLAN) launched in 2009 into the emerging world of services growing as and where interests and funding aligned. The idea was simple and attractive. Services would be invited to join a network, for a fee, from which peer reviewers would visit the member services and describe the quality and effectiveness of what they found. In addition, the review teams would include experts by experience and focus on aspects of culture in hospital emergency departments, the safety of facilities for making mental health assessments with dignity and the other aspects of clinical governance that make for a high-quality, safe and effective service. Accreditation by PLAN quickly added status to the services participating and, over time, this process has helped liaison psychiatry services prepare for formal regulatory inspection.

It would be fair to say that even with all the work in the preceding 10 years, the policy-makers at the Department of Health and latterly at NHS England remained concerned that liaison psychiatry might not deliver the return on investment as promised. Leaders in liaison psychiatry shared concerns that these new services might not be implemented correctly (poor 'model fidelity') and so not deliver the promise. This had been part of the challenge for the implementation of the Birmingham model, which was essentially an enhanced version of Core24. In its purest form, it had delivered beyond its commissioners' expectations, but when the 'badge' was applied to more limited, single-discipline, self-harm-focussed services, it is not surprising that it did not achieve the same economic impact.

It is embedded within the culture of medicine and clinical science to debate and challenge one another's ideas, testing truths and identifying new research opportunities. This can be unhelpful to those who simply want to know what it is that we want done about a problem which we all agree needs solving. While we have many examples of exemplary pioneering services within liaison psychiatry for the politician, policy-maker or future commissioner looking in, we risked that all they would see would be debate and disagreement. It was helpful to recognise this and to adopt a consensus approach; asking for the same thing, simply and consistently, while at the same time including systems that could address the issues of uncertainty. Examples include building in an outcome framework (see Chapter 20), a national quality improvement framework (see Chapter 24), a curriculum framework and credential training for psychiatrists in other specialties moving to work in these new services (see Chapter 2).

Monitoring Progress

In any large system implementation, there will remain professionals and commissioners who wish to accept the investment but deliver something other than the specified service. It is critical that thought leader and peer influence is brought to bear to help local managers within the provider adhere to the model.

It has long been problematic to ascertain exactly what economic impact liaison psychiatry services might be having. Despite efforts to find all the relevant services, formal research by academics and policy-makers was thwarted by inconsistent nomenclature and lack of agreement about what actually constituted a liaison psychiatry service. Electronic systems and lay researchers had found 'psychiatric liaison', 'liaison psychiatry', 'liaison mental health', 'psychological medicine' and other services, many of which were doing different things with different staff across different working hours, sometimes intertwined with crisis resolution and home treatment teams, at other times confused with health psychology services in general hospitals, sometimes seeing outpatients and sometimes not.

Research based on tracking investment allocated for these services found the trail going cold in regions and local commissioning groups. Response rates were less than 20% and little data of any use had emerged. The implementation of Core24 services led to change. Right or wrong, there was now a model of liaison psychiatry that the Department of Health and NHS England had agreed to commission, and it came with sufficiently detailed specification in terms of hours of work, staffing and location that useful metrics could be extracted, at least in theory. There is a target of having 70% of all hospitals in England with emergency departments to have Core24 liaison psychiatry services by 2023–4.

Another successful initiative for data collection to help drive change was the Liaison Psychiatry Surveys of England providing a regular census. The survey contacted every English hospital with an emergency department and asked any 'reasonably well-informed clinician' within the service to respond to the survey. The Liaison Psychiatry Faculty of the Royal College of Psychiatrists was mobilised to look out for the call. Senior leaders in the faculty and at NHS England were martialled to push awareness of the work. There was a live map on the web showing which centres had responded and those which had not. This map was shared at conferences. 'Regional Champions' were appointed and requested to call centres that were slow to respond. With each survey iteration, more useful information has been collected on the size, shape and model fidelity of these services as they have grown towards the Core24 standard.

This had a significant effect. Around the UK there is evidence of wholesale change and investment in liaison psychiatry services to support the urgent and emergency care pathways. The surveys of liaison psychiatry services undertaken so far in English hospitals achieved census level (100% response) and showed the growth of liaison psychiatry services in England. Wales, Scotland and Northern Ireland are making similar investments.

Challenges Created by the Recent Changes

Rapid Expansion of the Workforce

It was quickly apparent that delivering the staffing model for Core24 liaison psychiatry services to all English hospitals with an emergency department would quickly exhaust the supply of consultant psychiatrists with appropriate sub-specialist training in liaison psychiatry. The principal concern was that consultant psychiatrists from other areas of psychiatry would require further training to work in liaison mental health services. Similar constraints and concerns applied to liaison mental health nursing.

Staffing, educating, training and supervising the new workforce that would be needed to fulfil the Core24 roll-out became the number one issue. Health Education England needed additional help from the Royal Colleges to work out how this might be achieved and the Royal Colleges found themselves limited by the pace at which the professional councils could react. From these conversations, a connected agenda was found. Other areas of medicine were also wrestling with an interim mechanism that might allow consultants previously trained in one area of medicine or surgery to be reskilled to a new or emerging area of medicine that was currently short-staffed. The ideal was to offer a 'credential' from the relevant Royal College and that the credential would be underpinned by a competency-based curriculum and delivered by clinicians with the relevant endorsements or experience. The liaison psychiatry credential was piloted with the support of the Royal College of Psychiatrists and subsequently approved by the General Medical Council.

Consultant psychiatrists are now being offered new training routes into the speciality with the support of the 'credentialing scheme' described above and the current endorsement previously offered to general adult psychiatry trainees is available now to those training in old-age psychiatry.

Rebalancing: Maintaining and Developing Specialist (Non-Acute) Services

The recent expansion in liaison psychiatry has come entirely through investment in staff to allow comprehensive coverage in the acute response part of the service. For example, despite the staffing increase noted earlier, there has been no increase in provision of specialist clinics, which are only provided by about a quarter of English liaison psychiatry services. Helping patients manage the co-existence of physical and mental health problems and medically unexplained or functional disorders is part of the core remit of liaison psychiatry. The main challenge now in the UK is to develop and sustain a high-quality specialist workforce able to work in these areas. Nursing numbers need to grow to manage the growth in services and many more psychologists, occupational therapists and social workers will be needed if these teams are to be genuinely multidisciplinary.

Integration within Mental Health Services

Limitations within the NSF to address the disability resulting from untreated depression and anxiety were observed by psychologist Professor David Clark and economist Lord Richard Layard. They suggested designing, marketing and selling an evidence-based model of psychological care with a well-defined outcome and performance framework and associated research and quality improvement frameworks (17).

They succeeded in shifting policy to bring about 'Improving Access to Psychological Medicine' (IAPT) in primary care. Their model consisted of high-quality psychological therapy services delivering evidence-based interventions with clinical outcome measures and underpinning information systems. It has transformed the care of people with anxiety and depression in primary care in England. High-quality data from these services showed that not only did people presenting with depression and anxiety do well but this approach also helped people with physical symptoms where the underlying cause is depression or anxiety and those with physical conditions associated with depression and anxiety. More recently, they have been able to take referrals for treatment of disorders such as ME/chronic fatigue syndrome and fibromyalgia, albeit at the less complex and severe end of the spectrum.

At the same time, many general hospitals have a clinical health psychology service, and (less universally) non-clinical health psychology services. In most places in the UK, these services work independently of each other so that it is by no means rare to find centres in which all three function independently of each other. There are differences in the cases seen – for example, in medical complexity, in suicide risk or in the existence of severe mental illness. But nonetheless it is desirable that we move towards more integration than currently exists.

Final Word: Persistence and Taking Action

The political landscape has undergone several iterations since the concept of Core24 liaison psychiatry services was conceived. Anything which might be described about the approach to implementing Core24 liaison psychiatry services is entirely contextual to the period of government and policy across which it has happened.

To be precise, the programme found pace in the era of the coalition government (2010–15), negotiated the period of competitions and markets in the subsequent Five-Year Forward View for Mental Health and now continues as part of the NHS Long-Term Plan. The push for integrated mental healthcare in all acute hospital settings is at a fairly early stage. It needs clinicians, opinion leaders, document writers, clinical leads, psychiatrists, primary care physicians, hospital doctors, nurses, allied healthcare practitioners, patients, carers, politicians, commissioners, academics, educators and more.

The opportunity is still there to influence and contribute. Do not wait for permission: write to that person who spoke at the conference; write a letter to a journal; respond to requests for comment; make the ideas from that informal conference conversation a reality; stand for election to your faculty. Soon you will be part of a loose coalition consisting entirely of interesting, passionate people such as yourself. And you will have a chance to change things for the better.

References

1. Walker A, Barrett JR, Lee W et al. Organisation and delivery of liaison psychiatry services in general hospitals in England: Results of a national survey. *BMJ Open*. 2018;8:e023091.

2. Cooksey D. HM Treasury. A review of UK health research funding. 2006. https://assets.publishing.service.gov.uk/government/uploads/system/uploads/attachment_data/file/228984/0118404881.pdf.

3. Black N. The Cooksey review of UK health research funding. *BMJ*. 2006;333 (7581):1231–2.

4. https://healthinnovationmanchester.com/our-work/mental-health-research-domain.

5. www.bristolhealthpartners.org.uk/health-integration-teams.

6. Aitken P, Perahia D, Wright P. Psychiatrists entering the pharmaceutical industry in the UK. *Psychiatr Bull*. 2003;27(7):248–50.

7. CNBC. Three tips for building personal and professional success, according to Billie Jean King. 2017. www.cnbc.com/2017/11/16/billie-jean-king-on-how-to-balance-personal-and-professional-success.html.

8. Aitken P, Drury J, Williams R. *Social Scaffolding: Applying The Lessons of Contemporary Social Science to Health and Healthcare*. Cambridge; 2019.

9. Hansard. https://hansard.parliament.uk/commons/2013-05-16/debates/13051646000001/MentalHealth#contribution–13051646000031.

10. Ministry of Health. A hospital plan for England and Wales. Cmnd. 1604. London; 1962. http://hansard.millbanksystems.com/lords/1962/feb/14/the-hospital-plan.

11. www.crisiscareconcordat.org.uk.

12. National Institute for Health and Care Excellence. Achieving better access to 24/7 urgent and emergency mental health care – Part 2: Implementing the evidence-based treatment pathway for urgent and emergency liaison mental health services for adults and older adults: Guidance. 2016. www.england.nhs.uk/wp-content/uploads/2016/11/lmhs-guidance.pdf.

13. Intellectual Property Enterprise Court. *APT Training & Consultancy Ltd & Anor v Birmingham & Solihull Mental Health NHS*

Trust. 2019. www.bailii.org/ew/cases/EWH C/IPEC/2019/19.html

14. House A, West R, Smith, C et al. The effect of a hospital liaison psychiatry service on inpatient lengths of stay: Interrupted time series analysis using routinely collected NHS hospital episode statistics. *BMC Psychiatry.* 2020;**20**(1):27.

15. Care Quality Commission. Assessing mental health care in the emergency department. 2022. www.cqc.org.uk/sites/default/files/202 2-09/Brief_Guide_Assessing_mental_health_ in_the_emergency_department.odt.

16. Care Quality Commission. How are people's mental health needs met in acute hospitals and how can this be improved? 2020. www.cqc.org.uk/sites/default/files/2 0201016b_AMSAT_report.pdf.

17. Clark DM, Layard R, Smithies R et al. Improving access to psychological therapy: Initial evaluation of two UK demonstration sites. *Behav Res Ther.* 2009;**47**(11):910–20.

18. Department of Health and Social Care. Saving lives: Our healthier nation. 1999. www.gov.uk/government/publications/ saving-lives-our-healthier-nation.

19. The Health Foundation. The nation's health. 2019. www.health.org.uk/ publications/long-reads/the-nations-health.

Consultation-Liaison Psychiatry
Four International Perspectives

Gregory Carter, Wolfgang Soellner, James Levenson
and Kathleen Sheehan

This chapter provides an overview of the evolution of consultation-liaison psychiatry services across three continents, including service configurations and scope, training and research, and what the future holds for these services.

1 Consultation-Liaison Psychiatry in Australia and New Zealand

Gregory Carter

Introduction

This chapter will present a highly selective and therefore likely non-representative set of milestones, opinions, achievements and highlights of the practice of consultation-liaison psychiatry in Australia and New Zealand over the past 50 years or so, with a lesser emphasis on the historical and a greater emphasis on more recent developments. I will refrain from mentioning any person by name, even the giants of history, to reduce the sense of invalidation to those that are not recognised.

History

The history of the first 200 years of (non-Indigenous) Australian psychiatry 'and the struggle for psychiatry to find an honourable place in Australian history' (1) have been published (3), as well as other excellent historical accounts of psychiatry (2) and the Royal Australian and New Zealand College of Psychiatrists (RANZCP) in the early years. An early journal review article examined the practice of psychosomatic medicine in Australia (4) and a comprehensive history of consultation-liaison psychiatry (not psychosomatic medicine) in Australia can be read in an equally excellent book chapter (5).

The practice of consultation-liaison psychiatry in Australia as a sub-speciality began in the 1970s, with emergent foci in Melbourne and Sydney in Australia (5) and in Dunedin in New Zealand (6). The initial developments were born out of a clinical need by patients, as perceived by their treating physicians and surgeons in the general hospital system, which were neither the clinical responsibility nor within the clinical interest of most psychiatrists employed in the public mental health systems. Development was driven initially by a small number of interested clinicians with dual training as physicians and psychiatrists employed in specific general hospitals or by psychiatrists connected in other ways with the general hospital system, often by university teaching appointments.

In addition to the clinical need and the implications for the identification of a clinical workforce, the requirements for psychiatric training were instrumental in sustaining the initial development of consultation-liaison psychiatry. In 1978, the RANZCP training guidelines required a minimum of six months' registrar training in consultation-liaison psychiatry during the first three years of training, an obligation that was maintained in the 2003 and 2012 Training Guidelines (5). Professional developments followed training requirements. In 1992 the RANZCP Special Interest Group was formed and this became the Section of Consultation-Liaison Psychiatry in 1995. The Section was established with 225 members, which by 2018 had grown only to 364 members (5). The number of trained consultation-liaison psychiatrists across the two countries is small, and their services tend to be delivered by small, often multidisciplinary departments, concentrated in metropolitan centres, operating mainly during office hours and using a variety of funding models and governance systems (5, 7).

Scope of Practice

In the 1970s the call for the development of consultation-liaison psychiatry services identified the consultation aspect where psychiatrists were involved in the care of patients who are admitted under the direct care of specialities other than psychiatry, and the liaison aspect was aimed at improving communication and functions between the psychiatrist and the other general hospital specialist teams, hopefully to the advantage of the patient (8).

At the time of formation of the then Section of Consultation-Liaison, the RANZCP defined a clinical population of interest: 'those who are physically ill or who somatise and who are in medical settings of care, particularly the general hospital' (9). This definition did not specifically include or exclude emergency department patients (e.g. self-harm, intoxication, behavioural disturbance) and the inclusion or exclusion of these populations as part of the clinical responsibilities is still disputed. Later the Faculty of Consultation-Liaison Psychiatry of the RANZCP offered this definition: 'Consultation–liaison psychiatry is a psychiatric sub-specialty focusing on the practice of psychiatry in collaboration with a range of other health professionals, usually in a hospital setting' (10). Recently the Victorian branch of the RANZCP offered this wider description and functional role: 'Consultation-Liaison Psychiatry teams provide the mental health services for those patients admitted to Victorian general hospitals who require greater expertise than can be provided by the parent unit. A minimum of 1% of general hospital admissions require specialist mental health services. Adequate mental health services are required in order to provide quality care, ensure patient flow and maintain safety' (11).

Whatever the specified minimum percentage should be, the low rate of referral to consultation-liaison psychiatry has been challenged as being inadequate on the grounds that physical and psychiatric co-morbidity is very common and has serious consequences in terms of morbidity, mortality and healthcare costs. The Royal Melbourne Hospital (Victoria) reported a referral rate for general hospital inpatients and the emergency department of 2.9% and 2.1%, respectively. A recent systematic review of 35 studies suggested that despite evidence of the benefits of consultation-liaison psychiatry, referral rates were too low, with referrals more likely for the young, with previous psychiatric history, living in an urban setting or with functional psychosis. Systemic factors that improved referrals were a dedicated consultation-liaison psychiatry service, active consultation-liaison psychiatry consultant and collaborative screening of patients.

Clinical Service Models and Funding

Departments of consultation-liaison psychiatry, or multidisciplinary teams or networks, often include members of other clinical disciplines, especially consultation-liaison nurses, clinical psychologists and social workers. The most common current clinical model is a for a direct clinical consultation service provided to the treating medical, surgical, paediatric or oncology clinician or treatment team member, acting as the referring agent, when requested for an individual clinical case. The referring team retain full clinical responsibility and decision-making power and as such may or may not choose to implement all, some or none of the consultation advice provided. These consultation requests cover many different areas of clinical relevance including: diagnostic issues, management advice, pharmacological issues, competency assessments, suicidal patient assessments, psychotherapy assessments, discharge planning and requests to facilitate transfer of a patient to the mental health services. In recent years the changes in the general hospital of the case mix to older, sicker patients and the move towards shorter lengths of stay in general hospitals have been paralleled by increased numbers of referrals, a higher proportion of single assessments, more transfers to inpatient psychiatric care and increased demand on available consultation-liaison resources. (12). In 2018, New Zealand conducted their first national survey of consultation-liaison services. Most were funded and managed by the mental health division, and had psychologists and other allied health staff external to the service; however, there was significant heterogeneity in structure and function, particularly for the coverage of emergency departments and younger and older clinical populations (7).

The liaison component is mostly focussed on communication and coordination of services across several important boundaries or relationships: general hospital consultants and teams, patients, families, *whānau* (extended families), private sector clinical, social and welfare service providers and inpatient and community-based mental health services. The older notion of specific liaison services or activities, usually aimed at specifically teaching non-psychiatrists psychiatric and interpersonal skills, is still practised in some locations.

Early Paradigms

Early review articles outlined the need to consider psychosocial issues in the care of the medically ill and emphasised the contribution this approach could make to medical cost containment (13), while surveys of general hospital patients confirmed high levels of co-morbidity of physical illness with common mental disorders (14–16). During this period the shift in clinical practice in Western psychiatry from a dominant 'biomedical' model to a 'bio-psycho-social model' (17) was widely embraced by Australasian consultation-liaison psychiatry, although there were also trenchant criticisms of this model (18). Patients often appreciated these early psychiatric consultations in the general hospital, with anxiety or depression symptoms usually associated with a positive response; however, those with a diagnosis of psychogenic regional pain, alcoholism or drug dependence felt negatively about the consultation and obtained no benefit from it (19).

Losing Out to Severe Mental Illness

Changes came in the 1990s, whereby the prioritisation of mental health funding was predominately for 'serious mental illness' at the expense of medical-psychiatric co-morbidity, which was nonetheless considered to be the most common form of mental illness, having widespread impacts on morbidity, mortality and healthcare costs (20). Funding and administrative responsibility for consultation-liaison services showed marked variability by health division, state or territory and nationally, with the main funding exemplars being no funding, fully funded by mental health, fully funded by general hospitals or some form of joint funding, and hence responsibility. There were calls for the development of a systematic approach to consultation-liaison mental health service delivery and funding to help meet the clinical demand and to reduce this variability in service provision and funding models (21). Later writers anticipated the possible demise of consultation-liaison and identified a dialectical struggle characterised by general hospital specialities that appreciate the service but are reluctant to pay for it versus mental health service managers in under-resourced systems who do not see the value of providing funding for an expert service provided to general hospital patients (22).

Digital Experiments

During the 1990s there were attempts to develop a variety of digital clinical recording systems to demonstrate the service provision and funding requirements for consultation-liaison services. In Melbourne, the development of a system of clinical indicators for consultation-liaison psychiatry was undertaken in response to changing service delivery: more patients, shorter lengths of stay, closure of specialist general hospital psychiatry units (co-morbidity), reduced funding by formulas disadvantageous to consultation-liaison services and increased general adult psychiatric services being delivered from the emergency department due to the advent of co-location of psychiatric and general hospitals (23). A semi-structured diagnostic interview linked to a computerised database (MILP) was developed at Monash to better characterise psychiatric illnesses (especially somatic diagnoses) in the medically ill (24), which was accompanied by the development of the MICRO-CARES clinical database system (25). In Sydney the use of handheld computers was explored as an aid to continuing medical education and embedding evidence-based medicine in clinical practice (26). In Newcastle the development of the Hunter Area Toxicology Service case register was used to demonstrate the cost-effectiveness of the clinical model of care for self-poisoning patients (27).

A Risk of Stagnation

By the early 2000s it was widely recognised that the consultation-liaison psychiatry services in Australasia were suffering from erratic and slowed growth, disorganised funding models and a lack of political and health bureaucracy support, and were considered to be struggling for survival, which was likened to a mid-life crisis (28). Perhaps the speciality as a whole was content to simply maintain the status quo, with recognition of the RANZCP training requirements for a compulsory six-month rotation during the first three years of training being the main protection against being removed entirely during periods of budget restraint and efficiency gains. A recent report from the Victorian branch of the RANZCP made the case, which would be similar throughout Australasia. Consultation-liaison psychiatry funding through the Victorian Department of Health and Human Services' mental health branch has remained stagnant over the past 20 years, despite major growth in acute health services. The resulting inadequacy in consultation-liaison psychiatry has impacted upon quality of care, length of stay, preventable behaviour disturbance and safe discharge planning (94). The ongoing attempts to develop standards and systems to measure the efficiency and effectiveness of consultation-liaison psychiatry are still continuing in the face of growing clinical, economic and systemic arguments, addressing the mental health needs of patients with physical presentations in adult (29) and youth populations (30).

A Shift to Firefighting

During the last 20 years in Australia, there were also important changes in clinical service provision outside of the boundaries of the general hospital, which had implications for service demand within the general hospitals. While the growth of acute care and chronic care medical services has increased, the general psychiatric services have not kept pace. Underfunding for inpatient and community mental health services has been accompanied by service fragmentation and disorganisation. The large psychiatric hospitals were progressively closed and the corresponding programme of co-location of psychiatric hospitals with general hospitals was implemented. The impact has been felt by increased mental health presentations at the emergency department, which was traditionally the geographical province of consultation-liaison services rather than general adult psychiatry services. A recently commissioned report for the Australasian College of Emergency Medicine (ACEM) reported a failing mental health system, with too few services to meet community need, and with emergency departments being the only access point for many to the mental health system, particularly in times of crisis. To highlight a specific example of unacceptable service delays, a recent joint statement from the RANZCP and the ACEM called on the South Australian Government to find a systemic solution to the significant waiting periods experienced by mental health patients in emergency departments in Adelaide, South Australia. The immediate implications are for general adult psychiatry services to be provided by emergency department and consultation-liaison psychiatry clinicians for patients presenting to the emergency department for mental health services. An audit of a 10-year period at an Adelaide hospital quantified this increase in attendance for primarily mental health concerns. A 10-fold increase in the number of patients attending the emergency department was reported, within the context of relatively stable total emergency department presentations. The increase was observed in all diagnostic categories, and length of stay, with the greatest increase for psychotic disorders (31). There have been some centres that have made a decision to embrace these developments and to explore the provision of psychiatric services to emergency departments of tertiary hospitals in Australia, with the establishment of specialised in-reach or liaison services as well as various forms of short-stay units attached to emergency departments, including innovative attempts to deliver psychological therapies via digital platforms to emergency department patients.

The Current Situation

Governance

The RANZCP currently has seven faculties with accredited training programmes. Consultation-liaison psychiatry is one of those faculties, and it in turn has five sub-committees representing New Zealand, New South Wales, Queensland, Victoria and Western Australia. A graphical representation of the complex system of the governance structure of the RANZCP has been recently presented on the RANZCP website.

Staffing

To date there are no agreed standards for staffing by medical, nursing and allied health staff. In 1994, a study was undertaken to establish the then current and desired levels of staffing and funding of the 52 consultation-liaison psychiatry training units in Australian and New Zealand general hospitals. The referral rates and staffing levels were lower than those reported in Europe and the USA, and were considered sub-optimal. The large variation in referral rates and workload was considered to have implications for the type of clinical activity conducted and the quality of training experience (32).

In 2011, a survey of three hospitals over a five-year period in Victoria reported the average clinical staffing at 0.84 equivalent full-time (EFT) clinicians per 100 beds, servicing 2.4 referrals per 100 hospital admissions. The authors concluded that in order to provide a minimum level of service for consultations to the expected range of serious and immediate psychiatric disorders present in the general hospital, 1.0 clinical EFT was required per 100 beds. To address more complex elements of illness behaviour, provide education, conduct research, contribute to comprehensive care in specialist areas and undertake other liaison activities, more multidisciplinary EFT would be needed (33).

Most of the evaluations have focussed on general hospital inpatients and less is known about non-inpatient services. In some centres there are outpatient clinics that follow up discharged inpatients and service patients referred from the community. Some centres have specialist non-inpatient services for neo-natal, substance use, somatising or medically unexplained symptom populations, for example, or specialist psychotherapy services such as psycho-oncology populations. Outside of the hospital boundaries there have been various outreach programmes usually based on palliative care, rehabilitation or primary care populations.

Nursing

In large urban centres, consultation-liaison psychiatry services are commonly staffed by nurses as part of a multidisciplinary team, while in smaller and peripheral hospitals nurses may be the only staff members. Mental health nursing roles in consultation-liaison psychiatry have developed rapidly since the mainstreaming of mental health services within the general healthcare system. A wonderful overview of the development of the role of the nurse and the many successes of nursing in consultation-liaison psychiatry is available (34). A very early description of the concept and the role came from the Royal Prince Alfred Hospital in Sydney (35), while a liaison model (36), and the identification of the different characteristics of liaison referrals came from Westmead Hospital in Sydney (37). An article reporting the development of a model of practice in Victoria also detailed the history, components of the role, consultation-liaison culture brokering, quality improvement and research (38), and was propagated in other jurisdictions. A later survey of 56 psychiatric consultation-liaison nurses across Australia showed that these nurses were usually experienced psychiatric or mental health nurses who worked primarily in general hospital wards or emergency departments and used a range of titles to identify their role. Consultation requests came predominantly from other nurses and educational inputs were provided to a range of staff groups (39). Later suggestions were made on how to translate the traditional educational experiences for non-mental health nurses into a capacity-building approach for knowledge, skill and confidence leading to improved patient outcomes (40).

Speciality nursing contributions have been made in: perinatal services in the community (41); child health depression screening in the general hospital (42); antipsychotics and breastfeeding in perinatal services (43); electroconvulsive therapy (ECT) for Parkinsonism in neurology (44); ethical dilemmas (45); health policy (46) and medicolegal issues including mental health law and human rights (47); knowledge, attitudes and behaviours relating to patient capacity to consent to treatment (48); and duty-of-care decisions (49).

The emergency department has been a particular focus for consultation-liaison nurse activities: the development of a triage scale for psychiatric patients (50), the application of triage scales for psychiatric patients (51), the development and validation of the Emergency Triage Education Kit (52), violence risk screening (53), a team management approach including a senior nurse for the management of behavioural disturbance (54), a training programme on nurses' attitudes for prevention of aggression (55), and a nurse practitioner-led liaison service for general adult psychiatry patients in the emergency department (56), which has been further evaluated in a multicentre trial (57).

Indigenous Populations

The consideration of consultation-liaison psychiatry in relation to Indigenous populations is challenging, although typical metropolitan units have reported on service use and clinical characteristics (58, 59). Perhaps the most important feature is that the nature of illness in Indigenous populations needs to be understood through the context of language, culture, family, tradition and a deeply felt sense of connection to the land and life in community, which is a rather different context when compared to a traditional Western model of 'co-morbid physical and mental illness' or 'physical illness and psychological distress' in the general hospital.

Historically, this has been perhaps best recognised by the RANZCP in New Zealand. The Eighth Annual Congress of the Australian and New Zealand College of Psychiatrists was opened at Auckland on 18 October 1971, the first College Congress to be held in New Zealand. The conference title was 'Māori Traditions'. Dr Henry Bennett, FANZCP, who by age and qualification was the senior Māori psychiatrist in the world, provided the following exhortation (59):

> Recite a spell
> Recite a spell
> over this canoe
> Recite magic
> Recite magic
> to clear the gloomy South!
> It floats
> It floats
> this canoe
> It floats
> It floats
> upon the Home-of-the-Wind!
> All together!
> Pull together!

Inclusion of *whānau* in Māori culture is particularly important and interventions have been developed locating the *whānau* within their own culturally determined knowledge systems and optimising their role in the delivery of culturally required intervention in traumatic brain injury and other rehabilitation settings (61). The context of Indigenous life in rural and remote locations and the differences to life in urban settings are also relevant, particularly in Australia where the physical distances are great and social isolation and physical limitations on access to health services more pronounced. There have been some excellent developments in trying to build workable connections between these different ways of understanding and treating illness.

New Zealand has developed collaborations between Māori healers and psychiatrists (62, 63), including the recognition of culture-bound syndromes (64), while in Australia the appointment of Aboriginal liaison officers in metropolitan hospitals is becoming a required standard (65, 66) following the well-recognised principle, established decades earlier, of the benefits of direct involvement by Indigenous health workers (67). In Australia, non-Indigenous scientific methods have been used to develop best practice guidelines for the psychosocial assessment of Aboriginal and Torres Strait Islander people presenting to hospital with self-harm and suicidal thoughts (68), and an expert committee has acknowledged the negative effects of colonisation and trans-generational trauma while advocating for a renewed emphasis on improving access, cultural orientation and trauma-informed care (69).

There have been multiple specific studies and a few examples are provided: rates of mental illness in non-Māori and Māori women in late pregnancy in New Zealand (70), and the relationship between severe mental illness and the physical health of Māori (71). A quality improvement study of Aboriginal and Torres Strait Islander peoples referred to an inner-city general hospital psychiatry service found that Aboriginal ethnicity was variably identified and Aboriginal health workers, primary care physicians and families were not routinely involved in consultation-liaison psychiatry assessments (72).

Research

The *Australian & New Zealand Journal of Psychiatry*, first published in 1967, has for over 50 years been home to many publications focussed on consultation-liaison psychiatry; while the *Australasian Psychiatry Journal*, first published in 1993, has been a keen publisher of articles concerned with training standards and experiences; and of course consultation-liaison psychiatry authors have been published in various international journals. A highly selective review of some of the Australasian research areas of interest follows.

Abnormal Illness Behaviour and Abnormal Treatment Behaviour

South Australia was the site for development of the Illness Behaviour Questionnaire (IBQ), a 62-item self-report instrument identifying a patient's attitudes, ideas, affects and attributions in relation to illness. The concept of abnormal illness behaviour from Adelaide and the complementary concept of abnormal treatment behaviour from Newcastle have been useful contributions in understanding the complexities of health behaviour by patients and their treating clinicians.

Somatisation

Nevertheless, studies of 'illness behaviour' have shown that patients with a strong somatic focus were less likely to be referred for psychiatric assessment despite the presence of significant psychiatric morbidity (73), a pattern of under-recognition and under-referral that remains little changed today. Abdominal pain and somatisation has been a topic of interest for several decades (74); similarly for chronic pain (75). Even in very recent times common somatic syndromes such as undifferentiated abdominal pain continue to be a focus of study (76).

Psycho-oncology and Palliative Care

A recent review identified the large collaborative programmes of psycho-oncology clinical care and research in Australia (77). Some notable achievements include: the concept of demoralisation, the development of the demoralisation scale, clinical practice guidelines for the psychosocial care of patients with cancer, key features of the Distress Thermometer, systematic screening to reduce pain and psychological distress, and the diagnostic accuracy of instruments used to measure depression and anxiety in cancer populations. There have been effective interventions developed to reduce fear of cancer recurrence (78, 79) and to reduce malnutrition in head and neck cancer (80).

In the palliative care area multiple topics have been covered: the response of doctors who have participated in euthanasia and physician-assisted suicide, patient attitudes to euthanasia and physician-assisted suicide, palliative care for schizophrenia patients and the measurement of psychological distress in palliative care.

Suicidal Behaviours

Hospital-treated deliberate self-harm (or suicide attempt) is common, costly and often serviced by consultation-liaison staff. Increasing rates of 'parasuicide' were noted in the period preceding 1973 and 1986, although it was unclear if this was due to a real increase in these behaviours, better recording or better use of early consultation-liaison services (73). The problem of accurate measurement of self-harm is still well recognised and the known underestimate of intuitional data has been reported in New Zealand (81, 82) and Australia (83, 84). Various epidemiological studies of hospital-treated deliberate self-harm have tried to more accurately estimate the true rates. The RANZCP Clinical Practice Guidelines have been published in several iterations.

Eating Disorders

Most Australian states have developed integrated treatment models for the spectrum of common eating disorders, using specific, integrated treatment programmes delivered in the general hospital, psychiatric hospital and the community. These programmes are predominately aligned with the recommendations of the most recent RANZCP Clinical Practice Guidelines.

Implementing Novel Study Designs, Analyses and Interventions

Despite the relative stagnation of funding for clinical position and services in recent years, the output for research activity has continued to increase steadily. Consultation-liaison researchers have utilised novel study designs in observational studies and interventional trials and have developed novel interventions for evaluation. In hospital-treated self-harm and self-poisoning populations, observational studies have used self-controlled case-series designs (85); and for interventional trials, double-consent Zelen designs have been used in New Zealand (86) and single-consent Zelen designs in Australia (87). Multicentre trials have included cluster-randomised designs for multilevel interventions in suicide prevention (88) and stepped-wedge cluster-randomised designs for nutritional status in head and neck cancer patients (80) and depression in cancer (89), while novel interventions have included online self-guided psychological interventions (90), a combination of motivational interviewing and cognitive restructuring (91), a culturally informed intervention for Māori (92), measurement of treatment adherence by dieticians trained as therapists (93), the measurement of treatment fidelity in translational research (93), a combined intervention of psychological intervention, screening behaviour and values-based goal-setting (89), and training oncology staff as therapists (89).

Conclusion

The future directions of consultation-liaison psychiatry are not clear. There will likely be forces outside consultation-liaison psychiatry that will shape future directions. The recent COVID-19 pandemic and past HIV pandemic remind us that psychological impacts on patients, families, staff and service delivery can arise from novel and unexpected sources. The increasing digitalisation of investigations, interventions and data recording will have impacts on service delivery and staff training. People are living longer with multiple chronic diseases and disability, and dementia prevalence increases with the ageing of Western populations; inpatient care will not be sufficiently available to service these needs and it is possible that intermediate services filling a gap between inpatient and community care will be developed. Greater contributions will come from nursing, psychology and social work-trained professionals, probably with specific training and accreditation; and in some speciality areas such as Indigenous health, paediatrics, perinatal and palliative care, novel professional roles will be developed. Staffing and funding models for Australian and New Zealand services will always be insufficient to meet the demonstrable need and so mental health clinicians will need to continue their tradition of curiosity, innovation, evaluation, collegiality, cultural partnerships and advocacy in meeting the challenges ahead.

Acknowledgements

My thanks to the many colleagues who assisted me with advice, source materials and suggestions.

2 Consultation-Liaison Services across Europe

Wolfgang Söllner

Structures

Types and Organisation of Consultation-Liaison Services

In the 2009 second edition of the *Oxford Textbook of Psychiatry*, Huyse and co-workers wrote, 'The European Consultation-Liaison Workgroup (ECLW) collaborative study made

:lear that C-L psychiatric service delivery is primarily an emergency service' (1). Our clinical impression is that this is still true, although no recent systematic study or survey investigating the organisation of consultation-liaison (CL) services throughout Europe was performed since the ECLW study (2).

In the last 20 years, nationwide surveys on the organisation of CL services have been performed in some European countries (Eastern European countries) (3), Norway (4), Sweden (5), Spain (6) and the UK (7). Two surveys focussed on CL services for old-age patients in Ireland and the UK (8, 9). All these surveys showed an expansion of CL services but a lack of personal resources resulting in a failure to provide adequate assessment and treatment of mental disorders in medically ill patients. The authors of the surveys stated a lack of outpatient CL clinics for the provision of follow-up support for patients diagnosed and treated by the CL services during acute hospital care.

The surveys show that care provided by CL psychiatry and psychosomatic medicine varies widely across Europe and on a local level too. Most services are *core services* for the acute care of hospitalised patients offering 24/7 availability of a psychiatric consultant. In such services, referral rates vary between 1% and 3% of patients admitted to the general hospital. Multiprofessional services including CL nurses exist in larger hospitals only. In some countries (Austria, Germany, Italy, the Netherlands, Norway), health psychology services have been established for the care of certain patient groups, for example in the field of psychosocial care for cancer patients.

Only a minority of services offer enhanced or *comprehensive care* including ambulatory follow-up sessions and specialised treatment for specific disorders, although the number of such services seems to have increased since the ECLW study in 2001. These services are usually multiprofessional including nurses, clinical psychologists and sometimes social workers. In tertiary-care centres, CL services are combined with outpatient clinics (general mental health or specialised on targeted disorders). In such comprehensive CL services, referral rates are higher depending on the contracts with the hospital administration for the care of specialised patient groups. In countries with a specialisation in psychosomatic medicine, such comprehensive services are provided more frequently (10, 11).

Case Mix

According to the above-mentioned surveys, the case mix of core services for the acute care of medical and surgical inpatients seems to be identical to the one reported in the ECLW study 20 years ago. The most prevalent disorders in these services are:

- anxiety and depression in the medically ill
- adjustment disorders
- delirium/dementia
- functional disorders/somatic symptom disorders
- alcohol and substance misuse
- intentional self-harm.

Less prevalent are psychotic disorders, eating disorders and personality disorders (e.g. borderline personality disorder complicating medical treatment).

In comprehensive CL or psychosomatic services, the case mix may be quite different depending on the existence of specialist services (e.g. in oncology, palliative care, transplantation medicine, chronic pain treatment and bariatric surgery; in some countries psychosocial assessment is mandatory before living-donor transplantation or bariatric surgery).

More recently, CL services for migrant populations (often suffering from functional disorders and chronic pain) or refugees (often suffering post-traumatic stress disorder) were set up in some countries (12).

CL in Primary Care/Collaborative Care

- CL services in primary care were established on a local basis; see examples from Italy, Switzerland, the Netherlands and the UK (13–15).
- Collaborative care is still an exception in public healthcare in Europe. This care model was developed in the USA for the treatment of complex, chronically ill patients. It is a collaborative model between general practitioners and CL psychiatrists. The central role is played by a case manager (in most cases a specifically trained nurse or social worker) who regularly contacts the patient by phone or online, carries out a screening of psychological and/or somatic symptoms and, if necessary, provides psychosocial advice and support (e.g. motivational counselling). The CL psychiatrist supervises the case manager weekly and even sees therapy-resistant cases in the general practitioner's office. Some projects of collaborative care for the treatment of patients with affective disorders, anxiety disorders and somatic symptom disorders were established in the framework of research projects in the UK (16, 17), Germany (18–20), Denmark (21) and the Netherlands (22, 23). British working groups effectively tested collaborative care in medically ill patients suffering from depression (24, 25). Although these projects showed a reduction in symptoms, an increased quality of life and, in some cases, a reduction in overall health costs for the population included in the trials, implementation in routine care is pending (26–28).

Med-Psych Units/Psychosomatic Units

- Med-psych units were established to provide care for complex patients suffering from both physical and psychiatric disorders and who were too ill to be treated by CL services on medical wards. While such units have existed in the USA for 30 years, only a few exist in European countries (most of them psychiatric-geriatric patient units), with one exception. Based on newly agreed quality standards for the care of complex patients suffering from medical and mental illness, med-psych units were established in 30 of 90 Dutch hospitals (29). The main reasons for referral were psychiatric symptoms or disorders or behavioural problems accompanying medical illness (most prevalent were mood disorder, suicidal behaviour, aggressive behaviour and catatonia) (30). Patients admitted to med-psych units showed a decrease in medical service use and an appropriate increase in exposure to psychiatric interventions compared with complex patients treated in usual medical units (31).
- In German-speaking countries, psychosomatic inpatient or day hospital units were established in general hospitals (combined with CL services) and in rehabilitation centres. Patients with psychosomatic disorders (often with a chronic course) who need more intensive treatment are referred to these wards either by the CL service or by resident doctors. The most common diagnoses are mood disorders, anxiety disorders or post-traumatic stress disorders, in most cases combined with medical disease, somatisation disorders and eating

disorders (32). Some psychosomatic units focus on geriatric patients (33) or chronic pain patients (34). Treatment in such units is multimodal and multiprofessional, combining pharmacological and other somatic treatment with psychotherapeutic approaches (individual and group therapy, art therapy, relaxation and movement therapy). Therefore, the length of stay in such wards is longer than in med-psych units, which are focussed on the treatment of acute psychological crises in medically ill patients. A systematic review and meta-analysis of 81 trials investigating the effectiveness of psychosomatic inpatient treatment published in 2014 showed high effect sizes for the reduction of symptoms and low effect sizes for changes in interpersonal behaviour (35). Inpatient or day-clinic multimodal psychosomatic treatment is an effective option for the treatment of severe psychosomatic illnesses when intensive outpatient treatment approaches are lacking or inadequate. Close coordination with CL services is advantageous in order to quickly move patients from one-sided somatic treatment to specific psychosomatic treatment. This is particularly important in the case of somatoform disorders and eating disorders (36).

Training of Specialists/Specialisation

Experts and professional societies unanimously demand a specific expertise and training of mental health specialists who care for medically ill patients with co-morbid mental disorders. In 2007, the European Association of Consultation-Liaison Psychiatry and Psychosomatics (EACLPP; since 2012 merged with the European Network of Psychosomatic Medicine to the European Association of Psychosomatic Medicine EAPM) published Guidelines for Training in CL Psychiatry and Psychosomatic Medicine (37). Based on these guidelines, different training programmes for psychiatric and psychosomatic residents as well as advanced training (fellowship) were established throughout Europe (see a summary in (38)). In some European countries, this led to the establishment of a sub-specialisation in psychiatry (in Switzerland and the UK with a mandatory rotation to a CL department of at least 12 months) or a specialisation in psychosomatic medicine. Such a specialisation can either be acquired by physicians of all medical specialisations (in the Czech Republic and in Austria, with a rotation to a psychosomatic department of at least 18 months), or it is a distinct specialisation (in Germany and Latvia) with a full resident training programme lasting five years.

Process and Outcome

In some European countries (the Netherlands, Germany), practice guidelines based on systematic literature research have been established. They documented a blatant lack of resources in the field of CL psychiatry and psychosomatics and called for more intensive care of particularly complexly ill and stressed patients with physical and psychological co-morbidities. Among other recommendations, the guidelines advocated for (a) mental health services to be better integrated into medical care, (b) more direct interventions of CL psychiatrists instead of solely recommending interventions to the team of the medical ward and (c) the introduction of nurse specialists in the field of CL care (39–41).

In 2009, Frits Huyse and co-workers wrote in a chapter on CL psychiatry in the *Oxford Textbook of Psychiatry*: 'The organization of psychiatric services for general hospital departments might change in far-reaching ways in the next decades. Whereas the focus was primarily on reactive services for inpatients on medical and surgical wards, the future should focus on more proactive integrated service delivery for the complex medically ill' (1).

Since the ECLW study published 20 years ago, the number of CL services and patients treated by these services has increased in most European countries (except for countries such as Greece, where mental healthcare has deteriorated because of the economic crisis). However, the number of mental health specialists in these services has not kept pace with this increase. This was accompanied by a significantly increased workload and a reduction in the time spent per patient. Team-related activities (the so-called liaison aspects), such as communication with the referring doctors and nurses or training for health professionals in the medical and surgical departments, had to be reduced. This led to a reduction in satisfaction among consultants and consultees. There were exceptions to this development where public quality assurance programmes provided psychosocial care for the treatment of special patient groups and there was an associated increase in resources, such as in the field of psycho-oncology or transplant medicine.

Studies in the USA showed that so-called proactive CL services, which did not passively wait for referrals but instead actively identified patients with increased psychosocial treatment needs using screening methods and providing active and timely delivery of care, showed better effects in terms of reducing symptoms in the patient, enhancing the satisfaction of the referring physicians and nurses and reducing the length of stay. However, most of these studies showed methodological shortcomings (small sample sizes and non-randomised design) (42). The case finders were either short questionnaires included in the routine medical admission, with which depression or stress were recorded, or short, semi-structured interviews, which assess the psychosocial burden and the need for treatment (e.g. the INTERMED interview carried out by trained nurses or case managers) (43). A randomized-controlled multicenter trial of the effects of proactive CL services was recently conducted in the UK (47) and we are eagerly awaiting the publication of the results.

A recent systematic review concluded that traditional consultation services are unable to significantly reduce patients' psychological complaints even when screening methods are used (44). A second more extensive systematic review, in which CL services were also included, which provided integrative and collaborative care for certain patient groups, showed that CL services with more pronounced integration of the mental health team into medical care sharing responsibility for the patients with the medical team enable better effects in terms of reducing anxiety and depression of medically ill inpatients (45). Study groups in Switzerland (46), Germany (33) and the UK (47, 48) showed how such models of integrated CL services can be effectively established in clinical practice.

The effects of CL interventions on length of stay in hospital has been the subject of controversial debates for years. While conventional consultation services show no effects here (44), there is limited evidence from a few studies that proactive and integrated services may to be able to shorten the length of stay and to reduce readmissions of special patient groups with pronounced psychological co-morbidities (42, 49).

CL services differ greatly in the various European countries depending on historical, cultural and health policy developments. Basically, two main currents can be distinguished: (1) CL psychiatry, which has developed from the psychiatric departments in general hospitals and whose focus is the treatment of medically ill patients with psychiatric co-morbidities, and (2) psychosomatic medicine, which has often developed from general and internal medicine and represents a broader approach in the sense of a holistic bio-psycho-social model of all diseases. In clinical practice, the two models overlap, but depending on the historical development the concrete forms in the different countries are different.

German-Speaking Countries

In these countries, a specialisation called 'psychosomatic medicine' has developed from general medicine and internal medicine in addition to psychiatry. In Germany, a distinct specialisation with this name was established in 1992 and in Austria and Switzerland a specialisation which all clinical specialists can acquire as an additional title. There are around 5,000 specialists in psychosomatic medicine (besides 11,000 specialists in psychiatry) in Germany, half of them in hospital and half in private practice (11, 50). They work in research, in the training of medical students and healthcare professionals and in the clinical sector. In the past 30 years, clinical psychosomatic departments have been set up at most of the large general hospitals and in numerous rehabilitation clinics in Germany (about 220 departments with a total of more than 10,000 beds (50)). In Austria and Switzerland, the number of psychosomatic departments is still small.

These departments focus on the treatment of the medically ill with psychological co-morbidities and of patients with functional syndromes and eating disorders. They offer multimodal therapy programmes with a focus on psychotherapeutic methods. The vast majority of these hospital departments carry out CL services for the other departments of the hospital in addition to inpatient and day hospital treatment in psychosomatic wards. The ECLW Collaborative Study (10) showed that psychosomatic CL services differ from psychiatric CL services in terms of the type of patient treated and the form of treatment. Psychosomatic services focus on the treatment of chronically medically ill patients suffering from anxiety disorders, post-traumatic stress disorder and depression, and of patients with somatic symptom disorders. Psychiatric CL services primarily care for patients with acute mental disorders (delirious syndromes, psychoses and attempted suicide). Accordingly, the forms of treatment are also different. While psychiatric services are mainly active as consultants and offer pharmacological treatment, psychosomatic services more often carry out liaison cooperation with more frequent visits, more psychological treatment approaches and a focus on training the ward teams. They integrate screening of stressed patients more often and work more proactively.

One wonders why psychosomatic specialisation and healthcare services have become established in Germany and Austria alongside general psychiatry. Three factors are likely to play a role:

- a long-lasting separation between psychiatry and medical/surgical health care
- a strong tradition of holistic approaches in internal medicine and family medicine with the aim of integrating medical and mental care for every patient
- the misuse of psychiatry by National Socialism in Germany and Austria and the resulting reservations about psychiatry among the population.

Eastern European Countries

Since the fall of the Iron Curtain and the opening and democratisation of the Eastern European states, existing psychiatric CL services have been expanded in these countries and psychosomatic societies, and training curricula and clinical facilities have been established in some countries (3). In Latvia, as in Germany, a stand-alone specialisation in psychosomatic medicine and psychotherapy has been established alongside psychiatry. In the Czech Republic and Romania, a specialisation in psychosomatic medicine can be acquired by doctors of various specialist fields. Inside the Czech Medical Society, a multiprofessional

Psychosomatic Society with currently about 250 members has been established and organises annual scientific conferences.

It might be that similar factors as in Germany and Austria contributed to the development of psychosomatic specialisations in these countries, in particular the involvement of psychiatric institutions in the Stalinist regime of oppression.

Southern Europe

Since psychiatric care was largely integrated into general hospitals in Italy, Spain and Portugal, psychiatric CL services exist in almost all hospitals. A minimum of three months' training in CL psychiatry became compulsory for all residents. The ECLW Collaborative Study stimulated the research and formation of national societies for CL psychiatry. There are also smaller, multiprofessional societies of psychosomatic medicine. However, the economic crisis in southern Europe has led to a significant setback and loss of staff for clinical CL care in recent years.

French-Speaking Countries

The strong psychoanalytic tradition within psychiatry in France has for many years contributed to the withdrawal of psychiatry from mental healthcare in general hospitals. Renowned CL services have only emerged in a few university hospitals (Paris, Nantes, Toulouse). However, there has been a positive development here in recent years. Empirical research on effects of CL interventions on the length of stay of general hospital inpatients and other economic impacts has been conducted (51, 52). A French CL psychiatry network was established in 2018 and a textbook on CL psychiatry in French (*Psychiatrie de Liaison* by Lemogne and colleagues) with more than 100 authors was published the same year.

Switzerland

In Switzerland, CL psychiatry is strong and clinically and scientifically active with a pronounced psychoanalytic tradition in the French-speaking part of the country. A subspecialisation in CL psychiatry has been established in psychiatry.

There is also a strong and active group of primary care physicians who have completed advanced training and a degree in Psychosocial and Psychosomatic Medicine and have joined forces in an academy of the same name, which has around 1,000 members.

Benelux States

In the Netherlands, a strong section of general hospital psychiatry was founded inside the Dutch Psychiatric Association. A growing number of med-psych units have been established in the last 10 years, which offer CL services in general hospitals and, in some cases, collaborative care programmes in the outpatient area. The general hospital psychiatry section agreed practice guidelines for CL psychiatry (39, 40). Within this section there is a strong research interest with large, multicentre and Europe-wide networked studies in the field of functional syndromes. At the University of Groningen, a PhD programme on Functional Disorders across Europe (ETUDE) has been recently awarded for 15 students per year by a European Union grant. Besides CL psychiatry, there are separate psychological services in the hospitals for the psychological care of the chronically ill.

Scandinavia

CL psychiatry is clinically and scientifically well developed in Norway, with a professorship and department of psychosomatic medicine at Oslo University. Most CL services are multiprofessional, including senior psychiatrists, residents, psychologists and CL nurses. The most prevalent diagnoses are suicide attempts, somatic symptom disorders and affective disorders accompanying somatic illness (51).

In Finland and Denmark, CL psychiatry is established in most major hospitals. Since 1999, Finnish psychiatrists can achieve a special competence in general hospital psychiatry after a two-year training in specialised centres of CL psychiatry (52). They are organised as a special section within the Finnish Psychiatric Association.

A globally unique multiprofessional centre for the research and treatment of functional disorders has developed at Aarhus University, Denmark. Training courses and practice guidelines for primary care physicians have been developed for the treatment of these disorders.

In Sweden, CL psychiatry is less well developed. Consultation services are organised according to the principle of acute intervention on demand. In primary care, models of collaborative care are spreading. Recently, the Swedish Association of Consultation Liaison Psychiatry was reactivated and now allows membership also for healthcare professionals who share a common interest in bio-psycho-social healthcare.

What's Coming Next?

One of the pioneers of CL psychiatry in Europe, Frits Huyse, titled his speech at the award ceremony for the Tom Hackett award in 2009 'Farewell to C-L? Time for a change?' (53). He advocated for the development of more proactive care models, better integrated into somatic medicine, in order to be able to treat patients with complex medical and psychological disorders more adequately and to reduce deficits in patient care. In the meantime, research results show that proactive and integrative models of CL in hospitals and collaborative care in the outpatient area are not only feasible and better accepted than traditional on-demand consultation services but also show a better outcome in terms of patient quality of life at acceptable costs. It is now necessary to establish this in practice, especially in areas in which many complex patients are treated. The task now is to convince those responsible in the healthcare system and representatives of patient organisations and to establish such models, especially in areas of the healthcare system in which many complex patients are treated. We need more cross-sectoral, multiprofessional and integrative models of care and accompanying methodologically sound research.

The long-term consequences of migration and flight on mental health, as well as the long-term consequences of the COVID-19 pandemic, pose serious challenges for CL psychiatry and psychosomatics. Specially tailored treatment programmes need to be developed and evaluated. With the support of the European Association of Psychosomatic Medicine a number of multicentre research projects on long COVID have been started. When developing new models of care and training programmes for health professionals, we have to overcome national borders and learn from one another.

The increased use of digitalisation and artificial intelligence in medicine will provide better medical diagnosis and more sophisticated treatment and offer new possibilities to bring treatment to patients via apps and telemedicine and to better network the practitioners. On the other hand, the use of artificial intelligence will also bring new challenges for medicine and especially for the treatment of mental disorders. In the course of rationalisation in the healthcare system, the interpersonal relationships between doctors, other healthcare professionals, patients and their relatives could increasingly be replaced by elaborate digital programmes. The role of CL psychiatry and psychosomatic medicine as advocates of patient-centred medicine could become even more important.

3 Consultation-Liaison Psychiatry in the United States

James Levenson

History

Intellectual Ancestry

In the United States, the origins of consultation-liaison psychiatry largely lie in the period between the First and Second World Wars, alongside the development of psychosomatic medicine and general hospital psychiatry. The roots of all three can be traced to the influential American psychiatrist Adolf Meyer (1866–1950), the first psychiatrist-in-chief of the Johns Hopkins Hospital and president of the American Psychiatric Association (APA) in 1927–8. His theoretical approach known as 'psychobiology' considered mental disorders as due to dysfunctional personality resulting from psychological, social and biological factors over a lifetime, not solely from neuropathology. George Engel's bio-psycho-social framework for understanding all disorders, medical and mental, is a later extension of psychobiology [1]. Lipsitt has written a comprehensive account of the history of consultation-liaison psychiatry in the USA [2] and a brief summary is provided in this chapter.

Other important historical influences include the American physiologist Walter B. Cannon (1871–1945), whose studies of the somatic effects of emotional states, the fight or flight response and homeostasis were the foundation on which psychosomatic medicine was built. Helen Flanders Dunbar (1902–59) had degrees in psychology, theology, philosophy and medicine, and published psychosomatic studies including a cardiac personality type very similar to the later concept of type A personality [3]. She had studied with psychoanalysts in Europe including Helene and Felix Deutsch (who coined the term 'psychosomatic medicine') and Carl Jung. Dunbar and a group of analysts founded the American Psychosomatic Society in 1936 and she was the first editor of its journal, *Psychosomatic Medicine*, in 1939. Another European psychoanalyst, Franz Alexander (1891–1964), emigrated to the USA and developed a psychoanalytic psychosomatic medicine centre at the Chicago Psychoanalytic Institute. While Dunbar had focussed on personality as predisposing to particular medical disease, Alexander stressed the importance of unconscious conflict in underlying specific medical disorders. There are many other scholars in the USA worthy of mention in the evolution of psychosomatic medicine and consultation-liaison psychiatry, such as Grete Bibring, Ralph Kaufman and Zbigniew Lipowski [1, 4–6].

The Birth of a National Consultation-Liaison Psychiatry Organisation

New York City was the early epicentre for consultation-liaison psychiatry. A small group of psychiatrists there founded the Society for Liaison Psychiatry (SLP) in 1973. The SLP played a key role over the next 30 years in promoting consultation-liaison psychiatry, including an unsuccessful effort to convince APA and the American Board of Psychiatry and Neurology to officially recognise CL as a psychiatric sub-specialty. A first national conference on consultation-liaison psychiatry was held in 1981, bringing together a small group of leaders to advance the field. This led to greater involvement of CL psychiatrists in the APA, resulting in the formation of the APA Committee on Consultation-Liaison Psychiatry and Primary Care Education. Convinced of the need for a national organisation specifically devoted to CL, leaders from the SLP met with the Academy of Psychosomatic Medicine Council to advocate that the Academy of Psychosomatic Medicine (APM) transform itself into such an organisation.

The SLP's call for the creation of a national CL organisation led to a second national conference in 1989, bringing together 39 leaders from organisations in which CL psychiatrists were active, including the APM, American Association of Child & Adolescent Psychiatry, APA (including the medical director and deputy medical director), American Psychosomatic Society, Association for Academic Psychiatry and Association of Directors of Psychiatric Residency Training. The goal was to seek consensus on creating a new national CL organisation. The APM representatives indicated that if such consensus could not be reached, the APM would transform itself into such an organisation. No consensus was reached, perhaps because each organisation feared losing members to a new one. In 1989–90, the APM followed through with its conditional intention, declaring itself the 'national organization for C-L psychiatrists'. Regular voting membership would only be open to psychiatrists who were actively engaged in CL psychiatry. Non-psychiatrists were eligible for associate membership. The annual meeting programme now focussed entirely on clinical, research and educational issues of relevance to CL psychiatry.

The APM also then launched a campaign to make CL psychiatry an officially recognised sub-specialty of psychiatry. The APM developed standards for CL training during psychiatric residency (7) and for fellowship training and started its own fellowship programme approval process. The APA Commission on Subspecialisation approved the proposal for CL to be a recognised sub-specialty, but it was opposed by the APA Committee on Graduate Medical Education who feared fragmentation of the specialty. This did not prevent the APA Assembly, its governing representative body, from approving the proposal, but the American Board of Psychiatry and Neurology turned it down on a split vote. Before this could be appealed, in 1992 the American Board of Medical Specialties (ABMS) declared a moratorium: no more sub-specialties would be approved. Geriatric psychiatry had managed to get through the approval process as a sub-specialty just before ABMS closed the door.

There were a number of reasons why some leaders in psychiatry opposed making CL psychiatry a sub-specialty. They pointed out that all psychiatrists provide consults or should be able to. The name itself was unacceptable to many. Minutes of the APM Council document that the name had been debated at every meeting since 1964. Sub-specialties were supposed to be defined by a specific patient population (e.g. children, geriatric or forensic populations). CL psychiatrists were told, 'Your knowledge base is one all psychiatrists should know.' There was concern that creating CL fellowships would detract from residency training of general psychiatrists. Some feared that general psychiatrists would lose business. CL psychiatrists' answers to these concerns were that their specific patient population was the medically ill, that specialised skills and knowledge were necessary, that it would enhance general residency training and that general psychiatrists were not interested in leaving their private offices and psychiatric hospitals to come and see patients in general medical hospitals.

The APM did not give up and published practice guidelines for consultations in the hospital in 1998 (8). That same year, the APM started an International Consultation-Liaison Committee as efforts to organise the European Association of Consultation-Liaison Psychiatry and Psychosomatics (EACLPP) were just beginning. A new campaign to achieve sub-specialty status was launched in 2000. Approval was required sequentially from the APA, the American Board of Psychiatry and Neurology and the ABMS, with final approval in 2003 (9). However, the American Board of Psychiatry and Neurology had refused to approve the name 'consultation-liaison psychiatry', insisting instead on 'psychosomatic medicine' on historical grounds, noting the correspondence to the names of the national organisations and journals devoted to the field.

Renaming the Sub-specialty

The APM conducted multiple surveys of its members starting in 2015 regarding their preferences for the name of the sub-specialty. This reawakened a debate that had never really ended. Younger members in particular disliked 'psychosomatic medicine' and voted overwhelmingly for 'consultation-liaison psychiatry'. The change was accomplished by obtaining the sequential approval of the APA Council on Psychosomatic Medicine, the chief executive officer of the APA, the APA Board of Trustees, the American Board of Psychiatry and Neurology, the American Council on Graduate Medical Education and finally in 2018 the ABMS. The APM formally changed its name to the Academy of Consultation-Liaison Psychiatry (ACLP) in 2017 (10).

The Current Situation

Governance

In 1930, psychiatrists in the USA were located in mental hospitals, with little interaction with their medical colleagues. There could be no consultation-liaison until they moved into the general hospital, which was just beginning in the 1930s. G. W. Henry in 1929 outlined the concept of liaison psychiatry in advocating that every general hospital should have a psychiatrist who would regularly visit the wards, direct a psychiatric outpatient clinic, teach house staff and attend meetings with non-psychiatric colleagues. Accomplishing that meant a major change in healthcare delivery. The Rockefeller Foundation invested a huge amount of money to develop a modern American psychiatry in the 1930s, which included funding nascent CL services at the University of Colorado, Massachusetts General Hospital and Duke University.

The National Institute of Mental Health (NIMH) began funding psychiatry in the general hospital shortly after the Second World War, but most significantly in the 1970s by the director of the psychiatry education branch of the NIMH, James Eaton. Under his leadership, multiyear training grants in CL psychiatry were funded, birthing fellowship programs all over the USA. An institutional step backwards occurred when the American Board of Psychiatry and Neurology eliminated the requirement for a medical internship in 1969 to become board-certified in psychiatry, reflecting a move to 'de-medicalise' psychiatry by psychoanalysts and social psychiatrists. This was soon recognised as a bad decision; the internship requirement was restored in 1977 and psychiatry was 're-medicalised'.

A number of national organisations showed increasing interest in CL, including the American Psychosomatic Society, the APM (founded in 1954), the American Association of General Hospital Psychiatrists, the APA and the Association for Academic Psychiatry. In 1977, the Association for Academic Psychiatry established a special section for those who were devoted teachers of CL psychiatry.

In the mid-1980s, the NIMH made it a priority to develop outcome research in CL and invested in nurturing the field (11). While most CL psychiatrists consider themselves primarily clinicians or clinician-teachers, major growth in US CL research followed NIMH's intervention, exemplified by Wayne Katon, the first recipient of the ACLP Research Award, for whom it is now named.

The ACLP now has 1,846 members (James Vrac, personal communication, 18 May 2020). Its annual meetings are attended by larger numbers each year, now over 1,200. The ACLP has 23 Special Interest Groups, ranging from Addiction and Toxicology to Women's Health. ACLP publishes a clinically orientated journal, *Psychosomatics*, started by the APM in 1960. For fundraising, a non-profit foundation was established by the Academy in 2009, now named the Foundation of the Academy of Consultation-Liaison Psychiatry. There are 53 approved one-year CL fellowships in the United States, with programmes in 24 of the 50 states (14 of the 53 are in New York), the District of Columbia and Puerto Rico. Applicants must have successfully completed residency in general psychiatry. Certification in the sub-specialty is granted by the American Board of Psychiatry and Neurology following passing a written examination.

Current CL Service Delivery
Service Configuration

Since US healthcare is not nationally organised, the nature of CL services varies greatly. There are no national uniform protocols or standards for psychiatric consultation. All large teaching and tertiary-care hospitals have CL services, but other hospitals usually rely on general community psychiatrists or psychiatric nurse practitioners to provide consults when needed.

At some but not most major hospitals, CL psychiatrists cover the emergency department. CL psychiatrists serve as the attending physicians on medical-psychiatry inpatient units at some teaching hospitals, providing care to patients with co-morbid mental and medical disorders that are too difficult to manage on regular medical or psychiatric units. A growing number participate in collaborative primary care.

Consultation is far more available than liaison because both federal and private health insurers provide reimbursement for the former but not the latter. The role of clinical health psychologists varies, but they generally function independently of CL psychiatrists. The number of psychiatric nurse practitioners is rapidly growing but most are practising in general psychiatric outpatient practice or on inpatient psychiatric units.

Because there is no single electronic medical record used by all hospitals and outpatient practices, communication between systems must rely on telephone, fax and regular mail, hindering consultation and liaison between hospital-based CL psychiatrists and community-based providers, or when a patient is transferred from one hospital to another. Where available, child psychiatrists provide psychiatric consultations for patients under age 18, but there is a national shortage and they are scarce in rural areas far from cities.

The racial and ethnic makeup of physicians in general and CL psychiatrists in particular does not match the patient populations they serve in the USA, with under-representation of Black and Latinx (the two largest minority groups), but this is beginning to be better addressed. Too few CL psychiatrists speak Spanish, which is prevalent throughout the United States, as immigrants from Central and South America have come for decades for economic opportunity and to escape violence. The USA is a very multi-ethnic country, despite the previous national administration's attempts to stop immigration.

Scope of Clinical Practice

CL psychiatrists at major hospital systems often participate in more specialised interdisciplinary services, such as transplant programmes, cancer centres and HIV clinics. Over the last 35 years, the severity and complexity of illness in US medical-surgical hospitals have increased, while the average length of hospital stay has signifi-cantly fallen. The national average for a hospital stay in the USA is now 4.5 days. As a consequence, the most common reasons psychiatric consultations are requested have changed.

The most common reasons now are for suicidality, delirium, dementia with behavioural disturbance, substance abuse/withdrawal and capacity for making decisions about medical care or discharge disposition. Some CL services provide substance abuse/withdrawal con-sults, while other hospitals have separate addiction consult services.

4 Consultation-Liaison Psychiatry in Canada

Kathleen Sheehan

As a clinical discipline, consultation-liaison psychiatry (CLP) has developed more slowly in Canada than in other countries (1). The field and its practitioners have faced numerous challenges in being recognised, which limited its expansion in clinical practice, medical education and research. CLP is not a sub-specialty in Canada as designated by the Royal College of Physicians and Surgeons of Canada (RCPSC) which oversees medical education and examinations for specialist physicians across the country. This stands in contrast to the USA, UK, Australia and New Zealand, where CLP is a sub-specialty with specific training programmes. The history of CLP is maintained through oral history, publications and organisational artefacts. While numerous people have made important contributions to the development of CLP in Canada, I will focus on the process of CLP development rather than the individuals who drove these changes (2).

Development of a Discipline (Pre-1980)

While there were psychiatrists interested and engaged in caring for medical and surgical patients prior to this, the first CLP service in Canada is believed to have been started in 1959 at the Royal Victoria Hospital in Montreal, led by Dr Z. J. ('Bish') Lipowski, a prolific writer about the history and practice of CLP (3, 4). The first empirical paper about the work of a

CLP service was a pilot study of the Psychiatric Consultation Service at the Montreal General Hospital, investigating referral patterns, diagnoses and suggested management from 1 July to 31 December 1961 (5). It described a service with a consultant physician, a research fellow, a resident in psychiatry and two medical students consulting on referrals received from medical and surgical teams. The team assessed 205 patients over this six-month period with the majority of referrals from internal medicine.

CLP featured prominently in the 1967 and 1968 meetings of the Canadian Psychiatric Association, suggesting an increased interest in this area of practice (6). This included both general and plenary sessions, including one entitled 'The Aims and Techniques of Psychiatric Consultation in Medicine'. Gagnon refers to a significant shift during the period between the Second World War and 1970, by which time CLP/psychosomatic medicine had moved from being a 'field of interest', restricted to major urban centres such as Montreal and Toronto, to becoming a 'discipline' across the country (2).

By 1972, 5–10% of Canadian general hospitals had departments of consultation psychiatry (7). In the 1979–80 academic year, 15/16 Canadian psychiatry residency programmes were offering training in CLP psychiatry in a total of 54 teaching general hospitals, with 33% of residents receiving CLP training as part of a general inpatient or specific CLP rotation (8). However, half of the teaching hospitals did not have a formalised or organised CLP service. The majority of programmes (13/16) had core teaching on CLP and psychosomatic medicine, although only two offered post-residency fellowship in CLP. At that time, 12/16 Canadian medical schools offered some CLP to medical students through didactic teaching, clinical experience and case conference discussions. By 1977, training and experience in CLP was required for certification in psychiatry by the RCPSC, although this was not operationalised as a mandatory CLP rotation block until 2007 (2).

Specialisation without a Sub-Specialty (1980s–1990s)

In their paper about CLP training in Canadian residency programmes, Agbayewa and Perez comment that 'the trend to develop consultation liaison psychiatry as a sub-specialty in the United States through post-residency fellowships has not caught on in Canada, probably due to lack of funding' (8). Their statement foreshadowed the next two decades, with limited growth in fellowship opportunities and challenges in having CLP recognised as a sub-specialty of psychiatry in Canada.

Through the 1980s and 1990s, educational, clinical and research endeavours in CLP expanded across the country. By 1984, 14/16 medical schools offered CLP teaching, 10/16 offered CLP clinical electives and 8/16 included CLP as part of a core clerkship rotation (9). The majority of directors of undergraduate psychiatric education across the country felt that CLP should be included as a mandatory part of the undergraduate curriculum. At a residency level, CLP was discussed at a national conference on 'Key Issues in Postgraduate Psychiatric Education in Canada' in October 1985 (10). While a mandatory experience in CLP during the residency general hospital rotation was proposed, 'either six months continuously or a total of 60 consultations', this was narrowly defeated. A summary of the conference's activities reported that 'this decision should not be interpreted as minimizing the importance of consultation-liaison ... it seems like a large number of residents already chose it as an elective ... some programs have internally decided to require a consultation block' (10). Further evidence of CLP's popularity with trainees included a survey of psychiatric residents where over 40% reported CLP as one of their top three career choices (11). With more limited training opportunities in Canada, some residents went on to complete formal fellowship training in the United States (12, 13).

During this time, numerous CLP services were established throughout Canada. While some were general CLP services, others focussed on particular patient populations, such as obstetrics and gynaecology, renal dialysis, transplant, surgery, somatisation, cardiac, and cancer (14–16). Several papers described these services and aspects of clinical care, such as patient characteristics, referring service and psychiatric diagnosis (17, 18). These enabled comparisons of CLP services in Canada with those in the USA and UK. CLP research was also described, outlining how it had evolved from being 'initially descriptive and evaluative in nature … toward the delineation of the mechanisms which mediate psychopathology in the medically ill' (19). Psychiatric services also became embedded within outpatient family practice and specialist clinics (20, 21). Although the growth of CLP was frequently noted to be less rapid than that in the United States, it was becoming a much more developed area of practice in Canada (18). In May 1988, *Can J Psychiatry* published a special issue dedicated to CLP, with the editorial indicating that it would be the first devoted to this topic (it remains the only issue focussed on CLP to date) (2, 22).

During this time, the Canadian Psychiatric Association (CPA) established a Section on Psychosomatic Medicine. Canadian psychiatrists also joined and became actively engaged in the European APM, as well as the APM (renamed the Academy of Consultation-Liaison Psychiatry in 2018) and the American Psychosomatic Society in the United States (13, 23). With increased interest in the idea of sub-specialisation, a survey was sent to all members of the CPA's Section on Psychosomatic Medicine. Over half (55%) were in favour of CLP as a sub-specialty, with increased proportions of recent residency graduates and those working in CLP being in support (24). Swenson and colleagues highlighted features unique to Canada as likely shaping the discourse about sub-specialisation in Canadian psychiatry, such as geographic distribution, centralised government funding and educational priorities (24).

Self-Organising to Set the National Agenda (2000s–2010s)

Through the early 2000s, there was a growing desire for recognition of psychiatric sub-specialties and to have dedicated residency and post-general psychiatry residency training in these areas. Psychosomatic medicine/CLP was granted sub-specialty status in the USA in 2003 by the American Board of Medical Subspecialties.

In 2005, the Canadian APM (CAPM) was founded, joining three other academies of the CPA (Child and Adolescent Psychiatry, Geriatric Psychiatry and Psychiatry and the Law). The academies 'represent and advance the special interests of subspecialty areas of psychiatric practice' (2). The choice of name caused great debate (2, 13, 23). Many supported 'psychosomatic medicine' to parallel psychosomatic medicine's recognition as a psychiatric sub-specialty in the USA, while others preferred CLP, which reflected the name of most hospital-based clinical services and medical school and residency rotations in this area. In the end, psychosomatic medicine was the chosen term.

Concurrently, there was a major review of general psychiatry residency training, with collaboration between the CPA and RCPSC (2). This culminated in a revision of the general psychiatry training programmes which started to require a mandatory 'supervised experience in Consultation and Liaison Psychiatry (Psychosomatic Medicine) in a specific rotation no less than the equivalent of 3 months and no more than the equivalent of 6 months duration in which the experience is with medically and surgically ill patients' for all psychiatry residents in 2007 (25). Prior to 2007, the RCPSC guidelines required psychiatry residents to have 'supervised experience, not necessarily in a dedicated clinical rotation, sufficient to assure competence in consultation and liaison psychiatry' (26).

In 2008, with the support of the CPA, all four academies prepared applications for the RCPSC Committee on Specialties, proposing that each should become a recognised sub-specialty of psychiatry, with additional residency training being required for this designation. Child and adolescent, geriatric, and forensic psychiatry were all successful in their applications; however, CLP was not. It was reported that the Committee on Specialties felt that all psychiatrists should be able to perform the activities associated with CLP rather than this requiring additional training. Since that time, the RCPSC has indicated that they likely will not be designating any further psychiatric sub-specialties and recommended a focus on applications for Area of Focused Competence (AFC) Diploma, which represents additional 'competencies that enhance the practice of physicians in an existing discipline or a highly specific and narrow scope of practice that does not meet the criteria of a subspecialty' (2, 13, 27).

A Question of Competence (2010s–2021)

With sub-specialty status no longer a likely possibility, the CLP community in Canada re-grouped with its national activities focussed around CAPM, which hosts an annual meeting and other educational activities. Discussion shifted from whether CLP should apply to be a sub-specialty to whether CLP should apply to be an AFC Diploma. Led by a group of CL psychiatrists from across the country, an application was developed and submitted to the RCPSC in September 2019. A survey conducted for the AFC application found that there were approximately 270 psychiatrists working full- or part-time in CLP at academic health sciences centres and five universities offering up to 12 post-residency CLP fellowship training positions annually (British Columbia, Toronto, Queen's, Montreal and McGill). As previously noted, all Canadian psychiatry residents complete a mandatory CLP rotation of at least three months' duration.

In May 2020, an AFC in CLP was formally approved by the Committee on Specialty Education, RCPSC. The AFC is focussed on the provision of psychiatric care to complex medically ill patients. It meets an important societal need, bridging the gap between physical and mental health given the poor outcomes for patients with co-occurring mental and physical health conditions. A national AFC working group is developing programme objectives, with a provisional plan for launch in 2023.

In the autumn of 2021, following approval of the CLP AFC, CAPM changed their name to the Canadian Academy of Consultation Liaison Psychiatry (CACLP). The change in name ensures alignment between the national academy and the RCPSC AFC Diploma. These developments have led to a sense of reinvigoration and optimism about the future of CLP in Canada. Since the name change, CACLP has seen a substantial increase in applications for membership. As a CL psychiatrist, and member of the CACLP executive, I believe this reflects a growing recognition of this field in Canada and a renewed sense of professional identity – as clinicians, educators and researchers.

Acknowledgements

Thank you to Susan Abbey, Nancy Brager, Fabien Gagnon, Donna Stewart, Adrienne Tan and Louis Van Zyl for participating in interviews on this topic and/or reading drafts of this piece. Thank you also to CAPM/CACLP (Susan Adler, CPA Administrator) and the RCPSC (Anna Marrello, Administrator Specialties Unit; Kimberly St. John, Chair of the Specialty Committee; Peter Smith, Special Collections Administrator) for administrative and archival support.

Australia and New Zealand

1. Dax EC. The first 200 years of Australian psychiatry. *Aust NZJ.* 1989;**23**(1):103–10.

2. Kirkby KC. History of psychiatry in Australia, pre-1960. *Hist Psychiatry.* 1999;**10**(38):191–204.

3. Rubinstein WD, Rubinstein HL. *Menders of the Mind: A History of the Royal Australian and New Zealand College of Psychiatrists 1946–1996.* Oxford; 1996.

4. Kalucy RS. Psychosomatic medicine: A review of the discipline. *Aust NZJ.* 1979;**13**(2):85–101.

5. Gribble R. Australia: Consultation-liaison psychiatry not psychosomatic medicine. In Leigh H (ed.), *Global Psychosomatic Medicine and Consultation-Liaison Psychiatry.* Cham; 2019.

6. Smith GC. Obituary: Wallace Ironside. *Med J Aust.* 2002;**176**:593.

7. Hopkins J, Cullum S, Sundram F. The state of play: The first national survey of consultation-liaison psychiatry services in New Zealand. *Australas Psychiatry.* 2020;**28**(4):448–53.

8. Evans L. Consultation-liaison psychiatry. *Aust NZJ* 1977;**11**:95–100.

9. Royal Australian and New Zealand College of Psychiatrists. By Laws for the Section of Consultation-Liaison. 1995.

10. Royal Australian and New Zealand College of Psychiatrists. Faculty of Consultation–Liaison Psychiatry. 2020. www.ranzcp.org/membership/faculties-sections-and-networks/consultation-liaison.

11. Royal Australian and New Zealand College of Psychiatrists. *Service Model for Consultation-Liaison Psychiatry in Victoria.* Melbourne; 2016.

12. Devasagayam D, Clarke D. Changes to inpatient consultation-liaison psychiatry service delivery over a 7-year period. *Australas Psychiatry.* 2008;**16**(6):418–22.

13. Mendelson G. Psychosocial factors and the management of physical illness: A contribution to the cost-containment of medical care. *Aust NZJ.* 1984;**18**(3):211–16.

14. Clarke DM, Minas IH, Stuart GW. The prevalence of psychiatric morbidity in general hospital inpatients. *Aust NZJ.* 1991;**25**(3):322–9.

15. White W, Bloch S. Psychiatric referrals in a general hospital. *Med J Aust.* 1970;**1**(19):950–4.

16. Tiller JW. Psychiatric consultations from public wards of a Melbourne metropolitan teaching hospital. *Med J Aust.* 1973;**1**(9):431–5.

17. Engel G. The clinical application of the biopsychosocial model. *Am J Psychiatry.* 1980;**137**(5):535–44.

18. McLaren N. A critical review of the biopsychosocial model. *Aust NZJ.* 1998;**32**(1):86–92.

19. Hughson B, Lyons R. Patient response to psychiatric consultation in a general hospital. *Aust NZJ.* 1973;**7**:279–82.

20. Smith GC. From consultation–liaison psychiatry to psychosocial advocacy: Maintaining psychiatry's scope. *Aust NZJ.* 1998;**32**(6):753–61.

21. Huyse FJ, Smith GC. Consultation-liaison: From dream to reality. A systematic approach to developing C–L mental health service delivery. *Psychiatr Bull.* 1997;**21**(9):529–31.

22. Ellen S, Gray C, Selzer R et al. Is consultation liaison psychiatry doomed? *Aust NZJ*. 2007;**41**(1_suppl):A20–A.

23. Holmes AC, Judd FK, Lloyd JH, Dakis J, Crampin EF, Katsenos S. The development of clinical indicators for a consultation-liaison service. *Aust NZJ*. 2000;**34**(3):496–503.

24. Clarke DM, Smith GC, Herrman HE, McKenzie DP. Monash Interview for Liaison Psychiatry (MILP): Development, reliability, and procedural validity. *Psychosomatics*. 1998;**39**(4):318–28.

25. Smith GC, Clarke DM, Handrinos D, Dunsis A. Consultation-liaison psychiatrists' management of depression. *Psychosomatics*. 1998;**39**(3):244–52.

26. Ryan C, Kotze B. Hand-held computers and consultation-liaison psychiatry: A practical tool for the information age. *Australas Psychiatry*. 2001;**9**(3):203–6.

27. Whyte IM, Dawson AH, Carter GL, Levey CM, Buckley NA. A model for the management of self-poisoning. *Med J Aust*. 1997;**167**(3):142–6.

28. Macleod S. Consultation–liaison psychiatry hits a midlife crisis. *Australas Psychiatry*. 2002;**10**(3):229–31.

29. Wand AP, Wood R, Fossey MJ, Aitken P. Standards, efficiency and effectiveness in consultation-liaison psychiatry. *Aust NZJ*. 2015;**49**(2):104–5.

30. Allison S, Baune BT, Roeger L, Coppin B, Bastiampillai T, Reed R. Youth consultation-liaison psychiatry: How can we improve outcomes for young people with chronic illness? *Aust NZJ*. 2013;**47**(7):613–16.

31. Kalucy R, Thomas L, King D. Changing demand for mental health services in the emergency department of a public hospital. *Aust NZJ*. 2005;**39**(1–2):74–80.

32. Smith GC, Ellis PM, Carr VJ et al. Staffing and funding of consultation liaison psychiatry services in Australia and New Zealand. *Aust NZJ*. 1994;**28**(3):398–404.

33. Holmes A, Handrinos D, Theologus E, Salzberg M. Service use in consultation-liaison psychiatry: Guidelines for baseline staffing. *Australas Psychiatry*. 2011;**19**(3):254–8.

34. Sharrock J. Perspectives on psychiatric consultation liaison nursing. *Perspect Psychiatr Care*. 2006;**42**(2):137–9.

35. Meredith L, Weatherhead R. Psychiatric consultation liaison nursing: 18 months later. *Lamp*. 1980;**37**(6):19.

36. Anderson G, Hicks S. The clinical nurse specialist role, overview and future prospects. *Aust Nurses J*. 1986;**15**(8):36.

37. Hicks S. The psychiatric nurse in liaison psychiatry. *Aust NZJ*. 1989;**23**(1):89–96.

38. Sharrock J, Happell B. The psychiatric consultation-liaison nurse: Towards articulating a model for practice. *Aust N Zeal J Ment Health Nurs*. 2000;**9**(1):19–28.

39. Sharrock J, Bryant J, McNamara P, Forster J, Happell B. Exploratory study of mental health consultation-liaison nursing in Australia: Part 1. Demographics and role characteristics. *Int J Ment Health Nurs*. 2008;**17**(3):180–8.

40. Brunero S, Lamont S. Mental health liaison nursing: Taking a capacity building approach. *Perspect Psychiatr Care*. 2010;**46**(4):286–93.

41. Harvey ST, Bennett JA, Burmeister E, Wyder M. Evaluating a nurse-led community model of service for perinatal mental health. *Collegian*. 2018;**25**(5):525–31.

42. Downie J, Wynaden D, McGowan S et al. Using the Edinburgh Postnatal Depression Scale to achieve best practice standards. *Nurs Health Sci*. 2003;**5**(4):283–7.

43. Usher K, Foster K, McNamara P. Antipsychotic drugs and pregnant or breastfeeding women: The issues for mental health nurses. *J Psychiatr Ment Health Nurs*. 2005;**12**(6):713–18.

44. Pridmore S, Pollard C. Electroconvulsive therapy in Parkinson's disease: 30 month follow up. *J Neurol Neurosurg Psychiatry*. 1996;**60**(6):693.

45. Mohan I, Wendelborn K, Politis B. Ethical dilemma in consultation-liaison psychiatry. *Aust NZJ*. 2014;**48**(3):291–2.

46. Wand TC, Coulson K. Zero tolerance: A policy in conflict with current opinion on aggression and violence management in health care. *Aust Emerg Nurs J.* 2006;**9**(4):163–70.

47. Wand A, Wand T. 'Admit voluntary, schedule if tries to leave': Placing Mental Health Acts in the context of mental health law and human rights. *Australas Psychiatry.* 2013;**21**(2):137–40.

48. Lamont S, Jeon YH, Chiarella M. Health-care professionals' knowledge, attitudes and behaviours relating to patient capacity to consent to treatment: An integrative review. *Nurs Ethics.* 2013;**20**(6):684–707.

49. Lamont S, Stewart C, Chiarella M. The misuse of 'duty of care' as justification for non-consensual coercive treatment. *Int J Law Psychiatry.* 2020;**71**:101598.

50. Smart D, Pollard C, Walpole B. Mental health triage in emergency medicine. *Aust NZJ.* 1999;**33**(1):57–66; discussion 7–9.

51. Happell B, Summers M, Pinikahana J. The triage of psychiatric patients in the hospital emergency department: A comparison between emergency department nurses and psychiatric nurse consultants. *Accid Emerg Nurs.* 2002;**10**(2):65–71.

52. Gerdtz MF, Collins M, Chu M et al. Optimizing triage consistency in Australian emergency departments: The Emergency Triage Education Kit. *Emerg Med Australas.* 2008;**20**(3):250–9.

53. Daniel C, Gerdtz M, Elsom S, Knott J, Prematunga R, Virtue E. Feasibility and need for violence risk screening at triage: An exploration of clinical processes and public perceptions in one Australian emergency department. *Emerg Med J.* 2015;**32**(6):457–62.

54. Downes MA, Healy P, Page CB, Bryant JL, Isbister GK. Structured team approach to the agitated patient in the emergency department. *Emerg Med Australas.* 2009;**21**(3):196–202.

55. Gerdtz MF, Daniel C, Dearie V, Prematunga R, Bamert M, Duxbury J. The outcome of a rapid training program on nurses' attitudes regarding the prevention of aggression in emergency departments: A multi-site evaluation. *Int J Nurs Stud.* 2013;**50**(11):1434–45.

56. Wand T, D'Abrew N, Barnett C, Acret L, White K. Evaluation of a nurse practitioner-led extended hours mental health liaison nurse service based in the emergency department. *Aust Health Rev.* 2015;**39**(1):1–8.

57. Wand T, Collett G, Cutten A et al. Evaluating an emergency department-based mental health liaison nurse service: A multi-site translational research project. *Emerg Med Australas.* 2021;**33**(1):74–81.

58. Wand APF, Corr MJ, Eades SJ. Liaison psychiatry with Aboriginal and Torres Strait Islander peoples. *Aust NZJ.* 2009;**43**(6):509–17.

59. Kowanko I, De Crespigny C, Murray H et al. Better medication management for aboriginal people with mental health disorders and their carers: Final report. Adelaide; 2003.

60. Gluckman L. Maori traditions and the eighth Congress of the Australian and New Zealand College of Psychiatrists. *Aust NZJ.* 1972;**6**(1):6–8.

61. Elder H. Te Waka Kuaka and Te Waka Oranga: Working with whānau to improve outcomes. *Aust N Z J Fam Ther.* 2017;**38**(1):27–42.

62. NiaNia W, Bush A, Epston D. Huarahi Oranga: An introduction to Māori concepts informing a Māori healing and psychiatry partnership. *Australas Psychiatry.* 2019;**27**(4):334–6.

63. Bush A, NiaNia W. Voice hearing and pseudoseizures in a Māori teenager: An example of mate Māori and Māori traditional healing. *Australas Psychiatry.* 2012;**20**(4):348–51.

64. NiaNia W, Bush A, Epston D. He korowai o ngā tīpuna: Voice hearing and communication from ancestors. *Australas Psychiatry.* 2019;**27**(4):345–7.

65. Hunter Headline. Aboriginal Hospital Liaison Officer appointed at Calvary Mater Newcastle. 2019. https://hunterheadline.co

m.au/blog-post/aboriginal-hospital-liaison-officer-appointed-calvary-mater-newcastle.

66. New South Wales Ministry of Health. Aboriginal health worker guidelines for NSW Health. 2018. www.health.nsw.gov.a u/workforce/aboriginal/Publications/abori ginal-health-worker-guidelines.pdf.

67. Kahn MW, Henry J, Cawte J. Mental health services by and for Australian Aborigines. *Aust NZJ*. 1976;10(3):221–8.

68. Leckning B, Hirvonen T, Armstrong G et al. Developing best practice guidelines for the psychosocial assessment of Aboriginal and Torres Strait Islander people presenting to hospital with self-harm and suicidal thoughts. *Aust NZJ*. 2020;54(9):874–82.

69. Balaratnasingam S, Chapman M, Chong D et al. Advancing social and emotional well-being in Aboriginal and Torres Strait Islander Australians: Clinicians' reflections. *Australas Psychiatry*. 2019;27 (4):348–51.

70. Signal TL, Paine S-J, Sweeney B et al. The prevalence of symptoms of depression and anxiety, and the level of life stress and worry in New Zealand Māori and non-Māori women in late pregnancy. *Aust NZJ*. 2017;51(2):168–76.

71. Cunningham R, Stanley J, Haitana T et al. The physical health of Māori with bipolar disorder. *Aust NZJ*. 2020;54(11):1107–14.

72. Moloney J, MacDonald J. Psychiatric training in New Zealand. *Aust NZJ*. 2000;34 (1):146–53.

73. Clarke DM, Minas IH, McKenzie DP. Illness behaviour as a determinant of referral to a psychiatric consultation/liaison service. *Aust NZJ*. 1991;25(3):330–7.

74. Joyce PR, Bushnell JA, Walshe JWB, Morton JB. Abnormal illness behaviour and anxiety in acute non-organic abdominal pain. *BJPsych*. 1986;149 (1):57–62.

75. Pilowsky I, Spence ND. Is illness behaviour related to chronicity in patients with intractable pain? *Pain*. 1976;2(2):167–73.

76. University of York. Somatic symptom disorder: Prevalence of somatization in primary and secondary care populations.

2020. www.crd.york.ac.uk/prospero/dis play_record.php?ID=CRD42020125353.

77. Butow P, Dhillon H, Shaw J, Price M. Psycho-oncology in Australia: A descriptive review. *BioPsychoSocial Med*. 2017;11(1):15.

78. Dieng M, Morton RL, Costa DSJ et al. Benefits of a brief psychological intervention targeting fear of cancer recurrence in people at high risk of developing another melanoma: 12-month follow-up results of a randomized controlled trial. *Br J Dermatol*. 2020;182(4):860–8.

79. Shih ST-F, Butow P, Bowe SJ et al. Cost-effectiveness of an intervention to reduce fear of cancer recurrence: The ConquerFear randomized controlled trial. *Psycho-Oncology*. 2019;28 (5):1071–9.

80. Britton B, Baker AL, Wolfenden L et al. Eating As Treatment (EAT): A stepped-wedge, randomized controlled trial of a health behavior change intervention provided by dietitians to improve nutrition in patients with head and neck cancer undergoing radiation therapy (TROG 12.03). *Int J Radiat Oncol Biol Phys*. 2019;103(2):353–62.

81. Hatcher S, Sharon C, Collins N. Epidemiology of intentional self-harm presenting to four district health boards in New Zealand over 12 months, and comparison with official data. *Aust NZJ*. 2009;43(7):659–65.

82. New Zealand Health Information Service. Suicide and self-inflicted injury: Selected morbidity data for publicly funded hospitals 1998/1999. Ministry of Health. Wellington; 2001.

83. McGill K, Hiles SA, Handley TE et al. Is the reported increase in young female hospital-treated intentional self-harm real or artefactual? *Aust NZJ*. 2019;53(7):663–72.

84. Steenkamp M, Harrison J. *Suicide and Hospitalised Self-Harm in Australia*. Canberra; 2000.

85. Dassanayake TL, Jones AL, Michie PT et al. Risk of road traffic accidents in patients discharged following treatment for psychotropic drug overdose: A self-

controlled case series study in Australia. *CNS Drugs.* 2012;**26**(3):269–76.

86. Hatcher S, Sharon C, Parag V, Collins N. Problem-solving therapy for people who present to hospital with self-harm: Zelen randomised controlled trial. *BJPsych.* 2011;**199**(4):310–16.

87. Carter GL, Clover K, Whyte IM, Dawson AH, Este CD. Postcards from the EDge project: Randomised controlled trial of an intervention using postcards to reduce repetition of hospital treated deliberate self-poisoning. *BMJ.* 2005;**331**(7520):805.

88. Collings S, Jenkin G, Stanley J, McKenzie S, Hatcher S. Preventing suicidal behaviours with a multilevel intervention: A cluster randomised controlled trial. *BMC Public Health.* 2018;**18**(1):140.

89. Butow PN, Turner J, Gilchrist J et al. Randomized trial of ConquerFear: A novel, theoretically based psychosocial intervention for fear of cancer recurrence. *J Clin Oncol.* 2017;**35**(36):4066–77.

90. Beatty L, Kemp E, Coll JR et al. Finding my way: Results of a multicentre RCT evaluating a web-based self-guided psychosocial intervention for newly diagnosed cancer survivors. *Support Care Cancer.* 2019;**27**(7):2533–44.

91. Britton B, Baker A, Clover K, McElduff P, Wratten C, Carter G. Heads Up: A pilot trial of a psychological intervention to improve nutrition in head and neck cancer patients undergoing radiotherapy. *Eur J Cancer Care.* 2017;**26**(4).

92. Hatcher S, Coupe N, Wikiriwhi K, Durie SM, Pillai A. Te Ira Tangata: A Zelen randomised controlled trial of a culturally informed treatment compared to treatment as usual in Māori who present to hospital after self-harm. *Soc Psychiatry Psychiatr Epidemiol.* 2016;**51**(6):885–94.

93. Beck AK, Baker A, Britton B et al. Fidelity considerations in translational research: Eating As Treatment – A stepped wedge, randomised controlled trial of a dietitian delivered behaviour change counselling intervention for head and neck cancer patients undergoing radiotherapy. *Trials.* 2015;**16**:465.

94. Royal Commission into Victoria's Mental Health System. A new approach to mental health and wellbeing in Victoria. 2021. https://finalreport.rcvmhs.vic.gov.au/wp-content/uploads/2021/02/RCVMHS_FinalReport_Vol1_Accessible.pdf.

Europe

1. Huyse F, Kathol R, Söllner W et al. The organization of psychiatric services for general hospital departments. In Gelder MG, Andreasen NC, López-Ibor Jr. JJ, Geddes JR (eds.), *New Oxford Textbook of Psychiatry*, 2nd ed. Oxford; 2009, pp. 1144–8.

2. Huyse FJ, Herzog T, Lobo A, et al. Consultation-liaison psychiatric service delivery: Results from a European study. *Gen Hosp Psychiatry.* 2001; **23**:124–32.

3. Rymaszewska J, Söllner W. Training in consultation-liaison psychiatry in Eastern Europe. *J Psychosom Res.* 2012;**72**:460–2.

4. Weisser KW, Diseth TH, Boye B et al. Examining the organization and quality of the psychiatric consultative service in Norway. *Nordic J Psychiatry.* 2019;**73**(1).

5. Wahlström L. Psychiatric consultation-liaison in Sweden surveyed: A patchwork of reimbursement schemes, organizational structures and levels of ambition. *Lakartidningen.* 2003;**100**(3):120–4.

6. Lobo A, Rabanaque I, Blanch J et al. The development of psychosomatic and liaison psychiatry units in Spain: A national enquiry. *J Psychosom Res.* 2019;**125**:109784.

7. Walker A, Barrett JR, Lee W et al. Organisation and delivery of liaison psychiatry services in general hospitals in England: Results of a national survey. *BMJ Open.* 2018;**8**(8):e023091.

8. Holmes J, Bentley K, Cameron I. A UK survey of psychiatric services for older people in general hospitals. *Int J Geriatr Psychiatry.* 2003;**18**(8):716–21.

9. Reidy J, Kirby M. A survey of old age psychiatry consultation/liaison services in Ireland. *Ir J Psychol Med.* 2008;**25**(2):66–8.

10. Herzog T, Creed F, Huyse FJ et al. Psychosomatic medicine in the general hospital. In Katona C, Montgomery S, Sensky T (eds.), *Psychiatry in Europe: Directions and Developments.* London; 2004, pp. 143–51.

11. Zipfel S, Herzog W, Kruse J et al. Psychosomatic medicine in Germany: More timely than ever. *Psychother Psychosom.* 2016;**85**(5):262–9.

12. Gramaglia C, Gambaro E, Delicato C et al. Pathways to and results of psychiatric consultation for patients referred from the emergency department: Are there differences between migrant and native patients? *Transcult Psychiatry.* 2019;**56** (1):167–86.

13. Menchetti M, Tarricone I, Bortolotti B et al. Integration between general practice and mental health services in Italy: Guidelines for consultation-liaison services implementation. *Int J Integr Care.* 2006;**6**:e05.

14. Saillant S, Hudelson P, Dominicé M. The primary care physician/psychiatrist joint consultation: A paradigm shift in caring for patients with mental health problems? *Patient Educ Couns.* 2016;**99** (2):279–83.

15. Creed F, Marks B. Liaison psychiatry in general practice: A comparison of the liaison-attachment scheme and shifted outpatient clinic models. *J Royal Coll Gen Pract.* 1989;**39**:514–17.

16. Coupe N, Anderson E, Gask L et al. Facilitating professional liaison in collaborative care for depression in UK primary care: A qualitative study utilising normalisation process theory. *BMC Fam Pract.* 2014;**15**:78. www.biomedcentral.com/1471-2296/15/78.

17. Taylor AK, Gilbody S, Bosanquet K et al. How should we implement collaborative care for older people with depression? A qualitative study using normalization process theory within the CASPER plus trial. *BMC Fam Pract.* 2018;**19**:116. https://doi.org/10.1186/s12875-018-0813-7.

18. Gensichen J, Torge M, Peitz M et al. Case management for the treatment of patients with major depression in general practices: Rationale, design and conduct of a cluster randomized controlled trial – PRoMPT (Primary care Monitoring for depressive Patients Trial). *BMC Public Health.* 2005;**5**:101. doi: 10.1186/1471-2458-5-101.

19. Magaard JL, Liebherz S, Melchior H et al. Collaborative mental health care program versus a general practitioner program and usual care for treatment of patients with mental or neurological disorders in Germany: Protocol of a multiperspective evaluation study. *BMC Psychiatry.* 2018;**18**:347. https://doi.org/10.1186/s12888-018-1914-5.

20. Löwe B, Piontek K, Daubmann A et al. Effectiveness of a stepped, collaborative, and coordinated health care network for somatoform disorders (Sofu-Net): A controlled cluster cohort study. *Psychosom Med.* 2017;**79**(9):1016–24.

21. Curth NK, Brinck-Claussen UØ, Hjorthøj, C et al. Collaborative care for depression and anxiety disorders: Results and lessons learned from the Danish cluster-randomized Collabri trials. *BMC Fam Pract.* 2020;**21**:234.

22. de Jong F, van Steenbergen-Wejenburg KM, Huijbregts KLM et al. The depression initiative: Description of a collaborative care model for depression and of the factors influencing its implementation in the primary care setting in the Netherlands. *In J Integrated Care.* 2009;**9**.

23. van der Feltz-Cornelis CM, van Oppen P, Adèr HJ et al. Randomised controlled trial of a collaborative care model with psychiatric consultation for persistent medically unexplained symptoms in general practice. *Psychother Psychosom.* 2006;**75**:282–9.

24. Camacho EM, Ntais D, Coventry P et al. Long-term cost-effectiveness of collaborative care (vs usual care) for people

with depression and comorbid diabetes or cardiovascular disease: A Markov model informed by the COINCIDE randomised controlled trial. *BMJ Open.* 2016;**6**(10): e012514.

25. Sharpe M, Walker J, Holm Hansen C et al. Integrated collaborative care for comorbid major depression in patients with cancer (SMaRT Oncology-2): A multicentre randomised controlled effectiveness trial. *Lancet.* 2014;**384**(9948):1099–108.

26. Richards DA, Bower P, Chew-Graham C et al. Clinical effectiveness and cost-effectiveness of collaborative care for depression in UK primary care (CADET): A cluster randomised controlled trial. *Health Technol Assess.* 2016;**20**(14):1–226.

27. Krauth C, Stahmeyer JT, Petersen JJ et al. Resource utilisation and costs of depressive patients in Germany: Results from the primary care monitoring for depressive patients trial. *Depress Res Treat.* 2014: Article ID 730891.

28. Grochtdreis T, Brettschneider C, Shedden-Mora M. Cost-effectiveness analysis of a stepped, collaborative and coordinated health care network for patients with somatoform disorders (Sofu-Net). *J Ment Health Policy Econ.* 2018;**21**(2):59–69.

29. van Schijndel MA, Jansen LAW, van de Klundert JJ. Empirical types of medical-psychiatry units. *Psychother Psychosom.* 2019;**88**:127–8.

30. Caarls PJ, van Schijndel MA, van den Berk G et al. Factors influencing the admission decision for medical psychiatry units: A concept mapping approach. *PLoS ONE.* 2019;**14**(9):e0221807.

31. Leue C, Driessen G, Strik JJ et al. Managing complex patients on a medical psychiatric unit: An observational study of university hospital costs associated with medical service use, length of stay, and psychiatric intervention. *J Psychosom Res.* 2010;**68** (3):295–302.

32. Steinert C, Kruse J, Leweke F et al. Psychosomatic inpatient treatment: Real-world effectiveness, response rates and the helping alliance. *J Psychosom Res.*

2019;**124**:109743. doi: 10.1016/j .jpsychores.2019.109743.

33. Wunner C, Reichhart C, Strauss B et al. Effectiveness of a psychosomatic day hospital treatment for the elderly: A naturalistic longitudinal study with waiting time before treatment as control condition. *J Psychosom Res.* 2014;**76**:121–6.

34. Wulsin LR, Söllner W, Pincus HA. Models of integrated care. *Med Clinics North Am.* 2006;**90**:647–77.

35. Liebherz S, Rabung S. Do patients' symptoms and interpersonal problems improve in psychotherapeutic hospital treatment in Germany? A systematic review and meta-analysis. *PLoS ONE.* 2014;**9**(8):e105329.

36. Fink P, Burton C, de Bie J et al. Current state of management and organisation of care. In Creed F, Henningsen P, Fink P (eds.), *Medically Unexplained Symptoms, Somatisation and Bodily Distress: Developing Better Clinical Services.* Cambridge; 2011, pp. 97–123.

37. Söllner W, Creed F, EACLPP Workgroup on Training in C-L. European guidelines for training in consultation-liaison psychiatry and psychosomatics: Report of the EACLPP Workgroup on Training in Consultation-Liaison Psychiatry and Psychosomatics. *J Psychosom Res.* 2007;**62**:501–9.

38. Söllner W, Guthrie E, Berney A. Training in consultation-liaison psychiatry and psychosomatics: Insights from psychosomatic medicine and consultation-liaison psychiatry. In Grassi L, Riba J, Wise T (eds.), *Person Centered Approach to Recovery in Medicine.* New York; 2019, pp. 303–19.

39. Herzog T, Stein B, Söllner W et al. Konsiliar- und Liaisonpsychosomatik und-psychiatrie. In *Leitlinie und Quellentext für den psychosomatischen Konsiliar- und Liaisondienst.* Stuttgart; 2003.

40. Leentjens AF, Boenink AD, Sno HN et al. The guideline 'consultation psychiatry' of the Netherlands Psychiatric Association. *J Psychosom Res.* 2009;**66**:531–5.

41. Leentjens AF, van Baalen A, Kuijpers HJH et al. The revised guideline on

consultation-liaison psychiatry of the Netherlands Psychiatric Association. *J Psychosom Res.* 2018;**110**;12–14.

42. Oldham MA, Chahal K, Lee HB. A systematic review of proactive psychiatric consultation on hospital length of stay. *Gen Hosp Psychiatry.* 2019;**60**:120–6.

43. Stiefel FC, Huyse FJ, Söllner W et al. Operationalizing integrated care on a clinical level: The INTERMED project. *Med Clin N Am.* 2006;**90**(4):713–58.

44. Toynbee M, Walker J, Clay F et al. The effectiveness of inpatient consultation-liaison psychiatry service models: A systematic review of randomized trials. *Gen Hosp Psychiatry.* 2021;**71**:11–19.

45. Stein B, Müller MM, Meyer LK, Söllner W for the C-L guidelines working group. Psychiatric and psychosomatic consultation-liaison services in general hospitals: A systematic review and meta-analysis of effects on symptoms of depression and anxiety. *Psychother Psychosom.* 2020;**89**:6–16.

46. Stiefel F, Zdrojewski C, Bel Hadj F et al. Effects of a multifaceted psychiatric intervention targeted for the complex medically ill: A randomized-controlled trial. *Psychother Psychosom.* 2008;**77**:247–56.

47. Sharpe M, Toynbee M, Walker J. for the HOME Study Proactive Integrated Consultation-Liaison (Proactive Integrated Psychological Medicine group). Proactive integrated consultation-liaison psychiatry: A new service model for the psychiatric care of

general hospital inpatients. *Gen Hosp Psychiatry.* 2020;**66**:9–15.

48. Baldwin R, Pratt H, Goring H et al. Does a nurse-led mental health liaison service for older people reduce psychiatric morbidity in acute general medical wards? A randomized-controlled trial. *Age Ageing.* 2004;**33**(5):472–8.

49. Hussain M, Seitz D. Integrated models of care for medical inpatients with psychiatric disorders: A systematic review. *Psychosomatics.* 2014;**55**:315–25.

50. Deter HC, Kruse J, Zipfel S. History, aims and present structure of psychosomatic medicine in Germany. *BioPsychoSocial Med.* 2018;**12**:1.

51. Vulser H, Vinant V, Lanvin V, Chatellier G, Limosin F, Lemogne C. Association between the timing of consultation-liaison psychiatry interventions and the length of stay in general hospital. *Br J Psychiatry.* 2021;**218**(4):204–9.

52. Yrondi A, Petiot D, Arbus C, Schmitt L. Economic impact of consultation-liaison psychiatry in a French University Hospital Centre. *L'Encephale.* 2014;**42**(1):112–15.

53. Ekeberg O. Consultation liaison psychiatry in Norway. *J Psychosom Res.* 2006;**60**:651–2.

54. Hiltunen PM, Leppavuori A, Männikkö T et al. Training model for special competence in general hospital psychiatry in Finland. *J Psychosom Res.* 2006;**61**:737–8.

55. Huyse FJ. Farewell to C-L? Time for a change? *J Psychosom Res.* 2009; **66**(6):541–4.

United States

1. Engel GL. The need for a new medical model: A challenge for biomedicine. *Science.* 1977;**196**(4286):129–36.

2. Lipsitt DR. *Foundations of Consultation-Liaison Psychiatry: The Bumpy Road to Specialization.* New York; 2016.

3. Dunbar HF. *Emotions and Bodily Changes.* New York; 1935.

4. Bibring GL. Psychiatry and medical practice in a general hospital. *N Engl J Med.* 1956;**254**(8):366–72.

5. Kaufman MR. The role of the psychiatrist in a general hospital. *Psychiatr Q.* 1953;**27**(3):367–81.

6. Lipowski ZJ. Consultation-liaison psychiatry: The first half century. *Gen Hosp Psychiatry.* 1986;**8**(5):305–15.

7. Gitlin DF, Schindler BA, Stern TA et al. Recommended guidelines for consultation-liaison psychiatric training in psychiatry residency programs. A report from the Academy of Psychosomatic Medicine Task Force on Psychiatric Resident Training in Consultation-Liaison Psychiatry. *Psychosomatics*. 1996;**37**(1):3–11.

8. Bronheim HE, Fulop G, Kunkel EJ et al. The Academy of Psychosomatic Medicine practice guidelines for psychiatric consultation in the general medical setting. *Psychosomatics*. 1998;**39**(4):S8–30.

9. Gitlin DF, Levenson JL, Lyketsos CG. Psychosomatic medicine: A new psychiatric subspecialty. *Acad Psychiatry*. 2004;**28**(1):4–11.

10. Boland RJ, Rundell J, Epstein S, Gitlin D. Consultation-liaison psychiatry vs psychosomatic medicine: What's in a name? *Psychosomatics*. 2018;**59**:207–10.

11. Larson DB, Kessler LC, Burns BJ et al. A research development workshop to stimulate outcome research in consultation-liaison psychiatry. *Hosp Community Psychiatry*. 1987;**38**(10):1106–9.

Canada

1. Lipowski ZJ. Consultation-liaison psychiatry: Toronto. *Can J Psychiatry*. 1988;**33**(4):247–8.

2. Gagnon F. Canadian consultation-liaison/psychosomatic medicine: A discipline still waiting for official recognition and patient care accessibility. In Hoyle L (ed.), *Global Psychosomatic Medicine and Consultation-Liaison Psychiatry: Theory, Research, Education, and Practice*. Boston, MA; 2019, pp. 529–88.

3. Lipowski ZJ. Current trends in consultation-liaison psychiatry. *Can J Psychiatry*. 1983;**28**(5):329–38.

4. Lipowski ZJ. Review of consultation psychiatry and psychosomatic medicine. *Psychosom Med*. 1967;**29**(2):153–71.

5. Marcus AM. A pilot study of the psychiatric consultation service in a general hospital setting. *Can Psychiatr Assoc J*. 1964;**9**:19–27.

6. Association Des Psychiatres Du Canada Congrès Annuel de 1968. *Can Psychiatr Assoc J*. 1968;**13**(1):90.

7. Krakowski AJ. Consultation psychiatry: Present global status. *Psychother Psychosom*. 1974;**23**(1–6):78–86.

8. Oluwafemi Agbayewa M, Perez E. Consultation liaison training in Canadian psychiatric residency programs. *Can J Psychiatry*. 1982;**27**(6):482–5.

9. Voineskos G, Hsu K, Hunter RCA. The teaching of consultation-liaison psychiatry in the undergraduate curriculum of Canadian medical schools. *Gen Hosp Psychiatry*. 1984;**6**(2):117–22.

10. Paris J, Kravitz H, Prince R. Report: Conference on key issues in post-graduate psychiatric education in Canada. *Can J Psychiatry*. 1986;**31**(8):705–7.

11. Leichner P. Opinions of psychiatric residents regarding the educational aspects of consultation-liaison psychiatry. In Krakowski AJ (ed.), *Psychosomatic Medicine: Theoretical, Clinical and Transcultural Aspects*. Boston, MA; 1983, pp. 633–40.

12. Swenson JR, Abbey S, Stewart DE. Consultation-liaison psychiatry as a subspecialty. *Gen Hosp Psychiatry*. 1993;**15**(6):386–91.

13. Abbey SE, Brager N. Letter to K. A. Sheehan. April 2021.

14. Rodin GM. Renal dialysis and the liaison psychiatrist. *Can J Psychiatry*. 1980;**25**(6):473–7.

15. Taerk G. Psychological support of oncology nurses: A role for the liaison psychiatrist. *Can J Psychiatry*. 1983;**28**(7):532–5.

16. Stewart DE, Lippert GP. Psychiatric consultation-liaison services to an obstetrics and gynecology department. *Can J Psychiatry*. 1988;**33**(4):285–9.

17. Mainprize E, Rodin G. Geriatric referrals to a psychiatric consultation-liaison service. *Can J Psychiatry.* 1987;**32**(1):5–9.

18. Pablo RY, Lamarre CJ. Psychiatric consultation in a general hospital. *Can J Psychiatry.* 1988;**33**(3):224–30.

19. Rodin GJ, Craven C, Littlefield G et al. Research in consultation-liaison psychiatry: The Toronto general hospital experience. *Can J Psychiatry.* 1988;**33**(4):254–8.

20. Turner T, de Sorkin A. Sharing psychiatric care with primary care physicians: The Toronto doctors hospital experience (1991–1995). *Can J Psychiatry.* 1997;**42**(9):950–4.

21. Kates N, Lesser A, Dawson D, Devine J, Wakefield J. Psychiatry and family medicine: The McMaster approach. *Can J Psychiatry.* 1987;**32**(3):170–4.

22. Yatham L. Letter to K. A. Sheehan. 1 September 2021.

23. Gagnon F, van Zyl LT. Letter to K. A. Sheehan. 17 May 2021.

24. Swenson JR, Lam RW, Morehouse RL. A psychiatric fellowship in the United States. *Can J Psychiatry.* 1990;**35**(3):243–7.

25. Royal College of Physicians and Surgeons of Canada. Specialty Training Requirements in Psychiatry. 2007.

26. Royal College of Physicians and Surgeons of Canada. Specialty Training Requirements in Psychiatry. 2005.

27. Tan AO. Letter to K. A. Sheehan. 20 December 2021.

Index

Please note: page numbers in **bold type** indicate figures or tables.

acceptance and commitment
  therapy, 264–5
accreditation, national process,
  41, 394–6
acquired brain injury
  and the MHA, 169
  in children, 241
  psychosis and, 161
active listening, 261
acute behavioural disturbance
  (ABD), 172–86
  aetiological
    considerations, 174
  affective disorders and, 174
  assessment, 175
  case example and overview,
    172–3
  debriefing, 185
  ethnography and impact
    studies, 185–6
  management, 175
    preliminary steps, 175–6
    de-escalation, 177–8
    indicators of heightened
      arousal, 176
    initial observations, 176–7
    pharmacological, 185
      administration route, 179
      antipsychotics,
        180–2
      aripiprazole, risperidone
        and quetiapine, 181
      benzodiazepines, 179–80
      choice of medication, 182–4
      dexmedetomidine, 182
      droperidol, 180–1
      'black box' warning, 180
      haloperidol, 180
        plus lorazepam, 181
        plus promethazine, 181
      ketamine, 182
      loxapine, 181
      olanzapine, 180
      promethazine, 182
      rapid tranquillisation, 179
        during pregnancy, 184
      health monitoring, 184–5

post-de-escalation and
    medication, 185
  restraint and restrictive
    practices, 178–9
  personality disorders and, 175
  psychosis and, 174
  risk factors, 173
  self-harm as driver of, 173
ADHD (attention deficit
    hyperactivity disorder),
    potential impact on care
    of chronic physical
    illness, 233
Adults with Incapacity
    (Scotland) Act 2000, 272
affective disorders, and
    ABD, 174
age of patient, as triage criteria
    for CL services, 2
Agenda for Change (NHS), 33
alcohol misuse, 117–31
  alcohol-related brain damage
    (ARBD), 131
  facts and figures, 117–18
  intoxication, 120–1
    and suspected head
      injury, 122
    and Wernicke's
      encephalopathy, 123
    characteristic features, 121
    common associated
      complaints, 118
    common reasons for
      requesting CL team
      assessment, 122
    co-morbidities to look out
      for, 123
    initial assessment scaffold,
      122–4
    mimics, 123
    stages of, **122**
  liaison mental health nursing
    and, 38
  pharmacology of alcohol,
    118–20
  percentages and units,
    119–20

reference guide for alcohol
    units, **119**
  role of CLP in chronic cases,
    130–1
  screening for, 120
  withdrawal, 124–6
    and Wernicke's
      encephalopathy, 129–30
    delirium tremens, 126, 127–9
    diagnostic criteria, 125
    management of, 126–7
    monitoring
      requirements, 126
    severity, **125**
Alexander, Franz, 430
Alzheimer, Alois, 189
anticonvulsants, depression
    and, 86
antidepressants, risks of
    prescribing in
    pregnancy, 222–4
antipsychotics
  in management of ABD,
    180–2
  prescribing in pregnancy, 224
anxiety disorders
  epilepsy and, 199
  MS and, 206
  perinatal, 213–16
  presentation to the ED
    with, 378
anxiety, post-stroke, 194
anxiety/depression in physical
    disease, 253, **259**
anxiolytics and hypnotics,
    prescribing in
    pregnancy, 226
assessment process
  overview, 1
  basics, **12**
  feedback provision to
    medical/surgical team,
    13–14
  follow-up
    inpatient, 16–17
    on discharge, 17
  formulation, 15–16

bio-psycho-social approach, **15**
case example, 15–16
'Five Ps', **16**
gathering collateral information, 12–13
high-risk assessment room, PLAN requirements, 391–2
parallel assessment argument, 3
patient handover, 11
preparation, 5–9
  current presentation, 6
  GP care record, 8
  investigations, 7–8
  medical status and barriers to progress, 8
  medication chart, 8
  multidisciplinary team notes, 7
  review of medical notes, 5
  understanding the patient's hospital journey, 7
psychiatric notes, 9
recommendations, 16
referrals
  alternative sources, 4–5
  helpful requests criteria, 3
  organisational aspects, 3–5
  prioritising and allocating, 3
  SBAR principles, 3
  triage criteria, 1–3
specialist circumstances, 13
suitable location, 10–11
the process, 11
attachment theory, health outcomes and, 53
attitude change, liaison psychiatry teaching and, 309
autistic spectrum disorders (ASD)
and self-harm, 65
antidepressants in pregnancy
  as risk factor for, 223
liaison nursing and, 39
medication and, 223
potential impact on care of chronic physical illness, 233
autoimmune encephalitis (AIE), 202–4

balneotherapy, for treatment of FSS, 112
Bennett, Henry, 419
benzodiazepines, 142–4
  acute intoxication, 143
  dependence syndrome and withdrawal state, 143–4
  harm minimisation, 144
  in management of ABD, 179–80
  mechanism of action, 143
  prescribing in pregnancy, 226
  toxicity, 143
    management, 143
beta blockers, prescribing in pregnancy, 226
Bibring, Grete, 430
biofeedback and relaxation techniques, for management of FSS, 113
biopsychosocial treatment, of FSS, 112–13
bipolar affective disorder
  and ABD, 174
  in MS, 205–6
  intoxication and, 124
blood tests, role of, 8
bodily distress disorder, 103
bodily distress syndrome, 104
brain damage, alcohol-related. see under alcohol misuse
'Bridging the Gap' (RCPsych/ CMH), 406
Brief Illness Perception Questionnaire (Broadbent et al.), 51

cancer
  and suicide risk, 85
  CBT and, 323
  children's psychosocial adjustment, 237
  common analogies, 48
  psychosocial care, 421
  trials of psychological treatment, 253, **257**
cannabis, 150–2
  acute intoxication, 150–1
  associated risks, 152
  harm minimisation, 152
  mechanism of action, 150
  toxicity, 151
  withdrawal syndrome, 151
capacity

assessment in patients with symptoms of psychosis, 168
assessment of by liaison mental health nurses, 35
assessment of in the ED, 377
cardiovascular disease, relationship between depression and, 84
Care Quality Commission (CQC) hospital inspection programme, 390
catatonia
  diagnosis and treatment, 87–8
  in the context of schizophrenia, 159
children and adolescents 40
  We Can Talk training package, 40
  see also paediatric CLP
chronic disease
  adjustment to, 49
  differential effect, 52–3
  most common conditions, 52
chronic fatigue syndrome, trials of psychological treatment, **254**
chronic pain, understanding, 361
chronic primary pain, 105
Clark, David, 410
cocaine, 147–9
  acute intoxication, 148
  'crack', 148
    risks specific to, 149
  mechanism of action, 147
  risks of chronic use, 149
  routes of administration, 147–8
  toxicity, 148–9
  withdrawal state, 149
cognitive analytic therapy, 266
cognitive behavioural therapy (CBT), in management of FSS, 113, 252, 262–3
cognitive impairment
  alcohol misuse and, 130
  as a risk factor for delirium, 378
  assessment and, 13, 177, 338
  autoimmune disease and, 191
  capacity to refuse treatment and, 277
  depression and, 195
  in MS, 206

cognitive impairment (cont.)
in older adults, 305
Parkinson's disease and, 197
perinatal mental illness
and, 220
use of restraint and, 280
Whipple's disease and, 190
cognitive therapy, inclusion
criteria for trials, **251**
Collaboration for Leadership in
Applied Health
Research
(CLARHC), 401
common mental health
disorders, education of
hospital staff, 305
communication
impairment of and its
impact, 57
potential required
modifications during
assessment process, 13
communication skills,
education of hospital
staff in, 306
congenital malformations,
antidepressants in
pregnancy as risk factor
for, 222–3
consultation-liaison services,
common referrals to see
also under referrals to
CL services
Convention on the Rights of
Persons with
Disabilities
(CRPD), 271
Cooksey report, 401
COPD (chronic obstructive
pulmonary disease),
trials of psychological
treatment, **258**
coping, psychological reaction
to physical illness, 50, **51**
Core model of liaison
psychiatry, 323, 405,
407–9, 411
counselling, 265–6
COVID-19 pandemic,
challenges for CLP, 429

de-escalation of patient
agitation
recommended response, 374
verbal, 177–8
delirium tremens, 126, 127–9

delirium, presentation to the
ED with, 378
dementia
depression as risk factor for
development of, 82
education focus, 304
intoxication and, 124
liaison nursing and, 36,
38
potential impact on discharge
planning, 9
'This Is Me' tool, 38
depot injection medications,
risk of being missed in
review of prescribed
medications, 8
depression
overview, 78
associated outcomes, 83–5
emergency hospital
admission, 83
interactions with medical
staff, 84
maladaptive effects, 84
mortality and suicide, 84–5
physiological effects, 84
quality of life, 83
response to drug treatment
for physical
condition, 83
bi-directional relationship
with physical disease,
78, 80
catatonia, 87–8
course of in physical
disease, 82
determining difference
between a psychological
reaction to illness and
depression, **80**
diagnosis and detection,
78, **80**
epidemiology, 81–2
in medical settings, 78–94
inflammation and, 85
medication-related
anti-inflammatory drugs, 87
antiretroviral drugs, 87
chemotherapy agents, 87
epilepsy treatments, 86
hepatitis C treatments, 87
hypertension treatments, 86
rheumatoid arthritis
treatments, 86
treatments Parkinson's
disease, 87

older adults, 82–3
pathogenesis, 80–1
people's understanding of,
79–80
post-stroke see under stroke
prevalence estimates in
general medical and
surgical inpatients, 82
screening for, 85
symptoms in people with
physical disease, 79
treatment/management
antidepressants, 92
collaborative care, 88–90
exercise, 90
general approaches, 78–94
NICE guidelines, 92
primary/community care,
92
psychosocial
interventions, 90–1
response of physical
symptoms to
psychological/
psychotropic
treatment, 92
understanding contributing
factors, 5
deprivation of liberty 347
detention powers of liaison
teams under MHA, 347
see also under legal and ethical
issues
Deprivation of Liberty
Safeguards (DoLS),
279–80
expected replacement,
280, 285
hospital treatment under
DoLS, 280
Deutsch, Felix, 430
Deutsch, Helene, 430
developing CLP services,
401–11
challenges
integration within mental
health services, 410
maintaining and developing
specialist services, 410
rapid workforce expansion,
409–10
evidence-practice
alignment, 401
marketing, strategic, 402
nurses' influence, 41
policy into practice

expertise by experience and
the role of patient
advocates, 407
implementation, 407–8
monitoring progress, 408–9
NHS commissioning
framework, 406
PLAN, 408
quality assurance, 408
policy-making
case study, 405–6
co-production and
partnerships, 405–6
linking to other
developments in acute
care, 406
political perspective,
404–5
role of relationships, 403
taking action, 411
diabetes
impact of depression on self-
care regimes, 84
in young people, 234
trials of psychological
treatment, **259**
diagnostic overshadowing,
mitigating the risk
of, 374
disability, UN Convention on
the Rights of Persons
with Disabilities
(CRPD), 271
discrimination and abuse, in
the ED, 376–7
dissociative disorders, 103, 104
distress 97
functional somatic symptoms
as indicator of, 97
see also functional somatic
symptoms
managing, 37
domestic violence, and
assessment in the
ED, 380
droperidol
'black box' warning, 180
in management of ABD,
180–1
Dunbar, Helen Flanders, 430
Duty of Candour, 36

eating disorders
Australian perspective, 421
co-occurrence with
self-harm, 62

legal and ethical issues, 285
education of hospital staff
attitude change and, 309
audience
medical staff, 302–3
nursing staff and allied
health professionals,
303–4
curriculum planning, 304–5
feedback and evaluation of
teaching, 314
general psychiatry
common mental health
disorders, 305
history-taking and
communication
skills, 306
psychopharmacology, 307
psychotherapeutic
interventions, 306
risk assessment of suicide
and self-harm, 305–6
liaison psychiatry-specific
teaching
medically unexplained
symptoms, 307
mental and physical health
co-morbidity, 307
mental health law and
ethics, 308
practical aspects of teaching,
308–9
teaching environments
clinical supervision
groups, 311
digital content and social
media, 312–13
learning groups, 310
lectures, 310
reflective practice
groups, 311
simulation, 312
small group teaching, 310
teaching rounds, 312
video conference versus face-
to-face teaching, 313–14
the case for liaison psychiatry
teaching, 301–2
education, training, research
and supervision, liaison
mental health nursing
competencies, 40
electroconvulsive therapy
(ECT), catatonic
schizophrenia and,
170

emergency department
psychiatry, 373–84
assessments for patients in the
ED, 3
heroin toxicity management,
138–9
legal and ethical
perspectives, 286
liaison mental health nursing
and, 41–2
principles of ED care, 373–7
consent, capacity and leaving
the department, 377
de-escalation, 374
diagnostic
overshadowing, 374
frequent attendance, 375–6
optimising patient
experience, 374
rapid tranquillisation, 375
restraint, 375
stigma, discrimination and
abuse, 376–7
triage and side-by-side
working, 373
psychosis, 161–2
service configuration,
381–4
ED facilities, 382
follow-up clinics, 382
governance, 381
integration with mental
health services, 381
mental health emergency
centres/psychiatric
decision units, 382
onward care, 383
outcome measurement,
383
staffing, 382
training, 383
specific conditions, 377–80
alcohol and other drugs,
379–80
anxiety disorders, 378
crisis and adversity,
380–1
delirium, 378
factitious disorder and
malingering, 380
intellectual disability 379
mania and psychosis, 377
suicidality and self-harm,
379, 392
suicidal ideation and referral
to CL team, 4

emergency departments, 373
and 'place of safety' policy
development, 404–5
assessment of domestic
violence, 380
evaluation of CLP in ED
settings, 350–1
frequent attender services,
351–2
managing distress in, 37
'Morbidity & Mortality'
reviews, 381
PLAN standards
for high-risk assessment
room, 391–2
requirements for
accreditation, 397
violence reduction strategies,
185–6
Engels, George, 430
epilepsy, 198–202
anxiety disorders, 199
depression in, 198–9
forced normalisation, 201
psychosis, 161, 200
assessment tips, 201
ictal, 200
interictal, 201
post-ictal, 200
treatment, 201–2
Equality Act 2010 (England
and Wales), 275
European Consultation-
Liaison Workgroup
(ECLW) Collaborative
Study, 345
European Convention on
Human Rights
(ECHR), 271
evidence base for CLP, 345–53
activities, 345–6
common clinical problem
scenarios, 346
evaluations, 348–53
emergency department
settings, 350–1
frequent attender services,
351–2
hospital in-patient settings,
349–50
primary care settings, 352–3
specialist clinics, 352
impact, 347–8
exercise
in management of FSS,
112, 365

in treatment of depression, 90

factitious disorder
and presentation to the
ED, 380
functional somatic symptoms
and, 105, 111
vulnerability of children
to, 241
families, role in collateral
information provision,
12–13
'Four Habits' framework for
teaching and assessing
communication
skills, 306
framework for routine
outcome measures in
liaison psychiatry, 41
Framework of Health Services
Utilisation (Andersen
and Newman), 52
frequent attendance in the ED
and evaluation of CLP in ED
settings, 351–2
recommended responses,
375–6
functional neurological
disorders
body changes, 360–1
chronic pain, 361
mechanisms, 360–1
options for follow-up on
discharge, 17
trials of psychological
treatments, 256
functional somatic symptoms
(FSS), 97–114
overview, 97
acceptable terminology,
99–100
aetiology and
psychophysiology, 100
background of somatic
symptoms, 97–8
barriers and prospects, 102–3
classification, 103–5
bodily distress disorder, 103
bodily distress
syndrome, 104
chronic primary pain, 105
dissociative disorders, 104
functional somatic
disorders, 105
functional somatic
syndromes, 104

other symptom
categories, 105
somatic symptom
disorder, 103
somatoform disorders, 103
clinical presentation and
impact, 102
diagnosis
conditions, contexts and
consequences, 108
examination and workup,
106, 108
informing the patient, 108–9
screening, 106
disambiguation, 99
key points, 114
management in CLP, 105, 107
points to discuss with
patient, 260
risk factors and predictors,
100–1
symptom phenomenology
and narration, 98
syndromes, 104
treatment
balneotherapy, 112
biofeedback and relaxation
techniques, 113
bio-psycho-social treatment,
112–13
communication,
cooperation and
commitment, 110
complementary
therapies, 112
development of an
individual explanatory
model, 110
expectations and goals,
110–11
hypnotherapy, 113
occupational therapy, 365–6
pharmacological, 112
physiotherapy/exercise
therapy, 112
psychotherapy, 113–14
self-help, 111
gamma butyrolactone see
GBL/GHB
gamma hydroxybutyrate see
GBL/GHB
GBL/GHB, 144–7
acute intoxication, 145
harm minimisation, 146–7
mechanism of action, 145
onward referral, 146

toxicity, 145–6
typical dosage, 145
withdrawal state, 146

haloperidol, in management of
ABD, 180–1
Hart, Chris, 33
Health and Social Care Act
2012, 407
healthcare staff, relationships
with, 56
heroin/opioid misuse,
137–42
acute intoxication, 137
dependence management, 139
buprenorphine, 140
methadone, 140
naltrexone, 141
mechanism of action, 137
toxicity, 137
emergency management,
138–9
treatment in a liaison setting,
141–2
onward referral, 142
withdrawal states, 139, 140–1
high-risk assessment room,
PLAN requirements,
391–2
history-taking, education of
hospital staff in, 306
homelessness, and attendance
in the ED, 381
hospitals
environmental challenges, 56
responsibilities under
MHA, 281
Human Rights Act 1998, 271
humour, value of for
recovery, 57
Huyse, Frits, 425, 429
hypnotherapy, for
management of FSS,
113, 265

identity, and the impact of
a disability, 58
illness
experience of and responses
to, 55
illness perception and
common-sense model
of self-regulation, 50–2
meaning of, 48–9
personal experience of illness
and recovery, 57–8

potential benefits, 49
Illness Action Model, 52
illness perception
core constructs, 50
measuring, 51
patient drawings, 52
relationship to health
outcomes, 52
illness perceptions, 50
Improving Access to
Psychological Therapies
(IAPT), 92, 339, 352,
357, 410
independent prescribing,
liaison nursing and, 37
intellectual disability 233
potential impact on care of
chronic physical illness,
233
see also people with
intellectual disabilities
international perspectives
Australia and New Zealand,
413–22
current situation, 417–20
governance, 417
Indigenous populations,
419–20
nursing, 418–19
staffing, 418
history of CLP, 413–17
clinical service models and
funding, 415
digital experiments, 416
early paradigms, 415
prioritisation of 'serious
mental illness', 415–16
scope of practice, 414
stagnation risk, 416–17
solution, 417
research, 420–2
abnormal illness/treatment
behaviour, 420
eating disorders, 421
novel study designs and
interventions, 421–2
psycho-oncology and
palliative care, 421
somatisation, 421
suicidal behaviour and
self-harm, 421
Canada, 434–7
history of CLP
a sense of professional
identity (2010s–
2021), 437

Canada, history of CLP
development of the
discipline (pre-1980),
434–5
specialisation without
subspecialty
(1980s–1990s), 435–6
self-organising to set the
national agenda
(2000s–2010s), 436–7
Europe, 422–30
case mix, 423
future developments,
429–30
med-psych/psychosomatic
units, 424–5
primary/collaborative
care, 424
process and outcome,
425–6
regional perspective
Benelux states, 428
Eastern European
countries, 427–8
French-speaking
countries, 428
German-speaking
countries, 424, 427
Scandinavia, 429
Southern Europe, 428
Switzerland, 428
training, 425
types and organisation of CL
services, 422–3
United States, 430–4
current situation, 432–4
CL service delivery, 433–4
governance, 432, 433
scope of clinical
practice, 434
history of CLP, 430–2
birth of a national CLP
organisation, 430–2
intellectual ancestry,
430
name change, 432
interpreters, in the assessment
process, 13
intoxication, 120–1
presentation to the ED with
intoxication-related
injuries, 379–80
see also under alcohol misuse
irritable bowel syndrome, trials
of psychological
treatment, **255**

Jung, Carl, 430

Katon, Wayne, 433
Kaufman, Ralph, 430
ketamine, 153–5
  acute intoxication, 154
  harm minimisation, 155
  in management of ABD, 182
  mechanism of action, 154
  risk of acute use, 154
  risks of chronic use, 154
  toxicity, 154
King, Billie Jean, 403

Lamb, Norman, 404
Lasting Power of Attorney
  (LPA), capacity
  assessment, 278
Layard, Richard, 410
legal and ethical issues, 271–86
  benefits of LP-specific
    teaching, 308
  challenging areas of practice
  capacity to end one's own
    life, 284–5
  eating disorders, 285
  core principles of LP
    practice, 271
  human rights legislation and
    mental health law, 271
  in liaison mental health
    nursing, 35–6
  legislative changes, 285–6
  mental capacity 271
  concept and practice, 271–2
  assessment, 273
    setting up an assessment,
      274–5
    setting up an assessment,
      pre-assessment
      considerations, 273–4
    conducting an
      assessment, 275
  decision-making
    advance, 278–9
    best-interests decisions,
      277–8
    eating disorder
      example, 285
    Independent Mental
      Capacity Advocate
      (IMCA), 279
    limb amputation
      example, 279
    documentation and record-
      keeping, 277

example of an MCA
  assessment,
  275–7
Lasting Power of Attorney
  (LPA), 278
capacity to end one's own
  life, 284–5
deprivation of liberty
  the concept, 280
  Deprivation of Liberty
    Safeguards (DoLS),
    279–80
  expected replacement,
    280, 285
  example, 280
  hospital treatment under
    DoLS, 280
  Liberty Protection
    Safeguards (LPS),
    280, 285
Kerrie Wooltorton case,
  284–5
Mental Capacity Act, 272–3
Mental Capacity
  Amendment Act
  (expected 2023),
  280, 285
  US perspective, 272
Mental Health Act, 280–1
MHA detention versus MCA-
  DoLS, 283–4
see also Mental Capacity Act
  (MCA); Mental Health
  Act (MHA),
liaison mental health nursing,
  32–45
overview, 32
Australian and New Zealand
  perspective,
  418–19
competencies, 33–41
  overview, 33–4
  capacity assessments and
    advice, 35
  child and adolescent/
    paediatric services,
    39–40
  clinical interventions, 36
  education, training, research
    and supervision, 40
  ethical issues,
    35–6
  evaluation and improvement
    of nursing provision, 41
  learning disabilities and
    autism, 39

mental health nursing
  assessment and
  consultation, 34–5
nursing advice
  on care of patients with
    complex needs, 37
  on legal issues, 36
  on medication and non-
    medical prescribing, 37
  older adults, 38
  patient admission and
    discharge, 36
  patient advocacy, 35–6
  perinatal services, 39
  persistent physical
    symptoms, 38
  record keeping and report-
    writing 36
  risk assessment including
    self-harm, 35
  specific physical
    illnesses, 37–8
  substance misuse including
    alcohol, 38
development history, 32–3
informal education
  opportunities, 40
in-house staff development
  ('growing your
  own'), 44
key points, 44–5
leadership roles
  emergency department and
    wider hospital, 41–2
  service development and
    influence, 41
nurse consultant roles
  education, training and
    development of staff,
    agencies and services, 43
  expert clinical practice, 43
  leadership and consultancy,
    including clinical
    supervision, 43
  research into service
    provision and
    evaluation, 44
liaison psychiatry services,
  interventions, main
  types, **347**
liaison psychiatry teaching, the
  case for 301–2 see also
  under education of
  hospital staff,
Liberty Protection Safeguards
  (LPS), 280, 285

Lipowski, Zbigniew, 48, 56, 430, 434
lithium, prescribing in pregnancy, 225
London Wide Liaison Nurses Special Interest Group, 33
loss, view of illness in terms of, 48–9
low mood
 and failure to engage in rehabilitation, 79
 as key symptom of all depressive states, 79
 exacerbated by communication impairment, 57
 potential impact on engagement with physiotherapy, 5, 8, 15, 16

malingering, and presentation to the ED, 380
manual restraint
 NICE definition, 178
 rapid tranquillisation as alternative to prolonged restraint, 179
medical fitness, as triage criteria for CL services, 2–3
medical notes, reviewing, 5
medically unexplained symptoms (MUS)
 liaison psychiatry specific teaching, 307
 psychological treatments for see psychological treatments for PPS/MUS
medications, psychiatric consequences, 8
mental and physical health co-morbidity, liaison psychiatry-specific teaching, 307
Mental Capacity Act (MCA)
 capacity determination process, 273
 example of an MCA assessment, 275–7
 key principles, 272
 main function, 283

Mental Capacity Amendment Act (expected 2023), 280, 285
mental disorders
 association with self-harm, 64–5
 impact on physical health outcomes, 1
Mental Health (Care and Treatment) (Scotland) Act, 281
Mental Health (Northern Ireland) Order, 281, 282
Mental Health Act (MHA), and patients in ED settings, 286
 decision-making aid, 283
 detention powers of liaison teams, 347
 hospital responsibilities, 281
 legislative history, 280–1
 liaison nursing and, 36
 likelihood of errors in application and use in the general hospital, 308
 main function, 283
 'places of safety', 281, 404, 406
 psychosis management and, 168–70
 reform proposals, 286
 Section 136 (place of safety), 281
 Section 5(2) (doctor's holding power), 282
 Sections 2 and 3 (assessment of mental health), 282
 see also under legal and ethical issues
Meyer, Adolf, 430
migration and flight, long-term consequences on mental health, 429
mindfulness, 264
mood stabilisers, prescribing in pregnancy, 225–6
Mosely, Lorimer, 361
motor neurone disease (MND), trajectory of disease, 189
multiple sclerosis (MS), 204–6
 anxiety disorders in, 206
 bipolar affective disorder in, 205–6
 cognitive impairment in, 206
 depression in, 204–5
 epidemiology, 204

psychosis in, 206
self-harm, risk factors, 204

National Confidential Enquiry into Patient and Outcome and Death (NCEDPOD), 390
Network Episode Model, 52
neurodevelopmental disorders, associated with increased prevalence of physical comorbidities, 234
neuroleptic malignant syndrome (NMS), 88, 198
neurology, 189
neurology–psychiatry interface, 189–206
 assessment approach to a known neurological diagnosis, 189–90
 autoimmune encephalitis (AIE), 202–4
 differential diagnosis, 190–1
 historical perspective, 189
 mental state examination, 191–3
 neurology topics for CL teams 195
 epilepsy, 198–202
 neuroimmunology, 202–6
  see also anxiety disorders; bipolar affective disorder; cognitive impairment; psychosis
 Parkinson's disease, 195–8
 stroke, 193–5
  see also under individual topics
NICE (National Institute for Health and Care Excellence)
 definition of manual restraint, 178
 guidance on self-harm, 305
 guidelines for management of depression in chronic physical illness, 85
 guidelines on suspected head injury patients, 122
 guidelines on treatment of depression, 92

NICE (cont.)
screening recommendations
for alcohol misuse, 120
self-harm
definition of, 61
guidelines for management
of, 66
nitrous oxide, 155–6
acute intoxication, 155
chronic use,
consequences, 156
harm minimisation, 156
toxicity, 155
'No Health without Mental
Health' (RCPsych
campaign), 404
Northern Ireland, mental
health legislation, 272
novel psychoactive substances
(NPS), 152
nurse consultant roles see
under liaison mental
health nursing
nursing education, revised
standards, 40
nursing in CL settings 32–45
see also liaison mental
health nursing,

occupational therapy, in
management of FSS,
365–6
older adults
cognitive impairment in,
305
depression in, 82–3
liaison mental health nursing
and, 38
multimorbidity and
coordinated care, 92
physical illness and risk of
suicide, 83, 84–5
opiate substitution therapy
(OST), 139
outcome measurement,
328, 343
at different levels of service
activity, 329–39
case mix and, 340–1
ED attendance and, 383
evaluation design, 339–40
Framework for Routine
Outcome Measurement
in Liaison
Psychiatry, 383
in context, 328–9

individual-level clinical
outcomes, 334–8
choosing outcome measures,
335, 338
outcomes to measure
following liaison
psychiatry contact, 334
non-psychiatric staff
responses, 338
organisation level,
330–3
early readmission rates, 331
inpatient length of stay, 330
limitations of organisation-
level outcomes, 333
patient complaints/
satisfaction, 332
serious/untoward
incidents, 331
specialist referral rates,
331
waiting times, 331
planning checklist, 342
population level clinical
outcomes, 333–4
condition-specific measures,
333–4
frequent attendance, 333
limitations, 334
TIDieR intervention
description and
replication
template, 330

paediatric CLP, 232–47
chronic illness and
adversity, 234
clinical aspects
developmental view of
assessment and
intervention, 237–8
Piaget's stages of
development and
conception of illness,
237–8
interviewing children and
adolescents and
working with paediatric
teams, 238
parental involvement and
working with
families, 239
psychiatric presentations in
paediatric settings,
239–43
case examples, 242–3

diagnostic difficulties, 234
intersection between physical
illness, educational and
social opportunities and
mental health, 233–4
legal aspects, 243
Children's Act (2004), 244
competence, capacity and
consent, 243–4
safeguarding, 244
liaison mental health nursing
competency, 39–40
need for paediatric liaison
services, 234–7
improving access to care, 235
improving outcomes, 236
reintegration, 236
risk assessment, 235–6
specialist and holistic
approach, 235
specialist assessment and
interventions, 236
relationship between physical
illness and psychiatric
disorders in young
people, 232–3
service development
interface work and the PL
team, 244–5
models, 245–7
research and audit, 247
parallel assessment, argument
for, 3
'Parity of Esteem' (RCPsych
campaign), 404
Parkinson's disease (PD)
anxiety symptoms, 196–7
depressive symptoms, 195–6
psychotic symptoms, 197–8
trajectory of disease, 189
patient admission and
discharge, liaison
mental health nursing
and, 36
patient advocacy, as liaison
mental health nursing
competency, 35–6
patient advocates, role of in
developing CLP
services, 407
people with intellectual
disabilities, assessment
in the ED, 379
people with learning
disabilities
and self-harm, 65

increased mortality, 39
liaison nursing and, 39
perinatal mental illness 219
  anxiety disorders, 213–16
  baby blues, 210–11
  bipolar disorder, 216–18
  care planning, 228
  complex PTSD, 216
  depression, 211–13
  eating disorders, 221–2
  generalised anxiety disorder
      (GAD), 214
  liaison nursing and, 39
  mood disorders, 210–13
  percentage of fathers
      experiencing postnatal
      depression, 210
  postpartum OCD,
      214–15
  postpartum psychosis, 218–19
  preconception counselling,
      228–9
  risk assessment, 227–8
  schizophrenia, 219–20
  tokophobia,
      215–16
  see also prescribing in
      pregnancy
perinatal psychiatry see
      perinatal mental illness
persistent physical
      symptoms (PPS)
  liaison mental health nursing
      and, 38
  psychological treatments for
      see psychological
      treatments for
      PPS/MUS
persistent pulmonary
      hypertension in the
      neonate (PPHN),
      antidepressants in
      pregnancy as risk factor
      for, 223
personality disorders
  and ABD, 175
  association with self-harm,
      65
physiotherapy/exercise
      therapy, in management
      of FSS, 112, 365
Piaget, Jean, stages of
      development and
      conception of illness,
      237–8
Pick, Arnold, 189

'places of safety', 281, 404,
      406
PLAN standards, 391–9
  accreditation process, 394–6
    key stages, 394
    collection of feedback, 394
    compilation of initial
        report, 395
    peer-review visit, 395
    revision of report, 395
    self-assessment, 394
    submission of report to
        Accreditation
        Committee, 395
  achieving accreditation,
      396–8
    preliminary review of
        standards, 396
    collecting feedback, 396–7
    ED assessment room, 397
    peer-review visit, 397
    policies and protocols, 396
    publicising
        accreditation, 398
    team involvement, 396
  categorisation, 392
  core standards, 393
  development, 391
  ED high-risk assessment
      room, 391–2
  examples, 393
  learning from PLAN, 398–9
  relevant additional
      standards, 393
planning and delivery of CLP
      services, 318–26
  clinicians' perspective, 323–4
  commissioners and senior
      managers' role, 322–3
  current picture
    patterns of activity, 320–2
    service provision, 318–20
  economic arguments, 323
  factors to consider, **321**
  implementation plan, 326
  model service configuration,
      324–6
  patients' perspective, 324
  service description
      framework, **325**
  stages, 318
police, and referrals to CL
      team, 5
polypharmacy, potential
      impact, 38
pregnancy 184

psychosis and, 163–4
rapid tranquillisation during,
      184
see also perinatal mental
      illness; prescribing in
      pregnancy
prescribing decisions in
      psychosis
  arrythmias, 167
  liver disease, 166
  renal disease, 166
prescribing decisions, liaison
      nursing and, 37
prescribing in pregnancy
  antidepressants, 222–4
    risks to the fetus
    autistic spectrum disorders
        (ASD), 223
  antidepressants, risks to the
      fetus
    congenital malformations,
        222–3
    PPHN, 223
  antipsychotics, 224
  anxiolytics and hypnotics, 226
  benzodiazepines, 226
  beta blockers, 226
  general principles, 222
  lithium, 225
  mood stabilisers, 225–6
  psychotropic medication, 222
  risk versus benefit, 223
  'Z-drugs', 226
primary care model of CLP
      services, 356–72
  overview, 357–8
  case examples
    Carol, 356, 362–4
    Isaac, 356,
        368–9
    Neil, 357, 369
  data analysis and, 367
  diagnosis and medication,
      367–8
  dos and don'ts for primary
      care physicians and
      juniors, 362–4
  evaluation, 352–3
  facts and figures from
      Nottinghamshire CLP
      teams, 369–72
  function of the service, 359
  functional neurological
      disorders, 360–1
    body changes, 360–1
    chronic pain, 361

primary care model (cont.)
initial assessment and
psychoeducation,
364
interventions, 365
occupational therapy,
365–6
physiotherapy, 365
psychological input, 367
support workers, 366
location of patient
assessment, 362
symptoms, 359–60
systemic approaches, 367
team make-up, 361
team meetings, 362
psychiatry, historical blurring
of the boundaries
between neurology,
neuropathology and,
189 see also neurology-
psychiatry interface
psychodynamic-interpersonal
therapy (PIT),
treatment of PPS/MUS,
263–4
psychological reaction to
physical illness, 48–58
overview, 48
adaptive coping and
emotional regulation
strategies, 51
chronic disease
adjustment to, 49
differential effect, 52–3
most common
conditions, 52
formulation, 55–6
family, 56
meaning of the illness, 56
nature of the distress, 55
personality, 56
previous experience of
illness, 56
prior history of mental
health problems or
childhood adversity, 56
illness perception and
common-sense model
of self-regulation, 50–2
maladaptive coping and
emotional regulation
strategies, 51
meaning of illness, 48–9
personal experience of illness
and recovery, 57–8

previous experience of illness
and, 55
psychological and social
models of health
behaviour, 52
relationships, importance
of, 53
resilience and, 54–5
spirituality and religious
faith, 53–4
stress and coping, 50, 51
psychological treatments for
PPS/MUS, 250–67
cognitive therapy, inclusion
criteria for trials, 251
determining patient
suitability for, 266
evaluation challenges,
250–2
evidence base, 252,
259
anxiety/depression in
physical disease,
253, 259
functional somatic
syndromes, 253
reviews of non-
pharmacological
interventions, 252–3
generic aspects
active listening, 261
clear rationale for
treatment, 261
empathy, 261
engagement, 261
expertise/understanding of
physical health
problems, 261
healthy lifestyle advice, 262
matching intensity to
severity and chronicity
of symptoms, 253–60
points to discuss with
patient, 260
referral process, 260
shared model, 261
therapeutic alliance, 261
individual approaches, 262–6
acceptance and commitment
therapy, 264–5
cognitive analytic
therapy, 266
cognitive behavioural
therapy, 262–3
counselling, 265–6
hypnosis, 265

interpersonal therapy, 265
mindfulness, 264
psychodynamic
interpersonal therapy,
263–4
psychological treatments, trials
cancer, 253, 257
COPD, 258
diabetes, 259
functional
neurological
disorders, 254
IBS, 255
psychopharmacology,
education of
hospital staff
in, 307
psychosis
and ABD, 174
assessment and diagnosis, 159
assessment and treatment in
general hospital
settings, 158–69
distinguishing between
schizophrenia and other
causes, 160
epidemiology and the role of
the CLP team, 158
factors prompting
consideration of organic
drivers for, 160–1
likely presentations
emergency department,
161–2
ICU, medical and surgical
wards, 162–3
liaison outpatients, 164–5
maternity department,
163–4
management
biological aspects, 166–7
clinical aspects, 165
depot injections and
clozapine, 167–8
medicolegal aspects
capacity assessments, 168
Mental Health Act (MHA),
168–70
prescribing considerations,
166–7
arrythmias, 167
liver disease, 166
renal disease, 166
psychological factors, 165
side effects, 167
social aspects, 165–6

organic drivers, examples of, 161
post-stroke, 195
presentation to the ED with, 377
presentations in different general hospital settings, 161
psychosocial care of patients with cancer, Australian perspective, 421
psychosocial interventions, for chronic disease and depression, 90–1
psychotherapeutic interventions, education of hospital staff in, 306
psychotherapy for treatment of FSS, 113–14
teaching requirements, 306
psychotropic medication, prescribing in pregnancy, 222

Quality Outcomes Framework (QOF), 333

rapid tranquillisation
as alternative to prolonged restraint, 179
during pregnancy, 184
health monitoring, 184–5
in management of ABD, 179
in the ED, 375
referrals to CL services
alternative sources, 4–5
common reasons for, 6
helpful requests criteria, 3
organisational aspects, 3–5
prioritising and allocating, 3
SBAR principles, 3
triage criteria, 1–3
refugees and asylum seekers, and attendance in the ED, 381
relationships, importance of, 53
religion/spirituality, and psychological reaction to physical illness, 53–4
resilience
and psychological reaction to physical illness, 54–5
measures of, 54
restraint
in management of ABD, 178–9

removal in the ED, 375
role of peer to developing CLP services, peer influencers, 402

safeguarding and protection, responsibilities of hospital staff, 380
schizophrenia
diagnostic criteria, 159
distinguishing from other causes of psychosis, 160
intoxication and, 124
management, 165
physical health and the role of the CLP team, 158
pooled lifetime prevalence and life expectancy, 158
presentation with ABD, 174
Scotland (Mental Health (Care and Treatment) (Scotland) Act, 282
SEGUE framework for teaching and assessing communication skills, 306
self-harm, 61–77
overview, 61
definition, 61–2
age and, 63
as driver of ABD, 173
assessment
overview, 61
diversity and, 69–70
of needs, 68–9
of resources and assets, 70
of risk, 66–7, 71
associations
life events and difficulties, 65–6
mental disorder, 64–5
personality disorder, 65
psychological characteristics, 65
by swallowing objects, 380
epidemiology, 62–4
ethnicity and, 64
function, 68
gendered perspective, 63
in the NEET population, 64
leading to hospital admission, 70, 72
case examples, 72
lifetime prevalence in UK adult population, 61

main risks for suicide or repetition, 67
management guidelines, 66
NICE guidance, 39
outcomes following, 64
overlapping phenomena, 62
personal experiences, 76
positive feelings generated by, 68
relationship with substance misuse, 64
relationship with suicidal behaviour or intent, 61–2, 64
risk assessment as liaison mental health nursing competency, 35
risk factors in MS, 204
socio-economic status and, 63
sources of information, 62–3
therapeutic responses
assessment, 73
brief interventions, 74
CBT and PIT, 74
intensive and longer-term therapies, 74
safety plan, 75
safety planning, 74
supported self-management and the internet, 71
talking therapies, 73
UK statistics, 63
see also suicidality and self-harm
self-regulation, common-sense model, 50–2
severity of mental health problem, as triage criteria for CL services, 2
social aspects of CLP, 288–98
the concept, 288
assessing the patient's social situation see social history of the patient
social history of the patient
liaison psychiatrist's role, 290–1
place of in an assessment, 288–90
questions to ask, 291–6
regarding debt, 292–3
regarding employment, 294–5
regarding housing, 293, 294
regarding social isolation, 295–6

social history (cont.)
sources of information, 297
using the information, 297–8
social support, relationship
to health outcomes, 53
somatic disorders, functional 105
see also functional
somatic
symptoms (FSS),
somatic symptom disorder, 103
somatic syndromes,
functional, 104
specialist clinics, evaluation of
CLP services, 352
SPIKES framework for
teaching and assessing
communication
skills, 306
standard-setting 391
CQC hospital inspection
programme, 390
measures of a good LP
service, 389
Psychiatric Liaison
Accreditation Network,
391–9
Treat As One report (National
Confidential Enquiry
into Patient and
Outcome and Death),
390
see also PLAN standards
stigma
depression and, 80
liaison nurse's role in
breaking, 34, 36
stimulants, misuse of, 152–3
Strathdee, Geraldine, 404
stroke, 34, 43, 44, 57, 58, 84–5,
88, 100, 103, 189, 191,
192–5, 328
benefits of outcome
measurement, 328
post-stroke anxiety, 194
post-stroke depression, 193–4
assessment, 193
predictors, 193
treatment, 194
post-stroke mania, 194
post-stroke psychosis, 195
substance misuse, 134–56
addictions assessment, 134–6
benzodiazepines,
142–4
cannabis, 150–2
cocaine, 147–9

considerations for, 156
DVLA restrictions, 156
examples of patient
presentations in
a liaison setting, 136–9
GBL/GHB, 144–7
heroin (diamorphine), 137–42
ketamine, 153–5
liaison mental health nursing
and, 38
nitrous oxide, 155–6
novel psychoactive
substances, 152
occupational restrictions, 156
relationship with self-harm, 64
stimulants, 152–3
see also under individual
substances
suicidality and self-harm
and referral to CL team, 4
assessing risk in the ED,
379, 392
Australian/New Zealand
perspective, 421
education of hospital staff in
risk assessment, 305–6
Indigenous populations, 420
Kerrie Wooltorton case, 284–5
suicide
capacity to end one's own life,
284–5
increased risk in perinatal
period, 39, 210, 227
physical illness and risk of in
older adults, 83, 84–5
prevention role of liaison
staff, 347
relationship with self-harm, 64
support workers, in
management of FSS, 366
suspected head injury,
intoxication and, 122

'This Is Me' (Alzheimer's
Society), 38
TIDieR (Template for
Intervention
Description and
Replication), 330
training 383
ED staff, 383
see also education of hospital
staff
training pathways
CLP curriculum structure, 20
Foundation Programme, 19

framework for post-CCT
credentials in CLP, 20
from graduation to consultant
psychiatrist,
19–20
international examples, 26
Australia and New
Zealand, 27–9
Canada, 27
USA, 27
mapping curriculum
objectives to workplace
assessments, **24**
"must see" cases, 26
personal development plan
(PDP), 22
construction, 22
evidence collection,
23–6
placement, 20
Treat As One report (National
Confidential Enquiry
into Patient and
Outcome and
Death), 390
treatment adherence, social
support associated
with, 53
triage in the ED, through a LP
lens, 373

UK Psychiatric Liaison
Accreditation Network
standards see also under
PLAN standards,
UN Convention on the Rights
of Persons with
Disabilities
(CRPD), 271

violence, emergency
department reduction
strategies, 185–6

Wernicke's encephalopathy,
123, 129–30
Whipple's disease, 190
WHO (World Health
Organization),
definiton of self-
harm, 61
Wooltorton, Kerrie,
284–5

'Z-drugs', prescribing in
pregnancy, 226

Printed in the USA
CPSIA information can be obtained
at www.ICGtesting.com
LVHW080423110124
768603LV00003B/61